Pre-Employment Background Investigations for Public Safety Professionals

Frank A. Colaprete

CRC Press
Taylor & Francis Group
Boca Raton London New York

CRC Press is an imprint of the
Taylor & Francis Group, an **informa** business

CRC Press
Taylor & Francis Group
6000 Broken Sound Parkway NW, Suite 300
Boca Raton, FL 33487-2742

Printed in the United States of America on acid-free paper
Version Date: 20120330

International Standard Book Number: 978-1-4398-9385-2 (Hardback)

Library of Congress Cataloging-in-Publication Data

Colaprete, Frank A.
Pre-employment background investigations for public safety professionals / Frank A. Colaprete.
p. cm.
Includes bibliographical references and index.
ISBN 978-1-4398-9385-2 (hardcover : alk. paper)
1. Employee screening. 2. Public safety. I. Title.

HF5549.5.E429C66 2012
363.10068'3--dc23 2012009683

Visit the Taylor & Francis Web site at
http://www.taylorandfrancis.com

and the CRC Press Web site at
http://www.crcpress.com

Dedicated to the loving memory of my Father

Frank Louis Colaprete
Tech Corporal
United States Military Police
World War II

If God, in his divine and infinite wisdom should someday shine his countenance and grace upon me and grant me the blessings of a single prayer, I would ask only for the solemn comfort and lasting peace of knowing you have always been proud of me, while you were here with me and for all the time you have been in Heaven watching over me.

Contents

Foreword

If you are asking yourself, "Why a book on pre-employment background investigation is needed?" stop for a minute to consider your organizational life, reviewing all those who were employed and the behaviors and work performance you have observed over the years. It takes only a moment to see a face or remember a name of someone who caused you to ask, "How did that person ever get hired?"

Those early days were frustrating and clearly pointed out to Dr. Colaprete that a better method of hiring excellent employees required a more informed approach. Hiring is a multistep process, with candidates progressing to the next level, or being dropped for any number of reasons. Each step had to use best practices and the right screening criteria. The process had to be sensible, smart, and with confirmation at each juncture along the way that correct information was being gathered and carefully reviewed. As Dr. Colaprete conceptualized basic hiring needs, based on past successes and by comparing these with those less than positive outcomes, his experience led him to more serious research into the hiring process in general, which then led to the development of this book.

This book, *Pre-Employment Background Investigation for the Public Safety Professionals*, is the most comprehensive book available today on the topic of hiring practices. It serves as a guide to all levels of management and human resources, a reference for questions related to the topic, and offers a process that is thorough, thoughtful, and will help any person or group charged with hiring employees to consider how they can improve what they are currently doing. One bad hire, one aberrant employee, can, and often does, result in liability issues that are frightening and costly, at multiple levels. This is a critical responsibility for any organization and is especially true with public safety operations.

In my own career, when the hiring of employees was necessary, there was always that certain individual who was offered employment yet left us with a feeling of lingering doubt. We followed a script that examined a variety of traits, characteristics, experience, and other indicators of who the person was, but it was not comprehensive to the point where we never felt any consternation for our hiring decisions.

Dr. Colaprete's book leaves no hiring criteria unexamined. He uncovers and sheds light upon the process in great depth and with the critical and professional guidance you will not find in any other single reference. In time, it will represent a well-worn referenced book, as its use to the individual and the organization has no equal in today's field.

What makes this book stand out? Simple: It is a thorough and comprehensive compilation of information assembled by the author, who always applies exhaustive research and examination. If it exists, Dr. Colaprete has found it, and it is part of his database that becomes the document you are holding in your hand.

The reader is walked through six macro-topics, including (1) practical implications of pre-employment investigation, (2) pre-employment screening process, (3) legal issues in the hiring process, (4) medical and psychological standards, (5) informational sources and the final investigative package, and (6) the past predicting the future of pre-employment investigations. Each of these major categories is broken down into well-organized and easily referenced subcategories of information to make your task, if you are charged with hiring employees, almost fail-safe. I say "almost fail-safe" based on the following experience.

We were all set to hire someone for a police officer position, based on the hiring process of the day, when the fingerprint results were faxed to us. It seems that the individual had officially changed his name, eliminating a previous drug conviction and prison sentence. When asked, he said the person who sold the drugs and served the time no longer existed and we could not hold that against him. We naturally refused to hire his "previous" or "new" self.

There are so many important aspects to this book that to discuss them all here is not feasible. Suffice it to say, as you read through or look up a particular aspect, you will know this to be true. For example, in Chapter 5, Dr. Colaprete discusses personal and professional references, specifically written recommendations, something we ask for and generally do not process appropriately. He says, "The background investigator should verify the veracity of all written recommendations, as they may have been forged by the applicant, generated by the applicant and signed by the reference, and may even contain fake electronic signatures. Letters of recommendation should not be taken on their face value as often serious underlying issues may be present. All of the submitters of letters of reference should be interviewed personally by the background investigator to verify the information contained as well as seek new information not revealed in the written recommendation."

If that sounds like a step too difficult to make, consider the liability implications for not being thorough versus the hours, days, and weeks spent in documenting and attempting to fire an employee who turns out to be problematic. We often accept past practices as if they were valid and sacrosanct. This book offers a check and balance to current procedures and helps guide restructuring where needed. It is not something to be taken lightly.

The book is unique in its completeness. If you have a question about hiring and need an answer to guide your actions, this is the book to have on the shelf. In today's world, we often seek a quick answer to make the process as simple and easy as possible, and in so doing, we may stumble from the path into the swamp for not properly charting our journey. It is completely referenced, indexed, and with a compilation of supporting information and useful tools. There is no comparable book available to you.

And, most importantly, this topic matters. Organizations are filled with people who make it successful or bring harm in some cases. We want to avoid the person not well suited for what we do, who we are, our values, our mission and goals, and the value we place on employees. To make the best decisions, we must act from an informed position, up-to-date with all manner of direct and indirect influences we are sorting through, in the quest to hire the right individual for the job at hand. *Pre-Employment Background Investigation for the Public Safety Professionals* is one book that is critical for the organization's responsibility to hire the best possible people. That single decision will result in tremendous benefit or perhaps costly negative outcomes. One thing is for sure, we can minimize the negative outcomes if we use the information contained in this book.

Richard C. Lumb, PhD

Preface

Rhetoric and hyperbole aside, we are truly facing a very difficult situation in the recruitment, selection, and retention of the nation's public safety officers. This seems to be a timeless issue in organizations, one that often defies logical reason in even the simplest of forms. As the gateway to the criminal justice organization, the background investigator serves as the filtering agent between the efforts of recruiting officers, who measure success by numbers and not quality, and the flawed predictive abilities of formalized cognitive and psychological testing processes. Serving as the nexus between recruitment and selection, the background investigator occupies a crucial role in the hiring system of the organization, a role that is all too often marginalized and scapegoated for budgetary and political reasons.

Brought into the role of commanding officer of my department's backgrounds and recruitment unit, the learning curve was quite difficult as the pre-employment investigations process shares only a few parallels to the criminal investigations process. The process for which I was versed in, however, ill-equipped me for the myriad issues I would face in the role of hiring manager. My growth in the role, as painful as it was, led me to the conception of this type of book for those who are either voluntarily or involuntarily assigned these types of investigations. As my exposure to the topic area widened through practice, research, and teaching, the development of this book became my sine qua non. This drive was fueled for two reasons: To ensure the edification of those charged with the completion and oversight of these types of investigations and to hopefully assert a positive impact on the entire profession. We often face watershed moments in our careers. For me, the development of a comprehensive examination of the entire discipline of pre-employment background investigations became mine, primarily because of the lack of such a work and the detrimental impact it had on my entry into the field. Hopefully, this book will assist those fledgling and tenured investigators, administrators, and human resource professionals in developing the enhanced knowledge, skills, and abilities to conduct these types of investigations to the highest levels of quality and integrity. This book is intended for use in a ground-up systems design as well as for existing systems analysis and change. The numerous legal issues are not intended as a strict legal analysis or for legal advice to a specific individual, issue, or agency. The issues of local, state, and federal laws as well as collective bargaining agreements are addressed to present a national view of patterns, trends, and similarities in the issues discussed in the book as they narrowly relate to pre-employment investigations and the vetting of new applicants for these positions of trust.

As a background investigator, you may never have the prominence of Sherlock Holmes, the glamour of a big city homicide investigator, or the privilege of being the chief or sheriff who swears in those who pledge to serve the agency and their respective communities with the highest levels of honor and integrity. Often, the background investigator's work is a thankless role with the best work never being acknowledged, let alone rewarded. Analogous to a CIA agent, you will work behind the scenes to do the organizations' most critical intelligence gathering so the organization can make strategic human resource decisions. You will operate in secrecy for the protection of all you have sworn to uphold, including the preservation of every applicant's privacy rights. Most assuredly you will be questioned and second-guessed by your most favored and supportive colleagues on those who slip through the cracks, decisions that will likely be beyond your control. And, in spite of all of this, one of the advantages is that you may be fortunate enough to be in the wheelhouse and actually have the opportunity to steer the organization along the correct course in making hiring decisions. The only comfort you may have is sleeping at night knowing you had some positive impact on the future of the organization and the safety of those you serve, citizens and applicants alike.

DISCLAIMER

This book is designed to provide information and general guidance in regard to the subject matter covered. It should not be interpreted as legal advice. The author assumes no responsibility or liability to any person or entity with respect to any loss or damage caused or alleged to be caused, directly or indirectly, by the information and illustrations in this book.

In regard to federal, state, and local statutes, case laws, court rulings, labor laws, and agreements, it should be noted that different jurisdictions must abide by all applicable legal and procedural requirements. Readers and users should examine their own requirements as well as seek legal counsel when needed.

Incorporated statutes and case laws are from around the country and are meant to demonstrate patterns, trends, and concepts. Check state of processing and consult counsel prior to making adverse decisions.

Acknowledgments

At the outset, Carolyn Spence, Laurie Schlags, Kyle Meyer, Remya Divakaran, and the support, editing, and design teams of Taylor & Francis Group/CRC Press deserve much credit for their support in the development of this book. Absent their dedication and desire to expand the knowledge base of the field of criminal justice and the skills and knowledge of professional investigators seeking to grow, works like these would not be possible.

I have been truly blessed with the opportunity to serve in two professions that I love: policing and higher education. Policing has given me the experiential foundation to speak with credibility on the topic, but higher education and research have added the depth and breadth of topical analysis that were so critical to the comprehensive approach to this book. As I reflect on my time in both fields, there have been numerous administrators, academics, and scholars who have shaped me into the researcher, teacher, and mentor that I am today. Their support affords me the endless opportunities of professional growth that are driven by the force of my dreams of what can be. Dr. Richard C. Lumb and Dr. Charles P. Nemeth were principal guides at my entry point into higher education and my pursuit of developing the capacity to publish. As I have moved through the evolutionary processes of the higher education system, several others have provided me with the motivation and insights that ensure a level of success that is tempered with sincere humility. I have grown personally and professionally from their sage advice and unwavering patience. My thanks extend to all those in academia who have consistently provided a support structure that allows me to complete these types of works: Dr. Anne Weed, Dr. Gary Smith, Dr. Richard Quest, Dr. Thomas Tremer, Dr. Donal Hartman, Dr. Amy Rafferty, Dr. Nelly Lejter, Dr. Tammy Kushner, Dr. Robert McKenna, Professor Richard V. Martin, Assistant Director Chris Ormsby, and Assistant Director Denise Owens. They have all given me very wonderful and fulfilling opportunities in the field of higher education, and I hope I have always been able to fulfill their trust in me every time I have the privilege to stand at the lectern.

To Dr. Art Amann, one could not find a better colleague and confidant in the field of higher education. I have had the benefit of his humor-laced and timeless wisdom that has grounded me from when we were aspiring doctoral classmates to the lasting friendship we enjoy today.

Throughout my years in law enforcement, I was equally blessed with working with the finest and most talented cops one could ever hope to meet. What better group to engage as technical editors for this type of work. I most appreciate their tireless efforts and thoughtful feedback that have led to the refinement of the final edition of the manuscript: Captain Joseph J. Davis (ret.), Lieutenant Michael Vanroo, Lieutenant James Noble (ret.), Professor Joseph Mariconda (police sergeant, ret.), Sergeant Brian P. DiSalvo, Senior Parole Officer Kathleen McDonnell, Investigator Gary A. Galetta, and Investigator Jonathan Tahara. Also of note are the contributions of proofreaders who assisted in the final development of the book: Detective Frank P. Tona, Deportation Officer Vincent Pulcini, and Senior Analyst Todd Longstreet.

As a special note, for Mike, Gary, and Jon—they truly are the best investigators I have ever had the privilege and honor to work with during my professional career. Every time

I talk to them, I always learn something new that continues to help me grow personally, professionally, and academically. I do not know what I did that was so right to bring all three of them into my life. They are far more than professional colleagues—they are part of my family.

I would also like to thank Deputy Chief Jason Moen and Lieutenant Scott Watkins of the Auburn Maine Police Department and Chief Richard Boyan and Captain Martin Corbett of the Irondequoit New York Police Department for offering their investigative packages and forms for use as guides in the book.

Author

Dr. Frank A. Colaprete, AAS, BS, MS, EdD, CLS, is an associate professor of criminal justice administration at Keuka College, Keuka Park, New York. He is also an adjunct faculty member of Norwich University, Nova Southeastern University, New England College, and the Justice and Training Research Institute at Roger Williams University. Dr. Colaprete has served for 20 years in law enforcement in such roles as patrol officer, evidence technician, sergeant, detective sergeant, and lieutenant. During his career, he was assigned to Patrol, the Evidence Technicians Unit, the Central Criminal Investigations Division, Field Criminal Investigations and Coordination, Research and Evaluation, Professional Development (Training), Professional Standards (Internal Affairs), and the Recruitment and Background Investigations Unit. He currently teaches, consults, and conducts independent criminal justice research in myriad topics as the owner and lead consultant of Justice Systems Solutions, LLC. Dr. Colaprete has published two textbooks, *Internal Investigations: A Practitioner's Approach* and *Mentoring in the Criminal Justice Professions: Conveyance of the Craft*, both released through Charles C Thomas Publisher, Limited. His publications also include numerous journal articles on police management, training, and criminal as well as administrative investigations. His work has garnered him the finalist award from the IACP/Motorola Corporation Webber Seavey Award process. He has also been featured in the National League of Cities database for successful municipal programs. In 2009, the administration of the Norwich University School of Graduate Studies conferred upon him the Distinguished Faculty of the Year Award. He holds an AAS in criminal justice–police science, BS and MS in organizational management, and an EdD in higher education leadership, with a specialization in adult education. He also holds the title of certified litigation specialist (CLS) through the Americans for Effective Law Enforcement (AELE) and is a master instructor and instructor evaluator certified by the New York State Division of Criminal Justice Services Office of Public Safety.

1 Practical Implications of Pre-Employment Investigations

LEARNING OBJECTIVES

- To develop a historical understanding of the issues that both positively and negatively impact the pre-employment investigation process for public safety organizations
- To develop an appreciation for the importance of the pre-employment investigation process in a public safety organization
- To develop an understanding of the predominant factors affecting applicant attrition rates as well as the predictive factors of the pre-employment investigation process
- To develop an understanding of the transitive nature of recruitment, selection, and training in the organization's future success and how they impact succession planning processes

KEY TERMS AND CONCEPTS

- Objectives of a pre-employment investigation for public safety personnel
- Applicant attrition rates
- Recruiting process needs
- Social and organizational issues of the public safety personnel selection processes
- Risk management

INTRODUCTION

Throughout the history of American law enforcement, there has been a requirement to screen applicants for the characteristics and behaviors of service, dedication, and integrity. Born from heated discussions of the causes of police corruption that have continued since the early nineteenth century, the need for law enforcement personnel who are devoid of corrupt behaviors is self-evident.[1] There is unilateral agreement that the screening processes of law enforcement applicants must include disqualifying parameters that include those who have arrest records and poor employment histories.[2] While the issue of police corruption and abuse of power had been an ongoing discussion as evidenced by the *Wickersham Report* and the *Report on Lawlessness in Law Enforcement* since the early twentieth century, little was accomplished until the mid-twentieth century at the dawn of the civil rights movement.[3] The most sweeping changes began to occur as a result of the findings of the report of the *President's Commission on Law Enforcement and Administration of Justice* (1967) that among other recommendations advised law enforcement to make significant changes to their selection processes.[4] This is a direct result of the *Omnibus Crime Control and Safe Streets Act of 1968* and the precursor of the Law Enforcement Assistance Administration (LEAA) all put in motion the methods to improve police effectiveness in controlling crime and improving community relations.[5]

Fast forward a few decades, and in the post-9/11 era, society has been forced into a newly heightened and galvanized awareness that also constructively mandates mainstream American businesses to require criminal records checks on prospective employees.[6] The background investigation, and more appropriately titled *character investigation*, is the predominant method used to ascertain if these positive traits exist in the applicant's character.[7] Sadly, that has not been the result in many, many instances. For law enforcement, the background or pre-employment investigation is the most critical step in assessing the prospective applicant's fit for entry into what still is the most honorable of positions one can serve in, a police officer charged with the responsibility of protecting the free society we have all come to enjoy. There is an expectation, and rightly so, that those who are brought into the ranks will enforce as well as comply with the laws they are sworn to uphold.[8] The social contract between the police and the public has never changed, and it is within the purview of the background investigator's responsibilities to see that the terms of that contract are strictly enforced.

Simply stated, the most profound impact a law enforcement manager can have on an agency is the hiring of an effective officer to add to the ranks.[9] The success of a police officer is primarily based on their ability to effectively manage human relations issues, thus calling for police officers to be human relations specialists.[10] This makes the responsibility to hire the best qualified applicants of the utmost importance to law enforcement administrators as well as those who have political control over their respective agencies. That responsibility requires an unwavering commitment to the legal, procedural, and ethical issues that transcend the hiring of the nation's centurions. In contrast, bad politics leads to irreparable damage to a law enforcement agency's ability to recruit, retain, and motivate the rank and file in proper fashion.[11]

To provide some perspective to the issue, in 2004 there were more than 800,000 full-time sworn law enforcement officers working in the United States, the bulk of which, approximately 450,000, were employed in local police departments.[12] With respect to attrition rates, between 2002 and 2003, 34,474 officers were processed by local police departments: 28,791 at the entry level and 5,323 as lateral transfers.[13] Over the last 20 years, a mass exodus has been observed in law enforcement officers migrating through lateral transfers, from large agencies to smaller ones.[14] Reversing the trends of the previous era when smaller agency officers sought to gain the ability to be involved in more police work and promotional opportunities that larger agencies had come to be known for. However, since most police departments in the country employ 10 officers or less, the task of quickly replacing lost human resources becomes that much more critical even as the shift in employment demographics has tended to favor these smaller agencies.

While the overwhelming majority of law enforcement applicants are hired and have successful and lengthy service-based careers, the inevitable cracks always seem to be wide enough for a few of the unfit or corrupt to slip through. The effects of such errors polarize the ranks and create high levels of distrust and sometimes hostility from the public we are responsible to protect. The pressures created by short staffing, political influence, and the like can severely compromise the selection process of an organization. The return of political influence to the police realm can be accredited to the period of civil unrest during the 1960s that led to primary control of police agencies being placed under local political structures.[15] Moves to centralize the political organization and structure of municipalities have yet to eliminate corruption in state and local governments wherein corruption is starkly characterized as an infestation.[16] Political pressures often unduly and negatively impact the operational effectiveness of a law enforcement organization.[17] Political pressures are also more intense in the elected ranks of law enforcement such as in the case of sheriff's departments.[18] The most disturbing factor is that the issues of the abuse of political power by those elected officials have been the subject of controversy for nearly two centuries. The only proven answer is to have formal legal controls in place to maintain the necessary and proper administration of any law enforcement process.[19] This includes the pre-employment screening process.

Political trends are cyclical with respect to affirmative action initiatives in the United States.[20] Political influences due to attempts to meet affirmative action goals have led to several devastating scandals in law enforcement organizations throughout the country.[21] These deficits in the hiring process lead to public outcries, external body oversight, and further constriction of the police chief's ability to hire and manage their own staff. Politics will also enter the process when elected officials will consider themselves somehow qualified to question the veracity of the hiring practices and systems of the organization.[22] The irony of it all exists in the theory that bureaucratic corruption can also be interpreted as a direct reflection of society's morality.[23] Elected officials must be educated about the requirements for becoming a police officer in order to abate these types of issues.[24] Any type of reform must first emerge from changing the undue influence the political structure has over the police function in a free society.[25] A means v. ends analysis must not be maligned to justify these types of actions.[26] Political influence is truly the single most damaging bane of the law enforcement officer hiring process. Regardless of these pressures, law enforcement administrators must demonstrate a level of civic integrity that is beyond reproach.[27]

Accountability is also felt at the highest levels of the organization when these hiring problems are uncovered.[28] Not only are police managers being held accountable, but also those key figures who work in the supportive human resource functions.[29] Worse yet, these likely episodic lapses may be perceived, whether real or imagined, as indicating patterns of flaws and abuses in the hiring process rather than as isolated incidents.[30] Managers will also privately extol situational justification for these ethical lapses.[31] However, in the light of the public eye, they will deny such allegations in an attempt to insulate themselves from the decision that has gone wrong.

Compounded by nepotism and cronyism, which are somehow still tolerated by law enforcement and municipal administrators, but never by the American public, the problem grows ever worse with a real-time media that froth at the mouth for its next virtual meal. This plays out daily in the press reminiscent of a Greek tragedy where the histrionics of the media members act in the finest traditions of Aeschylus, Sophocles, and Euripides, using the virtual theater to bask in the paradoxical joy of watching others suffer. Yellow journalism is alive and well in the Internet and cable television conduits that are directly wired to all of our homes.

Research has consistently demonstrated that the press has a penchant for reporting decadent news events in lieu of other less controversial news events.[32] And if law enforcement and municipal administrators are still holding on to the belief that this information will not be found by the media, they are dangerously deluding themselves.[33] From seeing the *Pentagon Papers* to the publishing of some 400,000 secret war documents on the Internet should put a damper on any hope of anything being secret anymore in this age of lightning fast information dissemination.[34] For example, one media investigation uncovered that a county child protective services agency had employed 68 CPS workers with criminal histories that ranged from drug possession, illegal weapon possession, domestic violence, prostitution, and repeatedly drunk driving charges.[35] Another media report revealed the hiring and promotion of a law enforcement officer who was terminated from his previous police employment. Despite the written objections of the background investigation unit command, the allusion was the hiring was done because of a relationship the applicant had with the chief executive and his administration.[36]

A spate of legacy officers who were arrested for serious crimes in the Buffalo and Niagara region of New York State led to the media's questioning of screening and hiring practices with the connotation of nepotism being the driver of the hiring rather than the qualifications and backgrounds of the applicants.[37] In yet another case dubbed the largest police corruption scandal ever uncovered and prosecuted in the state of New Jersey, officers were involved in bribery and extortion, admitting to beginning their criminal careers the moment they were sworn in.[38] The results of poor hiring practices have forced many law enforcement agencies to reevaluate their personnel selection and employment practices and standards.[39] How much change has been implemented is apparently a question for another day.

While we can lay blame on the waning quality of candidate pools and a host of other issues that would on the surface seem out of our control,[40] the reality is that many agency administrators bring these problems on themselves. And for a discipline that prides itself on doing what is right, how do we consistently make such monumental mistakes as these? For this statements' seeming hyperbole, there is no exaggeration in the examples that will be presented throughout this text. One clearly poignant example emerges from the analysis of the pre-employment investigations of the officers involved in the Los Angeles Police Department Rampart Division scandal. The investigation revealed that four of the involved officers had highly questionable issues in their backgrounds indicating that they should have never been hired as police officers in the first place.[41] Had they not been hired, at least the conduct attributed to their criminal actions under the color of law could have been avoided.

Corruption in local government that transcends law enforcement is seen as the most damaging influence to our strongly rooted American values.[42] My charge is to use this text to move forward and create lasting organizational change that enhances your screening and selection processes. The use of these materials can help you avoid the situations that have plagued many agencies that have had a naïve or, worse yet, fully cognizant and palpable role in their faulty or illegal hiring processes.

OBJECTIVES OF THE PRE-EMPLOYMENT INVESTIGATION

Background investigations, like any organizational initiative, need a vision, mission, goals, and objectives to ensure the process is aligned with the overall organizational mission. The background investigation process contributes to providing the human resource needs that will help fulfill the macro-level mission of the organization. At the micro-level, the pre-employment investigation focuses on the individual applicant. Background or personnel investigations are designed to determine as best as possible, the applicant's character, background, and suitability for positions in the law enforcement field.[43] For example, good judgment under tense situations is a critical behavior that is required of law enforcement officers in order to avoid improper and, at times, criminal behavior in their day-to-day actions.[44] The background investigation should include tests and measures of good judgment in previous roles as a demonstration of the applicant's ability to make the right decisions in a variety of situations. These objectives are also specific. For example, the objectives of the background investigation include such areas as the presence of a criminal record and undesirable as well as desirable behavior patterns of the applicant.[45] Also at the macro-level, the objectives include securing the future of the organization by selecting employees to fill key and vital roles, for example, "The investigations play an important role selecting employees for positions of high trust. The focus is on the trustworthiness and integrity of the applicants, as evidenced by their behavior and relationships with others over a long period of time."[46] The objectives of the process must be developed with the long-term human resource needs of the organization in mind, communicated to those responsible for filling these goals, supported through the issuance of policy, and guided by the leaders at the highest levels of the organization to achieve fruition.

In addition, the objectives of the pre-employment investigation are to determine the fitness of the applicant for the role of a law enforcement officer. As part of the investigation, several information targets should be examined. The following list represents those relevant targets of the process:

1. Biographical data
2. Employment history and discipline
3. Relocation attitude and commitment
4. Shift attitude, availability, and commitment
5. Retention and permanency
6. Financial responsibility
7. Integrity
8. Drug behaviors
9. Alcohol behaviors
10. Criminal activities
11. Military history and discipline
12. Driving history
13. Reliability
14. Service attitude and response
15. Certification/education history
16. Perjury/falsification of official reports/records
17. Bribes and gratuities
18. Excessive force/violence
19. Child abuse[47]

WHY DO WE DO A BACKGROUND INVESTIGATION?

The question may seem rhetorical, but some discussion is required to gain a perspective on the contemporary issues facing organizations that deal with this question at varying levels. The most rudimentary answer is to maintain a set of high professional standards that are required to meet the demands of these types of positions that require trust and integrity in the public safety officer field.[48] The ideological answer is to prevent the criminals and treasonists who have disgraced the names of local, state, and federal agencies from entering the ranks.[49] In other venues, the mere asking of some simple historical questions could have led to the discovery of some of the greatest impostors and charlatans ever to walk the face of the earth and quite possibly have prevented the defiling of the sacred soil of Ground

Zero.[50] From no investigation to a complete investigation, and intervening levels on the continuum that strive to give the appearance of complete investigations, the variation is wide in the conduct of pre-employment investigations. Even when the process has been followed to the letter, some applicants will escape discovery by the background investigator, and the entire unit will be afforded symbolic rather than founded blame for matters which may be well beyond their control.[51]

Not solely the bane of law enforcement organizations, the fire service has not gone untouched as the need for background investigations has taken on a heightened awareness in the wake of incidents of firefighters across the country being arrested for numerous types of crimes, ironically among them the crime of arson.[52] The Transportation Security Administration (TSA) can also attest to the issues of hiring glitches in bringing on unqualified applicants to protect our nation's airways in a post-9/11 world absent adequate hiring checks. Federal statistics from an audit revealed that in their rush to fill positions created by the 9/11 attack, TSA had hired 85 screeners who had felony convictions and another 503 who had failed to disclose an arrest or conviction.[53] Background inquiries that are substandard or inadequate are one thing. Agencies have also been called to question for hiring without any background check at all. In one such case, information later came to light of an applicant's potential misconduct in their previous law enforcement command position that included dishonesty, providing false information, insubordination, and improperly following department procedures. In this specific case, the city administrators were presented with a 1000-page investigative document detailing the allegations of misconduct from the previous agency that was not sought prehire since no investigation was even conducted.[54] Another incident of failure to properly screen led to one of the most high-profile cases in the country when a questionable appointment to the position of police executive led to a senior governmental cabinet nomination that ultimately resulted in embarrassment and scandal for all involved.[55] An analogous case involved the failure to check the background of a security officer who had a criminal record. Subsequent to his employment, he sexually assaulted a female tenant of the apartments he was assigned to protect, and the court found a proximate cause between the security company's failure to conduct a proper background investigation and the victim's subsequent assault.[56]

The good news is that recent estimates are that over 90% of all employers conduct background checks on prospective applicants.[57] Also on the positive side, from the agency level, aggressive hiring and training practices heighten the likelihood of capturing qualified candidates that in turn bring needed levels of trust and competence to the organization.[58] From the level of the applicant, a background investigation can reveal qualities such as honesty, ability to make good judgments, and suitability to fill the role of a police officer.[59] An intangible, yet esoteric value can be had through the rigor and thoroughness of the screening process which impresses upon the applicant that final acceptance into the organization is the highest honor that can be bestowed.[60]

On the negative side of the equation, pre-employment investigations often do not rise to high priority levels in many enforcement organizations. In point of fact, inadequate screening which includes incomplete background investigations has led to egregious acts such as drug-related police corruption.[61] The City of Philadelphia was the subject of a study on their pre-employment hiring processes. The study revealed that in a 6-month period, picked at random, 17 of the department's officers were arrested and charged with crimes that included homicide, rapes of underage girls, off-duty assault, and theft.[62]

A recent report concerning the pre-employment screening of air marshals revealed that since the 9/11 hiring drive, dozens of federal air marshals have been charged with committing crimes while hundreds more have been accused of varying levels of misconduct. Some of the crimes have involved drug smuggling, child sexual abuse and pornography, and murder for hire.[63] Government agencies that have very strict entry level requirements are also very vulnerable to mistakes being made in the screening process. For example, a foreign national took advantage of those glitches in the screening process by fraudulently gaining U.S. citizenship. As a naturalized citizen, she was subsequently hired for sensitive positions in the FBI and CIA. Able to defeat the rigorous screening processes, she gained access to vital government secrets and confidential information as a result of being hired. U.S. Attorney Stephen J. Murphy asserted that, "This case highlights the importance of conducting stringent and thorough background investigations."[64]

Terrorist organizations plan years in advance to use operatives planted in key sectors to do their bidding. The breakdowns at the local and state levels have also been observed in the federal hiring process; however, the risks are much higher as we progress through the hierarchy of the law enforcement field. While the argument can be made that these are, for all intents and purposes, isolated occurrences, a disturbing trend has emerged in the levels of investigation committed to the pre-employment screening process for law enforcement officers. According to a study by the U.S. Department of Justice Bureau of Justice Statistics, research has revealed the following percentages of police departments in the United States use the various stages and components in their pre-employment screening processes. Table 1.1 is a comparison of the differences in percentages from the year 2000 to 2003.

TABLE 1.1
Longitudinal Analysis of Differences in Pre-Employment Screening Steps by Percentage of Departments

Pre-Employment Screening Stage	2000[65]	2003[66]	Percent Change + or (–)
Criminal record	98	99	1
Background investigation	97	98	1
Driving record	97	96	(1)
Personal interview	96	98	2
Medical	94	85	(10)
Psychological evaluation	91	67	(26)
Drug test	89	73	(18)
Credit history check	78	55	(30)
Physical agility	77	50	(35)
Written aptitude	76	43	(43)
Polygraph	61	25	(59)
Personal inventory	53	26	(49)
Voice stress analyzer (VSA)	10	4	(60)
Volunteer/community service check	7	8	14
Second language ability test	4	1	(75)

In review, while departments have shown a slight increase in the numbers of criminal record checks and background investigations as a whole (an approximate 1% increase), there have been drastic decreases in other more crucial components. For the use of truth detection devices, there was a drop of 60% and 59% for the use of the voice stress analyzer (VSA) and polygraph, respectively. Several other key components have also been cut back substantially. Specifically, written aptitude tests which assess cognitive ability, a significant and proven predictor of success, fell by 43%. Other stages that have been historically and empirically proven to predict success in police officer candidates that have fallen off substantially are ranked in order such as physical agility exams (35%), credit history checks (30%), psychological evaluations (26%), drug testing (18%), and medical examinations (10%). In context, 75% do not use polygraph, 57% do not use written aptitude tests, and a full one-third does not use psychological evaluations! What possible explanation can be offered for such a deviance in operational policy on a national level? Especially when we cannot view the national media on a daily basis without being subjected to at least two or three incidents of officers across the country who have been implicated in some wrongdoing. Spates of increased hiring have been eclipsed by mass terminations wherein the so-called isolated incidents will be prophesized as being related to systemic issues in the hiring processes of the organization.[67] In contrast, private sector screening processes have steadily gained momentum due to threats of terrorism, employer liability, and workplace violence which are all ominous issues facing the selection of new employees.[68] How does this disconnect make any sense to public safety administrators?

One explanation may rest in the argument that despite the elaborate and thorough selection processes used to hire employees, those same methods really may not produce the desired results of identifying the best employees for the position.[69] For example, what testing process or background screening could have predicted an incident where two seasoned corrections officers would be involved in an on-duty fight over a bag of potato chips?[70] Can such arguments truly justify the scaling back of the only methods to establish the fitness of an applicant for the position of police officer? The pyramid of public safety, liability, and organizational integrity must be the driving force to maintain the highest levels of applicant screening for our organizations to continue to be successful in servicing the American public.

For public safety, the LAPD Rampart scandal[71] and the tragic case of Abner Louima[72] are but a few examples of the need to effectively and consistently screen-out unfit and criminal officers who will present a danger to the public they are sworn to protect. Many of the behaviors that have been found to precipitate misconduct and corruption in serving police officers, such as drug use and sales, sexual impropriety that escalates to criminal culpability, and aberrant/violent behavior, are all subjects of intense exploration during the pre-employment screening process. In relation to the background investigation, Early Warning Systems (EWS) (also referred to as Early Intervention Systems) have been implemented in law enforcement agencies in order to identify and determine patterns of complaints of performance, criminal behavior, poor judgment, and the like. These systems are intended to identify aberrant behavior in a serving police officers' career early on so that some type of intervention can be used to correct those behaviors before they become chronic and acute.[73] In a perfect world, these systems would be superfluous. In reality, they are necessary as a system of checks and balances to maintain the integrity of the entire system of monitoring officer behavior. In a continuous improvement environment, the EWS would be a feedback loop to the pre-employment process, funneling information on identified aberrant behavior patterns so that these characteristics could be more closely scrutinized in the background investigation of the applicants. For example, an agency that struggles with complaints of excessive force can build into the process closer scrutiny of applicants who may demonstrate those patterns of behavior that are possibly manifested in other forms like aggression, inappropriate control of emotions, temperament, and physical demonstration such as fighting. While this seems to be an overly simplistic concept, when do we ever do this in law enforcement? Often, we function in the business-as-usual mindset and do not endeavor to make these connections that will serve to better enhance our selection processes.

Civil and criminal liability is the next level in the hierarchy. For example, the City of Chicago endured a very painful investigation of homicide detectives who were accused of torturing homicide suspects to gain confessions.[74] Other major jurisdictions such as Miami; Washington, DC; the New York State Police; and Los Angeles County have all endured very public and very damaging scandals related to police corruption.[75] The New Orleans Police Department was also embroiled in a scandal that was related to their inadequate and negligent hiring standards. As a result, numerous officers were arrested for crimes including rape, homicide, and drug trafficking.[76] The Dallas Police Department, under new leadership, terminated over 30 officers for misconduct in a 2 year period.[77] Specifically linked to flaws in the selection process, the *Miami River Cops* scandal of the 1980s was directly related to relaxed screening mechanisms for police applicants under consent decrees and affirmative action policies.[78] The Philadelphia Police Department scandal was actually precipitated by a forced diversity mandate through a consent decree wherein officers were hired who were so unfit that they did not need to have the negative influences of policing to change their behaviors, opting to commit crimes at the outset of their employment.[79] The costs of these scandals are incalculable. In the Rampart scandal alone, a conservative estimated cost to the City of Los Angeles was $125,000,000.[80] The U.S. Border Patrol is also wrestling with numerous high-profile misconduct cases that some believe are related to the immense post-9/11 hiring buildup.[81] The *Violent Crime Control and Law Enforcement Act of 1994* pledged funds to add 100,000 new officers across the country.[82] Yet another example of a rush to hire that cannot be accurately evaluated in terms of the damage caused by bad hires. There is no method to accurately calculate the effects of such massive hiring processes and where flaws may have been experienced in the background investigation processes of the agencies that chose to increase their ranks. The pre-employment screening process is perhaps one of the only viable methods to help mitigate future problems of this nature.

Organizational integrity and image are the final level. When these issues are discovered, internal organizational dilemmas are faced by the rank and file. When they are made public, the problems are taken to an entirely new arena. With much of the contemporary thought in gearing the work in law enforcement toward voluntary transparency, often these types of incidents set the calendar back decades on many of the positive changes that have been implemented over time. Transparency is also a forced issue when background investigations frequently come to light in the wake of officer involved incidents.[83] Some jurisdictions have reacted by imposing "antinepotism" ordinances to preclude relatives from being hired even if they are fully qualified for the position in the agency.[84] Major jurisdictions have also been forced by federal consent decrees to curb political hiring practices.[85]

Further exacerbating the problem is a real-time, market-driven media. As a consequence, negative media attention to officer misconduct often results from the failures of an organization's hiring processes. A profound example of this can be found in the failure of a past New York City mayor to properly vet a police commissioner appointment with the ensuing scandals and revelations unfolding for close to a decade.[86] The media attention also drives public opinion, and the events of 9/11 were no different. Public opinion and approval of the police was elevated during this period. One comforting note is that a Gallup poll conducted in 1998 revealed that police officers ranked quite high on the scale of professionals with respect to the characteristics of honesty and integrity.[87] Image in the public also brings with it the public's opinions on the factors they see as important to the screening of law enforcement personnel. A recent study of air travelers revealed that two of the top three recommended requirements to serve as an air marshal that are included in screening were psychological testing and polygraph examinations.[88]

Alternative models of policing that challenge the paradigm of the traditional or professional policing model also are in need of consideration in the move to improve the image and integrity of the police function. For example, the onset of community policing has had significant influence on the discretionary powers of police officers.[89] This change in philosophy has taken the discipline away from policy-driven and strict command-and-control models to one of empowerment and autonomy. Other studies have shown the need to adjust hiring criteria that match the requirements of identifying officers that have the ability to develop community engagement and build trust through their actions.[90] With these constructs comes latitude of decision making and freedom not enjoyed in the professional model. The change also requires the selection of applicants who will be comfortable, adept, and far more resilient to the temptations of law enforcement than those hired in the past.

Due to a real-time mass media, in-service law enforcement officers are exposed to the daily reporting of officers somewhere in the country being suspended, arrested, indicted, and terminated for acts of misconduct and corruption. Despite this continual and patent reminder, many are still not deterred from engaging in the same or similar deplorable conduct and suffering the same consequences. For example, the tragic story of a K-9 officer who was convicted of felony animal cruelty for starving his own personal dog to death fills the press and enrages an online community to develop a social networking page to protest his actions.[91] We then question the thoroughness of the selection process for a K-9 officer who subsequently kills his own personal dog! This is truly a different time requiring a different response. This is certainly not a time for pusillanimous law enforcement administrators and background investigators to take the path of least resistance and hope for a different outcome, hence the true meaning of the definition of insanity!

When the question is posed, "Why do we do a background investigation?" the response should be "Why not?" If history teaches us anything, it is that we live in a circular environment and history will undoubtedly repeat itself. We cannot influence history or attempt to rewrite the past, as often happens when these situations rear their ugly heads! We can, however, take the necessary steps to change the future and avoid these mistakes, or at least vitiate the prospect of poor selection practices for our organizations, for the honest and dedicated officers that work beside us, and for the communities we are sworn to serve and protect. The simple reason we do background investigations may be eloquently summed up in the *California Government Code* that states the reason a background is completed on an applicant for the position of peace officer is to determine if the person is of "good moral character."[92] We can usually train for the rest of the requirements needed (see pages 11–14).

EXAMPLE OF A FAULTY PRE-EMPLOYMENT PROCESS[93]

Screening for Police is Called Lax in Phila.: The Department's Anticorruption Office Found "Minimal, if Any, Standards" for Hiring.

The applicant failed the entrance exam. Sometime later, he tried again and passed—barely. But he washed out when he twice failed lie-detector tests on questions related to drug use and sales.

Again, he took the exam and passed. Again he flunked the polygraph—three times.

Once again he passed the exam. And finally, on three more tries, he cleared the polygraph.

He can't spell simple words or write basic sentences. His credit rating is abysmal.

And he was appointed to the Philadelphia Police Department.

That's a case study from a scathing new report by the Police Department's anti-corruption office, which looked at police recruiting and hiring and drew a sobering conclusion:

You don't have to be the best or the brightest to join Philadelphia's police force.

In fact, the report says, you can be a chronic deadbeat, a near-illiterate, a high school screwup. You can have an awful job history, owe back child-support payments, and be the subject of protection-from-abuse orders.

You can be so ill-suited for police work that you commit crimes soon after joining the department.

"The core problem we are finding," said James B. Jordan, the department's integrity and accountability officer and the report's coauthor, "is we're hiring people who should not be allowed to carry a gun and wear a badge."

Jordan and his deputy, Ellen H. Ceisler, undertook the study as part of a wide-ranging review of police corruption and misconduct. Their office, created under a court settlement after the 39th Police District scandal, is charged with bringing deficiencies in the department to public attention and recommending change.

The 43-page report, scheduled for release today, concludes the department does a poor job of screening out potential bad apples at the earliest stages.

"Instead of high standards of selection and screening," Jordan said in an interview, "we're seeing dangerous evidence of minimal, if any, standards."

"It's a recipe for disaster." And he said the failings were responsible for the most startling of the report's statistical findings:

From May to November 1997, a 6-month period picked at random, 17 officers were arrested and charged with crimes that included homicide, rape (of a 16-year-old girl), statutory rape (of a 15-year-old girl), off-duty assault and theft.

Jordan said the alleged misdeeds represented "a crime wave of startling proportions" for a law-enforcement agency.

Jordan and Ceisler focused on the personnel records of all 322 Philadelphia officers fired between 1987 and 1997. They found a majority were relatively young and new to the force. Fifty-two percent were 25 or younger. Half had less than 6 years on the force.

How did such people become police officers in the first place?

After examining scores of personnel and performance records and interviewing nearly 200 members of the department, Jordan and Ceisler said they found abundant evidence of breakdowns in recruiting and hiring.

Among the problems, the report asserts:

1. A 1990 federal consent decree intended to bring more African Americans onto the force has put disproportionate emphasis on getting large numbers of blacks to apply for police positions, without regard to whether they have the qualifications to get hired.
   a. The result has been to flood the hiring process with ill-qualified candidates. This places an untenable load on the police investigative units that do background checks, with the result that many candidates of dubious quality—both black and white—slip through, the report says.
   b. Jordan said his point in criticizing the consent decree was not that the black officers hired are less capable than whites, but that recruiters and investigators are diverted from their true task of seeking out the best candidates because the hiring process has become a "numbers game."
   c. The 322 fired officers whose records were studied included 131 whites and 172 blacks. Jordan said this shows that "racially, corruption and misconduct are integrated."
2. By law, applicants must live in Philadelphia for a year before taking the entrance exam. This "substantially limits the department's recruitment efforts," the report states—especially in attracting qualified minorities."
   - The Police Department's five-person recruitment unit is isolated, unmotivated, unimaginative, inadequately funded and badly supervised.
   - Some officers in the Internal Investigation Unit, which conducts background checks, have little or no investigative experience.

In addition, the unit's polygraph equipment is antiquated, the testers are ill-trained, and candidates can learn to beat the machine by taking the polygraph several times, the report says.

Investigators don't examine school records. Before 1997, they didn't conduct credit and financial investigations. Now they do, but the results are given little weight, the report states.

Many criticisms in the report have been voiced before, but not in such detail. Similar findings were sounded in a report released last week by the nonpartisan Committee of Seventy.

They come at a time when Police Commissioner John F. Timoney, on the job 6 months, is attempting to dramatically improve recruiting, training and accountability. Timoney said he welcomed Jordan's report.

"There's nothing in it that I disagree with," he said.

Richard B. Costello, president of the Fraternal Order of Police, said the report missed the central issue: police pay, which was slashed for recruits by $6,000 during the city's fiscal crisis. Pay for recruits fell to $22,000 in 1992, Costello said. It has risen gradually to $28,500.

The department's Integrity and Accountability Office was created 2 years ago in the wake of the 39th District scandal, in which officers framed, robbed and beat suspects, and committed perjury to obtain convictions. Six officers went to federal prison, nearly 200 criminal convictions were overturned, and the city paid out almost $5 million in wrongful-arrest settlements.

A lawsuit by the NAACP, the American Civil Liberties Union and the Police-Barrio Relations Project led to a package of reforms, including the creation of the anti-corruption office, which has access to virtually all departmental records and personnel.

David Rudovsky, an ACLU lawyer long involved with criminal justice issues, praised the Jordan-Ceisler study as "an important report."

"It highlights a very critical problem that we've been concerned with for a very long time," Rudovsky said. "There's probably nothing more critical to the department's mission than to hire good recruits, and then, when they're on the force, to effectively evaluate them."

J. Whyatt Mondesire, head of the Philadelphia NAACP, said neither he nor the organization's lawyers had seen the report.

Some of the most vexing problems in recruiting and hiring for the department have arisen from the 1990 consent decree, a legacy of the W. Wilson Goode administration, when 22% of police officers were black in a city whose population was 39% black.

The decree stemmed from Freeman v. City of Philadelphia, a lawsuit brought by black officers that argued the police entrance exam was a poor predictor of police performance—and racially biased to boot. Evidence cited in the lawsuit showed whites were passing the test at four times the rate of blacks. And among those who passed, whites dominated the highest-scoring brackets, giving them first crack at job openings. Of the top 200 scorers in 1990 and 1991, 163 were white.

To settle the suit, the city agreed to develop an improved test. As a stopgap until that happened, the city would use the existing exam. But it would hire black police recruits in the same proportion as blacks who take the test, regardless of the scores.

Eight years later, that stopgap is still in effect.

Although the city has hired a consulting firm to develop a new exam, it is not finalized, said Linda Seyda, the city's personnel director.

Under the present formula, the more African Americans who take the test, the more must join the force. One result has been a lopsided emphasis on boosting the numbers of African Americans who take the exam, regardless of the individuals' fitness or desire for police work, Jordan said.

As an indication of how the recruitment unit sees its role, Jordan said, "the only recruiting is exclusively focused on minorities and women, so there's no recruitment of whites."

A common practice of the police recruitment unit is to send notices of forthcoming tests to people who have previously flunked, Jordan and Ceisler said. Predictably, mediocre prospects end up taking the exam over and over.

There is little effort to recruit at local college campuses or other sites where better-qualified candidates might be found.

Before the consent decree, police exams were given roughly every two years. Those who passed would be placed on a list, in descending order of test score. Police hires for the next couple of years would be plucked from the list, from the top down.

Under the current process, so many people fail the background-check stage that, typically, there are too few African Americans on the list to fulfill the hiring goal tied to the percentage who took the exam. That forces the city to conduct another exam; this time, though, only the African Americans in the testing room have a realistic shot at making the police force. At times, the city has had to give three tests to list enough African Americans eligible for hire.

Not surprisingly, white applicants commonly complain they must wait for long periods to be called for hire, despite scoring well on the exam.

Timoney said: "You go to these community meetings," and they say, "I've taken the exam, I'm on the list two or three lists ago, I haven't been called yet, and you're giving another exam."

"You've got people questioning this thing, and I mean, there's no way to kind of explain it. It's just a bad situation."

In the years of the consent decree, African American participation in the police force has risen. Blacks now make up 35% of the force.

The report proposes that a new, race-neutral entrance exam be quickly implemented. That would end the consent decree.

It also urges that the city relax its pre-employment residency requirement to allow recruiting at military bases, colleges and other law enforcement agencies.

The report joins with reformers who have urged that the entry age be raised from 19 to 21 or higher, the educational levels stiffened (a high school diploma is now all that's needed), and the scrutiny of candidates' backgrounds tightened.

Without steps like these, Jordan said, there will be more cases like that of Jorge Pedraza, who joined the police force in December 1996. Last September, he was walking by a convenience store in uniform when he was spotted by his former employer. The man was shocked.

According to Jordan's files, his former employer told police he had fired Pedraza for stealing.

Police took another look at Pedraza's background. In October, he was suspended with intent to dismiss.

THE MOST IMPORTANT INVESTIGATION

As a barometer, the background investigation must be considered as the most important investigation conducted by the public safety agency. Integral to the selection and deselection of potential law enforcement applicants, the process must adhere to the highest nondiscriminatory standards while accomplishing the goal of hiring the most qualified of the applicant pool.[94] One research study revealed a near 40% failure rate of applicants in the background investigation process alone excluding all other screening methods.[95] Even if we consider homicide, child abuse, and police corruption cases, the importance of the pre-employment investigation supersedes all of these very serious examples of heinous conduct. Thinking of the entire process, if we fail to properly screen applicants, a caustic chain reaction occurs. The chain of events includes an unfit or substandard applicant who is welcomed into the ranks of the organization, who now has the authority to deprive others of their civil liberties, responds and is charged with investigating to varying degrees, major crimes, to having the susceptibility to engage in serious crimes, and given the opportunity by virtue of employment and sworn authority acting under the color of law, to become a corrupt police officer. Given this example, the experts agree that with respect to the hiring of police officers, the background investigation has been characterized as the most important component of the entire selection process.[96]

Take, for example, the Christopher Commission's findings concerning the issues in the Los Angeles Police Department hiring process prior to 1991. The Commission findings revealed, among other things, that even though 40% of applicants were disqualified based upon the results of psychological testing and the background investigation, these components were still ineffective at predicting an applicant's predilections toward violent behavior. The Commission also specifically noted that the background investigation afforded minimal attention to the applicant's history of violence.[97] Despite these findings, the principle of *Occam's razor* holds true in that the diametrically opposed theories of the effectiveness and lack of effectiveness of the background investigation. In these competing theories, the simplest answer is the truest; the responsibility to conduct a thorough pre-employment investigation of the applicant is an unquestionable principle. The Commission supported this theory in their assertion that, "The background investigation offers the best hope of screening out violence-prone applicants."[98] Consequently, to reduce the levels of corruption in an organization, an aggressive and exhaustive background investigation must be conducted.[99]

From all of the supportive research that exists, we know that to be successful, organizations develop long-term human resource philosophies that are aligned with the goals of the organization.[100] Unfortunately, law enforcement has consistently failed to effectively use this model. The marginal successes in advancement can often be attributed to happenstance or divine intervention rather than by design and execution.

Some argue that the investment the organization makes in a police officer is not enough to prevent them from engaging in behaviors that result in misconduct.[101] This assumption, on the surface, would obviate the need for such investigations. For all intents and purposes, quite the opposite is true though. If the assumption is correct, then we are provided with one of the strongest arguments for having stringent pre-employment screening in order to prevent as many of those into the discipline who will acquiesce to such pressures and feelings. Methods to thwart these problems must include the integration of applicants to the highest values of police work and to reconnect applicants to the notion of law enforcement service as a calling rather than just a job. "Back in the day," kids dreamed of being a policeman or a fireman, and now these jobs just are not the attraction they once were to the young.[102] We also need to reawaken the nobility of policing in our society, and consequently, the by-product will be the rewards drawn from our future applicant pools.[103]

Another salient factor concerning resources is that in many agencies, the thoroughness of the investigation may depend on the available human, physical, and budgetary resources, as well as the immediate and often competing human resource demands of the organization.[104] And thinking in the long term, would this ever be an acceptable excuse for failing to conduct a thorough review to those who will have the authority to question the decision? Or worse yet, to those who have no authority to question our decisions but, by virtue of having the media on their side, are somehow miraculously empowered. Case law, the media, and public opinion all have historically not given such generous leeway. If faced with these situations, we are often forced to seek for forgiveness elsewhere.

Lastly, as we travel through the hierarchy, much like vicarious liability, if we are ever to be truly perceived as a profession, we cannot be influenced by the insidious onslaught of politics. The issue of political intervention has been responsible for many of the catastrophes experienced by cities that have been wracked by police scandals in places like New Orleans; Washington, DC; and Miami, Florida. As a profession, we have apparently never learned from as early as the days of Tammany Hall[105] to the aforementioned scandals that politics has no place in the hiring of police officers.[106] Those who hold offices at all levels of politics either are naïve or knowingly and intentionally choose to totally disregard the causal connection of the impact of their decisions and the breakdown of the law enforcement organizations they interfere with.[107] A classic example is the appointment of a police commissioner who displayed numerous warning signs of character flaws yet was still appointed by the sitting mayor despite admonishments from his senior cabinet members.[108] Some argue that because of political influence, the process is mismanaged and results in discriminatory practices that not only hire unacceptable and corrupt applicants but also worse yet work against the hiring of otherwise qualified applicants.[109] This problem is also compounded when managers are aware of flawed systems and practices that lead to hiring personnel of questionable character.[110] This also impacts political administrators who are later made aware of these system failures by the news media investigations rather than their own police administrators.[111] As evidenced by the countless examples we can find, and the immeasurable number of examples that we will never be made aware of, public safety administrators and politicians have taken an oft-recreant view to set aside their responsibilities to protect the public in lieu of the advancement of their political and personal agendas. In light of all of this, the strongest argument for the importance of the background investigation emerges from the thought that someone you are responsible for bringing onto the job will conceivably have the life of a colleague and friend, a family member, or maybe even your life, hanging in the balance.

THE BEST PREDICTOR OF BEHAVIOR

When we think of the power of prediction, we often conjure up images of infamous prognosticators like Nostradamus and Edgar Cayce. While we cannot definitively argue for or against the validity of premonition, absent real psychic ability, Tarot cards, mediums, divination, or the background investigator with planchette in hand spelling out "*BAD CANDIDATE*" on a Ouija board, we are caught in the trappings of the conventional methods to guide us in our decision-making processes for hiring. Even the various conventional and accepted predictors of behavior are often controversial. Each has its own strengths and weaknesses with respect to validity. Testing processes, in spite of eons of research and validation, are frequently flawed methods of accurate assessment. Flaws come from the initial construct designs as well the fact that they are vulnerable to compromise through cheating and political influence such as "racial gerrymandering" as one researcher has determined.[112] Often the true power of accurate prediction comes from tacit or experiential learning and a visceral sense that something is wrong or will go wrong. Prediction in the background process can also be an oxymoron when those who are not involved in the process and silent in the selection stages become a prophetic wellspring when they proudly claim shortly after the fact, "I knew he'd be a problem!" Hyperbole aside, the process and investigator must be concerned only with the legally valid and ethically acceptable methods of prediction.

For the purposes of this chapter, this discussion is limited to the predictive merits of background investigations. This topic will be treated in three other forms, cognitive and personality testing processes (Chapter 2), psychological battery testing processes (Chapter 4), and polygraph testing processes (Chapter 5). Suffice it to say at the outset that prediction should rely on multivariate analyses rather than a single aspect of the selection process schema.

In vocational settings, predictions are based on the "behavioral consistency principle – that the most reliable predictor of future behavior, such as job performance, is past behavior."[113] Valid predictions of occupational success emerge from the historical chronology of an applicant's past dealings. The primary purpose of the background investigation is to discover those dealings and compare them to the occupational requirements in order to make an informed decision on proper fit. Research has revealed that an applicant's educational acumen, disciplinary matters related to employment and military history, criminal arrests, and the recommendations of the background investigator all have strong correlations to an applicant's subsequent job performance.[114] In particular, higher education as a predictor of posthire behavior has a direct correlation to law enforcement officers who have lower reported rates of misconduct than their counterparts possessing only a secondary education.[115] With respect to the quality of an investigation, thorough background investigations often lead to the identification of applicants who have the tendencies to become corrupt officers after they are hired.[116] Therefore, the predictive value of future behaviors is often contingent upon the quality of the background investigation.[117]

In contrast, others argue that predictions at the time of selection may not be as accurate until after the candidate is hired and exposed to the rigors of an unsympathetic police environment. When the candidate enters the police service, they will be subjected to the stress and temptations of police work which may develop into corrupt behavior that may not have been detected in the background or even manifested in the applicant.[118] As evidenced by numerous examples used in the development of this text, even the highest quality and most deeply probing background investigation may result in a complete failure to predict critical personality deficits such as lack of integrity, substance abuse, pathological behavior, and the lack of control of violent behaviors. Racism is another difficult character flaw to discover. Consequently, racist attitudes have been a difficult issue to overcome even when so many advances have been enjoyed and yet we have isolated incidents that still lurk in the discipline.[119] Another example involves officers who have been indicted and convicted of murder as they certainly did not display this level of behavior prior to being hired—we would hope! But, in the absence of a crystal ball, the background investigation has time, and time again proven to be the best available and accepted predictor of the future behavior of a police applicant.

If we ascribe to the theory that our history may not always be the best predictor of our future, we must also accept that it does define who we were in our past endeavors. Those past behaviors stand as a testament to when we really decided we wanted to be a police officer. That may have been, when we were carrying a cap gun and wearing a plastic badge, or quite possibly the moment we were being connected to the sensors of the polygraph. In the interim, what we hope to discover during the background are positive characteristics and behaviors that have proven to be those demonstrated by successful police officers as well as those undesired performances and behaviors which, by the nature of their deviance, may require too much risk for us to trust a person with the protection of our communities and, quite possibly, our loved ones (see the following example).

Past behavior as a predictor of future behavior[120]

January 11, 2009

WARNING SIGNS: Falls Officer Ryan Warme was in Trouble Long Before he Became a Cop

By Rick Pfeiffer

A federal prosecutor has called him "the poster boy for detention."

An ever lengthening list of witnesses has appeared before a federal grand jury in Buffalo to detail their complaints against him.

Now, a Gazette investigation has revealed that suspended Niagara Falls Police Officer Ryan Warme was getting into trouble long before he became a cop.

Warme, 27, already faces charges on a federal criminal complaint that include cocaine trafficking, violating the civil rights of two women and using his police-issued firearm while committing those crimes. Prosecutors have hinted that when the grand jury finishes its work, the list of felony charges will be even longer.

While the three and a half year veteran of the Falls police force had admitted to having sex with at least two women while he was on duty, he has pleaded not guilty to the charges he currently faces and is being held without bail by the U.S. Marshals.

Warme's arrest by his fellow officers and federal agents on December 2 was not the first time he'd felt handcuffs on his wrists. In the fall of 2000, while he was attending Western New England College and playing on the school's football team, Warme was arrested on an assault charge.

Law enforcement sources tell the Gazette the charge stemmed from a fight following a football game. Warme was suspended from the team for four games and was given an adjournment in contemplation of dismissal on the assault charge.

That disposition meant that if Warme "stayed out of trouble," the charge would be dismissed and removed as a criminal record.

When Falls police detectives investigated Warme's background prior to his appointment to the Niagara County Law Enforcement Academy in August 2005, they were aware of the arrest but did not disqualify him for it.

"He was given an ACD, if you translate the charge to New York state law, (it's relatively minor)," Falls police Superintendent John Chella said. "At that time, it didn't alert us to the point where he was disqualified."

Chella also said Warme's father's former position as a captain and chief of detectives in the Falls Police Department played no role in the determination not to disqualify his son from a police appointment.

"We would have handled it the same way for any candidate at that point," Chella said. "We did with him what we've done with others."

The Gazette investigation has also shown that a post football game fight wasn't the only trouble Warme got into during his college days. During the course of a federal court hearing, prosecutors revealed that Warme had been expelled from his college ROTC program "for cheating on an exam."

Federal investigators learned of the ROTC incident from U.S. Air Force criminal investigators who had handled a probe into Warme's application to attend Officer Candidate School while he was a member of the Air Force Reserves. On his application for the officer's school, Warme "checked the (no) box that asked if he had ever been rejected for military service for any reason."

"The Air Force determined he had lied," Assistant U.S. Attorney Anthony Bruce said in court. "That is a flat out lie."

Yet that lie was never uncovered by Falls police during Warme's background investigation.

"There was no evidence of the ROTC issue in his (police) application," Chella said. "We only verified that he had 60 hours of college credit to come on the job."

Warme's father, testifying in federal court, admitted that his son had been kicked out of ROTC "for violating the honor code." However, he said his son never told him he had cheated on an exam.

Warme had another run-in with the law, roughly a year before his appointment to the Falls police force.

"We have had contact with [Warme] in the past," Cheektowaga Police Captain John Glascott told the Gazette. "It was in early August 2004 and it had to do with a domestic situation."

Glascott declined to comment any further on Warme's case. Other law enforcement sources indicted that Warme was arrested, though the exact charges were not known.

Like the college assault charge, the Cheektowaga incident apparently resulted in another adjournment in contemplation of dismissal and the case was ultimately sealed. It's unclear if Falls police were aware of the Cheektowaga incident before Warme's appointment to the force.

Chella said Warme passed both a psychological evaluation and a polygraph test prior to joining the force.

"We put a lot of weight in those," he said. "He passed the psych evaluation and he was given a lie detector test to determine if everything on his application was truthful and he passed that."

Federal prosecutors have suggested that Warme is proficient at lying. Even after his arrest, they say he lied to federal probation officers about why he left the Air Force Reserve in the spring of 2008.

Warme told federal pre-trial services investigators he left the reserves "based on the fact he could make more money working part-time jobs." However, Warme's resignation letter indicts that he left the military prior to the start of discharge proceedings against him.

The discharge proceedings followed an incident at a Texas Air Force base where Warme had reported for training in December 2007. Warme was scheduled to be in training until May or June 2008, but in April went AWOL for a period of roughly seven hours.

According to sources with knowledge of the incident, Warme was scheduled to report for drills at 8 a.m., but failed to show up at the base until 3 p.m. Warme told a superior officer that he had "been out drinking the night before, passed out and missed the drill."

He also told the officer that he "had been afraid to report after waking up, because he knew he would be in trouble."

By the time of the military incident, Falls police had already begun their investigation into Warme.

There was still another warning sign, prior to Warme's working on the street, that the young officer might not be qualified. While Warme was attending the police academy, he was the subject of a criminal complaint filed with Amherst police.

In a November 2005 incident in the parking lot of the Marriott hotel, Warme was accused of stealing a woman's cell phone after a domestic dispute. Chella said Falls police became aware of the incident but had trouble investigating it because the victim was uncooperative.

"She didn't want to get (Warme) in trouble," Chella said. "She said she was mad, but didn't want to get him kicked out of the academy."

STUDYING APPLICANT ATTRITION RATES

The private sector effort to hire talented employees does not come without a very high price. Worse yet, their approaches to replenishing the talent supply chain are relatively unsophisticated and often of minimal value.[121] One disturbing trend in private sector job screening deals with prospective employers who fail to consider applicants who are not currently employed.[122] Mistakes and barriers abound to the selection process.

Applicant attrition rates for law enforcement personnel have always been high. Some departments report an attrition rate as high as 96% of the applicants who have sought employment.[123] Attrition occurs as a result of many factors both within and outside of the organization's control: the quality of the applicants; length of the application process; rigor of the application stages of processing; better job offers from the military, government security, and the private sector;[124] and loss of interest once an applicant begins to realize the requirements of the position are not like what they see on TV (working 1 hour a week and always making a great arrest in that exciting hour long drama!). Statistics reveal that approximately 5%–10% of all applicants ever get the chance to raise their right hand to be sworn in. To put applicant attrition rates into perspective, one study presented a categorical analysis of applicant attrition rates from the applicant pool's processing during the background investigation. This analysis excludes candidates who were removed from the process for failing medical examinations, did not meet minimum qualifications, or voluntarily withdrew from consideration. These figures represent the trends identified in the larger candidate population:

1. Over 88% had violated an average of five or more laws, rules, and regulations.
2. Over 68% had been untruthful on an average of four or more occasions regarding a material fact of their background history.
3. Over 47% had a poor financial history averaging four or more delinquent accounts.
4. Over 39% had poor employment histories amounting to two or more poor employment references.
5. Over 36% had on average two or more at-fault motor vehicle accidents.
6. Over 9% had violated the drug policy.
7. Over 8% had been involved in a domestic violence offense averaging two or more incidents.
8. Over 3% had issues of inappropriate control of emotions on five or more occasions.
9. Over 76% of all applicants had violated three or more categorical civil service hiring standards.[125]

Grim figures in our continued trek to locate and acquire human capital to replenish the ranks. These figures underscore the depth and breadth of issues candidates bring to the table. In this group, only 12% of the applicants that were decertified had a clean criminal and driving record. In the analysis of integrity, only 32% of these applicants were truthful in the process. What is far more disconcerting is that those who were caught lying, on average, had lied on four or more occasions pertaining to material facts in their processing documents or in their utterances during interviews. This analysis proved consistent with previous research that revealed an average of 65% of police applicants are untruthful in the screening process.[126] This factor is crucial to the investigative process as often it is the candidate who is the source of the disclosures necessary to determine fitness for duty. The lack of candor unduly impedes the investigation and forces the commitment of precious and limited resources toward needless investigative follow-up had the candidate just been honest. Also dispelling a popular assertion by applicants that they are excluded from the process for some minor issue, the analysis revealed that over 76% of all applicants had violated *three or more* categorical civil service hiring standards. And there are those who say that we are the problem!

This analysis may also prove to be of very high value in the selection process in the development of a typology of applicant attrition. These figures give perspective and focus to the pathology present in the applicant pools—not only in how they have deviated from societal norms to the point of application but also, more importantly, the steps they will take to conceal their inappropriate and often criminal conduct.

These issues are reflective of a society that refuses to accept boundaries and, more importantly, any semblance of responsibility for personal actions. A viable study in social control theory, the concept of controlling, restraining, or directing human behavior by way of legal sanctions,[127] could be had in these candidate pools as the irony is that they are applying to be the arbiters of the rules of law and justice they have so frequently disregarded. Had these applicants slipped through the cracks, the cumulative amount of damage they could have caused in the way of liability, lost community trust, substandard performance issues, and organizational strife are truly inestimable.

As an aside, like many who have said it was a curse to win the lottery and have subsequently squandered and lost it all, those who finally enter police service and feel the sense of winning their lifelong dream feel after a short period of time that it was a curse to become an officer in the first place. Sadly, if we do not screen as many of these individuals as possible, we will own them for a very long time.

RELATIONSHIP BETWEEN RECRUITING AND SELECTION

The transitive connections of recruitment, background investigation, and selection are irrefutable. For recruitment to be effective, it must also share a transitive relationship with high-quality training and congruently shaped performance standards.[128] A parallel goal of selection is finding applicants who have the capacity to be trained to meet the needs of the position.[129] Major organizations throughout the globe use an integration of recruiting, pre-employment screening, and human resource processes to select the best applicants for the position—a form of talent management.[130] Attrition statistics from one major department reveal that on average, 10% of those candidates who are hired fail to graduate from the basic academy and an additional 10% fail to successfully complete the field training program.[131]

The executive team in the organization becomes a critical component in light of this information. Senior executives must select recruitment directors and supervisors who have a process management background to lead their talent acquisition efforts.[132] This cohesive recruiting effort is necessary for the organization to set in motion long-term plans to meet the organization's human resource needs.[133] Other goals of recruiting in law enforcement should identify applicants who have a common bond with the community and people they will eventually serve.[134] Ethical arguments also reveal support for the theory that recruiting those of high moral character will eliminate corruption in law enforcement organizations.[135] The only method of addressing a systemic problem is by using systemic approaches to solutions.

Recruiting qualified applicants in law enforcement is particularly problematic, especially in times of department buildups. As a result of the riots of the 1960s, departments across the country increased in size to handle the pervasive civil unrest. The late 1980s experienced a cyclical bailout during good economic times when officers were able to find alternative employment after retiring. The *Omnibus Crime Control Bill of 1994* filtered $5.3 billion for the hiring of additional police personnel with a goal of adding 100,000 more police officers in addition to those lost through attrition.[136] Many organizations have experienced steady and significant declines in applicants over the years as well.[137] Sadly, these issues were brought to the attention of police administrators across the country during the 1980s and 1990s, much to no avail though as there always seems to be something else in the works that is of a higher priority.[138]

This problem does not affect only one segment of the discipline as small and large agencies struggle with the specter of attracting qualified applicants to the role.[139] Minority recruitment has also been impacted severely despite decades of work to build the diversity levels in police organizations.[140] Female recruitment is also suffering similar issues wherein not only the number but also the quality of applicants is a barrier to replacement.[141] This problem is not unique to the criminal justice professions as the military has also come under the microscope for their perceived stifled efforts at increasing the gender and racial diversity in the ranks to reflect equitable levels of these protected populations in the United States.[142] Other assumptions are the deterrent effects of the negative portrayals of police by the popular media.[143] A seemingly eternal issue exists both in hiring and maintaining capable personnel at every level of law enforcement.[144] Departments have reported as high as 75% less applicants applying for law enforcement positions.[145] Declines in those interested in promotional advancement are also straining organizations in developing succession plans that guarantee solid and competent command structures to take these organizations into the future.[146] In agencies where there is an interest to rise in the ranks, promotions are delayed as departments do not have sufficient applicant pools to backfill the openings that will be created.[147] From all of the classical and contemporary research, the only conclusion that can be drawn at this point is that the problem will continue long after we have all retired from the field. This does not mean we should give up trying to make a difference in our organizations.

The quality and interest of the applicant pool are only part of the dilemma. Recruiters often focus on the size rather than the quality of the applicant pool, touting successes by showing the raw numbers of those who apply rather than the numbers that are qualified for certification and able to be considered for hire. Department leadership is also an issue following a model of reactive management wherein law enforcement managers count numbers rather than proactive management where they examine the quality of the applicant pool during the recruitment process.[148] Another problem recruiters face is that their work to harness as many prospective applicants as possible may produce larger applicant pools, but their ability to recognize the qualified persons is extremely dismal.[149] Rapid recruitment drives top the list of problems when the fast hiring of applicants has led to widespread drug-related police corruption.[150] This exemplifies the issues active recruiters face who work for police organizations. We also need to consider ineffective and unmotivated recruiting practices. For example, one research study in California revealed that only one in eight applicants was positively influenced by a department recruiter.[151] We struggle to find the proper balance in all of these issues and competing interests.

Simply stated, the symbiotic relationship between recruitment and retention must be a priority for the law enforcement agency.[152] For profit entities have acknowledged the connection between delivering value that attracts and retains customers, however, that only occurs when we create the value chain starting with capturing high-quality talent in our human resource ranks.[153] In law enforcement, our credo should be to develop and hold the line to the highest recruiting standards in order to prevent officer misconduct that leads to widespread scandals.[154] We need to realign the diametrically opposed concepts of recruiting for numbers with the concept and practice of hiring for quality! We need to reengineer the process and think differently in order to solve this problem. In the preceding discussion concerning the study of applicant attrition rates, the issues of why candidates fail were painfully clear from a theoretical and categorical analysis. To turn this situation around, maybe we should develop an ideology that examines applicant retention rates. Instead of the provincial mindset of why applicants fail, our efforts should be directed at learning why applicants are successful and target recruiting efforts toward those qualities and characteristics in those we recruit in order to increase the prospect of attracting the most qualified applicants to our profession.

SOCIAL AND GENERATIONAL INFLUENCES OF LAW ENFORCEMENT ORGANIZATIONS

Police work by its very nature is a social activity. Studies of the police culture and subculture have portrayed police groups as highly closed environments open only to those who are *on the job*. Arguments have existed both for and against the notion of the police subculture throughout the history of police research.[155] Theorists believe that a culture of corruption in law enforcement agencies emerges from varied factors, including primary attribution to the failure of recruitment processes.[156] The New Orleans Police Department wracked with scandals and, under federal investigation, has attributed much of this aberrant behavior to the enduring culture of the organization.[157] While there is some validity to this assumption, it is most likely a product of previously observed social norms. The precedent that was set may not be the self-fulfilling prophecy after all though. One observation that supports this is that the heady days of choir practices have waned significantly in lieu of officers finding different priorities such as family and other diversionary endeavors to provide balance to their lives. The paradox is that we still want officers completely dedicated to police work, but *not too dedicated* that they return to the embarrassing behaviors of days past. Police departments are still highly social organizations, but from an organizational underpinning, that often have limited extensions into the private lives of the cop on the beat.

Cultural theory is a structured concept that explains how society interprets threat levels and the resultant levels of trust afforded to an organization that regulates risk.[158] In the application of cultural theory to law enforcement, the community and the officers are both affected by this relationship. From the officer's perspective, you will find extremely low levels of social trust in their organization and often no trust in the organizational command structure. No confidence votes by the line of their chiefs are becoming far more common and publicized. This phenomenon is also passed from generation to generation further perpetuating the problem.

The resilience of the police culture has always been an amazing phenomenon. Organizational development managers and organizational psychologists will estimate that it takes upwards of 7–10 years to turn an organization around. With the cyclical nature of policing being about 20–25 years, many organizations that date back to the early nineteenth century have turned over dozens of times have yet to substantively demonstrate a metamorphosis of any sort. A theory of this phenomenon occurs through occupational socialization or police socialization wherein the new officer enculturation is based on the social values, skills, and behaviors of those already serving in the ranks.[159] The police culture endures because the indoctrination is powerful enough to overcome most levels of resistance. However, even with this lasting legacy, there is a noticeable difference in the characteristics of the law enforcement officers of the past and those who serve today. Despite the enduring cultural demands, officer attitudes and behaviors have changed as they will transform into police officers, but they will only be police officers for 8 hours a day, not the 24/7 mindset of old. Those differences may be metaphorically characterized as the difference between *policeman* and *policeman light!*

Interestingly, one study in a large municipal police department in New York State revealed an inverse relationship on motivation between traditional policing or the professional model and community-based policing. Analysis of the officer responses concerning preferences of policing models and motivation revealed that the motivation levels to engage in community policing activities actually increased over time.[160] This is in direct contrast to traditional or professional policing models wherein new officers begin their careers highly motivated and then scale back their proactive and reactive activities over time. This speaks to the potential of transformational leadership models that espouse alternative methods of policing that have multiple benefits for the internal as well as external stakeholders of the law enforcement organization.

The relevance of this discussion emerges from the sometimes unrealistic expectations of old guard administrators and old school background investigators that have assimilated the historical dedication to the nobility of policing and have the same or even higher expectations of those being courted for the ranks. The disconnect may be such a chasm that we refuse to look beyond the leading edge of the applicant into exploring where their true potential lies. In contrast, applicants who may be already attuned to such high levels of dedication prior to hire may also turn out to be very problematic employees the moment we give them a gun and a badge.

The generational issues have been bantered about for a few decades or so in the law enforcement field. As a point of fact, the issues of generation X were ignored for so long that when they finally came to the attention of those in the field, this group was already penetrating the supervisory and management ranks. The irony is they were often complaining about employees born in this generation, hence complaining about themselves. Constructively, there are four generations serving in law enforcement: veterans (born before 1946), baby boomers (born between 1946 and 1964), generation X (born between 1965 and 1980), and generation Y or the millennials (born after 1980). Age or generational cohorts are distinguished by a common foundation of historical or socially structured life experiences.[161] The research is often conflicting. Some researchers characterize the younger generations in very positive terms such as being highly motivated, often well educated, and a desire to develop marketable job skills for career advancement.[162] Others present starkly different interpretations. For example, some trends in applicant pools are disturbing at best when departments are faced with groups that have disciplinary problems, literacy issues, do not accept the incongruent nature of police work, and often focusing on self-serving and materialistic interests.[163] Sparsely published literature paints a picture of hope for the younger generation; however, these opinions seem to be mostly of conjecture as at the time of this writing, they really have not had enough time to prove themselves yet. What we do know is that less and less people are drawn to the police service, and compounding that problem is that even fewer of those are willing to pursue positions of higher responsibility in competing for and attaining supervisory and command ranks.[164]

The fact of the matter is that this disconnect of generations has existed, in a recorded fashion, since the days of Babylon, some 1000 years before the Common Era. Socrates (470–399 BC) complained of the youth of the day being unmotivated, recalcitrant, and lacking proper respect for their elders. A more contemporary example occurred during the 1950s when veterans complained of the same issues with the youth of the 1950s, perhaps the greatest time our country has ever experienced. Were the 1960s, 1970s, and the arrival of the third millennium any different? Is this a product of a temporal birth period or a natural phenomenon that has withstood the historical test of time? I think the latter theory is the answer to this seemingly timeless and yet unanswered question.[165]

While there are differences between the generations, the linkage to the law enforcement environment is crucial to understand at this point. At the onset of this discussion, several points were made concerning the influence of the social networks and organizational or occupational psychology issues of those who enter the law enforcement field. The "cop mentality" seems to prevail in spite of the purported differences in the generations. A research study of over 500 law enforcement, corrections, and community corrections officers has revealed some trends that are consistent and inconsistent with the contemporary thought on the behavior patterns of these unique groups:

1. In general, some behavioral patterns in law enforcement are consistent with those identified as being primary motivators in the private sector. For example, (1) veterans were motivated by job satisfaction, (2) baby boomers were motivated by job security and benefits, and (3) generation X and generation Y were motivated by pay.
2. Other behavioral patterns emerged that are anomalies and therefore inconsistent with the general population such as generation Y is primarily motivated by job security and also by job satisfaction (service and community).
3. Other behavioral patterns also emerged that were consistent with the classical and contemporary research on behavioral theory, however, inconsistent with the anecdotal and empirical evidence related to specific generational behavior patterns. For example, with the variable of ascending rank, behaviors and motivations significantly shifted for all generations from salary, job security, and benefits, in the ranks of officer, investigator, and sergeant, to such self-actualizing behavioral patterns like autonomy, opportunities for substantive input into the organization's policy and operational decisions, and job satisfaction (both pride and excitement as well as service and community) in the ranks of mid-level manager through chief executive officer.[166]

This research buttresses more a theory of normalization of the generations in the law enforcement ranks which is one of balance in the environment rather than an overriding theory of developing a strict *cop mentality*. It also speaks to the misnomer of individualism and cohort mores and behaviors being the controlling or dominant factor of how the different generations respond to the varied stimuli of the profession. At the end of the day, we must still recognize the value of those social networks as well as the diversity that exists in our law enforcement organizations and work to increase the capacity of others through these very important constructs.

Finally, policies for recruitment, selection, training, and socialization do not guarantee alignment of the expectations of the candidate.[167] They are merely implements of the process to use best practices methods to identify the best candidates for the positions to be filled. There is also a parallel responsibility of the selection process to manage the social and generational expectations of the incoming guard so they are aware of the road ahead. A concurrent legal test is taking place in the courts concerning applicant expectations that are consistent with the reality of the position hired for based upon the communications of the employer. Truth-in-hiring litigation is being filed in both state and federal courts where employees are claiming fraud, fraudulent inducement, misrepresentation, negligent hiring, and failure to disclose pertinent facts and information relative to the position to be held.[168] This will likely be a continuing area of debate in the social, organizational, and legal realms.

BACKGROUND INVESTIGATIONS AS A RISK MANAGEMENT TOOL

The history of risk management dates back to the evolution of new risks that emerged in a post-WWII society. The concept was introduced into the business world during the 1960s as a methodology of managing these types of risks to minimize financial exposure and maximize business continuity when severe incidents occurred.[169] The process of organizational risk management allows an organization to assess potential risks of financial loss and prepare to manage these types of risks if encountered.[170] Risk management has a darker side though when minimizing exposure equates to more an examination of the bottom line as opposed to the ethical and moral issues that underscore the events that have transpired, such as in the case of the Ford Pinto scandal and the LAPD Rampart scandal where settling claims after the fact was thought to be more cost efficient than resolving the original problems.[171] Law enforcement is no stranger to the concept of risk, in both its execution of services as well as the consequences of those actions. From the execution of services, officers are exposed to the dangers of police work in maintaining public order and arresting violent offenders which are the physical risks of the occupation. In relation to this, the police officers of this country wield the powers entrusted to them from the federal and state constitutions to legitimately deprive persons of their civil liberties. That level of power also has attached to it a very high level of discretion. Valid arguments are often posed concerning both power and discretion as being on opposite ends of a scale that requires an equitable balance to ensure the public safety needs of those who are policed are met.[172] The landmark cases of *Tennessee v. Garner* (1985) and *Graham v. Connor* (1989) are examples of the court's intervention in regulating the behaviors of the police.[173] In order to balance this level of risk, we must ensure that we have officers who have the proper behavioral patterns to fill these decisive roles in the criminal justice system. Risk management concepts focus on many areas of exposure, including the potential liability of the wrongful acts of an organization's employees and management.[174] Self-insured agencies enjoy some latitude in the issue of liability coverage, while agencies and municipalities that must use private insurance carriers run the risk of losing their coverage if they knowingly allow an employee to engage in potentially litigious acts.[175] In order to reduce the potential liability of an agency, police managers must use an array of sanctioned selection techniques in the hiring of new employees.[176]

Consequently, to minimize the potential for risk, the applicant's entire history must come under microscopic examination for the hiring authority to determine if the applicant will have the potential to fill these decisive roles.[177] Minimizing risk includes the adequate exploration of an applicant's history and background as well as the use of layered psychological screening procedures prior to hire.[178] The difference between minimizing risk and managing risk is delineated by the timelines of the stages of prehire and posthire, respectively. The quality and depth of our selection processes minimize our exposure to risk when we reject candidates who are unfit while management of risk occurs after we hire a candidate who reveals themselves to be unfit and the actions we take to control any damage. To minimize risks, departments will use multiple screening techniques in order to develop the best profile of the applicant possible given the nature, depth, and breadth of the process. Risk management is also the posthire process of training standards, field performance measurements, probationary periods, and disciplinary processes. Many managers, however, believe the cost is too high to conduct a proper background investigation.[179] History has taught us that we cannot arrest our way out of the drug and violence problems facing this country. What makes us believe we can discipline our way out of police misconduct and corruption problem? Those who are charged with managing the selection processes must give great consideration to the fact that the costs associated with a negligent hiring or retention claim will far outweigh the costs incurred from simply screening unfit applicants at the outset.[180] Risk managers must think and act in these terms. We will never be able to wholly avoid the onus of risk in the hiring process; however, we can take steps to minimize the risk involved in the decisions that we make.

SECURING THE FUTURE OF THE ORGANIZATION

Policing is as much about tradition as it is about transformation. While we espouse models of policing that fight crime, engage the community, and keep pace with the technological advancements that improve policing methods and operations, we also reflect on the venerable history of the profession. This history is our anchor in this veritable sea of opportunities. While this anchor provides stability and keeps us from going adrift, we can also lift anchor and move further toward our destination when we choose. Even as our free society has evolved, the fundamental concepts of policing have been quite stable. Since the days of Sir Robert Peel, we still work to protect the public, prevent crime, maintain public order, and marshal those who would bring harm to others. The way we underscore the importance of these concepts is by holding them as value systems that withstand the test of time.

How we can secure the future of our organizations is by ensuring those who come after us will have those same values. A return to the core values of policing is an essential component of the ability to maintain who we are as a discipline and why we joined the service. The Auburn, Georgia Police Department very adeptly places its value statement at the beginning of their application package in order to begin inculcating prospective employees in the fundamental and yet requisite organizational values that are required of every department employee:

1. *Honesty and integrity*: All department employees should be honest and ethical, on duty as well as off duty. Always!
2. *Have regular and prompt attendance*: You cannot be productive and fulfill our purpose and our commitment to the public if you are not there. Those people that are here are the only ones that are contributing and adding value to our community.
3. *Positive attitude*: Your attitude and demeanor are infectious. When it is positive, both you and the department can accomplish great things. That is our standard and our expectation. If you have a problem, let us get it addressed through the proper channels quickly. Negativism is nonproductive and harmful. It is inconsistent with our mission.
4. *Be courteous and helpful to the public*: Not one of us should ever forget that our customers and citizens provide us our jobs. They deserve excellent service and to be treated with respect.
5. *Be productive*: Use all your abilities, every day, to accomplish our mission. Our work is too important, and our standards too high to spend our time doing anything other than our best. Expect excellence from yourself.
6. *Respect yourself and each other*: The department will not allow bias with regard to race, gender, religion, or cultural diversity. Jokes and language that are ethnic oriented, vulgar, or of an offensive nature, even without a complaint from the public or a coworker, offend the department and are not appropriate and will not be tolerated.
7. *Be safe*: Most of us work with tools of the trade and drive vehicles under conditions that expose us and the public to safety hazards. Accidents hurt everyone. Be careful and use safety equipment.
8. *Work smart*: Be responsible for your own performance and set high standards for yourself. Be creative. If some rule or process is in the way, bring it to the attention of those that can change it. Always try to do the right thing.
9. *Be accountable*: Make yourself responsible for your own performance. Do not make excuses or blame others when problems arise. Take it upon yourself to solve problems.
10. *Be committed*: We all spend a significant part of our lives at work. Let us make it count for something. Let us all make a difference.[181]

Succession planning is about selection processes, continuous professional development, and instilling an organizational culture of service and integrity that survives the test of time. As the monitors of the social contract, we must ensure that the people we put in place to be the watchmen do not need to be watched! Since integrity and character are not concepts that can be taught to any degree of certainty, our screening processes must be effective to remove those who have questionable character from the process as early as possible.[182] Once hired, we find that an officer's value system is significantly influenced by the occupational culture.[183] During the screening process, we must identify the correct people who fit into the positive aspects of the culture.[184] We must also screen out those who do not fit into the specific organizational culture of the agency or department as well as those who we can predict will succumb to the more pernicious drivers of the culture. As a job hazard, our law enforcement officers are presented with an abundance of opportunities to engage in corruption.[185] Hiring applicants who have patterns of aberrant behaviors only ensures that our organizations will have future problems.

Therefore, a fundamental shift in organizational philosophy must occur where we change our search parameters from finding applicants who demonstrate the minimum required skills and knowledge to applicants who have the congruent behavior, ability, and skills necessary to fit the long-term needs of the organization.[186] This requires a significant investment of human resources and budgetary capital in finding an organization's human capital needs.[187] This also requires every member of the organization to become actively involved in the selection process and take ownership of those others who will be the future of the organization. The applicants that we hire will not only be the next generation's hope but will also shape the future of the organization with their values and beliefs.[188] When we examine our history in policing and the documented cases of catastrophes that have occurred because of poor hiring decisions, we can clearly see that the future has the same potential if we do not raise the standard and keep it there.

CONCLUSION

This chapter has examined the foundational issues and objectives of why a law enforcement agency must exercise due care in recruiting, investigating, and processing applicants to their organizations. Investigative importance is highlighted using numerous examples of where the process went bad for many agencies, emphasizing the procedural, political, legal, and ethical issues of applicant screening. Ethical professionalism as a background investigator is an inextricable component of the background investigation process.[189] Several other areas were discussed including applicant attrition rates, the need for connecting recruiting to the background investigation process, and the social and generational influences of law enforcement organizations on those we hire. This chapter closes with a discussion on how background investigations are used as a risk management tool to minimize a department's exposure to liability and with the use of the background investigation as part of an organization's overall succession planning process.

DISCUSSION QUESTIONS AND EXERCISES

1. Discuss in detail how your department's objectives for the hiring process link to the organization's strategic planning process.
2. Review your department's history and discuss the issues that have arisen from hiring any poor quality candidates. Do not use names, but discuss what could have been done to remove the applicant from the process before they were hired.
3. Have components or a combination of components of the screening process accurately predicted applicant successes or failures in your organization? Review these issues and develop recommendations for change.
4. Would proper background investigation be an effective risk management tool in your organization? Examine the risk management program or process your agency uses and determine if the pre-employment investigation process is considered part of the formula used for managing risk.
5. Looking at your organization's projections for future attrition, how important is the background process for securing your organization's future?

2 Pre-Employment Screening Process

LEARNING OBJECTIVES

- To develop an understanding of how the entire process impacts the pre-employment investigation
- To develop an understanding of the linkages between the foundational development of job task analyses and how the results will impact every component of the pre-employment selection stages to and including evaluation in continuous employment
- To promote an awareness of the need for collaborative and not competitive efforts of all support services to meet one goal, the hiring of the best qualified candidates
- To develop an understanding of all of the roles and support services to the process of pre-employment selection of public safety officers

KEY TERMS AND CONCEPTS

- Job task analysis, criterion, and standards
- Testing and screening processes
- The conditional offer of employment
- Roles of the principal contributors to the pre-employment selection process
- Organizational and process components

INTRODUCTION

The pre-employment screening process has numerous components in the public safety realm. Beyond entry level cognitive testing, applicants may also have a physical agility test, medical examination, polygraph examination, drug testing, psychological examination, personality testing, various levels of interviews, and a background investigation. A public safety agency can have varying levels of components and penetration into an applicant's past in their investigative process as well.[1] The courts have supported this depth and breadth of analysis of a law enforcement applicant's history as found in the decision of *Fraternal Order of Police v. Freeman* (1978) wherein the exploration and evaluation of an applicant's financial history, results of polygraph testing, and psychological screening were all found acceptable areas to question and the inquiry resisted legal challenge.[2] The goal of the process is to either screen in or screen out the applicant based upon their qualifications and fit for the position.[3] Research has revealed that the average screening time for small agencies is over 6 weeks while the average for large agencies is over 11 weeks.[4] Agencies that have fallen behind in revamping their hiring processes can take upwards of 6 months to process an applicant.[5] This delay in processing can significantly limit the applicant pool as one department study revealed that approximately 25% of applicants withdrew their candidacy from the hiring process because of the delays in processing.[6] Usually progression of the process begins with the lowest cost components for screening, for example, the written exams are upfront, while the most expensive components of professional evaluations and the background investigation scheduled later for those who survive the initial screening process.

No matter the variation of process though, the administrator or person who is the hiring authority must have consistently valid selection criteria that they use as the guide for making their organization's hiring decisions. For example, the U.S. Department of the Interior outlines the requirement as, "Elements used in a selection process must be job-related, requiring criteria used to determine the candidates referred and selected be related to the job to be filled."[7] Large organizations will have the resources and breadth of processes to conduct these validation procedures; however, small organizations may have limited options in terms of practical and defensible selection procedures making the issue all the more critical.[8]

There must not only be this level of requirements, but the organization must also apply a high level of consistency to the selection process for every applicant who is processed.[9] Not treating each and every applicant fairly can expose the agency to unnecessary and often expensive litigation. In addition, unfair treatment that is uncovered by the media is usually quite embarrassing to the chief executive of the agency.

Consistency, fairness, and valid criteria are but part of the requirements. The organization must also have a logical progression to the personnel selection process in place to make the process efficient and effective.[10] Haphazard approaches lead to mistakes and claims of unfair treatment. Wasted time or resources in the hiring process are things that need to be avoided at all costs given the often limited resources agencies have available. These factors of limitation will not be considered in a negligent hiring or negligent retention claim as agency size, lack of available resources, or exorbitant costs to process a candidate do not diminish the agency's responsibility to hire the fittest applicants for the position. There is most often a direct link between the quality of the process and subsequent quality of the certified and hired applicant.

CRITERIA FOR SELECTION AND HIRING STANDARDS

Many local and state level systems allow for patronage types of positions in the public realm.[11] Clearly, these types of systems invite problems. The criteria for performance- and meritocracy-based selection and hiring standards of the process are built upon a foundation that empirically examines the requirements of the position of a police officer. For example, in the federal system (e.g., General Schedule or "GS" rating), testing processes are augmented with the applicant's educational and experiential levels in order to develop a standardized rating system in order to fairly select for positions as well as justify the selection to any oversight group.[12] In order to develop these types of criteria though, the first level in the process is the job task analysis (JTA).

Job Task Analysis

JTA, also referred to simply as job analysis (JA), is the basis for all entry level requirements, entry level and continued training needs, and a performance measurement tool for those who are hired into the public safety professions. JA is used to design valid instruments that allow the assessment of the match between key job characteristics and applicant capacity to meet those knowledge, skills, and abilities (KSAs) required of the particular job classification.[13] The U.S. Department of the Interior describes the purpose of JTA as follows:

> Job analysis is information about a position to be filled that helps to identify the major job requirements (MJR) and links them to skills, education, training, etc., needed to successfully perform the functions of that job. The purpose of the job analysis is to identify the experience, education, training, and other qualifying factors, possessed by candidates who have the potential to be the best performers of the job to be filled. It can also be used to identify documents and other elements vital to the candidate evaluation, referral and selection process, such as measurement methods and interview requirements.[14]

The elements of JTA include (1) identification of major job requirements (MJRs) and (2) identification of KSAs required to accomplish each MJR.[15] In its simplest form, JTA identifies all of the job-related tasks for a specific position. From that identification, those serving in the roles would assess these responsibilities using two separate scales to measure the task frequency and task importance. Some examples are tactical situations that may be rated infrequently, but are highly important or critical. Testifying in judicial proceedings may also share the same levels of ranking. Normal driving of a police vehicle would likely be frequent and only moderately important as less danger exists in normal operation as opposed to emergency operation. Tangible and intangible KSAs are then statistically analyzed to reveal the highest priority and frequency tasks that must then be tested for, trained in, and assessed in performance. Entry level testing processes must include valid and replicable job task analyses. The testing validation process is underscored in the decision of *Swearer v. Karoleski* (1989) wherein an appellate court decided that the rejection of an applicant based upon test results that indicated the applicant had a 15% chance of failure due to unacceptable performance was unjust.[16]

Examination processes using JTA also incorporate general behavioral constructs that target specific aspects of the police function. Darany and Associates have developed a process entitled DELPOE that screens candidates for the following characteristics and behaviors of job performance:

1. Service orientation
2. Accountability
3. Professional ethics
4. Problem-solving orientations
5. Job knowledge
6. Written communication skills
7. Observation skills
8. Oral communication skills[17]

For law enforcement officers, many additional behaviors are required as integral characteristics of the position. While considered the softer science of JA, they are critical characteristics which require measurement. Police officer orientation measurement parameters with respect to attitudes and personality characteristics should include the following areas:

1. *Interpersonal ability*: To communicate and interact well with others
2. *Assertiveness*: To present ideas positively and to demonstrate appropriate command presence
3. *Stress tolerance*: Ability to deal effectively with the day-to-day stressors of criminal justice work
4. *Team orientation*: Ability to work effectively with others
5. *Ethics and integrity*: Ability to uphold both the letter and spirit of the law; to deal honestly with others and uphold a strong moral code.[18]

Additional research into this area through the Ohio Law Enforcement Foundation on entry level hiring for law enforcement officers revealed 12 traits that are desirable to varying degrees at all law enforcement agencies regardless of size or type:

1. *Integrity*: The candidate has high moral and ethical standards and possesses integrity in all matters, public and private.
2. *Human diversity*: The candidate has the ability to act in an unbiased manner and must have an understanding of human diversity issues.
3. *Service*: The candidate has a service orientation: A desire and commitment to service above self.
4. *Team compatibility*: The candidate has a team orientation. The candidate has the ability to work with others in a cooperative, caring, and supportive manner to achieve the goals of the group.
5. *Oral communication*: The candidate has the ability to communicate well orally. The candidate is a good listener and can clearly transmit thoughts and ideas to others.
6. *Written communication*: The candidate has the ability to communicate well in writing and the ability to convey an idea, concept, or information in a clear, concise, and appropriate format.
7. *Motivation*: The candidate has the ability to be highly motivated while working independently.
8. *Decision making and problem solving*: The candidate has the ability to be a good decision maker and problem solver.
9. *Human relation skills*: The candidate has the ability to interact with people, effectively, demonstrating good human relation skills.
10. *Self-control*: The candidate has the ability to maintain self-control under stressful circumstances. Self-discipline is critical to responding properly.
11. *Planning and organizing*: The candidate has planning and organizing skills.
12. *Performance driven*: The candidate is performance driven and has the desire and motivation to be successful in achieving group and individual goals.[19]

The changing face of policing may also require additional measures be built into the testing process. For example, there are varied models of policing including the traditional or professional policing model, the community policing, and the like.[20] JTA must include the policing model that the organization's mission is geared toward. Current trends and needs should be balanced against emerging issues as well. For example, a peace officer JTA in the State of Ohio revealed emerging trends to handle calls for biological weapons, bomb threats, emotionally disturbed persons, and hatred against foreigners.[21] The vehicle for testing must be valid in the general methodologies of policing as well as the specific needs of the organization. These requirements are fulfilled with a comprehensive and valid JTA.

Accurate analysis and validation may be difficult in such small populations with limited taxonomy or unique job responsibilities though, and the organization must use accepted validation techniques like synthetic validity that allows pooling of occupational parameters of positions that have overlapping responsibilities and work behaviors.[22] Synthetic validity uses an inferential model to identify common job elements and uses those elements to design selection instruments that are predictive of future performance of the individual job. The fundamental theory is that myriad jobs include the same KSAs, but the process can validly predict those little used or unique characteristics of specialized positions, for example.[23] Synthetic validity can be used to effectively defend an organization's selection instruments and process.[24]

Criteria and Standards

The development of job-related criterion is the foundation for codifying job-related standards. The JTA is used for determining pre-employment selection criteria.[25] From criterion, we can make the next evolutionary step to forming selection standards. Selection standards can range from the minimally acceptable to superior background characteristics, behaviors, and performance. While we have acceptable standards, we must pay equal attention to those exclusionary standards that address the issues of moral turpitude that would make an applicant unfit for the position of public safety officer. Public safety officers are held by society to much higher standards of conduct—conduct that is scrutinized in both their professional and private lives. Consequently, untoward and deviant conduct that may be tolerated or excused on the part of a private citizen may, in contrast, be an intolerable deviation that would require exclusion from the selection process. The vetting process must produce applicants who are able to meet these high standards.

The question of standards in public safety officer hiring has been a heated discussion for many decades. As discussed in Chapter 1, hiring applicants without proper investigation and those revealed through investigation to be unfit become ominous issues. Some additional examples of this point include the New York Police Department's (NYPD) struggle with replacing positions lost through massive attrition. As a result, NYPD hired at a rate of one-in-five applicants who should have been disqualified based upon their own hiring standards, some for such crimes as laundering drug money, assault, grand larceny, and weapons possession.[26] Another example comes from the findings of the Christopher Commission concerning weak application of hiring standards that allowed risky candidates to become Los Angeles police officers.[27] Some jurisdictions have decided to hold the line in order to maintain standards in their hiring processes. For example, in spite of the constraints of a federal consent decree, the administrators of the Buffalo Police Department strongly advocated for higher educational standards in order to appoint officers who could meet the continuing needs of contemporary officers, emphasizing that skills learned in college include enhanced communication abilities, technological savvy, judgment and decision-making skills, and knowledge of the relevant laws that will need to be enforced.[28] Another example comes from a Dallas County, Texas, scandal that has led to the development of stricter hiring standards regarding lateral transfers.[29]

Lowering standards can be attributed to several driving forces. Some examples include departments that have trouble finding drug-free applicants that will resort to lowering these types of standards in order to meet their hiring quotas.[30] Hiring standards were lowered in places like New Orleans and Miami, the cause of which was through political interference. This was linked to the rampant corruption in those same cities.[31] Nassau County, New York, became yet another department caught up in the maelstrom created by the U.S. Department of Justice's ill-conceived efforts to address the issues of racial disparity by forcing a political solution to the problem that resulted in a disaster.[32] Dayton, Ohio, also became embroiled in a controversy over lowering test scores due to pressures from the U.S. Justice Department concerning the lack of African American applicants who could not successfully pass a fully redesigned entry level examination process.[33] A similar case also unfolded concerning the same issues in the New York City Fire Department where the lowering of standards has raised concerns over a sympathetic effect on compromised safety of fire fighters and citizens alike.[34] Studies have also revealed that lower age and education requirements may be related to incidents of police corruption.[35] And if these examples are not sufficient to cause concern, the City of Chicago administration actually proposed the entire elimination of an entry level examination for police officers and attempted to justify this by citing failures of previous examination processes to net higher levels of minorities as well as the cost of legal challenges to the existing screening process.[36] One state level human resource conference held some years ago was themed, *What standards are left for police hiring?* Certainly a sad commentary on how this state's hiring processes has been eroded at the macro-level. The Transportation Security Administration (TSA) has undergone severe scrutiny over its hiring practices. One airport was ordered by TSA to issue the highest level security access to a screener who had been convicted of a felony robbery.[37] TSA still suffers from image problems as incidents such as two of their agents stealing tens of thousands of dollars from a passenger's luggage plaster the news.[38] Transgressions such as these are rooted in part in the inadequate language used in criterion and standards development for exclusion of applicants. In this example, TSA considered the crime as an offense committed by a juvenile under federal law as the screener was 17 at the time he committed the robbery. TSA also has a 10 year rule in place, and information that falls outside of those boundaries, no matter how serious the violation, does not need to be reported on the application.[39] The rhetorical question then becomes, "How much more shock value is necessary before someone says this is insane?"

Arguments emerge from both sides of the table concerning the assertion that question if the hiring standards of public safety officers have been lowered over the years or are they a response that meets the needs of an evolving society and available candidate pools.[40] Irregardless of which argument is correct, the fact remains that compromises in the hiring standards will often lead to heightened and unnecessary risks for all those involved.

Research has shown that some law enforcement agencies are working to upgrade the existing standards for officers to increase the levels of professionalism among the ranks.[41] Support has also been garnered from the courts as in the ruling of *Davis v. City of Dallas* (1985) where the decision supported a law enforcement agency's right to require college education as an entry level requirement.[42] The benefits of college-educated officers include advanced communication skills, the ability to properly exercise discretionary powers, and higher moral and ethical values.[43] Dichotomous research exists that suggests that many law enforcement organizations, while reducing the standards for clean criminal records, are also raising standards regarding drug use discovered through drug testing.[44] Raising standards, though, brings with it a new set of complex issues. For example, the NYPD's efforts at raising the standard application requirements from 20 years of age and a high school diploma to 22 years of age and either 60 college credits or 2 years of military service reduced the applicant population from a high of almost 60,000 to less than 4,000.[45] Departments are fighting for a candidate pool with the existing standards; any deviation could prove catastrophic to the process. Also for consideration is that higher standards lead to the need for greater legal justification.[46] Standards that are too high or too restrictive may lead to adverse impact in the protected classes and significantly impair an organization's efforts to increase diversity in the ranks. Residency requirements, while found legal in the ruling of *McCarthy v. Philadelphia Civil Service Commission* (1976), often have a devastating impact on the ability to recruit the best and most diverse applicants.[47] Therefore, law enforcement agencies must have valid screening and selection processes that enhance the ability to diversify the ranks instead of lowering standards to fill arbitrary quotas.[48]

As a system of checks and balances, the individual states will often have at least a minimum standard for entry level requirements for law enforcement officers as well as minimum training requirements. With respect to training requirements, the Commission on Peace Officer Standards and Training (POST) was established by the California Legislature in 1959 to set minimum selection and training standards for law enforcement personnel.[49] Many other states have a POST model in place including Tennessee,[50] Alabama,[51] Wyoming,[52] Missouri,[53] and Nevada,[54] to name a few. Some states vary in title of their certifying bodies like the Texas Commission on Law Enforcement Officer Standards and Education (TCLEOSE),[55] the Oklahoma Council on Law Enforcement Education and Training (CLEET),[56] and the Washington State Criminal Justice Training Commission.[57] Training requirements are part and parcel to the hiring process as applicants who successfully complete the screening process and are hired must also successfully complete the training process to be certified. In setting hiring standards, these issues must be considered.

As an example of state level entry level requirements, the New York State Department of Civil Service is the controlling body for all such minimum requirements in the state. Disqualification under New York State standards may include any number of factors including the following:

> Lack of established requirements for the position, inability to perform the job duties due to a disability, history of criminal conviction, dismissal from employments due to poor performance, falsifying a material fact on the application, or practicing fraud in the examination or appointment.[58]

The *New York State Civil Service Law* also requires officers to be of good moral character.[59] While some standards are definitive, others require some interpretation. With the inexact nature of each applicant's history, there are some absolutes of immoral behavior translating to engaging in felonious conduct, deviant sexual activities, and the like, as well as conduct that must be interpreted including infractions, violations, and minor offenses of alcohol use, and acts committed as a youth, to name a few of those ubiquitous gray areas. Some state laws allow for a case-by-case assessment wherein a conviction for a crime or an offense may be disregarded on the basis of some mitigating circumstance.[60] The trouble arises when no clear precedent is in place and the line gets pushed back further and further. Realistically, there really is no such thing as a case-by-case basis when having to justify to a federal judge or a consent decree oversight committee why one candidate was given preference over another, especially when the new hire was substandard to the plaintiff. Often we fail to acknowledge that all candidates must clear the lowest hurdle, not the highest or worse yet, a floating bar!

And as mentioned earlier, police chiefs and administrators are being held more and more accountable for the integrity of the hiring process.[61] Policies and standards must be maintained consistently and uniformly despite any pressures of politics, community, special interest groups, or such malevolent issues as cronyism and nepotism. Definitive standards must be delineated, so guidance is provided and justification for actions is afforded. These standards will provide the height of the bar and also exclude candidates even when the applicant has a multitude of strong characteristics. No matter how educated, experienced, or connected an applicant may be, these and other factors would not overcome a lifetime disqualifier of a felony conviction or admission to an uncharged felony. In fact, the Auburn, Georgia, Police Department also lists in its criteria any crime under investigation by its agency, or another at the time of processing may also lead to rejection of the applicant.[62] Those in the field clearly recognize that these are very difficult issues to resolve to everyone's satisfaction.

Perhaps some prophetic guidance can be found in the Customs and Border Patrol definition of suitability to serve as an agent. Suitability is, "A determination based on an individual's character or conduct that may have an impact on the integrity or efficiency of an agency's mission."[63] Echoed in the *Code of Federal Regulations* are several criteria-based standards that reflect these fundamental principles.[64] For example, a *suitability determination* means a decision by an agency with delegated authority that a person is suitable or is not suitable for employment.[65] Suitability is determined through several means consisting of *risk designations* (i.e., low to high) in the potential of the applicant's hire, leading to adverse impact on a federal agency's efficiency or integrity.[66] These risk designations are measured against *public trust* positions involving those of public safety and law enforcement that could provide access to power or information that could lead to compromising the integrity of the organization.[67] These are excellent examples to follow when developing program standards and criteria.

Translating Standards into Organizational Policy

One method of translating standards into policy is by means of an *adjudication module*.[68] This type of decision-making tool is developed as a matrix or grid that is used to classify applicants based upon exclusionary standards. They are effective at demonstrating fairness and consistency as long as they are adhered to. An excellent example of criteria and standards for entry level law enforcement officers can be found in the Washington State Patrol's posting for minimum requirements and qualifications. Among the numerous requirements are the following standards with respect to the applicant's history:

1. Have no felony convictions. Have no misdemeanor convictions involving theft, crimes of violence (e.g., domestic violence, assault on a family member, etc.), larceny, moral turpitude, controlled substances, or hit and run
2. No conviction of driving under the influence of alcohol and/or drugs or reckless driving within the last 7 years
3. No conviction of two or more major moving violations (DUI, reckless driving), regardless of the time frame
4. Be free from the use of narcotics or controlled substances
5. Knowledge between right and wrong and demonstrate it by example and lifestyle
6. Pay one's bill and meet financial obligations[69]

Another excellent example can be found in the policy of the Warwick Police Department in Warwick, Rhode Island, which includes in their *General Orders Manual* policy that sets forth the specific qualifications of new applicants:

1. Must be a U.S. citizen.
2. Must be at least 21 years old.
3. Must possess a valid motor vehicle operator's license.
4. Must possess at least 60 college credits from an accredited institution or proof of 3 years continuous active duty in the U.S. military in lieu of the 60 credits.
5. Cannot have been convicted of or otherwise admitted to having committed any felony in a court of law. A conviction or admission to a misdemeanor may be considered a disqualifying factor depending upon the totality of the circumstances (i.e., sentence, facts, and circumstances surrounding the incident, distance in time, nature of the incident).
6. Must be of good moral character and habits and successfully pass a background investigation.
7. Must be in good health and meet physical, medical, and psychological requirements for entry into the Rhode Island Municipal Police Academy.[70]

The Federal Bureau of Investigation (FBI) very succinctly presents their qualification standards posted on the website so interested candidates may conduct a personal assessment at the outset to determine initial eligibility. Titled as FBI Employment Disqualifiers, the exclusionary factors include the following:[71]

1. Conviction of a felony.
2. Use of illegal drugs in violation of the FBI Employment Drug Policy:
   a. Have used any illegal drug (including anabolic steroids after February 27, 1991), other than marijuana, within the past 10 years, or engaged in more than minimal experimentation in their lifetime. In making the determination about an applicant's suitability for FBI employment, all relevant facts, including the frequency of use, will be evaluated.
   b. Have used marijuana/cannabis within the past 3 years, or have extensively used marijuana/cannabis or over a substantial period of time. In making the determination about an applicant's suitability for FBI employment, all relevant facts, including the recency and frequency of use, will be evaluated.[72]
3. Default of a student loan (insured by the U.S. Government).
4. Failure of an FBI-administered urinalysis drug test.
5. Failure to register with the Selective Service System (for males only).

The South Carolina Highway Patrol posts their minimum qualifications for applicants to review prior to submitting their application:

1. At least 21 years of age.
2. U.S. citizen (South Carolina residency is not required).
3. High school graduate or GED.
4. 20/20 vision or no more than 20/100 corrected to 20/20.
5. No criminal record.

6. Driving record shall be clear of any suspension for the last 5 years as a result of alcoholic beverage or dangerous drug violation, or leaving the scene of an accident. The overall driving record will be evaluated placing emphasis on the severity, date and age, time span, and number of violations accumulated.
7. Must be able to perform all of the essential and marginal job functions of a state trooper.[73]

The Washoe County Sheriff's Office uses this set of exclusionary standards for applicants to their agency:

1. A person may not be appointed to perform the duties of a peace officer if he or she has
   a. Been convicted of a felony in this state or of any offense which would be a felony if committed in this state
   b. Been convicted of an offense involving moral turpitude or the unlawful use, sale, or possession of a controlled substance
   c. A documented history of physical violence[74]

The New Hampshire State Police have developed a very comprehensive and definitive list of the offenses that would result in automatic disqualification of an applicant for the position of probationary trooper (see below).[75]

New Hampshire State Police Examples of Automatic Disqualifiers[168]

Abuse of a corpse
Advertising drug paraphernalia
Aggravated DWI
Aggravated felonious sexual assault
Aiding criminal activity
Arson, or attempt
Attempt to commit abduction
Attempt to commit extortion/blackmail
Attempt to commit larceny
Attempt to commit welfare fraud
Attempt to commit wire fraud
AWOL/desertion
Bail default; driver's license suspension resulting
Bail jumping
Bail jumping, interstate
Bigamy
Boating while intoxicated
Bribery; official/political matters
Burglary, or attempt
Capitol murder
Carrying a loaded handgun without a license
Changed or removed VIN
Changing marks on a firearm
Child abuse
Child neglect
Commercial bribery
Compensation for past action
Computer-related crime: ATM/credit fraud
Computer-related crime: damage resulting
Computer-related crime: fraud
Computer-related crime: theft of data
Computer-related crime: wire fraud
Concealing death of a newborn
Concealing identity of a vehicle
Consolidation; general theft or larceny
Contributing to the delinquency of a minor
Criminal defamation of character
Criminal liability for conduct of another
Criminal mischief, or attempt
Criminal restraint
Criminal threatening

Cruelty to animals
Deceptive business practices
Desecration of U.S. flag
Disobeying an officer
Disorderly conduct
Distribution of drug paraphernalia
Domestic violence act
Driving after revocation or suspension
DWI
Driving without giving proof of financial responsibility
DWI of commercial vehicle
Escape
Exposing a minor to harm
Fail to answer a court-issued summon
Fail to appear; default to recognizance
Fail to report injuries
Failure to pay court-ordered judgments
False fire alarm; aiding and abetting
False fire alarm; injury/death resulting
False imprisonment
False report of a stolen vehicle
False report of accident
False report to law enforcement
False reports—explosives; bomb threat
False statements on vital records
False swearing/statements
Falsifying physical evidence
Felon in possession of a dangerous weapon
Felonious sexual assault, or attempt
Felonious use of body armor
First-degree assault, or attempt
First-degree murder
Forgery
Fraud on creditors
Fraud on depositors
Fraudulent communications paraphernalia
Fraudulent execution of documents
Fraudulent handling of legal documents
Fraudulent issue of nonnegotiable bill
Fraudulent sales/purchases of securities
Fraudulent use of credit card, or attempt
Fugitive from justice
Gambling equipment violations
Habitual offender
Harassment
Hindering apprehension or prosecution
Illegal night hunting
Illegal possession of a hypodermic needle
Illegal sales of securities
Impersonating a police officer
Implied consent
Improper influence
Incest
Indecent exposure and lewdness
Inhaling toxic vapors for effect
Insurance fraud
Issuing bad checks
Manslaughter, or attempt
Negligent discharge of firearm/crossbow
Negligent homicide
Nonsupport
Obscene matter/materials
Obstructing government administration
Obtaining controlled drug by forgery of prescription
Obtaining controlled drug by fraud or deceit
Obtaining controlled drug by misrepresentation
Obtaining controlled drug from two or more doctors
Obtaining noncontrolled drugs by fraud or deceit
Odometer tampering
Operating after suspension
Operating boat after suspension/revocation
Operating OHRV while intoxicated
Perjury
Possessing bomb
Possessing infernal machine
Possessing loaded firearm in vehicle
Possession/use/display of false ID card
Possession controlled drug/narc drug with intention to distribute
Possession of burglary tools
Possession of child pornography
Possession of controlled drug in boats

- Possession of controlled narcotic/drugs
- Possession of explosives
- Possession of false or forged controlled drug prescription
- Possession of forgery tools or writing
- Possession of more than one driver's license
- Possession of property without a serial number
- Possession, sale, etc., of wiretap device
- Prohibited vehicles on highway
- Prostitution and related offenses
- Prowling
- Purchase of public office
- Receiving stolen property
- Receiving unsolicited merchandise
- Reckless conduct; placing another in danger
- Reckless operation
- Resisting arrest or detention
- Retail selling of drug paraphernalia
- Robbery, armed
- Robbery, or attempt
- Robbery, unarmed
- Sabotage against the state or United States
- Sale of controlled/narcotic drug
- Sale of handguns to minors
- Sale of hypodermic needles
- Second degree assault, or attempt
- Second degree murder
- Sexual assault, or attempt
- Shoplifting
- Simple assault, or attempt
- Stalking
- Taking without owner's consent
- Tampering with public or private records
- Tampering with witnesses and informants
- Theft by deception
- Theft by extortion
- Theft by misapplication of property
- Theft by unauthorized taking or transfer
- Theft of lost or mislaid property
- Theft of service
- Theft of utility services
- Theft; from a building, or attempt
- Theft; from a motor vehicle, or attempt
- Theft; motor vehicle, or attempt
- Theft; of motor vehicle parts/accessory, or attempt
- Theft; pocket-picking, or attempt
- Theft; purse-snatching, or attempt
- Unauthorized use of propelled vehicle/rented property
- Unlawful dealing in prescription drugs
- Unlawful gambling
- Unlawful manufacture of a controlled drug
- Unlawful possession of alcohol
- Unlawful wiretapping—felony
- Unlawful wiretapping—misdemeanor
- Unlawfully conducting a lottery
- Unsworn falsification
- Use and possession of slugs; fraud
- Use of Molotov cocktail
- Uttering false/forged prescription
- Violation and contempt of protective order
- Violation of privacy
- Violation of probation or parole
- Weapons possession (during other crime)
- Willful concealment

Scores of offenses are listed so that the new applicant can see what the standards are prior to applying. In addition, background investigators are provided with a clear and unequivocal guide for their investigative questions that will arise during the process.

Care must be taken in using terms that often are difficult to articulate and define. For example, the term *moral turpitude* needs some definition if to be defended as a deselection criterion. In the search for guidance in this issue, other professions that require higher than normal levels of public trust, teaching, for example, bring with them these same types of standards that are designed to regulate and sanction conduct that rises to the level of those involving conduct that is deemed to be moral turpitude.[76] The courts have historically failed to provide a definitive standard of proof that can be used as a guide to this nebulous concept.[77] Even where the concept is used as a regulatory term for those who professionally practice and interpret law, the term is highly discretionary in nature and execution, for which it consistently escapes definitive meaning.[78] The law in the State of Alabama defines moral turpitude as, "Conduct contrary to community standards of justice, honesty and good morals."[79] With respect to immigration matters, the U.S. Department of State Foreign Affairs (2010) defines the foundational elements of moral turpitude as (1) fraud, (2) larceny, and (3) intent to harm persons or thing.[80] While no statutory definition currently exists, the courts have endeavored to elucidate the issue for those who will be involved in using the concept to exact sanctions. For example, the language in the ruling of *Itani v. Ashcroft* (2002) reads:

> An act of baseness, vileness, or depravity in the private and social duties which a man owes to his fellow men, or to society in general, contrary to the accepted and customary rule of right and duty between man and man. Generally, a crime involving dishonesty or false statement is considered to be one involving moral turpitude.[81]

Additional light on the topic is provided in the language cited in the decision of *Kellerman v. Holder* (2009):

> Moral turpitude has been defined as an act which is per se morally reprehensible and intrinsically wrong or malum in se [wrong or evil in itself], so it is the nature of the act itself and not the statutory prohibition of it which renders a crime one of moral turpitude.[82] Among the tests to determine if a crime involves moral turpitude is whether the act is accompanied by a vicious motive or a corrupt mind.[83]

With respect to a specific act and the requirements to meet the application of a moral turpitude standard, the *Itani v. Ashcroft* (2002) decision clarifies:

> Whether a crime involves the depravity or fraud necessary to be one of moral turpitude depends upon the inherent nature of the offense, as defined in the relevant statute, rather than the circumstances surrounding a defendant's particular conduct.[84]

While many obvious crimes can come to mind that fit these requirements, some are not so obvious. For example, tax evasion can be interpreted as a crime involving moral turpitude as it involves some fraudulent act such as filing false tax returns.[85] Applicants who work off the books or have businesses with an income that is not reported on their annual return may be considered as committing an act involving moral turpitude. Clearly articulating the act and its application to this standard will be central to the ability to exclude an applicant for the inclusion of such a standard in the hiring policy of the organization. Researchers argue that in the employment realm, the attainment of clear and convincing evidence is enough to substantiate sanctions in cases where criminal offenses and moral turpitude are involved.[86] The employment realm is a civil proceeding involving not quite the quantum of proof of the criminal courts, but, needless to say, must be met at the level of a preponderance of the evidence in order to establish the burden of proof in the case of an employment action.

Selection vs. Deselection

Careful selection to maintain integrity in the ranks of the public safety organization is a timeless concept.[87] Selection is defined as a process that includes evaluation, testing, screening, and interviewing applicants who have applied to the organization.[88] Others have delineated the process of selection as the entire process of recruitment, hiring, basic academy training, and job orientation.[89] The process is also viewed as a deselection methodology that provides the ability to vet applicants who are not fit for the role based upon validated and nondiscriminatory disqualifying factors.[90] Take note that the selection process is onerous for both the organization and the applicant.[91] The U.S. Equal Employment Opportunity Commission (2010) lists the myriad testing processes used to select and deselect job applicants as follows:

1. Cognitive tests assess reasoning, memory, perceptual speed and accuracy, and skills in arithmetic and reading comprehension, as well as knowledge of a particular function or job.
2. Physical ability tests measure the physical ability to perform a particular task or the strength of specific muscle groups, as well as strength and stamina in general.
3. Sample job tasks (e.g., performance tests, simulations, work samples, and realistic job previews) assess performance and aptitude on particular tasks.
4. Medical inquiries and physical examinations, including psychological tests, assess physical or mental health.
5. Personality tests and integrity tests assess the degree to which a person has certain traits or dispositions (e.g., dependability, cooperativeness, safety) or aim to predict the likelihood that a person will engage in certain conduct (e.g., theft, absenteeism).
6. Criminal background checks provide information on arrest and conviction history.
7. Credit checks provide information on credit and financial history.
8. Performance appraisals reflect a supervisor's assessment of an individual's performance.
9. English proficiency tests determine English fluency.[92]

The intent of the selection process is to use information from the applicant's history that will have predictive value on their job success.[93] Consequently, strong companies invest in the hiring process hiring only those who will fit in the organizational schema and have the prospect of success.[94] Succinctly stated, the quality of selection process often translates into the overall quality of the organization.[95] The goal of the selection process should then be to hire the most qualified and appropriate people from the candidate pool available. Yet another issue to consider in the selection process is that workforce development plans depend heavily on the quality of entry level hires who will be the future leaders of the organization.[96] Selection, therefore, is concurrently a short-term and long-term strategic initiative in the succession planning process. Common sense prevails when we recognize the simple fact that a plethora of performance and behavioral problems occur when we fail to select the right people for our organization's needs.[97]

Organizational psychologists began their earliest works in the employee selection process with the Army in order to design processes and testing that would identify those individuals who had the characteristics needed in the military complex.[98] More recent work has postured for composite testing processes in order to use multiple assessment methods to identify candidates with the right mix of characteristics that would lead to success as a public safety officer. Research into the characteristics of successful police officers has revealed correlations to the characteristics of the general working population as well as unique characteristics required of law enforcement personnel. The results of the research have led to the need for selection and deselection criteria be developed in order to guide the process for making decisions on whom to hire and whom to reject. To effectively screen, organizations need to develop a set of defined behaviors called criteria that directly measure these unique characteristics.[99] In order to do so, the need exists to identify those characteristics that lead to unproductive and unhealthy officer behaviors.[100] Disqualifiers and qualifiers must, therefore, be directly linked to work performance in order to be valid and enforceable.[101] The components of a selection process must be valid and predictive of the job-related performance requirements for the position tested for.[102] To accomplish this, selection/deselection criteria must be based upon qualified job dimensions. For example, there are 15 job dimensions used for selection/deselection in the Sacramento Police Department:

1. Communication skills
2. Problem-solving ability
3. Learning ability
4. Judgment under pressure
5. Observation skills
6. Willingness to confront problems
7. Interest in people
8. Interpersonal sensitivity
9. Desire for self-improvement
10. Appearance
11. Dependability
12. Physical ability
13. Integrity
14. Operation of a motor vehicle
15. Credibility as a witness in a court of law[103]

Supporters of selection criteria argue that the assessment constructs for law enforcement officers have resulted in applicant attrition rates of about 10 rejections for every one candidate hired.[104] Other opinions vary widely with respect to the predictability and validity of the selection process. For example, in spite of the extensive research into the issue of criteria, notable errors can occur in the process wherein *reject errors* (rejections of qualified applicants) are turned away while *accept errors* (hired and subsequently have disciplinary and performance issues) are consequently accepted into the ranks.[105] Some also believe the only predictor of job success occurs during posthire job performance and not from any prehire or employment screening methods or processes.[106] Classical research supports this assertion in part by analysis that demonstrates the strongest predictors of performance are posthire and in the infancy stages of the officer's career with such indicators as police academy grades and evaluations during the probationary period as measures of success.[107] Still others argue for the strength of behavior modification through the quality and rigor of basic academy programs. The training vs. selection argument falls short of the goal when training fails to appropriately and efficiently modify the behavior of the marginal or substandard recruit.[108] For example, with respect to ethical drivers, research has revealed that an overwhelming majority of serving police officers were predominantly influenced by their own personal ethics rather than a professional law enforcement code of ethics.[109] In this case, training may have an insignificant impact on how ethical the officer will be in their performance of duties making the identification of high ethical standards even more critical in the background investigation process.

Lastly, several legal precedents affect the use of selection criteria for police officers. For example, the court affirmed that selecting competent police officers is a daunting task. This fact was identified in the decision of *Davis v. City of Dallas* (1985) wherein the courts language concerning the role of police officer as a professional type position was articulated as follows:

> The job related skills of which are especially difficult to precisely define, test for, and quantify... characteristics which must be found in an applicant and rookie officer are not easily measured in terms of statistical analyses, such as individual judgment, ability to make important decisions, or presence and performance as a witness in court. The problem is one of measuring maturity and the ability to handle tough decisions with a gun.[110]

The court further defined the problem by asserting the inexact science of selection techniques by stating, "Even if appropriate skills could be accurately tested, the combination of skills that would be found in a successful officer would vary from one policeman to the next."[111] This makes the issues of selection and deselection even more problematic when clear answers cannot be had even after litigation has been adjudicated.

STEPS IN THE PROCESS

This section discusses the steps in the process from initial testing to hiring. The pre-employment screening process requires the consideration of several divergent issues. Among the driving issues are cost considerations and budgetary limitations, local organizational and political demands, legal and civil rights requirements, and finding applicants that meet the minimum qualifications of the organization, just to name a few.[112] A concept of note that deserves mentioning at this stage is the *Theory of Constraints (TOC)* which contends that the background investigation process may be constrained by the least effective process in the system.[113] In lieu of these many and often conflicting interests, the process must be designed in a series of strategic stages or steps in order to meet all of these needs in the most effective and efficient manner possible. A brief description of each is provided as well as the recommended chronology of the different stages. Note that some departments may not use some of the stages, and this list is meant to supplement and not supplant systems designed in departments that are currently legal and effective. In addition, hiring must be made contingent upon passing all pre-employment tests and screenings. An early note in this discussion is that the steps must be consistently followed in order to have a valid hiring process. Attempts to alter or circumvent necessary stages are looked upon very unfavorably by the courts. For example, accelerating the hiring process due to the need to fill positions and even to make the process more convenient for the applicant is neither an acceptable nor legal reason to circumvent the steps and requirements of the pre-employment selection process.[114] An example of this can be found in the ruling of *Leonel v. American Airlines, Inc.* (2005).[115] Finally, departments must endeavor to continuously improve their selection processes. Research has revealed that hiring processes in most law enforcement agencies have failed to keep pace with advances in the technological applications available for employment selection.[116]

Examinations and Civil Service Testing

Civil service testing has its roots in ancient China. Development in the United States was based upon the *Pendleton Civil Service Reform Act of 1883*. The Act required that federal hiring must be based on the qualifications of the applicant in relation to the needs of the position. The purpose of the *Federal Civil Service Reform Act of 1978* was to provide a guideline for fair and impartial hiring practices that is worded as follows:

> In order to provide the people of the United States with a competent, honest, and productive federal work force reflective of the Nation's diversity, and to improve the quality of public service, federal personnel management should be implemented consistent with merit system principles and free from prohibited personnel practices.[117]

Reformists in policing began infusing testing processes and minimum requirements for police officers in the early twentieth century in order to have minimum standards for performance so they would be capable of doing the job they were hired to do. Testing process has significantly evolved over the last century to include many variations as discussed later. Research has revealed though that a disturbing trend has occurred in the last part of the twentieth century wherein law enforcement agencies have significantly reduced the use of written and intelligence tests as a part of entry level requirements.[118] Testing is broadly defined as psychological and educational instruments that are designed to develop inferences about those who are vying for a specific position or role.[119] Testing process must also be criterion related, have content and construct validity, be accurate and standardized, and must not produce disparate results.[120] Testing validation can emerge from the use of a single measure or series of measures such as criterion validity, content validity, or construct validity.[121] While validity is one factor, tests must also be reliable or replicable as valid predictors of behavior to compare the test takers knowledge to that required of the ideal employee.[122] The courts closely scrutinize this area, and in the landmark decision of *Washington v. Davis* (1976), the court stated, "It appears beyond doubt by now that there is no single method for appropriately validating employment tests for their relationship to job performance."[123] In the later decision of *Watson v. Fort Worth Bank and Trust* (1988), the courts entertained certiorari and ruled that this type of analyses can be applied to testing processes.[124]

In addition, according to the *Uniform Guidelines for Employee Selection Procedures* (1978), any selection instrument that is used which may adversely impact the hiring of protected class individuals must be validated.[125] Actions that constitute discriminatory practices for protected classes as well as nonminority applicants can result in discrimination and reverse discrimination claims. A recent U.S. Supreme Court decision on reverse discrimination found in favor of nonminority candidates.[126] This ruling will quite possibly have a significant effect on future hiring and promotional practices throughout the country. Other reverse discrimination claims have resulted in multimillion dollar awards for plaintiffs in class action lawsuits.[127] One component of a proposed solution to the problem is to recruit larger pools of qualified minority and female candidates in order to increase the ability to compete on entrance and promotional examinations.[128]

Civil Service, Organizationally Based, and Private Testing Contractors

Civil service testing is widely used for law enforcement positions across the country. Departments either have their own civil service process or use a county or state level process to test applicants. These processes are often valid and defensible, but may not fully meet the needs of the organization as they test for general skills and knowledge. Organizationally based examinations usually are civil service sanctioned, but are expensive to develop and may be subject to much higher levels of scrutiny and litigation. There are also private contractors who do police testing for those agencies who need an alternative, and this method is acceptable to any local or state requirements. An example of an organizationally based examination process can be found in the Washington State Patrol's two-part written testing methodology:

1. The first examination evaluates an applicant's judgment and common sense using situational questions and multiple choice answers.
2. The second examination is designed as a learning ability test that evaluates observation skills, written communication skills, and reading comprehension. Additional information is captured concerning the applicant's background and personality.[129]

A fundamental tenet of testing process, no matter who designs or administers them, is that they should be nondiscriminatory in form and structure, test only job-related criteria, and voluntarily comply with fair employment laws.[130] Testing processes, specifically written examinations that have been found to be discriminatory, have led to multimillion dollar settlements to plaintiffs.[131] Much effort has been placed in increasing racial parity in organizations to reflect that of the communities served. Testing processes have been experimented with over the years that have produced marginal and, at times, questionable results at best. Practices such as quota hiring are also being questioned for their efficacy as a means to an end.[132] Opinions vary widely on what testing methodology, type, or battery will produce desired results. Care must be exercised when using the *magic bullet* as it may morph into a *silver bullet* if we do not do our homework correctly.

Types of Pre-Employment Testing and Screening Process Stages

There are numerous types of pre-employment testing processes. Screening instruments can be designed to measure behavioral traits such as cognitive abilities, job-specific skills, emotional stability, personality, and self-control.[133] Three major types of tests exist: (1) intelligence, (2) personality, and (3) simulations.[134] As a system, the remaining types are also addressed in physical agility testing, medical examinations, psychological evaluations, and polygraphs. Woven into this discussion are the steps to the process in logical order.

Failure to Cooperate with the Investigation/Meet Processing Requirements

At the outset, applicants are required to cooperate fully with all stages of the pre-employment screening process. Communicating this clear and unequivocal expectation should start at the moment of application. Applicants should sign an acknowledgment of this requirement especially in the processing stages where personality and psychological testing will be used.[135] Resources, availability of testing stages, administrative and legal timelines, and the like will all drive the process. A department should make reasonable efforts to accommodate an applicant's needs and schedules, but the applicant is fully responsible for all stages, timelines, and testing requirements. Applicants must be advised that they are responsible for every component of every phase. For example, an applicant is given a final due date and supplies all requested documentation except for their credit report, the applicant should be advised that they are being removed from consideration. This equates to a failure to meet investigative and processing requirements, and the applicant has made the choice on their own to fail to provide the required documents in a timely fashion. Another example is an applicant who sits for the psychological testing portion of the examination and answers intermittent questions or does not finish the exam with enough responses to provide valid analysis. They should not be allowed to retake the exam because their actions were the cause of the invalid analysis. The department should not be burdened with additional expenses for applicants who attempt to circumvent, practice fraud, or delay the process.

Intelligence or Cognitive Testing

Intelligence tests are used for measuring an applicant's ability to think and solve problems and can be used in two forms: (1) verbal intelligence testing and (2) nonverbal intelligence testing.[136] Intelligence tests are also referred to as cognitive or aptitude tests. They can be further categorized as general intelligence tests or aptitude tests that include (1) mechanical aptitude, (2) clerical aptitude, and (3) spatial aptitude.[137] Cognitive testing measures memory skills, reading comprehension, math skills, reasoning, and the like.

Intelligence tests have been proven to provide significant predictive validity with respect to the productivity and success of employees in an organizational setting.[138] For use in the police testing environment, cognitive ability is a highly valid indicator of an officer's performance during the academy training and through subsequent job performance measures of success.[139] A diametrically opposed court decision in *Jordan v. City of New London* (1999) allowed a police department to reject an applicant for being too intelligent though![140] To be effective, cognitive skills testing must include the entire spectrum of knowledge and behaviors required to fulfill the functions of a police officer.[141] One of the problems associated with testing entry level police officers though has been attributed to the candidate pool's lack of abilities at both reading comprehension and writing skills.[142] These areas weigh heavily in assessing cognitive ability.

Personality Testing

Personality testing is used to evaluate the traits and characteristics of an applicant in order to provide some level of prediction of the future behavior or conduct of the applicant. This area is discussed more fully in Chapter 4.

Simulations

Simulations are testing and training exercises built into assessment centers that allow for comparison of current skills and decision-making ability against practical scenarios that may be encountered. These scenarios are also defined as job task simulation testing[143] and sample job tasks.[144] From in-basket exercises, to role-plays, to the current technological capacity of the organization, simulations can be used for most any scenario. Scenarios for the simulation can be designed with elements that are common to many of the actual situations encountered by the organization and will subsequently be faced by the officer in the street.[145] Simulation testing is a process that when used effectively in the selection process enables the employer to make better hiring decisions that are based upon actual job-related tasks.[146] These systems also produce more accurate predictions of future job success.

Simulation technology for law enforcement allows for the assessment of decision-making capabilities.[147] Video-based scenarios incorporate a series of professionally acted and produced video simulations, wherein the candidate watches and then responds verbally as if they were at the scene. The applicant's responses are videotaped and scored using validated criteria.[148] Interactive technological advances such as those used in firearms training allow for sophisticated computer control to simulate force-type scenarios and accurately gauge the officer's decision making and response skills in a controlled environment.[149] Simulated computer scenarios used in promotional examinations take the applicant through a decision model or tree, and test takers are automatically scored based upon the different options they exercise to resolve the scenario.

One caution with simulations is the validation process. Simulations, like all other testing used to qualify or disqualify an applicant, must withstand court scrutiny if subjected to challenge. Simulations must be based on the JTA, reasonable expectations, and grading systems that mirror unacceptable, acceptable, and superior responses that are accurate and reflective of the needs of the position. Assessors must also be trained in fair and impartial assessment techniques and use them during their evaluations.

Physical Agility Testing

Physical agility testing attempts to assess an applicant's physical ability against the job-related physical needs of the position.[150] There are two types of physical screening tests used by law enforcement agencies to screen applicants: (1) physical qualification test (PQT) and (2) job standards test (JST).[151] Validating a physical agility test for law enforcement involves the same steps for the normal functions of the role. A JA must include the assessment of the frequency and importance of physical tasks in order to justify the standards used to decertify applicants who cannot meet the minimum standards through testing. Some states have their own standards that are a statewide requirement for all departments. Some states allow individual departments to have their own standards in place and can vary widely from agency to agency. Many states and individual departments throughout the country have adopted the Cooper Standards[152] to use as a validation for their physical fitness requirements.[153] This move was to justify the standards that can and are often challenged in the courts. Examples of these types of challenges can be found in *Powell v. Reno*.[154] *Peanick v. Reno*,[155] and *Lanning v. South Eastern Pennsylvania Transit Authority—SEPTA* (2002).[156] While *Powell* and *Peanick* addressed the issues of cutoff scores, the *Lanning* decision related more to job simulation which was believed to be a better barometer than physical fitness for justifying the need for disparate impact. In practice, law enforcement physical fitness testing has traditionally excluded females at a disproportionate rate to males.[157] In order to level the playing field, age and gender norming is a method used to reduce adverse impact and apply a measure of fairness to the myriad applicants who are testing for the position. One interesting note is that one study revealed that in spite of the difficulty of the physical agility test, applicants preferred them and employments interviews over the psychological examination process.[158]

The physical fitness test is not a test that is covered under the *Americans with Disabilities Act of 1990*.[159] Applicants can be required to perform job-related tasks or physical fitness tests prior to the need to issue a conditional offer of employment (COE). This test measures job-related functions that do not ask the applicant to divulge confidential medical or psychological information prior to a bona fide job offer.

Departments should adopt a practice that requires applicants to have a physician's clearance prior to engaging in the physical agility test. Because of confidentiality and patient rights, the medical statement must not include any information about the applicant's health status other than their physician either recommends or does not recommend the participation in the test. This type of form should be issued to the applicant by the department, signed by the applicant's physician, and presented prior to taking the physical agility test. If the physician does not recommend the participation, the applicant must indicate they are voluntarily disregarding the physician's recommendations and agree to hold the department and all its agents harmless prior to participation. At a minimum, department policy must include a waiver of liability that the applicant signs prior to the testing process. This is done to release the department of any liability that may accrue from an injury sustained during the test.

Preliminary Background Investigation Recommendations

The preliminary background investigation is used as an early screening process. This process is also entitled the preliminary review, early disqualification process, and early out. Preliminary screening is a method to establish early on if the applicant meets the minimum qualifications for the position.[160] Civil service laws will include the review of the application and preliminary background investigation (e.g., valid driver's license, exclusionary arrest record, minimum qualifications, automatic disqualifiers) as a sanctioned process to obviate the need to waste resources in cases where the applicant does not qualify for the first level of review.[161] There are several reasons to do the preliminary background investigation.

Failure to Meet Minimum Qualifications

First, a review of the application materials may reveal the applicant does not meet the minimum qualifications (e.g., age, education, lack of a valid driver's license) for the position. If they do not meet the minimum qualifications, then we have no responsibility to continue with any further review of the applicant at this stage. If they are able to meet the requirements at a later time (e.g., regaining their driver's license after a suspension is lifted) *and* within the processing time frame, the investigation can be reinitiated. But, there is no right or entitlement to an investigation by virtue of mere application and passing of an entrance examination.

Automatic Disqualifiers

If the applicant meets the minimum qualifications, then the recommendation is to investigate as much as legally possible at the preoffer COE stage.[162] This stage would include basic local record checks and an in-depth interview.[163] Automatic disqualifiers can be revealed early on by review of the criminal record check, driving record, license check, credit history, collection of educational records, and employment history. Departments have also taken a hard line on immediate disqualification of applicants who have tattoos, body art, and piercings that are considered highly unprofessional when displayed by those in uniform.[164] Personal history statements/background questionnaires can be completed absent any medical or psychological questions being asked and reviewed in this stage.

Automatic disqualifiers include felony and certain misdemeanor convictions, admissions to crimes, violations of drug policy, and pending civil judgments. The New Hampshire State Police publish quite an extensive list of criminal offenses that if committed by the applicant qualify for automatic disqualification for those who apply to be probationary troopers.[165] Discrepancies found are also sufficient grounds for removal from the process considering the entire issue of integrity.[166] An applicant can also fail to meet investigative requirements by not cooperating fully with the investigation, policy and procedural needs, directions of the background investigator, and timelines for submissions of investigative documents. These all amount to factors that can be used for early disqualification. The South Carolina Highway Patrol translates policy into practice by providing the applicant with a series of automatic disqualifiers and advising the prospective applicant to complete a self-assessment before they apply. Their precursor info reads: "Please read the following information carefully before applying. The following list includes the South Carolina Highway Patrol's automatic disqualifiers. If you meet any of these, **DO NOT APPLY**."

1. Under 21 years of age, at the time, when recruits report to Training Academy
2. Not a U.S. citizen
3. No high school diploma or GED
4. Dishonorable discharge from the military
5. Convicted of any crime punishable by imprisonment in a federal or a state prison
6. Have been arrested for driving under the influence of alcohol and/or drugs within the past 5 years
7. Any conviction of criminal domestic violence
8. Driver's license currently suspended, revoked, or more than six points currently assessed against your license
9. A tattoo, brand, or body art that can be seen while in uniform (short sleeve shirt)
10. Cannot meet minimum vision and hearing standards
11. Sold marijuana or controlled substance
12. Any felony conviction (whether convicted as a juvenile or an adult)
13. Used and/or experimented with marijuana within the past 2 years
14. Used and/or experimented with steroids within the past 5 years
15. Used and/or experimented with controlled substance within the past 10 years[167]

Quite often you reach a point of diminishing returns where no amount of investigation can overcome a mandatory exclusionary act or event. For example, no amount of additional investigation of an applicant who has strong family ties, an advanced degree, and superb work record can diminish or overcome a felony driving while intoxicated (DWI) conviction. Discovery of applicant crimes is a different issue discussed further in Chapter 5, and pursuing criminal investigations is different than the background investigation. Unless there is a compelling reason to continue in these cases, the case should be a preliminary review and the candidate deselected from the process, so the resources can be diverted to processing more viable candidates.

Candidate Motivation

The applicant has the responsibility to educate themselves about the process before they apply for the position.[169] The candidate also has the responsibility to be thorough in their submissions and respond to the stages of the process without being prompted.[170] How the candidate communicates their knowledge of the process speaks to their motivation to enter the law enforcement field. A candidate's intent should also be used as a qualifier or disqualifier from the process. With the exorbitant and unrecoverable costs of processing and training new law enforcement officers, a determination needs to be made early on if the candidate is truly interested in working with the agency doing the processing to consider them for employment.

Candidate Withdrawal

A candidate can also exercise their option to withdraw from the process for any reason. If information is revealed at any stage of the process that is of a nature where the applicant may not believe they are viable, do not wish to continue for fear of having more negative information revealed, or simply lose interest along the way, that is their right. The applicant should complete a release form that indicates their voluntary desire to withdraw from further consideration, and this document is made part of the official case file.

Efficacy of Early Hires

Some agencies face such deficits in their ranks that they feel the need to hire early and commence with the training and on-the-job experience process in order to meet their personnel needs. This certainly is not a recommended practice and should be avoided in every case possible. From the costs of hiring to the potential liability, these types of hires can turn very badly very quickly, and the agency is left to defend itself as the applicant's past unfolds without any control afforded. If this does happen, agencies still can terminate and exercise some levels of protection. Probationary periods are one remedy wherein the applicant can be terminated from employment for no stated cause. In addition, case law supports these types of terminations wherein an applicant has made it into the ranks, but is later determined to be unsuited for the role. This was the case in *Brown v. Benton* (1978) where a probation officer was hired subject to satisfactorily passing the background investigation which was commenced shortly thereafter.[171] The background investigation revealed that the newly hired employee was considered unqualified for the position and was discharged from his conditional employment. A subsequent lawsuit was dismissed by the courts finding in favor of the agency.

Pre- and Post-Conditional Offer of Employment Stages

The COE will be discussed in depth later in Chapter 4. This section is being provided to recommend a timeline of screening process events. Briefly, the *Americans with Disabilities Act of 1990* prohibits the discovery of any medical or psychological information prior to the offering of a bona fide COE.[172] In the pre-COE stage, an employer can ask questions regarding the applicant's ability to perform a specific job functions and may assess personality traits, KSAs as they apply to job qualifications. Any inquiry into any medical or psychological information that falls under the *Americans with Disabilities Act of 1990* must be preceded by the COE in order to be legal.[173] In relation to the processual issues, the timeline included in Table 2.1 frontloads all of the processes that can be completed with minimal cost and without the issuance of a COE. Post-COE, and if applicable and legal in your state, the polygraph or voice stress analysis (VSA) should be used. In-house personnel are often used with minimal expenditures. If the applicant survives these stages, they should advance to the medical and psychological examinations, which are much larger expenditures. Contemporaneous to these examinations, the continued background investigation is conducted. Candidates must pass the first or pre-COE stages in order to be viable. Once past that stage, a significant resources and financial commitment can then be invested in their processing.

TABLE 2.1
Pre- and Post-COE Process Stages

Pre-COE	1. Preliminary testing or screening qualifier (civil service, etc.)
	2. Physical agility test
	3. Oral interview and review of personal history statement/background questionnaire, truthfulness statement
	4. Explore illegal drug use
Post-COE	1. Integrity examination (polygraph/VSA)
	2. Medical examination and drug screen
	3. Psychological and personality examinations
	4. Completed background investigation
	5. Review and approval of completed case by authorized personnel (department, HR, legal, etc.)

One last point on this topic is that the COE is not a guarantee of a job, but rather a reasonable expectation. One of the most fundamental requirements is that the COE is conditioned upon the applicant successfully completing every stage of the process. If the applicant fails at any stage, then the COE can be automatically voided. The burden is upon the applicant to be successful in the process based upon all of the steps and standards of the agency.

Medical Examinations

Medical examinations are used to evaluate the applicant's physical health in relation to the requirements of the position. This area is discussed more fully in Chapter 4.

Psychological and Personality Evaluations

Psychological and personality examinations are used to evaluate the applicant's mental health and suitability in relation to the requirements of the position. These areas are discussed in depth in Chapter 4.

Integrity Examinations

Integrity examinations are used to evaluate the applicant's propensity for truthfulness in relation to the requirements of the position. This area is discussed in depth in Chapter 5.

Continued and Final Background Investigation

The background investigation can be categorized into three broad stages: (1) preliminary background investigation, (2) continued background investigation, and (3) final background investigation. Each stage has distinctly different yet related purposes. The preliminary background investigation has been previously discussed. The next stage is the continued background investigation. This is the post-COE stage where all of the investigation begins concerning the applicant's history. The U.S. Customs and Border Patrol gives a clear explanation to aspiring agents concerning the inquiries that will be made during their background investigation process for new hires:

> The background investigation will include credit and criminal history checks, records checks to verify citizenship of family members, verification of birth, education,

employment history, and military history. Interviews will be conducted of sources who know the candidate and of any current or former spouse (divorced within the past ten years). Residences will be confirmed, neighbors interviewed, and public records queried for information about bankruptcies, divorces, and criminal or civil litigation. Additional interviews will be conducted, as needed, to resolve any inconsistencies or developed issues.[174]

The final background investigation is the stage wherein all of the investigative information culled during the continued background investigation is coalesced with the information developed during the medical, psychological, and personality testing, and the results of the integrity testing. The screening team examines every piece of information developed, assesses whether or not additional investigation needs to be conducted, compares the information and responses on every investigative document and professional evaluation, and develops the strategy for the final interview of the applicant. The final interview is discussed in depth in Chapter 5. The results of this process will lead to the recommendation for decertification or certification and then offer the applicant a ride-along or series of ride-alongs to gain a commitment from the applicant on their true interest to join the ranks of the agency.

Candidate Ride-Along

When the continued investigation is completed, those applicants who have passed all of the stages and show promise as a prospective department member should be offered at least two ride-alongs with a field training officer (FTO) or supervisor if possible. Those applicants who are marginal or clearly unacceptable should not be offered the ride-along as their candidacy is at issue. They will advance into the final interview stage for final disposition.

For those applicants who are offered the ride-along, there are numerous benefits to this stage. Benefits of the opportunity to do the ride-along are derived for both the applicant and the agency.[175] Fundamentally, the organization must manage the expectations of prospective and newly hired employees.[176] In order to manage the expectations of the candidate, a reasonable match between organizational policies and social practices must be aligned with human needs and organizational demands.[177] Second, the candidate ride-along can be used as a component of the selection process that can minimize unnecessary and time-wasting mismatches of employees and organizations.[178] Third, the ride-among provides the applicant with a realistic job preview (RJP) that communicates the actual job functions and responsibilities that the organization requires.[179].

Also during the ride-along, the FTO or supervisor can communicate realistic job expectations and assess the feedback from the candidate with respect to their continued interests as well as any concerns they may have about the position. Any information and assessment that is revealed as a result of the ride-along should be passed on in writing to the background investigator by the FTO or supervisor for continued evaluation of the candidate.

Final protocols include the applicant signing a liability waiver, ensuring they are not allowed to carry any firearm or weapon during the ride-along, briefed on safety procedures, and offered the opportunity to wear body armor during the tour. They must also be allowed to leave at any point that they desire. Any rescheduling or additional ride-alongs should be at the discretion of the background investigation supervisor or unit command.

Candidate Final Interview

The candidate final interview is used to review the cumulative findings of the investigation and selection process stages with the applicant, allow the applicant the opportunity to offer an explanation for any untoward or negative findings, and gauge the applicant's true desire for the position. This area is discussed in depth in Chapter 5.

Advising the Candidate of the Steps in the Process

Lastly, the candidate should be advised of all steps in the process so that nothing is a surprise to them. Oral advisement upon first contact and continually advising of remaining steps as each progressive step is completed. This information should be reduced to writing and given to the candidate either in person or by mail. The Auburn, Maine, Police Department provides an excellent example of such an advisement and is provided in Appendix G.

PHILOSOPHY, MISSION, AND PURPOSE OF THE INVESTIGATION

The philosophy, mission, and purpose of the pre-employment investigation are different than that of what most officers have inculcated as those of a criminal investigation. Criminal investigation is an entire process while pre-employment investigation is a component of the entire screening schema. Pre-employment investigation is not a stand-alone process, but rather, a complementary role to the selection process. That does not minimize its importance, but rather, accentuates it.

Both processes operate from a fundamental perspective that investigation is the systematic inquiry into any event in search of the truth of the matter.[180] Investigators collect, assess, and develop evidence for subsequent submission at some type of official or judicial proceeding.[181] These commonalities exist in both types of inquiries. However, the difference is that the mission and purpose of a pre-employment investigation is to identify qualified persons to hire in the organization. Qualified persons include those who have or can be trained in the required KSAs of the position sought.[182] This makes the process far less adversarial than that of attempting to identify and convict an offender. While a concurrent mission is to exclude applicants who do not meet these requirements, the process is intended to make a very positive impression on those candidates who are eligible for hire after completion of all of the stages of the screening process.

Consequently, the background investigator should view their role as an emissary of the organization. Their conveyance of the process should be as positive as possible at all times until the point where an applicant has not met the minimum criteria or standards. In these circumstances, the background investigator should allow the decertified applicant as much dignity as possible in relation to the reasons of the rejection. The philosophy, mission, and purpose of the investigation are to find qualified applicants. Rejection is a necessary by-product of the process, but not the primary goal.

SCREENING TOOLS AS A SYSTEM

Systems theory is an emergence of the ideology that organizational units are sensitive and responsive to stimuli through every part of the system, much like an organic structure. In this theory, each unit contributes to the operation of the organization and is dependent on the others for its own needs.[183] Systems theory focuses on the objectives of the entire system as opposed to those micro-level objectives of individual departments or units.[184] The impact of systems theory on organizational theory and the effectiveness of general management practices cannot be overstated.[185] Therefore, screening processes must therefore be designed as unique systems in the organization given the numerous components that are dependent upon each other for success.

A paradigmatic change is really necessary for this to happen in many law enforcement organizations. As the complexity and scale of hiring process activities continues to grow in modern public safety organizations, the demand grows for a successful administrator to integrate them within a framework.[186] This should be considered as an aggregate model of an enterprise system to assist the senior executive or hiring manager's ability to make strategic human resource decisions.[187] This connection leads to a quality chain, including the link between systems and quality, the quality judgment, and perception and quality.[188]

To develop this approach, all of the screening components must be coordinated through the highest level manager who has direct control over the process. All of the screening tools that include medical, psychological, and others must be coordinated and fully integrated with a complete and thorough background investigation. Since each component has its own fallibility factors, the others provide a supportive systemic structure to ensure success based upon the cumulative assessment culled from the entire screening process. This is no easy task as it requires training, policy, and most importantly cooperation with all components of the process including recruitment, professional evaluators in the medical and psychology fields, background investigators and their command, department command, polygraphers, human resources and legal advisors, and training. The cooperation of this value chain is critical to the success of the entire hiring process. Egos must be left at the door, and each entity must view itself as a supportive and lateral or equal element of the process rather than as the central figure of the process that must be supported.

CONFIDENTIALITY IN THE PROCESS

To place this issue in perspective, confidentiality of the process should be considered tantamount to the integrity of the process. The information revealed during the course of examining someone's entire life can be embarrassing, negatively impact employment prospects, and even have civil and criminal penalties. The entire selection staff must be sensitive to these needs and operate with the highest confidentiality rules in their daily operations. In spite of the high levels of security and confidentiality that should be the drivers of the process, surreptitious disclosures will occur.[189] These must be addressed immediately with the proper changes put in place to prevent future breaches of this trust.

Some of the historical foundation is revealed through the *Privacy Act of 1974*.[190] This Act protects government employees and certain government contractors from records releases without the written request or consent of the individual to whom the record pertains. The Act does however have provisions for release of information to law enforcement for legitimate purposes.[191] With the advent of technology and data-based information, the federal government responded by enacting legislation to protect computer files with the *Computer Security Law of 1987*[192] and the *Federal Information Security Management Act of 2002*.[193] These Acts were developed to increase the levels of security and privacy of sensitive information in federal computer systems. They are also intended to establish minimum acceptable security practices for all of the federal computer systems. The government also has provided a vehicle for transparency in the *Freedom of Information Law* which was designed to guarantee the public access to government records and meetings as a method of providing protections through open access.[194] Most states have these types of laws in place along with information privacy laws that prevent unwarranted use and disclosure of information on private citizens that is in the hands of the government.[195] These laws, however, do not provide carte blanche access to all records in the hands of the government. For example, federal law requires that an investigation conducted for the purpose of determining suitability may not be used for any other purpose except as provided in a *Privacy Act* system of records notice published by the agency conducting the investigation.[196] In addition, the requirements of the *Freedom of Information Act*[197] generally provide that any person has a right to request access to federal agency records, except to the extent the records are protected from disclosure by any of nine exemptions contained in the law or by one of three special law enforcement record exclusions (e.g., pertains to particularly sensitive law enforcement and national security matters). The nine exemption categories that authorize government agencies to withhold information are the following:

1. Classified information for national defense or foreign policy
2. Internal personnel rules and practices
3. Information that is exempt under other laws
4. Trade secrets and confidential business information
5. Interagency or intra-agency memoranda or letters that are protected by legal privileges
6. Personnel and medical files
7. Law enforcement records or information
8. Information concerning bank supervision
9. Geological and geophysical information[198]

An example under the *Freedom of Information Law* for New York State includes the ability to deny access to records or portions thereof that[199]

1. Are specifically exempted from disclosure by state or federal statute
2. If disclosed would constitute an unwarranted invasion of personal privacy under the provisions of subdivision two of section 89 of this article
3. If disclosed would impair present or imminent contract awards or collective bargaining negotiations
4. Are trade secrets or are submitted to an agency by a commercial enterprise or derived from information obtained from a commercial enterprise and which if disclosed would cause substantial injury to the competitive position of the subject enterprise
5. Are compiled for law enforcement purposes and which, if disclosed would
   a. Interfere with law enforcement investigations or judicial proceedings
   b. Deprive a person of a right to a fair trial or impartial adjudication
   c. Identify a confidential source or disclose confidential information relating to a criminal investigation
   d. Reveal criminal investigative techniques or procedures, except routine techniques and procedures
6. If disclosed could endanger the life or safety of any person

7. Are interagency or intra-agency materials which are not
   a. Statistical or factual tabulations or data
   b. Instructions to staff that affect the public
   c. Final agency policy or determinations
   d. External audits, including, but not limited to, audits performed by the comptroller and the federal government
8. Are examination questions or answers which are requested prior to the final administration of such questions
9. If disclosed would jeopardize an agency's capacity to guarantee the security of its information technology assets, such assets encompassing both electronic information systems and infrastructures
10. Are photographs, microphotographs, videotape, or other recorded images prepared under authority of section 11011-a of the vehicle and traffic law[200]

Pre-employment investigations and screening documentation are considered part of the personnel record. Several states like Nevada have laws that keep police officer personnel records confidential.[201] An example of a statute that exempts the release of such information can be found under the *New York State Civil Rights Law*[202] where the personnel records of police officers, firefighters, and corrections officers are confidential and may not be released unless with permission of the employee or by court order. Court challenges to these privacy rules have been met with ambivalent rulings. For example, a media lawsuit for police disciplinary records was denied in New York State.[203] Conversely, in an Ohio Supreme Court ruling, the background and investigation reports were ordered disclosed. In the ruling of *Suppan v. Kratzer* (1995), the court also found no liability in the failure to keep the plaintiff's application confidential.[204] The Ohio courts ruled in a similar case that investigatory reports used to make employment decisions, even such reports as medical and psychological information, can be released as they do not directly involve law enforcement.[205] Personnel records confidentiality laws vary from state to state, and the background investigator and administrator must be well versed in the regulations of their specific jurisdictions.

From a departmental policy and process perspective, confidentiality levels vary widely.[206] From faulty departmental policies to intentional disclosures of confidential information, the issue is an ominous one. Take, for example, an improperly disclosed police background investigation where the applicant's lack of fitness for hire launched both an internal and criminal investigation to identify the person conveying the information to the media and several municipal officials.[207] Care must be taken though in pursuing such actions in light of federal and state whistleblower statutes that protect an employee from retaliation when disclosing violations of the law, rules or regulations, gross mismanagement, gross waste of funds, an abuse of authority, or a substantial and specific danger to public health or safety.[208] Specifically, these types of records releases, even though confidential employment records, may allow the discloser to enjoy the protections of the whistleblower statutes.[209] Discipline or termination that is motivated by retaliation can result in the discipline or termination being vacated and employees returned to full work status with substantial compensation.[210] Another example can be found in *Gold v. City of College Station* (2001), where an employee who disclosed wrongdoing and was also a participant in the incident alleged disparate treatment through disciplinary actions taken compared to the others who had been involved in the same wrongful acts.[211] A 2006 U.S. Supreme Court ruling limited the protections of the *First Amendment* for firefighters, police officers, and sheriff's deputies, allowing disciplinary action for exposing wrongdoing in their official capacity, but individual state laws protecting these disclosures may still offer some level of protection.[212] Whistleblower cases are becoming more prominent, and these types of incidents should not be a surprise, nor treated improperly by agency officials.[213] This entire subject certainly underscores the principle of doing everything that is legal, proper, and justified in these cases so that if a disclosure is ever made, the agency's actions are not at question as was evidenced in these examples.

In mandating policy and practice, all background investigation and pre-employment screening records should be considered confidential in nature. Policy formation of this severity can provide expectations as well as protections when a violation occurs. For example, in an online college class, two students who were in-service police command officers from separate agencies began to exchange confidential information concerning an applicant's identity and the results of a pre-employment interview and truth verification exam in an open discussion room. They were immediately advised to refrain from disclosing this type of information in this forum. Policies would hopefully deter this type of exchange as well as protect the agency if this information caused any damage or came to light.

Background documentation, polygraph analysis, psychological evaluations, and medical examinations should all be secured and filed separately. The *Americans with Disabilities Act of 1990* mandates that all medical records (which include psychiatric examinations, medical information disclosed as part of the COE, and integrity testing results that also contain medical information) must be kept confidential and maintained in separate medical files.[214] While this info must be available to the processing agency, information concerning medical and psychiatric information should not be disclosed to other law enforcement agencies during their processing even with a waiver from the applicant. This issue is discussed in further depth in Chapter 4 (also see the Chapter 5 section, "Information Release Authorizations and Release of Liability Forms," and Appendix H). Accreditation standards, addressed later in this chapter, also require secure locations for these types of records. These are in addition to the requirements of state and federal laws. Above all, there is an ethical requirement and moral obligation to protect the confidentiality of these sensitive records.

This information must be kept confidential from everyone except those who have the authority or legitimate reason to view the records. One of the greatest demands placed on the background unit is requests for a case status from other police officers, police officers who are relatives or acquaintances of the applicant, other units and divisions, command officers with no connection to the process, politicians, and sometimes your own chief executive's curiosity. Policy and command fortitude must reign supreme in these cases. Until the final recommendation is codified, no one really can say with any level of certainty what an applicant's final status will be. Cases will also progress well for lengthy periods of time and then take drastic turns for the worst as different stages are completed. A sign of promise in the early stages may be met with an applicant who has violated, or violates, a standard that forces exclusion from the process. A poor rating on a professional evaluation may trickle in after the applicant has been given a green light on the background investigation. These situations all create consternation on the part of all the stakeholders, so the best practice is to never disclose case information to any unauthorized persons outside of the review and decision chain. Once the applicants receive their letter, they alone are free to disclose the contents to anyone they choose to.

The final issues of confidentiality deal with the dichotomy of care in promising confidentiality when it may be violated for legitimate or illegitimate purposes. We should only promise what we can deliver. Mistakes, leaks, and court mandate may force disclosure that is beyond our control, so the applicant needs to know that these issues may occur. Lastly, while the information may be exposed either intentionally or inadvertently, the candidate, unless required by a state law, has no authority or right to review the investigative documentation in the package that they did not complete or offer themselves. A policy to prevent release must be developed and enforced at the organizational level. Under these circumstances, unless through a release by applicant waiver to another processing agency or through litigation and a court order, the applicant should not be allowed to view or copy any of the investigative or screening documentation for their own edification or use.

ALTERNATIVE METHODS TO IN-HOUSE SCREENING

Most law enforcement organizations do not have the budget or expertise to employ the professionals for every component of the process. From psychologists, to medical doctors, and experts at cognitive testing development and interpretation, departments must use contractors for these specialized and varied testing processes. For the background investigation process, many agencies hire out these services through alternative methods. Agencies may use the services of larger agencies, private investigators, and other departments within a municipal or state agency. The following discusses some of those options available.

Contract private investigators: Private investigators are being hired by agencies with limited means as well as limited expertise in the background investigation process. Many retired police officers who were responsible to conduct backgrounds in their full-time law enforcement positions have retired and now do so as private contractors.[215] Fee structures vary from actual time invested, maximum fees with the option to approve additional investigation, or a set fee for every background investigation. Investigators should either be hired directly by the organization or work under the auspices of their own state investigative licensure structure. Minimum experience, training, bonding, and insurance should all meet the state level and organizational requirements.

In *U.S. v. Virginia* (1998), the FBI hired retired FBI agents to conduct background investigations.[216] As a requirement, they must follow the Federal Acquisitions Requirements (FAR) found in the *Code of Federal Regulations*.[217] In 1990, the FBI instituted the Background Investigation Contract Services (BICS) Program. As part of the compliance to FAR, the agency must affirmatively determine that the bidder is a responsible entity. In order to make that responsibility determination, the agency must conclude that the contractor has, among other things, adequate financial resources to perform the contract, or the ability to obtain them, a satisfactory performance record, a satisfactory record of integrity and business ethics, and the necessary organization, experience, and technical skills, or the ability to obtain them. In addition, the Statement of Work provides that BICS contractors must be former federal investigators who have experience conducting background investigations and who qualify for a top secret security clearance.[218] This series of requirements provides an excellent launching point for a department to develop standards and criteria for the selection and use of private contractors to do background investigations.

This fast developing cottage industry may seem like a viable option for an agency that has limited human resources and cannot afford personnel shortages that are created to conduct extensive background checks, but, in essence, you get what you pay for. One other issue is the lack of control over the investigation when contracted out. A contractor will only complete the services contracted for leaving the agency with some very difficult decisions to make when the investigation goes into cost overruns. Opponents argue that the industry is unregulated and does not give sufficient emphasis on compliance or on hiring quality people.[219] Many of the private companies that have compiled electronic databases purportedly capturing this type of information are also extremely inaccurate for the purposes of this type of investigation.[220] The screening practices are exceptionally perfunctory, allowing countless job applicants to slip through the cracks who would not have been hired had the proper investigation been conducted.[221] Most importantly, the choice to use a contractor may not avert but rather result in substantial liability on behalf of the hiring authority.[222] Several examples can be found on how contractors have failed to conduct thorough investigations on law enforcement applicants that results in not only embarrassment but also criminal and civil charges being levied. One example involves an applicant who was investigated by a contractor who missed information that should have been included in background concerning a history of domestic violence that led to an order of protection, restraining order, or any other type of court order. This same applicant, after hire and training, was alleged to have committed several sexual assaults on females during a series of traffic stops.[223] At the opposite end of the spectrum, agencies have been called to task for engaging in patently illegal questioning concerning such protected areas as alcohol and drug use, physical and/or psychological disabilities, financial issues, and sexual preference.[224] Cases like these serve the argument that this is not a recommended practice unless the agency strictly controls the process and holds the contractor civilly liable for the same requirements that the agency must live to. The standard of information that is either known or should have been known must be the guiding principle to ensure the contractor has more accountability than just the delivery of a written report at stake.

Private organizations known commonly as online data brokers also fall into this category. Companies are offering services to conduct computerized online searches of databases and providing background reports almost solely on the online information discovered. These types of searches can be valuable as a component of the process, but must be abutted by real investigative work to confirm or refute information provided by the company. Information developed should only be considered as a lead until such time that physical follow-up confirms the veracity.

Hiring agency retirees: Agency retirees who are familiar with the process can be brought back on a part-time or contractual basis and work under the supervision of a background investigation supervisor or commander. This option has better possibilities than the use of a private investigator as the agency can exercise more control over the quality of the investigation and hopefully these individuals will have a buy-in to the organization's needs for hiring quality personnel. International research has revealed that this concept has merit in the administrative investigation realm with the proviso that the investigators used be screened for the highest professional qualities and standards of performance.[225]

Internal entities: Law enforcement agencies will often do their own background investigations as discussed in detail later in the text. Current issues and emerging trends are forcing investigations to be far more comprehensive in public safety positions as well as expanding the scope of positions that the background investigation must be completed in. Public safety positions also include firefighters, corrections personnel, and emergency dispatchers. The use of law enforcement personnel to investigate the varied positions can enhance the process and provide an objective investigation as they are not members of the requesting department.

External entities: Law enforcement agencies can also use the services of external entities to conduct investigation on their prospective candidates. The U.S. Office of Personnel Management (OPM) is one example. OPM conducts background investigations for most federal agencies and their contractors.[226] Using other agencies to conduct your department's background investigations is also an option. A larger agency and state level divisions can offer personnel, resources, and higher levels of expertise in the process. The use of another agency can also go far to remove any claims of favoritism in the process of a department that may be under scrutiny or being challenged in some type of litigation.

Strategic alliances and multidepartment consortiums: Strategic alliances can be formed with other law enforcement organizations.[227] These multidepartment consortiums contribute to the development of an eligibility pool of candidates that all agencies can draw from.[228] There are several advantages, including the sharing of information, expertise, and resources to process groups of applicants who can be hired by any one of the agencies in the consortium. This also saves the duplication of efforts when an applicant applies to several agencies in the consortium and must be investigated by every separate agency. Problems may occur though if departments begin competing for the same candidates or inordinate responsibilities are placed on a single agency in the consortium.

These are all alternative methods for an organization to the background investigation. If well-managed and committed people are completing the background, then the alternatives may be very viable options for agencies that do not have the in-house resources to commit to these very lengthy and complex investigations. The recommended method is for the chief executive to have complete authority and access to the investigative process in order to make the best hiring decisions possible. This is best accomplished by the use of in-house, fully trained, and highly committed investigators.

TEAM APPROACH TO PRE-EMPLOYMENT SCREENING

To be efficient, effective, and serve the needs of the organization, the pre-employment screening process must be a team approach. As discussed in systems thinking, every component of the process must work in concert to achieve the ultimate goal of hiring the best-qualified applicants for the organization's human resource needs. The human capital of the organization can advance this goal through the sharing of their knowledge of culture, policy, and procedures of the organization.[229] The traditional hierarchical process must acquiesce to a more functional and process-driven model where department command; human resources; legal, medical, and psychological staff; and the background investigator all work as complementary and equal members of the selection process team. The background investigator should be considered an integral part of this team rather than subordinate to the process. All other roles in the process should be supportive of the background investigator's work.

A knowledge-based team must be built to fulfill the functional needs of this process.[230] Ultimately, this type of multidisciplinary and cross-functional team should be responsible for designing and improving the entire process.[231] Once assembled and in working form, the team members can identify missed opportunities and improvement points that will continuously enhance the process. The levels of cooperation in these types of teams must be high not only with the relationship between the horizontal ranks but also among operational staff as well as supervision and command.[232] Everyone on the selection team must take ownership of the process for the process to be successful.[233] Teamwork in its most valuable form brings balance to the complexities of the entire process.[234]

Role of the Background Investigator

The background investigator serves a pivotal role in the organization. They are the consummate link between the applicant and the department. While the applicant will have contacts with human resources, professional evaluators, and other key entities in the process, they will most likely put all of their faith and trust in the process in the background investigator assigned. As the veritable entry point to the organization, the background investigator has the enormous and dichotomous responsibilities of being both gatekeeper and greeter. An *Applicant Whisperer* of sorts, resolving processual issues and barriers faced by the applicant to keep them interested and motivated in gaining employment with the agency. The background investigator carries parallel responsibilities of ensuring only the best make it and those who do must have a level of comfort and acceptance bestowed on them throughout the process. The background investigator must work diligently to uncover all relevant facts of the applicant's history while also developing a relationship between the applicant and the organization. This is an extremely challenging balance to maintain to say the least. A thankless role, the background investigator's lot is often not a happy one.

Often a marginalized position in the organization, the background investigator's responsibilities are also complex and burdensome. The U.S. Merit Systems Protection Board describes the role as, "The investigations are performed by specialists trained to probe and analyze a great deal of information about each applicant."[235] This type of acumen is well beyond the scope of a criminal investigator's areas of job knowledge as the background investigator must not only be able to conduct the normal activities of a criminal investigator, but must also be a personnel specialist in order to fulfill their duties.[236] The background investigator must be a logical thinker, able to coalesce the volumes of information collected from significantly large data sources, and develop enabling relationships and networks both internally and externally in order to perform the functions both efficiently and effectively.[237] As evidenced by the information brought forward in this text, legal, procedural, ethical, and humanistic considerations are replete in most every background investigation conducted. The background investigator must view each and every investigation as a new challenge rather than falling into a mindless routine of punch list activities.[238] The background investigator must have not only technical knowledge and skill but also a blend of civility and savvy in dealing with the prevalent organizational and political culture and conflicts that will arise. Tenacity, strength of purpose, legal and ethical boundaries, and intestinal fortitude will all be tested at various points in the professional career, and those who believe in the process must rise to the challenges that lie ahead. The skills required of a background investigator make them specialists in their own right.[239]

The background investigator must possess numerous positive and driving characteristics. The characteristics that are predominant must be those of objective reasonableness in actions, logical thought processes that lead to efficient and effective task completion, and a high level of pragmatism.[240] For example, the background investigator must be able to fairly examine all of the evidence obtained in the investigation free from the influence of negative or preconceived paradigms.[241] With this thought in mind, integrity is paramount. Background investigators must live to a higher standard as evidenced by their personal history in the organization. Histories of discrimination, excessive force, sustained personnel complaints, or sexual harassment must be immediate grounds for rejection of applications for the position. The ramifications of falsifying employment records, for good or ill, can have civil and criminal implications as well as lead to employment sanctions cannot be overstated as well.[242] The background investigator's work product will be the legacy of the organization. When considering the higher standards placed on law enforcement agencies as a result of the requirements of countless, yet relevant federal and state laws that are buttressed by evolving case law decisions, the human resource function has become a far more complex process over the past few decades.[243] The background investigator's conduct must comply with all local, state, and federal standards of the proper methods and tactics of the investigative process (e.g., *ADA* compliance).[244] Screening and selection of the background investigator must comply with these types of standards so that no bias can be successfully claimed. Race and gender are commonly alleged bias claims in these types of processes. Alternative lifestyles and applicants who are gay and lesbian must also not face these types of prejudices. With the last organization to hold out in banning the admittance of gay and lesbian applicants to their ranks, the U.S. military is forgoing the requirements of forbidding this type of sexual orientation in the military; law enforcement agencies must also neither publicly nor privately discourage their candidacy.[245] The background investigators must also be screened for any propensity toward bias of any kind that may manifest itself in the selection process.[246] An organization can be held civilly liable if the selected investigator has some bias toward the subject of the personnel investigation who may be a member of a protected class.[247] Complaints of bias or impropriety of the background investigator must also be addressed in a timely and appropriate manner.[248] The background investigator must be the personification of the officer the agency is attempting to bring into the ranks as an example to those they are processing for the roles.[249] Consequently, investigator selection should be carefully designed, efficient, and validated in order to ensure the appointment of highly productive personnel.[250] Each agency should have its own unique and validated selection criteria for the position.[251] Application standards and screening should include the following basic parameters:

1. Integrity
2. Tenacity
3. Organization skills
4. Investigative acumen
5. Communication skills
6. Decision-making skills
7. Administrative skills
8. Knowledge of employment and hiring laws, rules, regulations, and departmental policies
9. Ability to testify with unimpeachable credibility in administrative and judicial settings
10. Minimum service, experiential, and educational requirements
11. Demonstrated desire to be an integral part of the screening and hiring process

Organizational administrators may also consider more in-depth testing processes of prospective background investigators. A basic written qualifier of cognitive knowledge of the process components and regulations or application essay that discusses their preparation, desire, and suitability to serve in the role can be required. Dependent upon the circumstances, state laws, and collective bargaining agreements, the organizational administrators could conduct psychological and polygraph examinations on those who apply to be background investigators. This would measure psychological fitness and truthfulness of the applicant in order to provide a higher level of screening to the background investigator application process. The position is highly influential to the future of the organization. Organizational managers and administrators should not assign investigations to anyone in the organization that is not qualified or not interested in the basic investigative needs as well as the future of the organization. The role is both technical and human, dealing with those who are in the organization and those who desire to be. Minimizing or marginalizing the position speaks highly to the lack of commitment of the organization's administration to the organization's future.

Role of the Investigative Coordinator

The background process should include the position of investigative coordinator. In agencies that process consistently, or when hiring drives occur, this position can be invaluable. In smaller agencies, a supervisor or command officer may have to fill both this role and their own; however, agency administrators should always consider the use of someone in this position as part of the quality assurance and control of the process.

An investigative coordinator can oversee the entire process offering guidance and technical advice to the background investigators. They can track status and develop statistics, handle scheduling of different components of the process, and perform supervisory functions in the absence of the background investigation supervisor. With respect to information and data, an investigative coordinator can collate, filter, and disseminate relevant information so that the overwhelming amount of information collected can be put to the best use. The law enforcement field has evolved from the most basic reactive functions to being driven by information that is developed by multiple sources.[252] An investigative coordinator is needed to assist in the effective cultivation and management of this type of information. Investigative coordinators can develop liaisons with other police departments, other background investigation unit staff, businesses, educational institutions, and the like. Research has revealed that a significant portion of an investigator's time is wasted in unproductive activities.[253] Coordinators can develop strategies to limit this amount of wasted time through assisting in case planning strategies and completing the front-end work for an investigator to build from. Much of the case preparation and groundwork requiring records checks, letters of request, and document collection are just a few of the tasks that this position can be responsible for. They can also analyze preliminary drafts and final packages for quality control purposes and act as another independent voice in case review for the recommending supervisor. A list of responsibilities could include, but are not limited to, the following:

1. Identify training needs and develop training programs for new and tenured background investigators. Field train background investigators in the administrative investigation process. Train investigators in the administrative proceedings process related to selection processing.
2. Act as a mentor to all officers in investigative techniques and administrative processes and requirements.
3. Assign officers to specific cases. Supervise and control major or lengthy background investigations with the permission of the unit supervisor. Track all cases to ensure equitable and fair investigative management.
4. Ensure that all investigation reports and documents are fully and accurately completed in a timely manner and presented as a total package for proper disposition.

5. Maintain all investigative and administrative records of ongoing investigations as to status, processing dates, and hiring or deselection decisions. Supervise and manage all records release requests and releases.
6. Ensure that the chain of command is kept fully apprised of the status of all ongoing and completed investigations.
7. Liaison for support services such as medical, psychological, human resources, legal, etc.
8. Act as the primary liaison for all accreditation efforts.

Role of the Investigative Supervisor

The pre-employment investigation process requires not only direct supervision but also, more importantly, a supervisor who is versed in the employment screening process and can focus their attention to ensure that the tenets of the process are being adhered to. Like the background investigator, the investigative supervisor should embrace and be a model of the characteristics and high levels of integrity and professionalism that the organization is seeking in the candidates to be hired.[254] The lack of proper supervision often leads to irreparable problems. Supervisors in these roles hold others accountable and can be held accountable for their actions and the known improper actions of their subordinates.

As difficult as this is, it is the reality. Legal action can be brought against a police organization and the agency's alleged improper hiring practices under *Title 42 Section 1983* of the *United States Code* and Title VII of the *Civil Rights Act of 1964*.[255] Supervisors and command officers who fail to take appropriate disciplinary measures when officers engage in conduct or behavior that contradicts the mandates of the law may suffer personal liability as well as allowing the organization to be unnecessarily exposed.[256] The background investigator must work to protect the civil rights of all those who apply to the organization in order to avoid these types of situations.

Investigative supervisors serve many additional functions in the process. Similar to investigative coordinators, they are monitors of quality control and assurance. Quality can be negatively impacted by many factors including faulty operations, lack of motivation, and excessive workload. Faulty operations can encompass the collective selection process or any of the components that can fail. A lack of motivation on the part of the background investigator may also be detrimental to the quality of the investigative process. Often, the process suffers from overload. The lack of sufficient physical and human resources takes its toll on the investigators managing large caseloads and in the process making mistakes in order to meet arbitrary deadlines. One finding of the Independent Commission on the Los Angeles Police Department revealed that background investigators were severely overworked lending in part to unqualified candidates who were able to slip through the selection process.[257] Consequently, to avoid these issues, investigative supervisors need to stay close to the process, monitor actions, and continuously guide their subordinates toward quality investigations.[258]

Supervisors and managers must ensure a process is in place to manage the continuing investigation process before there will be any measure of success in the system.[259] Managing the investigative process requires the ability to develop objectives for which individual and collective performance can be measured against.[260] The investigative supervisor must master three key areas of the supervision and management process: (1) motivation, (2) evaluation, and (3) inspection. With respect to motivation, supervisors should communicate through expectancy and equity theory the motivators of high performance. High performance must then be consistently rewarded through official and personal recognition, job satisfaction, empowerment, and additional more challenging and developmental responsibilities.[261] Through the supportive structure that performance evaluation systems provide, supervisors are able to positively modify behaviors by providing reinforcing feedback. The evaluation of work performance emphasizes measurements of behaviors against an objective job standard, identification of any gaps that may exist, and training or remedially training in the area of deficiency to raise performance to validated organizational expectations.[262] Staff inspections are the supervisors' method of assessing unit achievements, employee efforts with regard to the stated mission and design of the unit, and if the unit's efforts are in the furtherance of the organizational mission as a whole.[263] Having a grasp of these three constructs is a priority for the supervisor to effectively manage the efforts of others.

Supervisors must also maintain the free flow of information, acting as a conduit that connects line employees to command personnel. Policies, directives, and philosophies of management must be correctly filtered and interpreted for conveyance to line personnel, while the concerns and suggestions of line personnel must be fully developed and supported to command by the supervisor.[264] The background investigation process results in the culling of enormous amounts of information that must be analyzed and applied correctly. This only happens when everyone involved in the process can participate in the decision-making process and information flow provides for informed decision-making processes. One of the most positive intangibles of information transparency is the building of trusting relationships. Trust must then evolve into the high levels of reciprocity that continue to build the long-term relationships necessary for success between supervisor and subordinate. From this, supervisors must recognize and build upon the concept that each investigative team member contributes to the overall process of the investigation.[265] Teams are built through the strong ties of these types of relationships. The supervisor must master the art of managing people, not the science of managing situations.

This role is critical in communicating an independent assessment of the true character of the applicant to the administration and championing the role of preventing those who are unfit from entering the ranks of the organization.[266] The investigative supervisor brings a wealth of knowledge and experience that allows for common sense decision making to enter into the prudence of applicant selection.[267] Recommendations for candidacy or exclusion should come from higher authority than the investigator.[268] The background investigation supervisor or command officer should bear the responsibility of this task with the input of the background investigator as a guide.

Role of Administrator and Chief Executive Officer

The next link in the value chain is that of administrator and chief executive officer. Administrators can do much to advance the organization and improve performance by using recruitment and development as an integral part of the larger organizational strategy.[269] With respect to administrator input into this process, department administrators can do much to remove the barriers that impede maximum quality output of the selection process. This will require a commitment to rethink the current hierarchical and descending bureaucratic paradigms that are in place in most public safety organizations. Many of the problems faced on the criminal investigation side of the house are created by management miscommunication, conflicting policies, and faulty practices.[270] The lack of managerial control has been proven to cause numerous issues in the investigative process, to include inequitable caseloads, improper case assignment, unproductive prioritization, procrastination of investigations, and inconsistency in investigative techniques.[271] This holds true on the administrative investigation side as well. Management must make a commitment to perpetually examine the preliminary and continued investigation processes at all levels in order to ensure continued effectiveness.[272] What this section addresses is many of the overarching issues that organizational administrators and chief executives should consider as drivers and barriers in the process.

First up on the list is the organizational structure of centralization vs. decentralization of process argument, which is omnipresent with the question of should the department employ a specialized unit to complete these tasks or simply allow generalists with other responsibilities to perform these tasks. Specialization and singularly committed assignments seldom lend themselves to success with agencies of limited size and capacity.[273] The smaller the agency, the more balance is required between normal and specialized duties. Aligned with this concept is the issue of permanent vs. rotational assignments of the background investigator. On the criminal investigator side, there are arguments both for and against the concept. The proponents see this as an opportunity to cross-train and develop more flexibility in the organization as well as an opportunity to provide more professional development. Others see the role as one that requires a high level of skill and training that is augmented by practical experience, and rotation can prove to be highly detrimental to the quality of the investigative process.[274] This decision will be impacted by need, organizational size, and collective bargaining agreement that will influence permanency in the role.

Next on the list is that public safety organizations are extremely complex systems. As a component of the criminal justice suprasystem, they are also made of countless subsystems of police, courts, and corrections. Each entity also has a series of subsystems, for example, policing has patrol and investigations as well as operations and administration. The interplay between these subsystems has a consistent impact on the outcomes of the suprasystem. Organizational administrators must consider these affects and how their personal actions can influence the system from a positive perspective, rather than a stagnant or negative perspective. These types of systems are also complex adaptive systems that are in a constant state of change. Complexity and diversity make up the multiple interconnected elements of the system, and the continually adaptive nature of the components of the system allows for the capacity to change and learn from those continued experiences.[275] Complex adaptive systems may also have an indirect effect on the organization through mediating variables of organizational identity and social movements.[276] As discussed earlier, law enforcement organizations have strong organizational identities and are highly social organizations. The selection process must be considered as an integral part of the entire organizational schema. The selection process should also be geared to constantly adapt to the continued and changing human resource needs of the organization's short- and long-term succession planning goals. Senior administrators must embrace the concept of complex adaptive systems in order to place this process in the perspective that it rightly deserves.

Complexity science uses leadership concepts to enhance the dynamic interactions between all individuals in the organization. Through these interactions, innovation is often encouraged through opportunities to experiment. The support system is then formed through collective action rather than through any single employee.[277] Leadership at all levels is, quite frankly, obligatory. Quality leadership at this level, though, is a critical function that must be carried out by those who have risen to these policy- and decision-making authority positions within the organization. Leadership in its development in law enforcement has literally become the bane of the discipline though. Dozens of recognized models, hundreds of characteristics, and thousands of books and seminars have yet to infuse a substantive impact on the field. Sadly, in law enforcement, very poor, frequently divisive, and highly unethical management practices are portrayed as effective leadership skills. What many in positions of leadership fail to realize though is that *yelling like General George S. Patton doesn't make you General George S. Patton!* The intent of this part of the discussion is not to review what we have all learned in *Leadership 101*. The intent is to cover some advanced and forgotten perfunctory concepts that are necessary for the administrators and managers of the selection process to understand and embrace.

The predominant leadership taxonomies include administrative leadership, enabling leadership, and adaptive leadership.[278] Technical competency is, by far, shadowed by the leader's ability to enable organizational processes and adapt to the continually changing landscape of the field so that progress can never be bottlenecked. To do this, leaders must analyze their strengths and weaknesses as well as those of others in order to surround themselves with a competent and productive staff.[279] Leaders accomplish the goals of the organization with others *not through* others. One inescapable fact that is a measure of leadership quality is that leadership is a social process.[280] Research has revealed that motivation to engage in problem solving is often a product of the leader's perceptions, attention, and actions rather than being driven by an internal motivation of the employee.[281] Therefore, problem solving emerges from the leader's engagement with the employee rather than being the employee's sole responsibility. Leaders are a part of the solution, not the driving force of the proposed or speculated solution. Leaders must invigorate reengineering processes and prevent their impeded flow by keeping passive and active resistance from employees and managers in check as well as keeping organizational bureaucracy to a minimum, always focusing on process integrity, effectiveness, and customer satisfaction.[282] Managers demonstrate leadership qualities when they recruit and cultivate talent to fill the necessary positions of pre-employment selection team members.[283] They should also be masters of change management techniques. Leaders of change must recognize the stages of the change cycle: (1) realizing the need to change, (2) planning the change, (3) implementing the change, and (4) sustaining the change.[284] This process, as discussed in complex adaptive systems, will require constant change to stay ahead of the continuing needs of the selection process.

Leadership requirements do not end there! Leaders must have highly developed communication skills. Vertical and horizontal communication must be accurate and transparent for the leader to keep those in their sphere of influence informed as well as to develop credibility among their staff. Selection processes often suffer from unwarranted reputations—too tough or too lenient is the standard hue and cry from stakeholders and bystanders alike, and unit reputation must be managed in order to bring credibility and validity to the work of those directly involved in the selection process. Therefore, communication must also be designed to strategically manage the reputation of the unit.[285]

Leaders must have a prognosticator's ability to see the future. This is a much more complex characteristic than simply portending that substandard applicants will develop into poor quality employees. Leaders must develop a vision of the organization's preferred future that is inclusive of the best human resources available in the field. To do this, managers and administrators must ascribe to the concepts of visionary leadership wherein they develop a view of the future that is grounded in core beliefs and values.[286] Values and principles must be based on law and morality, not on self-advancement at the cost of all others.

As seers of the future, administrators and managers must also plan for the inevitable cyclical effects of budget ebbs. Invariably, departments will have highs and lows in the fiscal environment that continues to repeat itself through the life of our organizations. What transpires in the life of the organization are circular dialogues that accomplish virtually nothing. Leaders must plan for the inevitable budget cuts in advance as they often can translate to personnel cuts. The economy will rise and fall and so will the public's cry for sound fiscal management balanced against the needs of increased public safety. An ominous situation is created in the worst of times when budgets are cut that include the severance of public safety personnel, often the last positions cut from a municipal budget. Recent events in the economy have forced agencies from the east to west coast to drastically slash sworn positions in their agencies in order to balance their budgets.[287] This, coupled with massive retirements, will create enormous hiring needs when the economy rights itself. Consequently, agencies will scramble to meet these needs, accomplishing the goals through forced hiring processes that lead to long-term problems. Agency leaders must not relegate this process as a back burner or parking lot item until after times return to normal. By then, it is ultimately too late. The investments in keeping the process fluid and alive will reap substantial rewards when the cycle returns to the status quo.

Lastly, leaders of character and principle should occupy all roles in the process of selecting new employees for the organization.[288] They must demonstrate the highest levels of integrity in dealing with the professional futures of those who apply to occupy positions of trust in law enforcement as well as to those employees who are under their charge. They must also demonstrate this integrity to those who they follow in the organization and have the resilience to forbear those who would violate these principles for political expedience. Leaders must never lose sight of the fact that they are responsible to manage those negative forces in the organization as well as the positive. Administrators must avoid such damaging influences as bureaucracy, turf battles, and unnecessary administrative procedures in order to make the process efficient and effective.[289] Leaders must endeavor to bring civility to the workplace and take appropriate action against those who work to poison the work environment for others.[290] Intergroup conflict in these types of structures must be managed to focus the effort of all entities on the goal of productivity.[291] This will require a high level of introspection to measure whether or not the leader may be a significant contributor to the problem. The leader's responsibilities are to direct, develop, and, most importantly, to console those under their charge.[292] We have truly lost our way, and we need leaders of quality and character to guide us back. The challenge is not to look above you to see who fits the bill, because you will likely be highly disappointed and possibly suffer irreparable damage. The challenge is to be this leader in your organization! Rainmakers come in many forms. In this process, the leader must be that rainmaker to bring lasting and productive change to this often dysfunctional process.

In our knowledge-driven economy, tacit, not codified knowledge, is our most precious commodity. Knowledge management, knowledge transfer, and learning management are a part of the value chain that the administrator and chief executive must create. Collective works on the background investigation process are rare and frequently do not match the needs of an individual organization. Educational interventions, while an effective strategy for implementing knowledge, are different than knowledge translation which deals with contextual meaning, understanding, and application for the target audience.[293] Successful navigation of these waters comes mostly from experience. Rudimentary training or exposure is followed by trial and error experiences that will shape the background investigator's approach to the investigative and administrative process. Tacit knowledge is also termed institutional knowledge. Institutional knowledge exists in complex adaptive systems. Administrators and chief executives must develop systems and culture that allow permeation of the institutional knowledge through such theories as the Diffusion of Innovations model and the development of knowledge management systems.[294] Leaders should become aware of the stages of organizational learning diffusion: (1) agenda setting, (2) matching, (3) restructuring, (4) clarifying, and (5) routinizing.[295] Leadership models must be shaped around a knowledge-based economy and encourage this concept of knowledge diffusion. Complexity Leadership Theory fosters the enabling of learning, creativity, and adaptive capacity in knowledge-producing organizations.[296] Department administrators must consider the knowledge needs of the organization. Capturing the tacit knowledge base of background investigators should be a priority as often the toolbox of critical skills are not documented anywhere except in the investigator's mind.[297] Knowledge must become a business and social resource for the organization especially in a process that is so dependent upon tacit knowledge to function effectively.[298] Territorial knowledge hoarding must be ended in lieu of knowledge diffusion techniques. Naturalistic diffusion leads to the spread of innovation in an organization.[299] A science of dissemination can then be formed by adapting intervention techniques through evidence-based practices, programs, and policies used in the field.[300]

The administrator uses the screening process as a functional strategy to control the prospect of improper police behavior.[301] Quality management through innovation and change is also part of the administrator's and chief executive officer's responsibilities in this process of screening-out poor quality candidates. The quality of the investigation of an applicant's history often rests in the support provided by management to the background investigator and the investigation process.[302] Management must take an active role in the selection process to avoid hiring candidates who are found unqualified or ultimately terminate their employment because they were not the appropriate fit for the organization.[303] Managers must also identify and utilize all devices of quality at their disposal to ensure that an ever-improving level of quality encompasses the entire process.[304] Frequent reevaluation of the pre-employment screening process is required to accomplish all of these goals.[305]

Role of the Human Resource Department

The human resource department also has a central role in the process. Often turf battles ensue over who is in charge of the selection process. The reality is that everyone should own the process and work together to fight for the right candidates rather than fighting over who's in charge. Ironically, that person seems to disappear when a decision goes bad and fingers get drawn like six guns of children playing cowboys and Indians. And no matter how many times we have seen this happen, we never seem to learn how unproductive these practices are. Instead, we should work toward very high levels of cohesiveness with human resource professionals and consider them an equal partner in the process of selection.

The human resource department, section, or unit is charged with the responsibility of handling all personnel matters in fair and equitable terms as well as ensuring the organization is complying with all applicable laws, rules, and regulations.[306] Because of this, human resource professionals should have a key role in developing the organization's policies on pre-employment selection processes. As expert advisors to the process, human resource administrators also serve to assist and monitor the behaviors of other managers in the organization to ensure that compliance and quality is maintained.[307] Some agencies have elevated the roles of human resource managers to the same decision-making authority as high level law enforcement command officers in an effort to increase efficiency in the process that is often impeded by unnecessary multilevel command reviews.[308]

Human resources should be involved in all short- and long-term planning of the public safety organization. The overwhelming majority of processes in a public safety agency are driven by the human resources and thus have human resource process or function implications attached. Human resource planning is the path to connect strategic planning and management to the organization's human resource functions.[309] Human resource personnel should also assist in the development of the long-term organizational strategies in order to develop the policies that will be followed to keep the organization moving toward the chief executive's overall goals.[310]

Many other responsibilities and goals attach to the human resource function in a public safety organization. For example, the objectives of a human resource department should include several goals, including the stabilization of the organization's emerging employment needs as well as matching the identified human resource needs of the organization with qualified and capable applicants.[311] One proven method to meet this goal is to actively engage in human resource forecasting that is consistent with the future human resource needs of the organization.[312] All of the stakeholder's processes must be in alignment and not conflict with the ultimate goal of hiring the most qualified applicants.

Some recommended strategies to ensure alignment are focus groups and steering committees of all of the involved stakeholders to have input into the process rather than separate units developing policies and procedures in a vacuum as opposed to the open air of collaborative discussion. Another strategy is to employ the use of teams or human resource roundtables that can be used to reduce risk by infusing insight and continuous improvement methods to the selection process.[313] One of the best strategies is to create a culture in the organization where the human resource function becomes an integral part of everyone's job in the organization rather than being relegated to a single staff.[314] Ultimately, the primary goal of the human resource function must always be to ensure fairness, kindness, and efficiency of operations and purpose in the pre-employment selection process.[315]

Role of the Legal Advisor

Much like human resources, legal advisors must be considered equal partners on the selection team with the only caveat that they have the tie-breaking vote in personnel matters. The function of the legal advisor is necessary due to many factors that include continual changes in criminal and civil law, society's evolving needs, and the public's right to accountability and professionalism from their law enforcement officers.[316] Legal advisors serve an important role as part of the pre-employment selection team. They provide legal advice on employment law, assist in developing policies and practices, review applicant records to ensure compliance standards are met, and act as a liaison to hiring bodies like the civil service commission or alternate hiring authority.[317] Their work is highly valued and should be sought after in this very complex process.

Legal advisors have a broad range of professional responsibilities to the selection process including training program development, administrative duties, and advisory roles to support the process as well as the chief executive of the agency.[318] In developing their primary responsibilities in this role, one of the most important functions they fulfill is that of educator. Legal advisors should have a central role in the development of training and policy development in a public safety organization.[319] As a matter of fact, legal advisors should concentrate much of their work on being a trainer, educating those in the pre-employment selection process on the correct applications of employment law. Some techniques of training dissemination to consider would be the use of training lectures, newsletters, and direct access of the background investigator to the legal advisor.[320] They should also have several additional qualities such as some law enforcement experience, so they can relate to the issues they will face and be able to develop informed decisions and legal response strategies in this environment. They should possess highly developed facilitator skills as they will be exposed to all levels and ranks in the law enforcement organization as well as with supportive departments including human resources and other hiring authority entities. Also of critical importance is that they should be good communicators.[321] They will be dealing internally and externally with all stakeholders, including the applicants.

In-house counsel is the most preferred method. For larger agencies, a police legal advisor can work directly for the department. If a corporation counsel or municipal attorney structure exists for the municipality, an attorney or series of attorneys can be assigned direct responsibilities or as a liaison to the agency. For small organizations, one cost-saving measure would include the development of a consortium to hire an expert legal advisor who has the legal training and experience in employment law to advise all of the agencies.[322]

The police legal advisor should be welcomed into the process as opposed to being viewed and treated as a barrier to the process. In contrast, police legal advisors must enter the process with the motivation, legal acumen, and proper temperament to work effectively with this diverse group. The police legal advisor rounds out the entire pre-employment selection team to ensure a balanced and holistic approach to the selection process is constantly maintained.

Promoting Interagency Cooperation

Interagency cooperation is necessary in the pre-employment selection process. Developing information concerning applicant history and the evidence to certify or decertify the applicant may conceivably rest in the inaccessible files of another agency. Relationship building with other agencies both local and distance can help overcome the barrier of distance, time, and resources in order to complete the investigation.[323]

Many organizations in a specific area or region will cross-background applicants who are applying to multiple agencies within the region. Developing networks with background investigators, coordinators, and supervisors with those agencies will expedite the communication process as well as open the flow of records and documentation review. One of the most effective methods we miss in this process is likened to the crime analysis model wherein regional crime coordinators gather on a regular basis to discuss crime trends. Fusion centers are used to track regional patterns and trends of crime in order to develop intelligence information and strategies to address those identified patterns. In contrast, other than on an as needed basis, these background investigation entities do not collaborate in information or effort sharing. Applicants become more sophisticated in learning the process the longer they are in the process and the more agencies they apply to. A methodology like this could go far to prevent applicants from beating the system as it were. This would also go far to reduce duplication of efforts for investigators who have completed tasks that can be used perpetually in the process. Information and document sharing should also improve in this type of environment. We can choose to work harder or choose to work smarter.

Application Package Review Board

The chief executive, or by mandate of a consent decree or municipal policy, may authorize the use of an application package review board. This process is separate from a civil service commission or hiring authority review. The composite of the board would be that of the previously cited positions for the selection committee; however, this process is designed for more independent and not collaborative review of the applicant investigation package wherein each member has input by way of voting rights rather than equal or subordinate input to form a consensus. Care must be taken in these types of arrangements as they provide far too many opportunities for the advancement of personal agendas and to unduly lay blame on other doorsteps. As previously discussed, everyone in the process should have a vested interest in the process from their level or authority or expertise in selecting the best candidates. In contrast, no one person in the process should be allowed to use the process for their own personal, professional, or political gains. Board member selection may also impede the process as by virtue of someone occupying a position they will be required to serve on the board, whether they are committed or not. Strict policies, guidelines, and monitoring of the process by the chief executive officer become critical for this process to work. The board must have only one collective agenda, the hiring of the best qualified applicants.

ORGANIZATIONAL AND PROCESS INTEGRITY

The integrity of the process often equates to the integrity of the entire organization. The lack of process integrity has very broad implications that transcend image, liability, and morale all with equal impact. The process must be devoid of political influence so that the highest standards of recruitment, screening, and selection can be met.[324] Managers and chief executive officers must be resilient to these insidious detractors of quality in the process. In order to do so, managers must have strict control systems in place to manage and monitor organizational processes.[325] Those controls must extend to outside influences with a system of checks and balances that includes an oversight committee that must be advised of any attempted tampering to the process by those who are not directly involved. In addition, for the process to have internal integrity, there must be self and social regulation as well as formal regulatory mechanisms in place. From a systems perspective, all forms of regulation are interdependent and adaptive requiring coregulated systems to maintain the integrity of the entire process.[326] Many organizations have completely lost any semblance of integrity in their selection processes, and when these flaws are revealed, the damage is often irreparable. The road to recovery is long and takes much planning, work, and fortitude to restore the system to one of operational effectiveness and veracity.

THERE IS NO SUBSTITUTE FOR TRAINING

We recognize this fact but do a poor job of responding to it. There's no easy way to frame this issue. Working with numerous organizations over the years has taught me that training is the proverbial necessary evil. Most organizations will not train until mandated, and then beg, borrow, and steal what they can to give the appearance that they are fulfilling training obligations. A sad commentary on the adage, "If it's not free it's not for me!" Training is a diminishing skill set that requires initial investment and constant reinvestment in order to be effective. Skills and knowledge that are not practiced tend to diminish. For example, employment interviewing skills will be slow to develop and quickly diminish when the background investigator is only assigned to do these investigations on a part-time basis. In criminal investigations, interview techniques should be part of an organizational program of assessment, coaching, and ongoing development in order to maintain and increase the required skill sets.[327] Changes are also consistently made in law and best practices that should be built into new training so that the process can consistently be modified to meet the emerging needs of the organization. Skill sets also go stale in time and need refreshing. The lack of training can prove to be fatalistic as evidenced by the finding do the Independent Commission on the Los Angeles Police Department which revealed that the LAPD background investigators were inadequately trained leading to processing flaws of new applicants who were subsequently involved in gross misconduct after hire.[328] In contrast, effective training of background investigators can greatly improve the quality of a department's applicants.[329] One research study revealed that training significantly influenced the thoroughness of the background investigation.[330] Additional research examined preferred models of investigative training for criminal investigators. The highest-rated preferred models were in-house training and mentoring. Field training and hybrid programs also faired moderately as useful strategies for investigation training techniques.[331]

This is an area that organizational leaders must champion. There are myriad training philosophies and mediums. The following list encompasses the various methods that can be employed in the process.

Self-study, osmosis, and savants: This construct has been a long and well-established operating principle with a plethora of public safety administrators who believe that training is unnecessary because our ranks are apparently filled with those who routinely practice self-study, are natural born savants, or gather the requisite knowledge through the process of osmosis. There is some merit to this theory as there are those who will rise above it all and engage in self-study, professional research, and go as far as paying for their own training out of pocket in order to do the best job possible, but these people are certainly in the minority. More importantly, this must come from an organizational commitment to training investigators in the latest techniques, so they can work to identify the best candidates who will be the future of the organization. Self-study, osmosis, and savants (SOS) really are a distress signal in an organization that practices this philosophy. In litigation, the training record is the first document examined in an effort to attach liability to the organizational pocketbook. The U.S. Supreme Court decision in the *City of Canton v. Harris* (1989) laid the foundation for plaintiff's to attack hiring and training practices of law enforcement organizations.[332] Fending off these actions can be as simple as developing at a minimum an in-house program that foundationally develops a background investigator in the basic tasks of the position. Several more viable options are available to keep the solicitors at bay.

On-the-job: This is the least preferred option available. Large agencies have the ability to assign personnel full-time, but often lack in providing the proper training to the background investigator. Smaller agencies assign this task to an officer as parallel responsibilities wherein they may have to alternate between line services and the background investigation. In both cases, officers may not have the expertise to handle a background investigation case properly.[333] At a minimum, a basic guide or manual should be provided to the background investigator to outline policy, procedures, and investigative and reporting requirements. The investigator must also have a subject matter expert (SME) liaison to contact when issues and questions arise. This person can be a department level coordinator or supervisor who has this type of expertise and can offer the proper guidance when needed.

Traditional training: Traditional training methods are the most accepted and recognized technique of educational development for the background investigator. Training options include external seminars and in-service type opportunities; however, these must also be tailored to agency processes and needs. Generic training in the topic may be extremely informative, but often falls short when application to the specific environment is required. This leaves the investigator guessing at the needs and hoping their actions are correct. Training options should not only utilize adult education concepts and practices but also incorporate technology such as Web-based or CD-based options.[334] A critical area of training is the investigative interview. Criminal investigations require certain skill sets and have much more latitude. Employment interviews are quite different, and the investigator must discern the differences and act accordingly. Therefore, investigators must be made aware of the issues surrounding discrimination and equal employment opportunity, the types of questions that can and cannot be asked in relation to job qualifications, and the prevention of using overly intrusive or discriminatory questions in the interview process. Successes have also been realized in the use of neurolinguistic programming and interviewing skills in order to develop both employees and managers in recognizing and addressing the human factors of their roles in the organization in order to build both increased capacity and organizational excellence.[335] Another area of need is in document requirements and verification. Local experts similar to county clerks as well as national experts as in the use of field investigators for U.S. Immigration and Customs Enforcement (ICE) could provide invaluable knowledge on acceptable types of documentation. Risk managers recommend training in communication and behavior modification as tools to ensure high degrees of accountability in the process.[336] As experts, psychologists should teach police culture and psychological job descriptions used in the selection process, so the background investigator can grasp the need for such assessments as well as use the findings to assist in their investigations. A basic curriculum of 16 hours should include the topics and time frames depicted in Table 2.2.

TABLE 2.2
Proposed Background Investigator Training Program Curriculum

Day 1		Day 2	
9:00–9:30	Program intro/administrative time	9:00–10:00	Psychological examinations and reports
9:30–12:30	Background investigation process	10:00–11:00	Polygraph examinations and reports
12:30–1:30	Lunch	11:00–12:00	Administrative review process
1:30–3:00	Information sources and data mining	12:00–1:00	Lunch
3:00–5:00	Legal issues	1:00–3:30	Investigative package requirements
		3:30–4:00	Civil service commission standards
		4:00–4:30	Command and chief's expectations
		4:30–5:00	Program close, feedback, and critiques

Other considerations for the training process should include the development of delivery methods and criteria. For example, eclectic or blended approaches to training should include differentiated instruction, lecture, group and individual exercises, learning contracts, case studies, role-plays, and independent research, to name a few methods that are the innovative ways to stimulate thought, promote interaction, and further the learning process in the classroom.[337] The criteria for administrative investigation training delivery systems development could include the following:

1. The course should be delivered in an eclectic form, providing a combination of progressive and behaviorist teaching modalities. This methodology would allow for close interaction and communication in program delivery as well as satisfy state program delivery requirements.
2. The program should be delivered during a professional development seminar offered through the police training academy. This would ensure comprehension by delivering clarity of expectations and the implementation of a monitoring system to provide feedback through the normative reeducative approach to learning and employ reinforcement theory to meet organizational objectives of quality in the background investigation process.
3. The program could be delivered in six consecutive 2-hour blocks over a 12 weeks period to ensure utility in reaching all affected employees responsible for the administrative investigation process. The program could also be devised to integrate a distance learning component for frequent interaction by instructors and students during the 12 weeks program to enhance the learning and retention of the skills being delivered.
4. The instructors should be current police background investigators, supervisors, and/or command officers who have an extensive knowledge base and practical application ability in the background investigation process.[338]

Field training: FTO programs for officers have been in existence since the 1970s. Field training bridges the gap between the theoretical emphasis of police training concepts and theory to their practical applications in real-life situations.[339] Advanced methodologies include the recently developed police training officer (PTO) model. Unlike field training concepts which are more evaluation than learning based, the PTO concept cultivates lifelong learners who develop the capacity to effectively manage current and future complex problems that will be faced during their career.[340] The FTO and PTO style should be tailored to the trainee's adult learning needs.[341] Additionally, in the PTO model, the trainee, rather than the trainer, sets the pace of the learning.[342] These models have applications to many ranks and positions including investigators and supervisors. Modified versions of FTO and PTO programs can be directly applied to the training of background investigators.

Mentoring: Mentoring is a timeless knowledge transfer concept that also has direct applications to the development of a background investigator KSAs and behaviors. Experience is essential to the proper conduct of these types of investigations.[343] Mentors possess these types of experiences as well as the ability to develop relationships with the new investigator to create an adult-learning environment. Successes have been enjoyed in mentoring aspiring criminal investigators through the use of experienced detectives.[344] Research has revealed that mentoring not only works in a variety of criminal justice positions but also is a preferred methodology for knowledge transfer.[345] Mentoring new background investigators in their role is a viable alternative to formalized and regimented FTO and PTO programs.[346]

Professional associations and conferences: Many organizations exist that provide training and resources for background investigators and may be considered by the organization or individual investigator for membership. The Society for Human Resource Management[347] and Mid-Atlantic Personnel Assessment Consortium (MAPAC)[348] are a few major organizations that cater to the needs of public and private organizations. Other specific organizations that specialize in the background and pre-employment screening process include the National Association of Professional Background Screeners (NAPBS),[349] the Association of Certified Background Investigators (ACBI),[350] and the California Background Investigators Association (CBIA),[351] just to name a few of the major ones in the country. Research the organization to see if it meets the department's and screening unit's needs to select the most compatible organization for affiliation with. Yet another option is to develop a local, regional, or statewide organization of background investigators who can provide a network of information and professional development activities for those in need of this type of training.

Supervisory and command coaching: In the absence of the aforementioned alternatives, one final option is professional development through supervisory and command coaching. Coaching involves the assistance to individuals in clarifying their personal values, identifying their strengths and weaknesses, and developing priorities to work toward.[352] The guidance of a coach will lead the employee to conduct their own research in an effort to solve their personal challenges and build new professional capacities.[353] Supervisors and managers must seize all available opportunities to counsel and coach their employees.[354] Supervisors and command officers who are responsible for the process need to take an active role in coaching new and seasoned background investigators to ensure they have the proper guidance to appropriately complete their function.

PROCESS CHARTING AND REPORTING

Process charting and reporting is a method of tracking each candidate's progression through the various stages of the pre-employment selection process. Much like in the criminal investigations and the crime analysis process, methods used to mine data and develop predictive analytics can afford an opportunity for strategic characterization to understand and react to specific candidate typologies.[355] Individual and aggregate data can be developed to ascertain if the process is on track, to gauge if organizational objectives are being met, and to ensure the process adheres to policy-based and mandated requirements. The following is a list of uses for the charting process:

1. Parameters of assessment and real-time data capture for analysis purposes are developed prior to the initiation of the selection process.
2. Pre-COE and post-COE attrition rates can be tracked more effectively and efficiently.
3. Goal achievement can be measured and opportunities to adjust the process incrementally.
4. Decisions are based upon real-time data developed during the process, not at the completion of the process.

5. Ability to demonstrate the power of statistical analysis in driving the process toward improvement.
6. Monitor and adjust to issues of adverse impact that may emerge as well as monitor compliance with any consent decree that is in effect.

Dependent upon unit resources, budget, and legal restrictions, the data can be an immense benefit to justifying unit productivity, attrition rates, and the need for additional resources. These reports can be completed monthly, semiannually, and annually conveying the results of the process to the chief executive, affected managers, corporation counsel, and human resources for their review, advice, and support.

VALUE OF POLICY AND PROCEDURE

Policy and procedure acts as the anchor of law enforcement operational values. Policies ground our actions with the intent of giving us the best guidance possible for an array of foreseen and unforeseen incidents that can occur. Well-researched and formed policy not only guides our actions but also, when used in good faith, protects our organizations from unnecessary and unwarranted scrutiny as well as civil liability exposure. Policies also protect our employees from sanctions when they follow organizational policy in accordance with the scope of their sworn duties. Most importantly, policies protect the rights of all applicants who deserve to be treated fairly in this very rigorous and rarely forgiving process.

Policy and Standards

Policy is a rule or series of rules that constructively guide the decision-making processes within an organization.[356] That guidance should be directed toward the attainment of the agency's unique vision, mission, goals, and objectives.[357] Policy helps the organization define the role of its agents as well as control the practices in both operations and administration of the short- and long-term functions.[358] Policy also allows the agency to meet and exceed industry standards that have been set for the proper completion of operational and administrative functions.[359] Public safety agencies use policy to ensure that their hiring processes operate fairly on the basis of race, gender, and national origin and do not present any unnecessary barriers or result in disparate impact upon minorities and women.[360] Policy in these cases can provide protections against Title VII actions and negligent hiring and retention lawsuits. Organizational administrators must be proactive in forming policies and practices that can be defended when challenged at any level.[361]

Policy development should be based upon solid facts and research rather than individual belief systems.[362] The use of recognized experts to assist in developing policies on applicant rejection based upon business necessity and the connection to the job responsibilities is a method that should be employed by public safety agencies in designing standards and processes.[363] Policy must also have some flexibility to deal with exceptional situations and candidates who have mitigating circumstances as the need arises. The intent of employment policy holds an organization to a standard that prevents questionable activities, as well as avoids the appearance of questionable activities in allegations of racism, sexism, and nepotism.[364] Policies also stabilize the system by integrating local constraints to the practices of the organization.[365] Policies should have broad and specific implications wherever possible to allow an appropriate response to the range of issues that will surface during the pre-employment investigation. For example, in integrity issues, a policy must specifically establish that any employee who makes any false statement on his or her employment application will be discharged from employment.[366] Policy must be continually reviewed and updated. One example of a policy failure can be found in the hiring of a municipal employee whose initial background check was recorded as having no criminal record. A subsequent check after the employee had been arrested for committing a forcible rape while on duty revealed a record of numerous felony convictions.[367]

Policy and Procedural Manual

A policy and procedural manual should be developed for use in the pre-employment screening function. The background investigator should also have a guide to use in conducting the investigation.[368] A unit or section manual that prescribes the entire process as well as providing forms, exemplars, and checklists is very useful for all those responsible for the investigative process. Other options are to make policy a part of the department's general orders manual as opposed to having a separate document. An example of integrating policy into a general order is found in the *Warwick Police Department General Orders Manual*. Included in their *General Orders Manual* policy are the components of the background investigation process in their organization:

1. Background investigations will be completed on each candidate. Officers may be temporarily assigned to background investigations under the direction of the Inspectional Services Division.
2. Officers assigned to background investigations will be trained in collecting the required information and will be provided with an information packet detailing requirements of the investigation and providing a checklist for documentation.
3. Background investigations will include the following:
   a. Verification of qualifying credentials, that is, diplomas, degrees, driver's license.
   b. Criminal history record checks.
   c. Verification of at least three personal references.
   d. Health history inquiries.
   e. Credit inquiries.
   f. Neighborhood canvas and family interview.
   g. Employment record.
   h. Military history.
   i. Other histories or inquiries as determined by the Captain of the Inspectional Services Division and detailed in the selection procedure manual.
   j. Follow-up inquiries regarding any matter or incident discovered during the investigation.
4. The Inspectional Services Division will maintain a record of each candidate's background investigation in a secure file. Records will be maintained for at least 3 years.

5. *Rhode Island General Law* 28-6.1-1 expressly prohibits the use of polygraph examinations as conditions of employment.[369] Therefore, a polygraph examination will not be administered in the selection process.
6. Any polygraph examinations taken by the candidate in another jurisdiction and provided to this department by another agency will not be relied upon solely as a basis of determining truthfulness, deception, or a determinant of employment status.[370]

Another excellent example of an entire policy order can be found in the *General Order Manual* of the Auburn Police Department, Auburn, Maine (see Appendix D).

ACCREDITATION

The use of external mandates through accreditation bodies is meant to achieve the high standards of organizational professionalism through selection, evaluation, training, and retention and is a primary driver of the defense process in civil litigation cases.[371] Accreditation at the state and national levels is also a coveted distinction for an agency to attain. Beginning with national accreditation through the Commission on Accreditation for Law Enforcement Agencies, a move began in the country for credentialization of law enforcement to demonstrate a continued commitment to professionalism.[372] Accreditation is defined as "The process of considering or recognizing as outstanding, it gives official authorization to, and approval for, operations, recognized for conforming to, and maintaining, higher quality standards of performance."[373] Numerous states have developed independent commissions as well as coalitions to advance this very worthwhile goal.[374] Accreditation requirements include all aspects of an organization's function including operational and administrative practices. Accreditation requirements specifically include the development of policies on the pre-employment screening and selection process. Several requirements can be found in state level accreditation mandates concerning various components of the process.

Mandates include that all elements of the process, including administration, testing standards, evaluation, validation, and processing, must be conducted in a uniform manner.[375] Agencies are required to demonstrate through the documentation of standards that the components of their selection process are job related and nondiscriminatory.[376] One method that the agency demonstrates this consistency of application of requirements is by ensuring the investigative process in standardized.[377] Standardization methods provide a level of assurance that every applicant will be treated in the same fair and consistent manner as delineated.

Some variations will also be found in state accreditation bodies, for example, the setting of an absolute minimum standard in the verification of credentials, review of any criminal or noncriminal record, and verification of at least three personal references.[378] Because of the requirements of the *Employee Polygraph Protection Act of 1988* and the restrictions of individual state standards, very wide variations are observed in the administering of these types of truth detection devices.[379] For example, in Washington State, accreditation standards mandate that the hiring agency conduct a polygraph examination on the applicant prior to appointment.[380] In New York State, the pre-employment polygraph examination is administered at the discretion of the agency. And under *Rhode Island General Law*, the polygraph examination of law enforcement applicants is strictly prohibited and would impact this accreditation standard.[381] Records retention also becomes a requirement impacted by state law wherein there are often minimum requirements. New York State requires retention for a minimum of 6 years as mandated by the *New York State Education Law*.[382] Another example of the impact of state laws as they impact accreditation standards can be found in the mandates for applicants for sworn positions to meet requirements found in the *Code of Virginia*.[383] At the federal level, state accreditation standards are impacted by various legal mandates as the *Americans with Disabilities Act of 1990* that requires records confidentiality be maintained through the filing of medical and psychiatric evaluations separate from the personnel folder.[384] Washington State's accreditation requirements respond in kind by mandating that employee personnel files as well as medical, psychological, and polygraph results and reports are kept separate and secured from other files.[385]

Various other standards include mandates of proper training of background investigators[386] and that trained background investigators must conduct these types of investigations.[387] Background investigators must also have these policies and procedures issued to them and have helpful mechanisms in place in the manner of written instructions and checklists of tasks in order to effectively document the performance of their duties.[388]

Accreditation has had an extremely positive impact on the pre-employment selection process. Credentialization and the equitable treatment of applicants are important parts of the process. In addition, the development of policies and adherence to these strict standards assists an organization immensely in defending their employment actions in the civil courts as well as the court of public opinion. Organizations that have not sought accreditation should at least look to these standards for guidance in the development of their processes.

SPECIFIC TECHNOLOGY AND TOOLS

The background investigation process should have its own information management system. Because of the confidential nature of the cases and the requirement to strictly limit access, these systems should be proprietary. Record confidentiality is paramount to the process, and these records should not be available to unauthorized personnel.

Redundancy should be maintained in both electronic and written form if possible. For hard copy systems, some logical filing system should be in place with the applicant's name and case number that can be searched through a master or central registry. Record tracking should be built into the system showing any viewings, copying, or movement of the files. All previous applicants should be tracked electronically regardless if the case is purged and shredded. These previous applicant databases can offer at least minimal information should an applicant return to the process. They can also be of assistance when working with other agencies who are seeking information on the applicant. With the advent of technological databases, software packages can be purchased or designed to meet the specific needs of the unit.[389] Software packages can also be built to allow the entire capture of the file electronically through the use of document imaging and scanning so that hard copies can be purged frequently in order to save storage costs.

Purging dates are often a point of contention. Arguments for litigation potential vs. records storage costs should be moot. Purging dates should be based on the maximum allowable time period under applicable laws with purge dates only surfacing for applicants who age out of processing requirements. Applicants can return and have returned a decade later in the process, and because of purging requirements, information is permanently lost that could be vital to the case investigation. One example is an applicant who was permanently rejected for impropriety in the military later surfaced to reapply and was subsequently hired as he had lied about his status in the return application.[390] Records management systems are more about utility than about cost. Whatever works and is within the agency's budget should be used as long as the earlier-mentioned requirements can be met.

TIME COMMITMENT AND MANAGEMENT

Time is a commodity we all have very little of. With our ambitious agendas in the workplace, it is extremely hard to argue for more time than is believed necessary to investigate cases. We cannot get beyond the fact that quality takes time though and the background investigation process is like any other; for us to get quality, we must commit to the process. When we think of homicide investigations and internal investigations, we accept that they require inordinate expenditures of time and human resources to produce the desired results. The background investigation process should be no different in our thoughts. There is a definitive relationship between the importance of the background investigation and the time committed to completion.[391] A research study of those serving as background investigators revealed that time spent in the investigation significantly impacted the quality and thoroughness of the final case.[392] Conservative estimates of the time to complete a background investigation range from 72 to 80 hours on the average case.[393] More complex cases may take months of investigation. Administrators must make the commitment to support the work of the background investigator in affording the requisite time to conduct thorough investigations of quality that can withstand the scrutiny of any and all challenges that may be encountered.

DEVELOPING THE BUDGET

Those who think things in life are free realize too late that they usually get what they have paid for. Worse yet is that cost-cutting measures often have an inverse affect and can actually result in far higher expenditures than were originally anticipated.[394] Hard to believe, but there must be a budget line for this expenditure. Budgeting for the process is the first step in ensuring efficiency and effectiveness of the selection process. The budget can be considered as a primary driver of the operational plans that are designed to achieve the organizational goals set for the looming fiscal year.[395] Budgeting techniques are also a part of process management where the timeline is designed to screen-out unqualified applicants in the early stages as opposed to making substantial investments in money and time in those who will not be successful.[396] Large and small agencies should work to put in place a budget process that includes fiscal responsibility in reducing selection costs without reducing the quality of the investigation or increasing their exposure to potentially litigious situations. It is very simplistically a "*Pay me now or pay me later*" ideology. In order to maintain the highest quality of personnel, organizations must invest in people.[397] This is not always the case as too often we see people as a burdensome and exorbitant cost to our limited budgets rather than an investment in our organizations.[398]

Sufficient resources such as staff, supplies, time, and funding must be provided.[399] Budget lines include vehicles, overtime pay, travel expenses, training, equipment, and professional examinations, just to name a few. Because of the need to search for qualified applicants beyond our political boundaries, background investigations may cover many different jurisdictions and will consequently be quite costly to complete.[400] All of these are major considerations in developing a budget line for the process. If your organization has one in place, then a needs assessment should be conducted to ensure that the current budgeted expenditures adequately meet the needs of the process. If they do not, then as we all know, we need to start early in the budget process to offer our best arguments and data to allocate monies for the next fiscal year. Conducting attrition studies and projected vacancies and matching those voids with the needed selection process resources is part of the long-term or strategic planning process. Much forward planning is invested in properly financing this type of process.

FINAL STAGES OF THE INVESTIGATION

The final stages of the investigation are based primarily on organizational needs and processes. At a minimum, considerations for final case filing; file transmittance to interested parties of human resources, internal affairs, personnel, and corporation counsel; final analysis reports; and planning for the next process based upon the analysis of the current process are all a part of this closure-based function. A coordinator, supervisor, or project director should be named to ensure all of the final stage requirements are completed as per organizational policy and needs.

CONCLUSION

This chapter examined pre-employment screening as a process rather than a series of unconnected events, or as the background investigation being the primary driver of the process. From the very foundational understanding of how JTA develops the criterion for every subsequent stage of the pre-employment screening parameters to use in probationary and continuous employment evaluations, through the processual steps, specific roles and functions, and to the final stages of investigation, this chapter gives a schematic of the chronology of the various stages and steps. Many other areas are also treated such as accreditation, budgeting, and process integrity, so the user of this text can see the inexorable connections to each and every stage of the process.

DISCUSSION QUESTIONS AND EXERCISES

1. Determine when the last JTA was conducted in your agency for the entry level positions of law enforcement officer. How dated is it? In reviewing the analysis, have there been any substantive changes in the position requirements? Has the testing process been adjusted accordingly?
2. Is there a selection process calendar of recommended events in place in your organization? If so, after reviewing the recommended strategies, what changes, if any, would you recommend to your department to improve the process?
3. In reviewing the stages of the process, and after reviewing the recommended calendar of stages of the process, are you in compliance with the requirements of the ADA and the issuance of the COE? If not, what recommendations would you make to your organization to improve the process?
4. In reviewing the position responsibilities for the role of background investigator, are there minimum selection requirements in place? Does the department ensure that proper preappointment and in-service training is provided to the background investigator? Are there sufficient resources and flexibility for the background investigator to effectively function in the role? If not, what recommendations would you

make to the organization to improve the conditions for the background investigator to perform their functions appropriately and effectively?

5. Determine what entities are involved in the entire selection process. Is there a chain of command or hierarchy or do all supportive units work equally in the process? What barriers are encountered in most every selection process your agency begins and what can be done to improve the process based upon the cooperation and coordination of efforts?

3 Legal Issues in the Hiring Process

LEARNING OBJECTIVES

- To provide a functional understanding of the various federal-level laws, rules, and regulations of the hiring process
- To provide a functional understanding of the various state-level laws, rules, and regulations of the hiring process
- To provide a functional understanding of the concepts of negligence through hiring, retention, and entrustment
- To provide a level of synthesis to both bodies of law and how they are applied to the hiring process

KEY TERMS AND CONCEPTS

- Civil rights
- Equal Employment Opportunity Commission
- Affirmative action and reverse discrimination
- Human rights laws
- Negligent hiring

INTRODUCTION

Legal issues are addressed throughout the text. Where cited elsewhere, they are treated in the context of the specific component of the process they are applicable to. This chapter is provided to address the additional issues that also have a bearing on the selection process. This chapter and other references to legal issues in the text are provided not as legal advice, but rather to offer some guidance and to engage the thought process of the user to explore these issues in their own processes through the services of legal advisors who can shape policies and practices to meet the unique needs of the user and their organization. References throughout the text include constitutional, statutory, and common law examples, which often culminate in case law.[1] Criminal and civil law examples are also addressed both here and in their contextual settings throughout the text.

FEDERAL LAWS OF HIRING

Several federal laws are in place that govern the hiring process at the state and local levels. Their primary function is to ensure that a set of minimum requirements are in place to hold local entities accountable for fair and equitable hiring practices. State and local hiring officials must be aware of the requirements that are directly related to the hiring process in these mandates as well as those that are not applicable or are waived as a result of job necessity for law enforcement positions. The process must be legally sound and be consistency applied. A full understanding of due process rights is also required as one of the most basic tenets of the *United States Bill of Rights* and the *Fourteenth Amendment* to the *United States Constitution*.[2] Components must be validated so that decisions made with respect to hiring and rejection that result in legal challenges can be successfully defended. As a general rule, the discovery process for federal lawsuits is much broader than in state-level litigation. Applicants who are rejected need a much lower level of proof attached to a constitutionally protected right in order to file a claim. If successful, they can conceivably examine what was done in their investigation as well as with all others who were processed to determine if they have been treated unfairly. In the continued efforts of public safety administrators to hire the most appropriate applicants, state and federal court decisions have not always been kind, exposing public safety organizations to far more liability as compared to all other public and private organizations.[3] And even though the applicant has not risen to the level of enjoying a Property Right to the position, they will invariably have a modicum of rights that must be protected by the processing agency in order to ensure fair and equitable treatment for all. Disqualification from the hiring process must be based on more than anecdote, assumption, or opinion. One guide the agency can use can be found in the court's determination of *just cause* to discipline an employee as delineated in the *Enterprise Wire Company and Enterprise Independent Union* (1966) decision wherein a series of tests were involved:

1. Proper notice or warning was provided to the employee concerning the potential consequences of their conduct.
2. The company's rules, regulations, or managerial orders were reasonably related to expected performance of the employee and was aligned with efficient and safe operating practices for the company.
3. The company performed a full and fair investigation into the circumstances of the matter.
4. The investigation revealed substantial evidence of the violations investigated.
5. The company has applied all applicable rules and regulations equally to all employees in the organization.
6. The company weighed the evidence of the offense, seriousness of the aberration, and the employee's work record in order to mete out reasonable and equitable discipline.[4]

Constructively, the court mandated an equitable investigation in which the findings must be based upon substantial evidence and the punishment fits the employee's history as well as the crime. As an extension of this, while also a property interest case, the court's decision in *Cleveland Board of Education v. Loudermill* (1985) resulted in due process being enjoyed by employees who are confronted with dismissal.[5] Conceptually, both can be applied to the pre-employment investigations process as an applicant's candidacy is being explored and the proverbial skeletons emerge from the closet. Applicants should be allowed the opportunity to respond to the negative or exclusionary evidence presented against them that has been developed during the investigative process. Organizations must embrace a proper and justified process that mirrors this mindset of investigation and the sound development of just cause to act on the evidence revealed as a result of legal investigative techniques that ultimately further the concept and application of due process.

Federal intervention is often in the form of a consent decree to mandate nondiscriminatory hiring practices. consent decrees last for extended durations and can take on a life of their own in driving the hiring process.[6] Some cases have lasted decades and cost government entities tens of millions of dollars.[7] Testing processes that have been found to have disparate impact can also fall under the scrutiny of a consent decree.[8] Departments work to overcome these issues by using different practices such as band scoring to increase the viability of hiring protected classes of applicants.[9] Other tactics include progressive recruiting strategies and lifting residency requirements in order to meet the quota mandates set by consent decrees.[10] Even with consent decrees in place in numerous locations throughout the country, there is still a struggle to meet court-imposed mandates.[11] Still other jurisdictions have been ordered by the courts to abandon the use of sometimes decades-old consent decrees when hiring quotas have been met and then it becomes unconstitutional to continue following them.[12] Jurisdictions who are not under consent decree mandates should examine these court agreements as well as their local needs to increase racial and gender parity in order to take appropriate steps to avoid or, at least, adequately defend against such claims.

Civil Rights and Title VII

The birth of this body of protections under the law emerged in the *Civil Rights Act of 1871*.[13] Beginning as a civil remedy to abuses of human rights, the law has been the subject of much interpretation and revision by the courts over time. The *Civil Rights Act of 1964* was passed to outlaw, among other issues, racial discrimination in employment practices.[14] Title VII of the Act makes it illegal to discriminate against someone on the basis of race, color, religion, national origin, or sex.[15] The Act also defines the concept of a Bona Fide Occupational Qualification and extends sanctions for employment practices to also make the practice of discrimination in offering training programs to only prospective employees of protected classes illegal.[16] The law also makes practices illegal that retaliate against a person because the person complained about discrimination, filed a charge of discrimination, or participated in an employment discrimination investigation or lawsuit.[17] Title VII of the *Civil Rights Act of 1964* was first amended by the *Equal Employment Opportunity Act of 1972* to include public employees, granted enforcement authority to the Civil Service Commission (now the Office of Personnel Management) to ensure nondiscrimination in human resources actions and to establish affirmative employment measures.[18] The *Crime Control Act of 1973* was signed into law to prevent law enforcement agencies from discriminating against females in the employment process.[19] The *Civil Rights Act of 1991* was enacted to modify some of the basic procedural and substantive rights provided by federal law in employment discrimination cases. The Act provided for the right to trial by jury on discrimination claims, the ability to claim punitive damages, stipulates that employers may have to pay for legal costs of plaintiffs, introduced the possibility of emotional distress damages, and limited the amount that a jury could award a plaintiff in a case.[20] Further requirements are placed upon law enforcement based upon the ratification of the *Omnibus Crime Control and Safe Streets Act of 1968*.[21] Also under Title VII is the *Pregnancy Discrimination Act* which makes illegal the practice of discrimination against a woman because of pregnancy, childbirth, or a medical condition related to pregnancy or childbirth.[22] The law also makes illegal the retaliation against a person because the person complained about discrimination, filed a charge of discrimination, or participated in an employment discrimination investigation or lawsuit.[23]

Affirmative Action and Disparate/Adverse Impact

Affirmative action laws were put in place to create parity in hiring of protected classes of persons in the country who had been subjected to discriminatory hiring practices. The classic interpretation of prohibited employment discrimination is on the basis of race,[24] color, national origin, gender, and religion. Laws have been codified to make it unlawful to fail to hire or limit, classify, or segregate employees or applicants for employment in ways that would deprive them of employment and promotional opportunities in the workplace. One example includes the freedom to practice religion. While an inalienable right under the Constitution, these practices can be limited in certain employment situations. Under Title VII, the term "religion" includes all aspects of religious observance and practice, as well as belief, unless an employer demonstrates that he or she is unable to reasonably accommodate to an employee's or prospective employee's religious observance or practice without undue hardship on the conduct of the employer's business.[25]

A relevant police case of religious discrimination was brought forth in the decision of *Fraternal Order of Police Newark Lodge 12 v. City of Newark* (1997). In this case, the court determined that a departmental order banning the wearing of beards could not be enforced when the department officers of Muslim decent claimed they were worn in respect to religious beliefs.[26]

Additional requirements have been steadily put in place as the laws around civil rights and protections continue to evolve. The *Equal Pay Act of 1963* made it illegal to pay different wages to men and women if they perform equal work in the same workplace.[27] The law also makes it illegal to retaliate against a person because the person complained about discrimination, filed a charge of discrimination, or participated in an employment discrimination investigation or lawsuit.[28] In *Griggs v. Duke Power* (1971), adverse impact was found in the disparate treatment of minority employees.[29] Invalid job requirements were developed to pay minority employees less money than their nonminority counterparts for equal work. The case underscored the issues of overt discrimination (disparate treatment) and covert discrimination (disparate impact). In the ruling of *Albemarle Paper v. Moody* (1975), a similar set of circumstances was discovered during litigation in that the jurists examined the standards a district court should use in deciding back pay awards to employees who have suffered monetary losses because of racial discrimination and established the requirements placed upon an employer to develop pre-employment tests that have a discriminatory effect are sufficiently job related (business necessity) to successfully withstand a legal challenge.[30] *EEOC v. Dial Corporation* (2006) resulted in a physical testing process that was found to be highly discriminatory to females who were applying for positions in the organization.[31] *EEOC v. Daimler Chrysler Corporation* (2005) resulted in the organization having to extend the ADA and provide reasonable accommodations for those who needed assistance in reading the written examination.[32] In addition, according to the decision in *Robinson v. Lorillard Corporation* (1971), the burden of meeting the business necessity threshold was further strengthened by having to also satisfy the practice of the deselection of an applicant; the organization must also prove that the business necessity of the exclusionary criteria be necessary for the safe and efficient operation of the business.[33] Specifically related to law enforcement, the ruling in the *Commonwealth of Pennsylvania v. O'Neill* (1972) dealt with hiring and promotion disparities of minority police officers.[34] In the ruling of *Vanguard Justice Society v. Hughes* (1979), the courts found minimum height requirements to result in disparate impact against protected classes of persons.[35] These decisions provide a guide for the court's opinions and response to discriminatory practices in the hiring practice that have been brought to their attention.

Several other examples of laws that have been enacted to prevent discrimination against protected classes of persons are the *Age Discrimination in Employment Act of 1967 (ADEA)* that protects people who are 40 or older from discrimination because of age.[36] The law makes it illegal to retaliate against a person because the person complained about discrimination, filed a charge of discrimination, or participated in an employment discrimination investigation or lawsuit. The law also requires that employers reasonably accommodate the known physical or mental limitations of an otherwise qualified individual with a disability who is an applicant or employee, unless doing so would impose an undue hardship on the operation of the employer's business.[37] Several other laws are discussed later in their relevant applications to the pre-employment screening process.

For the purposes of this discussion, the pre-employment selection process requirements to avoid discriminatory hiring practices are delineated in the Uniform Guidelines on Employee Selection Procedures:

> Procedure having adverse impact constitutes discrimination unless justified. The use of any selection procedure which has an adverse impact on the hiring, promotion, or other employment or membership opportunities of members of any race, sex, or ethnic group will be considered to be discriminatory and inconsistent with these guidelines, unless the procedure has been validated in accordance with these guidelines.[38]

Further clarification for the justification of procedures that can have a disparate impact, but may be clearly justified with respect to job necessity, can also be found in this same body of law:

> The principles of disparate or unequal treatment must be distinguished from the concepts of validation. A selection procedure, even though validated against job performance in accordance with these guidelines, cannot be imposed upon members of a race, sex, or ethnic group where other employees, applicants, or members have not been subjected to that standard.[39]

Central to the justification of hiring actions is to develop practices that are valid and related to legitimate business necessity in order to have a different set of conditions in the workplace that are legally justified. Job task analysis leading to criterion, linked to validated testing processes, and legitimate performance evaluations of continuing job requirements will lead to legally defensible employment actions. Also important at this point is to note that adverse impact is related to the practices of job requirements that can be measured and their relationship to the position such as physical agility testing or math skills, for example. However, adverse impact is not a consideration for such areas as applicant integrity or truthfulness. This was the deciding factor in the case of allegations of race and gender bias for an applicant to the Department of Homeland Security. In the decision of *Crawford v. Department of Homeland Security* (2007), the court ruled that severe prior conduct used in the rejection of a minority female applicant did not amount to disparate impact upon either of the protected populations claimed.[40] In the decision of *Drayton v. St. Petersburg* (1979), a minority applicant who had a prior felony record and was an illegal drug user claimed the requirements that allow rejection of fire fighter applicants who had engaged in such activities disparately impacted African American candidates.[41] The court rejected the claim as no disparate impact could be proven for this race classification as no majority applicants had been hired with this type of felony arrest or illegal drug use history.[42] Adverse impact occurs in testing processes that are proven to be unfair to women and minorities; however, concepts like integrity and truthfulness are color and gender blind and not an issue of adverse impact theory. Integrity is a valid and timeless business necessity for which the applicant can ensure further consideration in the process by merely being honest on all facts, material and inconsequential.

In addition to federal, state, and local laws, organizations must also develop policy statements and definitions of the acceptable standards for an organization. Policies and definitions help to guide employees in their actions and provide an internal sanction process to correct and remediate problems that are discovered. The Kansas University Medical Center has an excellent definition combined to their policy statement on adverse impact:

> A form of illegal discrimination which occurs when a neutral policy or practice that is applied uniformly to all applicants or employees (e.g., word-of mouth recruiting, diploma requirements, intelligence tests, minimum height requirements) has the effect of denying employment or advancement to members of protected classes. Business necessity is the only justifiable reason for adverse impact.[43]

Several historical and contemporary cases have been cited that have highlighted the issues of adverse impact in pre-employment selection processes, many with relevance and direct application to the law enforcement field. This issue is one to be taken seriously given the budget crushing monetary awards and image issues of organizations, not to mention the inexplicable need to promote and practice fair and equitable hiring standards that treat all applicants equally.

Reverse Discrimination

Reverse discrimination has also become an issue with departments working to develop equity in the ranks. In several cases, affirmative action has led to reverse discrimination with nonminority candidates.[44] The U.S. Supreme Court has ruled that race can be a consideration but cannot be an exclusive or overriding factor in selection.[45] Disparate treatment has also come under fire recently as an issue of reverse discrimination for the U.S. Supreme Court.[46] For example, at one southern college, three white professors were successful in a reverse discrimination suit as the court found validity to their claims that they were all passed over for positions and terminated due to their race.[47] Interestingly, the lawsuit was filed by the U.S. EEOC.[48] In some instances, the courts have allowed reverse discrimination as a method of rectifying past practices.[49] In the final analysis, organizations must consider all applicants and treat each with equal dignity and consideration absent any bias that can be considered as discriminatory regardless of race, not at the behest of race.

Equal Employment Opportunity Commission

The EEOC is responsible for enforcing the federal laws of equal protection in employment. The EEOC has broad authority to investigate and sanction organizations that do not comply with the federal standards. One such area of enforcement is the *Americans with Disabilities*

Act of 1990[50] discussed further in Chapter 4. The EEOC has been the monitoring agency in most of the pervasive discrimination claims in the country since their inception. Sensitivity to individual rights has also been an emerging issue in the past decade wherein single employees are taking actions to protect their workplace rights and liberties. Because of revisions to the civil rights laws and *Americans with Disabilities Act of 1990*, discrimination suits tripled during the 1990s. In 1998, employment discrimination cases accounted for about half of all civil rights cases filed that year.[51] In 2009, the EEOC received an all-time record number of complaints from employees who alleged discriminatory practices by employers,[52] lawsuits that are, for the most part, alleged acts that include discrimination and wrongful terminations.[53] Upon the filing of a claim, several steps will take place that involve the investigation, the possibility of a settlement if some reasonable cause of wrongdoing is found, or referral of the complainant to an attorney for the commencement of civil action.[54] EEOC guidelines and case law indicate that the recommendations contributing to the selection process be arrived at independently. This information is what the organization can use to defend their actions in the hiring process.

Title 42 of the United States Code, Section 1983

Federal remedies for civil rights violations against those who violate a person's constitutional rights under the color of law are addressed in Title 42 of the *United States Code* Section 1983.[55] Litigation rights have been expanded to include the sanction of police officers who act under the color of state law and, while in that capacity, violate a constitutional or federally protected right of a citizen of the United States. The statute reads as follows:

> Every person who, under color of any statute, ordinance, regulation, custom, or usage, of any State or Territory or the District of Columbia, subjects, or causes to be subjected, any citizen of the United States or other person within the jurisdiction thereof to the deprivation of any rights, privileges, or immunities secured by the Constitution and laws, shall be liable to the party injured in an action at law, suit in equity, or other proper proceeding for redress.[56]

Section 1983 was broadened by the courts to include penalties against police officers and police executives who engage in the use of policies or practices that demonstrate deliberate indifference to the rights of the public through negligent selection, training, or supervision. These claims are historically used for violations or deprivation of civil rights in police actions regarding arrests, search and seizure, and intrusive or invasive police actions but may also be applied to the hiring process wherein a law enforcement organization violates a person's rights to employment under the color of law. The court decided in *Monroe v. Pape* (1961) that the federal government could exercise authority over state and local government officials who were misusing their authority to violate the federal constitutional rights of citizens.[57] In *Monell v. New York City Department of Social Services* (1978), the court decided that federal jurisdiction could be exercised when the acts of public employees violated a citizens civil rights as a result of an official custom, policy, or practice.[58] As an extension of this, in *Cunningham v. Gates* (1997), actions were brought against the municipality for engaging in a practice of settling lawsuits in order to avoid the costly legal battles to defend against claims of police abuses.[59] The court reasoned that these acts were tantamount to a "policy of indemnification" and included an extension of the liability beyond the police department to city council members and city attorneys.[60] Lastly, the court ruled in *Owen v. City of Independence, Missouri* (1980) that the good faith or legitimate motivations exemptions that led to such policies were irrelevant.[61] In the pre-employment screening process, these types of issues must be considered so that a sworn officer who violates the civil rights of an applicant may be held liable and the agency that condones and indemnifies these practices may follow in proper order.

Federal Immigration and Naturalization

A few miscellaneous acts that should also be considered are the *Immigration Reform Control Act of 1986* that made it illegal to knowingly hire or recruit illegal immigrants (immigrants who do not possess lawful work authorization) and required employers to attest to their employees' immigration status.[62] Since 9/11, this has been an issue of state security as well as legally being able to work in the United States. The *Homeland Security Act (HSA) of 2002* has numerous considerations for law enforcement agencies in pre-employment screening processes.[63] Registration forms, release forms, and verification of work status and citizenship requirements are all a significant part of the process (see Chapter 5).

STATE LAWS OF HIRING

After the federal law considerations, there are also state law considerations. Most states have enacted laws or have empowered independent commissions through state legislation to determine and enforce entry-level requirements for positions in law enforcement.[64] These standards will be the guiding factors for acceptable standards and criteria for hiring law enforcement officers. Cornell University Law School hosts an excellent website through their Legal Information Institute that includes links to the labor and employment laws of all 50 states as well as the District of Columbia and Puerto Rico.[65] For example, in New York State, the *New York State Civil Service Law* establishes the minimum state-level requirements that must be met to be eligible as a police officer in the state. State law also sets the criteria for disqualification of eligible candidates:

1. Lacks minimum requirements for admission to examination or for appointment to the position
2. Physical or mental disability which renders him unfit to perform necessary functions of position
3. Has been guilty of a crime
4. Has been dismissed (or resignation) from a permanent position in the public service upon stated written charges of misconduct
5. Has intentionally made a false statement of any material fact in his application
6. Has practiced or attempted to practice any deception or fraud in his application, in his examination, or in securing his eligibility or appointment
7. Has been dismissed from private employment because of habitually poor performance[66]

These are most often found in the form of the original job posting where departments advise the prospective applicant of the minimum standards as well as disqualifiers. Examples of this concept are provided throughout the text for referencing. State laws will have the predominant impact on hiring applicants and they should be familiar to the background investigator from both categories of qualifying and disqualifying behaviors so that they can target the issues as they progress through the investigative process.

Human Rights Law

Mirror laws are developed at the state level to reflect state-level protections for federal mandates. They afford state-level control and sanctions to ensure that these types of rights are also protected as a matter of sovereignty rights. Each state enacts its own set of laws in the hiring process that are often worded the same as the federal statutes. For example, likened to the federal laws, the *Rhode Island General Law* prohibits discrimination based upon race, color, religion, sex, disability, age, or country of ancestral origin.[67] Discriminatory practices are also prohibited concerning the same protections of civil rights and fair employment.[68] New York State was in fact the first state in the nation to enact these types of laws. The mission of this body of law reads as follows: "This law prohibits discrimination in employment, housing, credit, places of public accommodations, and non-sectarian educational institutions, based on age, race, national origin, gender, sexual orientation, marital status, disability, military status, and other specified classes."[69] The New York State Division of Human Rights was hence created to enforce this important body of law. The mission of the agency is to ensure that, "Every individual… has an equal opportunity to participate fully in the economic, cultural and intellectual life of the State."[70] In order to educate and enforce these principles, the *New York State Human Rights Law* provides the following protections:

> It shall be an unlawful discriminatory practice for an employer …, because of the age, race, creed, color, national origin, sex, disability, genetic predisposition or carrier status, or marital status of any individual, to … bar or to discharge from employment such individual or to discriminate against such individual in compensation or in terms, conditions, or privileges of employment.[71]

Different municipalities also have entities to provide protections beyond the scope of those afforded under federal and state laws. For example, New York City has a Human Rights Commission that serves an aggressive educational function to provide city residents with information on their legal rights and an assurance that discrimination will not be tolerated in any form.[72] This is another body of law and a concept the background investigator and administrator should be familiar with in order to effectively and fairly dispense their duties in the pre-employment selection process.

NEGLIGENCE CLAIMS IN THE HIRING PROCESS

The negligence in hiring laws are based on the legal principle that employers have a duty to use reasonable care in screening and selecting employees so that those who act on the organization's behalf are competent and trustworthy in the discharge of their assigned duties.[73] While claims have steadily increased over the years, this area of law also is an emerging one.[74] As this area evolves, the ever-ominous threat of skewed case law clouds the matter even more.[75] Organizational liability can be incurred if the employee's drug use, criminal behavior, or misconduct injures someone.[76] Once an employee is alleged to have engaged in some inappropriate or potentially liable conduct, the issue of negligent hiring and retention will surface.

Case law demonstrates that once an impropriety surfaces during the background investigation, the agency has an affirmative duty to explore the nature and seriousness of that impropriety prior to hire.[77] Because of the nature of the applicable legal doctrines, these cases can lead to liability on the part of the employer when an employee's transgressions even stretch beyond the scope of their assigned duties.[78] According to legal doctrines that penalize *negligent hiring* and *negligent retention*, an employer may be liable for an employee's wrongful acts even if such acts occur outside the range and scope of duty. Building the case against the agency requires the showing of liability on the part of the employee and the agency. This requires the demonstration of a failure to exercise reasonable care in the hiring process that was as a result of actual or constructive knowledge of the incompetence or unfitness for the position.[79] Therefore, much effort will be placed in demonstrating that the agency knew or should have known of the foreseeable conduct of the employee based upon the comprehensiveness of the agency's investigation of the employee's employment behaviors prior to hire.[80] An example of this can be found in the court ruling of *Ponticas v. K.M.S. Investments* (1983) where the jury found evidence that the employer had sufficient follow-up information on the application to conduct a background investigation, but the agency's failure to investigate led to the sexual assault of a third-party victim.[81] A companion case, *Hines v. Aandahl Construction Co. L.L.C.* (2006), involved a construction worker hired by a construction company whose already known history included felony arrests and chemical dependency issues.[82] No background investigation was conducted in spite of the known information. After hire, the employee committed yet another felony and was still retained by the company. The employee was subsequently involved in a burglary, robbery, and violent assault of one of the company's customers.[83] Negligent hiring was affirmed by the court as the imminent risk in this case was foreseeable by the hiring organization.

Ever-increasing liability is occurring for employers who fail to adequately check an employee's background prior to hire.[84] Yet another example of this involves a fast-food worker who, while on the job, sexually assaulted a 3-year-old boy. The restaurant had hired the applicant absent a complete background check, one that would have shown a history of sexually assaulting children. This resulted in a substantial jury award to the victim.[85] A similar case involved the inadequate investigation of a teacher who was a pedophile. The lawsuit revealed the school failed to conduct a criminal record check, did not require references, and did not ask the teacher to explain a 10 year gap in employment.[86] Such was also the case where information was revealed after a plane crash that killed 50 people that the pilot failed to disclose three failed pilot tests prior to applying for the job.[87] Another case involved a deadly airplane crash where the pilot most likely would not have been hired had the airline known his record. The previous employer had a policy of nondisclosure of employee records to the prospective employer.[88] In the latter airline cases, these are classic examples of the use of all three concepts in the law: negligent hiring, negligent retention, and negligent entrustment. The examples are numerous.

From a national perspective, the issue is not limited to a specific area or industry. The United States Department of Commerce estimates that 30% of business failures are due to poor hiring practices. A survey in California revealed that employers have lost 60% of negligent hiring cases. The average settlement was $500,000 in addition to the plaintiff's attorney fees.[89] A clear trend has emerged in employer liability that is directly related to the quality of the pre-employment investigation process.

With respect to law enforcement, a recent increase in the plaintiffs' use of the federal courts to protect their civil and constitutional rights requires that police departments adopt stricter hiring practices.[90] As a consequence, the burden of negligent hiring elevates the importance of the pre-employment investigation.[91] The courts have responded in kind by placing higher expectations on organizations to perform reasonable pre-employment investigations of prospective new hires.[92] In one court decision, while the level of evidence did not meet the burden of gross negligence, the court still found gross flaws in the department's background investigation. In the ruling of *Stokes v. Bullins* (1988), the court cited the following facts: (1) that the municipality hiring practices were actions taken under color of state law, (2) that as a matter of policy, the municipality's governing body does not conduct a minimally acceptable background investigation of police applicants, and (3) the municipality's governing body was grossly negligent in reviewing the applicant's application and in hiring the applicant as a police officer.[93] This case truly underscores the court's opinions on negligence in hiring practices, even if this case did not meet the current burden of proof.

Even where statutes do not mandate a pre-employment screening process, there may still exist a common law duty of reasonable care that may be required of the hiring agency to conduct such checks of their prospective employees.[94] Law enforcement agencies must therefore exercise due diligence/due care in the hiring process to avoid these types of liability issues in as much as they can be avoided.[95] Due diligence/due care places an affirmative duty upon the hiring agent to ensure that their selection and retention methods are designed to screen out applicants who may present a foreseeable danger to the organization, other employees, and the public.[96] The next three sections discuss negligent hiring, negligent retention, and negligent entrustment as they relate to the pre-employment investigations process. Addressed in Chapter 5 are the issues of negligent referral and defamation as they relate to employment references in the process.

Negligent Hiring

In negligent hiring litigation, the plaintiff must prove that through gross negligence, recklessness, deliberate indifference, or that some pattern and practice of the organization led to the hiring of the unfit employee. This is a common area of attack when bringing legal action against a law enforcement agency.[97] This tort action also allows for the recovery of damages caused by an employee that are not directly related to job performance.[98] Potentially, the employer is then civilly liable for the negligent placement of an unfit person in an employment situation that creates an unreasonable risk of harm to others.[99] One of the keys to this type of litigation is that the employer knew or should have known the background of the applicant and chose to hire the person in spite of their history of problems. The issue will involve making a determination if the appointing authority made a hiring or retention determination with deliberate indifference to the rights of persons with whom the police come in contact.[100] In the decision of *Scott v. Blanchet High School* (1987), the court cited this language in the decision which clarifies the concept of negligent hiring:

> An employer may be liable to a third person for the employer's negligence in hiring or retaining a servant who is incompetent or unfit. Such negligence usually consists of hiring or retaining the employee with knowledge of his unfitness, or of failing to use reasonable care to discover it before hiring or retaining him. The theory of these decisions is that such negligence on the part of the employer is a wrong to such third person, entirely independent of the liability of the employer under the doctrine of respondeat superior. It is, of course, necessary to establish such negligence as the proximate cause

of the damage to the third person, and this requires that the third person must have been injured by some negligent or other wrongful act of the employee so hired.[101]

Under the *Negligent Hiring Doctrine*, the injured party can sue for damages if it can be proven that a check of the applicant's background would have revealed factors that made the applicant unsuited for the position for which they were hired.[102] Negligent hiring lawsuits involve an examination of the employee's past negligence and reputation.[103] The employer may also be liable for an employee's negligent or intentional acts as well as other types of defined conduct.[104] Studies have shown that the average court-ordered award in a negligent hiring claim is over one million dollars.[105] Further exacerbating the issue is that the negligent hire theory of employer liability can extend beyond the scope of employment to acts that occur away from the worksite.[106] In addition, respondeat superior liability is where an employer is vicariously liable for an employee's misconduct that is committed within the scope of employment. In negligent hiring theory, the employer knew or should have known of the dangerous propensities of a candidate, and in hiring the applicant in spite of the information known, the hiring led to the proximate cause of the victim's injuries. An interesting twist in a negligent hiring claim involving the concept of respondeat superior emerged from the decision in *Matt v. Pressley* (2006).[107] An employee who assaulted a patient was ruled to have acted outside the scope of employment; however, the court also ruled that the employer could be held liable for the negligent hiring of the employee.[108] In a contrasting opinion, the appellate court decision of *Anonymous v. Dobbs Ferry Union Free School District* (2002) involved a claim of negligent hiring due to an employee who was the subject of an abuse case off school grounds. The court reasoned in this case that the district incurred no liability because the abuse occurred on a social visit away from school and was beyond the scope of employment. Numerous examples are provided in the subsequent case law citations. A recent example of potential liability through a negligent hiring tort involved a city employee who was hired to do in-home lead inspections. The employee committed a forcible rape while on duty. The initial background investigation revealed no criminal record. After the employee's arrest, a second check after the rape allegation revealed that the employee had several felony convictions including one for weapons possession.[109] Two analogous cases involved nonexistent to minimal background checks wherein employees in these cases also committed sexual assaults on customers, and the lack of the proper background investigation was considered to be the proximate cause of these assaults as decided in *McLean v. Kirby Co.* (1992) and *Read v. The Scott Fertilizer Co.* (1998).[110] The courts consider such jobs as law enforcement and public safety to be highly trustworthy positions that require the utmost in integrity in public contacts. These positions are considered by the courts to be positions requiring much more responsibility be placed on the hiring authority to ensure the public is safe from untoward acts of these types of positions.[111] Very simply, reasonable care in the hiring process must be used to protect third parties from injury or harm.[112]

Liability claims often focus on the sufficiency of the pre-employment investigation of the applicant's background in order to establish any shortcomings.[113] The amount of inquiry into the background of the prospective employee necessary by an employer really depends on the nature and importance of the position.[114] Central to such litigation of an employee's misconduct as a result of negligent hiring practices will be the level of inquiry conducted during the hiring process to determine the sufficiency of the investigation and if the employee was in some manner unfit for the position.[115] A classic parallel case involved a decades-old discovery wherein the background investigator was still held to answer for the failure to effectively screen an applicant who had committed a sex crime prior to hire.[116] In *Parker v. Williams* (1988), this theory was put to the test, and the court's ruling included these facts:

> In this case, defendant [Sheriff] Amerson hired Williams [Chief Jailer] as county jailer and subsequently promoted Williams to the position of chief jailer. As chief jailer, Williams had control over all prisoners, male and female, in the jail. By the time Amerson hired him, Williams had been convicted of indecent exposure; he had undergone treatment for a variety of mental problems, including memory lapses, talking to himself, and multiple personality experiences; and he had had a history of drug use. Amerson either knew of this background or could have discovered it through minimal investigation.[117]

To defend the agency against these types of claims, a complete and thorough background investigation must be conducted to minimize the exposure of the agency to major litigation.[118] Successful defenses against these types of claims have been achieved by inquiries that did not reveal any conduct that would indicate the applicant had a predisposition for the behavior alleged in the negligent hiring lawsuit as was determined in the ruling of *Saine v. Comcast Cablevision of Arkansas Inc.* (2003).[119] One of the ways to mitigate these types of claims is to use reasonable care in the background investigation process by checking as many sources of info as possible.[120] We must not lose sight of the fact that the investigation must examine both negative and positive aspects of the applicant's behaviors and previous work history. For example, one method of reducing liability is through the advanced interpersonal communication skills of the officer in quelling disputes and deescalating potentially violent situations.[121] It behooves us not to search for candidates who not only have acceptable histories but who also demonstrate positive characteristics that will minimize our exposure to civil liability.

There have been a series of cases that have been filed against organizations, both public safety and private, that have not risen to the level of substantiating a claim of negligence in hiring as no history of prior conduct could be directly linked to future behaviors.[122] Other cases have specifically examined the threshold points where negligence in hiring liability could be incurred that introduce the concepts of due care in the hiring process and the concept of considering the totality of circumstances surrounding the hiring decision.[123] For example, in the decision of *Ahern v. Odyssey Re (London) Ltd.* (2001), the plaintiff must prove that (1) the employer was on notice of the potentially harmful propensities of the employee, (2) the plaintiff was within the zone of foreseeable risks created by the employment, and (3) the employer's breach of duty was the proximate cause of the plaintiff's injuries.[124]

There have been an abundance of cases that have supported claims against organizations that have engaged in negligent hiring practices amounting to deliberate indifference to the rights of others.[125] A near-equal number of those types of cases involved the courts finding flaws, inadequacies, and incompetence in the pre-employment investigations that were never conducted, conducted poorly, or conducted after the fact.[126]

In addition to case law supporting the need for thorough background investigations of prospective employees of the organization, state legislatures have also passed laws holding organizations strictly accountable for the completion of a pre-employment investigation in order to provide some level of protection for their constituents. In point of fact, a majority of states hold an employer responsible for completing a thorough pre-employment screening of every job applicant prior to placing them in a position where they will have opportunities for public contact.[127] This type of legislation provides a defense for agencies who conduct a pre-employment investigation as there is a presumption the agency acted properly when compliance of the statute is found to be in order.[128] One example comes from the *Florida Statute* which requires that pre-employment investigations must include a criminal background investigation, a reasonable effort to contact references and former employers, completion of a job application that includes particular questions related to crimes and past intentional tort claims, driving record check if related to work to be performed, and an interview with the prospective employee.[129] *Florida Statute* 768.096, Employer Presumption Against Negligent Hiring, specifically reads as follows:

1. In a civil action for the death of, or injury or damage to, a third person caused by the intentional tort of an employee, such employee's employer is presumed not to have been negligent in hiring such employee if, before hiring the employee, the employer conducted a background investigation of the prospective employee and the investigation did not reveal any information that reasonably demonstrated the unsuitability of the prospective employee for the particular work to be performed or for the employment in general. A background investigation under this section must include the following:
    a. Obtaining a criminal background investigation on the prospective employee under subsection (2).
    b. Making a reasonable effort to contact references and former employers of the prospective employee concerning the suitability of the prospective employee for employment.
    c. Requiring the prospective employee to complete a job application form that includes questions concerning whether he or she has ever been convicted of a crime, including details concerning the type of crime, the date of conviction, and the penalty imposed, and whether the prospective employee has ever been a defendant in a civil action for intentional tort, including the nature of the intentional tort and the disposition of the action.
    d. Obtaining, with written authorization from the prospective employee, a check of the driver's license record of the prospective employee if such a check is relevant to the work the employee will be performing and if the record can reasonably be obtained.
    e. Interviewing the prospective employee.
2. To satisfy the criminal-background-investigation requirement of this section, an employer must request and obtain from the Department of Law Enforcement a check of the information as reported and reflected in the Florida Crime Information Center system as of the date of the request.
3. The election by an employer not to conduct the investigation specified in subsection (1) does not raise any presumption that the employer failed to use reasonable care in hiring an employee.[130]

This presumption is unavailable to organizations that fail to conduct a pre-employment investigation or, worse yet, a posthire background investigation. This tactic can not only create significant liability, but also, more importantly, this ex post facto or retroactive approach has led to extremely problematic and highly embarrassing situations.[131] The background investigator should refer to their specific state laws and consult with legal counsel to determine if any of these laws exist and are applicable. As evidenced here, compliance is a presumptive defense and can go far to mitigating any subsequent litigation.

We can always cast doubt and dismiss the issues of a bad hire to the wisdom of 20/20 hindsight. We can also look to hindsight as the convenient justifier, claiming if we had known, our hiring decision may have been different. However, when the standards for exclusion are clearly articulated, and we violate them, even if the act is unrelated, this is not hindsight as the problem would have never arisen if the proper action was taken at the outset of the hiring process. Since we do not have a magical crystal ball to see the future, we must always use the clarity of the present to drive our decision-making processes.

Negligent Retention

Negligent retention is the next layer of liability to follow negligent hiring. This legal claim involves the attachment of negligent, reckless, or intentional acts of employees to the employer's retention of an employee who is unfit for the position. This requirement includes both psychological and physical fitness as was decided in *Parker v. District of Columbia* (1988) wherein an officer who was in poor physical condition escalated to the use of deadly physical force in an arrest that was deemed by the courts as excessive in nature.[132] Employee incompetence arises when an employee is found unfit to meet job requirements and subsequently places the public at risk because of the condition.[133] Some cases of note concerning this issue as directly related to the public safety officer realm are the following:

1. *Battista v. Cannon* (1996): Involved a deputy who had previous complaints of trying to sexually coerce women wherein the sheriff failed to take action and the deputy sexually coerced and battered the plaintiff.[134] A similar set of circumstances also appeared in *Johnson v. Cannon* (1996).[135]
2. *Colon v. City of Newark* (2006): City held liable for negligent retention due to department management's failure to submit prior exam results or disciplinary record to the evaluating psychologist who erroneously found the officer fit for duty in spite of a demonstrated propensity for violence.[136]
3. *McCrink v. City of New York* (1947): City found liable for retaining an officer who had been disciplined for being intoxicated on three separate occasions and while intoxicated in a fourth off-duty incident was involved in a shooting.[137]

In *Peck v. Siau* (1992), the court defined the time frames for negligent hiring and negligent retention as, "The difference between negligent hiring and negligent retention is the time at which the employer's negligence occurs. With negligent hiring, it occurs at the time of hiring; with negligent retention, it occurs in the course of employment."[138] That time frame was critical in the court ruling of *Kenneth R. v. Roman Catholic Diocese* (1997) where it was determined that the diocese failed to act once it learned of molestation complaints against a priest; consequently, the victims had a viable claim for negligent retention.[139] Similar cases have been decided wherein the church failed to act on information of prior bad acts of its employees.[140] Key to this specific case was the assertion that a counseling memo had been written and was a part of the formal record, but allegedly never forwarded.[141] This is a classic case for the burden of proof wherein the agency had known or should have known of the prior bad acts of the employee. Information contained in the formal records, even if the information was not forwarded, is not a solid defense of the agency's actions as this would indicate an array of reasons such as poor policy, ineffective management, and intentionally hiding such pertinent information that would have adversely affected the employment status of the employee as well as the culpability and liability of the agency. Another example emerges from several high-profile cases filed against the Boy Scouts of America that have resulted in multimillion-dollar awards that include both compensatory and punitive damages.[142]

In revisiting the *Ponticas v. K.M.S. Investments* (1983) ruling, the implications are also clear here in that the court cited that the "Doctrine of Negligent Retention arose out of common law fellow-servant law that imposed duty on employers to select employees who would not endanger fellow employees by their presence on job."[143] In addition, the duty and breach elements of a negligent hiring claim do not require the specific type of injury to be foreseeable as was evidenced in the ruling that the jury "could have found, as it did, that it was reasonably foreseeable that a person with a history of offenses of violence could commit another violent crime, notwithstanding the history would not have shown him to ever have committed the particular type of offense."[144] As long as seminal connection can be made, the municipality may suffer extensive liability.

As an aside, while we are primarily speaking of outside or external contacts of public safety officers in this context, we are also cautioned to consider the issues of employee-on-employee violence. Negligent retention claims can also arise from these types of incidents in the workplace. Pre-employment screening is a highly recommended method for preventing incidents of workplace violence.[145] Sadly, workplace violence that results in a homicide claims on average 20 people per week in the United States.[146] Workplace violence in the United States accounts for approximately 1.7 million violent victimizations per year of people who are at work or on duty.[147] The *Occupational Safety and Health Act of 1970* describes the duties of employers: "Shall furnish to each of his employees employment and a place of employment which are free from recognized hazards that are causing or are likely to cause death or serious physical harm to his employees."[148] The General Duty Clause has also been interpreted with respect to workplace violence as holding an employer accountable for failures to prevent acts of workplace violence.[149] While we must demonstrate concern for those we police that is at a level which is beyond reproach, tantamount to this is our concern for the safety of our own employees. It is the employer's responsibility to provide a safe workplace for the employee.[150] This is a condition of employment we truly must consider given the nature of the work that is done, the stressors involved, and the accessibility to weapons.

Negligent Entrustment

Title 42 Section 1983 of the *United States Code Section* 1983 provides for redress in claims of negligent hiring, negligent retention, and negligent entrustment.[151] These claims emerge from the lack of supervision of supervisors and administrators to properly supervise and control an employee's use of government property or equipment such as a police vehicle or issued defensive weapon. Improper supervision is usually the foundation for these types of claims.[152] An example of a standard of care commonly known as the law of negligent entrustment applied in these types of claims is found in the ruling of *Kitchen v. K-Mart Corporation* (1997):

> One who supplies directly or through a third person a chattel for the use of another whom the supplier knows or has reason to know to be likely because of his youth, inexperience, or otherwise, to use it in a manner involving unreasonable risk of physical harm to himself and others whom the supplier should expect to share in or be endangered by its use, is subject to liability for physical harm resulting to them.[153]

The most common of these claims is due to the operation of a motor vehicle. An organization's administrators are legally responsible to ensure that every effort is made to screen those who will be authorized to use a company vehicle during the course of company operations.[154] Negligent entrustment claims can be the result of hiring an employee whose history of reckless or negligent operation of a vehicle as evidenced by previous moving violations and motor vehicle accidents is not revealed during the pre-employment screening or interview.[155] An example of this comes from a case where an applicant was rejected for medical reasons, hired by the law enforcement agency that disregarded the medical decertification, and was subsequently involved in a car accident due to his medical condition.[156] Organizations must not only examine and strongly consider previous driving records in the hiring of law enforcement applicants who will be responsible to operate a police vehicle in high stress and dangerous response modes, but must also have policies in place to set the organizational standards high enough to fend off these types of claims.[157]

Negligent Supervision

Negligent supervision can be a significant issue in the hiring process.[158] As with all negligence torts, several factors must be present, including a duty owed to protect, a failure to exercise reasonable care, proximate cause of the actions to the injury incurred, and the demonstration of an actual injury. This also includes the reckless acts of supervisors with regard to the tortious acts of persons under their control in the organization.[159] Negligence liability can result from a wrongful act or a failure to act. These elements can be met when the negligent supervision of background investigators in an organization is present and an applicant, or a third party such as someone injured by the applicant who is hired by the organization, suffers an injury and is able to successfully support the remaining components in a lawsuit.

Liability is incurred through the knowledge of the acts by the supervisor or the proximate or causal connection leading to injury, or the predictability of acts that result in civil rights violations. There have been numerous causes of action in these types of claims where the courts have supported further review or affirmed the claims of liability.[160] In contrast, numerous other cases have not met the test required to substantiate a negligent supervision claim.[161] The potential for successful claims looms though, and background supervisors as well as chief executive officers should pay due attention to these issues. Because of the dynamics of the field, many managers spend inordinate amounts of time concentrating on the daily tasks they are currently engaged in at the behest of tasks and responsibilities that are not short-term goals or pressing issues but have long-term and serious consequences when not addressed in a proper and timely manner.[162] Failure to supervise employees is consistently bantered about in the field, and serious efforts must be taken to vitiate these problems as well as abate or, at the very least, effectively defend against these types of claims.

LIABILITY IN COMPLETING THE BACKGROUND INVESTIGATION

As in any action taken by those who work in a public safety organization, there will always be frequent questions as to actions taken and concomitant measures of liability. The pre-employment investigations process is not immune to these types of allegations and challenges. The pre-employment investigations process must be supported by the concepts of due diligence and good faith in the investigation so that the organization can have the ability to seek and be granted qualified immunity and summary judgment when the cases meet the required legal and technical thresholds.

Not only are there substantive ethical considerations to completing the pre-employment screening of a prospective public safety officer, but more importantly, there exists statutory authority to conduct the background investigation in the first place.[163] Several cases have also been decided in favor of the background investigations process, which include *Bardin v. Lockheed Aeronautical Systems Company* (1999),[164] *Jensen v. Prudential Financial* (2005),[165] and *Ramos v. Equiserve* (2005).[166] Statutory authority is buttressed by the onus of liability when a background investigation is required by state mandate and is not conducted or deemed an inadequate exploration of the applicant's past as decided in *Mahan v. Am-Gard, Inc.* (2003) and *Mueller by Math v. Community Consolidated School District 54* (1989),[167] the primary deciding factor being a prospective applicant's knowing and voluntary signing of a waiver releasing the prospective employer from liability due to the negative information discovered that may lead to the candidate's denial of, or subsequent removal from, a position as decided in *Cox v. Nasche* (1996)[168] and *McCleskey v. Vericon Resources, Inc.* (2003),[169] respectively. Chapter 5 and Appendix H include a discussion and sample waiver forms, respectively. Most recently, privacy rights were challenged in the solicitation of information in the background investigations process relative to questions of government contractors. In *NASA v. Nelson* (2011), the U.S. Supreme Court supported the need to give broad authority to the investigation of a government employee or government contractor's background in order to fully protect the government's interest in hiring employees whom are honest and trustworthy as well as requiring full disclosure of illicit drug use or involvement.[170] This is not without concern over the fact that while the applicant can be forced as a term and condition of processing for employment to submit the waiver, the organization must also ensure that the privacy rights of the applicant are fully protected legally and ethically.[171]

As an extension of this concept though, while organizations have the statutory and case decision authority to conduct administrative investigations, they must also train investigators as well as develop and follow a comprehensive process and, if required and appropriate, afford applicants the ability to contradict or correct negative information developed. For example, in the decision of *Young v. Providence* (2005), one substantive component of the lawsuit dealt with the failure of the City of Providence Police Department to train a background investigator who was responsible for the investigation of the hiring of an applicant who was subsequently involved in an on-duty shooting.[172] Using the guidance of the decision of *Board of County Commissioners of Bryan County, Oklahoma v. Brown* (1997), the court noted that the standard of deliberate indifference could not be met as there must be a causal link between the hiring decision and any concomitant constitutional violation by the officer hired.[173] The most important point is that this standard does not prevent these types of allegations when a plaintiff's attorney is able to establish the shortcomings of the background investigation that led to the hiring as well as the underlying issues and transgressions of the applicant. While on the criminal side, case support has been found in challenges to inadequate police investigations based upon the theory of a property interest in the outcome as decided in *Harrington v. County of Suffolk* (2009), the lack of liability in a poor-quality investigation would only translate to increased liability in negligent hiring and retention claims.[174] These types of litigation will likely become more prolific for both civil as well as criminal proceedings in light of the move to challenge the integrity of officers in *Giglio* discovery proceedings for officer integrity which can include the results of the background investigation.[175]

A textbook example of the proper methods can be found in the decision of *Silva v. Lucky Stores* (1998); the court ruled that trained investigators who submit administrative investigations are a demonstration of an employer's good faith in reaching decisions in adverse employee actions.[176] Drawing a parallel to the law enforcement environment, police departments can be held liable for failing to train and displaying deliberate indifference to needed training as well as customs, pattern, and practice issues wherein the training is either inadequate or outdated.[177] The requirement of substantial evidence that leads the employer to the belief that the information was true is the barometer for action. Those decisions must also meet the burden of rising to the level of objective reasonableness in the decision for the adverse action to be supported by the courts. The concepts of good faith and reasonableness in the investigative process also led to the courts supporting adverse action against several employees in the ruling of *Simpson v. Western Graphics Corporation* (1982).[178]

With respect to developing policy and investigative guidelines for in-service employees, the court ruled in *Casenas v. Fujisawa* (1997) that a company's procedures for investigation of employee matters should include meeting with the subject, all potential witnesses, comparison of statements and evidence to any adverse allegations, discussing the information with the subject, and communicating the findings of the investigation to the subject by means of a letter.[179] This case represents a guide to the court's thoughts on the thoroughness of the administrative investigation process as well as inclusion of the subject's interview and statement in order to balance the information obtained and come to a reasonable and objective finding.

Case thoroughness will be key. The background investigator's diligence must translate into inclusion of all of the discovered facts in a memorialized form. The Final Investigative Package must include all positive and negative information related to the applicant that can be legally included. This is the only manner in which an applicant can be fairly assessed. Exclusion of information and facts may be grounds for a liability claim. In a criminal case example, officers are required to include all facts in a criminal case wherein the prosecuting attorney is bound by rules of discovery. The exclusion of exculpatory information on behalf of the officer cannot only compromise the case but can also lead to civil liability on behalf of the investigating officer.[180] While this is a criminal case example, it serves an excellent guide to the responsibilities of the background investigator in this process.

Lastly, the subject of the investigation may be allowed an opportunity to respond to any negative information that is revealed in the investigation and used in the adverse action. In both *Casenas v. Fujisawa* (1997) and *Cotran v. Rollins Hudig Hall International, Inc.* (1998), the courts ruled that the subject should be allowed to air any additional issues before the investigation is closed and provide an opportunity to correct or contradict such information.[181] While these are current employee cases, the rules vary for new applicants. State and federal laws of hiring, organizational policies that require the release of information to the applicant, and mandates by such instruments as judicial or administrative decrees that allow for civil and administrative appeals must be reviewed in the specific jurisdiction the organization conducts their business in.

As a concept, liability can be avoided once law enforcement organizations fully commit to completing unbiased and thorough investigations in a technically sound and timely manner. We must all commit to do it right the first time rather than rely on no one finding out, or when they do, point fingers and develop creative excuses why it wasn't done right! This is not the way business should be done, and the courts (and applicants!) realize this.

CONCLUSION

This chapter has examined the various legal issues in the hiring process. Exclusive of those that are addressed contextually in the various other components of the process, this chapter treats the many seminal areas that must be known to the background investigator, administrator, and human resource professional. Beginning with federal laws, rules, and regulations that demonstrate the impact of civil rights legislation, case law, and the myriad acts that affect the hiring process, the user of this text gains a foundational understanding of the minimum federal standards applied to the appointment of public safety officers. Next, this chapter progresses through several examples of the laws of hiring at the state level and offers several cases from across the country to provide an understanding of the trends and patterns in the law. Finally, this chapter closes with the ominous issues of negligent hiring, negligent retention, and negligent entrustment and blends both federal and state examples to provide a synthesis of the legal thinking in both bodies of law. In the final analysis, the process can be heavily weighted in either direction and the agency administrator bears the responsibility to ensure the highest level of procedural justice is afforded to the process as well as the applicant.

DISCUSSION QUESTIONS AND EXERCISES

1. Has your department ever been the subject of a discriminatory practice in hiring lawsuit? Based on the information concerning the requirements of state and federal laws, discuss the merits of the case in detail. What, if anything, could have been done differently by the department? What suggestions would you make now in your analysis of the incident?
2. Review your department's hiring processes. Based upon the requirements of Title 42 of the *United States Code* Section 1983, do you anticipate any potential for litigation against your agency? If so, what changes should be recommended to your administrators to protect the agency from such a claim?
3. Review the human rights–type laws in your state. In addition, review your agency's hiring process. Assess if your department is in full compliance with the requirements of these laws. If not, what changes would you recommend in order to bring your department's hiring process into full compliance?
4. Review the section on negligent hiring. Has your department ever been the subject of a negligent hiring lawsuit? Examine the facts and assess whether or not your agency acted properly in the case. Could the agency have done anything different to avoid the lawsuit or better guard against the claim at the time? What changes should be made to the process to avoid this situation in the future?

5. This is often a complex and confusing area. Identify your agency legal liaison as well as your human resource department contact person for these types of issues. With their assistance, develop an in-house guide that will offer policy and procedure to be followed for you and for future background investigators to use to ensure legal compliance to the process.

4 Medical and Psychological Standards

LEARNING OBJECTIVES

- To provide an understanding to the various federal-level laws, rules, and regulations related to medical and psychological testing of law enforcement applicants
- To provide an understanding of the terms and requirements of the Conditional Offer of Employment (COE)
- To provide an understanding of the concept of policy development in disqualifying drug use
- To provide an understanding of the psychological standards and evaluation procedures required of the pre-employment screening process

KEY TERMS AND CONCEPTS

- ADA and HIPAA
- The conditional offer of employment
- Testing for illicit drugs
- Psychological standards and evaluations
- Medical and psychological records security and retention

INTRODUCTION

This chapter reviews the issues surrounding the medical and psychological standards of pre-employment law enforcement screening. A review of the impact of the *Americans with Disabilities Act of 1990*[1] (ADA) and related laws will address medical evaluations, drug testing, and psychological evaluation processes. This chapter refers to the discussions of physical agility testing processes and timelines for the specific components, as well as the timeline for the issuance of the Conditional Offer of Employment (COE) already addressed in Chapter 2. In this chapter, the primary concern is the requirements and regulatory practices of these specific components of the pre-employment screening process.

AMERICANS WITH DISABILITIES ACT OF 1990

Beginning with the *ADA*, the bulk of the processing requirements insofar as applicant protections are concerned are born from this Act.[2] As a consequence, the requirements of the *ADA* have a direct impact on the pre-employment investigation process.[3] The *ADA* was enacted to provide a national mandate for the elimination of discrimination against individuals with disabilities.[4] Fundamentally, the law prohibits discrimination against a person with a disability in selection, promotion, or placement in an employment situation. The provisions of the Act prevent an employer from developing selection practices that screen out or have the effect of screening out persons with disabilities unless there is a clear job-related business necessity for the applicant's rejection.[5] The Act also protects an applicant who may have a relationship with a person with a disability and the inference could be drawn that this relationship would lead to the applicant not being able to perform the necessary job functions, such as an applicant who cares for a spouse with a disability and the assumption may be that the applicant may take excessive time off to care for the spouse.[6]

Available remedies for violation of the Act include hiring, reinstatement, promotion, back pay, front pay, restored benefits, reasonable accommodation, attorneys' fees, expert witness fees, and court costs. Compensatory and punitive damages also may be available in cases of intentional discrimination or where an employer fails to make a good faith effort to provide a reasonable accommodation.[7] The Act is also intended to be self-regulating as employers are responsible for self-evaluation practices that assess and modify policies and practices so they align with the provisions of the Act.[8]

The *ADA* prohibits the use of qualification standards, entry-level tests, or restrictive selection criteria that reject applicants with disabilities unless the criteria for rejection are job related and consistent with business necessity. Specific to this discussion, the *ADA* makes it unlawful to discriminate in all employment practices that include recruitment, hiring, and training.[9] The *ADA* is enforced by both the Equal Employment Opportunity Commission (EEOC) and U.S. Department of Justice.[10] As discussed in Chapter 3, the EEOC has broad investigative and enforcement powers in these cases. The specific laws for which the EEOC enforces are as follows[11]:

1. Title I of the *ADA*: This law makes it illegal to discriminate against a qualified person with a disability in the private sector and in state and local governments. The law also makes it illegal to retaliate against a person because the person complained about discrimination, filed a charge of discrimination, or participated in an employment discrimination investigation or lawsuit.[12]
2. Sections 501 and 505 of the *Rehabilitation Act of 1973*: This law makes it illegal to discriminate against a qualified person with a disability in the federal government. The law also makes it illegal to retaliate against a person because the person complained about discrimination, filed a charge of discrimination, or participated in an employment discrimination investigation or lawsuit. The law also requires that employers reasonably accommodate the known physical or mental limitations of an otherwise qualified individual with a disability who is an applicant or employee, unless doing so would impose an undue hardship on the operation of the employer's business.[13]

For the purposes of this discussion, under the terms of *ADA*, a *qualified individual* is a job applicant with a disability who meets legitimate skill, experience, education, or other requirements of the employment position they seek and is able to perform the essential and not marginal or incidental functions of the position either with or without reasonable accommodation.[14] If an individual has a "known" disability that would reasonably interfere with or prevent performance of job functions, that person may be asked to demonstrate how these functions will be performed, even if other applicants are not asked to do so.[15]

Tests that simply measure an applicant's ability to perform a job-related task are not considered to be medical examinations. However, job requirements that screen out or tend to screen out persons with disabilities are legitimate only if they are job related and consistent with business necessity.[16] The *ADA* protects individuals who have a record of a substantially limiting impairment and people who are regarded as currently having a substantially limiting impairment.[17] *ADA* also covers those with AIDS and HIV afflictions from discriminatory hiring practices.[18] These types of genetic issues require employers to refrain from discrimination solely on the basis of coworker or customer opinions.[19] However, one contrasting case example is found in the ruling of *Chevron v. Echazabal* (2002), where the court ruled unanimously that employers do not violate the *ADA* when they refuse to hire disabled individuals for jobs that would subject them to significant health risks.[20] The court has also determined that the *Direct Threat Standard* question is one for the medical community and constructively the rightful arbiter of the amount and types of health information that employers should legitimately be able to collect from employees under the *ADA*.[21] The Direct Threat Standard allows a prospective employer to establish job-related qualification standards that will exclude an applicant that poses a direct threat or substantial risk of harm to the health or safety of the applicant or of a third party if that risk cannot be mitigated by a reasonable accommodation.[22] The EEOC states that, "This requirement may be met when an employer has a reasonable belief, based on objective evidence, that: (1) an employee's ability to perform essential job functions will be impaired by a medical condition; or (2) an employee will pose a direct threat due to a medical condition."[23] These standards must be developed through an objective and medically valid method that establishes such a significant risk of substantial harm could occur in the workplace.[24] There are four standards that are used as the test for this threshold that can be assessed by answering the following questions: (1) How long can the risk conceivably last for? (2) what is the nature and severity of the potential to cause harm in the workplace? (3) is there a probability that the harm will occur? and (4) if the harm is probable, is the harm an imminent threat to the safety of the applicant or a third party?[25]

The court has, however, questioned how acute a condition must be before it can rise to the level of an acceptable rejection.[26] Another example of the court's thinking on this issue involves the ruling in the *School Board of Nassau County, Florida v. Arline* (1987) wherein the U.S. Supreme Court examined the case of a teacher with a potentially communicable disease and reasoned that allowing an employer to justify discrimination by distinguishing between a disease's perceived contagious effects on others and its physical effects on the individual would be unfair.[27] The *ADA* also protects those who have been rehabilitated or are in a rehabilitation program and are no longer engaging in such illicit drug use or alcohol use. In contrast, the *ADA* expressly defines the following excluded claims from protection:

1. *Homosexuality and bisexuality*: For purposes of the definition of "disability," homosexuality and bisexuality are not impairments and as such are not disabilities under this chapter.
2. *Certain conditions*: Under this chapter, the term "disability" shall not include
   a. Transvestism, transsexualism, pedophilia, exhibitionism, voyeurism, gender identity disorders not resulting from physical impairments, or other sexual behavior disorders
   b. Compulsive gambling, kleptomania, or pyromania
   c. Psychoactive substance use disorders resulting from current illegal use of drugs[28]

The *ADA* was primarily designed to cover disabilities that have an impact on a major life function; however, with a reasonable accommodation, the applicant or employee may still be able to successfully perform the essential job functions. Employers, however, can establish a prerequisite for physical or psychological requirements based on the requirements for safe performance of the specific job applied for.[29] In law enforcement positions, there are numerous essential job functions that severely limit the application of the *ADA* standards in hiring. In response, law enforcement agencies must demonstrate that the basis for any adverse employment action is job related and consistent with business necessity. Based upon the concepts of essential job functions as a business necessity, law enforcement is relieved of many of the restrictions that the *ADA* normally covers. The courts also recognize these essential job functions and generally support rejection of applicants who do not meet the essential standards to perform job requirements. Interestingly, as the law evolves, a court decision in 2002 narrowed the definition of disability to include that the disability must prevent or severely restrict major life activities.[30] With respect to reasonable accommodations, the fact that a disability exists generally does not require the employer to change the essential functions of a job in order to accommodate a person's disability.[31] In order to meet the accommodation threshold provided in the law, the applicant must first have the requisite knowledge, skills, and abilities to perform the job, and if that level of competence exists, then a determination is made if a reasonable accommodation would assist them in performing all of the necessary job functions.[32] However, under the *ADA*, "An employer is not required to reallocate essential functions of a job as a reasonable accommodation."[33] The lack of cognitive skill and capacity is also not an *ADA*-relevant claim. An example of this can be found in the federal appeals court ruling of *Miller v. City of Springfield* (1999) wherein an applicant was rejected for a low score on the MMPI-2. The court ruled that the applicant suffered no actionable claim of discrimination because the low score did not indicate a disability nor did the low score lead to the perception of a disability.[34] The Act was recently updated, and the changes are included in the *Americans with Disabilities Act Amendments Act of 2008*.[35] The reasons for these updates emerged from the U.S. Supreme Court rulings in three separate cases: *Sutton v. United Airlines* (1999),[36] *Murphy v. United Parcel Service, Inc.* (1999),[37] and *U.S. Airways v. Barnett* (2002).[38] In order to determine if a person has an eligible disability, consideration must be given to the use and effectiveness of any mitigating measure used to assist in overcoming the disability. If the mitigating measure provides the ability to substantially overcome or supplant the claimed disability, then the person will not meet the *ADA*'s first definition of "disability."[39] In addition, an accommodation is deemed "reasonable" if it "seems reasonable on its face, i.e., ordinarily or in the run of cases."[40]

An employment discrimination claim must demonstrate that the employee was qualified to do the job and was treated unfairly for an illegal reason.[41] The court has held that conditions such as poor vision and high blood pressure are not disabilities under the *ADA* if they are treatable.[42] Also protected is the eventuality of a condition that exists and is episodic in nature that leads to an impairment, but the individual can function normally when the condition is in remission.[43] The Supreme Court has concluded that where a person has taken steps to overcome, adjust, and adapt to an otherwise *ADA*-protected condition or disability, that person can no longer seek the protection under the Act.[44] Fairly and appropriately applying the provisions of *ADA* to all hiring decisions is key. Those who do not can face severe repercussions. For example, an appellate court affirmed that a reasonable jury could infer that an employer's inconsistent behavior and fluctuating justifications of the reasons for not hiring an applicant indicated that the prospective employer knew that the decision not to hire the applicant was in violation of federal law.[45]

In order to comply with the law, position descriptions developed based upon job necessity can allow an occupational physician the ability to compare an applicant's impairments against a clearly stated list of essential job functions.[46] Well-designed and articulated position descriptions allow for an occupationally related physical examination that can determine if an applicant meets the essential job function whether they have an impairment or not.[47] The U.S. courts provide an excellent example of articulating the business necessity of the position of federal probation officer provided as follows:

Federal Probation Officer and Officer Assistant Medical and Age Requirements[51]

The duties of probation officers, pretrial services officers, and probation officer assistants require the investigation and management of alleged criminal offenders or convicted offenders who present physical danger to officers and to the public. In the supervision, treatment, and control of these offenders, these duties require moderate to arduous physical exercise, including prolonged periods of walking and standing, physical dexterity and coordination necessary for officer safety, and use of self-defense tactics. On a daily basis, these officers face unusual mental and physical stress because they are subject to danger and possible harm during frequent, direct contact with individuals who are suspected or convicted of committing federal offenses.

Because officers must effectively deal with physical attacks and are subject to moderate to arduous physical exertion, applicants must be physically capable. Officers must possess, with or without corrective lenses, good distance vision in at least one eye and the ability to read normal size print. Normal hearing ability, with or without a hearing aid, is also required. Any severe health problems, such as physical defects, disease, and deformities that constitute employment hazards to the applicant or others, may disqualify an applicant. Examples of health problems that may be disqualifying are an untreated hernia, cardiovascular disorders, serious deformities or disabilities of the extremities, mental health disorders, fainting and/or seizure disorders, metabolic disorders, bleeding disorders, pulmonary disorders, and marked speech abnormalities.

First-time appointees to positions covered under law enforcement officer retirement provisions must not have reached their 37th birthday at the time of appointment. Applicants 37 or over who have previous law enforcement officer experience under Civil Service Retirement System or the Federal Employees' Retirement System and who have either a subsequent break in service or intervening service in a non-law enforcement officer position may have their previous law enforcement experience subtracted from their age to determine whether they meet the maximum age requirement.

In order to develop a compliance process, employers should examine and update job descriptions that distinguish between essential and marginal job functions, plan interviews to avoid the inquiry into expressly forbidden questions, and have copious records of all selection processes and actions.[48] Ultimately, the responsibility for compliance falls on the shoulders of the management of the organization.[49] Simply put, the only way to avoid and defend against *ADA* claims is to abide by the requirements of the law.[50]

Health Insurance Portability and Accountability Act of 1996

The *Health Insurance Portability and Accountability Act of 1996* (HIPAA) was signed into law to protect the privacy of a patient's records from general disclosure without certain conditions for release and use.[52] The Act empowers the U.S. Department of Health and Human Services to regulate organizations that maintain and transmit health-related information to other entities for any use beyond the purpose of their original collection.[53] Additionally, the *Health Information Technology for Economic and Clinical Health Act* has also been ratified to protect the electronic storage and transfer of these types of files.[54] The *Privacy Rule* of the Act covers several different responsibilities for health-care providers (HCPs) that prescribes the limits and requirements for medical records releases. The relevant stipulations of the Act are as follows:

1. Defining the covered entities[55] as all HCPs: HCPs are "providers of services" (e.g., institutional providers such as hospitals) and "providers of medical or health services" (e.g., noninstitutional providers such as physicians, dentists, and other practitioners).
2. The Privacy Rule defines and limits disclosure of Protected Health Information (PHI).
3. PHI includes any individually identifiable health information transmitted in any form or media, whether electronic, paper, or oral. PHI includes any individual's past, present, or future physical or mental health or condition.
4. Information must be released when directed by court order, for law enforcement purposes as required by law (including court orders, court-ordered warrants, and subpoenas) and administrative requests and for workers' compensation issues to comply with workers' compensation laws and other similar programs providing benefits for work-related injuries or illnesses.
5. For psychotherapy notes, disclosure exceptions are included for an agency to use the information for its own training and to defend itself in legal proceedings brought by the individual.
6. In all cases, information release can be authorized by the individual or their personal representative. An authorization must be written in specific terms. It may allow use and disclosure of PHI by the covered entity seeking the authorization, or by a third party. Examples of disclosures that would require an individual's authorization include disclosures to an employer of the results of a pre-employment physical or lab test. In addition, all authorizations must be in plain language and contain specific information regarding the information to be disclosed or used, the person(s) disclosing and receiving the information, expiration, and the right to revoke in writing.[56]

The PHI requirements extend to pharmaceutical type of information as well.[57] In pre-employment screening, the issue of information release is covered in the Act as an applicant's complete processing will require the release of this information to both the department's physician and psychologist of record. Consequently, the applicant must authorize the release of this information for the limited purposes of pre-employment processing in order for the agency to make a determination of fitness for the position. Medical records releases and waivers are obtained after the COE is issued to the applicant (See Chapter 5).

The *Code of Federal Regulations, Title 42* (2010), also includes requirements for obtaining patient records through consensual means.[58] Once the applicant authorizes the release of the protected and confidential information, all of these records should be obtained by the licensed medical or psychological professional conducting the examination and evaluation. The applicant is responsible to be completely truthful in disclosing all treatments, conditions, medications, and the entire spectrum of physicians who have seen or treated them. If the proper disclosure is enjoyed, then the physician and psychologist can offer an informed opinion based upon the totality of the circumstances that includes the assessment of previous records as well as the results of current medical and psychological testing batteries. While this is overly dependent upon applicant candor, hopefully the level of support will also be high to foster cooperation and communication between the professionals involved. For future information releases, one goal is to have a national health records management system by 2014.[59] This would greatly enhance the ability of the professionals involved to review all of the relevant records of the applicant to give the most informed and accurate predictive assessment possible.

Workers' Compensation Laws and Issues

Relevant to this discussion is the issue of workers' compensation. This is inherently a medical application to the use of this type of information for the purposes of pre-employment screening. Employers across the country are greatly concerned with fraudulent claims as well as workers that reinjure themselves and subsequently become a drain to the organization's resources. Workers' compensation is primarily handled by the individual states in the country. Since the information that can be accessed is of a medical nature, then the protections of the *ADA* applies to the use of that information. Extreme caution must be exercised though in the use of these records.[60] Federal law protects workers who file legitimate claims of workplace injuries, protection which extends to antidiscrimination laws in hiring practices.[61] The background investigator must be able to explore the issue without violating the applicant's federal and state civil rights. Several factors may be the reason for an applicant's disability claims, from innocent or legitimate accidents due to lack of training and experience, to more questionable issues that involve poor habits or marginal personality traits.[62] This type of information cannot be sought until a valid COE is provided to the applicant (see Table 2.1 for the recommended timelines). After the COE is provided and if a history of filing workers' compensation claims is discovered, the COE can be rescinded under the following limited circumstances:

1. The applicant has lied about a worker's compensation history or medical condition, usually during a medical examination.
2. The applicant has a history of filing false claims.
3. The past claims demonstrate the applicant is a safety or health threat to himself or others in the opinion of a medical expert.
4. The past claims demonstrate the applicant is unable to perform the essential functions of the job even with a reasonable accommodation.[63]

If this type of information is discovered either directly or indirectly through inadvertent disclosure, the background investigator should not pursue a line of questioning exploring the nature or extent of any such injury that led to the initial claim. The information should be given directly to the licensed physician who should be responsible to obtain the relevant medical records and make a medical assessment of fitness based upon business necessity.

The use of these types of records may be more helpful in determining the truthfulness of the applicant where they may have not revealed this information to the examining physician in order to conceal a medical problem or condition that may preclude them from employment in the public safety position applied for. The applicant may also fail to disclose former employers where these types of claims have been filed with in order to conceal the injury or illegal activity such as fraud. In these circumstances, an applicant could be removed from the process for their failure to be truthful. According to Rosen,

> If the applicant has lied on a medical questionnaire, or to a doctor performing a pre-employment physical, then the employer may be justified in rescinding the job offer based upon dishonesty. If an applicant has a history of multiple claims that have been denied, then an employer may be justified in rescinding the offer based upon a history of dishonest conduct. The reason is based upon an inference of fraud, not disability.[64]

Additional methods of scrutiny should also be utilized when assessing an applicant's proclivity for behavior that demonstrates malingering or fraudulent acts. One recommended method of screening for these types of problems is through personality and behavioral assessment testing methods.[65] Another is employment interviews that explore the results of such claims rather than the actual claims themselves. For example, applicant interviews should explore gaps in employment, workplace attendance history, and job-related injuries that may not have been reported to workers' compensation.[66] This comes with one caveat though; employment interviews in these circumstances must be strictly limited to ascertaining if the applicant, in spite of the injury that resulted in a workers' compensation claim, can still perform the essential functions of the position applied for. If the applicant makes a disclosure, no further questions should be asked, rather referring the disclosure to the medical professional who will be conducting the job-related physical examination for follow-up and expert assessment as to if the claim of injury resulted in a condition that would preclude the applicant from performing essential job functions without reasonable accommodation, if applicable to the position applied for.

Conditional Offer of Employment

The COE is a mandated component of the pre-employment selection process where the employer seeks to ascertain any medical or psychological afflictions pertaining to the applicant. The COE represents the line of demarcation between for the collection of any and all medical and psychological or pathology-based information that can, or can be inferred, to have been used in the selection process.[67] Prior to the issuance of the COE, an applicant can be asked questions about their ability to perform job-related functions as long as questions are not formed in terms of the disability.[68] The applicant can also be asked any questions through psychological examination processes that are limited to personality testing or non-disease-related screening tools prior to the issuance of the COE.[69] However, the applicant cannot be asked to submit to any medical examination or psychological examination that solicits health-related information prior to the issuance of the COE. This significantly limits the parameters of any inquiry at this stage. More importantly, the processing agency should not deviate from established policy and practices in issuing the COE prior to obtaining any medical information.[70] Chapter 2 reviews the timelines for the issuance of the COE as related to the stages or steps of the selection process. For the purposes of this discussion, the extent of the pre-COE medical and psychological questioning is limited to the following:

1. Pre-employment inquiries into the ability of an applicant to perform job-related functions. The background investigator may not inquire into applicant's worker's compensation history or any medically related reasons for missing work as discussed previously in the *Workers' Compensation Laws and Issues* subsection until after the COE is issued. The background investigator must avoid inquiries that would directly or indirectly (through the line of questioning) disclose information relating to a real or perceived disability in the pre-COE stage of the background investigation.
2. In light of this, any and all medical questions that cannot be asked of the applicant at this stage also cannot be asked of prior employers or others who may have this type of knowledge in the pre-COE stage.

In contrast, the *ADA* was not intended to protect illegal drug use. Consequently, the background investigator can inquire either verbally or through the written application process about any and all current illegal drug usage. Any past illegal drug use can also be obtained such as last date of use as there is no exploration of the extent of the illegal drug usage. Illegal drug use includes obtaining and using illegal drugs as well as illegally obtaining and using the prescription drugs of others. If an applicant obtains and shares or sells drugs, this is a separate issue not covered under the conditions of the Act. However, addictions often fall within the realm of protected information under the requirements of the *ADA*. Prior drug and alcohol addiction of those who are currently in a rehabilitation program are protected, and this type of information should not be elicited. Self-declaration is another matter. If an applicant self-declares this type of information, then the circumstances must be considered concerning rehabilitation and a decision made that involves medical, psychological, and legal professionals in order to protect the applicant's and organization's rights.

Failing to issue the COE at the proper time in the process can be extremely problematic. Research has revealed that a significant number of agencies routinely violate public policy guidelines in the pre-employment screening process in both the medical and psychological testing areas.[71] The lack of the issuance of the COE also significantly impedes the background investigator's ability to conduct the pre-employment interview in these areas as needed.[72] The absence of the COE may also precipitate the need for multiple interviews with the applicant which can negatively impact on the costs, investigative tactics, and the ultimate liability of the agency.

In order to explore these types of issues with an applicant, a bona fide offer of employment must be made to the applicant in good faith (see Appendix E). To achieve this level of evidence, the organization must first evaluate all nonmedical information available that can be legally reviewed prior to extending the COE. The COE is an assertion to the candidate that absent any job-related reason that would adversely affect the hiring decision, the applicant can be considered for employment.

The COE is not a guarantee of being hired. The purpose of the COE is to ensure that no discrimination is present in the consideration of an applicant that may have a disability but is otherwise qualified for the role. The job offer can and should be conditioned upon successfully passing a medical examination.[73] The conditions should also extend to the applicant successfully passing other types of exams if applicable, such as the psychological and polygraph examinations, as well as all other processing stages and provision of all information requirements. For example, the psychological examination has been deemed by the courts to fall within the realm of medical examinations. With polygraph examinations, the examiner must determine certain medically related issues through questioning insofar as the applicant's mental, physical, or medical conditions, as well as any recent or past drug use (also see Chapter 5). The absence of the COE would severely inhibit the examiner's ability to effectively conduct the polygraph.[74] Polygrapher guidelines also further require that if there is some doubt as to the applicant's medical status to proceed with an examination, the polygraph examiner should obtain release forms from both the applicant and their personal physician.[75] Some offers even include successful completion of the field training and full probationary period.[76] In certain cases, the COE is written for a finite period of time, for example, reserving a position for 6 months during the processing period.[77] One department reported expediting their hiring process to complete all pre-COE requirements and then providing only 10 days for the COE time limit for the applicant to complete the remaining processes.[78] In practicality, these types of timelines are far more obstructive than productive to the process.

The timeline for issuance is critical. One case that challenged the COE issuance timeline was *Leonel v. American Airlines, Inc.* (2005).[79] Under the *ADA*, all nonmedical prerequisites for employment must be examined prior to the issuance of a valid and real COE that will lead to any type of medical inquiry.[80] In this case, three HIV-positive applicants had been afforded a telephone interview at the outset. In the ruling of *Bragdon v. Abbott* (1998), the U.S. Supreme Court recognized AIDS as being a protected affliction under the *ADA* regulations.[81] Without conducting any additional pre-employment checking, the company issued COE's contingent upon passing a drug test, a background investigation, and a medical examination. Their next step was the medical examination wherein they were required to complete a detailed medical questionnaire and submit to a blood test. The questionnaire required that truthful answers be offered and none of the applicants admitted to their condition. Subsequent to the results of the blood test, the company rescinded the COE's using their lack of disclosure or untruthfulness in completing the medical questionnaire as the cause for withdrawal of the offers. In the facts presented by one of the applicants, the company had offered that the applicant had been untruthful on the application, but the company had no business necessity–supported policy in place that precluded hiring those afflicted with HIV and also admitted to hiring HIV-positive employees in the past.[82] The issue for the court was that since no other nonmedical information had been evaluated prior to the issuance of the COE, the job offer did not meet the level of evidence or burden of proof required to be a valid or real job offer. Another salient point made by the court in this case was related to the issue of truthfulness in the process:

> We do not suggest that, when a medical examination is conducted at the proper time and in the proper manner, an applicant has an option to lie, or that an employer is foreclosed from refusing to hire an applicant who does.[83]

Since the *ADA* covers medical information, this also translates to the stages wherein psychological examinations, polygraph examinations, applicant interviews, and the background investigation elicit medical information.

If these requirements are met, then the agency has options for rejection of the applicant should any of the examinations reveal information that negatively affects the applicant's viability. For example, if the results of a medical examination conducted at the post-COE stage reveal a disability that meets the exclusionary business necessity requirements, the employer may withdraw the offer in compliance with the provisions of the *ADA*.[84] This is also true if the COE is withdrawn based upon an admission from the applicant outside the scope of the medical examination. The department must demonstrate that the withdrawal of the COE is based upon a condition that is directly related to the position sought; otherwise, the department can incur liability for violating the *ADA*.[85]

Issuing the proper number of COEs is also important. In the perfect world, an agency would only have to issue as many COEs as there are openings in the organization. The reality is that applicant attrition rates in the background screening process are extremely high. Ranges of 4-1 to as high as 12-1 can be experienced in any given process. Depending on the organization's processes of issuing these offers, consideration should be given to issuing proportionate quantities that are consistent with the law. Because attrition rates run high, an organization is allowed to issue as many COEs necessary to effectively process a group of applicants to fill the vacant positions. There must be a historical analysis of the past attrition rates of the organization to reach a reasonable figure to apply to the number of offers issued however. Each organization will have a unique rate of attrition that must be determined through simple statistical analysis. For example, a midsize law enforcement agency offers a written test to fill a series of 20 vacancies. Those at the highest ranks on the examination are invited for a physical agility examination in proportion to the historical losses of applicants in the process. Often, the attrition rate at a physical agility is at the 50% rate or higher loss ratio. This must also be considered in context to the number of applicants lost during the completion of the background process. A historical analysis of this organization demonstrates that over a 5 year period, on average, six applicants will need to be processed to have one acceptable candidate in the pool. If the organization needs at least 20 acceptable candidates at the end of the process, we must then multiply that by 6, which equates to 120 COEs that can be legally distributed. This now brings the original invitation of applicants to the physical agility test to 240 as we traditionally lose half of the applicants due to poor physical conditioning. Each organization must justify their loss rates through a review of their records and once developed, they can support the issuance of the appropriate numbers of COEs to effectively process a class. In addition, the law allows for variation in this process. For example, hypothetically, 120 COEs are issued to process a class and through some anomaly, the top 20 applicants all pass every stage of the process, there is no obligation to process other applicants further down the list nor provide them a position in the agency. This scenario would never happen due to the loss ratios that have been experienced across the country, but is an appropriate example of how the law works. A final consideration is that other factors may be considered in the COE process that may be out of the control of the agency. Not uncommon is the incidence of beginning a process and through any stage of the process, including completion and publishing of a certified final list of applicants who have successfully completed all of the stages of a process, change occurs such as a department suddenly cuts the budget, reduces personnel, loses a grant, or similar situations where the positions simply don't exist anymore. In these cases, even though the department issued the COE in good faith, they may be rescinded without repercussions to the agency as long as these types of extenuating circumstances exist.

One final note is that the COE does not trigger an employment relationship and thus garner collective bargaining unit protections. The applicant is not a member of the organization until they have successfully completed all hiring requirements, been certified by the appointing authority, and officially hired into the ranks. Since no employment relationship exists and no property right has attached, the applicant is not protected in this manner.[86] This does not open the door for sloppy or illegal practices as the applicant always has the right to retain an attorney and seek redress through the courts.

Pre- and Post-COE Disclosures

A few additional issues that need to be considered with respect to *ADA*-protected information are disclosures of medical and psychological information that is revealed prior to the COE being issued. Also addressed is the information that is disclosed to the background investigator after the COE is issued and the departments that include the discovery of medical issues in the background investigation stage. Discussed in this section are (1) information request timelines, (2) pre-COE disclosures, (3) post-COE disclosures, and (4) using the background investigation to discover medical and psychological information.

Information Request Timelines

Table 4.1 provides a basic timeline where information can be requested. Table 2.1 provides an outline of the recommended process step timelines. This table delineates information request guidelines in order to comply with the *ADA*.

TABLE 4.1
Pre- and Post-COE Information Stages

Pre-COE	1. Any and all drug experimentation or use (including any and all amounts and frequency/number of times of use) 2. The sharing of any drugs 3. The sale of any drugs
Post-COE	1. Any and all drug experimentation or use (including any and all amounts and frequency/number of times of use) 2. The sharing of any drugs 3. The sale of any drugs 4. Participation in any substance abuse program 5. Counseling and/or treatment for any emotional or psychiatric problem 6. The use of any psychiatric medications 7. Alcohol use/frequency and most recent occurrence of intoxication 8. Vehicle operation while intoxicated or under the influence of any drugs or alcohol 9. Retrieval of any and all mental health records in state and local repositories of treatments and commitments 10. Ascertain if the applicant has had any workers' compensation claims for work-related injuries

Pre-COE Disclosures

As outlined in Table 4.1, pre-COE requests for information must be strictly limited to illegal drug use questions which are specific areas not protected under the *ADA*. Probing of information beyond the scope of these specific areas may lead to the discovery of disability-related information that is protected from discovery at the pre-COE stage of the screening process. The federal government cautions against practices that attempt or appear to attempt to elicit this type of information in the pre-COE stage. A "disability-related inquiry" is a question (or series of questions) that is likely to elicit information about a disability.[87] This type of questioning should be wholly avoided in order to comply with the federal guidelines.

Unintentionally and occasionally, unsolicited health-related information will be learned by the background investigator.[88] Since the information was unsolicited, if treated correctly, may still be of use to the medical and/or psychological screening investigation. If the background investigator did not directly ask or attempt to further elicit this type of information, the information that was self-disclosed as well as the circumstances of the disclosure can then be communicated to the medical or psychological contractor for their evaluation purposes. To reiterate, directly asking any medical questions prior to the issuance of the COE is illegal under the *ADA*.

Post-COE Disclosures

Postoffer disclosures of health-related information may be developed through routine questioning of an applicant. Lapses in employment, terminations or resignations from a position, and the need to explore these issues may lead to such a disclosure. Information that is developed of a health-related nature should not be documented in the Final Investigative Package. The proper handling of this information would be to forward the relevant information developed to the medical or psychological professional tasked with the respective evaluation and keep no documentation or reference of this information either in the package or even on site.

Another inadvertent discovery of health information may emerge from the follow-up activities of the background investigator. The background investigator will be responsible to interview supervisors, coworkers, family, friends, acquaintances, and others who know the applicant well enough to offer an informed opinion. During the course of these visits and interviews, the background investigator may be privy to health-related information whether by disclosure of the interviewee or by obvious evidence of a possible disability (e.g., the presence of mobility assisting devices like canes, crutches, and wheelchairs or the presence of medications that are in plain view). This type of discovery may also occur when the background investigator reviews performance and disciplinary records of the employee as well as evidentiary documentation provided by or forwarded by the applicant. An example is the records related to health care. In the wide variation of health plans that exist as well as the continuing trend to offer fewer benefits, applicants may have credit card debts, bank statements, and even credit history statements that may include these types of expenditures. Once this information is revealed in the post-COE timeframe, any documentation or information should not be explored further by the background investigator. Proper handling would include forwarding this type information to the appropriate medical or psychological professional. The background investigator must also remove any of these reports from the file unless the report contains other germane information, wherein the background investigator must redact the segments of the affected report that would or could be interpreted as having any influence in the hiring process.

Using the Background Investigation to Discover Medical and Psychological Information

The author has worked with several agencies that include as part of the background investigation a medical or psychological background. In the post-COE stage, this type of information can be solicited (see Table 4.1). Drug use, mental health issues, treatments, and records, as well as many other areas protected in the pre-COE stage by the ADA, can be solicited in the post-COE stage of the investigative timeline. However, since the background investigator and, for all intents and purposes, anyone in the review process other than a medical or psychological professional can render an informed and defensible finding, the practice of including this information in the background investigation should be wholly avoided. From a proper protocol perspective, any information obtained that is subject to the *ADA* information release restrictions should be a matter of review by the affected professionals. In addition, any inclusion of this type of information in the Final Investigative Package could lead to a claim that the real or perceived disability was the reason for rejection rather than the rejection being based on the legitimate discovery of an applicant who is unfit for the role based upon poor characteristics, criminal record, or other exclusionary factors allowed by the law.

Just take pause in the fact that we are empowered to collect this type of information; how we use the information is another story. Don't be tempted to make unqualified medical and psychological assessments that will expose you and the organization to unnecessary scrutiny and litigation. The best use of this information for the background investigator is in establishing applicant integrity. Applicants must be truthful in all responses, written and oral. Questionnaires that have been completed for the background investigation, medical, and psychological screening processes should all be compared side by side to ascertain if the applicant has been forthcoming in every stage and component process. Leave the professional evaluations to the experts in their respective fields to make qualified and defensible assessments that may lead to adverse impact on employment decisions.

MEDICAL STANDARDS AND EVALUATIONS

Medical standards are developed from the job-related tasks and responsibilities of the position tested for. Some states will identify certain afflictions as hurdles for employment. Under the *Florida Law*, applicants who suffer from maladies such as tuberculosis (TB), heart disease, or hypertension may not be employed in law enforcement or corrections positions.[89] Medical standards for law enforcement officers are necessary to ensure that those hired are capable of fulfilling the required public safety functions, as a screening tool for persons with chronic medical problems that predispose them to frequent sick absences, to ensure that applicants who are hired can function effectively during their appointment, and to identify and disqualify drug use or abuse that is beyond the scope of acceptability.[90] Medical standards for the justification of business necessity should be continually reviewed and updated to comply with the evolving needs of the *ADA*.[91] Medical evaluations then determine physical condition, general health, and medical afflictions that would preclude an applicant from filling the role. If the affliction or disability prevents the performance of a job-essential task or if the disability poses a substantial threat to safety, then the applicant can be excluded from further consideration.[92] An extreme case occurred where a medical diagnosis of an applicant concluded that the applicant suffered from a long-term medical illness that rendered him involuntarily unconscious. The physician asserted that this could lead to serious injury. The applicant was subsequently hired and later suffered a similar episode that resulted in a motor vehicle accident.[93] With this type of paper trail, cases like these are virtually indefensible. An excellent example of published standards for medical requirements that directly relate to essential job functions can be found in the position posting for federal probation officer shown below:

Federal probation officer essential job functions[94]

Officer and officer assistant essential job functions

Based on data collected and analyzed by the Department of Health and Human Services, Public Health Services, Division of Federal Occupational Health, and Law Enforcement Medical Programs, the following essential job functions have been established to reflect the work of probation and pretrial services officer and officer assistants. An essential job function is a specific job duty that is critical to the safe and effective performance of the job. The ability to perform essential job functions is measured by a physician during an examination of the following specific medical areas.

Cardiovascular, dermatology, endocrine, metabolic, musculoskeletal, neurological, and respiratory

- Respond with unplanned vigorous physical activity.
- Climb stairs in pursuit or in emergency.
- Attempt to physically subdue attacker.

Gastrointestinal and genitourinary

- Work extended hours.
- Travel that requires significant time.
- Ability to miss meals.

Hematology, musculoskeletal, neurological, and respiratory

- Drive vehicles on duty.
- Drive vehicles in the dark.
- Work in adverse weather.
- Work under stress.
- Walk on uneven surfaces.
- Stop, question, or detain individuals (unplanned interviews).
- Encounter individuals who display a violent or irrational temperament.
- Confiscate weapons from persons.

Head, nose, mouth, throat and neck, and hearing

- Comprehend speech during face-to-face conversations.
- Comprehend speech during telephone conversations.
- Comprehend speech when you can't see another officer.
- Hear sounds that require investigation.
- Ability to localize sounds.

Vision

- Use distant vision for driving.
- Use distant vision to monitor activities and/or defendants during interviews.
- Use distant vision to monitor exterior/interior home environment.
- Use distant vision to assess threats.
- Use near vision for reading.
- Visually detect peripheral movement and identify a threat.

Medical Examination

According to the U.S. EEOC, a *medical examination* is "a procedure or test that seeks information about an individual's physical or mental impairments or health."[95] The following factors should be considered to determine whether a test (or procedure) is a medical examination:

1. Whether the test is administered by a health-care professional
2. Whether the test is interpreted by a health-care professional
3. Whether the test is designed to reveal an impairment of physical or mental health
4. Whether the test is invasive
5. Whether the test measures an employee's performance of a task or measures his or her physiological responses to performing the task
6. Whether the test normally is given in a medical setting
7. Whether medical equipment is used[96]

The U.S. EEOC further outlines the types of procedures and tests included under this definition as

1. Vision tests conducted and analyzed by an ophthalmologist or optometrist
2. Blood, urine, and breath analyses to check for alcohol use
3. Blood, urine, saliva, and hair analyses to detect disease or genetic markers (e.g., for conditions such as sickle cell trait, breast cancer, Huntington's disease)
4. Blood pressure screening and cholesterol testing
5. Nerve conduction tests (i.e., tests that screen for possible nerve damage and susceptibility to injury, such as carpal tunnel syndrome)
6. Range-of-motion tests that measure muscle strength and motor function
7. Pulmonary function tests (i.e., tests that measure the capacity of the lungs to hold air and to move air in and out)

8. Psychological tests that are designed to identify a mental disorder or impairment
9. Diagnostic procedures such as x-rays, computerized axial tomography (CAT) scans, and magnetic resonance imaging (MRI)[97]

The U.S. EEOC also outlines the types of procedures and tests included under this definition that are generally not considered medical examinations:

1. Tests to determine the current illegal use of drugs
2. Physical agility tests, which measure an employee's ability to perform actual or simulated job tasks, and physical fitness tests, which measure an employee's performance of physical tasks, such as running or lifting, as long as these tests do not include examinations that could be considered medical (e.g., measuring heart rate or blood pressure)
3. Tests that evaluate an employee's ability to read labels or distinguish objects as part of a demonstration of the ability to perform actual job functions
4. Psychological tests that measure personality traits such as honesty, preferences, and habits
5. Polygraph examinations[98]

Examination terminology and law will dictate the processual components of the examination process. Terminology will be important when developing policy in alignment with the relevant legal parameters. For example, in *Cremer v. Macomb* (1996), an absence of statutory language, hence a lack of clear definition of a final "physical examination," resulted in a ruling that forced inclusion of the psychological examination into this realm.[99] Policy and legal statute must be developed to draw a distinct line between these distinctly different applicant screening methods.

A final note is that employers do not have the right to access non-job-related medical information.[100] The job-related parameters must emerge from validated studies and be administered through an examination by a licensed physician, and questions and tests must remain within the framework of those guidelines. The types of tests vary in different jurisdictions that interpret the federal guidelines. For example, the Washington State Patrol requires proof of a TB test and, specifically for females, a recent Pap smear test as part of their medical examination.[101] The background investigator should be familiar with the current guidelines used by their agency in order to avoid being placed in a difficult situation by asking questions or soliciting information that is illegal to explore.

Genetic Testing

Genetic testing has its share of controversy. Executive Order 13145 states, "Genetic test means the analysis of human DNA, RNA, chromosomes, proteins, or certain metabolites in order to detect disease-related genotypes or mutations."[102] One of the earliest legal challenges concerning the genetic testing controversy was addressed in the ruling of *Norman-Bloodsaw v. Lawrence Berkeley Laboratory* (1998). The court found that such testing, even with consent to a general medical examination or consent to providing blood or urine samples, abolishes the privacy right not to be tested for intimate, personal matters involving one's health. The issues cited were violations of the 4th, 5th, and 14th Amendments as well as Title VII of the *Civil Rights Act of 1964*.[103] While numerous states preclude an employer from hiring, terminating, or placing certain conditions on employment because of the presence of a genetic disorder, employers may however have immense leeway in obtaining genetic testing samples from the applicant.[104] As a result of litigation and controversy, the *Genetic Information Nondiscrimination Act of 2008* (GINA) was passed. The law is excerpted as follows:

> This law makes it illegal to discriminate against employees or applicants because of genetic information. Genetic information includes information about an individual's genetic tests and the genetic tests of an individual's family members, as well as information about any disease, disorder or condition of an individual's family members (i.e. an individual's family medical history). The law also makes it illegal to retaliate against a person because the person complained about discrimination, filed a charge of discrimination, or participated in an employment discrimination investigation or lawsuit.[105]

While this body of law is still evolving, agencies who are interested in this type of testing must develop the true need that is job related and of a business necessity in order to withstand the most certain legal challenges that will follow.

Vision Screening

Vision screening requirements have been the subject of constant change over the years. In part, due to the need for candidates to fill vacant positions, however, the changes were primarily driven by legal challenges to departmental requirements. At the outset, law enforcement maintains high vision standards as a matter of safety protocols that are intended to protect the officer and the public equally.[106] Research by the use of a job task analysis has shown that not only the quality of vision but also color vision are critical to the successful, safe, effective, and efficient functioning of a law enforcement officer.[107] Even moderate levels of visual impairment that limit an officer's ability to effectively perform their duties can increase a department's liability exposure.[108] Some departments have lowered the standards of uncorrected vision to 20/200 where in many states this is the definition of legal blindness.

Aside from the safety issues, legal issues also ensue. With the *ADA* as a primary driver for developing vision standards, departments must consider many issues in developing minimum vision standards. Blanket medical prohibitions are highly scrutinized by the courts under their interpretation of the terms of the *ADA*.[109] As an aside, these protections, as a matter of law, extend beyond screening qualifications into the employee's career. *ADA* also protects impairment of sight even after hired as was evidenced by a U.S. Supreme Court decision to reject a city's appeal for reinstating an officer who had been terminated due to the loss of sight in one eye from contracting glaucoma.[110] This issue has been the subject of much debate and litigation in the country. Case law both supports and refutes the issues of vision requirements, ultimately relegating this topic at times to the gray areas of decision making in the selection process. For example, *DFEH v. City of Merced Police Department* (1988) addressed the issue of monocular vision and the need for binocular vision in order to promote safety.[111] The ruling stated that a monocular applicant for a position as a police officer "posed a significantly greater risk to the health and safety of others than a police officer with binocular vision."[112] However, federal civil rights lawsuits have led to the relaxing of stringent vision standards for such public safety occupations as firefighters.[113] This specific decision transcended an earlier decision where minimum vision requirements were relaxed for police officers.[114] The federal class action lawsuit filed against the Philadelphia Police Department resulted in a settlement that included, among other concessions, the lowering of stringent vision standards and more use of corrective measures such as prescription glasses and contact lenses.[115] Applicants have also been allowed to undergo corrective procedures such as radial keratotomy in order to meet vision requirements.[116] Physicians, and more appropriately, optometrists or ophthalmologists, must make these types of vision-related assessments in comparison to the business necessity requirements of the position.[117]

While poor eyesight is a valid reason to reject an applicant, departments must consider the *Direct Threat Standard* included under the *ADA* in developing minimum vision requirements in addition to developing policy that is based upon validated job task analyses to defend variations in vision standards of comparable agencies and to justify the lack of retesting during an employee's career.[118] Sadly, only a limited number of law enforcement agencies have conducted vision-related job task analyses to validate the minimum acceptable critical vision tasks required for police officer job performance.[119] Job task analysis leads to job descriptions of validated vision requirements for law enforcement officers so as proper screening can be ensured.[120]

Translating this to policy has been accomplished by the Washoe County Sheriff's Office wherein they post their vision standards online so as applicants have the expectation at the outset and there are no surprises presented when an applicant fails to meet their minimum qualifications:

1. Visual acuity must be 20/20 in each eye with or without correction.
2. Wearers of hard and semirigid gas-permeable contact lenses or glasses must have 20/40 uncorrected visual acuity.
3. Successful long-term, soft daily-wear contact lens wearers are subject to no uncorrected standard, provided the following conditions are met:
   a. They have worn their lenses 6 months without complications.
   b. They will replace their lenses every 6 months to 1 year or more frequently if the lenses become uncomfortable or difficult to wear.
   c. They will clean the lenses on a regular basis as recommended by the manufacturer.
4. Visual acuity for corrected vision (surgery, orthokeratology, or radial keratotomy) to 20/20 needs individual evaluation.
5. Loss of color vision (color blindness) is an automatic disqualifier.[121]

Auditory Screening

Auditory (hearing) screening also presents some issues as departments must have defined standards in place for the screening physician to use as a guide. Tests should be performed by an audiologist in a clinical setting. Applicants must also have some expectation of what are the acceptable thresholds for performance within the position. The Washoe County Sheriff's Office again uses the department website to post their hearing standards so as applicants understand the requirements prior to testing:

1. Hearing loss attenuated by hearing aid is not acceptable.
2. Pure tone thresholds of audibility shall not exceed 25 dB HL in either right or left ear at the following audiometric frequencies: 25, 500, 1000, 2000, 3000, 4000, 6000 Hz. Thresholds shall be measured adaptively under headphones using standard audiometric procedures.[122]

Preexisting Injuries

Previous injuries present a quandary as the question remains: Does the previous injury present substantive limitations that would prevent the applicant from fulfilling job-related tasks? *ADA* protections include disabilities that impair a major life function and if the impairment may be reasonably accommodated. As a general rule, the applicant may not be asked if they have ever filed a claim for or suffered a work-related disability.[123] Concerns in this area emerge from the very just fear of administrators who discover that applicants who have submitted workers' compensation claims in the past are likely to reinjure themselves, leading to inordinate amounts of lost time.[124] Employee health plans, workers' compensation claims, and Social Security Disability Income (SSDI) are investigative resources, but should be limited to a medical professional's review. As discussed earlier in pre- and post-COE disclosures, this type of information should be solicited by the medical professional whenever possible. Any inadvertent disclosures by the applicant, observations of the background investigator, results of any investigative steps such as interviews or document reviews should be packaged for the medical professional and psychological professionals and not be included in any of the documentation the organization maintains as part of the screening process.

One final note with respect to medical examinations concerns the process itself. Case law exists where an employee may have their attorney present during a nonpsychological and independent medical examination. This was the determination in *Gensbauer v. The May Department Stores* (1999).[125] As an extension of this, an applicant for a position may also enjoy a similar if not equal right to do so.

DRUG AND ALCOHOL USE

Unlike integrity issues or felony convictions that draw a very distinct line of demarcation in candidate viability, drug use is a much less definitive distinction in most agencies and, as disturbing as this fact is, in the eyes of most onlookers! Illicit drug use plagues the country, penetrating every walk of life. From marijuana to heroin and crack cocaine, the problem grows perpetually with a purported war on drugs that continues to lose ground because of the market demand. Trends have revealed the progression of the use of marijuana to much more potent compounds is prevalent. A recent analysis revealed that in some states methamphetamine use has substantially outpaced cocaine use.[126] Because of the pervasiveness, the implications of illegal drug use on the pre-employment process are an extremely troublesome trend in the pre-employment investigation process.

Alcohol use is an even more complex and problematic area to draw some very distinct conclusions from. Alcohol represents pseudo accepted mores of our society as drinking is for all intents and purposes legitimate for those of the legal age to imbibe. In the past, illicit drug use was much more defined in a society that, while mildly understanding, also accepted the fact that certain roles in society should exclude those who have had any admitted or proven involvement in the use of illegal substances.

Sadly, illegal drug use has become far more a social phenomenon than a moral aversion. A recent study has revealed that drug use is currently at a decade level high in the United States.[127] Further statistics point to the increased use of marijuana as having a significant proportional impact on those statistics.[128] Expectations of ethics and integrity have taken on an oddly inverse interpretation. Applicants are sought for positions who have clean records and are devoid of succumbing to the prurient, paganistic, and primal temptations of life so as they may resist the proliferation of opportunities law enforcement roles present when they are placed in these positions that require complete and unwavering public trust. Applicant pools are now poisoned with droves of aspiring centurions who have failed to resist these temptations when there was no pressure to do so, but can now somehow magically commit to this level of abstinence for at least 20 years. Insofar as past behavior is a confident predictor of future behavior, this assertion has significant merit when examining an applicant's background that includes previous drug use or abuse.[129] This puerile behavior can be accepted throughout our lives as opposed to a single mistake that we apparently never learn from until the ubiquitous "experimentation" actually matters with respect to our livelihood. In placing this in context to the hiring of public safety officers, while illegal drug use is a major consideration, the predominant consideration is that illegal drug use is also an indicator of the applicant's view of the law and their blatant indifference to violating those laws.[130]

This really is a product of a weak and corrupt society. An American president had freely admitted to alcohol, marijuana, and cocaine use prior to his landslide election.[131] The office that conceivably requires the highest level of integrity and trust in the known free world has been diminished by the lack of morality of the voting American people. Not far behind was the newly appointed replacement governor of New York who freely admitted to cocaine and marijuana use prior to taking office.[132] Common reactions in the ascension to political office are feelings of entitlement and self-indulging behavior that often includes political corruption.[133] Countless examples that seem to stretch beyond the reaches of infinity can be cited: the mayor of Baltimore is convicted of perjury and embezzlement as a result of stealing gift cards that were intended for needy families;[134] the former governor of New York State stepped down in disgrace as he was linked to a sex scandal and prostitution ring[135] and his replacement embroiled in even more scandals;[136] and the mayor of Detroit was charged with misconduct in office, obstruction of justice, conspiracy to commit obstruction of justice, perjury, and assaulting a police officer also as a result of a sex scandal.[137] Research has shown that the lack of integrity on the part of our elected officials is a substantive cause of the failing moral health of society.[138] In the final outcome, bureaucratic corruption is often a product of the personal virtue of the society's leader.[139] In the structure of public safety organizations, that also equates to the integrity of the chief executive officers and their command staff.

Given this set of circumstances, we cannot continually sit in amazement when drug users, and at times, drug dealers, believe they have some inalienable level of entitlement when they apply for these positions of public trust as public safety officers. Given the chance, applicants will attribute drug use from casual episodes through the need to survive myriad life crises.[140] We are continually faced with the challenges of drawing the clear line when the line is consistently blurred. This political, social, and public health issue has caused irreparable damage to the prospective candidate pools.

While an issue of personal responsibility, this issue is also one of workplace safety concerns. The matter of workplace drug use has wide social implications.[141] An all too disconcerting pandemic can be characterized as a true silent killer. In 2001, a study of the rate of positive drug tests for employees was at 4.5% of the total employee population.[142] Other studies have placed drug use in the workplace, with marijuana as the most frequently used substance, as high as 15%.[143] An additional simple example is shown through a research study conducted in Texas that revealed that the majority of substance abusers polled in the study work for small businesses.[144] Specifically, when considering workplace drug use, another study revealed that up to 25% of the workforce aged 20–40 are involved in illicit drug use and abuse.[145] An issue that knows no racial or gender boundaries, DWI testing of oral fluids revealed that females returned positive results of substance use and abuse at a rate of 19% of those tested.[146] One company that conducts over 20,000 combined drug and alcohol tests per year found that 70% of positive drug or alcohol tests came from employees who have been with the company for less than 1 year.[147] In extremely difficult economic times, a wise move would be to heed the warnings of the research concerning the economic costs of substance use and abuse in the United States. The economic cost to society from alcohol and drug abuse was an estimated $246 billion in 1992. In 1995, those costs increased to $276 billion.[148] These are the cumulative costs. Direct costs in the manner of shortfalls in productivity and employment among individuals with alcohol or drug abuse disorders accounted for estimated losses of $80.9 billion.[149] Employee health, safety, and productivity are all negatively affected by the widespread substance abuse found in the workplace.[150]

The problem gained national recognition and became a public policy concern with the passing of the *Drug-Free Workplace Act of 1988* that requires recipients of federal contracts worth $25,000 or more to have a drug-free workplace program in place.[151] The drug-free workplace requirements include notification to employees of the actions and sanctions for violation of the requirements and training supervisors to properly identify and handle employees who have been identified as using illegal drugs in the workplace.[152] Since that time, employers have been forced to comply with these types of rules. The positive aspects have revealed that employers with successful programs find their employees have fewer accidents, have less absenteeism and turnover, and have also enjoyed associated benefits of discounted health and liability insurance rates.[153] An oft-challenged and controversial issue has brought forth legislation that is designed to ensure the safety of the public. For example, the *Omnibus Transportation Employee Testing Act of 1991* "Requires drug and alcohol testing of safety-sensitive transportation employees in aviation, trucking, railroads, mass transit, pipelines and other transportation industries."[154] The U.S. Occupational Safety and Health Administration provides assistance to companies in identifying potential hazards and to improve safety systems. Organizations have found models such as those required by the Department of Transportation as very effective. This model includes pre-employment, random, postaccident, return to duty, and reasonable suspicion testing of employees.[155] Many departments across the country have taken this concept to nontraditional areas as well by the institution of no smoking bans for new recruits in an effort to promote healthier organizations.[156] While this Act has seen some positive benefits, one of the shortcomings is that the provisions do not have mandates for entry-level hiring, only affecting existing employees in the organization. The Act does not put controls in place for these types of prior drug use or abuse.

Over the years, many public safety agencies across the country have lowered their drug use restrictions and standards due to the lack of applicants who meet strict requirements.[157] This mistake is often irreparable, and public safety administrators must proactively draw acceptable lines and hold to them in order to promote a drug-free workplace. The recommended practice is to drug test all applicants for the position of public safety officer.[158] Research has developed a typology of drug abusers in the workplace that, in part, has implications to the law enforcement position. In workplace studies, predominant levels of substance abuse are in young males influenced by substance-abusing peers and working in hazardous or risky positions,[159] an almost uncanny description of today's police officers. One promising piece of research revealed during a longitudinal study of workplace drug testing that employee attitudes toward the process are becoming increasingly favorable.[160] Acceptance is only a small win though. Compliance is the war to be won!

Drug Testing

The next section discusses the integral components of drug testing for public safety officer applicants. Drug testing is defined as a method of medically approved and technical analysis accomplished through various biological specimens such as blood, urine, sweat or perspiration, and oral fluids such as saliva. The purpose of drug testing is to determine the presence or absence of any existing illicit drugs or pharmaceuticals in the applicant's biological system. This includes the primary detection of these types of drugs as well as their chemical fingerprints identified as metabolites. Testing methods have evolved over the years and are producing higher validity rates as the technology advances.[161] This section is intended to provide general guidance and to present national and selected local trends in the handling of this issue. This section addresses (1) legal and procedural issues; (2) drug types and detection methods; (3) prescription and over-the-counter (OTC) drug misuse and abuse; (4) false-positive and false-negative drug tests; (5) policy issues of marijuana use; (6) drug possession, manufacturing, sales, and distribution; and (7) alcohol use and abuse.

Legal and Procedural Issues

Federal law and the *Controlled Substances Act of 1970* set the foundation for controlled and psychotropic substances.[162] State penal laws and codes also are guiding in these issues as they arise with applicants. An analysis of all 50 states laws, inclusive of federal laws, reveals that in the vast majority of court decisions, government employers will be permitted to do pre-employment drug testing.[163] As has been discussed previously, the *ADA* was intentionally written to exclude the problem of illegal drug use in the workplace. Current illegal drug use is not protected under *ADA*, and several courts have supported restrictions on drug use as a business necessity. A test for the illegal use of drugs is not considered a medical examination under the *ADA* and is not a prohibited pre-employment medical examination.[164] An employer may deny employment to current illegal users of drugs on the basis of such drug use.[165] A department can also disqualify an applicant for a life of casual drug use.[166] Positive test results for illegal drug use can also be explored with the applicant with respect to the use of any prescription medications that may have caused the positive result, even though the answer may disclose information about a disability.[167] If the results of a drug test reveal the presence of a lawfully prescribed drug or other medical information, such information must be treated as a confidential medical record.[168]

Several court cases have been decided that support this practice. For example, *Skinner v. Railway Labor Executives' Association* (1989) decided by the U.S. Supreme Court allowed for random drug testing of public employees in "safety-sensitive" positions.[169] *Buckley v. Consolidated Edison of New York, Inc.* (1998) affirmed the ability of the prospective employer to inquire about illegal drug use can be made at any stage of the hiring process.[170] This case is also supported by the decision in *NASA v. Nelson* (2011) wherein the U.S. Supreme Court affirmed the right of government to screen applicants for illegal drug use and for possession, supplying, or manufacturing of illegal drugs.[171] As applied to the processing of law enforcement applicants, in *The Shield Club v. City of Cleveland* (1986) decision involving a claim of disparate impact due to drug testing, the court upheld the department's right to test based upon job necessity to use drug testing procedures for positions such as those of police officers.[172]

In contrast, testing process and validity have also been met with several court challenges. Policy, technology, and care must be exercised in any current employee as well as applicant screening process. As screeners, this is a moral as well as legal obligation. Negligence in the drug testing process may lead to liability on behalf of the employer.[173] A few citations of note involve challenges to process wherein the employees prevailed. In the decision of *Willis v. Roche Biomedical Laboratories, Inc.* (1995), an employee's urine test revealed a false-positive result for methamphetamine use which was in actuality an OTC cold medication.[174] In *Ishikawa v. Delta Airlines* (2003), a negligently performed urine test and invalid results subsequently led to the wrongful termination of a flight attendant.[175] These cases underscore the importance of developing a keen understanding of the prevailing and contemporary legal precedents and their impact on policy, procedure, and the science of drug screening.

Drug Types and Detection Methods

This next section provides an overview of the types of illegal substances and detection methods. This section is not intended to be an all-encompassing presentation, but rather it is intended to present the issues, concerns, and considerations in the testing and disqualification of public safety applicants for certain types of illicit drug use. For testing processes and protocol, most are discussed with the exception of the use of blood as this procedure is considered an overly invasive process and not used by those responsible for the pre-employment screening process. With the perishable nature of drug use detection looming about, the efficacy of drug testing is severely limited within the scope of the prescreening process. Only a small percentage of applicants are disqualified for positive testing results. Therefore, drug testing and the subsequent interpretation of an applicant's toxicology analysis are often in question. The majority of applicants are discovered through independent investigation and self-disclosure (e.g., admissions on pre-employment forms and paperwork, investigative interviews, polygraph examinations).[176] Still in all, this area is of great concern and must be addressed with every applicant with all due diligence.

ADA Considerations

The *ADA* was never intended to be a shelter for illegal drug use of any kind. The law was, and still is, only intended to provide protections for those who have suffered from some type of disability and some disabilities involving addictions to be free from illegal discrimination in the hiring process. However, casual, experimental, or pattern illegal drug use that does not fall within these guidelines is not protected. A public safety agency can inquire about any illegal drug use, possession, sales, and sharing, as well as any arrests related to such activities. Candidates with a felony drug conviction, even though a former addict, may be disqualified as long as the exclusion is job related and consistent with business necessity.[177]

Applicants may self-declare an addiction; however, this would need to be investigated and reviewed for validity. Once determined, then the applicant would be afforded all of the protections provided by the law if they in fact did have a protected claim. Any postoffer withdrawal of the COE based upon disability-related inquires would be scrutinized by federal investigators wherein the agency would need to demonstrate that the reason for the withdrawal was job related and consistent with business necessity.[178] Prior to any adverse employment action, the agency should consult with their legal counsel to determine the best legal strategy to deal with the issue at hand. One final note is that someone who self-declares an addiction and is successfully completing a rehabilitation program may be protected.

Drug Types and Detection Ranges

The types of drugs to be tested for should be numerous. Because of the range of illicit narcotics available to the average person as well as the damaging effects of many types of drugs, the candidate should be subjected to a wide battery testing regimen. To validate testing processes as well as exclusionary parameters, agencies should adopt validated standards in practice in their respective states or utilize a panel of medical experts and toxicologists to help develop parameters for an agency-specific standard to adhere to. The type of prohibited drug use as well as usage patterns must be included in the policy to offer guidance in disqualification as well as support any agency actions in any subsequent litigation. A common testing panel that is used is the Substance Abuse and Mental Health Services Administration or SAMHSA 5 Panel that tests for marijuana, cocaine, opiates, phencyclidine (PCP), and amphetamines.[179] Other tests include the DOT 5 Drug Test Panel, the DOT 10 Drug Test Panel, and the NIDA 5 Panel Test.[180] Nicotine is also a panel being tested for in pre-employment screening.[181] The following list is demonstrative of a drug testing battery for an applicant:

1. Cannabinoids (marijuana, hashish)
2. Cocaine (cocaine, crack, benzoylecgonine)
3. Opiates (heroin, opium, codeine, morphine)
4. Amphetamines (amphetamines, methamphetamines, speed)
5. Phencyclidine (PCP, angel dust)
6. Barbiturates (phenobarbital, secobarbital, pentobarbital, butalbital, amobarbital)
7. Methaqualone (quaaludes)
8. Benzodiazepines (tranquilizers—diazepam, valium, librium, ativan, xanax, klonopin, serax, halcion, rohypnol)
9. Methadone
10. Propoxyphene (Darvon compounds)
11. Ethanol
12. LSD
13. Hallucinogens (psilocybin, mescaline, MDMA, MDA, MDE)
14. Inhalants (toluene, xylene, benzene)[182]

Steroid Use

Steroid use has gained considerable infamy through the high-profile antics of professional athletes, some incidents leading to arrests and allegations of perjured testimony.[183] Steroid use also touches the general population of those who desire to obtain physical attractiveness or reach new levels of physical strength and endurance.[184] Steroid use has also been posited as having grown to startling proportions in high school students who use performance-boosting drugs in order to distinguish themselves on the playing field.[185] A national study revealed that increased use was noted in 8th, 10th, and 12th graders across the country.[186] Research has also revealed direct correlations of steroid use and the use and abuse of other illicit drugs and alcohol in American teenagers.[187] In response to the growing public health concerns, the U.S. government enacted the *Anabolic Steroids Control Act of 1990* that allowed regulation under the *Controlled Substances Act of 1970*.[188] In accordance with the Act, anabolic steroids are defined as, "Any drug or hormonal substance chemically and pharmacologically related to testosterone (other than estrogens, progestins, and corticosteroids) that promotes muscle growth."[189] The Act was subsequently revised in the form of the *Anabolic Steroids Control Act of 2004*, wherein the definition was further defined as including "tetrahydrogestrinone (THG), androstenedione, and specified related chemicals."[190] Steroids can be taken both orally and intravenously. The varying methods and drugs are categorized as follows:

Oral steroids:

1. Anadrol® (oxymetholone)
2. Oxandrin® (oxandrolone)
3. Dianabol® (methandrostenolone)
4. Winstrol® (stanozolol)

Injectable steroids:

1. Deca-Durabolin® (nandrolone decanoate)
2. Durabolin® (nandrolone phenpropionate)
3. Depo-Testosterone® (testosterone cypionate)
4. Equipoise® (boldenone undecylenate) (veterinary product)[191]

Not strictly limited to professional athletes and body builders, anabolic steroid (anabolic-androgenic steroids or AAS) use has also extended into the law enforcement realm. The use of the human growth hormone (HGH) has surfaced in studies of police and firefighters who desire to cheat *Father Time* in their efforts to recapture their fleeting youth.[192] Steroid use was believed to have peaked in law enforcement during the 1990s.[193] Reports across the country paint a different picture that steroid use is still a dark part of law enforcement, corrections, and the fire service.[194] Some very poor arguments by users are that law enforcement officers need such enhancements to stay physically fit because of the rigorous and dangerous demands of the job.[195] Reports by users in an attempt to justify their use have also revealed that steroids were not only needed but were discussed openly in certain police realms in spite of the illegal nature of the possession and use.[196] The New York Police Department has discovered several officers who have actively used steroids to enhance their physical performance and appearance.[197] As a consequence, the NYPD now randomly tests and disciplines officers for steroid use.[198] Reports of steroid use and distribution in the corrections realm have also surfaced wherein federal and state charges have been pursued in the distribution of steroids in both inside and outside of correctional facilities by corrections officers.[199] In light of the affect of steroid use in law enforcement and corrections, applicants must be scrutinized for any similar involvement.

The testing process requires a sample of the applicant's urine and the use of a gas chromatography/mass spectrometry (GC/MS) and, because of costs, should be done on a limited scale.[200] In the case of pre-employment investigations, the scope of tests should be limited to the group most likely to be hired, but conducted just prior to their actual hire date. Many commercial products and flushing schemes exist to eliminate traces of steroids as well as other toxins from the system.[201] Saliva is also proving to be another effective method of testing for steroid use in athletes.[202] Applicants who self-disclose or are caught using steroids and are not excluded from the hiring process by policy should be checked by a specially trained endocrinologist, who would determine if the applicant would be fit for duty.[203] Prevention has shown some promise in reducing steroid use. One department conducts a random monthly test on five officers to determine if they have used steroids, and if they refuse, the refusal constitutes grounds for their termination.[204] Prevention also should be a part of the screening process where any steroid use should preclude an applicant's candidacy. Departments should at least consider random or for-cause testing even if the costs of testing prove to be high. Given that this problem is a national health concern with law enforcement, as we are well aware, problems discovered in the hiring process usually grow more acute after hire.

Untruthfulness Concerning Drug Use

Prehire testing, though, presents some very problematic concerns. This is an area that applicants are noted for unilaterally denying in spite of admonitions to the contrary. Independent research by the author revealed that initial admission rates of police applicants to illegal drug use were far lower than they were after the use of a truth detection device.[205] In this same body of research, of the double-digit-level applicants who admitted to use both pre- and postadministering of the truth detection device, none screened positive for any illegal substance during the medical examination drug testing phase by using urinalysis as the testing medium. An interesting companion research study of the timing of urine testing and self-reported drug use also found some consistent results. Group testing of research subjects who were asked about illegal drug use prior to a urine test self-reported illegal drug use at a rate that was far lower than those who were tested prior to being queried about drug use.[206] Underreporting illegal drug use is a common dilemma in many populations.[207] Much of the available research speaks of the lack of honesty of applicants when it comes to this type of disclosure.

Untruthfulness is only part of the equation though. While the analysis of urine may in fact be a sound scientific process, flaws in collection procedures, applicant tampering, methods of purging, and the simple biology of dissipation from the human body all call the results into question. Clean urine and a clean applicant are often mutually exclusive concepts. As previously discussed in this chapter, drug use has permeated most American companies, and in positions as sensitive as those in law enforcement, drug use is an unconscionable prospect. There are other options that have higher accuracy rates that are also discussed, along with layered testing processes combining multiple methods for drug screening that may prove to be far more effective in the face of all of the issues presented when using only urinalysis as the sole measure of testing.

Urinalysis

Urinalysis is a common testing method in the pre-employment screening process. Noninvasive, cost effective, and relatively simple to administer, agencies have used this method to satisfy policy requirements for screening. Urine testing reveals the use of different substances such as opiate (codeine) and marijuana, to name a few.[208] Urine testing processes can involve several different methods such as enzyme multiple immunoassay test (EMIT), the radioimmunoassay test (RIA), thin layer chromatography test (TLC), and the gas-liquid chromatography test.[209] Supportive research indicates that random and consistent in-service use of urinalysis to drug screen current employees has the potential for reducing workplace injuries and their associated medical costs.[210] Insofar as the validity of results are concerned, research has also supported that epidemiology-based drug testing processes will receive similar results when subjected to independent testing by separate and distinct laboratories.[211] Some continue to support the position that in practicality there is no viable substitute for urinalysis testing procedures.[212] In the absence of other testing methods, some research indicates that urinalysis results in the detection of drug use more often than interviews and self-disclosure in some environments.[213]

Oral Fluids/Saliva Testing

Oral fluid and saliva testing is growing in popularity in many employment sectors and should also be considered in the pre-employment screening process as a secondary or confirmatory method to the current testing methods used in the drug screening process. Drug compounds and pH levels after drug use will be present in the oral cavity and can be sampled for subsequent analysis.[214] Oral fluid testing is a valid detection method for the presence of several illegal substances including amphetamines, cocaine and metabolites, and opioids such as morphine, methadone and heroin, and cannabis.[215] Oral fluid/saliva testing analysis can also provide both qualitative and quantitative information on the test subject's recent drug use.[216] At last count, oral fluid–based testing methods have been permitted by legal statutes in over half of the United States.[217]

Oral fluid–based testing methods are continuing to gain favor in drug testing of employees as a method of detection as well as prevention.[218] The process is commonly lauded as providing a superior and alternate analytical matrix for the purpose of detecting foreign substances such as illicit drug use in a person's system. Oral fluid testing, in contrast to other means, provides a credible, replicable, and easy means of testing recent drug use.[219] This type of testing is believed to have several advantages over the testing of other bodily fluids that include blood and urine.[220] Oral fluid testing provides advantages over conventional means of collection that include ease of accessibility of the collection sample for analysis.[221] One convenient component of testing is that the sample can be collected by trained persons in the organization as collection does not require the need for trained medical personnel.[222] Oral fluid testing is recognized as the most objective medium for the diagnosis of recent drug use.[223]

Hair Testing

Hair testing (radioimmunoassay hair analysis) has been in existence for some time now and, except for a marginally higher cost to administer, has shown much greater promise in narrowing down and confirming an applicant's assertion they have not used illegal drugs, or refute such claims if they have. Hair samples can provide a quantum of evidence of an applicant's illicit drug use that is often not possible to determine by other accepted testing methods.[224] Standard hair tests can include analysis for cocaine, marijuana, opiates (including heroin, oxycodone, hydrocodone, and hydromorphone), methamphetamine, Ecstasy (MDMA), Eve (MDEA), and PCP.[225] The uniqueness of hair testing lies in the ability to determine long-term and chronic cocaine or morphine use as well as being an indicator of marijuana use.[226] Scientific research supports the efficacy of human hair sample testing as a procedure that can identify over a 100 pharmaceuticals as well as the use and abuse of illegal substances.[227]

Hair sampling has also proven to be far more definitive in establishing a historical record of a person's drug use or abuse. Human hair entraps drugs or their metabolites for much longer periods than other bodily fluids and provides an alternative method for estimating the use of illicit substances that are rapidly excreted from the human body.[228] Oral fluid and urinalysis have limited detection periods, usually confined to a time frame of less than 2–3 days, while hair can have as long as 90–100 days.[229] This certainly offers a greater window of opportunity than does urinalysis alone.[230] One promising research study of the effectiveness of hair sampling tested criminally involved youth and found that recent cocaine and crack cocaine use was self-reported at a rate of one-third that of actual use as determined through hair analysis.[231] Another study of juvenile offenders revealed a detection rate for the use of cocaine in hair samples that was seven times higher than corresponding urine samples.[232] More evidence supports the use of hair samples over urinalyses in the pre-employment screening process.

A concern that has been raised in the use of hair testing over urinalysis is the potential for disparate impact on minority populations and protected classes. Fears often abound when new processes are introduced. Thankfully, there is usually a balanced response that is evidence based. At present, there is no scientific or court-acceptable evidence to support this notion.[233] Two separate studies, one including both police applicants and in-service police officers, have rebuked this notion. In the first study, minorities who tested positive for cocaine use were higher than nonminorities. However, these findings were consistent with the self-reported claims of the research subjects; thus, the differential rates were consistent with the drug use of the tested populations.[234] A second and later study specifically targeted police applicants and serving officers. Urinalysis and hair analysis comparing marijuana and cocaine use in separate studies revealed no statistically significant race bias attributable to the use of hair analysis over urinalysis.[235]

The legal use of hair sampling has been established in the courts in a series of cases that have been decided in favor of this scientific process to determine drug use and abuse among job applicants. Furthermore, hair testing has been found to be superior to urine testing for the presence of cocaine and as a foundation for any subsequent legal proceedings that may be required by the detection of these illegal substances.[236] A case precedent was set in New York State, wherein the Appellate Division ruled in *Bernadette Brown v. the City of New York et al.* (1998) that the use of hair analysis (radioimmunoassay hair analysis) was of sufficient reliability in determining the presence of cocaine in a probationary officer. In this case, the reliability of this type of evidence was accepted by the court and was directly applicable to police applicants as they do not have any of the rights enjoyed by tenured employees. This specific area of case law has evolved and now extends to in-service police officers. Testing has been used on a for-cause basis with in-service officers who have subsequently been arrested for improprieties in handling drug evidence.[237] The New York State Court of Appeals ruled that using human hair samples is acceptable for random drug tests for officers as well.[238] In *The City of New York et al. v. The Patrolmen's Benevolent*

Association of the City of New York, Inc. et al. and The Sergeants' Benevolent Association of the City of York et al. (2009), the court used the following language in their ruling:

> If the Commissioner is not at liberty to use a particular drug test even after determining that [it] would be more effective at exposing drug use among police officers, then his ability to carry out his disciplinary 'authority' has been significantly limited. Similarly, decisions about when and where to use such a test – especially in the area of random testing – has an obvious bearing [on] how effective efforts to detect drug use will ultimately be.[475]

Testing process can be accomplished even if the applicant has shaven their head prior to the sampling as hair samples can be tested from any location retrieved from the body to include face, underarms, arms, and legs. In addition, no method has been found to date that can adulterate the sample taken. All things being equal, the great value of hair testing over urinalysis cannot be denied. With respect to the arguments of cost being a marginal obstacle, the lack of racial bias, and the legal acceptance of this method of testing, screening personnel who have a choice must strongly consider this option as a better measure of determining drug use than conventional urinalysis.

Prescription and Over-the-Counter Drug Misuse and Abuse

From the 1960s through the 1990s, a picture of illegal drug use by law enforcement applicants was a reflection of the times. In the 1960s through 1970s, marijuana use and the use of inhalants or "glue sniffing" (i.e., modern day whippets) graduated into heroin and cocaine use. The 1980s and early 1990s brought about stronger compounds that included crack cocaine and methamphetamines. For many, however, the drug of choice has switched from illegal narcotics to prescription and OTC drugs. Prescription drug abuse can be tracked as far back as the early nineteenth century.[239] For the past 20 years or so, a plethora of research into this issue has given rise to the great concerns for the public health threat this type of substance abuse has on a truly national scale.

The twenty-first century has brought us a decrease in the use of illegal drugs, tobacco, and alcohol, while also delivering an increased abuse of prescription pain medications, with the major drug types being hydrocodone, oxycodone, and codeine.[240] Prescription drug use is fast approaching the levels of illegal drug use as compared to cocaine use in the United States.[241] There are actually nine opioids that are commonly abused: hydrocodone, immediate-release oxycodone, tramadol, extended-release (ER) oxycodone, fentanyl, morphine, methadone, hydromorphone, and buprenorphine.[242] Another study revealed close to 5% of the sample participants had engaged in alcohol abuse and illicit drug use along with the nonmedical use of prescription opioids.[243] Period-based national studies have revealed that the abuse of prescription drugs including sedatives, tranquilizers, opioids, and stimulants still continue to rise as we move further into the Third Millennium.[244] Also of note in the research is that nonmedical users of prescription drugs are at a heightened risk for drug abuse.[245] Research has also revealed that nonmedical use of psychotherapeutic drugs has increased to staggering proportions in comparison to illicit drug use, with this type of drug use rating second only to marijuana use and three times that of the use of cocaine.[246] One seminal study of felony probationers in both urban and rural settings found that rural participants were almost five times more likely than their urban counterparts to have misused prescription opiates,[247] a truly troubling trend in the American public health realm.

The most disturbing research findings with relation to the abuse of prescription drugs and law enforcement positions is the proliferation of drug use in the nation's teenagers and young adults, those same prospective applicant populations for current and future positions of trust. Medical research has revealed significant increases in prescription-based drug abuse being observed in populations that are between the ages of 18 and 25, those who currently are, or will be, eligible for positions in law enforcement in the very near future.[248] Yet another study revealed that higher levels of reported stress and strain in college students have led to increased levels of nonmedical use of prescription stimulants.[249] Supportive research has also consistently reported nonmedical use of this type of substance abuse in high school and college age students.[250] Teens have taken to prescription opioid drug abuse with the predominant drugs of choice as OxyContin and Vicodin.[251] Opioid-based prescription drug use and abuse as of late has rivaled that of cocaine use in the nation's younger generations.[252] Strong evidence has also revealed the misperception of norms of nonmedical prescription drug use among college age students.[253] The effects are also observed in measuring the impact of nonmedical prescription drug misuse in studies linking abuse to delinquent behavior and conduct that has led to criminal arrests during adolescence.[254]

Yet another disturbing trend finds this type of drug abuse to be atypical to illegal narcotics use as gender-based differences also exist.[255] Research has revealed that females are also more likely than males to abuse prescription opioids.[256] Still other anomalies emerge as this problem is not limited to prescription pharmaceuticals but also OTC medications that include tranquilizers, stimulants, and pain relievers, also showing a steady rise over recent years.[257] Still another emerging problem can be found in prescription sharing as a growing public health problem, with the results of a medically based research study revealing prescription drug loaning and borrowing at rates of 22.9% and 26.9%, respectively.[258] This problem continues to grow in scope, necessitating specific attention in the pre-employment screening process.

With all of the contemporary research indicating this extremely disturbing emergence of behavior, pre-employment screeners, if they have not considered this element of the hiring process, must take measures to explore these issues with prospective applicants. This concept must be built into policy as exclusion of these types of applicants is supported by case law. For example, in *Roe v. Cheyenne Mountain Conference Resort, Inc.* (1997), the employer's policy requiring all employees to report all drug use, including legal and prescribed use, was found valid.[259] In *Krocka v. Branfield* (1997), a police department implemented policy that mandated employees report all occurrences of taking psychotropic medications.[260] Through the post-COE time frame, this type of abuse can be examined with the applicant. Addition of these types of questions to the post-COE drug questionnaire in order to seek self-disclosure of these types of behaviors is highly recommended. Polygraph examiners should also add these types of questions to their written questionnaires as well as through the actual examination given how pervasive this problem has become. With respect to the conditions of *ADA*, positive results of tests for any drug use can result in an inquiry concerning an applicant's use of prescription drugs. Since this is a legitimate inquiry in the essence of the *ADA*, any disclosure of a disability should not develop into violating an applicant's protections.

False-Positive and False-Negative Drug Tests

A few realities of drug testing are that most screenings do not definitively prove the applicant has not used drugs, in the past or even recently. Infrequently, some positive drug tests may be erroneous or result from the prescribed or legitimate use of certain controlled substances.

The Issue of Rapid Excretion

The first proverbial hurdle in the drug screening process is the rapid excretion of illicit substances from the system due to the natural functions of the human body. The difficulty arises when the process of applicant screening is lengthy and limited in opportunities to randomly or real-time test candidates for illicit drug use. Substances including cocaine, opiates, amphetamines, and methamphetamines have a high end duration of detection at 48 h from the time of use.[261] Applicants who will have months and possibly years of waiting to be processed can in many instances be "clean" in a matter of days, giving the appearance that they are within acceptable drug policy hiring guidelines. The following table provides some general guidelines for the amount of time a drug can be detected by most standard drug tests (Table 4.2).

Given the ease of elusion, screening processes must include myriad and alternative mediums of testing. Testing should also be repeated in the hiring process at random and unannounced milestones in the process. Applicants who have initially tested negative may well

TABLE 4.2
Estimated Excretion Rates for Selected Controlled Substances

Drug	Detection Time
Alcohol	6–24 h
Amphetamines	2–3 days
Barbiturates	1 day to 3 weeks
Benzodiazepines	3–7 days
Cocaine	2–5 days
Codeine	3–5 days
Euphorics (MDMA, ecstasy)	1–3 days
LSD	1–4 days
Marijuana (THC)	7–30 days
Methadone	3–5 days
Methaqualone	14 days
Opiates	1–4 days
PCP	2–4 days
Steroids (anabolic)	14–30 days

Source: CollegeGrad.com, Drug testing and other possible conditions of employment, Provided by QuinStreet, Inc., Retrieved on January 24, 2010 from http://www.collegegrad.com/jobsearch/New-Job-Preparation/Drug-Testing-And-Other-Possible-Conditions-Of-Employment/, 2009.

believe the testing, for all intents and purposes, is done and fall back into their patterns of drug use, providing the pre-employment screener intermittent opportunities to screen while also impressing upon the applicant the level of importance of being drug free. Applicants may use this as an opportunity to self-disclose previous drug activity not provided to the background investigator as well as voluntarily withdraw from the process if they believe they will eventually be discovered during independent and random testing in the process. Policies must not only be strict but also be enforced in order to avoid violators from being allowed to pass through the hiring system unfettered.

False Positives

False-positive tests are those results that indicate some type of illegal drug use when none may be present. Because of the chemical makeup of many prescription drugs, some testing processes may inappropriately label legitimate substances present in a sample as illegal. In addition, many OTC medications can produce false-positive results on drug tests.[263] For example, certain OTC antihistamines may test positive for amphetamines.[264] Antibiotics and anti-inflammatories, as well as certain headache and cold pills, have similar chemical structures to those of illicit narcotics and may produce false toxicology results.[265] Another example of some field research into roadside DWI tests revealed that while 75% of screenings indicated correct results, high false-positive rates for such substances as opiates and benzoylecgonine were also discovered.[266] Yet another study of outpatient children revealed a false-positive rate of 21% of drug use that was attributable to the legitimate use of different OTC drugs.[267] The following is a list of OTC medications that have been known to cause false-positives in drug testing:

1. Ibuprofen (Advil, Motrin)
2. Midol
3. Nuprin
4. Sudafed
5. Vicks nasal spray
6. Neosynephrine
7. Ephedra- and ephedrine-based products (often used in diet products)
8. Dextromethorphan
9. Vicks 44[268]

Some evidence indicates that extremely valid testing processes may still produce significant false-positive results.[269] False positives that are not subjected to alternate confirmatory testing may be the subject of severe problems of evidentiary reliability as the initial testing process is open for scientific and legal challenge.[270] Others have argued that flaws in the testing process have led to false-positive results that have concluded in questionable adverse actions against the employee.[271]

False Negatives

False-negative tests are those results that fail to indicate some type of illegal drug use when they are present in the system and could be detected by other means. Testing limits and flaws can be found in the resultant findings wherein a negative test may in fact be a false negative as there was a failure to detect drugs that were present in the system at the time of testing. The factors that affect false-negative results are numerous, including the issues that testing may prove less reliable due to the low or infrequent incidence of drug use.[272] One pilot study of military personnel who had tested positive for marijuana, cocaine, or both during a urinalysis test revealed some disparity with respect to a false-negative rate as discovered through admissions in subsequent polygraph examinations.[273] Field DWI screening research with some types of tests has also revealed a relatively small number of false-negative results; however, with cannabinoids, those numbers demonstrated a notable increase.[274] Contradictory research has also revealed that immediate testing of those driving under the influence of marijuana reveals failure rates of as high as 25% of those tested.[275] Because of the ambiguous nature of this process, concerns have been raised about the need for safeguards to minimize the occurrences of false-negative drug tests of subjects.[276] As addressed earlier, pre-employment screening regimens must include multiple mediums of testing as well as separate and distinct test dates in order to overcome, in part, the problems inherent in the drug testing process. False-negative findings can be the result of flawed process, inadequate testing materials, abstinence, or tampering and adulteration by the applicant. Screeners must consider all of the factors and work to minimize the error rates by investing in quality through the testing materials used and variant testing procedures.

Tampering and Falsifying Testing

This problem has grown to staggering proportions when considering the level of drug use in society as well as the proliferation of websites and products that provide an applicant with the means to mask or purge their illicit drug use with testing resulting in false-negative findings. The use of adulterants and flushing methods often leads to masking and defeating many drug screening processes.[277]

Diluting the foreign substance by flushing the system with fluids is the most common method. Applicants can dilute the sample by drinking large amounts of water prior to the test, thus flushing the system of residual drug substances and their metabolites.[278] Research of outpatient children from the ages of 13–21 revealed that 6% of all tests were found to be too diluted to be interpreted accurately, resulting in false-negative results; therefore, examining samples for high levels of dilution is necessary to avoid false-negative drug tests.[279]

Beyond dilution, applicants will introduce different substances such as pyridinium chlorochromate (PCC) into their systems as an adulterant of the urinalysis in order to purge the system of THC and opiates.[280] These types of adulterants mask the detection of abused drugs but cannot be detected by routine specimen integrity checks (pH, specific gravity, and temperature).[281] Cheating in the pre-employment drug testing process has necessitated the use of spot test and new developments in test strips.[282] Rapid spot tests are useful for detecting adulterated urine to avoid false-negative drug tests.[283] Testing protocols and security must also be strict in order to minimize tampering with samples that is intended to produce false-negative, or even false-positive results.[284] As an affirmation of the previous discussion on hair analysis, with all of the controversy and questions surrounding the efficacy of urinalysis, and the current research that indicates that hair tests cannot be altered, common sense must prevail in the consideration of alternative methods in order to heighten the probability of accuracy in the testing process.[285]

Confirmatory Testing

Confirmatory testing is a highly recommended practice given the multitude of variables in testing processes and the dubious outcomes possible of so many of the available drug test methodologies.[286] As previously discussed, rapid excretion, tampering, and the onus of false-negative and false-positive test results being the reality of some types of testing, as well as the inexact nature of singular and intermittent testing protocols, confirmatory testing should be an integral part of pre-employment screening policy and process. In the case of laboratory testing, usually a positive result means that the specimen has been subjected to two separate and distinct methods of testing and that the results were measured against a predetermined acceptable cutoff level of presence.[287] Drug testing programs should include the most advanced technology available in order to produce accurate, reliable, and defendable results.[288] For example, testing validity must be validated as was the case in one research study where testing for Ecstasy use in military personnel was found to be inaccurate and revealed false-positive results.[289] Battery testing, much like the ideology used in psychological testing, must be strongly considered as likened to testing for behavior and pathology, in toxicology testing, no single screening medium will give the most accurate analysis.

In the case of prescreening tests, all presumptive testing results must also be subjected to validated laboratory testing in order to confirm or refute the initial findings.[290] At a minimum, all positive drug test methods derived from urine, oral fluids, and sweat or perspiration should be subjected to a confirmatory test as well in order to validate and defend any pre-employment decisions that result in adverse employment actions.[291] Simultaneous testing of hair and urine is a recommended method for discovering opiates, cocaine, and metabolites and can increase the probability of learning the presence of patterns of drug use and abuse with an applicant.[292] These combined with random oral fluid testing should lead to the most accurate assessment possible.

Policy Issues of Marijuana Use

There is truly no topic that attracts more controversy than the policies surrounding acceptable limits of marijuana use for public safety applicants. The topic crosses all social, ethical, legal, and political boundaries analogous to a national contagion. The range of acceptance of use is almost as wide as the number of agencies who hire. And the future does not offer any promise of clarity in this issue.

From the 1960s' heyday of marijuana use through the dawn of the Third Millennium, public opinion polls have steadily demonstrated favoritism toward the legalization of marijuana.[293] Research has revealed that over 40% of Americans have used marijuana at some point in their lives.[294] Popularity often does not translate into a favorable caucus though as while legalization is peddled in the public opinion polls, hesitance is faced when the prospect of legalization materializes as the voting public shows up on election day to actually pull the lever.[295] However, many state legislatures are slowly moving toward decriminalization of at least smaller amounts of marijuana.[296] Because of this level of indecision, much resistance and hostility has been created on the topic, forcing continual public debate.[297] As of late, the legalization through regulation and taxation has become a motive in order to benefit the individual states and help close their ominous budget deficits.[298] Fraught with social, political, legal, and ethical questions, this dispute shows no promise of resolution for public safety administrators as they develop more tolerant thresholds for pre-employment screening policies that allow levels or frequencies of use. A recent arrival on the scene is the drug *Salvia divinorum*, which is an herb-like substance, similar to marijuana, with very powerful effects that when used mirror the symptoms of psychosis in the user.[299] Salvia is believed to be comparatively as powerful a drug as LSD.[300] Currently a legal intoxicant in the United States, several states as well as the Federal government are researching the need to make this substance illegal. Mephedrone, used in fertilizer, is yet another example of a synthetic stimulant being used in Europe as a currently legal, yet dangerous intoxicant club drug.[301] Substances like these further add to the complexities of developing workable policies around the use of narcotic substances by applicants. There are numerous toxicants that are legal in the United States that the background investigator should become familiar with in order to effectively screen applicants.[302]

The potency of marijuana varies depending upon manufacture, alteration, and additive. From low-grade Schwag, to chronic and hydroponic marijuana, to lacing the substance with cocaine, all present substantial health and safety risks. Debates still rage on that not only is the potency and potential health risk higher now than at the time of the drug's introduction to the mainstream, but more importantly, marijuana is still believed to be the gateway drug to more addictive and toxic illegal substance abuse.[303] Therefore, any admission of marijuana use warrants a deeper exploration of the type used rather than simply the assumption that the use was an archetypal "experimental" use admission. And, as if this topic was not complex enough, the battle for the medical use of marijuana has continued to rear its menacing head. The medical facts are still unrefuted as even when used as a recreational drug, marijuana creates the danger of arrested development leading to social and emotional issues in our nation's youth.[304] The most current medical evidence exists that smoked marijuana is harmful to a person's health. Legitimate medical research has concluded that no sound scientific studies support the medical use of marijuana for treatment regimens or general medical use in the United States.[305] To meet the restrictions of a Schedule I drug of the *Controlled Substances Act*, marijuana met three criteria for placement as a controlled substance in that the substance has "a high potential for abuse, has no currently accepted medical use in treatment in the United States, and has a lack of accepted safety for use under medical supervision."[306] Federal oversight emerges from the *Federal Food, Drug, and Cosmetic Act* which requires that all new drugs be shown to be safe and effective for their intended use before being marketed in the United States.[307] Public opinion and advocacy by special interest groups must not be allowed to exert undue influence over unbiased analysis of scientific evidence in the continued efforts to transform an illegal controlled substance into a legitimate pharmaceutical alternative to pain management.[308] Much of the motivation to scientifically legitimize the use of smoked marijuana for medical purposes can be deftly characterized as an insidious attempt at backdoor legalization.[309] In spite of the contradictory evidence, state-level officials continue to push the issue of medical marijuana to the agenda.[310]

Federal intervention has also met with some limits due to the U.S. Supreme Court rulings in both *United States v. Lopez* (1995) and *United States v. Morrison* (2000) wherein a precedent was set to minimize federal control of private conduct as these cases exceeded the limits of congressional powers.[311] However, a later Supreme Court decision in *Gonzales v. Raich* (2005) redefined the issue as Congress did have the right to control or ban marijuana for nonmedical uses as the ban would lead to prevention, or at least limited access to marijuana that may be used for illicit purposes.[312] The court reasoned that possession, cultivation, distribution, and sale of marijuana are illegal since the drug has no legitimate medical uses.[313] Despite the ambiguity of the issue, state-level attempts at legalization may not prevent federal prosecution under the *Controlled Substances Act of 1970*.[314] The debate to balance the rights of physicians to recommend the use of medical marijuana and the power of the federal government to regulate the distribution of dangerous drugs will be an ongoing battle.[315] Physicians who have an expertise should be allowed the latitude to treat patients within accepted therapeutic guidelines developed for medical and pharmaceutical science; however, the limit must be established in cases where the prescribed treatment is not only unproven but, more importantly, illegal. A license to legally practice medicine does not translate to a validation to sling dope from the comfort and safety of an examination room. If this is the mentality of a certain segment of the medical profession, then drug dealers should also be allowed to sell leeches and snake oil in the open-air drug markets of our cities, towns, and villages!

Much to the purported chagrin of the federal government, though, many states have passed legislation to statutorily enable the legalized medical use of marijuana as prescribed by a physician.[316] As of last count, some 16 states have legalized the medical use of marijuana, each having its own unique requirements and restrictions.[317] The current states are Alaska, Arizona, California, Colorado, Hawaii, Maine, Michigan, Montana, Nevada, New Jersey, New Mexico, Oregon, Rhode Island, Vermont, and Washington, DC. However, legalization has not solved the problem of criminal activity that takes place under the umbrella of sanctioned medical marijuana dispensaries.[318] Retail conglomerates are also capitalizing on this glitch in the law by opening retail sales locations for selling resources, equipment, and expert advice on the methods of growing hydroponic marijuana in residences and as operating businesses.[319] California has some of the most liberal interpretations of the medical use of marijuana with an estimated 250,000–350,000 people having been prescribed medical marijuana by a licensed physician.[320] Under the provisions of the *California Health and Safety Code*[321] (also referred to as the *Compassionate Use Act of 1996*),[322] the use of medical marijuana is not limited to serious or debilitating diseases. For example, medical marijuana can be prescribed for chronic pain, arthritis, migraine headaches, or any other illness for which marijuana provides relief.[323] This very loose language opens the door for many questionable cases of illegal use that are under the guise of medical treatment.[324] This body of law also precludes criminal prosecution of the patient and primary caregiver.[325] Interestingly, the political winds are shifting as several state legislatures that had voted for the legalization of the medical use of marijuana have not reaped the rewards that were originally projected, rather, resulting in very damaging outcomes of their uninformed and political posturing.[326] Discussions of repealing, or at least severely limiting, these laws are now in the forefront of many of these discussions. Other jurisdictions are taking very strong stances on the issuance of licenses to persons of questionable character who apply to open medical marijuana dispensaries.[327] In spite of this, California continues to force legislation that seeks to legalize the recreational use of marijuana.[328] Sadly, while many in law enforcement oppose this type of legislation, some actually support the legalization movement.[329] One codicil in the legislation, though, prevents the dangerous use or diversion of medical marijuana for nonmedical purposes.[330] In states that have developed this type of legislation, there may be an impact on screening practices given this type of exemption as well as the nature of the *ADA* which may protect this type of information from use in some hiring processes. Another issue may be had in the potential for states that legalize growing marijuana for medical purposes wherein an applicant could conceivably be licensed to grow marijuana but claim they have never used the controlled substance, presenting a new twist to this controversial issue. In spite of this, the International Association of Chiefs of Police strictly opposes the arguments to circumvent state and federal laws that marijuana use has some legitimate medical purpose.[331]

Law enforcement is still able to hold the line in this bona fide occupational qualification (BFOQ) or job requirement though, based upon the case law and past precedents. For example, in the ruling of *Davis v. City of Dallas* (1985), the courts upheld the department's use of restrictions on recent or excessive marijuana use.[332] Also mentioned in Chapter 3 was the U.S. Supreme Court ruling in *City of Canton v. Harris* (1989) which specifically identified the need to screen officers who have histories of drug sales and/or usage.[333] In Californian jurisprudence, the ruling of *Ross v. RagingWire Telecommunications, Inc.* (2008) upheld the right of an employer to terminate an employee for the use of medical marijuana.[334] The court ruled that

> The majority holds that an employer may fire an employee for such marijuana use, even when it occurs during off-duty hours, does not affect the employee's job performance, does not impair the employer's legitimate business interests, and provides the only effective relief for the employee's chronic pain and muscle spasms.[335]

In this case, the rights afforded under the *Compassionate Use Act of 1996* only applied to criminal prosecutions.[336] A companion federal court ruling in the state of Michigan in support of the aforementioned case upheld the termination of an employee who had used medical marijuana outside the scope of his employment as well.[337] In this case, the judge reasoned that the protections for the use of medical marijuana were an affirmative defense to a criminal prosecution but did not extend to protections in the employment relationship.[338] This type of situation, while sanctioned by a licensed physician, does not give rise to gratuitous protections in the employment law realm.[339] State laws will also provide some guidance in these areas. Even absent these rulings, the use of these types of substances that are known to the employer could result in a negligence claim if a third party suffers an injury that may be related to such use.[340] Again, some excellent examples of those who act before they think through the long-term consequences of implementing these types of decisions.

Policy, however, is frequently another story. Policy variations of exclusionary limits are almost as numerous as there are administrators who write them.[341] Policies can also range from highly restrictive to extremely lenient, as well as the ever ubiquitous case-by-case analysis. Arguments for publicly posting policies on drug use also cover this same spectrum. Candidates who have the standards at the outset may attempt to deceive the background investigator by admitting to marijuana use that is outside of the exclusionary time limits. In contrast, applicants who do not know the standards may fail to admit to any use, even use that would not disqualify them from consideration. Disclosure of standards may prevent many candidates from applying when they know the expectation and save much time and investigative resources. Having the expectation clearly defined at the outset also leaves no surprise to those who are excluded. Similar strength of arguments can be made wherein applicants who do not know the standard can be tested on time limits and levels of disclosure as a bifurcated measure of exclusionary drug use and their level of candor. Decisions like these must be agency specific and based upon best practices that have been successful in the specific organization.

Also of consideration is setting the bar so as, in either case, there are clear and defensible standards that are published within the agency when adverse employment actions are warranted based upon the candidate's history of marijuana use. Two agencies that have delineated specific standards of marijuana use are the Washoe County, Nevada Sheriff's

Office, and the South Carolina Highway Patrol. In the Washoe County Sheriff's policy, clear timelines are defined for an applicant's scrutiny and rejection parameters with regard to marijuana use:

1. Experimental use within 1 year immediately preceding the date of application (experimental use is defined as no more than two times in 1 year)
2. Use within 3 years immediately preceding the date of application if the use cannot be categorized as experimental[342]

The South Carolina Highway Patrol, while using different language, is also just as effective in accomplishing the goal of discovering and excluding applicants who are beyond the thresholds of excusable drug use behaviors that occurred prior to their application for a law enforcement position. The South Carolina Highway Patrol's Drug Usage and Experimentation Standards states that

> No applicant will be considered who has used or possessed a controlled dangerous substance or combination of controlled dangerous substances... This applies whether the illegal conduct was detected or admitted by the applicant... Controlled substances are those that are illegal to possess without a prescription as defined under all applicable Local, State, and Federal laws, to include the unlawful use and possession of prescribed drugs.[343]

Forewarned is forearmed! The complexity of this issue crosses all social, political, ethical, public health, and legal boundaries with equal zeal. Consequently, there will be a high level of zealotry that will be faced with every person and special interest group that is either pro or con. The strength of policy emerges from the decisiveness of the words used to define and sanction such behavior. Case-by-case is not a standard! Case-by-case wording allows for vacillation and pushing limits well beyond acceptable boundaries until the wrong person slips through the cracks and, at the most, seriously violates someone's constitutional rights. At the least, they can present an extremely embarrassing situation that could have been prevented had the correct action been taken prior to consideration for employment. In these scenarios, the choice is often yours to make and yours to live with! Good conscience must prevail.

Drug Possession, Manufacture, Sales, and Distribution

Drug use is the primary question that is on every background investigator's mind when reviewing an applicant's history and conducting the pre-employment investigation. The problem with thinking in this linear fashion is that drug possession, manufacture, sales, and distribution may not enter the thought process until the matter becomes an unwelcome surprise. Either through criminal record check, independent investigation, or applicant admission, this is also a growing problem that must be explored with law enforcement applicants. Physiological testing rarely reveals any measure of current drug use, and rarer still is the definitive test for drug possession, manufacture, sales, and distribution. Sophistication of testing simply may not always reveal these types of actions. As slaves to their criminal record and admissions in the interview process, these issues become far more critical in the ability to properly and accurately screen applicants.

From hard-core street-level drug dealers to college students who infrequently purchase marijuana and resell it or give it away to their dorm mates, the issue is the same, sale and distribution of dangerous drugs. One case exemplifies the gravity of this issue. A group of suburban high school students who began smoking marijuana developed an elaborate and self-proclaimed highly visible and lucrative marijuana distribution enterprise. The operation went undetected by law enforcement until a homicide-precipitated investigation led to their discovery and conviction.[344] Manufacture of illicit drugs by individuals has also seen a significant rise with hydroponic marijuana and methamphetamine labs being operated out of the average American home. In addition, arrest and conviction are not the sole determinant in using this behavior as an exclusionary act. In these cases, the applicant will most likely be disqualified based upon an admission rather than an actual possession, manufacture, or sale charge.

Hydroponic marijuana has shared in this move for the public's desire to get high and elude the cost and possible criminal action through a series of do-it-yourself websites that offer step-by-step procedures to cultivate home gardens that bear neither flora nor vegetation. The growth in the home-grown industry emerges from a few reasons. One is that the industry has been driven by the desire to elude detection risks that are inherent in drug importation.[345] Yet another is that the upsurge can be explained in the drug's high quality and high profit margins due to the hardiness ascribed to growth in these environmentally controlled settings. The multimillion dollar profits have attracted not only individuals seeking a stash for their personal use and sale but also international drug organizations who vie for a piece of these lucrative profits.[346] Many of the home growers have developed extremely sophisticated operations to enhance the number and quality of the plants in order to meet market demands.[347] Detection has been a vexing issue for law enforcement agencies, but there have been numerous examples across the country of seizures based upon opportunity of discovery, informants, or painstaking multijurisdictional investigations. One such investigation by the Drug Enforcement Administration in a drug sweep in Florida netted 135 arrests and 3400 plants being confiscated.[348] The country is full of examples of independent growers who are being arrested as a result of fortuitous discovery as opposed to direct detection.[349] Not beyond the stretch of the imagination, but an applicant could have a hardy stock and lucrative business and never have been discovered. The background investigator must review the applicants history with a keen eye and through their investigative experience establish the cues that may lead to further investigation (e.g., high electric bills, tall fences, areas of the home the applicant is reluctant to have the background investigator see during a home visit).

Methamphetamine production has also grown to epic proportions. Clandestine laboratories present significant social, health, and environmental issues in the United States.[350] With the research on methamphetamine production evolving, direct links have been drawn between production and use.[351] The proliferation of Internet sites that provide simple directions on the manufacture of the product through easily obtained household ingredients also adds to the difficulty in detection for law enforcement.[352] As with hydroponic labs, methamphetamine labs should also be a concern for background investigators as they explore an applicant's history, record of property rentals, and ownership of real property where the applicant either resides, works, or has access to.

Lastly, there is the matter of manufacture, possession, and distribution of false, fake, or counterfeit drugs. A famed tactic of street dealers is to substitute look-alike substances and pass them off as illicit narcotics to increase their profit margins. This is also a method to minimize their culpability if an arrest occurs. Depending on several factors, felony possession may be the appropriate charge due to possessed weight, intent to sell, or actual sale.[353] Most all states will have statutes that prohibit the illicit possession, distribution, and sale of fake or counterfeit narcotics.[354] Aligned with this is the possession, manufacture, sale, and distribution of false or counterfeit prescription drugs. Counterfeit prescription drugs are also presenting a nationwide health problem.[355] Law enforcement is wrestling with this emergent problem and the lack of training and resources to address this complex dilemma adequately. In both cases where applicants are found to have committed these types of violations, state and federal laws should prevail. Even if the state-level charge is substantiated in the background investigation, federal laws should also be used as a standard reference in the background investigation whenever applicable. In addition, laws vary from state to state, so out-of-state charges should be compared to the hiring state's standards to determine application to the department's hiring standards. From federal and state law, these parameters should also be built into an organization's pre-employment drug use policy that excludes applicants for any involvement in sale and distribution of any drugs.[356] If information is gathered either through arrest record or admission, the consequence should be a lifetime excluder or disqualifier. Other types of violations will be determined by state laws.

Alcohol Use and Abuse

Alcohol use presents an even more perplexing issue than does the ambiguity of marijuana use. For a very brief period in our nation's history during the 1920s and 1930s, the problem had a simple answer; due to the *National Prohibition Act of 1920* (*Volstead Act*), alcohol possession and use was illegal.[357] Unfortunately, no strict guideline such as this has ever been made available since that time. The opaqueness of the restrictions of the *ADA* also makes this a very problematic behavior to levy enforceable parameters against.

The *ADA* fundamentally offers protections for those who are alcoholics as the condition is defined as a disability.[358] The attachment of the *ADA* emerges from an employee's qualifications to perform essential functions of the job they are responsible for.[359] An employer can take action though if the employee fails to perform essential job functions or demonstrates any conduct that would be in violation of organizational rules when the behavior is attributable to alcohol use.[360] Once these alcohol-related behaviors adversely affect job performance or conduct, the employer may then discipline, discharge, or deny employment to an alcoholic.[361] Keep in mind that the courts will interpret the limits of these claims, and in the ruling of *Bailey v. Georgia Pacific Corporation* (2002), a workplace claim of alcoholism resulted in a ruling that called into question the condition being a disability. As cited from this case,

> While not specifically excluded from the *ADA*'s protections, alcoholism is nevertheless treated differently than other impairments and disabilities. For example, the *ADA* specifically authorizes an employer to prohibit the consumption of alcohol at the workplace and requires that employees not be under the influence of alcohol at work.[362]

Seemingly then there are limited applications of the protections of applicants with respect to the entire issue of claims of alcoholism. In the pre-employment investigation, the issue of alcohol use and abuse can be explored in depth under the protections of the

COE. Patterns of use may, for the most part, indicate irresponsible behavior rather than a textbook-defined addiction. Behavior patterns may have been manifested through illegal or dangerous behaviors that include bar room fights, DWIs, and workplace accidents just to name a few. The background investigator must also think beyond mere alcohol use as a singular event as there may also exist layered uses of illegal substances that are often associated with alcohol use. Research has revealed that in a small percentage of the population, alcohol use and dependence is accompanied by the nonmedical use of prescription opioids.[363] Marijuana and narcotic use is often accompanied by drinking as well, so the background investigator should consider the entire context of drug and alcohol use as they explore the applicant's history of digression from acceptable behavioral standards.

PSYCHOLOGICAL STANDARDS AND EVALUATIONS

The genesis of psychological testing of police officers was in the findings of the President's Commission on Law Enforcement and the Administration of Justice published in 1967.[364] Since that time, a plethora of research and challenge has been observed. For example, research supports arguments for the use of intelligence quotient (IQ) testing as a method to predict the potential for future violent behavior.[365] In spite of the evidence to support the use of psychological examinations for entry-level law enforcement officers, there still remain a substantial number of agencies across the country that do not avail themselves of this very useful tool, if not for prediction, at the very least for defense of hiring actions. In litigation, the plaintiff's counsel will most likely seek to learn if a psychological screening was ever done by the department.[366] In one example, an off-duty sheriff's deputy killed six people. Of note was that he had never been required to submit to a pre-employment psychological examination.[367] In another frightening example, an officer failed the psychiatric examination, was allowed to appeal, and, due to some discrepancies, was hired in spite of the questionable results. That officer was subsequently involved in an armed robbery wherein she brutally murdered several innocent people.[368] Concededly, there are those who possess criminal tendencies who are able to navigate the system, make it into the ranks, and continue their criminal paths until finally detected.[369] Others are brought into the ranks after a psychological examination has revealed no issues of concern and later engage in questionable conduct that this type of testing is specifically designed to reveal.[370] This should not dissuade the agency from doing everything possible to properly screen for these proclivities. Also, suicide rates for law enforcement officers are an area of concern as they are higher than the societal norm due to the stressors of the position.[371] Interestingly, the military has observed these same health issues and has begun advanced screening practices in predeployment to combat situations due to the higher rates of suicide experienced in recent years.[372] Smaller agencies and municipalities may not have a choice in pre-employment psychological screening requirements as they can be mandated to do so by their insurance carriers in order to be indemnifiable.

Some argue against the validity of psychological testing tools and protocols and their true ability to accurately screen applicants for undesirable behavior.[373] Critics of the science are balanced by the legal system in the country that requires prudence in selection processes. Several law enforcement agencies have faced serious ramifications for applicants who have either not been required to take a psychological examination or, worse yet, incidents where those who have failed the examination were still hired into the ranks.[374] For example, recent changes in the air marshals hiring process led to the suspension of a psychological written test and clinical interview for air marshals. However, demonstrated aberrant and disturbing behaviors have been noted of air marshals who have had delusional thoughts and engaged in such acts as fraud, abduction of a female escort, and child molestation.[375] Evaluations are a critical underpinning to the process of selection. Sadly, several cases exist beyond the aforementioned ones wherein departments have failed to use a psychological screening process which has led to the questioning of the hiring of law enforcement personnel who have engaged in violent and homicidal acts after hire.[376]

While many agencies have begun to appreciate the efficacy of this additional method of testing, some have administered the psychological examination process in violation of public policy and the best practice recommendations from the experts in the psychological field.[377] Practices such as these have led to much scrutiny in the psychological field as well as the courts. Suffice it to say that tantamount to psychological screening is the necessity for legal, proper, and accepted protocols for their administration.

There is an "intuitive appeal" to the use of psychological screening to determine if an applicant is fit for the position applied for.[378] The predictive value of the success of law enforcement candidates has been consistently demonstrated through the psychological battery testing process.[379] Psychological battery testing is used as a best practice approach to attempt to identify the propensity for immoral and violent behavior that may be latent in an applicant's personality.[380] Mental status tests establish if a disease or condition is adversely affecting an applicant's ability to process information as well as their ability to think and reason properly.[381] The psychological testing process can often predict the capacity for socialization and intelligence as well as the detection of any mental aberration that would impede the applicant's ability to perform the essential responsibilities of a law enforcement officer.[382] One stellar example of a success in the psychological screening process involved the rejection of a police applicant based on the results of a psychological examination wherein the applicant decided to pursue a career in the fire service and subsequently became a prolific arsonist and murderer.[383] The results, however indistinct, may still prove to be highly valuable in the prehire process as well a posthire analysis.

The *Diagnostic and Statistical Manual of Mental Disorders* (DSM-IV) (1994) offers psychological definitions in a multiaxial review to include such categories as clinical, major mental, personality, and learning disorders, mental retardation, as well as psychosocial and environmental factors contributing to a diagnosed disorder.[384] Psychological testing processes are designed to uncover these traits if manifested by the applicant. For example, standardized testing that includes the Substance Abuse Subtle Screening Inventory (SASSI, SASSI-2) has been used with success in predicting alcohol-related risks among law enforcement applicants.[385] This type of testing can also reveal positive traits and behaviors such as intelligence, habits, and motivation.[386] With respect to the process, fundamentally, psychological evaluations must possess certain psychometric properties to be used appropriately in personnel selection:

1. *Reliability*: consistency of a test to yield the same results when administered at different times
2. *Validity*: relates to the ability of the test to predict a real-life outcome
3. *Utility*: refers to the usefulness and incremental value of the test results within the context of the entire selection battery[387]

Application to the public safety officer pre-employment screening environment requires several additional considerations than the mere use of existing basic or general population testing processes. Testing ideology must combine a clinical and industrial model in order to meet the unique needs of the environment. To accomplish this goal, the testing process must include as a guide a set of behavioral indicators that are thresholds for acceptable and unacceptable characteristics, behaviors, and attributes for law enforcement personnel. This would require the development of a typology of acceptable behaviors of law enforcement officers to augment the psychological testing process for the psychologist to use when standardized testing fails to reveal problematic attributes or patterns of behavior.[388] Law enforcement testing should include the ascertainment of behavioral predispositions that may prove negative to the successful functioning of the law enforcement officer in fulfilling their responsibilities. For example, in order to avert incidents of excessive force, prevention would involve the deselection of applicants in the pre-employment screening process that have been identified by a police psychologist as having the propensity for this type of behavior.[389] One model suggests the use of seven components to measure an applicant's ability to perform to acceptable standards as a law enforcement officer:

1. Psychopathology
2. Substance abuse
3. Self-management skills
4. Team functioning
5. Impact of prior experience
6. Social influences
7. Intellectual abilities[390]

Application within the law enforcement realm can often predict officer orientation and interaction with members of the department and the community. The personality type of law enforcer compared to social worker may manifest itself in the testing process, giving the evaluator an opportunity to further explore the strengths and weaknesses of an applicant's psyche.[391] In addition, research exists that supports the theory that if an applicant demonstrates characteristics of high levels of conscientiousness, they will consequently demonstrate low levels of antisocial behavior.[392] Testing process can also be driven in part by the specific needs of the agency. For example, one statewide research study revealed that agency administrators place great emphasis on an applicant's skills of good judgment, their ability to communicate in this type of environment, and their responsiveness to supervision.[393] Law enforcement applicant attributes that should be tested for include cognitive ability, emotional stability, maturity, impulsivity, integrity, rule adherence, and judgment, just to name a few. Ideally, these types of evaluations should be linked to training academy performance, on-the-job performance, complaints and disciplinary actions, as well as supervisory and command observations in order to validate the initial pre-employment findings and predictions.[394]

Additionally, the theory of personality testing has also been added to the milieu of psychological testing processes. Personality tests (also referred to as talent tests) measure such characteristics as motivation, emotional adjustment, interpersonal relationships, integrity, and attitudes of the applicant.[395] Personality testing includes the ability to measure the interaction between personality traits and job requirements.[396] That interaction can lead to the identification of the human capital necessary to be successful within the organization.[397]

Other research has revealed that applicant character should be the predominant factors tested for in lieu of the applicant's ability to perform specific job tasks.[398] Research into the Inwald Personality Inventory (IPI) demonstrated predictive value in the scales of family conflicts, guardedness, and driving violations. Subsequent posthire supervisory review revealed the accuracy of these predictions in applicants who were assessed as having these as problem characteristics.[399] The California Personality Inventory (CPI) was also found to have validity in predicting officers who are unsuited for police works as well as having serious job performance issues.[400] Personality tests that do not test for mental disorders may also be used prior to the issuance of a COE.[401] The types of tests that are approved by the *ADA* to be administered at the pre-COE stage are tests that measure personality traits that include honesty, preferences, and habit.[402]

The introduction of personality testing into the testing field was based upon a recommended strategy to use composite exams that measure job-related cognitive abilities and personality traits to reduce adverse impact.[403] Their use was accepted in the courts in the decision of *Hayden v. County of Nassau* (1998) wherein the court recognized the use of personality testing to reduce adverse impact did not violate the equal protection clause of the Unites States Constitution.[404] However, evidence supports the rejection of this theory in that personality testing may not compensate for adverse impact claims that may be related to cognitive ability testing.[405]

Care must be taken though as while these tests are becoming a widely used phenomenon, their empirical predictive validity may be called into question as they may also lead to false interpretation and abuse.[406] The validity of these exams is also called into question when applicants are coached in their responses or simply adept at taking and defeating testing methodology and processes.[407] Some research also suggests less acceptance of this process by the test taker in lieu of more traditional or alternative verification methods.[408] Personality testing is not meant to be a replacement for other testing processes, rather one that works to validate the results of more comprehensive battery testing processes.[409]

Test Selection

Psychological tests are designed to identify a mental disorder or impairment.[410] Test selection is a matter of identified need within an organization. This should come from the staff of contracting psychologists, including those who have subject matter expertise in the organizational and industrial realms.[411] Industrial and organizational psychologists then work in consultation with the law enforcement agency's administrators, selection and training personnel, human resources, and legal staff to develop the best testing protocol to fit the organization's pre-employment screening needs. In addition, testing methodology should also emerge from the orientation of psychometric theory. Psychometric theory infuses a multidimensional testing process that assesses an applicant's psychopathology, cognitive ability, and personality traits through a series of tests. Evidence supports that the increased levels of accurate assessment are possible based upon this multidimensional view of an applicant's behavioral traits.[412] Research has also revealed significant correlations between academy performance as compared against cognitive ability as well as personally traits (e.g., neuroticism, extraversion, openness, agreeableness, and conscientiousness).[413] There are numerous psychological and personality tests available for use in the selection process:

1. Adult Neuropsychological Quest I
2. Adult Self-report Inventory

3. Automated Social History
4. Behavioral Personal Assessment Device (B-PAD)
5. California Personality Inventory (CPI)
6. Cognitive Stability Index (CSI)
7. Fundamental Interpersonal Relations Orientation (FIRO-B)
8. Inwald Personality Inventory (IPI)
9. Irrational Belief Test
10. Law Enforcement Assessment and Development Report (LEADR)
11. Mayo Clinic Alcoholism Screening Test
12. Minnesota Multiphasic Personality Inventory (MMPI and MMPI 2)
13. NEO Five-Factor Inventory (NEO-FFI)
14. OMNI Personality Inventory
15. Personality Assessment Inventory (PAI)
16. PsychEval Personality Questionnaire (PEPQ)
17. Revised NEO Personality Inventory (NEO PI-R)[414]
18. Shipley Institute of Living Scale
19. Sixteen Personality Factor/Clinical Analysis Questionnaire
20. State-Trait Anxiety Inventory (STAI)
21. Test of Adult Basic Education
22. Wide Range Achievement Test-3 (WRAT-3)
23. Wonderlic Personnel Test (WPT)
24. Wonderlic Basic Skills Test (WBST)

Battery Testing

The recommended and preferred testing methodology is one of battery testing, or using a series of psychological tests to examine several aspects of the applicant's psychological health, fitness, and personality. Standard battery testing by a significant portion of departments surveyed includes the MMPI and MMPI 2, the IPI, the CPI, and the WPT.[415] Research into pre-employment battery testing using just the MMPI and the IPI resulted in the accurate identification of problematic behaviors and predictions of future behaviors in a group of officers who were subsequently terminated from their respective agencies.[416] Battery testing should include not only the use of industry-accepted examinations, but also where marginal test results are produced, the applicant should be interviewed by separate psychologists or psychiatrists and an agreement of the recommendation be had by both.[417] This ensures a collective process of validated testing where the results are fairly decided by a team of experts rather than the individual influence of a single professional.

Clinical Interviews

After the testing phase is completed and scores analyzed by the reviewing psychologist or panel of psychologists, the next stage is the clinical interview. The clinical interview is augmented by not only the testing process but also by the use of a Pre-employment Psychological History Questionnaire completed by the applicant and by the use of all collected mental health records contained in local- and state-level repositories of any mental health–related treatments and commitments, both voluntary and involuntary. The interview attempts to clarify and verify the results of the comprehensive and objective testing battery. Specific characteristics should be explored in the interview to include emotional factors, behavioral stability, and social factors.[418] Clinical interviews allow for the examination of psychological variables related to job performance that include behavioral problems in social skill development, lack of maturity, and emotional instability that may have surfaced in the standardized testing or as a result of the follow-up questioning.[419] The clinical interview is a key component to having the applicant specifically address information that was culled from all of the components of the process including the battery testing results and the results of the background investigation.[420] Research has revealed that the traits of honesty, capacity for stress, and tendencies toward violence are key targets of the clinical interview process.[421] The clinical interview focuses on important criteria identified through prior research that are important to law enforcement officer success:

1. Social maturity and self-control
2. Social temperance
3. Emotional stability/stress tolerance
4. Confidence/assertiveness
5. Personal insight
6. Empathy
7. Effectiveness in work relationships
8. Conventionality and tendency to abide by rules
9. Nondefensiveness
10. Health
11. Achievement/motivation[422]

The recommended standard interview time period should range from 30 to 45 min.[423] During that time, the applicant should be allowed to explain circumstances surrounding incidents and behaviors (e.g., fights, arrests, drinking, and drug use habits). Responses and explanations should be measured against the results of the standardized testing to compare for consistency and discrepancies in the applicant's replies. A word of caution though as applicants may be adept at test taking and an interview may reveal this attempt at fraudulent practices. Applicants who have engaged in several iterations of the process, have accessed the various materials available, or have some higher education experience in the process may be able to present themselves in a far better light than what exists in actuality.

At the conclusion of the entire assessment, the psychologist should meet with the prescreening staff to discuss the findings. Comparisons should then be made between the behaviors and attributes discovered during the background investigation to the results of the psychological screening process in order to validate findings and explore any discrepancies for continued follow-up to resolve any differences. Lastly, psychological screening processes should not rely solely on a clinical interview of the applicant.[424] They should be based on the best practice recommendations of the industry in alignment with the specific needs of the organization. The courts have viewed this component of the process with a highly discerning eye. Because there exists an immense spectrum of variation in opinions that can be cast, the courts must view each set of recommendations with a warranted level of suspicion. For example, in the ruling of *Denhof et al. v. City of Grand Rapids* (2005), an analogous case dealing with Fitness For Duty Evaluations (FFDE), the court opined that the psychological evaluations process could garner as many opinions as there are psychologists conducting the examination.[425] These factors strengthen the argument for layered testing and review processes that bring validity and defensible practices to adverse employment actions.

Legal Issues of Psychological Testing

The legal issues of psychological testing are numerous. To comprehend some of the foundational issues of pre-employment screening, the cases for in-service and employed public personnel are made so as the reasons for pre-employment screening psychological examination processes can be more fully understood.

In-Service and Promotional Examinations

Psychological examinations have been used in the recertification and promotional processes of organizations. The courts have sided with departments who use the process in alignment with the intended purposes of the examinations. For example, in the decision of *Coleman v. N.Y.* (2007), the court agreed with the agency's use of the same psychological examination process that can be required for current employees as is used for applicants.[426] However, the courts have expressed divergent opinions in areas that explore protected information by the use of unnecessary questions related to religion, as was decided in *Bennett v. County of Suffolk* (1998).[427] Another court decision questioned the foundation for using a psychiatric examination in a promotional process. In *Karraker v. Rent-A-Center* (2005), the court reviewed the claim that the examination delved into restricted medical questions and, if intended for that purpose, would have been an invalid use of the instrument.[428] However, another court ruled in a promotional examination that business necessity and relevance allowed for the inquiry into issues of tattoos, engagement in teenage sex, sleep habits, and several other controversial matters.[429]

Random and Periodic Examinations

The courts have also been favorable to the idea of random and periodic psychiatric examinations of serving personnel. In periodic examinations, the decision in the matter of the *Police Benevolent Association Local 319 v. Township of Plainsboro* (1998) upheld the agency's use of periodic psychological testing of police officers.[430]

For Cause and Behaviors

The courts have routinely supported for-cause actions of agencies as well. In these cases, there is usually some potential threat to the officer or a third party. For example, in *Herman v. Commonwealth Department of General Services* (1984), the demotion of a police officer to an unarmed civilian employee after a suicide attempt was legally justified.[431] In the *City of Boston v. Boston Police Patrolmen's Association* (1979), the disarming and mandatory psychiatric examination of an officer involved in a shooting was also justified.[432] In *Kraft v. Police Commissioner of Boston* (1995), the agency can require psychological examinations for reinstatement as a condition of recertification to carry a firearm.[433]

Varying levels of cause can also be developed in order to subject a law enforcement officer to a psychological examination or sanction based upon the conduct. Noncriminal behaviors include a case involving a serving officer who was terminated due to a psychological diagnosis of being inflexible and overanxious as found in the decision of *Burge v. City of Dover, Kent County Chan. Ct.* (1993).[434] A similar decision was reached in *Tingler v. City of Tampa* (1981), where a mandatory psychological exam was the result of an observed mental instability.[435] Termination of an officer for excessive personality traits was also upheld as found in the decision of *Joseph v. Salt Lake City* (2003).[436] Justification was found in *Wertz v. Wilson* (1997) when a chief ordered the psychological and physical testing of an employee who demonstrated excessive absenteeism, tardiness, high use of sick leave, and rapid variations in mood.[437] A termination due to an unreasonable fear of job responsibilities was supported in *Sienkiewicz v. County of Santa Cruz* (1987).[438] In *Redmond v. City of Overland Park* (1987), the plaintiff officer's hostility and unwarranted suspicions of persecution warranted the termination of the employee.[439]

Psychological examination of an employee implicated in workplace thefts was also justified as the decision in *Wilson v. City of Baton Rouge* (2009).[440] cited an analogous precedent in *Benningfield v. City of Houston* (1998),[441] where a "referral for psychological testing was not an adverse employment action. Rather, the referral was designed to gather facts to form the basis for an employment decision."[442] However, in the ruling of *Dodd v. SEPTA* (2007), a federal court ruled that an involuntary psychological examination in this case had become part of the permanent employment record and thus rose to the level of an adverse employment action.[443]

In the for-cause realm, numerous cases can be cited where some type of aggressive or violent behavior toward coworkers or third parties was the foundation for the examination in which the courts all supported department actions.[444] These cases involved threats to coworkers and supervisors, abuse of citizens, domestic violence, and sexual misconduct.

Several cases have also been decided supporting agencies for insubordination charges and subsequent termination of officers who have failed to cooperate fully or refused to cooperate altogether with an order to submit to a department-related psychological examination.[445] Only rarely do the courts side with the employee as was later found in *Merillat v. Michigan State University* (1995) wherein a dispatcher who failed to cooperate with a mandatory psychological examination was reinstated as the department did not have a valid basis to order the examination as required by state law.[446] However, even in these types of cases, management can argue good faith as were the circumstances in the decision of *Caver et al. v. City of Trenton* (2005) wherein management acted in good faith in a termination based upon the results of a psychological evaluation even though the officer was later reinstated.[447] Management can still argue and often support any employment actions as was revealed in the decision of *Galas v. Ward* (1990) wherein the aberrant behavior of an officer that was disputed by psychiatric testimony was later proven by independent observations of aberrant behavior by the officer.[448] Lastly, claims of discrimination have also been successfully defended as was the case in the decision of *Reynolds v. Arizona* (1993) as a claim of gender disparity in the psychological examination process was rejected by court.[449]

Pre-Employment Examinations

The use of psychological screening is allowed under federal employment law as these types of tests are able to predict with relative certainty an applicant's potential for presenting a direct threat to the safety of themselves or others in the workplace. This allowance is defined as the *Direct Threat Standard* as previously discussed.[450] The courts have routinely supported applicant rejections based upon identified psychological problems that rise to the level of substantive personality disorders that would interfere with the prospective employee's work as decided in various cases that all have consistent themes.[451] This ideology is also supported in the federal courts that have upheld the use of psychological testing of applicants as found in the ruling of *McKenna v. Fargo* (1978).[452] Also clear in the law are the repercussions for failing to adopt a meaningful psychological screening process as was the court ruling in *Bonsignore v. City of New York* (1982).[453]

Lastly, there are legal precedents that may preclude the use of the psychological examination as the sole reason for disqualification of an applicant.[454] Interestingly enough, as a legal note, even though the psychological examination can be a significant deciding factor of rejection for employment, several cases have been decided concerning the court's assertion that there is no right to have an attorney present during a psychological examination.[455] More often than not, though, an applicant who is unacceptable or even assessed as a high psychological risk will have other factors in their background that will support this type of adverse employment action. Therefore, the department should endeavor to do complete investigations in these circumstances in order to develop a clear picture of the applicant's history and be able to confirm or refute through independent investigation the findings of the psychological examination. Psychologists also suggest that an applicant can be retested in as short a period of 6 months to 1 year and have different results, possibly even passing a screening process failed in that short window in time.

Psychological Evaluation Results and Reports

The psychological examination should produce a series of coalesced results that must be transmitted to the law enforcement agency in the form of a written document. The final psychological evaluation report is used as an informational, diagnostic, and investigative tool for the investigating agency. This document then becomes part of the formal background investigation package and is used in the screening process for decision-making purposes.

The information developed during the psychological evaluation as well as any reports that are produced also have numerous legal precedents that regulate and protect the content. General examples of psychological information related to these types of examinations that was not discoverable was due in part to patient-psychotherapist privilege, the results not being published, and the testing process created as a part of the hiring process.[456] In contrast, case law has also been established where either the components of the process or the entire process was discoverable by the applicant or other interested parties. These rulings were largely based on individual circumstances that deal with the lack of implicit or implied confidentiality in the process, examinations not being a part of a course of therapy, and the applicant voluntarily signing waivers of rights to apply for the positions, just to name a few.[457]

The report itself must be written for a wide range of audiences including lay persons, legal advisors, and other psychologists. Therefore, the language should be simple enough for the lay person to understand as well as technical enough to demonstrate a high level of analysis and validity. Test scores should be included along with short and cogent narratives that include specific examples related to the applicant's pathology. A specific rating system should also be included whether a pass/fail process or scaled process with ranges that may include language as 1 or A is acceptable while 5 or E is unacceptable. If issues of further concern or need for extended investigation by the department are not resolved before the report is submitted to the department, then a specific proviso should be included, advising the agency of this in the official evaluation report. These reports should be archived by the psychologist if the need for legal defense emerges from any subsequent litigation.

Dealing with the Contractor

Most agencies will not have the benefit of staff personnel who conduct these examinations and will need to seek the services of a contractor. In selecting and dealing with the contractor, the law enforcement agency should take into account and prepare for several issues that will affect the process.

The first is the choice of psychologist over psychiatrist. The preferred practice is the use of a certified and licensed psychologist who has an acumen in the law enforcement screening realm. Their research agenda should consist of job-specific research of this unique discipline. The psychologist must understand what the essential job functions are of a law enforcement officer and integrate that information into their interpretation of the standardized testing tools that will be used. Pre-employment psychological screening of law enforcement applicants must demonstrate business necessity and job relatedness that follows a logical rationale for assessment and decision making. This should lead to the psychologist giving an informed recommendation to screen applicants either in or out. The psychologist should not vacillate on their answers or commitment to the department as they conduct their independent and unbiased evaluation of the applicant. The evaluation should lead to a recommended status of the applicant that is either acceptable (fit), unacceptable (unfit), or if indeterminable based upon some aggravating or mitigating factor, deferred for further evaluation.[458] With respect to the classification system agreed upon between the agency and the contractor, research has revealed that pass/fail systems in lieu of rating scales (e.g., 1 through 5 or A through E) are preferred by some psychologists.[459] However, either is acceptable. The following is a list of considerations that should be used when developing the contractual agreement:

1. Department must clearly identify and define the tasks of the psychological evaluator/contractor.
2. Mutually agreed upon report formatting requirements and revisions.
3. Report turnaround time.
4. Rating system needs and requirements.
5. Contractor's work on conducting local validation and normative studies.
6. Contractor requests for additional investigation by the department in the continuance of the psychological evaluation.
7. Applicant testing and retesting limits.

With respect to the last point, the contractor should develop applicant testing and retesting limits in concert with the department's needs and requirements. Applicants who miss a component of the examination process, practice deception, are not cooperative, or attempt to circumvent the process in any manner should be sanctioned. On rare occasions, applicants will take the written examinations and skip around answering only the questions they believe will not reflect negatively on them. In these cases, not enough data can be developed from the test scoring and an applicant would have to retake the examination at the unnecessary expense of the agency. In these cases, all applicants should be directly advised at the outset of the testing process that they are to answer all questions fully and honestly. and if this situation occurs, the affected applicant should be rejected for failure to meet processing requirements and possible attempts at being deceptive.

The department should also invest in validation studies with the psychologist. Whether the same contractor, or if numerous contractors are used over time, the results and recommendations should be compared to the performance and disciplinary records of the officers in a longitudinal study. From this, a process validation could take place where correlations between psychologist ratings, or in essence, predictions, can be compared to the officer's job-related behaviors. This may also be an excellent defense mechanism wherein an applicant is rejected for being psychologically an unacceptable risk, possibly wins in a civil service or court appeals process, and later engages in the predicted behavior that results in litigation from a plaintiff. The department could argue that all reasonable measures were used to reject the candidate and thus potentially minimize culpability. The empirical validation studies would also be of use in defending the hiring decisions and adverse employment actions as they arise as well as offer some insight into the utility of the process where continuous improvement processes can be implemented. Lastly, with respect to litigation, contracting psychologists enjoy a level of protection of their recommendations as is found in the ruling of *Bopp v. Institute for Forensic Psychology* (1997) wherein a police applicant's defamation suit as a result of being rejected was decided in favor of the psychological testing firm as the applicant's statements were protected by qualified privilege.[460]

The psychologist should conduct their own examination based upon their work alone. They should develop their own questionnaires based upon the results of the psychological job task analysis for law enforcement personnel. These Personal Psychological History Questionnaires should be released to the law enforcement agency and used to compare against applicant responses on the law enforcement Personal History Statement/Background Questionnaire for inconsistencies. The results of the law enforcement agency's background investigation should be kept separate from the psychological examination so as the hiring agent can defend against allegations of a tainted review or collusion in the process. The strength of predictive value emerges from the combination of these two components as independent entities rather than as collaborative efforts. Therefore, the psychological screening process is used only as a segment of the screening process. The psychological examination should then independently and generally support findings of the background investigation. When conflicts are revealed, a more in-depth analysis should take place wherein the pre-employment screening personnel and psychological screening staff meet and specifically discuss the differences and develop a strategy to resolve any differences, whether through further follow-up investigation through the background investigation, with psychological screening staff, or both.

Lastly, agencies will be wrestling with costs as the depth of the psychological penetration and breadth of examination processes can be daunting and expensive. Needs assessment and best practices should prevail in the adoption of a battery testing and clinical interview process that meets the agencies' human resource and budgetary needs. The competitive bidding process will produce at least some relief in overall cost reduction. For smaller agencies, economies of scale are not possible. In these cases, reduced rates through volume referrals and collaborations with other agencies for group rates may be a method of keeping the fees manageable without sacrificing quality. A regional or collaborative bidding process with a consistent battery testing and clinical interview regimen can be developed to reduce costs and validate the process by utilizing at least a regionally accepted procedure.

Independent Evaluations and Appeals Processes

The psychological evaluation process brings with it some unique challenges. An applicant who fails the physical agility testing, is not medically acceptable, or has a disqualifying criminal conviction is definitely excluded. Applicants who fail the psychological examination are sometimes not as clear a case for exclusion. Many applicants can challenge these findings in a court of law. The psychological testing contractor and the department must be able to prove that there was a legitimate and business-related connection to the necessary skills tested for and the testing process as a whole was valid and unbiased.

With respect to the legal aspects, the psychological testing contractor will be held to the same standards as required under the *Federal Rules of Evidence*.[461] Having their foundation in the case of *Frye v. United States* (1923) the court defined the rule of "general acceptance" of scientific theory and expertise of a witness to offer opinion-based evidence.[462] Several other cases have impacted the use of expert testimony in the federal courts. These cases include *Daubert v. Merrell Dow Chemicals, Inc.* (1993),[463] *Kumho Tire Co. v. Carmichael* (1999),[464] and *General Electric Co. v. Joiner* (1997)[465] and have shaped the federal courts opinions on expert testimony. The *Federal Rules of Evidence* have also been modified to narrow the evidence admissible from witnesses called as experts as well as to apply more stringent tests directly to those opinions offered as expert testimony.[466] Valid standardized testing processes are the first hurdle to clear, and then the veracity of the psychologist becomes an even higher hurdle to clear in the eyes of the courts. The hiring authority is ultimately responsible to ensure the qualifications of the psychological testing contractor are valid and will withstand this level of legal scrutiny. The courts have been favorable in rendering a decision that an applicant's privately retained experts would not be a controlling factor in the final decision as cited from *Matter of Murray v. County of Nassau Civil Service Commission* (2007).[467] However, as is with most cases that make it to court, the decision may also depend on the dubious *Battle of Resumes*, where a jury or judge may find an independently hired testing contractor to have more veracity than the agency's contractor of record.

As an aside, the agency administrator should not place themselves in a position where they are challenging their own psychological screening contractor. Contractors are hired for their services and expertise. In their assessment of an applicant, the agency administrator should follow the recommendations unless some mitigating circumstances exist. For example, the severe disconnect between an applicant's behavioral patterns as discovered in the background investigation that may not align with the psychological contractor's assessment. In review of both, the administrator may choose to bring these discrepancies to the contractor's attention for further investigation and review to supply a more accurate assessment if that is possible. However, the administrator should not challenge or force the contractor to alter their assessment in favor of the administrator's caprice or as a result of political pressure to render a finding that is in contrast to the expert's assessment. This type of action can result in potentially damaging legal ramifications as well as a severely damaged image of the agency.[468] Worse yet, this type of backtracking calls the contractor's credibility into question as the qualified expert can be challenged in potentially every assessment they have done for the agency to that point as well as any future work they may be engaged to do.

Applicants may hire an independent psychological testing contractor in an effort to refute the rejection results of the agency's contractor. The majority of agencies do not entertain these types of unsolicited efforts. Some agencies afford an appeals process for applicants who desire to expend the effort and money to be independently tested. One research study of an individual state's appeals processes found about one-third of agencies allow an applicant to appeal the results of their psychological screening test.[469] These evaluations must be examined closely for consistency in the testing process. In order for an applicant to effectively challenge a process, they must be subjected to the exact same regimen as that which has resulted in their exclusion. The same battery testing, background questioning of the psychologist, and clinical interview must be used in order to present their rebuttal (if in fact there is one after they have completed the same process and the independent contractor finds them acceptable). Applicants who do not complete the same testing regimen should not be considered as they have failed to present a fully comparative rebuttal to the processing requirements of the hiring agency (see below).

Example of Failed Credibility in the Psychological Examination Process[470]

More Merritt Rahn misdeeds alleged ahead of trial
Gary Craig and Meaghan McDermott
March 28, 2010
Former Greece police chief Merritt Rahn ordered a psychologist to alter the findings of an examination of Gary Pignato to help ensure Pignato would be hired by Greece police, authorities allege.

In the spring of 2002, Rahn directed psychologist Jay Supnick to upgrade Pignato's evaluation from a "poorly suited" grade of D to a "conditionally suited" grade of C, prosecutors allege in a court document. Rahn told Supnick that, "It doesn't matter what you put in your report, we're going to hire him anyway," prosecutors allege.

Pignato would later become an embarrassment for the Greece department. He is now imprisoned on convictions of coercing one woman into sex and committing official misconduct by his actions with another woman who accused him of forcing her into sex.

According to the court document, Rahn told Supnick that town Supervisor John Auberger had directed Pignato be hired and "this is a political favor beyond his control."

The allegation against Rahn is contained in a document filed last week asking a judge for permission to use this evidence—and allegations of other "bad acts" by the former chief—at Rahn's criminal trial, which is scheduled to begin Monday.

Supnick declined to comment, saying he may testify at Rahn's trial.

Auberger denies that he encouraged the hiring of Pignato, who was fired from the Rochester Police Department in 1997 for disciplinary reasons.

But Rahn's attorney, John Parrinello, contends that the leadership of the town of Greece will be central at Rahn's trial. He maintained that Rahn is being used as a scapegoat for ineffective town leadership.

The trial "is going to be an exposé of Auberger's administration and his lack of control of what occurred in the Police Department," Parrinello said. Auberger was key to Pignato's hiring, Parrinello said. "I know Merritt did not hire Pignato."

Rahn faces 12 criminal charges—9 felonies and 3 misdemeanors—related to alleged involvement in falsifying a background check for Pignato's hiring, the 1999 theft of Rahn's department-issued gun, and the Greece Police Department's investigation of a 2008 crash involving Sgt. Nicholas Joseph, who was off duty at the time.

MEDICAL AND PSYCHOLOGICAL RECORDS SECURITY AND RETENTION

Medical and psychological records are confidential documents that can only be viewed by those who have a legally approved interest in their contents. Several federal as well as state laws protect record collection, storage, and dissemination.[471] Initially, as the investigation progresses, these records will be stored with the background package itself as the agency moves toward making a hiring decision. Once a decision is made, then the records should be removed from the Final Investigative Package and archived separately with strict limits to access. An alternate method is to mandate that the psychological and medical professional contractors be tasked with the storage of these records as well as providing a level of redundancy. As a general rule, pre-employment records must be kept at least 1 year.[472] Common sense dictates that these types of records be maintained far longer though.

CONCLUSION

The purpose of this chapter is to give some perspective to the issues that will be encountered in the applicant's screening for both medical and psychological issues. Beginning with the *ADA* and progressing through several other federal pieces of legislation, the impact of these laws is clear in how applicants must be processed in order to protect their rights as well as the rights of the hiring organization.[473] This chapter then progresses through the common areas of question and concern in both drug use and psychological standards and evaluations so as the background investigator can attain a level of clarity to the process as well as a range of viable options that can be used in setting and enforcing policy in these very difficult components of the pre-employment screening process. This chapter then touches upon the security and retention of medical and psychological records of the applicants. Lastly, medical and psychological examinations must be conducted and released to the organization prior to an applicant's hire, or even conditional hire basis. Otherwise, these types of tests may prove to be protected under collective bargaining agreements wherein the employee may not be terminated based solely upon the results.[474]

DISCUSSION QUESTIONS AND EXERCISES

1. Discuss in detail how your department's medical evaluation process complies with the various federal acts and statutes presented in this chapter. Determine if any discrepancies exist and outline a plan for change to bring your department's processes to acceptable standards.
2. Review your department's illicit drug use standards. Evaluate how they compare to the example department policies presented. Based on this comparison, would you recommend changes to the department's policy? If so, develop a draft policy that would work best for your agency's needs.
3. After your review of the issues surrounding policies on marijuana use, does your agency have an effective and definitive time frame for exclusion? What recommendations would you make based upon the review of the contemporary issues and policies presented in this chapter?
4. In reviewing the information concerning the COE, does your department meet the standards for issuance? If not, what needs to be changed in order to comply with federal law?

5. What type of relationship exists between the department and the psychological testing contractor? Examine the process that is in place in your organization on the collaborative nature of the contractor's relationships and communication with the background investigation staff. Determine if any improvement could be made and what recommendations you have for change.

5 Informational Sources and the Final Investigative Package

LEARNING OBJECTIVES

- To develop a full understanding of the various deselection issues including criminal behavior, drug use, credit record, and other salient factors of the process of the pre-employment investigations for public safety organizations
- To develop an appreciation for the various components involved in completing the pre-employment investigation in public safety organizations
- To develop an understanding of the issues of establishing the truthfulness and integrity of the applicant in the pre-employment investigation process
- To develop a full understanding of the various interview models, processes, and techniques for pre-employment investigations

KEY TERMS AND CONCEPTS

- Administrative vs. criminal investigation
- Reference checking and negligent referral
- Applicant integrity
- Employment interviews
- The Final Investigative Package

INTRODUCTION

The core operational knowledge of the pre-employment screening process is provided in the pages of this chapter. The previous chapters are intended to provide the historical, conceptual, and requisite direct and ancillary knowledge required to understand that conducting the background investigation is not simply a matter of searching criminal records and writing a final report. This chapter provides much of the operational knowledge required to complete all of the needed steps in the investigation as well as how the investigative report and final package requirements should be developed, structured, and submitted. Built into the structure is a recommended chronology of the report and process requirements that will ensure all of the necessary screening areas are appropriately addressed to give the most accurate picture of the individual applicant's suitability to join the ranks of the organization.

DON'T JUST REPORT; INVESTIGATE!

The tendency in reviewing this chapter would be to interpret the process as a mere matter of filling in the blanks when the reality is that this can be no further from the truth.

A fundamental flaw exists in the system wherein "administrative" investigations such as those dealing with human resource screening are not given proper attention or resources to thoroughly complete the required level of tasks with sufficient fervor. These types of investigations often require a much higher level of commitment and acumen to complete than most routine criminal investigations. The broad array of knowledge requiring the criminal investigator to become an erudite background investigator at screening techniques is an absolute if organizational administrators have any semblance of hope in hiring whom they deem are the very best. The aspiring background investigator must come to the position with advanced investigative skills, an undying commitment to see the case through to its logical conclusion, and a thirst for new professional knowledge and growth that are inherent to this process.

The word *investigation* is a derivative of the Latin word *vestigare*, which means to track or search out. An investigation can therefore be defined as "a detailed examination or search to uncover facts and determine the truth; a searching inquiry."[1] While definition is important, purpose must also be considered. The purpose of an investigation is the genuine attempt to reconstruct a historical event of some consequence.[2] The investigator plays a key role in this process as he or she is responsible to collect all of the available and ascertainable facts of the case being explored.[3] During this probing process, investigators and detectives will collect the facts of the investigation and make every effort to harness evidence that falls into one of several categories including direct evidence, indirect evidence, and circumstantial evidence in order to draw a conclusion on the probability that an incident or event has occurred, the identity of the person responsible, and the appropriate level of culpability involved.[4] Investigators require a mindset that includes an equitable balance of the components of logic, objectivity, and the ability to determine legal sufficiency to effectively conduct an inquiry into the matter in question.[5] Integrity of the process is everything that is held dear to the law enforcement profession, and violating this often results in grave consequences for the agency, applicant, and background investigator.[6]

Investigations in the administrative realm are much the same concept as in the criminal environment as the investigators are charged with the responsibility of conducting a lawful exploration of events, objects, and people in the ultimate search for the truth of the matter. Administrative investigations encompass much broader parameters than criminal investigations, and the background investigator must be prepared to adjust to the changing environment that will be faced in the process.[7] Pre-employment investigations, comparable to criminal investigations, also involve the thought processes of deductive reasoning (a definite conclusion following a given set of circumstances) and inductive reasoning (the acceptance that even if the given set of circumstances are satisfied, the conclusion may in fact be false or misleading). As the investigation develops from the known to the unknown, the background investigator is in a constant state of analysis and critical decision making as facts are progressively disclosed through contemporary investigative techniques. A single obvious path may unexpectedly flare out of control with the discovery of a new fact or lead. Depending on the timing, the weight of the information, the immediacy of needed response, and the corroboration of the evidence revealed, the background investigator is consistently called upon to make perfect decisions in an imperfect world that is in an often uncontrollable and constant state of flux. And, aligned with these issues, since "criminal investigations require a systematic inquiry to uncover facts and determine the truth, the investigator must possess the versatility to adjust his or her techniques to the particular crime and circumstances."[8] Neat, focused, and linear progressions are usually not the case in a background investigation, and necessity becomes the mother of invention as each fact is revealed that becomes yet another piece of a puzzle that the background investigator is trying to see take shape. There is no easy task for those who are assigned these roles.

As a result of these issues as well as the rapidly evolving social, political, legal, and technical concerns, current trends in investigations demand a multidisciplinary approach to addressing the issues related to continued investigation, including the use of problem-solving methods to improve the process.[9] Background investigators also have to consider the role of strategy as being tantamount to their professional skill sets. Multidisciplinary approaches and strategic thinking that is infused into the investigative process involve all players and components of the investigative process to be aligned toward a common outcome which should be considered at the outset of the process as well as through the entire progression of the investigation.[10] The contemporary investigator is called upon to be not only a "jack of all trades" but also a master of all trades in order to be effective in the role. Taking a multifaceted approach to the position and being willing to learn and grow in all of the requisite subject matter areas are crucial for success.

One axiom of the field is that the effectiveness of a law enforcement agency can be measured by the quality of the investigations that are completed by its members.[11] Criminal as well as administrative investigations must also be managed more from a business perspective considering process as the driver rather than functions.[12] A systems approach to case management, quality, monitoring, and disposition is essential to moving the organization forward toward the desired goals and measurable outcomes. Background investigations, not unlike criminal investigations, are often judged on their quality when the product of the pre-employment investigation is issued a badge and gun and subsequently acts in a manner that brings discredit and even incidents of disgrace to the organization as well as the law enforcement discipline as a whole. With this in mind, the background investigator holds the distinction of being in a position to make significant contributions to the investigative systems of the organization.[13] The background investigator has the opportunity to impact far more than a single transgression of a robbery, burglary, or even a homicide. Rather, they can have the long-term impact of being instrumental in the proper screening and hiring of a department member who will impact thousands of lives during the course of one single career in law enforcement.

SUCCESSFUL WRITTEN COMMUNICATION

While this concept seems obligatory, this is also an oft forgotten and frequently ignored basic tenet. In law enforcement, the overwhelming majority of our work is judged through the written word. This section endeavors to provide some insight and tactics that will refine the background investigator's use of the written word to convey the facts of the investigation in the most professional manner possible. While the background investigator may never bear the distinction of being a Rhodes Scholar, or win the coveted Pulitzer Prize, their work in protecting their communities by ensuring that the most suitable applicants are selected is a far more noble accomplishment than these public awards.

The written word is a very powerful medium of communication.[14] Examples such as *The Holy Bible*, the *United States Constitution*, and the *Gettysburg Address* have provided the foundation to shape religions, nations, and cultural belief systems of divergent groups of people. From the *Magna Carta* to the directions on a bottle of aspirin, we are enveloped in a world where actions are driven by the stated and underlying messages contained in the written word. Encapsulated in these dramatic examples is a simplistic concept: Audience plays a key role in the development of any form of written communication.[15] That audience will assess the meaning, purpose, and value of the message of those simple or complex words written in any communication. The recent trend of using digital media as a primary method of the distribution of messages through the written word as well as to distribute knowledge and learning is leading a revolution of how we access information and how we are able to learn.[16] E-mails and text messaging place us in interchanges where we need to ensure brevity in rapid real-time communication environments. Consequently, our skills continue to diminish as we move away from formal communication media. The test of time has brought us ambivalence toward evolution and regression of communicative processes. Technology has delivered unparalleled access to new worlds of communication wherein the formal and conventional methods are being lost in a milieu of coded syntax and the parlance of street jargon. In spite of all this, the written word still remains the most fundamental form of communication.[17]

Introspection must lead us to developing our own skill set to make the most use of this critical form of expression in order to ensure our message is clear and convincing to our intended audiences that include professionals and lay persons, legal scholars and vocational practitioners, supervisors and subordinates, alike. Best practice approaches include several basic rules to enhance our written communications. From form and structure, to drafting and outlining, to the use of software to enhance our final work product, the background investigator should use the entire spectrum of these helpful indices to improve upon their current skill sets. We must always operate from the perspective of what our writing depicts about us to others. Our writing skills are not only a direct reflection of our individual ability, but more often than not, they are a symbol of the professionalism and quality of the entire organization we work for as a whole.[18]

Preliminarily, enhancing the quality of writing skills begins with developing a clear thought in advance and then developing an outline for the work to be written to.[19] We must have a focused and thematic course for the development of the overall meaning and intent of the work to be produced. In order to meet these expectations, a full understanding of the target audience must be developed. Purposeful writing requires an understanding of the capacity of the audience, simplifying complex arguments by using evidence to present the reader with logic and reasoning in order for them to draw informed conclusions.[20] For the background investigator, this audience is a veritable endless series of groups from lay to expert and practitioner to onlooker. The background investigator must consider writing to the lay person while integrating the legal and technological terms in scientific as well as defined ways so that all audiences who will conceivably review the materials can comprehend the message. You must always avoid the use of work-based jargon at all costs and always define terms not commonly known to the lay person. Always scrutinize word choice and punctuation marks as they will have a significant impact on the interpretation of the message.[21] For example, "THANKS!!!," "Thanks," "Thank you for your assistance," and "I very much appreciate the help you have offered" all have distinct connotations from very positive and appreciative to extremely disingenuous and abrasive. In law enforcement writing, factual information must be used in lieu of emotional or symbolic writing. In law enforcement writing, shock value has no value.

Style and brevity also must be considered. There is a direct link between the use of style and consequent impact on the substance of a communication wherein the message can be lost or misinterpreted if the reader is not familiar with, or worse yet, offended by the writing style.[22] Even in factually based writing, style can emerge and be a deciding factor that works for or against the author, no matter how compelling the argument is that is delivered. An evolutionary sign of the times is indicated by the efforts of the legal profession to embark upon a path to use plain language in written works and communications.[23] Some fundamental elements of good writing are to write cogently and critically for the intended reader, using critical thinking skills and providing both structure and format to allow the reader to understand the content and message.[24] In order to avoid painfully long reports, the background investigator should spend more time in the planning and editing process in order to develop clear and persuasive messages in the primary and supportive documentation of the pre-employment investigation.[25] Writing in a succinct and cogent manner will go far in gaining the concurrence of the reviewer.[26]

Accept the notion that computers are our friends! Make the most advantageous use of software programs to edit and format your reports in order to avoid spelling and grammatical errors that will distract the reader from the message you are trying to convey.[27] Do not get caught in a trap though that presents a dichotomy that our friends can easily become our enemies. While software programs are effective at document development, they do not address the basic tenets of communication; therefore, the ability to navigate a software program is secondary to the ability to develop an effective communication style and design.[28] The quality of the writing is truly incumbent upon us as the writer to demonstrate those effective communication skills and techniques augmented by the advent of technology.

There are several additional considerations for developing the Final Investigative Report. First and foremost is that there is a direct connection between the exhaustive gathering of relevant information to the quality of report that will follow.[29] Writing skills will be overshadowed by the lack of comprehensiveness and quality of the information that is included, or not included when the information was available but not yet mined. The purpose of any report written in the law enforcement realm is to present the results of the investigation based upon the facts that have been uncovered and allow the reader to draw an informed conclusion.[30] To accomplish this task, you must use clear and supportive evidence and facts structured in a logical manner that offers a solution to the matter at hand.[31] You must also consider how the communication will be viewed by your superiors in order to develop the most effective method to persuade those doing the review to adopt your ideas or agree with your objective and unbiased findings.[32] Always remember that the final report is a direct reflection on your ability to communicate your acumen as a professional in the field.[33]

The review process is an auditing method to ensure quality control. One organization studied the effects of poor communication and determined that they had lost millions of dollars in revenue as well as had suffered significant damage to their corporate image because of these flaws.[34] The first level of review is accomplished by the writer. The writer must fully review and interpret their works to assess the potential implications of the message they are trying to convey.[35] The next level of review is from the supervisor or manager. In order to have the most effective system of review at this level, the supervisor or manager must take a proactive role in developing their own writing skills as well as taking every opportunity to mentor and professionally develop these skills in those who work for them.[36] Writing skills need to be continually refreshed, so there must be a strong consideration for the use of frequent writing workshops to keep skills at their peak.[37] Honing personal skills, developing supervisors to utilize best practice approaches, and an eye on continual professional development are a system that is geared for successful outcomes in the written communication realm.

Effective writing is a critical skill that must be mastered by the background investigator and background investigation supervisor alike. Consistency of purpose and message must be furthered through the command of the written word. You must always take every opportunity to develop your writing skills into models that demonstrate competence in the process.[38] Writing and revision then evolves into a process of galvanizing a document to ensure the safe and persuasive conveyance of your arguments through the entire approval process.[39] Skills development, templates, software applications, rigorous scrutiny, and revision will all provide the systemic support structure to withstand the challenges of any group charged with the responsibility for oversight and final approval.

SUPPORTING DOCUMENTATION REQUIREMENTS

Records are used in developing a trail to the applicant's past as well as to guide the direction of the entire investigation.[40] Each investigation will include the final investigative report or summary and a litany of supporting documentation. The background investigator must be concerned with three very salient issues: (1) the thoroughness of the records collected for each area of character and history of the applicant that must be investigated, (2) the accuracy of the records collected, and (3) the authenticity and veracity of the records collected. The information culled from these records and research documents will provide the foundation for the background investigator's recommendations that are communicated in the final investigative report.

As enumerated in the following text, each component will require the background investigator to collect the best evidence to verify the facts of the pre-employment investigation. The three requirements of thoroughness, accuracy, and authenticity can individually and collectively have an enormous impact on the pre-employment investigation as a whole. With respect to thoroughness, the Missouri State Highway Patrol Human Resources Division provides a basic list of application requirements:

1. Certified copy of birth certificate obtained from the birth states' Department of Health (an original birth certificate, photocopy of the original or certified copy, or a notarized copy are NOT acceptable)
2. Valid driver's license (photocopy)
3. Military service discharge papers, if applicable (DD214 and/or DD215)
4. High school diploma or GED certificate (photocopy)
5. High school transcript (official copy)
6. College diploma(s) (photocopy)
7. College transcript(s) (official copy)
8. Peace Officer Standard Training (POST) certificate[41]

As enumerated in this chapter though, these foundational application records are only the start of the evidentiary documents that will need to be collected in the furtherance of the pre-employment investigation. The background investigator will need to assemble the traditional and nontraditional documents that are collected as the investigation progresses. As the gatherer and presenter of these evidentiary facts, the best evidence ideology must be adhered to.[42] In these cases, evidence is most often information that has been memorialized in some form or fashion. Additionally, we are morphing into a *Going Green* mentality! Electronic documents and packages are filtering into the criminal justice system reflecting the same trends as private sector corporations. The administrator must consider all of the issues related to this as the integration of these concepts and processes moves forward in our organizations. The need for originals or "best evidence" to satisfy the courts, scalable software and hardware systems, and records security and access are all tantamount concerns for the future success of this process.

Records accuracy poses a vexing situation for the background investigator. In spite of the advancements in technology and required auditing systems, mistakes invariably will occur. No matter how advanced the criminal justice records systems are, they are still controlled and impacted by the fallibility of human error. Concerns of the accuracy of records repositories are a disturbing issue when deciding the fate of someone's livelihood. Care must be exercised when conducting records checks for inaccurate information contained in similarity hits, incidents of identity theft, and mismanaged or erroneous information entries.[43] The background investigator must endeavor to corroborate information from any hard copy or electronic source to verify the accuracy of the information obtained.

Records authenticity poses a very ominous situation for the background investigator and applicant alike. While records thoroughness may ultimately depend on availability and access, and records accuracy being open to challenge and correction by the applicant, falsified records present a very distinct challenge for the background investigator to authenticate as well as providing no viable avoidance of full intent, knowledge, and culpability on behalf of the applicant. Trends have strongly indicated that applicants supplying false documentation and credentials to gain employment are consistently maintained at an alarming level.[44] Pedigree information, as well as critical information concerning history and criminal records, is frequently omitted or minimized in order to conceal the true facts of the applicant's character and thus increase the viability for the position applied for.

Embellishing resumes is a common practice of those who desire a position and wish to impress; however, there are acceptable limits that need to be established between embellishment and resume fraud.[45] Applicants also frequently falsify or distort the true nature of their personal qualifications and, in many instances, their purported educational achievements in order to meet the requirements of the position "on paper."[46] The media have reported countless incidents of employee's whose false educational credentials have been later revealed causing immense embarrassment to the hiring agency that could have all been avoided had a proper verification process been in place at the time of consideration for hire.[47] Resume fraud not only is rampant but also, in some circles, has become a business.[48] Resume fraud is an international problem wherein one research study indicated that a majority of applicants studied in the research pool had lied about previous employment and educational qualifications.[49] Resume fraud is an issue in the United States but is being scrutinized more closely in information technology, executive, and managerial positions more so due to the rampant problems created in those industries by the hiring of unqualified applicants.[50] Resume fraud in assertions of work experience, educational accomplishments, and personal as well as professional references is often not checked, which perpetuates its incidence.[51] In a study of over five million resumes, almost half were found to contain misrepresentations across all of the key categories used by employers to identify qualified candidates for hire. Several methods have been suggested in the discovery of resume fraud. For example, conducting a complete background check can often avert the problems of hiring applicants who have lied on their resumes.[52] Some of the more common untruths deal with past employment wherein applicants will wholly omit bad employment experiences as well as try to conceal them in failing to fill gaps in employment history or claim self-employment during these periods of time.[53] Applicants will also offer falsehoods concerning the reasons for separation from previous employments in order to minimize or conceal forced terminations. The background investigator should strictly scrutinize all submitted resumes for gaps in employment, education, and other typical warning signs.[54] Internet searches of applicant to ascertain validity of claims may also be very helpful.[55] The background investigator should also endeavor to contact all of the references an applicant lists to verify that the relationship actually exists and the extent of relevant knowledge the reference has of the applicant.[56] Once the research process is complete, a follow-up through skillful and multiple interviews by pre-employment screener may overcome many incidents of resume fraud.[57] The bottom line is that public safety organizations should have a strong organizational policy that should require termination in cases of resume fraud for those discovered in the process.[58]

Several legal issues also come to the fore when we examine the issue of applicant falsification of their original applications for the position. At the outset, as a bright line rule, rejection of an applicant must be based upon their failure to meet the germane qualifications of the position. For example, integrity issues are critical to the role of a law enforcement officer. The integrity issues also should be directly related to the functions to be performed and be material to the nature and gravity of the incident omitted, concealed, or minimized (i.e., seriousness of the incident: minor discipline vs. commission of a crime). Responses to questioned information in an application package must be balanced against these types of requirements.

Agency liability must also be considered. For example, falsified documentation that is not fully authenticated by the hiring authority can lead to a negligent hiring claim if, as a result of the hiring, a third party suffers some type of injury or loss as a result of the employee's actions.[59] In this case, the standard is that the employer knew or should have known, and if the information would have led to rejection of the applicant, then the causal connection to the injury would have not been made. It behooves us to ask for original documentation in order to abate and defend against these types of claims.

As an aside, employee discipline often leads to an investigation that includes a review of the pre-employment investigation. Terminations and disciplinary actions for serving employees have frequently been based on a retroactive application of exclusionary issues not addressed or uncovered during the employee's original processing for employment in the organization. When untoward behaviors occur, a "complete" investigation may lead to the discovery of information that would have precluded the employee's hire in the first place. While supported on a case-by-case basis, the courts are also ambivalent about the origin of these types of adverse actions, especially after an employee has served the organization for any substantial period of time. There are numerous decisions that support termination of a serving employee based upon the later discovery of incidents of untruthfulness or concealment of material information of a negative nature in the initial application process.[60] In contrast though, many others have also been decided in favor of the employee wherein reinstatement was ordered, and in at least one case, excessive monetary compensation was the award to the claimant for a wrongful termination claim.[61] In posthire situations, the courts apply a level of scrutiny that may constructively close this perceived window of opportunity to take adverse action against the employee. The issue will be examined under the notion of clever and insidious conduct to conceal by the applicant versus sloppy and incomplete investigation of the agency. We must ask ourselves though, is this a character flaw of the employee, or more importantly, an investigative flaw of the organization for not fully exploring an applicant's preservice background? Most importantly, had the agency thoroughly completed the investigation and uncovered the facts that would have precluded employment, we likely would have avoided these situations altogether. The courts may not agree that the remedy for a poorly completed investigation is to sanction the entire employment relationship. The balance created may be the forced retention of a bitter employee.

The *Litmus Test* may very well be judged based upon the gravity of the untruth provided by the applicant as opposed to a strict definition of untruthfulness by either utterance, writing, or intentional and negligent omission. The question may in essence encompass not so much an analysis of the strict definition of truthfulness, but rather be that rejection for employment may not be the appropriate response if the applicant would have been hired anyways if they had just been truthful in their responses on the original application.[62] For the agency to pass the test, a strict set of standards must be applied when collecting and authenticating the various supportive documents required of the process.

The process and policy must then emerge from the local, state, and federal needs for documentation. In addition, some common sense rules must be applied. For example, an applicant who has served in the military will need to provide original documentation of their service discharge papers (DD 214) and any documentation relevant to their service. Where possible, these items can be ordered and mailed directly to the background investigator. If this is not possible, such as with certificates of training where these may be the only copy available, they can be brought to the background investigator by the applicant for examination for any alterations and photocopied personally by the background investigator for inclusion in the package. The applicant should also be required to sign an acknowledgment of the authenticity of all documents submitted as part of the final investigative package. The applicant should have all documents that can be ordered and forwarded by mail sent directly to the background investigator. College transcripts, credit reports, and other relevant and required documentation should be sent directly to the background investigator and can be considered original and official reports when they are conveyed in sealed envelopes through a postal service. Taking the few extra steps can go far in validating the entire investigative process.

Original Applications

An *applicant* is defined as "A person who is being considered or has been considered for employment."[63] Each organization will likely have a pro forma application for the prospective applicant to complete. This may be a separate human resource or personnel form than the law enforcement agency's pre-employment investigation process, or filed and maintained by the soliciting agency or department. A few issues to consider are if the form is updated on a routine basis and are the questions all legal to solicit from the applicant. Second, the application, even if filed through another department or entity, must be included in the final investigative package as a source of information for the investigation. This document can be compared to other documents filed for completeness and accuracy of corresponding information.

Some very basic requirements of the form should include pedigree information, work history, educational preparation, authorization and release of liability for checking references, previous employment history, statements that they understand the employment relationship is at-will where applicable, and a closing attestation that the applicant releases the agency and its agents of liability for the inquiries that will be conducted as a part of their consideration for employment, as well as their swearing to the truth and accuracy of all information they have submitted. These same requirements will be discussed in the section on Personal History Statement/Background Investigation Questionnaire; however, it is important to have all documentation aligned with the same requirements to avoid confusion on the part of all involved in the process.

With the advent of electronic media and the use of the Internet to search and apply for positions, authenticity and accountability of the information included in the original application must also be ensured. Applications may be submitted as an online form and may require a digital signature as proof. For the federal government, the *Digital Signature Act of 1999* authorizes the use of electronically signed documents where appropriate and available for use by an applicant.[64] In spite of the Act though, one study revealed that the majority of organizations surveyed have failed to comply with the federal requirements.[65] The best practice is to have the applicant sign all documents in the presence of the background investigator after the applicant has fully reviewed and acknowledged all information they are submitting in the forms.

Employment Eligibility Verification Form I-9

The Employment Eligibility Form I-9 is a required document used to verify a prospective employee's identity and to establish if they are allowed to accept employment and work within the United States. Through the passing of the *Immigration Reform and Control Act of 1986*, the federal government required employers to verify the identities and immigration status of all newly hired employees.[66] The Act was extended in scope with the passing of the *Intelligence Report and Terrorism Prevention Act of 2004*, wherein the federal government additionally mandated the standardization and consolidation of criminal records searches be extended to the noncriminal justice realm of employment applications.[67] As an outpouring from the war on terrorism, the Act is intended to heighten security by the use of stricter standards for issuing a state driver's license, nondriver identification card, and listing acceptable documents that can be used for identification purposes when applying for passports, Social Security numbers, and other official records. These requirements are also attached to applications for employment. Only limited exceptions are allowed as in the case of the U.S. Armed Forces who utilize certain aliens who are lawfully enlisted in the service and considered vital to the national security interests.[68] The I-9 must be completed without regard to national origin, which equates to all American citizens who must also complete the form when applying for new positions.[69] Employers are ultimately responsible for proper completion of the forms, verification of the acceptable forms of identification used by the prospective employee, and retention of the forms for the purposes of inspection by the government.[70] Copies of all original documents should be obtained including such items as a passport and enhanced driver's license so the background investigator can inquire about the travel habits of the applicant if needed.

As we move further into the technological era, electronic signatures and tracking systems are becoming the norm. The federal government has put the E-Verify system in place to streamline the process for businesses to meet these federal requirements of verification. E-Verify allows the exchange of information between the Social Security Administration and the Department of Homeland Security in establishing an applicant's eligibility for employment.[71] Both hard copy and electronic repositories are deemed acceptable by the federal standards.[72] The *Immigration and Nationality Act* also requires that the I-9 be maintained by the agency for a minimum of 3 years after the date of hire or at least 1 year after termination.[73] Social Security numbers can be checked against the Social Security Administration's database in a variety of manners to include (1) E-Verify, (2) Social Security Number Verification Service (SSNVS), and (3) Consent-Based Social Security Number Verification System (CBSV).[74] When the name and Social Security number do not match, physical verification should be requested of the applicant to establish if any discrepancies exist.[75] A classic law enforcement case emerged from an illegal alien who had been deported, reentered the country illegally, and was hired as a county jailer. A subsequent investigation during employment revealed the deportation record only because the systems are now all linked as a result of the changes that have occurred in information sharing since the 9/11 attacks.[76]

The federal government has also established an audit system to ensure compliance with these rules. Tasked with the responsibility, the U.S. Immigration and Customs Enforcement (ICE) division conducts periodic audits to monitor compliance procedures and enforce the Act when violations are discovered.[77] In order to prepare in the event of a Notice of Inspection from ICE, agencies should follow the technical compliance aspects of the Act.[78]

Online resources are available to assist the agency in proper form completion, procedures, and additional compliance requirements. The primary publication is the *Handbook for Employers: Instructions for Completing the I-9 (Employment Eligibility Verification Form) M-274* which is available as a resource for agencies.[79] One stipulation comes from the *Illegal Immigration Reform and Immigrant Responsibility Act of 1996* that mandates the use of the new forms and provides for penalties for those who fail to comply.[80] Examples of legitimate documents are provided in the handbook for employers to compare to the presented documents of the applicant. Any discrepancies or questioned documents should result in directing the applicant to present additional documents or proof of authenticity of the originals to the examiner.[81] These documents should also be photocopied and/or photographed to preserve them for the record and attached to the I-9. Care must be taken in examining these articles to identify if they have been falsified or altered in any way as well as documents that are presented as the applicant's but do not belong to the applicant. By statute, employers are required to log the numbers of the documents produced by the applicant such as in the case of a driver's license or Social Security card.[82] Agency representatives are also required to collect current documents and cannot accept expired documents for verification.[83] One final recommendation is that all I-9 forms should be kept separate from the personnel record in the event of an inspection so that the personnel record itself can remain confidential.[84]

Personal History Statement

The Personal History Statement, also titled as the Background Investigation Questionnaire, is a document used for self-disclosure of facts of the applicant's entire personal history (see, e.g., Appendices F and G). The purpose of the Personal History Statement is to provide a foundation for the background investigation to proceed from.[85] Every background investigation should always include some form of a Personal History Statement of the applicant.[86] The use of the document also provides structure to follow in verifying the applicant's self-disclosed information concerning required and significant events that have occurred in their personal history.[87] Because of the nature of the information, the background investigator relies heavily on the candor of the applicant's disclosures in the personal history statement. However, investigators burdened with heavy caseloads and lack of resources that have relied on the highest levels of disclosure have resulted in applicants slipping through the system who have committed egregious crimes.[88] For these reasons, the document's thoroughness, formatting, and procedural elements are crucial to the impending investigation as well as the ability of the background investigator to hold the applicant strictly accountable for their entries, statements, and most importantly, omissions.

The thoroughness of the document will depend heavily upon the formatting and structure of the document. Since the document will constructively be the focal point of the investigation, the questionnaire must be comprehensive in the formatting and structure to elicit the most complete and chronological delineation of the events in the applicant's life. The personal history statement/background investigation questionnaire is primarily a forced response document that requires entry of specific information, or written acknowledgment that the information does not apply to the specific applicant. Questions must be clear, and truthfulness statements attesting to the veracity of the package must be unequivocal. Each page must provide for adequate space to log all entries and addenda, or attachments must be available if the applicant needs additional space. Several examples can be found through an online search of law enforcement or corrections departments to use as models. Included in Appendices F and G are the personal history statements/background questionnaires of two separate departments that are provided as excellent examples of this type of document format and structure needs.[89] These types of documents should be reviewed and updated frequently to meet the needs of the respective organizations they are used in.

Document issuance, completion, use, and retention must also comply with a set of departmentally sanctioned procedures. Applicants who are identified as needing to submit the completed document should be notified 4–6 weeks in advance. This allows the applicant ample time to collect personal documents, clarify required information through independent means, and offer the most accurate and complete account of the information required. Conveyance of the document can be through electronic means and a web download, or preferably a hard copy mailed directly to the applicant's home address in the desired time frame. This will prevent applicants from needing Internet and printer access as well as the proverbial excuses of failing to have access to the document in the electronic form.

The personal history statement should include a form cover letter from the investigation unit or division/department head that stresses the criticality of thoroughness and truthfulness in all disclosures and responses in the entire process, inclusive of all disclosures made in the personal history statement. Sanctions of being denied employment and removed from the process at the outset as well as if falsehoods are discovered after employment has been offered are essential components of the letter. Directions should also include having the applicant complete the document truthfully, but not be required to sign the document until they have been preliminarily interviewed by an assigned background investigator. Contact information for any questions should also be provided, preferably and if available, with the background investigator who will be assigned the case. This will benefit the applicant and background investigator greatly in order to limit the possibility of confusing directions or answers to questions concerning the information that must be included on the statement.

Since the applicant has had an extended period of time to complete the personal history statement, the expectation of a thorough and honest submission should be relatively high on the part of the background investigator.[90] Clear directions, strict warnings, and ample time to collect the documents and recollect the information from their personal history should lead to many applicants who will fully disclose as many facts of their past as humanly possible. Many applicants will still attempt to mask, omit, or minimize information in the document prior to submission. There are a few schools of thought in this process, and while none are technically wrong, we must also consider the human factors of the process. Applicants who desire to be in the law enforcement field will often present themselves in the best light. This has been established in behavioral and psychological research. Some measure of this is actually positive. The first method is unequivocal removal from the process when any discrepancy of a material fact or facts is discovered. The opposite end of the spectrum is to treat each applicant on a case-by-case basis, which is extremely difficult to defend and patently unfair to all of the applicants in the process. A third option brings balance to the process. Applicants who have completed the document for presentation can be admonished on the day they arrive to submit the final information to the background investigator. In this scenario, the applicant is advised they have had ample time to complete the document thoroughly and truthfully. The applicant should be warned that if any untruths exist, they can make any changes they need to, up to completely rewriting the document if necessary. However, two provisos exist. The first is that the applicant should only be allowed a minimal and reasonable amount of time to make the corrections. This must also be enforced to its strictest limits; otherwise this is an empty threat of sanction. The second is that the applicant must attest to the complete truthfulness of the information submitted on the date presented. In some cases, you may be able to have the applicant waive any right to appeal if the information they have submitted is knowingly or intentionally false. Steps such as these allow for fairness to the applicant as well as placing the burden squarely where it belongs, on the applicant's doorstep to be entirely truthful.

In the aforementioned section, the applicant should be required to review and sign the entire personal history statement in the presence of the background investigator. As a matter of policy, the information derived from the Personal History Statement must be closely scrutinized only by responsible, experienced, and trained pre-employment screeners.[91] This will require a preliminary interview of the applicant wherein each entry will be reviewed in the presence of the background investigator and the applicant required to initial and date each and every page as verification of the review as well as their agreement with the accuracy of the information. This should not be left to a haphazard approach as a structured interview process should be used when reviewing the Personal History Statement with the applicant.[92] The applicant should be challenged in incidents where responses are vague or unclear, are obviously questionable, derived of falsehoods, intentionally or willfully omitted, or where the applicant has falsified any statement or required document used in the processing of their candidacy.

Once completed, the document becomes the primary source for the pre-employment investigative process. As delineated throughout this chapter, each section should not be merely considered as a checklist, but rather a series of comprehensive investigative steps for the background investigator that guides the exploration of the applicant's entire history. The document should always be protected in the original form, even if a department uses an electronic formatting process; these types of documents should also be archived and made part of the formal personnel record if the applicant is subsequently employed by the agency. If not employed, then they should be archived in accordance with the maximum period allowed by the prevailing legal records retention schedules and relevant organizational policies.

Pre-COE and Post-COE

Two additional questionnaires can be used in accordance with the requirements of the *Americans with Disabilities Act of 1990* (ADA). As discussed in Chapter 4, the ADA was not enacted to protect the use of illegal drugs; rather the law is intended as a protection for those otherwise qualified persons who may have a disability that can potentially be used to unfairly discriminate against them in the employment process. Therefore, the pre-employment screening process may include a questionnaire that can be distributed at the pre-conditional offer of employment (pre-COE) stage that solicits the disclosure of any illegal or illicit substances that have been used by the applicant (see Chapter 4). This questionnaire should be limited in scope to the type of illegal drug(s) used and their last use. Self-disclosures at this point can reveal automatic disqualifiers of applicants who have not met the prescreening drug use requirements set by agency policy.

The post-conditional offer of employment (post-COE) can be issued to the applicant soliciting all drug use, both legal and illegal, as well as many other types of information otherwise protected in the Pre-COE stage (see Table 4.1). This can be used for comparisons to previous disclosures, to establish patterns of use and abuse, and to determine if the applicant meets the prescreening drug use requirements set by agency policy. As in all forms completed by the applicant, these are strictly confidential and protected by the ADA. They can and should be shared only with those who have the authority or right to review them in the organization as well as with the medical and psychological professionals who will be responsible for the applicant's continued testing in these realms.

Information Release Authorizations and Release of Liability Forms

Independently developed information is the lifeblood of the investigation. While the applicant does incur a very hefty burden in self-disclosure as well as the collection and conveyance of numerous administrative and evidentiary documents, the background investigator is also tasked with the independent collection of documents relevant to the case, but not available to or provided by the applicant. In order to further that goal, the investigator is often hamstrung due to the lack of subpoena power and the bureaucracy encountered when seeking this type of information from any entity that has information relevant to the applicant's history and viability for employment. Worse yet are the fears of liability that may attach to the release of any information that is negative and defamatory to the applicant's character, work performance, and other measures used in assessing the ability to perform the functions of a public safety officer. In addition, while some may express concerns over the use of broadly worded waivers that seek to obtain far reaching and normally protected information, the reality is that these types of waivers are necessary to perform the functions of information gathering as well as protect the agency from frivolous claims.[93] For all intents and purposes, the release of information is for the most part voluntary, and the background investigator may need to use a blend of rapport building and tact with the use of a well-crafted and communicated information and release of liability waiver to achieve the goal of thorough information collection. This section provides some guidance and hopefully will allay many of the fears attached.

The legal issues were briefly discussed in Chapter 3 concerning liability issues in the processing of public safety officer applicants. There are two signature court decisions that provide a bright line rule for guidance in the use of Information Release Authorizations and

Release of Liability Forms. In the ruling of *McCleskey v. Vericon Resources, Inc.* (2003), a court ruled that both the current employer and independent screening company were not liable for any alleged damages caused by terminating an employee who was untruthful on his application concerning his arrests/convictions for crimes. The waiver language on the consent form released the organization, its agents, "and any person or entity which provides information pursuant to this authorization, from any and all liabilities, claims, or lawsuits in regard to the information obtained from any and all of the reference sources used earlier."[94] In the companion decision of *Cox v. Nasche* (1996), the court also found that liability waivers included in job application forms can protect former employers and superiors from claims of damages as a result of the information obtained. The court emphasized key points of language in the waiver and Authority for Release of Information as follows:

1. I Authorize any duly accredited representative of the Federal Government… to obtain any information relating to my activities from… employers…. This information may include, but is not limited to,… achievement, performance, attendance, personal history, disciplinary… information.
2. I Direct You to Release such information upon request of the duly accredited representative of any authorized agency regardless of any agreement I may have made with you previously to the contrary.
3. I Release any individual, including records custodians, from all liability for damages that may result to me on account of compliance or any attempts to comply with this authorization.[95]

Information Release Authorizations and Release of Liability Forms range from simple to complex in their development and scope of language. Much depends on the assistance of consulting legal counsel who will have input and possibly the final say in form development and use. Three excellent examples of the range of acceptable release forms are provided by the Auburn, Georgia Police Department (see below) as well as the forms used by the Irondequoit, New York Police Department and the Auburn, Maine Police Department (see Appendix H).

Sample Information Release Authorization and Release of Liability Form[96]

City of Auburn

Authorization for Release of Information

To whom it may concern: I am an applicant for a position with the City of Auburn. The City needs to thoroughly investigate my employment background and personal history to evaluate my qualification to hold the position for which I applied.

It is in the public's interest that all relevant information concerning my personal and employment history be disclosed to the City. I hereby authorize any representative of the City of Auburn bearing his release to obtain any information in your files pertaining to my employment records, and I hereby direct you to release such information upon request of the bearer. I do hereby authorize a review of and full disclosure of all records, or any part thereof, concerning myself, by and to any duly authorized agent of the City of Auburn, whether said records are of public, private, or confidential nature. The intent of this authorization is to provide full and free access to the background and history of any personal life, for the specific purpose of pursuing a background investigation that may provide pertinent data for the City of Auburn to consider in determining my suitability for employment. It is my specific intent to provide access to personnel information, however personal or confidential it may appear.

I consent to your release of any and all public and private information that you may have concerning me, my work records, my background and reputation, my military service records, my educational records, my financial status, my criminal history record, including any arrest records, any information contained in investigatory files, efficiency ratings, complaints or grievances filed by or against me, the records or recollections of attorneys at law, or other counsel, whether representing me or another person in any case, either criminal or civil, in which I presently have, or have had an interest, attendance records, polygraph examinations and any internal affairs investigations and discipline, including any files which are deemed to be confidential, and/or sealed. I hereby release you, your organizations, and all others from liability or damages that may result from furnishing the information requested, including any liability or damage pursuant to any state or federal laws. I hereby release you, as the custodian of such records, including its officers, employees, or related personnel, both individually and collectively, from any and all liability for damages of whatever kind which may at any time result to me, my heirs, family, or associates because of compliance with this authorization and request to release information, or any attempt to comply with it. I direct you to release such information upon request of the duly accredited representative of the City of Auburn regardless of any agreement I may have made with you previously to the contrary. The governmental organization requesting the information pursuant to this release will discontinue processing my application if you refuse to disclose the information requested.

For and in consideration of the City of Auburn, acceptance and processing of my application for employment, I agree to hold the custodian of such records, its agents, and employees harmless from any and all claims and liability associated with my application for employment or in any way connected with the decision whether or not to employ me with the City of Auburn. I understand that should information of a serious criminal nature surface as a result of this investigation, such information may be turned over to the proper authorities. I understand my rights under Title 5, *United States Code,* Section 552a, the *Privacy Act of 1974*, with regard to access and to disclosure of records, and I waive those rights with understanding that information furnished will be used by the City of Auburn in conjunction with employment procedures. A photocopy or FAX copy of this release form will be valid as an original thereof, even though the said photocopy or FAX copy does not contain an original writing of my signature. Should there be any question as to the validity of this release, you may contact me at the address listed on the rear of this form. I agree to indemnify and hold harmless the person to whom this request is presented and his agents and employees from and against all claims, losses, and expenses, including reasonable attorney's fees, arising out of or by reason of complying with this request.

Signed this day of 20________________________________
Applicant signature:________________________________

Print name:____________________________________
Notary public:__________________________________
Seal:____
Date:____

While there is variation in the examples, each serves the purpose of clearly conveying to the applicant the terms and conditions of the waiver as well as providing a method to defend the agency and those who release information against frivolous and unwarranted litigation. In developing a waiver, be sure to include the right to obtain information on the basic elements of the investigation that include criminal records, driving records, educational records, military records, employment records, financial records, and medical records. In addition, the waiver should include the request for the release of Internet records from all Internet service providers (ISPs) the applicant subscribes to as well as telephone and texting records given the examples provided in the text for use as an investigative avenue in these times where electronic evidence may preclude an applicant from consideration for hire. Also have the applicant sign (and if possible have the forms notarized) at least five originals for the file for agencies that require original releases as opposed to photocopies of the original. Use photocopies and faxes in every case they are accepted. Having additional original copies saves contacting the applicant to complete additional ones if originals are needed by the agencies contacted.

Fingerprints

Fingerprints are the most important component of the background investigation package. A classic case involved a convicted sex offender who had lied about his identity to gain a government position. The subsequent fingerprint check led to his identification and conviction for falsifying records and concealing material facts from the pre-employment screeners.[97] Their inclusion is self-evident, and every department has a process in place for collecting impressions, whether ink-rolled or electronically. Agencies will have a minimum number of cards that must be generated that include the Federal Bureau of Investigation (FBI) and National Crime Information Center (NCIC), respective state criminal justice services agencies, local criminal justice agencies, and for the processing agency to keep on file with the personnel records of the applicant. For official use in the employment process, applicants must be fingerprinted and all available records searches conducted. States also have independent records check systems in place through voluntary fingerprinting of applicants that are required to obtain records clearances for employment purposes as well as volunteer positions that are of a sensitive nature. The results confirm the existence or lack of Records of Arrest and Prosecution (RAP) as well as identification as a registered sex offender.[98]

For ink-rolled impressions, the FBI has an online resource for ordering the proper print cards.[99] The FBI also offers online guidance on the proper methods to take legible fingerprints for those agencies or individuals who need assistance.[100] In addition to inked prints, many states and several privately licensed companies have also adopted direct or live scan methods as the primary tool to capture fingerprints for the background investigation process.[101] A wonderful advent of technology, Livescan and Cardscan, in the capture of electronic images provides an effective and efficient point of contact process for capturing fingerprint impressions of the applicant.[102]

Two additional considerations are that the agency should also collect palm prints of the applicant and the use of the Integrated Automated Fingerprint Identification System (IAFIS) to search all existing databases for matches to the applicant. Palm prints are a routinely overlooked investigative tool. For current searches as well as future use if needed by the agency, taking palm prints will involve a minor investment of time that may later reap significant rewards.[103] The second consideration is the use of the IAFIS. Where practicable and appropriate, the system searches a database that includes a plethora of investigative information. The system accesses information on the following:

> Not only fingerprints, but corresponding criminal histories; mug shots; scars and tattoo photos; physical characteristics like height, weight, and hair and eye color; and aliases. The system also includes civil fingerprints, mostly of individuals who have served or are serving in the U.S. military or have been or are employed by the federal government. The fingerprints and criminal history information are submitted voluntarily by state, local, and federal law enforcement agencies.[104]

Active and cold case squads have had great successes in searching latent prints from selected crime scenes wherein thousands of cases have been solved that would have normally languished without resolution had it not been for the advances in technology.[105] An example of system capacity at the state level can be found in Missouri where the system stores and continuously searches over 50,000 latent prints collected from crime scenes.[106] As technology continues to advance, portable biometric scanners are being used in field investigations netting great successes in identifying and apprehending wanted persons.[107] The probability of a match in these types of searches is relatively low; however, given the ease of searching and cost-effectiveness of the process, this step would behoove us to not seize the opportunity to rule out involvement of the applicant in any unsolved crimes that are in the system. At the very least, this can be used as an interview technique in gauging the applicant's verbal, emotional, and physical responses when confronted with the prospect of these types of searches.

Photographs

The background investigation will require the use of photographs of the applicant for identification purposes and addition to the official records. Normal, portrait-type pictures that fill the frame with the applicants face from both the front and side should suffice. No real need exists for specialized or full body/extremity photography unless there is a specific purpose such as to document physical anomalies that include tattoos, piercings, and other oddities or clothing worn if the clothing is relevant to the applicant's candidacy. As of late, tattoos are becoming a useful source of intelligence information as well. An applicant's tattoos may reveal much about their affiliations and possibly criminal activities. Photographs can be obtained by plain view, permission if on private areas of the body, or from a licensed physician completing the physical examination provided the photo only depicts the tattoo and no other private parts of the applicant. These photographs can be shown to intelligence and gang experts as well as the psychological screener to establish applicant associations with street gangs or as an evaluation and interview tool during the psychological evaluation process to explore attitudes, mindset, and behavior patterns.

The applicant's face should be free of obstructions, and they should not be allowed to wear any type of headdress like a hat or scarf of any kind. If the applicant normally wears headdress, then photos should be taken in both modes in order to enhance identification purposes during a neighborhood canvas or other venue where identification will need to be made. Lastly, the background investigator should try to avoid the composition of the photograph as a traditional mug shot. Photos are primarily for employment purposes with the secondary purpose of confirmatory identification. They may potentially be used for temporary identification badges, media postings for hiring, noteworthy acts, or involvement in a critical incident, internal events, and for training, so they should be as flattering as possible. Think in terms of a point between a mug shot and artistic photographic portraiture to use as a frame of reference (FOR). Taking a few extra minutes may be very advantageous for the department and far less embarrassing for the applicant.

Standard 35 mm formats of 3×5 or 4×6 should meet the purposes of the investigation. Digital cameras are the preferred method though as they are reasonable, user friendly, and can provide electronic files that can be integrated into documents, communicated via technology with a great level of ease, and manipulated with simple photography programs if the need arises. Instant photography such as Polaroid formats are also available; however, most agencies have color printers for digital and scanned images which would suffice for this type of identification purpose.

Professional Licensure and Certifications

Trends and shifts in the job market often present opportunities for law enforcement recruiting. No matter how intense the educational and professional preparation may have been, positions in the desired or chosen field may be scarce which forces those in the job market to look to other fields for employment prospects. Worse yet is the person who has spent a significant amount of time and effort in their professional preparation for the "dream job" and later finds that the job is not quite what they thought it would be. Faced with this quandary, they will explore career options and many have found law enforcement to be a good match. If brought into the service, they bring with them many needed skills and knowledge bases that can be very useful to the public safety organization. Seeing the range from Emergency Medical Technicians and paramedics, nurses, engineers, surveyors, architects, teachers, accountants, paralegals, and attorneys just to mention a few, they can all be of value if welcomed into the ranks. Other licenses that are issued must also be collected and investigated (for example, taxi, liquor, private investigations, security, electrical, plumbing, as well as any others the applicant may hold).

Many of the positions mentioned require special professional and academic preparation to gain the roles they have chosen. With that comes the responsibility to obtain certifications and licensure to practice their professions and trades. With licensure, the tradesman, paraprofessional, and professional must pass a series of exams and steps, often apprentice, and annually maintain their skill sets through continuing education studies. Many also require that a high level of integrity be maintained as well. These are also all underpinning characteristics of successful public safety officers.

When applicants develop the interest to enter the public safety field, we must encourage more than question their motivations. Lack of interest or success in their current role does not automatically equate to the lack of potential success in the public safety realm. In addition, they will likely bring specialized knowledge, a renewed motivation, and tacit knowledge bases that can work to advance the field as a whole if developed properly.

When applicants present their Personal History Statement for review, this information should be listed (or should have a location for this information to be listed) in the package. All supporting documentation should be requested of the applicant including a copy of the original certificate or license, educational and continuing professional development records, and documentation of any awards. Censure and disciplinary actions should also be included, for example, the case of a medical doctor who was disciplined for writing prescriptions for drugs in exchange for sex.[108] Inquiries should also be made concerning any investigations that have been conducted where the applicant was the principal or if they had any collateral involvement. The use of these types of records can give some valuable insight into the applicant's characteristics, qualities, and commitment to a profession that can have predictive implications for their desired career in law enforcement.

Firearms Permits and Licenses

Two separate topics that need to be addressed are federal laws and Federal Firearms License (FFL) as well as the implications of firearms concealed carry permits at the local and state levels. Both have an impact on the applicant's candidacy for the position of public safety officer.

At the federal level, the laws are constantly evolving concerning the legal possession and carry requirements for citizens as well as public safety officers. Fundamentally, the *National Firearms Act* (1934) was codified to regulate the manufacture, transfer, registration, and taxation of the production and possession of certain firearms.[109] As an updated codicil of sorts, the *Gun Control Act of 1968* was codified to strengthen the conditions of the *National Firearms Act* (1934) by further regulating the activities of firearms transfers through licensed manufacturers and dealers on interstate commerce.[110] The Brady *Handgun Violence Prevention Act* (1993) was subsequently introduced, requiring a federal background check be conducted of every person purchasing a firearm in the United States as a method to prevent, in part, the possession of firearms by those who were precluded from possession by law.[111] Through records searched in the National Instant Criminal Background Check System (NICS), weapons possession can be immediately approved or denied based upon the results.[112] During the life of this process, hundreds of thousands of firearms applications have been denied due to meeting the threshold criteria for weapons possession in the United States and affected state jurisdictions.[113] Under this system, the background check queries similarity hits for names and descriptive features on criminal history records that would meet the federally prohibitive criteria or state law for denial. The standards for rejection are as follows:

1. Has been convicted in any court of a crime punishable by imprisonment for a term exceeding 1 year
2. Is under indictment for a crime punishable by imprisonment for a term exceeding 1 year
3. Is a fugitive from justice
4. Is an unlawful user of or addicted to any controlled substance
5. Has been adjudicated as a mental defective or committed to a mental institution
6. Illegally or unlawfully in the United States
7. Has been discharged from the Armed Forces under dishonorable conditions
8. Having been a citizen of the United States, has renounced U.S. citizenship

9. Is subject to a court order that restrains the person from harassing, stalking, or threatening an intimate partner or child of such intimate partner
10. Has been convicted in any court of a misdemeanor crime of domestic violence[114]

Federal law also allows for the correction of erroneous information that has led to the denial of a firearm based upon the provisions to conduct records checks prior to possession.[115] Those who intend to engage in the legal manufacture and sales of firearms and ammunition through interstate and intrastate transfers are required to possess an FFL.[116] The *Federal Gun Free School Zone Act of 1995* severely restricts the ability to legally carry a firearm within 1000 ft perimeter of any K-12 school in the United States.[117]

At the local and state levels, concealed carry permits are required for a person to possess and carry certain types of firearms in public. While numerous terms and definitions exist that are unique to each state, the concept is relatively uniform in the requirements for concealed carry.[118] Permit investigations and issuance are usually investigated at both the city and county levels with a county court magistrate who authorizes the final approvals. Regulation throughout a state can be regionalized as is the case between carry permits in New York City in contrast to the requirements in the remainder of New York State.[119] There are a series of emerging cases in the evolution of this issue that the background investigator should familiarize themselves with that impact the entire spectrum of permission to legally carry as well as compliance directives in the states where these privileges are being challenged in the courts.[120]

Interestingly, federal law that effects both intrastate and interstate concealed carry rights is the *Law Enforcement Officers Safety Act* (LEOSA) (2004) that provides a privilege to qualified active and retired law enforcement officers to carry a concealed firearm throughout the United States provided certain requirements of identification and training are met.[121] This is also an emerging body of law, and the background investigator should not only familiarize themselves with the existing decisions on restrictions but also continue to watch this issue evolve to stay abreast of the contemporary standards as they develop in the courts.[122] Of note is the matter of the *Federal Gun Free School Zone Act of 1995* that precludes the protections of the privileges contained in the *Law Enforcement Officers Safety Act* (LEOSA) (2004).[123] The significance of understanding these Acts relates to the applications of lateral transfer officers as well as law enforcement retirees who continue a second full- or part-time role in another agency and possibly another state.

As with any of these paper trail types of investigations, access to the original investigation and copies of original licenses and permits should be sought as part of the pre-employment investigation. The applicant should also be interviewed concerning the number and type of firearms, primary use, and any discrepancies or issues found in the records. Lastly and more a safety note, if the applicant discloses they have access to or possess and are licensed to possess a firearm, when the Personal History Statement is submitted, they should be given a clear and written directive that they are not permitted to carry or possess such weapon during any and all processing requirements with the agency and any of its agents or contractors.

PROFESSIONAL EVALUATIONS

The legal and procedural requirements of the series of professional evaluations have been discussed in Chapter 4. For the purposes of this section, the compiling of these reports and their subsequent addition to the final investigative report and final investigative package are addressed.

With respect to the investigation, they can be used as a resource along with any supporting documentation that is completed by the professional to compare to the information revealed during the background investigation. These types of reports can prove to be a great resource for comparing responses to drug use questions, admissions of unacceptable behaviors, activities, or incidents not revealed in the background investigation, and comparison to discovered behaviors as opposed to behaviors and testing results that lead to the assessment of the applicant's fitness for duty. Infrequently there will be severe disconnects between the results of the background investigation and the results of the psychological screening (e.g., inappropriate and violent acts in the background search and an acceptable psychological assessment). These can be used to bring the discrepancies to the attention of the psychological professional and to reevaluate the original findings. Medical issues may also surface wherein information was not disclosed to the medical professional that may have impacted the examining physician's assessment negatively can also be brought to light in this comparison review process.

With respect to filing, first and foremost, these are stand-alone documents. Because of the legal and ethical need for confidentiality, they must be secured for view only by authorized personnel. They may be maintained with the final investigative package to the point that a decision is made in the hiring process and, based upon that decision, can be archived in compliance with policy and law. If the applicant is hired, then the psychological and medical evaluations must be filed separately from the final investigative package and separately as psychological and medical reports as well in the department's personnel or human resources department or unit. They must be kept confidential and not reviewed unless for a specific legal and legitimate purpose. One method to ensure confidentiality would be to contract with the professional to archive all reports at their facility and destroy the department copies once their use in processing requirements has been fulfilled.

Since these reports will be available to make the hiring decision, stand alone on their merits, and must remain confidential, they should not be mentioned in any form in the final investigative report. Different agencies and their oversight bodies will have myriad requirements for medical examination processing. The psychological examination process is often far more wide ranging and, in many cases, convoluted. Variations in testing models, regimen, and evaluation can lead to starkly different outcomes. In addition, for psychological examination processing, some research suggests a testing iteration as minimal as 6 months apart may produce significant differences in the final evaluative assessment. With these reasons in mind, the medical and psychological evaluations should not be made available to any other agencies that are also processing the applicant for employment. Such a release could unduly influence an applicant's otherwise viable candidacy with another agency.

Another professional report that will be used in the final investigative package may be the polygrapher's final report if used by the agency. (Note: This also includes other truth verification devices such as the computerized voice stress analyzer [CVSA].) These types of reports and supporting documentation that include questionnaires and technological readouts may include protected medical and psychological information. Requesting agencies may also have restrictions on their use of the polygraph which may extend to other agencies that are authorized to use the device. Fundamentally though, the polygraph is used more as an interview tool with the subsequent admission or confession as the ultimate evidence. In these cases, the polygraph findings should not be mentioned in the final investigative report, choosing to only add if the applicant made any incriminating, inculpatory, or exclusionary statements during the process. The polygraph report can then, like medical and psychological examinations, become a stand-alone report where the protections of confidentiality can be ensured.

CONTENT, FORMAT, AND STRUCTURE OF THE FINAL INVESTIGATIVE PACKAGE

The remainder of this chapter addresses the content, format, and structure of the final investigative report and the contents of the entire final investigative package. Based upon a best practices approach, each section and subsection are presented in the most logical categorical representation as well as how each component should be investigated, documented, and supported with independent evidence that is accumulated as part of the investigative process. As this chapter progresses, several components will be treated independently with the relevant investigative techniques, legal issues germane to the topic area presented, and supporting evidence requirements. While such matters as legal requirements (Chapter 3) and medical and psychological topics (Chapter 4) are presented earlier in the text, the components of this chapter build on the previous generic knowledge gained and then specifically apply those concepts as well as any additional information needed to fully complete the investigation. In review of this chapter, variations may exist in how the specific agency chooses to present the final investigative product. Form and structure then defer to content as when all of the listed components are addressed, the organization can choose the manner and order in which they are addressed.

The content of the final investigative report should include all of the relevant facts discovered during the investigative process. Allowance for variation must be considered when blending departmental requirements with the individual techniques, practices, and style of the background investigator. The background investigator must adhere to some very fundamental principles though as they develop the report. Those principles include concentrating on material facts and how those facts relate to the selection and deselection criteria of the agency.

A material fact defined in reference to a statement is "One that is capable of influencing, affects, or has a natural tendency to affect, an official decision even if an agency does not rely upon it."[124] These facts would then lead to the ability to compare them to the deselection or exclusionary criteria for the position. These comparisons then need to be clearly articulated and later defended for their validity. The report then becomes the primary vehicle for this process. Several states have clearly defined what the requirements are for the final investigative report to meet this threshold. For example, in New York State, as a measure of deselection, the final report must include the following:

> The derogatory information that is provided to the municipal; civil service agency from the law enforcement agency must be sufficient to form the basis for disqualification under section 50(4) of the *Civil Service Law* and/or *Municipal Civil Service Rule* on Disqualification.[125]

Material facts of the background investigation run the gamut as these are administrative proceedings where the rules of evidence are not as stringent as those in criminal cases.

That range includes every aspect of the applicant's life that speaks to their fitness to fill the role. As in any investigation, the background investigator should purge themselves of the desire to include assumption, conjecture, anecdote, supposition, and flippant sarcasm as they compose these types of reports. Attempts at casting aspersions and trying to portray levels of facetious intellect usually have an inverse impact. With that, the facts should be reported by the background investigator devoid of any recommendation as to status or viability for employment or rejection.[126] This should be left to the purview of command and those involved in the process who must take responsibility for these types of hiring decisions, that is, the hiring authority.

As previously discussed, the final investigative report should also preclude information related to the medical and psychological examination processes as well as the conditions discussed concerning protected information revealed during a polygraph or CVSA.

A final note on content relates to process integrity. Integrity is everything as has been evidenced in numerous publicized situations where those involved in the pre-employment investigation and review process have compromised their personal ethics.[127] Such actions have led to, at a minimum, embarrassment for the organization and a maximum of criminal convictions for falsifying official records. These actions also stain the nobility of those who serve in the specific agency as well as the discipline as a whole.

Format and structure of the final investigative report will depend on the needs of the organization and the principles involved in their review, use, and defense. Existing, enhanced, or new models need to consider the structure and organization of addressing the key areas considered by the department in selection and deselection. The order of this chapter is one method of laying out the series of components for such a report. The format should take the form of an executive summary. Written in this manner, the summary refers the reader for further information to the attachments in the final investigative package by number designation dividers. For ease of development and arrangement, use a corresponding number system, for example, referring to criminal liability history as *Section 5.1* of the final investigative report and corresponding to criminal liability history as *Attachment 1.* All supportive evidence and documentation would be included in that corresponding attachment. An audit sheet or checklist should also be included for the background investigator to use in reviewing their final work in order to ensure all of the requirements are addressed and all components included.

CRIMINAL LIABILITY HISTORY

Criminal liability history is an issue that is neither uncommon nor unabashed no matter how sacred the environment.[128] Fundamentally, federal and state laws are designed to prevent undue discriminatory practices that are based upon criminal arrests and convictions alone that are not directly related to the job functions to be performed or if the offense can be connected to some unreasonable risk to other persons or property.[129] However, these same laws will exclude those positions in the law enforcement field from the normal regulations.[130] The discovery of crimes committed by the applicant is usually the first disqualifier. This issue composes the most basic and mainly valid defense in the final hiring decision or disqualification of an applicant. As clear as this issue can be, this matter can also be a very elusive one to the background investigator. A heightened awareness to this issue has surfaced since 9/11 but has always loomed over the entire process. From a process perspective, some competing issues come to light though. The specter of legislation passed in many states has placed a significant responsibility on employers who can be held liable for failing to fully explore the criminal propensity of prospective employees.[131] In the hiring process though, this must be balanced against the concomitant requirement that such disclosures of criminal information be related to job performance and have a business necessity to be legally authorized.[132] Add to this set of circumstances that hindsight is always 20/20 and we have a difficult burden to meet when vetting applicants for their published criminal records as well as their predisposition for committing future crimes. We cannot argue against a criminal records check though as this is a fundamental requirement of the background investigation process.[133] Categorically then, we must consider (1) discovered crimes: those crimes and offenses that have been discovered through criminal records checks and disclosed by the applicant or other sources close to the investigation; (2) undiscovered crimes: undiscovered and failure to disclose crimes and offenses that the applicant has committed; and (3) erroneous criminal records: erroneous records that inaccurately depict the applicant's criminal proclivities as nonexistent or existing in the wrong classification or form.

Discovered Crimes

The most straightforward of these categories is those crimes that have been officially recorded and those the applicant discloses during the investigative process. Sadly, there are few days per year that you cannot find some (or several) police officers in various locations in the country who are not implicated in some type of official misconduct or crime. Regardless of rank, these transgressions still continue. One assertion can be made that due to real-time media, we are exposed to more information and thus the reason for the inundation. Arguably though, the same officers who are considering such acts are viewing the same media reports and apparently not deterred! From violent assaults,[134] domestic violence,[135] robberies,[136] drug use, possession, trafficking, and sales,[137] robbing drug dealers,[138] facilitating violent felonies,[139] engaging in sexually explicit conduct with high school children,[140] commercial arsons,[141] multiple murders,[142] and police chiefs stealing pocket change from parking meters,[143] the 5% of our bad employees always seem to make the news. Sadly, the mere thought of any law enforcement officers engaging in these types of activities is unconscionable. Invariably these incidents cast aspersions on the one million plus police officers who serve their communities honorably and faithfully on a daily basis. However, their names are not mentioned when these transgressions occur. The mass media deluge the public with the limited and censored details, and an irrevocable stain is often left that blurs the entire image of the agency and the discipline as a whole. When faced with the sporadic examples around the country, there is no wonder or amazement when the average American citizen questions where all of the honorable cops have gone. The answer is they are all still out there, just not newsworthy enough to hold the same media attention as the bad ones.

During the screening process, federal, state, and local records checks are usually the strongest evidence that will reveal the applicant's failure to conform to the law of the land. Social and personal norms often translate to organizational norms, and when an applicant's behaviors fail to conform to those same social norms, it is extremely doubtful they will conform to the integrity-based organizational and structural norms required of contemporary public safety officers. Pre-employment records checks have run the gamut of applicants who have committed infractions and violations to serious felony crimes. More importantly, applicants have consistently disclosed involvement in criminal activities that may have never been reported to or investigated by the proper authorities. Even if these crimes were reported, the applicant may have never been listed as a person of interest or suspect. Such crimes also fulfill the range of larcenies, burglaries, drug dealing, and nurses and military personnel who were prostitutes in those work environments, again, just to name a few. And these are only the ones discovered through formal records searches, independent investigation, and voluntary disclosures of law enforcement applicants. In the pre-employment investigation process, these types of disclosures and admissions carry the same weight as if they were arrested for the crime. For example, if an applicant admits to committing a felony that was never discovered, reported, nor was the applicant even identified in the incident, the admission suffices as proper evidence to be a lifetime excluder from the process. Many other types of felonies and misdemeanors also fit into this category. For example, if an applicant admits to a felony burglary or sexual assault that may have not been reported and even if the criminal statute of limitations has expired on the original incident, the applicant can be disqualified from the hiring process. While the applicant may enjoy the criminal procedure right of the statute of limitations that may preclude prosecution, they do not enjoy the same rights in the hiring process. Note though that these types of admissions may require a full criminal investigation wherein the applicant would then be afforded those rights. In these types of cases where an admission or disclosure is of an egregious nature, the applicant should be turned directly over to the proper authorities to continue such an investigation.

Undiscovered Crimes

The second category includes those offenses that have not been discovered or disclosed voluntarily by the applicant. This is a much more insidious and elusive category. As difficult a problem that their discovery presents, it is critical that the possibility and existence of unreported or unidentified offenses the applicant has been involved in must be rigorously explored.[144] A reality we must face is that many applicants have committed crimes that they have never been apprehended for.[145] In one particularly gruesome and brutal home invasion that led to a homicide, the fact that the suspects were apprehended was due to their bragging of the crimes committed.[146] Absent their ignorance and bravado, they likely would have escaped detection and been able to apply for any job they desired. An axiomatic presumption is that crime rates far outpace arrest rates in the United States, with estimates of offenders being brought to justice at extremely dismal levels. Consequently, the lack of a criminal record is not the true barometer of an applicant's complicity in criminal activity. These types of offenses include grand larcenies, rapes, child abuse, child pornography, domestic violence, and many, many other serious crime classifications. Specifically, sex crimes are overwhelmingly never reported to police due to numerous reasons that include shame, fear, disbelief by law enforcement, and frustration with the legal system. Illicit drug involvement may also be skewed wherein drug sales are far different than drug use where an applicant may have never used drugs, but was complicit in drug possession and trafficking. Several incidents can be recounted where drug dealers admitted during a polygraph examination that they had dealt drugs through drug houses and open-air drug markets and were never investigated, arrested, nor did they admit to illegal drug use. Lower-level crimes may also not be reported to the police as in the case of employee thefts or in retail theft and shoplifting cases. Shoplifting falls into two primary categories: (1) casual or opportunistic shoplifting and (2) professional shoplifting committed by groups or gangs of thieves.[147] In order to save the embarrassment of reporting high levels of shrinkage, employers and retail outlets often handle these matters in-house with termination or restitution as the remedy. Companies fearing negative publicity will often forgo contacting the police when employees engage in untoward behaviors on site. Consequently, since no official record would exist in any place other than the organization's files, the need for disclosure becomes that much more critical.[148] Previous employers may be forthcoming in this type of incident, but tracking down retail outlets that have chosen to avoid prosecution is quite another matter. Another barrier we face is that historically, crime is significantly underreported, thought to be as high as over 50% going unreported. Discrepancies are always noted between the *National Crime Victimization Survey*[149] and the FBI's *Uniform Crime Report*[150] that are caused by numerous variables including victims failing to report crimes due to the lack of confidence in law enforcement as well as reclassification, and department cultures that refuse to take reports, to agencies that fraudulently lower crime statistics in order to make their communities appear safer.[151]

If that is not enough to frustrate the best-of-the-best background investigators seeking the most accurate information concerning an applicant's criminal history, those who are listed as persons of interest or even as clear suspects in criminal cases may also not be available to a background investigator depending on a department's record searching capability. Those listed as suspects or persons of interest in a criminal investigation, but never arrested, will never have a record or RAP sheet (Record of Arrest and Prosecution). As previously noted, less than half of all crime is reported to the police, and only an insignificant number of those investigations result in an arrest and prosecution. Countless cases where suspects are listed but not enough evidence exists to support a criminal arrest or conviction, or where a department does not move forward because a victim will not prosecute, will likely never come to light. The background investigator is also hamstringed by the inability to check every department where the applicant may have had contact with as well. And if that is still not enough, consider the transient populations we deal with today. Travel to foreign countries for pleasure or even employment that transcends borders where a criminal arrest or significant police contact occurs, military personnel that commit offenses in foreign lands that may be undiscovered or handled internally where no formal record may exist, or simply crossing domestic borders where crimes have been committed and undiscovered. This is an extremely vexing issue as if later revealed, hindsight will again be 20/20 and the armchair, *Monday Morning Quarterbacks*, will be the all-seeing eyes who have retroactively predicted something would happen. People will emerge from the woodwork who will ask how those in the department did not know the info, or the skeptics will wail, "Everyone knew it, why didn't the department know it?" Unfortunately, the courts do not allow this anthropomorphic assignment of blame.

Erroneous Criminal Records

The final category in this area is the existence of erroneous records. These are records that have inaccurate or false entries as well as nonexistent records that should exist to evidence culpability in criminal activity, but are not available due to several reasons.

Inaccuracies can occur for any number of reasons including the lack of complete information, inaccurate information, faulty auditing systems, failure to properly complete records regarding dispositions of cases where no entry is made, improper entries of original arrests and final dispositions, and misleading plea bargains that result in downgrading of far more serious original charges. This is extremely common in driving while intoxicated (DWI) and impaired cases as well as sex offenders who plead to lower-level classifications of sex crimes in order to receive lower-risk classifications on the National Sex Offender Registry (NSOR).[152] Final dispositions in criminal records are also not always kept up to date due to faulty communication systems, lack of proper staffing, and lack of proper oversight.[153] One specific case dealt with an applicant whose record check revealed an arrest for grand larceny from his workplace. The applicant denied being arrested and blamed the incident on his brother. Corporate records searches revealed all of these records had been purged. A follow-up with the applicant revealed the attorney's name who handled the case, and although the criminal records had been purged due to a plea agreement and restitution, the attorney, through a liability and information release form, turned over the fingerprint cards he had archived which allowed for positive identification of the applicant as the felony larcenist as well as his untruthfulness in the process.

A move is also taking place across the country to change legislation where criminal records may be wholly purged due to plea agreements and state laws allowing for removal of many types of offenses after certain term limits.[154] Other states that include Massachusetts, Connecticut, New Mexico, and Minnesota are banning some public and private employers from even asking questions on the initial application concerning any criminal history.[155] Add to this problem, organizations that are relying on private vendors for the culling of criminal records. Countless incidents have been reported where faulty data have led to employment being denied for blatant errors reported in an applicant's record.[156] More importantly, an employer can be held liable for these types of adverse employment decisions even when they are based on information provided by an outside source such as a contractor hired to conduct the records search.[157]

Nonexistent records also add to this problem wherein agencies have failed to make the initial crime information computer entries, cases and records mysteriously disappear for political or nefarious reasons, departments misfile and consequently lose official reports, departments that purge records due to limited storage capacities, or departments that outright refuse to release records.

Erroneous records can produce a quagmire of problems for the background investigator who is making an honest effort at establishing the true nature of the applicant's criminal liability history. Both ends of the spectrum can be experienced in the process, and each has grave repercussions. For example, one woman has been the victim of a similarity hit to a known criminal on numerous occasions while crossing the Canadian border wherein she is consistently stopped and beleaguered for no legitimate reason other than having similar identifying information as a male offender from another state.[158] In the court case of *Socorro v. IMI Data Search, Inc.* (2003), a records check resulted in the erroneous reporting of a criminal record that led to the employee being terminated unjustly.[159] As a collateral issue, some records systems may have protections in place in the way of laws and policies that preclude such records checks to protect the applicant. This is the case for the New York State Police Information Network (NYSPIN) which prohibits records checks for employment purposes due to the probability of similarity hits causing erroneous identifications and subsequent denial of a position.[160] At the opposite end of the spectrum is a municipal employee whose record check during the background investigation revealed no criminal record. A subsequent record check after an arrest for forcible rape, after hired, and while on duty, revealed a criminal record of numerous felony convictions including one for weapons possession.[161] Given the often ambiguous nature of records systems, limited capacity in searching out every possible source available, and an applicant's surreptitious concealment or lack of disclosure in their criminal history, this behavioral anchor must be given the highest priority in the pre-employment screening process. From a macro perspective, these conditions all work against the information flow required of the pre-employment screening process. The standard of *known or should have known* creates an extremely heavy burden on the organization's final placing of the seal of approval to hire the applicant.

One additional caveat relates to the ability of the applicant to handle sensitive and confidential information if they join the ranks of the law enforcement agency. The applicant's integrity must be measured against any ties to the criminal element as later discussed in the intelligence gathering section. For the purposes of this section though, being employed in confidential positions that include public safety, law enforcement, and in the other criminal justice professions, the applicant must be trusted with information that cannot be divulged to the general public, let alone the targets of criminal investigations. Law enforcement officers have been investigated and charged for divulging intelligence and confidential information to known criminals for various reasons including bribery.[162] History all too often repeats itself, and these types of ties prior to hire will likely continue after hire creating opportunities for these types of situations to arise and flourish.

In order to fully prepare for such events that are fraught with both barriers and ambiguity, the organization must employ two salvos: (1) strong policy and (2) selection of unrelenting and tenacious background investigators. Strong policy can be formed from legal precedents that are augmented by organizational precedents. For example, state laws will have minimum standards that automatically preclude applicants if they have committed certain types of offenses. A general hiring clause included in the *New York Correction Law* provides some guidance on how certain mitigating factors of previous offenses should impact policy statements:

1. In making a determination pursuant to Section 752 of this chapter, the public agency or private employer shall consider the following factors:
   a. The public policy of this state, as expressed in this Act, to encourage the licensure and employment of persons previously convicted of one or more criminal offenses
   b. The specific duties and responsibilities necessarily related to the license or employment sought or held by the person
   c. The bearing, if any, the criminal offense or offenses for which the person was previously convicted will have on his fitness or ability to perform one or more such duties or responsibilities
   d. The time which has elapsed since the occurrence of the criminal offense or offenses
   e. The age of the person at the time of occurrence of the criminal offense or offenses
   f. The seriousness of the offense or offenses
   g. Any information produced by the person, or produced on his behalf, in regard to his rehabilitation and good conduct
   h. The legitimate interest of the public agency or private employer in protecting property, and the safety and welfare of specific individuals or the general public

2. In making a determination pursuant to Section 752 of this chapter, the public agency or private employer shall also give consideration to a certificate of relief from disabilities or a certificate of good conduct issued to the applicant, which certificate shall create a presumption of rehabilitation in regard to the offense or offenses specified therein.[163]

In the decision of *Soto v. New York State Office of Mental Retardation and Developmental Disabilities* (2010), the court cited the need to use all eight factors listed earlier as a means to establish an applicant's eligibility for a position was obligatory under the statute.[164] The aforementioned codicil to New York State law also provides a caveat of not applying to law enforcement positions; however, many lower-level offenses that are of consideration in the background investigation and not an automatic excluder such as the commission of a felony will likely need to endure an analysis of this nature in order to survive any legal scrutiny. Based upon this, departments can and should have stricter standards as long as they can show a bona fide occupational qualification to exclude the applicant that is germane to the offense committed and consistent with the concept of business necessity. Strong and well-articulated policies enhance the department's ability to effectively explore an applicant's criminal history and disqualify those who do not meet the required standards. Policy failures, however, have led to the hiring of felons prior to a complete criminal records search.[165] Policy is the first step to avoid these types of situations occurring in the organization.

State laws are also supported by case laws. For example, in the decision of *Douglas El. v. Southeastern Pennsylvania Transportation Authority* (SEPTA) (2007), the court found that an employer's unilateral exclusion of applicants who have prior convictions for violent crimes is legal and justified under the concept of business necessity.[166] The court rejected the claim that the hiring policy "unnecessarily disqualifies applicants because of prior criminal convictions - a policy that he argues has a disparate impact on minority applicants because they are more likely than white applicants to have convictions on their records."[167] In *Silvera v. Orange County School Board* (2001), the firing of an employee who was convicted of child molestation and who also had multiple arrests for violent felony assaults was upheld.[168] The key was the matter of the series of assault arrests; while they did not result in convictions, they demonstrated the plaintiff's propensity toward violence.[169] Cases related to the criminal justice and public safety professions are also consistent with these legal opinions. In *Commonwealth of Pennsylvania Department of Corrections v. Krempowsky* (1997), for the position of Corrections Officer, the applicant's disqualification was based upon an expunged criminal record of resisting arrest as the conduct indicated "a disregard for authority and for rules, an inability or lack of inclination to comply with orders, a lack of self-discipline, and poor judgment."[170] In the decision of *United States v. Baer* (2003), a court ruled that due to the need for certain police officers to have security clearances, the hiring agency was allowed to ask questions concerning relevant misdemeanor and felony convictions.[171] These types of statutory and case laws are combined to support policy decisions and language.

A barrage of legislation has also been introduced over the past few decades in order to strengthen the accessibility and veracity of records checks for criminal justice and noncriminal justice purposes that are enhancing the ability to obtain accurate and timely information. For example, the *National Crime Prevention and Privacy Compact of 1998*[172] and *Crime Identification Technology Act of 1998*[173] both provide for numerous policies and upgrades on a national level for the sharing of these types of information.[174] Systems that provide a plethora of information include the Criminal History Record Information (CHRI) or Criminal History Record Information System, the Interstate Identification Index (III), the FBI's NCIC, the Master Name Index, the NCIC Protection Order File, the NICS, the NCIC, the National Fingerprint File (NFF), Positive Identification, Rap Back, the Statistical Analysis Center (SAC), the Juvenile Justice Record, and the NSOR.[175] Existing legislative acts have been modified to accomplish these same types of objectives in targeted areas of screening that include the *National Child Abuse Protection Act of 1993*[176] that was modified by the *Volunteers for Children Act of 1998*: Public Law 105-251[177] in order to strengthen the use of records checks for those who have direct contact with children. The standard of known or should have known applies as if a volunteer or employee has been convicted of a relevant crime, and is subsequently hired by the agency, and then sexually molests a child, the agency can be held liable for negligent hiring. This Act also requires the organization of electronic information sharing of criminal history records for noncriminal justice purposes, specifically authorizing the use of these records in background checks for employment.[178] The law also defines the term *Criminal History Records* as "Information collected by criminal justice agencies on individuals consisting of identifiable descriptions and notations of arrests, detentions, indictments, or other formal criminal charges, and any disposition arising therefrom, including acquittal, sentencing, correctional supervision, or release."[179] These systems also use common language to define various relevant terms including *felony* or *serious misdemeanor* which "Is defined to exclude certain minor offenses, such as drunkenness or minor traffic offenses."[180] The National Incident-Based Reporting System also continues to grow and may be of future use in this process.[181] Significant progress in information sharing has been born in the wake of tragedy. Individual states also have open records policies that can be accessed by request in conducting the background investigation.[182] As an aside, some systems do not allow criminal history records information checks due to concerns over similarity hits and inappropriate denial of employment based upon false-positive results.[183] When conducting these types of computer searches, be aware of the guiding regulations in the affected state.

All of these are components that must be considered when codifying an organizational policy on the use of the criminal records histories of public safety applicants. Local, state, national, and quite possibly, international records checks will need to be further solidified in the organization's policy mandates for pre-employment screening. Once the most accurate information possible is captured, then the treatment of this information also needs to be a part of the same policy that mandates the culling of the information. All information that is developed that is either positive or negative should be verified if possible, even if the verification comes from a candidate's disclosure and/or an independent source. While not always possible, the efforts must be made and documented so that good faith can be shown in the accurate foundation of the information and the absence of any malice in its subsequent use. Not only should the information be verified if at all possible, but also the organization should not "publish" the results in communications in any manner to anyone other than those who have the decision-making authority for hiring or the candidate and their legal representatives (note: see the discussion under *Issue of Defamation in Employee References: The Concept of Publication* later in this chapter).[184] Lastly, policy should include compliance with any and all state laws of notification to the applicant for rejection based upon the existence of a criminal record. For example, many states require the applicant be officially notified of the reason for rejection. Some states also make this an affirmative requirement of the applicant to request this information. One example is included in the *New York State Correction Law* wherein the law requires both public agencies and private employers to "Provide, within thirty days of a request, a written statement setting forth the reasons for such denial."[185]

Crime classifications and definitions will vary from state to state. So too will be the consequences. The processing state must decide if the standards adhered to will be their own state standards or use of the published standards of the state of occurrence. This can result in both upgrading or downgrading, and the agency must have a policy in place that demonstrates consistency of purpose and application of the standards used. The final investigative package should always include copies of the relevant sections of law or codes from where and when the offense was committed as well as any comparative state level laws where the applicant is being processed if the locations are different. Crimes defined by jurisdiction committed in as well as the jurisdiction where application is made can also be significantly impacted by events that occur in foreign lands. We are a diverse and growing population in the United States. Consequently, we have people who frequently travel, people who are naturalized citizens with ties to their homelands, and first and second generation Americans who visit their foreign relatives. This transitory lifestyle may result in police contacts and arrests while vacationing or conducting business abroad. Every effort must be made to determine if the applicant has these types of travel patterns and if any conduct they have committed can be considered for disqualification purposes. If these incidents are uncovered, an assessment must be made of the type of crime or offense in comparison to the laws of the United States and of the processing agency's state laws. For example, sex with minors in some Asian countries is tolerated while mere kissing in public in Dubai is a crime punishable by a prison sentence and fine.[186] In countries like Afghanistan, the crime of rape is minimized, tolerated, and often condoned.[187] In these situations, the offenses must be placed in the context of their domestic implications. In these countries, civilian national's cases have been discovered where child victims have been discouraged from reporting crimes and threatened with arrest themselves.[188]

In addition, military personnel also fall into this category wherein a comprehensive exploration of their service overseas should be reviewed in depth, along with comparisons of any transgressions to the laws of the foreign land of occurrence, as well as the domestic and military law implications. For example, having consensual sexual intercourse with a female who is under 16 years of age is the offense of carnal knowledge in the military, while most states consider the minimum age for nonconsensual intercourse under 18 years of age and classify the offense as rape or statutory rape.[189] Allegations of misconduct and criminal conduct abound concerning the actions of a small number of personnel who serve in foreign countries.[190] This is not intended as an indictment on the nobility and integrity of all who faithfully serve, but this issue must be fully explored when those from the military are applying for domestic law enforcement positions. This is not an effort to minimize their contributions to providing the defenses to our country, rather the overarching need for properly matching applicants to the role of law enforcement officer.

The aforementioned information deals predominantly with criminal records checks. Information developed from formal records checks should be verified, if possible, by obtaining the physical records as well as any additional documentation that exists in the form of criminal investigation reports, witness statements, and victim statements. Departments with advanced computer systems can also reveal all police contacts with the applicant.

From a crime perspective, the crime investigation report should be collected, if possible, when the applicant is listed anywhere, including those cases where they may be categorized as suspect, person of interest, or even as a witness. The content of these reports may prove to be very revealing and while no criminal charges may have been pursued, may indicate conduct that would preclude the applicant from acceptance as a candidate.

Just a few words on behaviors and conduct. Conduct in and of itself is generally not protected. Violent or aberrant behavior wherein an applicant is arrested for assault or criminal mischief that may demonstrate incapacitated mental behavior is generally not protected. All states have laws in place that allow for the arrest and detention of persons who, through temporary or permanent incapacitation, may be a danger to themselves or others.[191] Information of an applicant who was arrested under a mental hygiene law would likely be information with limited protections that should be conveyed to the psychological contractor and not included in the package as a mental hygiene arrest per se. The behaviors may be documented excluding the mental hygiene issues though. An applicant who is arrested for a crime and claims mental incapacity would likely not have a right to have this information excluded for consideration depending on the results of the trial. The behaviors though can be documented even if the outcome of the criminal case is favorable to the applicant.

The prospective employer must consider the direct relationship of the criminal activity as well as the frequency, nature, egregiousness, and distance in time from the commission of the crime or offense. The *direct relationship* of an offense can be generally defined as follows:

> The nature of criminal conduct for which the person was convicted has a direct bearing on his fitness or ability to perform one or more of the duties or responsibilities necessarily related to the license, opportunity, or job in question.[192]

According to the U.S. Equal Employment Opportunity Commission (EEOC), to establish a policy of employment rejection based upon business necessity that can exclude an applicant due to involvement in criminal activity, the organization must not unfairly discriminate against protected classes of individuals in the process. To accomplish this, the organization must consider these factors:

1. The nature and gravity of the offense or offenses
2. The time lapse that has passed since the conviction and/or completion of the sentence
3. The nature of the job held or sought[193]

Citing the ruling of *Green v. Missouri Pacific Railroad Company* (1975), in certain circumstances, a criminal record may not be used as an absolute factor in exclusion of an applicant; however, prior criminal record can be a factor that is considered in the hiring process when the prospective employer weighs the aforementioned factors. Law enforcement and public safety positions are unique in that these roles require higher job-related standards than most other positions in the country.[194] However, these factors should be considered when developing standards for policy and procedural development in the exclusion of applicants to the criminal justice professions.

Policies should support decertifying candidates when the criteria meet the delineated thresholds. For example, one department's standards strictly include that the applicant will have "No criminal record."[195] Policy must also have flexibility when dealing with the various types of events that may have some ambiguity attached as well. Fairness and equity in application must reign supreme. We are a nation of laws. Laws that are intended to bring order to chaos and mayhem. The principles of Social Control Theory are deeply rooted in our response as a nation to what behaviors can and will be tolerated.[196] For the employment screening process, ultratolerance cannot be abided.

Some basic precepts for the background investigation into the applicant's involvement in criminal activities must include the following steps of records and information searches:

1. Contact all agencies that may have had contact with the candidate, mailing releases to every police agency in jurisdictions where the candidate has lived and worked.
2. Establish if candidate was arrested, convicted, a traffic violator, a suspect, witness, victim, or even stopped as a suspicious person in any incident.

Intelligence Information Gathering and Sharing

A very powerful tool that can be used in the pre-employment screening process is that of cultivating criminal intelligence and analysis information. Linking applicants to times, places, vehicles, groups, and individual persons can be a very helpful method of screening for activities and behaviors. Field stops that tie an applicant to criminal associates, suspicious and wanted vehicles, and problem locations that include drug houses and bars can be of immense value when examining an applicant's behavioral and travel patterns as well as identifying their known associates. These types of investigations are consistently used to link serving police officers to inappropriate and illegal associations with known criminals such as active drug dealers.[197]

For intelligence and analysis to be useful, they must first be defined in the context of their intended use. Intelligence can be generally defined as "Raw information that is analyzed to provide a synthesis of knowledge about a specific person, group, or incident."[198] The combination of temporal and spatial information is combined with sociodemographic information to predict patterns and draw informed opinions on the propensity for future crime as well as possible identifications of offenders. Tracking crime information and analyzing trends to minor crimes has also led to identification models that predict precursors for major crime involvement.[199] However, specific definition of the term intelligence is required to provide significance, value, and relevance to the purpose the information will serve to clarify.[200] For example, general crime analysis is different than specialized crime analysis such as in sex crimes or terrorism. Each will have a specific purpose and mission to achieve. Intelligence is drawn from varied sources including "Informant information, surveillance, travel records, CCTV videotapes, banking transactions, undercover work, pen registers, document evidence, forensic evidence, 'dumpster diving,' wiretaps, and trap and trace methods."[201] Intelligence and analysis are also further defined into the categorical purposes of each. For example, intelligence amasses information on offenders and subversive groups while analysis places this information into an environmental context.[202] Intelligence and analysis are concepts dependent upon each other as they share a symbiotic relationship wherein one cannot advance or grow without the other. Beyond mission and purpose, the orientation of crime analysis can be categorized into three major areas and functions: tactical, operational, and strategic.[203]

As a knowledge management tool, crime analysis can assist in the efficient retrieval of valuable information.[204] From the availability of information and the retrieval process, the potential for identifying possible suspects in reported offenses is increased.[205] As used in crime detection, crime analysis works to further a decision-making ideology for several areas that include offender targeting, resource deployment, and concentration of efforts to increase efficiency.[206] Information culled from these types of systems advances the missions of problem-oriented and intelligence-led policing models.[207] Make no mistake; there is an immense value and importance to the sharing of crime and intelligence data in a structured and real-time manner.[208]

There are numerous resources and organizations that can be tapped for this purpose. Beginning within the processing agency's information network, information can be developed based upon the comprehensiveness of the agency's network. Regional crime analysis and fusion centers are also showing promise in crime and intelligence information sharing.[209] Specific information sharing task forces have also been formed to combat various serious offenses including sex crimes wherein a multijurisdictional response is needed to effectively and efficiently identify and track sex offenders.[210] Computerized pawn records may also be of help in identifying applicants who have pawned inordinate amounts of property.[211] For example, the FBI's Law Enforcement National Data Exchange (N-Dex) "Supports multi-jurisdictional task forces - enhancing national information sharing, links between regional and state systems, and virtual regional information sharing."[212] The FBI's National Center for Analysis of Violent Crime (NCAVC) and Violent Criminal Apprehension Program (VICAP) can also be a source for the process.[213] Federal assistance in regards to the onslaught of terrorism is provided to state and local fusion centers and also available for use in the process.[214] Regional Information Sharing Systems (RISS) are supported by the federal government to enable the sharing of criminal intelligence and investigative information throughout disparate agencies. The following is only a partial list of agencies that can be tapped for intelligence and analysis information concerning applicants:

1. Bureau of Alcohol, Tobacco, and Firearms
2. Central Intelligence Agency
3. Drug Enforcement Administration
4. Federal Bureau of Prisons
5. National Auto Theft Bureau
6. NCIC
7. State Motor Vehicle Departments
8. State Police Departments
9. U.S. Postal Inspection Service
10. U.S. Customs Service/U.S. Immigration (ICE)
11. U.S. Department of Justice
12. U.S. Marshals Service
13. U.S. Secret Service

Open-Source Intelligence (OSINT) is also an emerging area to mine information from.[215] These types of sources can reveal information on the applicant from simple searches of the electronic media, web-based networking communities, social networking sites, video sharing sites, blogs, and varied public data sources. Despite the value of knowledge sharing through collaboration, there are still significant challenges that must be overcome. Those obstacles include current and emerging legal issues, the protection of confidential information, advancing technological needs, and territorial or turf wars.[216] Files must be consistently monitored to prevent abuses in order to continue to focus on the value of information as being accurate and relevant to the needs of the organization.[217] Civil liberties and politics also have an adverse effect on the process. For example, in spite of the value of street stop information being used for crime analysis and the solving of hundreds of cases in New York City, a state law was passed that abolishes the retention and use of street stop interview reports.[218] All things being equal, intelligence and analysis can be a rich source of information in the pre-employment screening process. Since this type of information can be used in the application process for law enforcement, background investigators should make every effort to collect and utilize the information for the purpose of making informed decisions on the applicant's character and fitness for the position.

Domestic Violence and Child Abuse

Domestic violence is referred to in many ways: interpersonal violence, domestic abuse, and Intimate Partner Violence (IPV). IPV is defined as involving an "Allegation of intentional physical violence committed, attempted, or threatened between spouses, ex-spouses, common-law spouses, boyfriends or girlfriends, present or past."[219] Domestic violence is only one issue presented in the family violence realm which also includes parent abuse, child abuse, child sexual abuse, elder abuse, sibling violence, and domestic violence by police officers.[220] Approximately one million violent crimes are committed each year in the United States in this category of offense.[221] Included in this crime category are violent offenses committed against women that include murder, rape, sexual assault, and aggravated assault, accounting for 21% of all violent crime committed against women.[222] Research has revealed that on average only 60% of family violence incidents are ever reported to the police.[223] The occurrence of domestic violence has been accepted as being a common cause of long-term psychological and physical injury to women.[224] Violence against women has reached pandemic levels in most known societies where the issue has been studied.[225] For example, studies in the United Kingdom rate domestic violence as being as high as 25% of all reported crime.[226] Domestic violence is not gender driven with research indicating that women in heterosexual relationships may demonstrate equitable levels of violence toward their spouse or significant other as do male offenders.[227] Another study revealed that 46% of these types of cases involved a defendant with a prior history of abuse toward the same victim and approximately 25% of all cases also involved the use of some type of weapon.[228] Only 20% of reported cases of abuse result in an arrest.[229] In addition, an overwhelming majority of offenders engage in violent acts and behavior with multiple targets.[230] Alcohol and drug use and abuse seem to contribute greatly to the precipitation of these types of incidents. Cultural issues also have an impact where domestic violence is accepted in some cultures. Several theories of domestic violence, which include (1) psychological theory (violence emanates from some past or current psychological issue or trauma), (2) sociological theory (violence is inherent in all social systems or is a learned behavior), (3) feminist or societal-structural theory (violence is used to dominate or control female partners), and (4) the violent individuals theory (that the propensity for violence and criminal behavior transcends domestic violence as opposed to being an individual category or driver of the behavior), all should be known theories to the background investigator as they explore an applicant's history.[231] Physical abuse is not the only factor involved wherein victims also suffer from harassment, threats of violence, and stalking. In addition, police and corrections officers have been arrested and convicted of menacing and reckless endangerments, violent assaults, kidnapping, rape, and murdering their spouses, family members, and significant others.[232] Specific to policing, psychological testing in this area has not led to definitive methods of predictability.[233] Domestic violence attacks know no boundaries, occurring in public and private places, at work, and at home.[234] Domestic violence also crosses all social, ethnic, cultural, and class boundaries.[235]

Domestic violence is consequently a serious crime that must be treated as such by law enforcement, prosecutors, and the courts.[236] Police responses over time have been mixed with conciliation and mediation leading to the need for pro-arrest and mandatory arrest policies to ameliorate the problem. Federal legislation in response to this problem led to the *Violence Against Women Act of 1994* (VAWA) being ratified.[237] Numerous states have mirrored the federal response in enacting legislation to use state laws to enforce domestic violence sanctions. Police departments have also followed along by developing numerous successful domestic violence problem-oriented policing programs to address these issues in their respective jurisdictions.[238] As an ancillary crime to domestic violence, stalking has also been recognized as a serious issue requiring the attention of police enforcement. With the first state level stalking law enacted in 1990, every remaining state has followed the example in an effort to address the issues that stalking involves.[239] Each year, there are approximately 1.5 million female and male victims of stalking incidents.[240] While the obvious concerns of assaults and violations of orders of protection should be considered, other harassing behaviors that include repeated phone calls, unwelcome contacts through e-mails and cards, following the person, waiting in or around the vicinity of their residence or place of employment would all be considered stalking-type behaviors.

Child abuse is another difficult problem facing society. There also seems to be no age limit that an adult will have to abuse children, from infants to teenagers; the abuse issues seem to defy all senses of norm.[241] Child abuse can take many forms from excessive corporal punishment to homicide. Shaken baby syndrome/abusive head trauma is still a prevalent issue in American society that is being argued by both legal and medical experts.[242] Some research suggests that the effects of child abuse can last a person's entire lifetime.[243] Children are often involved as either victims or witnesses to much of the domestic abuse that occurs.[244] Child abuse often results in a pathology of violence toward other children, pets, and other types of animals, and is accentuated later in life when the abused becomes the abuser. Research also indicates notable increases in child-to-parent abuse cases predominantly with male children abusing their mothers.[245] Similar to the problems facing victims of domestic violence, the government has stepped forward to develop legislation that works to protect children caught in these untenable situations. The *National Child Abuse Protection Act of 1993* provides for the reporting of incidents of child abuse to centralized state agencies and entry into the national criminal history system.[246] Child abuse can be classified in four categories: (1) physical abuse, (2) neglect, (3) sexual abuse, and (4) emotional maltreatment.[247] The presence and potential for both domestic violence and child abuse issues must be examined when conducting the background investigation.

During the background investigation, the background investigator must be willing to explore these issues with a high degree of tact and sensitivity that is balanced against determining the truth. While these are pervasive issues, they are also bottlenecked in the discovery process due to the lack of reporting for numerous reasons. This makes the job of the background investigator all the more difficult, relying on observations, overt behaviors, and witness statements in lieu of hard documentation of official investigations.[248] Domestic violence is also not limited to male vs. female abuse. Cases are found in female vs. male and in same-sex couples, so the background investigator should not stereotype in lieu of conducting the proper and thorough investigation. Violence occurring in same-sex relationships is also of serious concern for the background investigator to explore if warranted.[249] Research has revealed that nearly half of the domestic violence cases studied involved a witness so seeking out a third party may be a viable alternative to proving or disproving these types of allegations.[250] Also, the background investigator must consider if the applicant is an abuser or has been abused either as a spouse or significant other or as a child growing up. Exploring how the applicant was raised and the tenor of their parents may be very enlightening when delving deeper into the conduct or behaviors of the applicant. Interviews of the spouse or significant other should be augmented by interviews with relatives, friends, neighbors, and those who have known the applicant personally throughout their lives. In addition, viewing the home environment first hand and interviewing any children of the applicant is well-advised. In interviewing the children, indicators may be noted on how they are treated by the applicant. Research has revealed that child abuse can be manifested in the behaviors of chronically violent children of the offenders and is a sign to look for when conducting the background investigation follow-up into the family life.[251] Records checks of immediate family and children may either demonstrate the lack of problems or give cause to investigate further.

Traditional investigative techniques may also prove fruitful as checking with social services and child protective units directly as well as state registries can garner the needed information to make a determination of the existence of any allegations of abuse. This search should include past as well as open investigations to be thorough. Searches of civil and criminal restraining orders and orders of protection through the NCIC's National Protection Order File may reveal the information needed to make an informed decision.[252] These steps coupled with criminal records check form the foundation to make a case concerning any failure to comply with the terms of the *Domestic Violence Offender Gun Ban* and *Lautenberg Amendment* (1997) which prohibits the possession of firearms by persons who have been convicted of domestic violence misdemeanors.[253] This law is a primary consideration given the incidence of domestic violence incidents involving serving police officers who have used their service weapons to threaten their domestic partners.[254] One dichotomy noted in the amendment is that with the public interest exception in place, which applies to police and military personnel, felonies are excluded from the Act allowing for weapons possession by only these groups.[255]

Lastly, even though all states have adopted a no-fault divorce decree process, examining the documentation of any divorce proceeding may reveal this type of information.[256] While the decree must be viewed with a discerning eye, issues for instance that allege abandonment and adultery should not have a substantive effect on the hiring decision; however, allegations of abuse and violence to any family member as well as the failure to pay child support may have a significant impact on the hiring decision. If this is the case, much investigative work needs to be invested, and legal counsel review sought before an adverse decision is made. This is done to protect all of the parties involved and to give a fair and equitable review for the applicant to prevent undue prejudice in the process.

Sex Crimes

The growth in sex crimes across the country is particularly disturbing. A study in 2001 revealed that both California and Texas had the largest populations of registered sex offenders with a cumulative total of over 110,000 offenders.[257] The level of brutality in many cases defies any sense of logic.[258] Added to this is the fact that the majority of sex crimes go unreported and the issue of pre-employment screening for these types of aberrations becomes far more complex and elusive than other salient issues such as discovering previous illicit drug use. Even when discovered or reported, the criminal justice system's response is often dubious. The levels of evidence required for convictions are a burden infrequently met requiring plea bargains that favor the defendants far more than the victims of these atrocious crimes of personal and physical violation. In repeat victimization analyses, 46% of the sexual assault victims studied had reported being victimized multiple times by a sexual assailant.[259] Some additional research that the background investigator should be aware of is that one study revealed a causal linkage was found between habitual unrelated criminal behaviors and that of sex offenders.[260]

Interestingly, in the severest of cases where the prosecutorial framework has failed, civil commitments of offenders have proven effective. The civil commitment of sex offenders and sexual predators has to date withstood the scrutiny of the U.S. Supreme Court, albeit in a civil rather than criminal or punitive setting.[261] From a pre-employment screening perspective, plea bargains in efforts to gain some type of criminal record for an offender often result in the minimizing of the seriousness of the original offenses and possibly exclusion from a Sex Offender Registry based upon the crime plead to or the terms of the plea deal itself. While sex offenders take pleas that reduce their level on the Sex Offender Registry, some conflicting research suggests that pleas did not increase due to the level a person would be assigned on the registry.[262] Courts are also holding the line in these cases in many parts of the country refusing to allow offenders to divest themselves of the identification as a sex offender.[263] The fact remains that pleas still occur and lower-risk classifications are enjoyed by sex offenders.[264] For example, one analysis of a group of sex offender dispositions in New York State revealed that over 80% of the defendants accepted pleas to lesser offenses; 37% of that group pleaded to non-sex-related offenses precluding their entry into the Sex Offender Registry.[265] With many state legislatures taking a liberal stance on records purging, serious offenses may slip away from detection when the only avenue of discovery may be voluntary applicant disclosure absent the evidentiary documents and court records to corroborate that these offenses even occurred in the first place. The most fundamental issue though is that sex offenses committed by criminal justice professionals are analogous to the *Black Death* or *Bubonic Plague* on the profession as a whole. Research suggests that a history of sexual deviance is an accurate predictor of the probability for future sex offenses.[266] Consequently, this is an area that must be subjected to the closest of scrutiny in the histories of the applicants for these types of positions. The next section is divided into four substantive areas of exploration and discussion: (1) adult-to-adult sex offenses, (2) adult-to-juvenile sex offenses, (3) juvenile sex offenders, and (4) criminal justice professionals involved in sex offenses.

Adult-to-Adult Sex Offenses

From a pre-employment screening perspective, those who are arrested and have a discoverable record can be easily excluded from the process based upon the nature of this type of crime. Mitigating circumstances may exist in some cases where there was a consensual relationship such as in the case of teenagers within certain age parameters. Adultery may also be a mitigating circumstance as this is still against the law in some states.[267] These are black letter law cases that are open to interpretation though, and justification based upon business necessity may prove to be an impossible standard to develop.

Cases that are not open to interpretation are those that may not have been reported, discovered, or definitively linked to an applicant in a manner that can be available to the background investigator. Sexual predators often have sophisticated methods to lure multiple victims wherein shame may keep them from reporting the crimes.[268] Unreported rapes, sodomies, and deviant behaviors may require the background investigator to probe more deeply with friends, acquaintances, and previous relationships in order to determine if this type of behavior has been demonstrated by the applicant. Prostitution and the sex trade industry also fall into this category. Reports of strip club dancers engaging in prostitution and drug trade activities, prostitutes who join the military and sell their wares until detected and then get pregnant and are medically discharged to avoid criminal charges, nurses who have sold sexual favors to patients, and the like are just some of the aberrations that can be revealed. Prostitutes are also using the anonymity of the Internet to solicit clients for money as well as other payments of value including narcotics trades for sex.[269] Some indicators may be rather innocuous in nature but have much deeper motivations. Low-level sexually harassing behaviors in the workplace may be an indicator for a much more comprehensive investigation into this aspect of the applicant's character. Personal comments, unwelcome or sexual contacts, e-mails, "sexting," and sexually suggestive acts will all be indicators of the applicant's proclivities for this type of unacceptable and offensive behavior.[270] They must not be ignored in the investigative process.

Beyond the workplace, dating relationships and patterns should also be investigated. Interviewing previous individuals who have had an amorous or sexual relationship should be a priority for the background investigator in order to determine if any of these untoward characteristics exist. The entire problem of date rape should be a consideration for the background investigator to pursue when vetting the applicant. As an outpouring of the *Drug-Induced Rape Prevention and Punishment Act of 1996*, the federal government intervened in order to pass stiff penalties for the crime of drug precipitated date rape.[271] Date rape has become pervasive enough to be considered a social concern rather than one of an isolated nature.[272] Date rape drugs are frequently used by sexual predators to facilitate involuntary sexual contact.[273] The numerous drugs used in date rape scenarios include gamma-hydroxybutyrate (GHB), Rohypnol (flunitrazepam), ketamine, Soma (carisoprodol), Xyrem, lorazepam, Ativan, Klonopin, Librium, Valium, Xanax, Ambien, chloral hydrate, Flexeril, and Transderm Scop.[274] Arrests and intelligence information that reveal possession of these types of drugs as well as methylenedioxymethamphetamine (MDMA) or Ecstasy may not be simple possession cases but rather have a more sinister meaning and interpretation than just personal use. Alcohol is also a factor to consider in date rape cases where the intoxicant may be entirely legal and the same outcome is realized in having a targeted victim drink to excess, losing the capacity to make proper decisions and ultimately be raped, subjected to aggravated sexual abuse, sodomy, or even gang rape.[275]

Adult-to-Juvenile Sex Offenses

Pedophilia has taken a drastic and exponential rise in the global arena. For example, child sex abuse in foreign lands like several Asian countries is a common occurrence.[276] In the

United States, there exist a plethora of federal laws and federal acts that have been designed for the protection of our innocent children. They include on the federal level the following: *Adam Walsh Child Protection and Safety Act* (2006), *Jacob Wetterling Crimes against Children and Sexually Violent Offender Registration Act* (1994), *Megan's Law (the State's Sex Offenders Registry System), Pam Lychner Sexual Offender Tracking and Identification Act of 1996*, and *Violent Crime Control and Law Enforcement Act of 1994*.[277] The U.S. Department of Justice has been charged with the investigation of these crimes on a national level through the Criminal Division's Child Exploitation and Obscenity Section (CEOS).[278] Project Safe Child is also a national initiative to investigate and prevent exploitation of children through the use of the Internet.[279] As both federal- and state-level mandate, designated professionals are also required to report these types of offenses so that they may be properly investigated and adjudicated.[280] The National Sex Offender Registry System augments federal, state, and local efforts to combat this most vicious crime that has become so prolific in our current society.

Yet, in spite of the national response, concerted efforts, and substantial commitment of resources, the problem seems to continue to plague our children. The levels of depravity that continue to shock the conscience of American society never seem to reach a limit. Intrafamily sexual abuse wherein parents sexually assault their own infant children, abduction-unlawful imprisonment and rapes, sexual abuse and molestation, and murder of children are all acts we are consistently exposed to in the print and electronic media.[281] Forced sex acts with children seem as sickening as they are endless in examples found almost daily in the national news.[282] If these episodic or singular acts are not enough to raise concern, then the research into incarcerated sex offenders who submitted to a polygraph examinations should be. The research revealed that there was an exponential difference between the number of victims of crimes they were convicted of and the number of admissions to unreported sex crimes to multiple victims; an approximate 2700% difference in the number of victims that they were convicted of and the number of victims they sexually violated prior to incarceration.[283] Other investigations have revealed similar results.[284]

"Voluntary" (in reality, coerced due to the lack of ability to consent based upon age) sexual relationships are also a quite devious and widespread problem.[285] One horrendous case involved the gang rape of an 11 year old girl wherein the 18 adult and teenage suspects tried to justify their actions by asserting the victim consented to the brutal and vicious violations.[286] Another involved the gang rape of an 11 year old by what has been postulated as a gang initiation rite.[287] As previously stated, pedophiles will likely have multiple victims. Many of these cases occur in the child's own household. Research has revealed that close to 60% of child sexual abuse and pornography victims were prepubescent. In addition, more than one-third of the abusers are the victim's parents.[288]

The next stop on the line occurs in our schools. For example, high school teachers having sex with underage students is something consistently occurring across the country.[289] Social networking has added a new spin to the problem where offenders are emboldened by a sense of pseudoanonymity in making connections to children for the purposes of engaging in illegal sex acts.[290] The cases of online enticement of underage children to send sexual and pornographic photos to sexual predators are making the news consistently.[291] Texting has also lead to the development of full sexual relationships between adults and children. One case of note resulted in a statutory rape charge that could carry a possible life sentence.[292] These crimes are not strictly limited to offenders who emerge from the underbelly of society. Countless prominent professionals, politicians, and executives have been arrested for engaging in sex acts with children. For example, a pediatrician was charged with possession of pornography and inappropriate acts with his child patients.[293] Yet another was a dentist attempting to develop a relationship with what he believed to be a 14 year old girl during an online relationship developed through an Internet chat room.[294] Federal cases are consistently being made against an entire range of sex offenders.[295]

Child pornography seems to surpass the issues being dealt with when considering forced and involuntary sex acts with children as this is often the precursor for the sexual abuse and exploitation. For example, one shocking act involved the rape of a 2 year old at an amusement park where the suspect photographed the act with his cell phone.[296] Child pornography is a crime that includes both innocent children as the individual victims and a crime against society.[297] While explicit sexual acts with children are well defined, categorizing images used to classify child pornography offenses needs to be refined.[298] Production, distribution, and sale are a global problem as can be noted in the efforts of countless foreign countries that are working to combat the problem since the advent of the Internet. Because of the Internet, child porn rings have become extremely pervasive and a global problem through the real-time distribution of photographs and streaming video.[299] Key-in "child pornography" and the Internet lights afire with criminal cases around the country and around the world. The levels of depravity have no bounds, depths, or heights; and the relative anonymity of the Internet seems to fuel pushing the boundaries to new and more depraved limits. Estimates place the number of commercial websites in the hundreds while private websites are over 100,000 that contain conservatively millions of photographs of child pornography, and those figures continue to grow on a daily basis.[300] Child pornography is not limited to the secretive or black market sites but has also been posted and solicited on several social networking, free video, and educational research sites with open access.[301] Child pornography is also not limited to the commonly perceived criminal element of society as professionals, members of the clergy, and sports executives have been equally investigated and charged with the possession of prepubescent images of child sex acts.[302] Several cases have involved the arrest of college students who have downloaded hundreds of images and videos.[303] The crime is not gender specific as females are also being charged in cases of possession of child pornography.[304] Countless examples can be cited for those who manipulate children into performing sex acts either overtly or who have surreptitiously recorded these types of gross sex acts.[305]

A true pathology, collectors of child pornography will go to any lengths in order to knowingly and intentionally possess these illegal images. Documented cases have been revealed where child pornography has even been smuggled into secure detention facilities and later confiscated as contraband from detainees who will coerce and bribe personnel to violate the rules and commit additional felonies.[306] Individual predators will search the Internet for free access, share these materials with other pedophiles, buy black market printed and electronic copies of photographs from others, and access pay sites that sell the images around the world. Child pornography cases usually involve mixes of the possession of videos and often thousands, sometimes millions, of illegal images.[307]

The investigative techniques are varied and fairly resourceful from a law enforcement perspective. First and foremost is the legal support for the investigation and prosecution of these types of cases. For example, in the decision of *United States v. Knox* (1993), the photographs need not include graphic images of naked children engaged in sexual activities but rather may merely need to be sexually explicit, lascivious, or suggestive in order to support a criminal conviction.[308] Federal- and state-level laws often mirror each other in the seriousness of these crimes and sentencing requirements. In the matter of electronic images accessed over the Internet, they merely need to be viewed or accessed to be prosecuted as a crime obviating any requirement for download, storage, or distribution to support the case.[309] In lieu of the pressure and heightened media attention, cyber-pedophiles will use sophisticated techniques in order to thwart detention and arrest. They will use any electronic means available to them to avoid detection, use software that will allow computer and Internet access through unwitting victim's computers, alternate physical locations and addresses, encrypt computer files, use false identities in social networking sites, and many other methods that may have not been invented or even envisioned yet in the nanosecond real-time computer industry evolution.[310] Law enforcement is endeavoring to keep pace with this evolution by using numerous creative methods to detect and combat the problem. For example, investigative spyware is being used internationally to investigate child porn cases, successfully resulting in numerous identifications and arrests of child porn collectors.[311] The ability to track the offender's digital fingerprint is being refined through defeating the protections being used by the peer-to-peer child pornography networks that are rampant on the Internet.[312] Law enforcement personnel are also using fake hyperlinks to attract child porn Internet surfers in an effort to proactively address the problem.[313] Much of the basic investigative need is to provide specialized training, the commitment of personnel, and federal assistance leading to aggressive investigation and pursuit of these types of offenders.[314] Unfortunately, seasoned investigators will assert that the problem is so pervasive and resources so limited that only the worst of cases are investigated in many areas of the country. This only heightens the need to go beyond the basic records check to ascertain if the applicant has shown up on the child pornography radar screen as it were, with the investigative units and task forces that may have information but do not have the resources to investigate further to make an arrest.

Sending or receiving sexually revealing electronic images via cell phones and other electronic media or *sexting* is yet the latest concern being wrestled with in contemporary American society. High-profile sexting cases among teenagers and children as well as adults and teenagers have emerged across the country leading to the filing of criminal charges and much controversy.[315] Some cases of sexting have led to the teenager committing suicide over the embarrassment when the explicit photos went viral within the receiver's social network.[316] Predators will use any and all means to possess these types of images no matter the cost, effort, or harm they may cause.[317]

Juvenile-to-Juvenile Sex Offenses

Juvenile predatory sex offenders are also an issue to consider. Juvenile sex offenders are showing increasing trends as well as numerous and ambiguous state laws that treat them as less important than adults, some not listing them on state sex offender registries while other states treat the juvenile offenders more strictly mirroring the laws and prosecutorial treatment of adults.[318] This concern is a matter of great consequence when we combine the low reporting rates of sex crimes as compared to the high levels of these types of crimes in comparison to those that are disclosed and investigated. For example, the overwhelming majority (95%) of the victims of sexual assaults by juveniles were younger than age 18.[319] For 2001, juvenile arrests accounted for 12% of all forcible rapes.[320] Trends have also been cited in juvenile sex offenders that indicate that they are offending at younger ages than as reported in the past as well as demonstrating far more violent tendencies in their acts.[321] These violent trends are disturbing to say the least. More disturbing is that these deviant characteristics may manifest themselves throughout a juvenile offender's lifetime. This propensity to commit sex offenses may include victimizing not only others of the same age but also children as the offender grows older. Even though it is difficult to predict pedophilia in juvenile sex offenders, the potential remains for them to engage in these types of acts later in life.[322]

Criminal Justice Professionals Involved in Sex Offenses

While corruption, excessive force, and egregious misconduct can all be cited as unacceptable, in contrast to policy and law, and certainly an obvious violation of a very strict code of ethics, conduct that crosses the line of sexual violations of victims under the color of law is unconscionable. In the wildest stretch of the imagination, no other conceivable violation can be more despicable to the uniform of the criminal justice professional. Much like the mark Cain wore as he was banished to the land of Nod for killing Abel, this indelible image follows everyone in the field, even those who serve the profession with the highest professional ethics. The problem is so pervasive, rising to the level of taking on its own identity and being defined as Police Sexual Violence (PSV).[323] Considered a global issue, other countries are also dealing with incidents of police officers involved in rapes and sexual assaults.[324] Understanding that this problem is not unique to the United States does not lessen the gravity of the issue. An endemic problem in American law enforcement and corrections, this is an issue that must receive the greatest attention in the vetting of prospective applicants to the criminal justice professions.[325] The documented examples force us to give a moment of pause when considering who will be the next applicant we trust with policing our society.

From a categorical perspective, at the lowest, albeit no less serious levels, sexual harassment and unwelcome sexual comments and behaviors that lead to hostile work environments are likely the least reported of these types offenses. Rank-and-file examples of this occur on a daily basis and are usually discounted as the byproduct of working in a male dominated profession.[326] The framers of *Title VII*, however, did not have such an open-minded view of the problem, recognizing the damage these types of behaviors cause on a personal as well as organizational level.[327] The government sector experiences a substantial share in the areas of sexual harassment in the workplace wherein male to female persecution is the predominant issue; however, same-sex harassment is also on the rise.[328] Numerous incidents can be cited of high-level public safety and law enforcement executives and officials who have engaged in sexually inappropriate conduct and have either resigned or been terminated as a result.[329] These types of claims also involve the soliciting of sexual favors to gain promotions or quid pro quo exchanges that involve sexually harassing behaviors.[330] Extremely disturbing incidents involve high ranking sheriff's officials and a police deputy chief of internal affairs who had been involved in alleged sexually harassing behaviors.[331] High-profile sexual harassment cases are leading to immediate terminations due to not only the damages caused to the victims but also the notoriety and tarnishing of the agency's image in the public's eyes.[332] Sexual harassment and hostile work environment lawsuits are far more prevalent now than a decade ago, and some are resulting in multimillion dollar settlements to the victims.[333] Again, these cases are no less important than the following incidents and arguably more important to identify as they are often the precursors for more serious and violent behaviors. One incident involved videotaping a police partner's inappropriate sexual activities.[334] Other incidents have involved serving male police chiefs sexually harassing and, in some cases, becoming progressively more violent by sexually assaulting other male employees leading to their resignations and criminal charges.[335] These are but a few examples of the current state of this problem in the public safety arena.

As discussed earlier, electronic media of communication have added an entirely new quandary to the schema. The sexting rage is taking root in the police environment wherein discipline and termination cases are being brought internally as well as adjudicated in the lower courts as well as U.S. Supreme Court.[336] Law enforcement personnel are also being caught for using their work computers to download various types of pornography.[337] These types of behaviors also include law enforcement personnel who are not only downloading but also distributing racially and sexually inappropriate police computer messages.[338] The problem will continue to grow as the technology becomes more affordable and more accessible to those in the field.

Voluntary sexual relationships in contravention of departmental policies continue to appear in the field as well. Officers continue to develop sexual relationships opting to engage in normal and deviant sex acts while on-duty including exhibitionism, bestiality, and other paraphilias.[339] These types of issues extend to relationships with sex workers and sex with prostitutes while on-duty.[340] These types of incidents have led to officers being convicted and sentenced to jail time for their on-duty indiscretions.[341]

Involuntary or coerced relationships that lead to criminal charges also wreak havoc on an agency's morale as well as image. This, however, is in the shadow of the damage caused to the individual victims of sexual predators who commit these vile and atrocious acts under color of law. The brunt of these cases in the law enforcement realm center on inappropriate and criminal sexual contacts during traffic stop.[342] One underlying theme in many of these cases is sexual bribery.[343] Many reported cases have become progressively more violent involving gunpoint rapes, sexual batteries, and sodomies during traffic stops, as well as burglaries, kidnappings, and carjackings.[344] These types of predators who wear the uniform often target those marginal individuals in society including runaways, prostitutes, drug addicts, transsexual-transgender persons, and migrants, where several cases have led to scores of felony counts in state and federal indictments.[345] Rapes of the temporarily incapacitated also are routinely reported of those who have been intoxicated and subjected to some type of police contact that has led to a sexual violation, some occurring within law enforcement facilities.[346] Off-duty cases carry similar gravity in incidents where officers have used date rape drugs and have even raped fellow officers.[347] Corrections and community corrections are also not immune to these aberrations of professional conduct. Regardless of detention status as well as during field supervision, on-duty and off-duty incidents have included such crimes as rapes and robberies of those supervised.[348] These types of cases led to the *Prison Rape Elimination Act of 2003* (PREA) as a method to deter and punish corrections officers for developing sexual relationships with those who are incarcerated.[349]

Child pornography seems to cross all walks of life including blue-collar and professional worker, civilian and military, and even law enforcement.[350] The most disturbing of all of these issues though is criminal justice professionals who solicit sexual relationships and sex acts from minors. Again, the social networking generation rears its ugly head resulting in law enforcement officers and administrators using online and electronic methods to solicit relationships and illegal sex acts with minors.[351] Numerous documented cases have also revealed officers possessing child pornography for purposes other than legitimate criminal investigations.[352] Deviate sex acts, rape, molestation, incest, fetishes, and inappropriate sexual contact ranging in hundreds of criminal counts on indictments and with some victims being under 11 years old have been reported.[353] One permanent stain on the profession has been the proliferation of officers having illegal and inappropriate sexual relationships with Police Explorers and Scouts, resulting in the sexual exploitation of both male and female children.[354]

In the pre-employment investigation process, any sex-related deviation from the norm must be taken seriously and investigated with the full rigor possible within the agency's abilities. Law enforcement personnel have engaged in sexual misconduct in previous public safety positions that has been uncovered during the investigative process and still hired by the processing agency.[355] In contrast, as a result of one state trooper's arrest for committing numerous sex crimes against several minors and adults while on duty, the agency responded by tightening their pre-employment screening processes.[356] Criminal records checks will be the primary source along with the numerous databases available to the background investigator to include NSOR, National Directory of New Hires (NDNH), and state departments of motor vehicles and commercial databases.[357] Federal, state, and local crime analysis resources including individual agencies, databases, fusions centers, and specialized task forces should also be contacted concerning active investigations where suspects have been implicated but not yet arrested should also be reviewed. Interviews with references, employment sources, family, and friends, permission requests (and warrants if they evolve into criminal investigations) to review websites searched by the applicant from the ISP, developing false identities and photographs to use for social networking sites and chat rooms in order to gain greater access to an applicant's history are just to name a few of the techniques the background investigator should use to more fully explore an applicant's fitness for the position. Of the myriad issues explored in an applicant's history, this one should rise to as close to the top of the priority list as possible.

Future Use of DNA

Public safety administrators must also strongly consider taking these investigations to much higher levels than have been considered the proper convention of the past. Deoxyribonucleic acid (DNA) sampling is an additional recommended method of the pre-employment screening process. DNA is a molecule that encodes genetic information and is used for the identification of human beings.[358] Considered the biological fingerprint, DNA is used to definitively identify individuals who are involved in crimes where they are a primary suspect or through comparison database searched where a suspect is unknown.[359] DNA is commonly collected now at most major crimes scenes including homicides and sex crimes. With respect to violent sex crimes such as rapes, a significant proportion are committed by unknown offenders wherein DNA may be the only method to identify an offender who can be charged and stand trial for the offense.[360] Several high-profile cases have been solved solely with the use of a DNA match.[361] One such case was that of the rape and murder of Chandra Levy. Absent the collection and comparison of DNA in the case, the true offender would have never been identified casting a omnipresent and lifelong shadow on the original suspect in the case.[362] The use of DNA is growing substantially across the country and around the world.

In support of the use of DNA as a primary tool for crime fighting, much federal legislation has been passed concerning the use of DNA to investigate crimes, bring justice to the victims, and exonerate those wrongly convicted to include the *Justice for All Act of 2004*.[363] State governments are following in the federal footsteps by enacting legislation that includes all adults, youthful offenders, and sex offenders convicted of criminal law violations be mandated to submit DNA samples to assist in solving current as well as cold cases.[364] The test for efficacy has been played out consistently in the courts of the United States. DNA has met the burden of scientific proof required by the Daubert ruling and subsequently is accepted scientific proof in the eyes of the courts.[365]

In a national effort to collect and track this type of evidence for investigative purposes, the federal government uses the Combined DNA Index System (CODIS). CODIS is a software program that operates national-, state-, and local-level databases of DNA profiles from convicted offenders and missing persons. The database also stores DNA profiles of unsolved crime scene biological evidence.[366] The CODIS and National DNA Index System (NDIS) are both administered by the U.S. FBI.[367] Accessibility is made to law enforcement agencies for numerous investigative purposes.

From a pre-employment investigation perspective, several cases have been solved involving the use of DNA to identify, charge, and convict law enforcement and corrections personnel in such crimes as sexual assaults and rapes of a transsexual prostitute and elderly women as well as a homicide cold case.[368] With these incidents in mind, as well as the evidence provided concerning the issue of detecting those involved in violent assaults and sex crimes, the use of DNA in the pre-employment process appears promising. Law enforcement screeners must avail themselves of this very powerful and definitive investigative tool whenever possible. Especially when an applicant's profile is not in the existing databases for unsolved crimes, this can be an excellent defense in any future claims of negligent hiring or negligent retention as related to efforts to establish if the applicant had been involved in any criminal activity. More importantly, the collection process with a voluntary and cooperative subject requires minimal intrusion through noninvasive or, at worst, the use of minimally invasive sampling technologies. The benefits to the screening process could far outweigh the costs. The first year's costs of a law enforcement applicant including recruitment, testing, screening, hiring, outfitting, equipping, training, and other ancillary costs of pay and benefits that can reach ranges of $50,000–$100,000. The costs could possibly be avoided with the simple use of one DNA test and comparison. In these lean fiscal times, this expenditure should rightly be considered an investment in the future of the agency. Implementation would require legal review and approval, policy development, job announcement, and strict consistency of application to every applicant in the hiring process.

Identity Theft, Forgery, Fraud, and Embezzlement

Identity theft, forgery, fraudulent acts, and embezzlement are all areas of concern for the background investigator. Because of the low incidence of reporting and insulation provided by the various methods of anonymity afforded in these criminal acts, they may be very difficult to discover if the applicant has engaged in these types of activities. The advent of the Internet has given rise to new and extremely creative methods to commit crimes in the shadow of virtual anonymity for the offenders.[369] Internet fraud involves numerous types of crimes including auction fraud, nondelivery of merchandise, credit card fraud, investment fraud, Nigerian letter scams, business frauds, and various e-mail scams.[370] Fraud and white-collar crime are very pervasive in the world today and are perpetrated by an array of individuals and organizations. These players include organized crime, drug dealers, and juvenile offenders committing a broad assortment of crimes that include health-care fraud and money laundering schemes.[371] Fraud and embezzlement can also be committed through various other acts that include involvement in settling estates, caretaking for the elderly, real estate and service scams, just to name a few others. A 2004 study revealed that over 3.6 million households in the United States had at least one member who had been the victim of identity theft with the most common type being credit card theft.[372] Experts have also asserted that workplace fraud has demonstrated a consistent rise over the years.[373] Therefore, applicants may come into the process as suspects or as victims, which necessitate a high level of sensitivity if the latter is the case.

Identity theft can take on a range of low-level to high-level implications. False impersonation and false personation cases are an example when using someone else's name to gain some type of benefit including the avoidance of being issued a traffic ticket or trying to gain access to an age restricted venue. By and large, the primary motivation for identity theft though is to access another person's accounts and credit lines.[374] Other nefarious reasons include access to otherwise restricted opportunities to gain prestigious employment positions and admission into high end colleges.[375] Of the populations discussed, college students seem to be highly susceptible to these types of crimes including credit card fraud, check fraud, false identification, student loan fraud, and obtaining false degrees and credentials.[376] Fraud is for all intents and purposes a relatively easy crime to commit in the realm of counterfeit and altered credit cards.[377] Credit card applications appropriated through mail delivery is common even with the act being a serious fraud concern and crossing over into federal- as well as state-level criminal acts. Federal legislation was enacted to deal with the symptoms of fraud by way of the *Fair and Accurate Credit Transactions Act of 2003*.[378] Unfortunately, there is a very limited instance of reporting credit card and check fraud to the police.[379] Banks usually make restitution for fraudulent credit card uses, and law enforcement agencies do not view this as a priority item in lieu of other more serious crimes.

While illegal drug use is a global problem, prescription drug fraud is also rising to the forefront.[380] Prescription fraud is defined as pharmaceutical diversion for the purposes of some personal use or illicit profit.[381] Prescription fraud can occur in several different manners: illegally possessing and forging a doctor's prescription, altering dosages on legitimately written prescriptions, or using several doctors to write individual prescriptions for the same drugs.[382] In lieu of illegal drug markets, addictions are being transferred to prescription-type drugs creating a black market for pharmaceuticals in quantities.

Other types of fraud include welfare fraud which has been a timeless issue throughout the country.[383] False claims for workmen's compensation, disability, and unemployment insurance while an applicant works off-the-books may all be encountered at one point or another in the processing of applicants. Another type of fraud occurs in falsely reporting of thefts during burglaries and robberies for ulterior motivations in covering up some other criminal offense, nefarious activity, or the commission of insurance fraud.[384] False reporting of serious or violent crimes may have motivations to gain notoriety or public recognition and sympathy.[385] Finally, the ubiquitous tax fraud concerns with applicants who are failing to claim income and avoiding paying income taxes at their required rate and income level. Rarely, the applicant may be involved in fraud and embezzlement through interstate commerce which falls under the sanctions of the *Racketeer Influenced and Corrupt Organizations Act* (RICO) used for prosecutions of individuals and organizations.[386]

Professionals in the criminal justice field are not immune to these types of criminal acts. Interestingly, they span the entire spectrum of rank in organizations, from line personnel to executives. At the lowest levels, personnel are being terminated and convicted of internal fraud issues that include using department credit cards to obtain personal services and products as petty as gasoline.[387] Other lower-level charges include fraud through filling ghost positions in departments.[388] The embezzlement and fraud of major department funds is the next level observed.[389] These types of incidents then graduate to higher-level crimes with embezzlement as the start, and then bribery, racketeering, and wire fraud in one noted case involving the majority of one department's command staff.[390] External issues emerge from forgeries,[391] tax fraud cases,[392] usury and income tax evasion cases,[393] insurance fraud,[394] mail fraud,[395] pension fraud,[396] wire fraud,[397] loan fraud,[398] high-end Ponzi schemes,[399] and even officers involved in identity theft cases.[400] There is a common thread found in that municipal and state officials are consistently being charged and convicted of fraud and embezzlement.[401]

In the pre-employment field, fraudulent practices are also being routinely discovered in the applications processes of all types of organizations. The primary motivator is to gain employment through the use of false or fraudulent documents.[402] One vehicle used is through the commission of identity theft. Identity theft can be used by an otherwise unqualified person to gain employment in a desired position.[403] Much of these instances are being addressed through the enhanced federal I-9 process as previously discussed, but the possibility remains that applicants will attempt these types of deceptive practices at varying levels and degrees.

There are numerous investigative resources to tap when investigating an applicant's background. The obvious sources are local, state, and federal law enforcement agencies (e.g., FBI, Secret Service, U.S. Postal Inspectors, U.S. Marshals). Nationwide consortiums also exist for the purposes of assisting in these types of investigations. For example, the National White Collar Crime Center (NW3C)[404] and Internet Crime Complaint Center (IC3)[405] may be of valuable assistance in this process. Private sector organizations may also prove to be valuable resources including the International Association of Financial Crimes Investigators[406] and the National Insurance Crime Bureau,[407] that is, a consortium of over 1000 insurance companies who collaborate on insurance fraud investigations. The background investigator should not discount these types of activities simply because the applicant does not have a criminal record. Interviews, investigation techniques through the listed alternative sources, and the use of truth detection devices may prove to be very effective at discovering an applicant's involvement. Engaging the assistance of a Certified Fraud Examiner or Certified Financial Examiner may also be very advantageous to the background investigator who is unfamiliar with this very specialized field of expertise.[408]

Juvenile Offenders, Delinquency, and Status Offenses

Juvenile issues are often difficult to discover and even more difficult to sort out in the pre-employment screening process. Because of society's and the legal systems' views toward disallowing acts committed as a juvenile as being, in most cases, excusable behavior due to the purported limited capacity to grasp the concepts of right and wrong, most offenses consequently go unreported and are handled in alternative manners more likened to rehabilitation and counseling, alternative courts, and records sealing or purging when adulthood is reached. Federal legislation used as edicts at the state level have included the *Federal Youth Corrections Act* and the *Crime Control Act of 1990* that have impacted how juveniles are treated in the courts, distinguishing the levels of offenses seen as germane to unique treatment, and guidelines on treatment and rehabilitation as opposed to strict punishment.[409] Only in the most serious of offenses are records maintained. In 1992, the FBI was tasked with the responsibility to accept and disseminate information concerning juvenile records as is done with adult records; however, the reporting process by the individual states is still strictly voluntary.[410] An example of state-level sovereignty can be found in New York State wherein the *New York State Penal Law, New York State Criminal Procedure Law*, and *New York State Family Court Act* all have provisions on the requirements for handling juveniles in the legal system.[411] Even in these cases, the records may enjoy the strictest of protections under applicable state laws. Notwithstanding, while societal tolerance may discount or wholly dismiss the occurrence of criminal acts as a juvenile, pre-employment screening processes may not enjoy this same level of clemency. Age and the type of offense as well as many other factors must be considered in the final decision; however, the acts cannot be considered obligatorily useless in nature and consequence solely because the acts were not committed in a statutorily defined period of adulthood.

The threshold of adulthood varies from state to state, with some drawing the line at the age of 16 while others the age is 17 or 18.[412] In addition, those who are below the threshold point may also have distinctions for age ranges and more serious crimes making the offenses prosecutable as adult crimes when certain conditions and aggravating factors are met. One particularly horrendous case occurred in New York State where a 13 year old brutally murdered a 4 year old and has been made to answer for the offense with the maximum penalty provided in spite of being a juvenile at the time of occurrence.[413] Another particularly vicious case involved male teens, both residents of a youth home, who savagely beat a female youth counselor to death to cover up a theft.[414] Trends have been identified in children committing criminal acts at progressively younger and more violent rates. For example, in 2001, juvenile arrests accounted for 12% of all violent crimes including 5% of all murders, 12% of all forcible rapes and aggravated assaults, and 14% of all robberies.[415] One case that gives significance to the statistics involves a 10 year old girl charged with the violent murder of an 11 month old baby.[416] In addition, some 9% of violent crimes that are committed against adults are perpetrated by juveniles.[417] The phenomenon of "flash mob attacks," the use of social media in rallying teenagers to engage in coordinated and unprovoked violent attacks and robberies, is on the rise in the United States.[418] Several large cities have experienced high levels of violence where youths are involved in serious assaults that for the most part are motivated solely by race.[419] Mob violence seems to be gaining in popularity at public and sporting events as well wherein the perpetrators feel free to commit these mass assaults and then flee.[420] In these cases, while hundreds are involved in these crimes, only an insignificant number are identified and charged criminally. Again, we must also realize that these are only the reported rates where an arrest has been made. In reality, the true rates are likely staggering.

Street crimes, physical crimes, property crimes, and sexual assaults are but part of the problem.[421] As previously mentioned, sexting has become the avant-garde method of communication that is leading to acts that are considered innocent by the offending child but are leading to serious crimes being charged and inclusion on sex offender registries. Bullying has also fallen into the mainstream. An act that was for the most part tolerated in decades past has now become a national problem. Bullying is considered a pervasive crisis that is not only underreported but also growing in scope and severity.[422] Bullying occurs at all grade levels with particularly acute effects on high school freshmen.[423] Specific and vicious incidents of bullying at the local level have gained national attention and reaction.[424] Again, we can also observe the physical bullying problem being augmented by technology as cyber bullying, texting, and social networking sites becomes the norm.[425] Teenagers are using these media as a means to permeate the social network of the child victim in order to apply a spherical environment of intimidation. The pathology is reaching frightening levels in our society.

For the background investigator, reaching back to grade and high school may prove to be quite arduous and may produce minimal if any valuable information. Depending on an applicant's age at the time of processing, this type of inquiry may be decades removed. Even with the obvious limitations that this inquiry may involve, efforts must still be made even if to simply rule out any of these types of issues. Primary and secondary educational records archives may need to be searched and collected as evidence that supports or refutes involvement in any of the listed activities. Criminal and juvenile records checks should be conducted in current computer systems as well as with agencies where the juvenile may have had contact, including those jurisdictions where the juvenile has resided and attended school. Actual criminal records can be supplemented by the physical reports and statements filed in cases, intelligence and street stop information, and personal interviews may all be used in determining involvement and level of criminality in incidents of this nature. Once all of the information has been culled and assessed, then an informed decision can be made as to the weight the information will carry in the vetting process.

Expunged and Sealed Records

Criminal record expungement, sealing, and statutorial eradication presents some precarious issues for the background investigator. Criminal history records in the system are used for law enforcement criminal investigations as well as noncriminal justice purposes that include professional licensing for the varied professions of nursing and health- and child-care workers, pharmacists, engineers and architects, positions in the investment industry, adoption applications, applications for citizenship, firearms purchases, and pre-employment background checks.[426] Federal law allows for the preservation and reporting of the existence of a person's criminal record indefinitely.[427] Dispositions of arrests are available through the National Criminal History Record File and include, if any, arrest charge(s) that have been modified in any manner, disposed of, or dropped, or any diversionary actions ordered by the adjudicating court.[428]

A person will seek to have their criminal record expunged for numerous reasons that may include personal embarrassment, the desire to regain rights that involve the ability to vote or possess a firearm, to obtain some type of professional licensing, and, in the case of this text, to gain employment in selected vocations that prohibit employment of convicted criminals.[429] In one case, a police officer was petitioning to have sex crimes expunged from his own records.[430] By simple definition, an expungement is a deletion of a single arrest or an entire criminal record.[431] Expunging a record can involve many different outcomes including the complete destruction or erasure of records to varying levels of retention that include merely sealing the records from public access or returning the records to the defendant. For all intents and purposes, when the criminal record is sealed or expunged, the entire incident is considered to be nonexistent. Expunction and sealing laws vary from state to state where an applicant may be allowed to wholly deny an arrest or conviction to a prospective employer.[432] An example of state law that regulates prospective employer boundaries in these issues can be found in the *California Code of Regulations Fair Employment* regulations under specific practices:

1. Criminal records. Except as otherwise provided by law (e.g., 12 U.S.C. 1829; *Labor Code* Section 432.7), it is unlawful for an employer or other covered entity to inquire or seek information regarding any applicant concerning:
   a. Any arrest or detention which did not result in conviction.
   b. Any conviction for which the record has been judicially ordered sealed, expunged, or statutorily eradicated (e.g., juvenile offense records sealed pursuant to *Welfare and Institutions Code* Section 389 and *Penal Code* Sections 851.7 or 1203.45); any misdemeanor conviction for which probation has been successfully completed or otherwise discharged and the case has been judicially dismissed pursuant to *Penal Code* Section 1203.4.
   c. Any arrest for which a pretrial diversion program has been successfully completed pursuant to *Penal Code* Sections 1000.5 and 1001.5.[433]

A basic set of guidelines are the necessary precursor for applications or petitions for the expungement of a criminal record. The Maryland Department of Public Safety and Correctional Services provides an excellent example of their state laws and policies as they relate to the eligibility of persons who have been charged with a crime (including traffic violations) for which a term of imprisonment may be imposed:

1. You were found not guilty.
2. The charge was dismissed.
3. The charge resulted in probation before judgment (excluding charges of driving while under the influence or driving while impaired).
4. The State's Attorney did not prosecute (Nolle Prosequi) your charge.
5. The court indefinitely postponed your case (stet).
6. Your case was compromised (settled).
7. You were convicted of only one non-violent criminal act and you were granted a full and unconditional pardon by the Governor. For a Pardon packet contact the Parole Commission's Office at 410-585-3200.
8. Juvenile Waived.[434]

Expunction is allowed in most states for arrests not resulting in a conviction as well as misdemeanor and felony convictions with some waiting period requirements that may need to be met prior to eligibility. Each state has its own set of rules though. Consequently, no universal protocol exists for the process of criminal records expungement. Many variations in process, definitions, dispositions, and thresholds exist from conservative to liberal for the erasure of criminal records in all but the most violent or excluded types of crimes related to homicides, serious or aggravated assaults, sex offenses, child abuse, and DWI or impaired. Other examples include states that vary in the number of arrests as well as convictions for crimes that can be expunged, the level or severity of crimes allowed for expunction, removal in time from the offense, successful completion of rehabilitation, lack of subsequent contact with the law, gubernatorial and presidential pardons, and inactive court proceedings known as stet dockets.

In the extreme, some state legislatures refuse to allow expungement unless very strict conditions are met where the defendant was found not guilty at trial or the prosecutor dismisses the charges with prejudice or will not reprosecute the case (e.g., there may have been probable cause for the arrest but the grand jury failed to indict on the available evidence).[435]

However, expungement may occur under certain circumstances when the case is found "in favor" of the defendant. For example, arrests and formal charges that are later dismissed by the prosecuting attorney, the defendant never pleading guilty, and successful completion of pretrial or rehabilitative diversion programs may all apply.[436] Expungements for convictions may also occur in rare cases. Pleading guilty/found guilty at trial and pleading guilty and receiving a stay of imposition, stay of adjudication, and adjourned in contemplation of dismissal where charges are later dismissed are all considered convictions in the eyes of the courts.

Exceptions may also be had in certain types of cases involving juvenile delinquency or drug cases; however, any plea of guilty or conviction is not considered as a disposition that is in favor of the defendant.[437] One requirement is that the sealing or expungement of the record will not have a negative impact or present a potential threat to public safety.[438] In addition, in the decision of *United States v. Flowers* (2004), a balancing test to determine whether judicial records can be expunged must be met. In this case, the court asserted that "If the dangers of the unwarranted adverse consequences to the individual outweigh the public interest in maintenance of the records, then expunction is appropriate."[439] Business necessity, as discussed in Chapter 3, also significantly impacts the ability to screen for a previous criminal record in several ways including the nature and severity of the offense, the removal in time from the final disposition of the conviction, and the type of position being applied for.[440]

Legislative bills are consistently being sponsored in numerous states across the country that are intended to expunge a much broader array of criminal convictions from an offender's record than are currently being allowed by statute.[441] For example, not only offense types but also other considerations are being used that include more forgiving limits on temporal relationships to the offense committed. Many states are moving toward expunging records for offenses when perpetrated by those who have committed nonviolent felony offenses when they were less than 25 years old due only because of the age of the defendant when the criminal act was committed.[442] A select number of states are taking extremely tolerant positions and allowing many crime categories that include murder, DWI, drug charges, and domestic violence incidents are all being approved for expungement by the courts of these jurisdictions.[443]

Lastly, juvenile records also have special rules attached that regulate their use. As a general rule, juvenile records are automatically sealed or sealed after a certain period of time is passed when the person reaches adulthood. Society's recognition of acts committed during the years leading to adulthood may carry minimum culpability due to these being considered the formative years of a person's life. Carrying these scars throughout life is considered an unjust burden for many low-level offenses and police contacts. Availability for review and use is consequently affected when the records have, for all intents and purposes, disappeared.

In processing applicants for the criminal justice professions, much more latitude is afforded to local, state, and federal governmental agencies in accessing records that have dispositions alternative to convictions. In general, criminal records can be used in the screening process; however, each state has its own laws and rules which must be adhered to. For example, in the states of Rhode Island and Maine, the use of expunged records is permitted in the background investigation process, and the law requires the law enforcement applicant to disclose the fact or existence of the conviction.[444] In contrast, New York State allows only the use of sealed records and mandates the exclusion of expunged records from the pre-employment investigation so that they cannot be used as a determinant for eligibility for hire.[445] The background investigator must defer to their own state's standards in the process. For example, in this scenario, an applicant who resides in a state that requires such disclosures (Rhode Island) subsequently applies to a New York State agency for hire. The information on expunged charges that may have been disclosed by the applicant must be redacted. The opposite is also true as an applicant who resides in New York but applies to a state similar to Rhode Island must disclose any expunged record in the application process.

One comforting fact for the background investigator to consider is that most records do not simply vanish from existence. For that reason, expungement does not always lead to total destruction or erasure of a record in most cases, and the event may still be recorded in not one but many protected as well as public access records systems.[446] The records may exist in various forms in both formal and informal repositories. At a fundamental level, criminal records may not be wholly obliterated as they may serve many other purposes for the police, FBI, immigration officers, and other public officials who may still be allowed access to sealed court files for certain purposes beyond establishing if the person has been arrested or convicted in the criminal system.[447] At the level of inception, records will exist in the form of field contacts or interviews (FIs), general or incident reports, crime investigation reports, motor vehicle accident reports, CAD systems, and all department databases for contacts. Personal files of contacting officers may also reveal vital information related to an applicant that may not have made their way to the formal recording system in the organization. For arrest and detention, records can still exist in the arresting agency, local, state, and federal records systems and repositories, the presiding courts, corrections, and community corrections (i.e., probation and parole) agencies. Often, expunction of agency records is a separate process than that of official court records depending on the conditions and allowable state and federal laws. In these cases, sending letters and release forms directly to the agencies that would have had a high probability of contact with the applicant (e.g., agencies with jurisdiction of locations of residence and work) may prove fruitful.

Expunged information may also be routinely available through vendors who have accessed or purchased criminal records information and have not updated their repositories when the records are ordered removed from the police files by a presiding court.[448] The news media are also an excellent source as well as the plethora of databases that electronically store news articles can be accessed where an arrest may have made the local or even national news. Applicants are often admonished concerning the government's right to ask such questions and, as a rule, admit to any and all arrests, noting the conviction has been dismissed.[449] The processing agency is then responsible to provide all protections afforded to the applicant and redact information that would illegally and negatively impact candidacy for the position. One caution though is that even if this type of information is disclosed by the applicant or located through an independent source or alternative source, state law may still require exclusion or redaction. Unlike a criminal court proceeding, the rules are generally applied from an administrative or civil proceeding where the rules of evidence are much more forgiving. As long as the agency can provide a preponderance of evidence through the use of legally obtained documents, there should not be a forbidden use issue raised. Even if a criminal case is lost in prosecution, unless some state law precludes using the information from a specific case status (expunged), then the evidence can be presented to decertify and reject an applicant based upon business necessity.

Drug and Alcohol Use

As previously treated in Chapter 4, the issues of drug and alcohol use must be addressed from a legal as well as policy-based perspective. Chapter 4 delineated the laws and protections of applicants as well as the ability of the background investigator to solicit information concerning the use and abuse of illegal substances as well as the abuse of legal substances. Drug use has permeated American society like no other disease known to modern man. As this malady continues to infect the youth of our nation, we are faced with future applicant pools that will be excluded from entering the ranks of the criminal justice professions. Individual and group use in schools and at social dealings that include sporting events and teen parties is growing in scope and severity. For example, rave parties are the craze for youth to gather for entertainment and the accessibility to licit and illicit drugs.[450] The range of drugs used at these types of parties boggles the mind. Drug use at rave parties includes the following:

1. Ecstasy or MDMA
2. Ketamine ("special K"), LSD (or "acid")
3. Rohypnol, GHB, MDEA (or "Eve") (MDMA)
4. MMDA
5. PMA (para-methoxyamphetamine)
6. Fentanyl, PCP (or "angel dust") (phencyclidine)
7. Psilocybin (or "magic mushrooms")
8. Methaqualone
9. DMT (dimethyltryptamine)
10. Over-the-counter drugs such as pseudoephedrine, ephedra, caffeine, menthol inhalants, and vaporizing ointments
11. Prescription drugs such as Viagra, Prozac, and DXM (dextromethorphan, a cough elixir)
12. Legal substances such as nitrous oxide (or "laughing gas" or "whippets")[451]

Drug use in preparatory, secondary, and postsecondary institutions is also making headlines where drug dealing rings are being cracked by law enforcement that include college students dealing to their classmates.[452] Also addressed in Chapter 4 are the issues of casual use to the additional problems created in drug use issues in the workplace. Law enforcement has not escaped these concerns. Illicit drug possession, use, sales, and heavy trafficking have been realized in departments across the country irregardless of size, location, or rank of the offender.[453] The problem extends to prescription drug use and abuse, fraud, and illegal sales by law enforcement personnel.[454] As a consequence, agencies must take a very strong approach to drug use policies in the pre-employment screening process. Decisions of the courts that include *City of Canton v. Harris* (1989), *The Shield Club v. City of Cleveland* (1986), and most recently, *NASA v. Nelson* (2011) affirm the right of the government to screen applicants for illegal drug use, possession, supply, and manufacturing.[455] Screening can lead to rejection; however, the agency must have a well-articulated and tough policy in place that can withstand the scrutiny of meeting the threshold of a business necessity.

For exemplar policies, one need not look any further than the model developed by the FBI. The organizational Employment Drug Policy is divided into three sections: (1) policy statement, (2) criteria, and (3) applicant self-disqualification. The policy statement is presented as follows:

> The FBI is firmly committed to a drug-free society and work place. Therefore, the unlawful use of drugs by FBI employees is not tolerated. Furthermore, applicants for employment with the FBI who currently use illegal drugs will be found unsuitable for employment. The FBI does not condone any prior unlawful drug use by applicants. We realize, however, some otherwise qualified applicants may have used drugs at some point in their pasts. The following policy sets forth the criteria for determining whether any prior drug use makes an applicant unsuitable for employment, balancing the needs of the FBI to maintain a drug-free workplace and the public integrity necessary to accomplish the FBI's intelligence and law enforcement missions. Applicants who do not meet the listed criteria should not apply for any FBI position.[456]

The second codicil of the Employment Drug Policy very distinctly provides definitions and criterion for disqualification from the process as an extension of their policy. The policy informs the applicant that they will be found unsuitable for employment if they

1. Have used any illegal drug (including anabolic steroids after February 27, 1991), other than marijuana, within the past 10 years or engaged in more than minimal experimentation in their lifetime. In making the determination about an applicant's suitability for FBI employment, all relevant facts, including the frequency of use, will be evaluated.
2. Have used marijuana/cannabis within the past 3 years or have extensively used marijuana/cannabis or over a substantial period of time. In making the determination about an applicant's suitability for FBI employment, all relevant facts, including the recency and frequency of use, will be evaluated.[457]

The third codicil of the Employment Drug Policy affords the applicant information that would allow them to self-disqualify from the application process if they have violated any of the delineated thresholds. An affirmative response to any of the questions would automatically disqualify the applicant from processing with the FBI:

1. Have you used marijuana at all within the last 3 years?
2. Have you used any other illegal drug (including anabolic steroids after February 27, 1991) at all in the past 10 years?
3. Have you ever sold any illegal drug for profit?
4. Have you ever used an illegal drug (no matter how many times or how long ago) while in a law enforcement or prosecutorial position or in a position which carries with it a high level of responsibility or public trust?[458]

This example can be compared and contrasted to the policy examples provided in both Chapters 2 and 4 to use as benchmarks to develop new, or revise current, organizational policies that will withstand legal scrutiny. The existence of policies, even strongly worded and highly restrictive policies, however, cannot be practiced as an empty threat. For example, policies must be enforced where an applicant may claim an unwitting or inadvertent use or ingestion as then this would be analogous to the infamous "never inhaled" claim.[459] Consistent and equitable application must be afforded to all applicants no matter the circumstances involved. Disparate treatment must never unfairly favor one population over another for any reason. More importantly, the moment we make concessions is the moment we no longer have a policy. This is not an issue of gender, race, or culture, but simply one of resounding responsibility. In spite of the issues faced with dwindling candidate pools, necessity should never be the driver of lowering standards especially with drug use and abuse. We see this issue transcending criminal justice organizations across the country and around the globe causing a plight of circumstances and repercussions for all of the stakeholders in this process.

Alcohol use and abuse is a far more compound issue. Alcohol is legal in the overwhelming majority of jurisdictions in the United States. Drinking to excess, unless attached to some criminal behavior such as DWI, drinking under age, and public open container laws, or a policy issue forbidding alcohol use in one's workplace, is, for the most part, activity that is condoned. Research has demonstrated though that alcohol use and abuse accounts for approximately 4% of deaths worldwide.[460] Discussed in Chapter 4 in depth with relation to addictions and the protections afforded under the law, alcohol use and abuse must also be closely scrutinized. Incidence of underage drinking is on a steady rise while binge drinking during special events, college attendance, to simple imbibement may individually and collectively have a negative impact on fitness for selection as a law enforcement officer or criminal justice professional. Incidents involving officers with alcohol problems have led to compromising situations for the agency and officer alike.[461]

Policy development and deselection becomes problematic though in this area that can be very ambiguous and does not lend itself to strict guidelines and interpretation. Usually the primary methods of attaching this type of drinking behavior to a disqualification are folded into some type of illegal act or behavior (e.g., a DWI accident, a drunken bar fight, a domestic assault where the applicant was intoxicated at the time) and through the cumulative psychological or medical examinations that may indicate the problem of alcohol use is acute to the point that it would negatively affect performance as a criminal justice professional. Another method is the issue of serving alcohol to minors. Recent developments in the *social host liability* laws have prompted enforcement in these areas wherein party hosts, fraternities, and even parents are being charged criminally and held civilly accountable for serving alcohol to minors.[462]

Terrorism, Gang Affiliation, and Hate Crimes

As of the last decade, international and domestic terrorism, gang affiliation, and bias or hate crimes have been brought to the limelight. From a pre-employment investigations perspective, these issues deserve to be brought to the attention of those conducting the background investigations due to the potential they now carry in persons who are involved in subversive actions attempting to gain entry to the field. For the process, these broad categories have both parallel and direct connections to each other.

Terrorism

Since the events of 9/11, the term terrorism seems to be on the lips of every concerned citizen, military, and law enforcement officer of the United States. A global problem that was largely ignored domestically resulted in a cataclysm of events that have deeply strained this great nation's solvency, infrastructure, and resolve. More importantly, this very real threat to our national and international interests has predominantly garnered a political rather than planned approach to resolution. The results of the *9/11 Commission Report* as well as countless other sources have both galvanized and polarized the public on the identified flaws in the pre- and postresponse to the series of events of that day that shattered the nation.[463] These events were the genesis for several changes in how we approach the entire issue of terrorism in the United States. For example, legislation was targeted in the form of the *Patriot Act* and the *Intelligence Reform and Terrorism Prevention Act of 2004*.[464] Investigative procedures for detection and tracking were implemented through various means that include the Terrorist Screening Database (TSDB) or "Terrorist Watch List" administered by the FBI.[465] Local initiatives have been sporadic across the country in an effort to prepare for an impending attack again on home soil.

Penetration has been accomplished by these groups in various forms. One of the earliest post-9/11 examples was the detection and arrest of terrorist cell members in a rural town in western New York in 2002.[466] There has also been an emergence of U.S. nationals who are now being discovered as having direct involvement in terrorist activities to solicit funds and extremists to support a Jihad War in the United States.[467] An ever-growing concern of U.S. counterterrorism officials and analysts has been the sudden emergence of Islamic radicals who are U.S. nationals.[468] In the wake of this is the apparent rise in domestic terrorism as well. Domestic terrorism is also an issue of great concern as a result of numerous destructive and violent acts in the country including those of Timothy McVeigh and the Oklahoma City bombing as well as splinter groups that include the Ohio Christian Militia that plotted to kill numerous police officers.[469]

While on the surface, these are distinctly separate issues the country is facing; they are in effect tantamount when considering the potential impact on pre-employment investigations for criminal justice positions. For example, a U.S. national who was known to U.S. law enforcement as having ties to Al Qaeda was employed at several nuclear power plants before being detected and arrested by Yemenise officials for ties to this terrorist organization.[470] Immigrants have also obtained citizenship and have deeply infiltrated high-level law enforcement and military positions and were only discovered as being active terrorists with terrorist organizational ties long after they were placed in these sensitive positions.[471] Foreign nationals who use the American educational system through student visas are also of grave concern to analysts.[472] And we can never forget the unconscionable tragedy that occurred when a military officer who was a known supporter of terrorist beliefs massacred numerous innocent victims at the Fort Hood military base.[473]

These types of events underscore the importance of recognizing and responding to the potential for homegrown terrorists who are able to enter the ranks of or, in some way, influence those who are in the ranks of the criminal justice professions. By direct belief or by influence through direct contact, these are very real concerns for the contemporary and future criminal justice administrator to consider and prepare for in the eventuality that these types of individuals may be plotting to enter the ranks of criminal justice organizations throughout the United States.

Gang Affiliation

Gangs have been around in some form or another for centuries. At any given time in the United States, there are over 30,000 youth gangs with over 800,000 members.[474] Primary involvement seems to be closely linked to the illicit drug trade.[475] Youth gangs know no conventional boundaries as they are spreading to small cities and rural counties throughout the country.[476] Gang affiliation also knows no gender or racial boundaries as members are males and females as well as African Americans, Hispanics, Asians, and Whites alike.[477] They are also morphing into adult gangs and becoming far more organized than they are perceived as, like their counterparts in Asian Triads, the La Cosa Nostra, Hells Angels, and many others. Gang members have penetrated the U.S. military structure with reports of activities around the world where military operations show a presence.[478] While a growing operational and enforcement concern, they are also an emerging concern in the pre-employment screening process. Gang members are reported to be successfully infiltrating the ranks of police departments.[479] Sworn and nonsworn personnel alike may have either direct or indirect connections to criminal organizations and gangs. Similar to the aforementioned examples in terrorism, these groups may be molding individuals who can enter the ranks of police organizations and operate with minimal constraint.

Bias or Hate Crimes

Bias or hate crimes are also a concern to be investigated because of the often surreptitious nature of the incidents. An average of 200,000 hate crimes are reported annually in the United States.[480] Statistically, the majority of hate crimes committed were motivated by race followed by religion and the sexual orientation.[481] Unprovoked attacks in hate crime cases know no bounds, and targets can be of any protected class inclusive of race, wherein whites have moved from the atypical to typical victims.[482] Federal law was passed through the *Hate Crime Statistics Act of 1990* to better track these types of incidents as well as having each state follow by enacting their own laws to protect their constituencies.[483]

Any of the aforementioned categories may or may not be discovered during the basic records check process. However, interviews with family, friends, references, coworkers, and all other affiliates will be necessary to establish if the applicant has ever been involved in any of these activities. Interfacing with the various intelligence agencies will also be necessary to either confirm or refute any information of involvement in these types of criminal or subversive activities.

Compulsive Gambling

Compulsive gambling should also be an area of interest to the background investigator. Gambling or gaming in the United States, when under control, is a normal and entertaining past time for over 100 million Americans. When the desire to gamble takes on the need to gamble is when the problem can become extremely damaging to one's life. According to a recent study, approximately 15 million Americans present a moderate risk for developing into problem gamblers.[484] Of these figures, only the top 3% of gamblers are considered to be either problem or pathological in their pursuit of gambling opportunities.[485] This problem is not only endemic to adults as children are also participating in gambling activities at alarming rates.[486] As a matter of fact, research of pathological gambling has been demonstrated at even higher rates in adolescents as they are manifested by adults.[487] This should concern pre-employment screeners as these adolescents are the future candidate pools for the criminal justice professions. One exacerbating issue is that Internet gambling is on a steep rise due to the accessibility to anyone who has a computer and a credit card.[488] The problem of accessibility continues to grow exponentially when revenue-strapped states approve the building of casinos across the country and within reasonable driving distances to many major metropolitan areas.

As a concern for the background investigator, there are numerous examples of officers and criminal justice professionals who claimed that gambling addictions have brought them to violate their oaths of office.[489] Charged with numerous crimes including grand larceny, fraud, and embezzlement, a common theme is stealing from the agency where they managed or had control over grants, funds, and cash which fueled their ability to gamble at compulsive and uncontrollable rates.

Gambling may also only be a symptom of several additional layered dependencies. In many cases, there are multidependence personality traits demonstrated by the compulsive gambler.[490] Quite frequently, there are additional chemical dependencies attached to the compulsive gambling problem as well.[491] Alcohol use and abuse, illicit drug use, and prescription drug abuse may be attached to the compulsive gambler's multiple problems that would be a determinant for their proper fit to most positions, let alone to those in the criminal justice professions.

Most importantly, gambling is not a protected addiction as defined by the ADA.[492] There are specific mental disorders for which there are no statutory protections, namely, compulsive gambling, as well as substance use disorders resulting from past or current illegal use of drugs, if any, that are discovered or disclosed as part of the gambling problem.[493]

The background investigator should make these types of questions surrounding applicant and reference interviews a normal component of the vetting protocol by contacting coworkers, independently developed sources, and self-disclosures through social networking venues. Additionally, the background investigator should examine available computer and financial records, credit reports tax forms, significant discrepancies in living expenses, and other indicators in order to either confirm or refute if the applicant has any involvement in gambling. If any gambling involvement is discovered, the extent of that involvement and the potential impact on the applicant's viability for a position where they will be exposed to numerous temptations and opportunities that would make them violate their oath of office must be considered in the balance of all other factors discovered.

CIVIL LIABILITY HISTORY

Civil liability history can encompass many areas from negligence to intentional torts that involve claims of breach of contract, injuries and damages through an automobile accident, and workplace liability, are just to name a few. Defaulted child support, garnished wages, and unpaid federal and state taxes are also others that fall into this category. Every state will have legislation and case law in place that will regulate the process of civil litigation, and the background investigator should be familiar with the concepts as well as the mechanics of the process.[494]

Civil litigation may arise from torts filed in the aforementioned categories and can be of great guidance to the background investigator. Civil liability is usually incurred when three standards are met that include the existence of a legal duty between parties, a breach of that duty between the parties, and an injury or damages occurs from the breach of duty as a proximate result. Many criminal matters are relegated to civil cases so that reparations can be made and the criminal case can be dismissed. Contractual agreements, loans, purchases, and services rendered may all be subject to civil suits for which the background investigator can use to make a determination as to whether the applicant can successfully meet their contractual obligations to others. The background investigator must establish if the applicant has been a plaintiff, respondent, or defendant in these types of civil actions in a civil or small claims court. Numerous databases exist for the search of personal injury, class action lawsuits, and commercial litigation. The background investigator should also check with all local and state courts, including small claims courts to ascertain if the applicant has been listed as plaintiff or respondent as well as any court-ordered outcomes and compliance to the court orders.

Child support is also another area that should be examined closely.[495] These issues demonstrate an applicant's commitment to meeting parenting and societal obligations. Child support or maintenance can also lead to indications or evidence of economic abuse wherein payments are held back or denied in order to gain some type of control over the child or parent. The background investigator must establish if the applicant has any children, stepchildren, is responsible to pay child support, and if those support obligations are being consistently met. The background investigator should also determine if the applicant has been the subject of any paternity lawsuits and if there has been any determination as to the status of the action. The background investigator should be aware of cases involving paternity fraud wherein the applicant may be the unwitting victim of a scam artist whose intent is to fleece the purported noncustodial parent or cover up an illegitimate pregnancy.[496] The applicant in the role of obligee will need to be established in order to fully understand their fitness for the position. The *Bradley Amendment* (1986), in spite of the continuing controversy surrounding codification, federally mandates child support without regard for many lower court controls, capacity of the obligor to pay, and automatically provides for nonexpiring liens whenever child support is in arrears.[497] Each state will have a department that handles these matters, for example, the Arkansas Department of Finance and Administration, the Florida Department of Revenue, the New York State Department of Taxation and Finance, and the Idaho Department of Health and Welfare.[498] The background investigator needs to research the applicable rules and databases for searches in their respective states.

Income taxes are also matters of concern for the background investigator to examine. Numerous previous examples were provided in how serving law enforcement officers have been charged with and convicted of income tax fraud and evasion. As a matter for review in the pre-employment investigation process, if state law allows, applicants should provide a series of Internal Revenue Service tax return forms, whether for individual returns that include the Form 1040 and accompanying forms (Schedules) as well as for any businesses, limited liability companies, S corporations, and corporations if the applicant is a principle and they are applicable to the screening process. The background investigator can also opt to have the applicant file an IRS Form 8821 (submitted 60 days in advance for reply—should be sent out at the beginning of the background investigation) so that official copies can be had as opposed to those the applicant may have altered prior to submission for investigative review. These reviews should be undertaken by someone adept at tax issues and common fraudulent practices if at all possible. If not, the background investigator should scrutinize the forms for discrepancies of income to lifestyle, bank accounts and financial records, and allow the applicant the opportunity to answer for any discrepancies discovered.

DRIVING HISTORY

The operation of a motor vehicle under normal driving conditions brings with it certain hazards that are sometimes unavoidable. Driving record is often a good barometer of an applicant's ability to safely operate a motor vehicle under normal conditions. Motor vehicle accidents, contributing factors that include driver inattention, alcohol or drug involvement, speeding, reckless driving, cell phone use, and texting are but a few of the issues that may indicate an applicant does not demonstrate due regard for the safe operation of a motor vehicle. Many state legislatures are toughening their traffic laws in order to reduce the number of accidents that occur due to driver distraction as a contributing factor. For example, New York State has responded by adding penalty points to the driver's license of any person who has been cited for texting while driving.[499] This was in response to a number of fatal accidents wherein the driver was texting just prior to the accident.

Alcohol has also plagued the operation of motor vehicles since the very first automobile hit the road. One elusive factor that fuels drinking and driving is the reality that there is a low probability or risk of apprehension of those who choose to drink to excess and then operate a motor vehicle in violation of the traffic laws.[500] The use of alcohol contributes to the primary factors of fatal auto accidents, and the number of fatal accidents that occur in the United States each year is comparable to the country's high homicide rates.[501] In fatal injury accidents where a driver's blood was tested, some 18% revealed the presence of some type of drug use.[502] State legislatures are also taking DWI far more seriously. For example, the legal blood alcohol concentration (BAC) limit in New York State was recently reduced from 0.10 to 0.08. Another extension of how seriously DWI is being considered in New York state is the passing of *Leandra's Law* (*Child Passenger Protection Act*) (2009) wherein a first time DWI with a child passenger under 15 is an automatic felony.[503] This was in response to numerous high-profile incidents that led to the passing of the law, and subsequently hundreds of DWI arrests have been made in New York State since the new legislation was signed into law.[504] The ability to safely operate a vehicle for the average person is of paramount importance. To provide a guide, BAC levels to support a DWI charge are consistent throughout most states. A general set of examples and definitions can be found in the New York State laws that control this type of behavior by vehicle operators:

1. *DWI*: .08 BAC or higher or other evidence of intoxication. For drivers of commercial motor vehicles, .04 BAC or other evidence of intoxication.
2. *Aggravated DWI*: .18 BAC or higher.
3. *DWAI/alcohol*: Driving while ability impaired (by alcohol); .05 BAC to .07 BAC or other evidence of impairment.
4. *DWAI/drug*: DWAI by a single drug other than alcohol.
5. *DWAI/combination*: DWAI by a combined influence of drugs or alcohol.
6. *Chemical test refusal*: A driver who refuses to take a chemical test (normally a test of breath, blood, or urine) can receive a driver license revocation of at least 1 year (18 months for a commercial driver).
7. *Zero Tolerance Law*: A driver who is less than 21 years of age and who drives with a .02 BAC to .07 BAC violates the zero tolerance law.[505]

Emergency operation of a vehicle in the worst of traffic and weather conditions brings with it an extremely higher responsibility for the safe operation of a vehicle than is required of the average civilian driver. More importantly, good judgment must be demonstrated at all times when faced with emergency response to high priority calls for service and the ominous police vehicle pursuit. These types of situations fall under some very famous cases on the use of force including *Tennessee v. Garner* (1985)[506] and *Graham v. Connor* (1989)[507] which both set the standards at the federal review level. While there are cases that support police actions in vehicle pursuits, as found in the decisions of *Scott v. Harris* (2007)[508] and *County of Sacramento v. Lewis* (1998),[509] the courts have adopted a "reckless disregard" standard for measuring the reasonable and safe operation of a police vehicle during a pursuit. However, in the decision of *City of Canton v. Harris* (1989), the court fundamentally forebodes the hiring of a police officer applicant who demonstrates an unsafe driving record.[510]

These justifications in the law are positioned, however, in the shadow of countless incidents across the country wherein law enforcement officers have been involved in questionable driving behaviors as well as serious traffic law violations both off duty and on duty. Law enforcement officers are being apprehended for off-duty as well as some on-duty DWIs that involve felony charges for alcohol, illicit drug use, speeding, and multiple other vehicular violations.[511] Analogous to an applicant's criminal record, a safe driving record is constructively a prerequisite to hire. As the timeless adage forewarns us, the past is the best predictor of the future. Applicants who have had difficulty in the safe operation of a motor vehicle, or who have had consistent brushes with the law, will likely be emboldened by the ability to operate an emergency vehicle with minimal supervision or repercussions for daily operation.

One benefit of driving records over criminal records is that traffic offenses are most always maintained on the permanent driving record or abstract. Unlike criminal records which can be removed or sealed, driving records are often permanent in some form or other. From simple traffic tickets to DWIs and motor vehicle accidents, the records can be obtained, assessed, and used as part of the screening process. Driving abstracts can be obtained from Secretary of State or appropriate motor vehicle agency from each state the applicant has lived or worked. These are obtained with permission of the applicant, and the use of any specific forms is mandated by the specific state motor vehicle agency. This is mandated by federal law in the form of the *Driver's Privacy Protection Act of 1994* as well as the requirements of the *U.S. Code* that prohibits release of certain types of personal information.[512]

Applicant disclosures in the application package and personal history statement are also important to the background investigation for accidents or charges that have not been located by conventional records searches. Motor vehicle accident reports are also an excellent source of information and can be obtained from the investigating agency, state motor vehicles department, or insurance agencies who have handled the claims. In addition, in the absence of formal charges, admissions of driving under influence during interview of candidate, polygraph, witness statements, and indications on motor vehicle accident reports where no charge was lodged are also very valuable to the investigation. The original driver's license application and any requests for reciprocity may also be examined for accuracy of statements made or for any untruths offered by the applicant in their request for a driver's license. This is not only a critical area for review but can also be a very revealing part of the screening process in determining if an applicant can meet this qualification for hire.

Finally, the type of driver's license is also important. Generally, the individual states issue driver's licenses for general classes that include personal vehicle operation, chauffeurs, taxi and livery, motorcycle, and commercial purposes.[513] Driver's licenses will include identifying information as well as any restrictions that may be in place for the applicant. Identification number and matching the information included as well as obtaining a photocopy for the official records should be completed when the applicant is present so that any discrepant information can be explored and verified.

CREDIT HISTORY AND REPORTS

Credit history of the applicant is a topic of both legal and cultural controversy. Debt ratios for the average American citizen have been on the rise for decades with bankruptcy filings reaching epic proportions in many locations across the country.[514] Debt settlement companies are exacerbating the problem by falsely making segments of the American public believe that debts can be incurred and dissolved with little, if any repercussions.[515] As this problem permeates American society, so does it equally permeate our applicant pools. The problem is growing far more complex as the federal government and the individual states are working to create a balance between the need to forgive these matters when faced with the prospect of dwindling opportunities for employment where a poor or bad credit record is a deciding factor for rejection. For example, the states of Illinois and Oregon have passed legislation to ban the use of credit reports in all but a limited number of circumstances.[516] The federal government and many other states are considering the modification of existing legislation, or passing of similar limited legislation.[517] This is important to note that each state will also have their own set of laws governing this process, and the background investigator must be familiar with those apparently ever-evolving regulations as well.[518] Lastly, race and gender issues are also of concern as research has revealed that these protected populations are more prone to have challenged credit histories which put them at a higher risk for rejection for employment.[519]

Credit history can reveal many indicators concerning the applicant's behavior patterns when it comes to the acquisition of credit and fulfilling contractual agreements. For example, bad credit may be an indicator of the applicant's lack of ability to manage critical tasks which may transcend their work ethic.[520] In contrast, good credit may be an indicator of other positive types of behaviors sought after in new employees that include such traits as honesty, integrity, and commitment.[521] However, opponents argue that credit history may not be a completely reliable indicator of an applicant's personality.[522] Prospective employers have consistently recognized the value of such assessments in gauging an applicant's ability to meet forced and self-imposed financial responsibilities. The private sector has extolled the need for the evaluation of credit history in hiring for sensitive positions within organizations with the contemporary research demonstrating that credit checks of prospective applicants have almost doubled over the past decade.[523] The use of credit history is an obligatory recommendation where an applicant would be handling, be responsible for, or have access to money or funds as a part of their job.[524] While the estimates vary greatly, at least 50% of employers use credit screening in the pre-employment investigation process.[525] With this information in mind, the onus also falls upon the applicant to take a proactive approach to locate and address discrepancies and defend concerns prior to application and interview for a position where their credit record may become a factor for consideration and rejection.[526]

In spite of the ensuing and, at times, vexing discussion, credit history must be considered a vital aspect of assessing an applicant's fitness for positions in the criminal justice professions. Navigating the complex landscape may be difficult; however, arriving at the proper assessment will be highly rewarding. This section reviews (1) credit reporting and consumer reporting agencies, (2) the implications and use of bankruptcy, (3) the intersection of the FCRA and ADA, and (4) procedural issues for use in the criminal justice professions.

Credit Reporting and Consumer Reporting Agencies

Credit Reporting

Based upon the history of abuses that were rampant in the credit reporting industry, in 1970, the federal government developed the *Fair Credit Reporting Act*.[527] The Act was designed to prescribe rules and guidelines for consumer/credit reporting agencies to follow to accurately collect and disseminate private information concerning the credit records of consumers. The Act is also designed to proscribe discriminatory practices in the employment process. The Act is ultimately enforced by the Federal Trade Commission. Subsequent legislation followed in the form of the *Fair and Accurate Credit Transactions Act of 2003* that further defined the need for the accuracy of information supplied to consumer reporting agencies as well as the prevention of identity theft.[528] Several contemporary studies, however, have found that credit reporting practices are still rife with mistakes. Research has revealed that defect rates have ranged from 60% to 100% of the reports issued by any given agency studied.[529] Errors can run the gamut from mistakes in biographical information to reporting the wrong types of credit the applicant has been approved for, to the types and number of loans had, and erroneous open and past due accounts. One court decision that accentuates this point can be found in *Smith v. Hireright Solutions, Inc.* (2009), wherein single poor credit incidents were reported multiple times on a credit report that were misleading to the potential employer.[530] These types of mistakes can lead to an adverse action and must be of great concern to the background investigator who should be earnestly interested in accurately assessing the applicant's credit history.

A codicil of the Act makes the use of credit information in employment (i.e., for "employment purposes") possible as long as certain conditions are met.[531] The U.S. EEOC allows the use of credit history when the threshold of business necessity for the position applied for has been reached.[532] For example, in the court decision of *Robinson v. City of Dallas* (1975), the use of a poor credit record in an adverse employment action withstood an adverse impact claim involving minority status as the organizational policies were race neutral and of business necessity.[533] The relevant laws, however, place much responsibility on consumer reporting agencies as well as prospective employers to use the information judiciously and without undue prejudice. As a mandate from the U.S. Congress, prospective employers have a legal responsibility to ensure that the information used from a consumer credit report (e.g., consumer report or consumer investigative report) is as complete and accurate as possible prior to making adverse impact (adverse action) decisions on the employability of an applicant.[534] Employers must provide prior notice to the applicant that the credit history can be used and that, if used, must also provide a preadverse action notice to the applicant that the rejection was based upon poor or bad credit reports as was decided in *United States v. Imperial Palace Inc.* (2004) and *United States v. Quality Terminal Services, LLC* (2009).[535] Applicants who are injured in the process can claim that negligence, intent, and malice were involved in the adverse employment decision and seek both compensatory and punitive damages for their injuries.[536] Interestingly, reporting restrictions are lifted where the position compensation is at a pay scale of $75,000 or higher.[537]

There are several matters to consider when collecting and using credit-related as well as other historical information included in a consumer credit report for the purposes of denying employment.

Credit History Reporting

The first type of consumer reporting agency reports only on the credit history of the applicant. These types of reports are prepared for third parties.[538] The major companies are Equifax, Experian, TransUnion, and AnnualCreditReport.com. Payment history, credit activity, credit cards, payment patterns, bad debts, court judgments, liens, bankruptcies, and credit ratings should all be available in the report sent. These reports should also include any history or information of overdue child support or maintenance requirements.[539]

Consumer Reporting Agencies

There exists a distinction in the law between Consumer Reporting Agencies and the conduct of investigations by the prospective employer or proprietary/in-house investigations. The structures and regulations for both are categorized and discussed later. Consumer Reporting Agencies can be categorized as those organizations that provide only credit histories as well as those that conduct background checks on a prospective applicant to include the credit history. In addition, the staff of the Federal Trade Commission views the term "employment purposes," as used in the *Fair Credit Reporting Act*, as being not only broadly interpreted but also broadly applied in the same manner in the context of the information sought and included.[540] Other relevant information that can be reported under the *Fair Credit Reporting Act* includes criminal convictions, which can be reported indefinitely to the prospective employer.[541] Any unpaid tax liens will also be a part of the record for 15 years. In fact, the term "consumer report" is defined as follows:

> Any written, oral, or other communication of any information by a Consumer Reporting Agency bearing on a consumer's credit worthiness, credit standing, credit capacity, character, general reputation, personal characteristics, or mode of living which is used or expected to be used or collected in whole or in part for the purpose of serving as a factor in establishing the consumer's eligibility for employment purposes.[542]

In addition, the *U.S. Code* further defines the term Investigative Consumer Report as follows:

> A Consumer Report or portion thereof in which information on a consumer's character, general reputation, personal characteristics, or mode of living is obtained through personal interviews with neighbors, friends, or associates of the consumer reported on or with others with whom he is acquainted or who may have knowledge concerning any such items of information. However, such information shall not include specific factual information on a consumer's credit record obtained directly from a creditor of the consumer or from a consumer reporting agency when such information was obtained directly from a creditor of the consumer or from the consumer.[543]

The *U.S. Code* further defines a *Nationwide Specialty Consumer Reporting Agency* as one that compiles and maintains files on consumers on a nationwide basis relating to the following:

1. Medical records or payments
2. Residential or tenant history
3. Check writing history
4. Employment history
5. Insurance claims[544]

As discussed earlier, there are numerous categories of information that are collected and reported in the consumer report. In contrast, under the *Fair Credit Reporting Act*, there are several categories of information that are forbidden to be reported by the consumer reporting agency.[545] These categories or types of information include the following:

1. Bankruptcies after 10 years (Note: While bankruptcies are a public record, employers cannot discriminate against applicants because they have filed for bankruptcy)[546]
2. Civil suits, civil judgments, and records of arrest, from date of entry, to after 7 years
3. Paid tax liens after 7 years
4. Accounts placed for collection after 7 years
5. Any other negative information (except criminal convictions[547]) after 7 years

Of note in credit reporting is that the consumer reporting agency can be found civilly liable if proscribed or inaccurate information is provided to the prospective employer via the report. A claimant can claim they were injured under the decision of *Philbin v. Trans Union Corporation* (2001) if the consumer reporting agency failed to maintain reasonable procedures for verifying and reporting information, which leads to the inclusion of inaccurate information being reported to the prospective employer, and the nature of the information resulted in an adverse employment action that translates to an injury to the applicant.[548] The courts have supported claimants in their allegations when the lack of reasonable procedures to verify information is not in place or followed by the consumer reporting agency's representatives. For example, in the decision of *Wilson v. Prudential Financial* (2009), an erroneous report of pending criminal charges against an applicant led to illegal withdrawal of the job offer.[549] In a similar case, erroneous information from a court clerk concerning a felony conviction was not confirmed by the credit reporting agency and was found to be improperly reported based upon the decision in *Dalton v. Capital Associated Indus., Inc.* (2001).[550] The culpability is borne by the consumer reporting agency if the prospective employer rejects an applicant or rescinds the job offer. In contrast, the prospective employer is not obligated to reinstate the original offer of employment if the consumer reporting agency provides a corrected report subsequent to the rejection.[551] One favorable case involved a consumer reporting agency that inadvertently reported a dismissed conviction. In the decision of *Obabueki v. Choicepoint, Inc.* (2002), the contractor disclosed a dismissed criminal conviction of the applicant.[552] While this information should not have been reported by the contractor, the prospective employer acted on the information by withdrawing the COE based upon the applicant's failure to disclose the original charge in the application. The court found the rescinding of the offer was proper based upon the applicant's untruthfulness in the process. It is also important to note that the *Fair Credit Reporting Act* does not limit or prohibit the types of questions that can be included in an employment application, for example, references or questions concerning criminal activity.[553] Consequently, exploring this type of information in the original application can be most revealing about an applicant's willingness to be forthcoming when a comparison is made to the available records.

Background Investigation Contractors and Proprietary Investigations/In-House Reporting

Contained in the *Fair Credit Reporting Act* is a distinction between third party and proprietary investigations.[554] A Consumer Reporting Agency is considered a third party, and most of the aforementioned regulations apply. The *Fair Credit Reporting Act* does not apply to background checks conducted by the employer when the employer conducts the investigation in-house or with their own employees.[555] The Federal Trade Commission has taken the position that the *Fair Credit Reporting Act* requirements do not apply when an employer directly obtains criminal background and other investigative information about employees.[556] When the employer uses a third party to conduct the investigation, that is when the investigation falls under the requirements of a Consumer Reporting Agency. The individual states may also have stricter laws as well. Federal, state, and municipal agencies are not considered consumer reporting agencies as their responsibility to conduct background checks comes from statutory authority.[557] However, if the public agency hires an outside investigator, then the background investigation would fall under all of the requirements of a Consumer Reporting Agency.[558]

Implications and Use of Bankruptcy

The concern of bankruptcy is yet another quagmire in the process of screening applicants based upon credit history. Poor life choices, as well as unforeseen difficulties that include the onset of severe illnesses, economic downturns, marriage dissolutions, or sudden job loss, frequently lead to excessive debt. Excessive debt leads to unpaid credit cards and loans that are often referred to debt collection agencies, and finally, bankruptcy is perceived as the only option. Bankruptcy options were enacted in the law to allow a consumer an opportunity to gain a "fresh start" at life by disposing of these incurred debts.[559] As codified in the *Bankruptcy Act of 1978*, employers are prohibited from engaging in discriminatory practices in employment screening based solely upon an applicant's declaration of bankruptcy.[560] Additional legislation was passed through the *Bankruptcy Abuse Prevention and Consumer Protection Act of 2005* designed to further limit the abuses that are rampant in the industry.[561] Proscribed under the *Bankruptcy Code*, a prospective employer may not discriminate against a job applicant solely because the applicant has filed for, and gained the protections of, bankruptcy.[562]

There are several different types of bankruptcy filings that an applicant may avail themselves of. For example, in a *Chapter 7 Bankruptcy* (Straight Bankruptcy), the debtor sells assets in return for the discharge of the pending debts. In a *Chapter 11 Bankruptcy*, the debtor company reorganizes under the supervision of the presiding court with jurisdiction. A *Chapter 12 Bankruptcy* filing relates to family farms where the debts are repaid. Lastly, in a *Chapter 13 Bankruptcy* (Wage Earner Plan), the debtor develops a plan to repay the pending debt. Under the bankruptcy laws, debts are divided into dischargeable and non-dischargeable categories for the purposes of the bankruptcy. Most debts are dischargeable except for the following:

1. Alimony and child support
2. Some student loans
3. Certain federal, state, and local taxes
4. Debts from fraud, larceny, and theft
5. Fines and penalties for violating the law, such as traffic tickets
6. Luxury goods or services purchased within 60 days of filing for bankruptcy, with a value of $1000 or more
7. Debts not listed on bankruptcy papers[563]

Depending on varied policies and state regulations, a Consumer Reporting Agency is required to remove a bankruptcy filing from a consumer's record from anywhere between 7 and 10 years after the date of the discharge, not at the point of the filing of the original petition. The background investigator must make themselves aware of not only the federal laws but also state laws that may be more restrictive of the use of bankruptcy filings as a method consideration for pre-employment screening. While federal law prohibits the sole use of a bankruptcy filing as a method of screening an applicant, several cases have been decided that support the use of this information, whether wholly or in part. This position was affirmed in the decision of *White v. Kentuckiana Livestock Market, Inc.* (2005), wherein a bankruptcy filing by a current employee could not be used as the sole determinant for decision to terminate.[564] In the decision of *Rea v. Federated Investors* (2010), a federal court set a precedent in allowing private employers to reject job applicants for filing for bankruptcy paving the way for more conservative positions in the law concerning the previous protections enjoyed by job applicants.[565] Specifically to policing, there were rulings in favor of the use of bankruptcy as a means of screening police applicants. For example, in the decision of *Marshall v. District of Columbia Government* (1977), the prospective employer may consider bankruptcy as an indicator of an applicant's fit for the position applied for.[566] Another supportive ruling can be found in the decision of *Detz v. Hoover* (1982), wherein the information from the bankruptcy can be used to determine if the police applicant has been unable to properly manage personal financial matters.[567] Therefore, the prospective employer can consider the circumstances that led to the bankruptcy when screening police applicants.[568] Based upon the variations in positions, bankruptcy may be used as long as the use is not overly discriminatory (i.e., the sole reason for the rejection) to an applicant and in compliance with all federal and state laws. One tactic that can be used is the redaction of any bankruptcy filings in lieu of the supportive case law that allows the use of the circumstances and actual debts that led to the bankruptcy filing. This would present a more objective presentation of the facts of the applicant's credit behaviors without the ominous presence of the bankruptcy filing being made available for review by the key decision makers in the process.

One final note concerning bankruptcies relates to the issue of cosigners. Bankruptcy may be brought on by the unwittingness or benevolence of a cosigner or guarantor. A third party with challenged credit may convince an applicant to assist in gaining credit through a cosigning situation. Cosigners can be required to pay the third party debts in both Chapters 7 and 13 filings. As discussed later, this may be a consideration for understandable debt if the applicant was burdened with the third party's failure to repay the debt or filing for bankruptcy.

Intersection of the FCRA and ADA

With respect to medical information, the Consumer Reporting Agency may report information of a medical nature in the credit report. This may be directly or indirectly revealed as delinquent medical bills for medications, examinations, and procedures that are all subject to reporting to a credit agency can be included in the consumer report. This type of information may also be relevant to the position applied for. However, great care must be taken in the interpretation of certain types of delinquent medical bills that include protected issues of medical privacy.[569] Protections for this type of information exist through the ADA and through workmen's compensation laws and regulations.[570] Under the *U.S. Code*, certain restrictions apply to the sharing of medical information, medical products, and medical services.[571] Further defined, medical information includes "information or data, whether oral or recorded, in any form or medium, created by or derived from a health-care provider or the consumer," that relates to the following:

1. The past, present, or future physical, mental, or behavioral health or condition of an individual
2. The provision of health care to an individual
3. The payment for the provision of health care to an individual[572]

Consequently, the metaphor of an intersection, absent traffic control in place, can result in a collision of sorts. The discovery of medical information absent the issuance of a COE can have such consequences. Therefore, prior to requesting the credit report from the applicant or directly from the consumer reporting agency with the applicant's permission, the applicant should be issued the COE.

Procedural Issues for Use in Criminal Justice Professions

The *Fair Credit Reporting Act* does not mandate that a background investigation be conducted on job applicants; however, when an agency decides to engage in such an inquiry, the Act mandates that certain standards be adhered to.[573] The rules of using consumer reports for the assessment of applicants to the criminal justice professions are far more liberal than to non-law enforcement positions. However, there are still several requirements for their legal and nondiscriminatory use in the selection process. As previously mentioned, each state will have their own fair employment agencies, and a search for the applicable laws and regulations is a required task for the background investigator.[574] Most importantly, credit information that is not statutorily prohibited from use must be used only as a part of all of the factors considered in the hiring process to make the most informed and objective decision possible as opposed to a stand-alone document in the process; therefore, credit history must never be the only component of the screening assessment process.[575]

Federal law requires that the job applicant be given written notice and provide authorization or permission to the agency to obtain the consumer report. This notice must be a single writing that advises the applicant that the report may be used in the selection process. The agency must also have this permission before requesting a report from a Consumer Reporting Agency. The applicant can also be requested to obtain the report on their own and deliver a sealed copy to the agency or have a sealed copy delivered by mail to the agency. This must be done subsequent to the issuance of the COE so that any protected information such as medical information may be used in the investigation. As a result of the review of the report, if the hiring agency intends to use the information to deny the application, prior to any adverse action, the agency must

> Give the individual a Pre-Adverse Action disclosure that includes a copy of the individual's consumer report and a copy of "*A Summary of Your Rights Under the Fair Credit Reporting Act*," a document prescribed by the Federal Trade Commission.[576]

After the adverse action has been taken, the agency must notify the applicant either orally, in writing, or electronically that the action has been taken in an Adverse Action Notice. The notice must include the following:

1. The name, address, and phone number of the Consumer Reporting Agency that supplied the report
2. A statement that the Consumer Reporting Agency that supplied the report did not make the decision to take the adverse action and cannot give specific reasons for it
3. A notice of the individual's right to dispute the accuracy or completeness of any information the agency furnished, and his or her right to an additional free consumer report from the agency upon request within 60 days[577]

To reiterate, the Act ensures (1) that individuals are aware that consumer reports may be used for employment purposes and agree to such use and (2) that individuals are notified promptly if information in a consumer report may result in a negative employment decision.[578] For a consumer investigative report, the applicant can request the information that led to the denial of employment. These documents are subject to discovery motions and proceedings if the applicant files a discrimination claim with the Federal Trade Commission, the EEOC, the state human rights boards and bureaus, or with the state and federal courts that have jurisdiction.

In practice, several issues will need to be considered in order to accurately and fairly assess an applicant's credit history to the point that the personal habits and debts of the applicant lead to an adverse employment action. Fundamentally, most every applicant will have some type and level of debt. Debt management through adjusting lifestyle is a benchmark to look for in reviewing an applicant's credit history. Understandable debt is also for consideration. Mortgages, car loans, and similar encumbrances will be normal as long as the applicant, under their normal circumstances, has not intentionally extended themselves beyond their financial means. Also for consideration are student loans that are accruing from several thousand to hundreds of thousands of dollars, a growing specter that is reaching epic proportions across the country.[579] Other credit conditions for consideration are cosigning loans where the primary debtor has defaulted and the applicant who is a cosigner is unwittingly burdened with the debt. Also be wary of clean or nonexistent credit which may be another area of concern. All cash transactions, debts paid off by a third party, parent–sibling situations wherein the applicant has been irresponsible with their credit (however, the acts and behaviors have been covered up), and, finally, the legal regulations requiring redaction of bad debts after certain time periods have been met should all be considered.

Excessive debt and bad debts must then be considered in the context of the position applied for (e.g., financial responsibility, opportunities for corruption, failure to pay child support or alimony, etc.). The background investigator must then follow-up to confirm or refute these debts to demonstrate that a reasonable procedure was in place to verify the veracity of the information supplied. The applicant must then be allowed to respond to the adverse information and given the opportunity to correct any inaccurate or erroneous information supplied by the consumer reporting agency. Once the best information is obtained and the applicant has had the opportunity to answer to any issues revealed, then excessive debt, bad debts, and the like must be considered in the context of the applicant's life (i.e., job loss, illnesses, divorce, etc.). This will allow a fair and equitable assessment that will meet federal and state standards.

One final note is that the organization should have a policy in place to justify any adverse employment actions taken. Fair and equitable policy that meets legal standards and is impartially applied to all candidates is the only manner in which the organization should function. Lack of policy leaves the door open for interpretation by the decision makers in the organization as well as the governing administrative bodies and the courts, who may all have quite varied interpretations of the same applicant. One example is provided by the FBI as the policy provides for rejection of applicants who have defaulted on student loans.[580] Another excellent example is demonstrated through the South Carolina Highway Patrol's posted credit standards for new applicants to the agency. At the outset, the policy asserts the following:

> The credit history and financial conditions of the applicant will be reviewed. Credit history will not be a sole basis for disqualification, except that an applicant may be denied for employment if he or she is indebted to the extent that their salary as a law enforcement officer would be insufficient to pay his or her debits.[581]

The policy then provides very specific examples for two reasons, to advise applicants that the screening process will encompass a review of these issues and that if minimum standards are not met, the applicant will be rejected, as well as providing a court defensible policy when adverse actions are taken based upon issues revealed in the applicant's credit history. The posted minimum standards are as follows:

1. An unsatisfied judgment
2. An unpaid state or federal tax lien
3. Accounts written off as bad debt with a remaining balance
4. Accounts turned over to a collection agency with a remaining balance
5. Voluntary or involuntary repossessions with a remaining balance
6. A student loan in default
7. An account with a payment 120 days past due with a remaining balance
8. A foreclosure account with a remaining balance
9. An account "included in bankruptcy" with a remaining balance[582]

Lastly, the policy includes a codicil for the applicant to remedy any issues that may be inaccurate, erroneous, or may have been resolved in the applicant's favor by including the following language:

> Applicants who are given the opportunity to review their credit reports may submit documentation which indicates that they have taken responsibility for the accounts in question (e.g., paid in full receipts/letters, payment plan letters).[583]

At the outset of this section, the issue of credit was portrayed as a very complex and ambiguous parameter used in the assessment of an applicant's fitness for a position in the criminal justice professions. The milieu of statutory acts, case law, and interpretation by federal and local authorities in review adds both lucidity and opacity to the application of these concepts. Fundamentally, credit history cannot be ignored as long as state and federal legislations allow the use of such information in the process of screening applicants who may be unduly influenced by past credit patterns or behaviors as they fill the positions of trust in the criminal justice professions.

EDUCATION AND TRAINING HISTORY

Educational and training history should include all available records of the applicant's attendance in grade schools, training and professional development seminars and programs, and higher education. This section discusses (1) confidentiality of educational records, (2) primary and secondary education, (3) postsecondary education, (4) training and professional development, and (5) procedural issues for use in the criminal justice professions.

Confidentiality of Educational Records

Educational records confidentiality is a federal mandate that is covered under the *Family Educational Rights and Privacy Act* (1974).[584] Parents of students under 18 have primary control over any records review and releases. At the age of 18, or if a student attends any school beyond high school, then the rights for records review and release transfer to whom the Act defines as the "eligible student."[585] A summary of the relevant components of the Act in relation to the pre-employment process is as follows:

1. The rights to inspect and review personal educational records.
2. The right to petition to correct inaccurate or erroneous records, to appeal through a formal hearing contested inaccuracies, and to have a letter of dispute placed in the educational file if the formal appeal fails.
3. Affected schools are not required to copy records for the eligible student; however, the issue of substantial distance from the school may be considered to release copies, or a charge for copying services may apply.
4. Written permission must be obtained from the eligible student for release of any and all records. The only other applicable method to this process is through judicial order or lawfully issued subpoena.
5. Information that may be released by the school without the consent of the eligible student includes only "directory information" which includes the student's name, address, telephone number, date and place of birth, honors and awards, and dates of attendance, except the eligible student may request the school to not disclose this type of information.[586]

All states will have their own educational laws and records release requirements and restrictions in place as well. Records releases are usually covered in the COE, and the applicant should be required to obtain the records from the affected schools or colleges and have them forwarded directly to the agency conducting the background investigation. The applicant can also bring sealed copies in official envelopes marked as such. Records that are not sealed should not be accepted unless mitigating circumstances exist. If this becomes necessary, then scrutiny of the records along with contacting the educational institution personally may be necessary to verify the veracity of the records submitted.

Primary and Secondary Education

Primary and secondary educational records should be accessed and added to the background investigation whenever possible. Much of the early documentation will demonstrate the formative years of learning, and information gleaned must be considered in context with the age of the applicant at that time in the applicant's life. Middle and high school, or secondary education, must be examined with a much more discerning eye. As the applicant advances to the teenage years, commitment to studies through grade reports and teacher observations, indicators of aberrant behavior, drug or alcohol use, violence, absenteeism, and many other facets of the educational experience can reveal some telling clues.

The American system of education has been under the microscope for some time now due to the failures of properly preparing the youth of our country to meet the needs of the society they will be entering as young adults. For example, one study in a midsize urban school district revealed that less than 5% of the high school graduates were prepared to enter college or a career.[587] Examples of alcohol abuse through binge drinking and drug use for those youth classified as high-risk users are also at staggering proportions in our schools.[588] Sadly, our youths see experimentation with drugs and alcohol as considered an innocent act where these same youth have no conception of the concomitant long-term negative effects that relate to health issues, addictions, behavioral problems, and, in the case of pre-employment investigations, rejections for positions that require the absence of a drug history.[589] Alcohol use and abuse has also rivaled illicit drug and tobacco use with the nation's youth.[590] And while marijuana use has subsided slightly, other illicit and over-the-counter drug use has steadily risen by our children.[591]

Violence in our schools has also brought on significant attention across the country.[592] Images of Columbine as well as similar acts of violence directed toward our children still haunt us as a society.[593] School violence is underscored by the vulnerable nature of the victims. School violence can be defined as follows:

1. Bullying
2. Fighting (e.g., punching, slapping, kicking)
3. Weapon use
4. Electronic aggression
5. Gang violence[594]

These definitions also include homicides, assaults, and sex crimes that include rapes and sexual abuse. School violence occurs either on, en route to and from, or during any school sponsored events.[595] Bullying has been a rising concern among educational circles because of how acute the problem has become across the United States as well as around the world. Physical as well as cyber bullying facilitated by the increased use of social networks and sexting, as previously discussed, seem to be far more pervasive and deeply rooted than school administrators are willing to publicly admit.[596] The background investigator's records review, investigation, and subsequent interview with the applicant in exploring incidents of this nature must be thorough and objective. The applicant may be the aggressor or victim and must be treated according to their involvement. Incidents have been dealt with wherein the victim of bullying, in the act of defending themselves, is also suspended as a matter of policy.[597] Educational records, interviews with teachers, administrators, and witnesses, as well as records of security staff, must all be obtained and evaluated as weighed against the applicant's explanations for the events that have occurred.

Finally, collection of any and all relevant school records must be included in the investigation. Copies of transcripts, awards, the high school diploma or Graduate Equivalency Diploma (GED), disciplinary and attendance records, and any other information that gives insight into the applicant's primary and secondary educational performance, experiences, and conduct will be helpful in developing the fundamental components of the review.

Postsecondary Education

The postsecondary educational records can be far more revealing than is the case with primary and secondary educational records. Degree program, academic performance, and legitimate cocurricular and extracurricular activities will provide part of the picture. Filling in the remainder with respect to patterns and behaviors of conduct will likely come from college and university police departments and security records, interviews with professors, classmates, and domestic relationships with others.

Academic Preparation and Performance

Taken as axiomatic, the knowledge gained from attendance at a legitimate, state licensed, and regionally accredited college that leads to a degree is a primary indicator for success in any profession. The available research has generally revealed that the predominant indicator of success in a law enforcement position can be correlated to the possession of at least a bachelor's degree from an accredited institution. This includes the possession of a bachelor's degree in any field as one piece of research found that there was no difference in performance when comparing criminal justice majors to other academic majors insofar as performance and cognitive ability are concerned.[598] The fact that the officer had a college education was the deciding factor in the positive outcomes of their service. Another piece of research found that there was no difference as to the type of college degree being a predictor of such posthire concerns as the number of complaints filed against the officer.[599] In spite of the research, political influence still abounds in lowering college requirements to satisfy unsupported claims of raising diversity levels.[600] Applicants will apply to the position that have an array of college experiences that range from a single course to postgraduate degrees in varied professional fields. Because the field is becoming so diverse, those who enter the ranks with discipline-specific degrees in areas other than criminal justice may be of great value to the organization. After hire, their areas of academic acumen can be tapped to meet specific organizational needs. The background investigator should examine the type of degree program, college accreditation, and coursework taken to meet the requirements of the major area studied, determine if any minor concentrations were taken, and general grades, academic awards, and cocurricular/extracurricular activity involvement.

Academic Transgressions

A sense of reckless abandon seems to dominate the cultures of many college fraternities and sororities.[601] Campus-based offenses include the gamut of transgressions, from minor to serious.[602] In light of these issues as well as the propensity for serious crimes to occur on campus grounds, for example, the murder of Jeanne Clery, the federal government responded by signing The *Jeanne Clery Disclosure of Campus Security Policy and Campus Crime Statistics Act* (1990) into law.[603] The Act mandates police and security departments of colleges and universities to report and maintain records concerning crimes that have occurred on campus, in noncampus buildings or property, or public property. Those categories include the following:

1. Criminal homicide: Murder as well as nonnegligent and negligent manslaughter
2. Sex offenses: Forcible and nonforcible sex offenses
3. Robbery
4. Aggravated assault

5. Burglary
6. Motor vehicle theft
7. Arson
8. Hate crimes for the aforementioned crimes and any crime that includes a serious injury
9. Arrests and judicial referrals involving illegal weapons, drug, and alcohol violations[604]

The Act requires maintenance of statistical records for at least 3 years. Campus police departments should maintain these types of records for much longer though which will allow access by the background investigator. As a requirement of the *Higher Education Amendment Act* (1998), federally funded campuses must keep public crime logs that document the specifics of all incidents reported to the security or police departments including the names of persons cited or charged and the offenses they are charged with.[605] Campus safety records should only be a part of the search as police agencies have used such tactics as employing student informants to infiltrate the college drug trade which may produce information on an applicant's criminal activities as well.[606] Contacts should be made to college security/police as well as local-, regional-, and state-level intelligence and vice units to see if any arrests, active investigations, or intelligence information exists. Media reports are also helpful as demonstrated through an incident where several college students were involved in hate crimes while off campus.[607] These records may include alcohol and drug violations, to property damage, theft, domestic violence, assaults, hazings, and many other problems that would be relevant to the review of the applicant's history and conduct in college.

Beyond criminal records may be the records of these types of incidents that are filed in college disciplinary board proceedings as well as other sources that include reports and records filed by administrators, resident assistants, academic advisement, coaches, counselors, and others who have had direct contact with the applicant. The background investigator must also be aware that colleges may routinely downplay or try to secrete these types of incidents in order to project a safe and secure campus environment for current and prospective students.[608] As a requirement of the law, campuses must share this type of information with local police agencies with jurisdiction. Issues of records release and lack of cooperation can be reported to the State's Attorney General or Inspector General, local district attorney, or the U.S. Department of Education.

A review of the applicant's original application to college may also be revealing. There have been incidents wherein a person engaged in identity theft in order to enter college and gain financial and educational benefits.[609] Untruths may be found in the application materials regarding lies to meet minimum standards. Depending on the program of study and college regulations, criminals may be denied entry to school if they lied on their application or failed to disclose a criminal record. Residency, pedigree information, names of references, and much other information can be gleaned from these forms and entrance materials. Interviews of students, guidance counselors, professors, coaches, and others who have had contact with the applicant may provide significant insight not found in the official records.[610]

Fraudulent Degrees

Another concern may be found in the emergence of fraudulent or fake college degrees that are used by applicants to meet minimum qualifications or to merely bolster themselves as being more qualified than other applicants for the position. Estimated to be in excess of a billion dollar per year fraudulent enterprise, diploma mills (fake degrees from legitimate colleges) and degree mills (genuine degrees from illegitimate colleges) are growing across the country, with domestic and foreign entities fleecing students under the guise of attaining a college degree at an accelerated pace and bargain-based prices.[611] Many of these counterfeit colleges will adopt similar names of credible colleges so as to further deceive the recipients and employing organizations.[612] Some even go so far as to use fake professor names or, worse yet, include legitimate faculty names from other colleges and universities on their rosters who have never had any affiliation with the college in question.[613] The online proliferation of these types of scams also includes such fraudulent acts as citing nonexistent accreditation bodies for those who are unaware of the qualitative requirements of the legitimate existing higher education accreditation organizations.[614] The State of Mississippi has unfortunately been named as the hub for these types of institutions.[615]

Online and distance education programs have become so pervasive that they blur the traditional lines and call into question the many credible programs available where students have obtained legitimate degrees.[616] Some have postured that the number of diploma mills issuing graduate degrees has permeated the United States to such a point as to have significant negative societal issues.[617] Other cases were noted where fake medical and psychology degrees have been used that underscore the public health and safety issues involved in the bogus degree marketplace.[618] Numerous incidents can be presented where public officials have been called to task over phony credentials and educational certificates that are from degree and diploma mills and have been used to obtain positions, promotions, and incentive pay, all illegally.[619] A shocking example includes a major federal inquiry that involved hundreds of federal and public employees who were found to have purchased fraudulent college degrees to shortcut their way to pay and promotions.[620] A grave concern has been voiced in the lack of the verification process of the existence of college degrees by federal employers for their employees who occupy some of the highest ranks in the organizations.[621] Specifically, this is also an issue that has come to light for polygraph examiners who have bogus degrees that are used to meet the minimum qualifications for the position of polygrapher.[622]

There are also issues of colleges that legally operate, providing degrees, but they are not accredited by any of the major accrediting bodies in the country.[623] The lack of proper accreditation and quality for a college degree conferred on one police chief has led to embarrassing high-profile media coverage for the college and the officials involved.[624] This also includes legitimate colleges whose administrators buckle to political pressure to lower standards for admissions and graduation requirements. Anonymous e-mails and an investigation led to information revealed by a college official concerning how there was oppressive political pressure to award a degree to a police official who failed to meet the college's and accrediting body's minimum graduation standards.[625] In this specific incident, the investigation was actually hampered when investigators were faced with "conflicting statements, failing memories, unwillingness to explain situations, and unexplained loss of relevant documents and records."[626] These circumstances further cast a shadow on the legitimacy of the degree awarded to the police official.

Institutions of higher learning require state and federal licensing as well as regional accreditation in order to be valid. The individual states have aggressively responded to consumer and student complaints by investigating and closing these types of scams as well as offering information through public access websites to inform prospective students of the issues. Maine, Oregon, Texas, and Washington State are but a few examples wherein they have made available an exhaustive list of fraudulent colleges as well as information on legitimate accreditation and the like.[627]

Criminal justice organizations will list as requirements certain degree levels as well as the need for the degree to be granted from a regionally accredited university or college in order to meet minimum standards or qualify for specialized assignments and promotions. One example is found in the *Quinn Bill* (Police Career Incentive Pay Program), passed in Massachusetts to provide educational incentives for officers who complete higher education requirements and receive college degrees.[628] In spite of the good intent of the legislation, several scandals arose due to investigations into the quality of the academic credentials and allegations of rampant diploma mills.[629] This issue gained national attention and was the subject of a Congressional investigation in 2004.[630] This federal response has not abated the problem entirely though. A separate scandal uncovered in 2008 involved numerous state troopers who had allegedly purchased bogus college degrees in order to gain pay raises and incentives.[631] A federal investigation was also recently launched into a Department of Homeland Security official concerning a false degree that was presented as part of the minimum requirements for employment some 25 years prior.[632] In a very high-profile case, one large city police chief and college administration were called to task regarding the dubious circumstances of the college's awarding a police chief candidate a college degree conveniently timed to satisfy the minimum requirements for the position.[633] One particularly egregious case in the criminal justice realm involved the use of fake degrees of a purported forensic psychologist who testified as an expert witness in hundreds of criminal cases.[634] Cases that have all been called into question and likely resulting in the loss of many convictions as well as the exorbitant law enforcement and prosecutorial resources expended in the process.

Because of the widespread abuses, many states are responding by enacting laws to prevent and sanction these types of fraudulent entities. For example, the Washington State legislature has passed a law that criminalizes the use of fake academic credentials for the purposes of gaining employment, gaining a promotion, obtaining professional licensure, promoting a business, or gaining admission to a school.[635] Other states have responded by moving to criminalize the use of fraudulent degrees offered by the recipient by placing the onus of verification on the applicant. For example, in the State of Oregon, it is currently a misdemeanor to assert in an official document the possession of a postsecondary degree that has not been awarded by a regionally accredited college or university.[636]

The final example can be found in false claims of having a degree. Applicants may claim the attainment of a degree when none actually exists. These claims range from blatant lies to attendance and completion, or some course work as matriculated or nonmatriculated students where the full requirements have not been met at the institution to award a degree of any kind. A classic court case decision can be found in the ruling of *Gilty v. Village of Oak Park* (1990), wherein a police officer claimed to have a college degree in order to secure a promotion, a degree he in fact did not possess. The court subsequently ruled the following:

> In 1985, Selester Gilty misrepresented his academic credentials in order to gain a promotion. Now, some years and several misrepresentations later, he alleges racial discrimination in his employer's failure to promote him and later decision to discharge him. But Gilty's claims collapse of their own weight, and we affirm the district court's grant of summary judgment in favor of his employer.[637]

In this case, the fact that he had lied about his academic credentials was the key to the court's finding even though the possession of a college degree was not a base requirement for the promotion he had been seeking.[638] Given all of these variables, college degree verification is a priority for the background investigator to pursue vigorously. Legitimacy of the degree presented can be called into question at any time in the applicant's career, and the need to establish the veracity of the degree as well as the applicant who asserts the possession of the credential may save much embarrassment as well as civil litigation in the long term.

Training and Professional Development

Training and professional development records should also be obtained. Training seminars, conferences, and workshops may all be relevant to the applicant's qualifications for the position, especially for lateral transfers to the organization. External training opportunities are but part of the records that may be available. Internal training may also be of relevance and documented through letters of attendance, certificates, and curriculum. The military conducts consistent training in specialized assignments that should be captured and added to the official background investigation record. All other specialized and vocational training should be collected, reviewed, and, most importantly, verified as credible training. Training records can be much trickier and more elusive to verify than college and university records as in most jurisdictions, there are no real requirements for training organization licensure, accreditation, or standards. While law enforcement and other criminal justice professions academies that include corrections, parole, probation, and others may require state or federal approval, many other small to large training entities may not. Follow-up and verification will be necessary through the host organizations, establishing if any licensing is required and in place, and also the quality of the training involved. All of these should be checked when an applicant has submitted this type of information for review in their background investigation.

Procedural Issues for Use in Criminal Justice Professions

For a matter that should be cut-and-dried as it were, examination of the numerous problems in the field makes this not as simple a matter as would originally appear. Higher education is an important component of a public safety professional's success in the field. The quality of the education is then a driver of this truism. Verifying that quality then becomes the task of the background investigator. The quality of the education as well as the granting institution will be central to the investigation of these matters. More importantly, the background investigator must establish if the information provided by the applicant is accurate, if the applicant does possess a legitimate degree, and that the degree is not from a diploma or degree mill. The initial steps in this chapter call for the background investigator to obtain transcripts directly, examine and copy actual diplomas and degrees, and contact the college and interview security and police officials, professors, and other principals to the investigation, who can speak to learning ability, performance, and character. The background investigator should also fully review and document all bad behavior, disciplinary actions, and activities that have led to suspension or expulsion from all schools attended. As we consider the numerous examples and scandals presented in this analysis, the need is clear to ensure that the applicant's claims are accurate and that the quality of their education is a fundamental element of the applicant's character that will lead to high probabilities of success in their future careers.

MILITARY SERVICE

One cannot experience a moment of pause, a deep sense of humility, and an expression of the utmost respect for those who don an armed services uniform in order to protect the American way of life. There can be no more eloquent nor moving understanding of the nobility of American military personnel than as asserted by General Douglas MacArthur throughout his distinguished career that spanned over a half of a century in military service the entire time recognizing the sanctity of the soldier's service to the country.[639] For centuries, they have done this under the auspices of the singular maxim of freedom. We justly place an unparalleled level of our trust, veneration, and personal safety in the hands of those who faithfully serve. Our support should never falter no matter the adversity that may arise as they do an impossible job, under impossible circumstances, and pay the highest personal sacrifices for their devotion to the principles of the constitution they swear to honor, uphold, and defend.

As difficult a task as this is, we must consider though that the responsibility we have to defend their honor and commitment to preserving our free society is tantamount to our responsibility to maintain public safety within the confines of that very same free society. The Fort Hood massacre underscores the importance of screening techniques for those who will occupy trusted positions responsible for the security of our country.[640] With respect to military service, we must examine several factors of an applicant's past in order to make informed decisions on fitness for the role in domestic public safety. These factors and areas of investigation can be categorized as (1) spectrum of conduct, (2) psychological and behavioral issues, and (3) records access and retrieval.

Spectrum of Conduct

The overwhelming majority of those who serve in the military are altruistic, dedicated, and patriotic Americans who truly believe in the ethos of the American Constitution. Similar to public safety though, there will be those who are driven by personal agendas, are unfit for duty, or who are maladapted, who make entry into the ranks and do nothing but create a blight on the nobility of the profession. Strict standards of conduct are the defining quality of the American military institution. One example can be found in the U.S. Department of the Navy Core Values Charter. U.S. naval personnel pledge that "I am accountable for my professional and personal behavior. I will be mindful of the privilege I have to serve my fellow Americans."[641] They also swear as members of the U.S. Navy to

1. Abide by an uncompromising code of integrity, taking full responsibility for my action, and keeping my word
2. Conduct myself in the highest ethical manner in relationships with seniors, peers, and subordinates
3. Be honest and truthful in my dealings within and outside the Department of the Navy
4. Make honest recommendations to my seniors and peers and seek honest recommendations from junior personnel

5. Encourage new ideas and deliver bad news forthrightly
6. Fulfill my legal and ethical responsibilities in my public and personal life[642]

For the overwhelming majority of military actions, these values have been upheld and more importantly, demonstrated throughout our history as a nation as their purpose is that of a peacekeeping armada as opposed to a machination of war. When considered in the scope of global military operations that occur on a daily basis, sporadic and individual transgressions are inconsequential to the positive change that has been brought to the world by their actions to protect democracy domestically and secure democracy abroad. There are a few caveats to this though when considering screening applicants for the public safety professions. Reminiscent of policing, acts that occur during critical incidents are always dissected by those either dressed in pajamas and in the comfort of an armchair, from those sporting brass laden uniforms, and from those who put on the judicial garb, all far removed from the realities of the flawed and dynamic circumstances of the incidents in question. The military carries the same type of burdensome fishbowl mentality when reviewing duty-related conduct. In the face of confusing and often politically motivated rules of engagement, split second decisions with imperfect information may forever haunt the best intended actions of the finest military personnel.[643] In the screening process, these types of incidents must be taken in the context that they occurred and balanced against the opinions and variant motivations of those who have reviewed the event. Much as we would need to fairly assess the actions of a lateral officer to our agencies, the same must be considered for those who are in similar and unique situations that require action that will be questioned no matter how justified those actions were. As independent and impartial investigators, we must avoid the trappings of the ulterior motivators of that investigative process and concentrate on the behaviors and conduct in the context and moment of the incident.

A second category we need to consider in the screening process is intended conduct that violates military codes of ethics as well as those incidents that rise to the level of military crimes. At the lowest level are issues of excessive alcohol use and petty offenses. Other issues include some applicants who may lie concerning ever being in the military in the first place.[644] Recently, concerns were voiced by the members of Congress over the military's flaws in their vetting process as highlighted by a man who used false documents and claims of prior service to fake his way into the army.[645] The military, in the continuing battle to fill the ranks, has taken to lowering standards immensely by accepting otherwise unfit recruits who have committed serious crimes including misdemeanors and felonies into the ranks by the use of moral waivers.[646] A much graver concern is the penetration of the U.S. military by hate groups as well as numerous street and motorcycle gang members.[647] Undetected upon entry, an applicant's credibility and legitimacy can grow significantly by design by simply attending to the proper codes of military conduct. Service and traits that are highly sought after by law enforcement recruiters and valued by law enforcement administrators.

There is also a hierarchy to these incidents that reaches unconscionable heights though. For example, one navy officer was terminated for developing offensive videos that were claimed to be innocent attempts to raise morale for serving personnel.[648] The issue became one of a conflict between purported navy tradition and the perceived lapse of integrity in the high position held. Taking another step in the hierarchy, female military personnel have been sanctioned for posing nude for adult magazines.[649] According to proper military convention, the indecent exposure and posing bare for profit violates military codes of conduct and is a consequent abuse of their official positions.[650]

As we advance to another rung, domestic violence is often the topic of much controversy in military settings.[651] Research has revealed a high percentage of soldiers who abuse their spouses, and significant others will also have a high occurrence of substance abuse as well.[652] The expansion of the *Gun Control Act* (1968), titled the *Lautenberg Amendment* (1997), restricts the possession of a firearm if a domestic violence conviction occurs does not exclude any individuals or job classifications including those serving in the military.[653] This includes not only possession but also the transfer of a weapon such as in the case of a command officer knowingly issuing a weapon to a person with a disqualifying conviction under the amendment.[654] Pre-employment certification to verify the lack of a criminal conviction in this area is accomplished through completion of DD Form 2760—Qualification to Possess Firearms or Ammunition.[655] In cases of domestic violence, a commanding officer or base commander can issue a Military Protective Order (MPO) to the alleged victim of the incident.[656] Sanctions for this in the military could result in the change of Military Occupational Specialty (MOS) and an unfavorable discharge from service.[657]

Next is sexual misconduct and deviant sexual misconduct which have also become a focus of much media attention.[658] Sexual harassment is believed to be prevalent in the military as according to their own research, women are quite frequently the victims of hostile working conditions aggravated by sexual harassment and sexual assault.[659] The infamous *Tailhook Scandal* has left an indelible mark on naval history.[660] Not limited to normal operations, service in the various theaters throughout the world also brings with it similar scandals. A study of female veterans revealed that over 20% experienced some type of sexual trauma while serving in foreign countries.[661] Sadly, whether reality or misperception, the military has been described by some as promoting a culture of rape.[662] This is due in part to rape and sexual assault investigations alleged to have been mishandled and covered up.[663] This issue is an internal as well as external problem. Externally, an applicant's assignments abroad and travel habits to places like Asia as well as other countries where the underage sex trade is rampant may also require a more thorough exploration of the potential for this type of involvement.[664]

Child pornography investigations have also reached a pinnacle as a federal investigation dubbed Project Flicker revealed over 5000 military personnel who were identified as purchasing, downloading, and possessing child pornography.[665] Discussed in depth earlier in this chapter, the results of this investigation simply exemplify the potential of an applicant's involvement in these types of criminal activities and the difficulty of discovering such matters in the background investigation process when the military itself fails to properly investigate these incidents.[666] The Blackwater Security investigation also brings to mind the potential for criminal activities to occur in these situations wherein the extent of an individual's involvement may never be truly revealed.[667] Other incidents have surfaced of photographs taken depicting the alleged abuse of military prisoners perpetrated by military personnel.[668] Finally, convictions have been had for multiple murders during military service which have constituted war crimes.[669] Postmilitary service also brings with it media attention to subsequent bad acts committed beyond the scope of military service, for example, in cases investigated as sex crimes, drug smuggling, and homicides where past military service is a highlight of the current media story.[670] All of the aforementioned examples are in the realm of personal conduct as well as clearly demonstrating the problematic systemic issues that plague the military.

Behavioral and Psychological Issues

Another category that must be discussed is that of behavioral and psychological problems that may be manifested by the applicant. Quite different from intended or culpable conduct, behavioral problems and patterns as a result of the unique inculcation to the military mindset may cause behavioral issues that may be inconsistent with the needs of proper behaviors required of public safety personnel. While a certain amount of behavior modification is required of those who will serve in the military mindset, including discipline, structure, and complete dedication to cause, there are also those who have too fully adopted the mindset and cannot effectively transition back or, in essence, be deprogrammed to a level that is workable in the public safety realm. These may be voluntary to trained responses to situations and scenarios that may not be appropriate for contemporary public safety officers required to function properly in a free society. Certainly, in most cases, previous military training and discipline can have very positive effects on those who go on to serve as law enforcement and public safety officers. One limited study revealed positive correlations with the ability of police officers with prior military experience to have better coping skills during stressful police-related situations.[671] These situations may be limited but pose very real concerns for background investigators in determining those who will be the best fit for their agency's needs.

The involuntary behaviors caused by medical and psychological ailments are also of great concern with the research indicating the increased levels of psychological and behavioral problems that are manifested by those who have served in combat situations who are returning home and seeking positions in the law enforcement field. Prior to the 1960s, psychological trauma related to military service was commonly referred to as Battle Fatigue Syndrome or Combat Stress Reaction. As a consequence of the Vietnam War, psychological research led to the first diagnosis of posttraumatic stress disorder (PTSD) in veterans who returned home from this conflict.[672] The general definition of PTSD is that the malady is a response by normal people to an abnormal situation.[673] PTSD is the result of exposure to traumatic events that include the types of situations a law enforcement officer will routinely be involved in investigating that include violent assaults, sex crimes, sexual and physical abuse, serious injury and fatal car accidents, and catastrophic natural disasters just to name a few.[674] Research of the intervening conflicts that this country has been involved in has borne bitter fruit though. A consistent concern voiced in the research has been the predominant factor that PTSD has been diagnosed in those who have served in combat situations in the Gulf War, Iraq, and Afghanistan.[675] Another gender-based study of female veterans revealed that over 20% had experienced some type of sexual trauma while serving in foreign countries.[676] The highest-risk age groups were also identified as those from age 18 to 24, age groups that are normally recruited for law enforcement positions.[677] These types of figures cannot be ignored.

Post-deployment adjustment problems run the gamut of psychological, behavioral, and substance abuse issues.[678] Those suffering from PTSD may exhibit signs that can include trouble maintaining normal sleep patterns, temper and anger issues, trouble concentrating, and symptoms of hypervigilance.[679] These symptoms may also include multiple mental and psychosocial disorders as a result of combat service and lead to such afflictions as homelessness, marital problems that include incidents of domestic violence and high divorce rates, high rates of suicide, fights and civil disorder, layered addictions that include excessive alcohol use and illicit drug use as well as prescription drug abuse.[680] A significant number of soldiers studied revealed that preexisting psychological problems were further aggravated by trauma encountered during deployment.[681] However, due to political and budgetary reasons, returning soldiers have been misdiagnosed with preexisting personality disorders identified as adjustment disorders, instead of their true afflictions, which have been the symptoms of PTSD and directly related to their service in combat situations.[682] During the screening process of military applicants, the background investigator should be aware of the potential for these types of behavioral issues in order to understand them as well as use this information to establish if the applicant is fit for the role of law enforcement officer. Behaviors and acts will be the focus of the investigation as well as any concomitant medical or psychological information that may be revealed during records searches and interviews. This information must all be passed on to the medical and psychological contractors of record in accordance with the protections of the ADA as discussed in Chapters 3 and 4.[683]

Records Access and Retrieval

Military records present a dichotomy of sorts. While the military is known for their copious records collection and management, many violations and infractions are also handled informally and without entry to the official records that will be available to the background investigator. Records should not be the only reference for the background investigator to review. Whenever possible, interviews should also be conducted with those who have had contact with the applicant including supervisors and command officers. The applicant should be required to identify the names and billets of all those who they have served under. Telephone contacts and letters requesting a response may be required given these individuals will likely be spread throughout the United States, and if still serving in the military, throughout the world. Personal contacts in these circumstances have often revealed a wellspring of information that is directly relevant to establishing an applicant's fitness for duty. Other information should come directly from the applicant with respect to their duties, assignments, all awards and commendations, training, and any discipline received should be documented by the applicant in their Personal History Statement. The applicant should also be asked in the Personal History Statement if they were ever rejected for military service prior to or after the induction stage.

The medium of military records dissemination is the Form DD, 214 Certificate of Release or Discharge From Active Duty. Other forms are also important to the process of investigation including the DD 214C, Certificate of Release or Discharge From Active Duty, Continuation Sheet; DD 215, Correction to DD Form 214, Certificate of Release or Discharge From Active Duty; and DD 214, WS Certificate of Release or Discharge From Active Duty, Worksheet. These forms are all protected by law, and release is controlled under the *Freedom of Information Act* and the *Privacy Act of 1974*.[684] Records can be requested by the applicant through the National Archives and National Personnel Records Center by using Standard Form 180, which allows for the request of General Information, Personnel Records and Service Treatment Records (STR), and archival records.[685] The applicant should have these files sent directly to the background investigator or deliver such records in their original sealed envelopes.

The military records will reveal several pieces of information relative to the investigation. Applicant pedigree information, residence, Social Security number, and other personal information will be listed. The applicant's MOS, rank, promotions, and combat assignments, as well as service overseas and other deployment information, will also be listed along with any training, awards, and medals the applicant received as a part of their military service. The records should also indicate the applicant's status as currently serving, in the reserves, or if they have been separated from service. An applicant can receive one of five types of military discharges:

1. Honorable
2. General (under honorable conditions)
3. Other than honorable
4. Bad conduct
5. Dishonorable

The latter of these, bad conduct and dishonorable discharges, are considered punitive discharges under the *Uniform Code of Military Justice*.[686] The circumstances for receiving a discharge are quite varied and may include reasons that are favorable, unfavorable, or beyond the control of the applicant. These include the following:

1. Expiration of enlistment
2. Disability, dependency, or hardship
3. Fulfillment of service obligation
4. Convenience of the government
5. Unsuitability

Army Regulation 635-200 includes the comprehensive list of involuntary and voluntary separation requirements which should be reviewed by the background investigator.[687] The military uses a set of Separator Program Designator (SPD) codes that are three character alpha codes for the reasons and types of classifications for separation from the military.[688] If made available, this specific code may shed some needed light on the conditions of the applicant's separation from service. Other separation circumstances may also occur depending on conditions, length of service, and rank. Entry Level Separation (ELS) is also another classification wherein the applicant is discharged prior to completing a minimum 180 days service commitment. These discharges are historically considered uncharacterized, and thus, neither a positive or negative separation circumstance is presented. There is also a distinction between the enlisted and commissioned ranks in the form of discharge from the military. Commissioned officers have a different set of rules that limit the military's ability to dishonorably discharge and demote within these ranks; however, they are still subject to court martial proceedings and dismissal from military service. Negative separation status affects many areas for the applicant including student loan eligibility, federal employment, and certainly other forms of employment with both the public and private sectors. Veterans also enjoy reemployment and benefits protections under the *Uniformed Services Employment and Reemployment Rights Act of 1994* (USERRA).[689]

Lastly, care must be taken in the interpretation of these records. These types of records may present an overly positive or skewed picture of the applicant as previously noted, they may be incomplete insofar as disciplinary actions are concerned. In contrast, they may also present a negative view of the applicant that has been precipitated by any number of reasons including those cited earlier. One indicator may be found in the percentage of time an applicant has served. In some cases, the lack of serving a complete service commitment may be due to disciplinary matters or lack of adjustment, but the applicant has received a positive or neutral separation. One final note concerns the frequency of multiple separation papers that may be in existence due to the transient nature of an applicant's military service. These include switching from active to reserve status, transfers to different branches of the military and different units of the National Guard; each will have its own specific DD214. An applicant will need to not only declare these types of movements in their military career but also, more importantly, produce every DD214 that exists for the service.

As a postscript to this, ensure that the applicant has registered for Selective Service as well as this is still a requirement under the federal law.[690]

EMPLOYMENT HISTORY

Employment history is generally an area where much information on the applicant can be mined.[691] In essence, examining this type of information becomes the search for indicators of good character, interpersonal competence, and capacity to perform the functions of the position they were hired for.[692] Employment history, however, while being a good place to solicit relevant information, may not produce the expected results in many cases. Employers, as discussed later, are wary of disclosing information on applicants, opting to give neutral recommendations and providing very basic, and often sparse, nonprobative employment information only. This reaction is caused by the proliferation of defamation lawsuits that have arisen from providing negative employment references. Organizations, due to liability and the threat of repercussions from discontented workers, will offer nondescript references in order to avoid these difficult and potentially litigious situations.[693] When information can be culled, the range of areas can be examined that include work habits and patterns, motivation, interpersonal skills, and transgressions. Occasionally there will be information developed on applicants who have committed crimes at the workplace as well as their inability to maintain working relationships with others, some debilitating to arguments, fights, and an emerging issue of bullying in the workplace.[694] Workplace violence is cited as a national as well as international concern that is steadily increasing in many occupations and professions.[695] The security industry has given the issue of workplace violence a high priority with respect to the potential threats that face organizations around the country.[696] Beyond those who serve in law enforcement, some of the highest rated occupations that experience workplace violence are security personnel and those who work as bartenders.[697] Domestic violence and coworker violence have also permeated the workplace with women being the primary victims.[698] Violence against women, a concern with both domestic relationships as well as male coworkers, has revealed that women are the victims of homicide in the workplace at proportionately higher rates than their male counterparts.[699] The workplace certainly creates a melting pot for these types of activities.

The fact of the matter remains that an intelligent, experienced, and motivated lawyer engaged by a plaintiff in litigation of this nature will, as expected, file discovery motions to examine the background investigation process and the results of any previous employer contacts and interviews in order to establish the defendant's fitness for hire in the current organization. As discussed in Chapter 3, the standard of *known or should have known* will invariably rear its ugly head at the most inopportune time. Episodic as well as patterns of conduct that include any form of discipline such as remedial training, suspensions, demotions, or termination will be closely scrutinized and certainly attached in some form or manner to offer at the very least, circumstantial support for the allegations in the complaint. The lack of contact with the previous employer(s) as well as the failure to make multiple attempts to interview a range of coworkers, supervisors, managers, and human resource or personnel department representatives will be detrimental to the hiring agency in these circumstances even if no negative information existed as it will cast much unnecessary doubt on the quality and veracity of the background investigation itself. The following is a punch list of steps to consider when investigating employment history:

1. Signed releases from the applicant forwarded to the previous employer via personal delivery, mail delivery with a receipt, or fax directly to the organizational representative who can authorize the release of information as well as any concomitant employee interviews.
2. Verify contact information of the organization. Establish the legitimacy of the organization through Internet searches, contacts with consumer advocacy agencies, and if needed, criminal records checks.
3. Basic information should include employment dates, positions and titles held, locations where worked, and supervisor and manager contact information.
4. Personnel records of all kinds should be reviewed and copied if possible, including attendance, performance evaluations, awards and recognition, training and professional development, remedial training, reprimands, counseling, suspensions, demotions, and terminations. Also solicit any information concerning any required licensing for the position as well as if the applicant is current and in compliance with the licensing requirements.
5. If the applicant has left the current position, or in all occurrences of previous employment, establish the reason the applicant left. Determine the reasons for termination of employment whether they are voluntary (e.g., resigned for a better position, family or health issues) or forced (e.g., terminated, laid off, forced resignation). Also establish if the applicant is eligible for rehire by the organization.
6. Personally direct the applicant to provide at least three references from each work location along with their full contact information. Make every effort to interview all volunteered references. During the interview, specifically establish the following:
   a. The length and nature of the workplace relationship.
   b. What strengths, knowledge, skills, abilities, judgment, interpersonal skills, control of emotions, ability to work with supervision and management, honesty, integrity, ethics, and work habits the applicant demonstrates.
   c. What weaknesses, behavioral, and disciplinary issues the applicant has demonstrated.
   d. Solicit at least three persons unknown to the background investigator from the volunteered contacts who may have information concerning the applicant's workplace qualities and shortcomings. Contact those persons to establish any new information that may be had.
   e. If unable to personally contact the references by personal visit or telephone interview, send letters to those included in order to document the attempts to make contact.

With respect to a claim by any previous employer that the applicant is not eligible for rehire, this assertion will require significant follow-up, likely through independent sources and the applicant to verify the reason for such a rejection.[700] A few final considerations are as follows. First, many companies will refuse to cooperate with the background investigation.

For the most part, there exist no legal or compelling requirements in the states that do not have this type of legislation in place to mandate the delivery of the information to the prospective employer. As discussed in Chapter 3 and in this chapter under *Negligent Referral and Defamation Claims*, the concept of negligent referral should be brought to the attention of the agent of the organization in order to hopefully influence voluntary compliance in full information release. If the organizational representative fails to cooperate or give permission for records releases or interviews, the background investigator will likely not be able to force the issue. The matter may then be decided through rapport development and diplomacy. Use the tactics that are effective and legal to gain the needed information. Alternatively, the background investigator can also attempt to make contact with references and supervisors off company property and outside of company time. If these persons are willing and volunteer to offer information outside of the influence and control of the company, the background investigator is obliged to receive it. The background investigator may need to be innovative and creative in the approaches to soliciting this type of very valuable information necessary to make informed decisions on the applicant's fitness for employment.

A brief word on applicants who request the background investigator not contact the current employer. While the applicant's motivation may be to hide some untoward information from preventing their candidacy, the majority of the time, this is merely a request to prevent sanctions from the current employer. This is a valid concern in very tough economic times where we would not want to jeopardize an applicant's standing or livelihood in the current role absent a reasonable expectation of employment in our organizations. These "do not call" considerations must be balanced against the need and timing of the information and hiring process. As much latitude and courtesy possible should be extended to applicants for this purpose. In most cases, the entire background investigation can be completed, and a preliminary decision into an applicant's viability can be made prior to having to contact the current employer. In all cases where this is requested, the background investigator should make every effort to honor the request as is consistent with the needs of the investigation.

Lastly, copiously document every step and effort made with respect to the applicant's employment history.[701] This does not minimize the requirement for documentation in all of the other key areas of the screening process, but employment history and information attainment can be extremely ambiguous at best. Consistently document the information received as well as the efforts made to obtain information where organizations and individuals fail to cooperate with the process. This will only work to protect the background investigator and organization in any subsequent inquiry, review, or litigation that may arise from the applicant's employment with the organization.

Lateral Transfers: The Enigmatic Answer

Hard to imagine any agency in the United States that does not routinely receive applications for lateral transfer from serving public safety and corrections officers. Serving personnel will seek to transfer for numerous reasons that include pay and benefits, promotional opportunities, location, and working conditions. Lateral transfers are perceived, rightly or wrongly, as an enormous benefit to an agency when a quality candidate is hired into the ranks. Training is minimal in comparison to a new applicant as well as the learning curve is much shorter for those hired, especially if they come from the same area or have attended the same regional academy for training. Hiring from other public safety agencies in order to fill vacancies has long been a recommended and accepted practice.[702]

However, lateral transfers can turn into the bane of a hiring process though as people who often seek transfer to another agency present their own unique challenges and shortcomings. Lateral officers may have varying motivations to leave their current positions, both positive and negative.[703] A certain level of benign neglect seems to prevail as well when we take for granted the unrealistic expectations of the capacity and experience of laterals brought into our agencies and we are all too often disappointed with the frequent poor results. Used largely as a cost-saving measure for agencies that have severely limited training budgets, many of these officers develop a transient pattern of movement working for multiple agencies during their career. Cost savings are often lost, however, in the posthire problems these people present to our agencies.[704] Lateral transfers can pose very difficult problems for the new agency as evidenced countless times across the country.[705] Inappropriate and criminal sexual misconduct seems to be a common theme in many of these hires.[706] Interestingly, this disorder is not confined to the lowest ranks in organizations, but is also rather prevalent at the highest ranks as well. Numerous incidents have occurred across the country wherein lateral or transferring police chiefs with checkered histories have committed horrendous acts including criminal acts, acts of misconduct, and sexually deviant acts, and demonstrated harassing behavior, only to be welcomed into another agency as their new chief executive officer.[707] In one highly publicized incident of conduct which led to the arrest of a command officer, in spite of the municipality's knowledge of the situation, he was still hired as a chief in another agency.[708] Another example includes a police chief involved in inappropriate sexual behavior who was reported to have worked for 16 different law enforcement agencies over a period of 13 years.[709] Processing laterals has led to, among other things, the discovery of crimes they have committed while employed as a police officer with the current agency,[710] acts of misconduct that are often covered up and never formally reported or investigated.[711] Many departments have been called to answer for the hiring and promotion of unfit officers due to ineffective state laws and regulations that have been compounded by substandard and incomplete background investigations and hiring's that are ill-informed or politically driven.[712] Incidents of this nature give much credibility to the contention that "You can't make this stuff up!"

Minimum qualifications and certification have also become a question in several agencies across the country. For example, a constable who was hired with a dubious past record also did not meet the minimum qualifications of the hiring agency.[713] On a larger scale, one multidepartment merger found 54% of the current serving police officers in the dissolving department failed the background investigation requirements for the absorbing agency.[714] Requirements are in place in every state. For example, under the *California Government Code*, employment of persons who are not of good moral character or who are not fit to serve as peace officers is prohibited, and currently serving police and peace officers are not excluded from this requirement.[715] The *Texas Occupations Code* requires that any law enforcement agency that is considering hiring a licensed peace officer in the state must first request any employment termination reports that may have been filed on the applicant to ascertain if the applicant is eligible to be a peace officer.[716] Texas legislation also requires the Texas Commission on Law Enforcement Officer Standards and Education to suspend the license of an officer upon notification that the officer has been dishonorably discharged for a second time.[717] An example court decision in the corrections environment includes the ruling in *Farr v. State Civil Service Commission (Department of Corrections)* (2008), where a corrections officer was terminated from a previous corrections position and, as a result, was disqualified from being hired in another corrections position.[718] Yet, in spite of these examples, concerns have been consistently raised in many states where law enforcement officers revealed to have disqualifying transgressions are not often subject to losing their certification.[719]

The compendium of these problems has touched off a veritable firestorm across the country. The phenomenon of transient police officers, or "gypsy cops," has become a matter of intense discussion in many states across the country.[720] These transient officers bring with them very questionable and colorful histories that transfer from department to department despite their misconduct and criminal activity.[721] The aforementioned examples also include the highest-level administrators in law enforcement organizations as well which is an even greater concern given their high-profile positions and control over the operations and ethics of the agency. With all of these issues in mind, an exploration of the applicant's history is equal to their motivation to make this type of move. Several areas will need to be examined in the lateral applicant's background investigation to include (1) certifications and training records; (2) internal affairs, discipline, and integrity records; and (3) performance, work records, and supervisory/command recommendations.

Certifications and Training Records

Employability will be primarily determined on the requirements of each state, whether through Civil Service standing, POST, or other licensing bodies, continuous employment as opposed to separation and reapplication for the role. This information can be obtained from the applicant, current and past employing agencies, and the certifying or governmental bodies as keepers of these types of records. Ensure reciprocity of certification in order to afford the applicant the opportunity to make the seamless transfer if so hired by the agency. All training records should be obtained and made a part of the official record.

Internal Affairs, Discipline, and Integrity Records

Countless examples have been provided on the critical nature of establishing if an applicant is fit for duty and these types of records are a direct reflection of the applicant's capacity to meet the new agency's needs. Internal investigations and disciplinary records should be requested and obtained, if possible, in every case of a lateral transfer application. From the release of no records to a limited number of selected records is certainly suspect and an area of concern. Many states protect such records from access, and therefore, any request for release, even with a valid applicant waiver, is often strictly voluntary by the agency that is the subject of the request.[722] Some states are open access states where any personnel record can be released through a FOIA or FOIL request. In these states, records access may be accomplished through mandatory as opposed to voluntary means.

The number, type, and final outcome of these investigations will be a good indicator if the applicant is a problem employee to the current employer. History tends to repeat itself, and this information will most often allow for an informed decision on hiring or rejection of the applicant. A word of caution though: each organization will have their own unique standards, culture, and political problems. For all the good that internal investigations provide for an agency, they are equally used for ulterior motives of administrators, constructively designed as a good tool that is consequently used for evil purposes! When records are provided, they must be reviewed with a high level of circumspect. Information included should be placed in the perspective that there will exist different standards from agency to agency and on a more base level, from supervisor to supervisor.[723] Any disciplinary actions should be considered in both the context of the employing agency as well as the agency considering hiring the applicant. The applicant should also be allowed to address any issues discovered so that a fair assessment can be made for the final decision. In addition, review of the complaint history may reveal complaints with various investigative findings that primarily will be classified as exonerated, unfounded, not sustained, and sustained. In all fairness to the applicant, only sustained cases should be used in the decision-making process, and all others with the remaining findings attached should be redacted from the official record.

Lastly, any pending civil litigation against the applicant should be reviewed by the corporation or municipal counsel of the processing agency. As a general rule, applicants that are the subject of any pending civil matter should not be employed by the new agency until the matter is resolved. Exceptions to this rule can certainly be made as long as the new agency's legal advisors approve and do not anticipate any resultant issues related to the new employment.

Performance, Work Records, and Supervisory/Command Recommendations

Review of all available performance evaluations, work-related records, awards, honors, letters of recognition, and community correspondence as well as several of the other methods that can be used in the final analysis of the applicant's existing work product is required. This review should be accompanied by interviews with supervisory and command staff of the organization. As in civilian applications, the background investigator should interview references that are volunteered as well as those independently developed in the agency.

The background investigator should gain a general opinion of the applicant's characteristics and behaviors from the identified references as well as certain specifics concerning the opinions of those interviewed regarding the applicant's motivations to laterally transfer to another agency. The applicant may be voluntarily moving to another agency or may be in a position where they are being forced to leave. Another area of exploration is that while the applicant may be a law enforcement officer, substantial differences exist in police, sheriff, federal, state, and local agency missions, culture, and operations. The measure of previous law enforcement effectiveness or ineffectiveness may be a misnomer depending on the new agency's standard operating environment. Comparisons should be presented to the reference as well as the applicant to gauge if the applicant can transition to the new environment with minimal or reasonable adjustment.

Care must be taken in receiving oral or written recommendations that fall in all categories, including negative, neutral, and positive recommendations. All must be reviewed and assessed with a discerning eye as each may have contravening motives for submission. For example, a completely positive recommendation may be because the applicant is a stellar performer or because the agency desires to rid themselves of a problem employee. Negative recommendations may be founded on personality issues or a vindictive supervisor bent on undermining a good applicant's attempts to move forward in their professional careers. Neutral and nonresponsive recommendations are also red flags for concern as the typical "good guy" letter, basic employment specifics letter, or failure to provide a letter or recommendation will all require further exploration to establish the true facts.

Always remember, they are leaving for a reason—our job is to ensure that their reason is compatible to our agency's needs.

PERSONAL AND PROFESSIONAL REFERENCES

During the initial stages of the process when the applicant submits their personal history statement, they will be required to submit a list of references. These can include both personal and professional references that can speak to an applicant's personal and professional character, behaviors, and habits. References, while their value may reach varying levels in the application process, do offer another dimension to entirely applicant-biased offers of information and may work to confirm or refute information as well as establish the need for further investigation.[724] This subsection includes (1) foundational concepts of reference checking, (2) personal references, (3) professional references, and (4) anonymous letters and correspondence.

Foundational Concepts of Reference Checking

Provided at the outset of this discussion is the general definition of reference checking which "Focuses primarily on an applicants' past behaviors and accomplishments. The concept relies on the behavioral consistency principle—that the most reliable predictor of future behavior, such as job performance, is past behavior."[725] References are used to both certify and decertify applicants.[726] Therefore, employers should be encouraged to disclose both positive and negative information rather than non, neutral, or strictly positive recommendations.[727] References are classified as primary (direct knowledge or observations) and secondary (indirect or third party information) sources of information. The highest rated categories of information sought from references include the areas of work performance, disciplinary issues, and character of the applicant.[728] Since applicants will often endeavor to present themselves favorably in the application process, the substantive use of reference checks equally serves to substantiate or refute an applicant's assertions of their character and qualifications.[729] Just as in criminal investigations, all statements given by those who know the applicant, or of some material issue or event of a positive or negative nature in the applicant's history, must be subjected to careful evaluation and corroboration if possible.[730] In part due to scams that have been identified wherein job applicants will engage coconspirators to provide positive and supportive references as well as hire agents to sell them false employment verifications,[731] reference checking is the core principle of verification of information revealed during the background investigation process. The components of a properly conducted reference check are as follows:

1. *Job related*: The focus of a reference checking discussion is on an applicant's ability to perform the job.
2. *Based on observation at work*: The information provided by a reference must be based on experience observing or working with a job applicant.
3. *Focused on specifics*: The discussion must be focused on particular job-related information common to all job applicants to ensure fairness. Skillful probing and comparing of information ensures that the process produces more than a superficial evaluation.

4. *Feasible and efficient*: Because reference checking is focused, it can be conducted quickly. It provides a reasonable return for the small amount of time needed to do it well.
5. *Assessments of the applicant*: The information obtained from reference checking procedures may be used to determine whether an applicant will be offered a job. Reference checking procedures therefore are assessments subject to employment regulations, such as the Uniform Guidelines on Employee Selection Procedures, and they must conform to accepted professional measurement practice.
6. *Legally defensible*: It is necessary for reference checks to meet high professional standards; the reference checkers can meet these standards within the constraints of the law.
7. *Part of the hiring process*: The purpose of the reference check is to inform a decision about hiring. The results need to complement other assessments used in the process.[732]

The background investigator should verify the veracity of all written recommendations as they may have been forged by the applicant, generated by the applicant and signed by the reference, and may even contain fake electronic signatures. Letters of recommendation should not be taken on their face as often serious underlying issues may be present.[733] All of the submitters of letters of reference should be interviewed personally by the background investigator to verify the information contained as well as seek new information not revealed in the written recommendation. Reference interviews should proceed with a list of department generated consistent questions as well as follow-up questions by the background investigator to clarify information revealed as the interview progresses. The applicant must provide all needed contact information on the references offered. Those who are developed independently may require the background investigator to find current contact information through workplace contact, home visit, telephone number searches via white page and Internet queries.

Lastly, consider the credibility and motivation of the reference. Information may be provided innocently and factually, or the information may be maligned by motivations of the reference who has some personal issue with the applicant. Establish the relationship between the reference and the applicant (e.g., longtime friend, immediate supervisor, human resource representative providing only documentation who has had no personal contact with the applicant). One hint is to listen to what references say and do not say. Indicators can be had in a reference's avoidance of certain issues, talking around a question and their lack of response to direct questions. The "I've never seen this, but I heard that…" are statements that should raise red warning flags. In addition, whenever possible, information obtained from the reference or any subsequent letters of reference should be compared to the applicant's personnel records if made available.[734]

Clear in the records of civil and criminal cases is the need to accurately and honestly report on all information uncovered by the background investigator as well as not lying in the background process to make an otherwise unqualified or unacceptable applicant acceptable.[735] High-profile cases have gone so far as to uncover allegations of witness tampering in these types of investigations.[736] With these factors for consideration, the background investigator must seek out and interview those references that are volunteered by the applicant as well as independent references developed as a part of the investigation. References should always be checked, and results documented even when no information is offered in order to stave off any negligent hiring claims.[737]

Personal References

Personal references often lead to far more revealing information than do professional references. Outside of the controls that are in place for work and school environments, the personal reference can offer information on how the applicant conducts himself or herself beyond these types of restricted information flow environments. The applicant should provide at least three personal references for interview. The background investigator should work to identify three others from each volunteered reference. Depending on the information developed from these sources will dictate further searches and penetration into this category. Questions of the references must be consistent with business necessity based upon the qualifications of the position as previously discussed in this text.

Professional References

Professional references usually come from the work environment. Contacting previous employers for references provides a viable defense to negligent hiring claims.[738] Others can be found in schools and colleges, professional associations, or those from certain professions that the applicant may have contact with. Professional references are a dichotomy though as they are intended to add more evaluative weight than a personal reference; however, many are generated from persons who know little of the applicant's background. The knowledge of the applicant's background must be at a level far beyond a superficial acquaintance or third party referred reference for the information to have some probative value. Sometimes they are worthless appraisals as the applicant has had no direct connection or involvement with the recommender as the applicant has merely solicited a letter personally or through a third party from a judge, politician, police chief, command officer, or the like. In part, these are understandable and should not be considered a negative characteristic of the applicant in most circumstances. As previously mentioned, most applicants will try to put their best foot forward, and historic convention promotes a mindset where these types of letters will afford some advance standing in the process. In politically rife hiring systems, this certainly is the case, but in the overwhelming majority of cases, they are predominantly discounted. The average candidate is, more often than not, devoid or absent of ill intent in these submissions, and while they carry little, if any, probative value, unless some malice is involved, they should also not negatively impact the applicant's candidacy. The simple answer is that if the applicant has replaced one or more required references with this type of reference, direct the applicant to provide as many as needed to meet the stated requirements for processing.

Anonymous Letters and Correspondence

On occasion, the background investigator may receive information from an anonymous or confidential source. In a multimedia environment, these sources may include anonymous letters or other correspondence that include among other methods, e-mails from untraceable accounts. Kept in context, this type of information must be taken seriously as well as investigated to a logical conclusion. Anonymous correspondence in and of itself may not, and should not, be sufficient to exclude an applicant from the process. However, the allegations in these types of correspondence must be investigated fully and either corroborated or discounted based upon the lack of evidence revealed during the subsequent investigation.

A classic example involved several anonymous e-mails and an investigation that led to information revealing political pressure to award a college degree to a police official who had not met the college's and accrediting body's minimum standards for degree completion.[739] The number of letters may also be an indicator of issues with the candidate that may need further exploration and given higher credibility than a single letter.[740]

Confidential sources of information may have motivations of honestly bringing crucial information forward as well as those who have ulterior motives such as revenge or retaliation.[741] When investigating these types of correspondence, the applicant may be a good source for identifying the motivations and quite possibly, the author. If this method reveals those possibly involved, a follow-up should be conducted with those individuals to either confirm their forwarding and other information they can offer or, at the very least, rule them out and document these attempts at tracking down the validity of the disparaging information. They can also be of useful information if they deny any knowledge and later surface so that any new information may be challenged on the basis of the credibility of the person. As an aside, infrequently the background investigator may encounter an uncooperative volunteered or independently developed reference. Absent a compelling legal statute, the background investigator will have to depend on rapport building and tenacity to gain the information needed. Again, if these tactics fail, documentation is key to defending an organization's hiring decisions in the event that the denials and ambiguity of information suddenly turns to the Gospel of Judas in any posthire revelations.

NEGLIGENT REFERRAL AND DEFAMATION CLAIMS

These concepts are the proverbial double-edged sword of the hiring quagmire. Defamation claims are a fact of life in an environment where desperate people who have a knowledge of their rights are matched with desperate litigators searching for their next settlement. Defamation claims as a consequence of reference checking are an area the background investigator must be fully aware of. In addition, the concepts of negligence in the hiring process were explored in Chapter 3, absent the concept of negligent referral. Negligent referral is treated in this section to demonstrate the inextricable relationship between these two critical concepts. This subsection discusses (1) the concept of negligent referral and (2) the issues of defamation in employee references.

Concept of Negligent Referral

As a hierarchy, the primary concern is the issue of negligent referrals with defamation taking second chair to the argument. In the opinions of many of the courts in the country, concerns of employee safety and security may well supersede any claims of violations of rights to personal privacy.[742] This concept is based on a common law theory of negligence as applied to the hiring of new employees.[743] Theories of negligent referral and negligent misrepresentation of dangerous employees may give rise to significant liability where the employee injures someone in the new position and a causal connection can be made to the lack of providing relevant information concerning that employee's past issues. Consequently, the failure to share information about employees may actually increase the liability of the organization beyond the scope of the anticipation of a defamation suit rather than reduce it.[744] For example, the legal precedent in California is that a prior employer has a duty to provide relevant work-based information about an applicant when there is a foreseeable risk of harm to an innocent third party in the new position applied for.[745] This can occur when the reference employer fails to offer accurate information concerning an employee's transgressions or shortcomings and due to exposure or opportunity in the new role that failure results in financial loss or damaged reputation to the new company who hires the employee.[746] The lack of candor in providing reference information to the prospective employer often impedes the prospective employer's efforts to avoid making mistakes in the hiring process.[747] Beyond the scope of the legal issues, the concept of negligent referrals is also a social and ethical issue for the previous employer.[748] The background investigator must carefully wade through the morass of these theories to come to a workable model to follow.

In negligent hiring and negligent retention litigation, the new employer will be held to a standard that they either knew or should have known the employee was unfit.[749] When the new employer can argue that this information was not provided or available at the time of the inquiry, claims can then be preserved for redress concerning fraudulent misrepresentation and of negligence of the reference to provide the germane information. Mixed interpretations exist in the court rulings on the ultimate refusal to disclose any information as opposed to disclosure of all relevant and truthful information concerning an applicant's entire work history. For example, in the ruling of *Davis v. The Board of County Commissioners of Dona Ana County* (1999), the former and current employers may have a right to refuse offering any information on an applicant and no liability will attach; however, if a recommendation is offered, the agency must exercise reasonable care, which includes the absence of misleading statements or "half-truths," in the referral to avoid liability that would attach from a negligent misrepresentation or a negligent referral claim.[750] Analogous to this situation is the offering of a nondescript or nonreference communication or published record, which is equal to neutral recommendations. One tragic case can be found in the ruling of *Jerner v. Allstate Insurance Company* (1995) which involved the communication of a neutral reference for an applicant who was forced to resign based upon the fact he had brought a gun to work and threatened coworkers.[751] The prior employer failed to disclose in the recommendation the applicant's previous conduct and hence his propensities for violence.[752] Another aggravating factor of this case was that the employer gave the letter of reference in contradiction to an organizational policy that precluded any referrals.[753]

In the contrary ruling of *Richland School District v. Mabton School District* (2002), one school district sued another for negligence, misrepresentation, and nondisclosure for failure to provide information in reference letters concerning the applicant's charges of child molestation and inappropriate comments made to students at the former employer's school.[754] In this case, the courts disagreed that the duty was owed by the previous employer to the new employer.[755] A salient fact of this case was that the termination from the new employer was not based upon any similar conduct at the new workplace, rather learning of the misrepresentation in the plaintiff's original application.[756]

More importantly, the information provided must also not misrepresent an unqualified or unacceptable applicant as otherwise qualified. This was a predominant factor in the ruling of *Randi W. v. Muroc Joint Unified School District* (1997), wherein the failure to disclose information of past criminal misconduct that included sexual misconduct, as well as providing only positive recommendations, led to fundamental liability on behalf of the references.[757] In this case, the previous employer not only failed to disclose relevant information but also worse yet blatantly misrepresented the applicant's fitness for the new position.[758] The applicant's predilection for violent or sexual misconduct in the previous position was the same behavior that was repeated in the new position and thus led the courts to conclude that this behavior could have reasonably been predicted if the applicant was placed in a similar role. Specifically in law enforcement, if the information provided is favorable, but false, and the only source of the true information is contained in the records of the previous department where there exists no other readily available means to access the relevant information, the previous department's liability in the failure to release the information can increase immensely.[759] In yet another law enforcement case, an applicant's complaint history as a sex offender was not revealed to the hiring agency, and the applicant subsequently repeated the same type of offenses as an on-duty police officer in the new agency.[760] The examples are clear that negligent referral is a matter that is being seized by plaintiffs and contested in the courts with the majority of rulings weighing in on the side of disclosure rather than caution.

Each state is wrestling to address these issues in the form of legislation that provides for qualified or conditional immunity from liability in order to enhance the free flow of relevant information from the previous to the future employer. In addition, this area will likely see increasing litigation as attorneys are able to access information much more easily than was available through the information networks of the past.

Issue of Defamation in Employee References

Akin to negligent referral and negligent misrepresentation is the issue of defamation. Sharing a reciprocal relationship, one could not exist without the other in spite of their parallel functions in the pre-employment screening process. A commonly accepted benefit of contacting references is to freely exchange employment-related information regarding an applicant's past behaviors which can lead to many organizational as well as societal benefits.[761] The conventional wisdom of legal advisors in the management realm to not disclose information has slowly changed over time given the emerging developments in case law as well as the many societal and safety issues presented by the failure to disclose employment information.[762] There are several considerations when analyzing the issue of defamation liability that are discussed as follows: (1) defamation liability, (2) concept of publication, (3) defenses to defamation claims, (4) conditional and qualified privilege, and (5) efficacy of releases and waivers.

Defamation Liability

Defamation can be defined as the act of providing an unprivileged communication that damages a person's good reputation or name by disseminating negative or false information in the form of slanderous (oral or spoken statements) or libelous (written or published) statements. Both direct and indirect wording may be at issue as language or terms that may be inferred as derogatory may also be subject to claims of defamation.[763] In the example of pre-employment screening, defamation litigation can occur any time a reference negatively represents an applicant's inability to perform at a future job as well as communicate any information concerning an applicant's involvement in the commission of a crime.[764] This may also result in defamation liability wherein a reference communicates issues involving allegations of an applicant's moral turpitude, bad character, or lapses in morality and integrity.[765] The method of redress is by filing a claim that asserts a person's liberty interests have been damaged as a result of the defamatory communication. In the employment realm, the damage is usually demonstrated as the loss of the prospective job opportunity. In order to establish that a liberty interest has been violated, the plaintiff must demonstrate that there was a publication and dissemination of the defamatory information that the information led to some type of damage in the employment realm and that the information disseminated was of a false nature or origin.

In general, few defamation suits prove to be successful.[766] Many others are rejected based upon the inability of the plaintiff to support all of the required elements of such a claim.[767] The ones that are successful are usually based upon the circumstances of the information provided to the prospective employer was clearly malicious, intentionally false, or driven by some type of retaliatory actions.[768] Where the fear arises is from the ensuing legal fees to defend such claims. Consequently, organizations will take widely varying approaches to providing references that range from complete disclosure to disavowing all knowledge of the applicant. Across the country, organizational policies are severely lacking in resolving these issues of information sharing.

As a corollary, many states have enacted blacklisting statutes. Blacklisting statutes in several states outlaw the intentional interference of a former employer in an employee's applications to other organizations.[769] This has made organizations all the more leery of providing any derogatory information on an applicant for fear of misinterpretation of the intent of the offer. Clear in the law though, codicils exist where the offering of truthful statements regarding the reasons for any discharge of the employee is allowed.[770] An understanding of individual state laws will go far in convincing unwilling references of their rights and responsibilities in providing truthful information concerning the applicant.

From a policy perspective, factual statements are actionable under the defamation statutes. Opinions may not be actionable unless based upon a fact or set of facts surrounding performance issues. In addition, inconsequential or harmless errors in disclosures should not be a trigger to the attachment of liability on behalf of the discloser of the factual information. Some mistakes are certainly possible and understandable in the process. Once discovered though, they should be remedied as soon as practicable. Unless some relevant connection exists, information developed from an employer should be limited to work-related issues as information beyond the scope of work matters may lead to a claim of invasion of the employee's privacy rights.

In rebuttal of defamatory information, an employee and, in some cases, an applicant for a position may be statutorily allowed to add written explanations to the employment or background investigation record. For example, in the case of employees who have received a negative reference from the current employer, they may be allowed by law to review the employment file and respond to any derogatory or negative information. Some case law exists where applicants for a position may also be allowed the same privilege. For example, in the ruling of *Doe v. U.S. Civil Service Commission* (1980), applicants are entitled to an opportunity to refute the legitimacy and reliability of derogatory information discovered during the background investigation.[771] In the ruling of *Garcia v. Walder Electronics, Inc.* (1990), if the applicant makes a timely request, they must be allowed the opportunity for a name-clearing hearing concerning the derogatory information that has been provided by the reference.[772] These types of name-clearing processes should be a part of the organization's policy and made known to the applicants in order to foster the practice of transparency as well as defend the organization against these types of claims.

Concept of Publication

Publication in the context of defamation claims deals with the communication of information concerning the applicant. Publication in this sense does not necessarily connote to a medium of books, articles, or other readily recognized means of publishing information.

Rather, in the pre-employment realm, information is considered "published" when made available and read by any person who is not the applicant.[773] Internal employee communications are not generally considered published with the exception of the court's ruling in *Gibson v. Phillip Morris, Inc.* (1997) where an internal communication was considered to meet the requirement of publication.[774]

There also exists a *Doctrine of Self-Publication* where the employee may be required to disclose or publish that information with the prospective employer.[775] Under the theory of compelled self-publication, a former employee who is forced to divulge previous workplace misconduct to a prospective employer, even when an actual publication of the information has not been communicated to the prospective employer, may result in defamation liability.[776] Court rulings on compelled self-publication defamation have run the gamut of opinions either in support or rejection.[777]

In requesting information from the previous employer, all documents, letters of reference, and interviews would be considered published materials in this context. The fact that they are delivered and communicated to the background investigator from the previous organization establishes this threshold. Any and all of those materials would then be discoverable when this type of claim is filed with the courts.

Defenses to Defamation Claims

There are several defenses to defamation claims. Basic legal protections as well as policy-level protections should be used by the referencing organization as well as the processing organization in order to properly and effectively protect both entity's interests in referring and hiring the best employees while also properly dealing with unfit employees. The processing organization should make the referencing organization aware of the numerous defenses available as well as the following discussions concerning legal privilege to disclose employment information as well as the indemnification of waivers and releases if the referencing organization is not forthcoming. From a legal perspective, there are several defenses to defamation claims:

1. Truthfulness and accuracy in the assertions contained in the communication
2. Qualified, conditional, constitutional, or absolute privilege
3. Consent of the applicant

With respect to truthfulness, the concept is an absolute defense against defamation. Consequently, the referencing organization must explicitly know that all letters of recommendation must include truthful statements concerning the employment history of the applicant.[778] Good faith immunity is provided as long as the previous or current employer does not offer false or misleading information, but rather accurate, job-related information. There is also a distinction between the offering of facts from the employee's personnel files and the offering of opinions, which may not be considered as actionable under the defamation statues. Another defense involves the *Innocent Construction Doctrine* which allows relief of defamation liability if an innocent interpretation of the communication is reasonable.[779] Additionally, any information offered as facts from the personnel records must have been explored and verified by a reasonable and competent investigation of the incident in question.[780] Failure to properly investigate the derogatory information that has been added to an employee's personnel file only invites defamation liability.[781]

The most basic protection is a "no comment" policy by an organization. This severely limits the background investigator's ability to obtain vital information possessed by the organization. When this barrier is encountered, the background investigator must fully document the circumstances of the refusal. Referencing organizations may be well aware of the social and ethical considerations that are flouted in lieu of the compelling fear brought on by the potential liability involved. In these cases, the background investigator can only go so far in the investigation and will have to document their genuine efforts to gain the cooperation of disingenuous authorities from the organizations where employment information is sought.

Conditional and Qualified Privilege

Immunity from liability can also emerge from legal privilege. The foundational privilege in this process comes from a constitutional privilege.[782] Absolute privilege is the next highest level of protection wherein a complete defense is provided for any defamation claim of malice involving any statements a defendant in a case has made. Absolute privilege is defined as follows:

> An absolute privilege protects the speaker or publisher from any liability for defamation; the privilege is also referred to as "absolute immunity" because the speaker is immunized from liability. The doctrine of absolute privilege arose from the theory that there are certain circumstances in which the ability to speak freely—usually in the context of governmental functions—is so important that it outweighs the interest that an individual has in his or her reputation.[783]

As cited from *Shanks v. Allied Signal, Inc.* (1999), "Absolute privilege is not a defense. Rather, absolutely privileged communications are not actionable." Constructively used only in legislative or judicial settings, the concept has also been accorded to the pre-employment investigation process on unique occasions. Absolute privilege in the release of information was affirmed by the courts in the rulings of law enforcement cases including *Bardin v. Lockheed Aeronautical Systems Company* (1999), *Garcia v. Walder Electronics, Inc.* (1990), and *O'Shea v. General Telephone Company* (1987).[784] While rare, this concept is allowed by the courts due to the critical nature of public safety position requirements.

Qualified privilege or conditional privilege is the most common justification in occasions where a defense must be brought in a claim of defamation in a background investigation. Qualified privilege serves as an affirmative defense to defamation claims.[785] It is also referred to as business immunity as the concept relates to the issue of decision-making rights based upon business necessity.[786] Claims of defamation can be successfully defended when these privileges are invoked by the reference when state law indemnifies these types of disclosures, when the information is job related, accurate, and given to an authorized representative in good faith.[787] Qualified or conditional privilege requires a legitimate reason or purpose for the use of the information in order to claim the defense.[788] The qualified privilege or conditional privilege defense is allowed when (1) the information offered is in good faith and believed to be true when published or communicated, (2) the information was intended solely for a legitimate business purpose, and (3) the person who received the information was authorized to do so for a legitimate business purpose. The emphasis of indemnification consistently rests on truthful and accurate statements of the previous employer.[789] For example, in the ruling of *Bals v. Verduzco* (1992), an applicant's previous employer may provide information concerning the applicant's work history as long as the privilege to disclose is not abused in any manner such as malice, intentionally false information, or the information is unwarranted or disproportionate to the situation.[790] Numerous cases underscore the judicial support of the concepts of qualified privilege and conditional privilege cases where communication was made in good faith from the previous employer to the prospective employer on workplace and performance-related matters.[791] However, the courts still view the privilege to offer defamatory employment references by a former employer as a conditional rather than an absolute privilege afforded to previous employers.[792]

State legislatures have also moved to provide protections for previous employer references in order to provide a free flow of information from employer to employer so that the social, ethical, and public safety concerns may be more fully addressed in the respective states. States that have enacted legislation to protect a former employer providing qualified immunity from civil liability concerning a defamation claim when the information release is in response to an inquiry from a prospective employer seeking only job-related information concerning the applicant, the information released is in good faith, truthful, accurate, and emerges from credible sources of information concerning job performance and that knowingly false or misleading information can be rebutted by the applicant.[793]

Several law enforcement cases have been decided in favor of prior employers releasing derogatory information and negative references to the processing police agency. These include the rulings of *Bishop v. Wood* (1976), *Garcia v. Walder Electronics, Inc.* (1990), *Johnson v. Martin* (1991), *Ratliff v. City of Milwaukee* (1986), and *Susan M. Miron v. University of New Haven Police Department et al.* (2007), where the facts and circumstances of a termination communicated to the processing agency were found to be appropriate.[794] In the ruling of *Introini v. Richland County* (1993), it provided that a previous law enforcement official offered as the reference could exercise the privilege to offer not only factual information but also more importantly opinions on applicant to prospective employer.[795] In the cases of law enforcement, the courts are much more supportive of the release of information concerning the hiring of applicants who will be charged with public safety as opposed to applicants for other positions in private and public sector organizations not so assigned.

Efficacy of Releases and Waivers

Most, if not all agencies, use some type of release of liability form or waiver for the applicant to sign prior to the conduct of the background investigation. Several examples are included in this text (see Appendix H). There exists much case law that supports the use of waivers and, in many cases, finds the processing agency and reference fully harmless in any prospective litigation. In the ruling of *Wells v. Minor* (1991), a waiver is defined as either an express or implied voluntary and intentional relinquishment of a known right.[796] In numerous cases, the knowing and voluntary signing of the waiver or giving consent to release information is generally a bar to a defamation claim and not actionable on the part of an applicant.[797] In fact, in the ruling of *Smith v. Holley* (1992), the court asserted that not only does consent create an absolute privilege to defamation but also, interestingly, in knowingly and voluntarily signing the waiver, the applicant has constructively consented to the possibility of being defamed.[798] However, release forms do not vitiate defamation liability where the statements made are intentionally false or malicious and the result is defamatory.[799]

A few situations to also consider are involuntary and voluntary separations from employment. There may exist a difference in the release of information due to any prior agreements in both situations that the background investigator should also explore in the investigation. In one distinguishing and limited ruling, the court reasoned in *Siegert v. Gilley* (1991) that a voluntary resignation would not fully serve to protect the release of derogatory information to the prospective employer.[800] For a voluntary or involuntary separation from employment, there may be an agreement in place that may limit or wholly prevent a previous employer from releasing information about the applicant. For example, the applicant may have a separation agreement in place that limits what a former employer can divulge which was upheld in the ruling of *Resnick v. Blue Cross and Blue Shield of Missouri* (1995).[801] In the ruling of *Nadeau v. County of Ramsey* (1979), there was a valid agreement in place between the former employer and employee to not provide unfavorable recommendations to future employers.[802] If the background investigator learns of these types of agreements, legal advice should be sought in order to determine how to proceed in the access and use of any information that may be developed in the process.

RESIDENCE AND THE NEIGHBORHOOD CANVAS

The conduct of a residence check and neighborhood canvas should be a part of every background investigation. These types of investigative activities can reveal information of value concerning the applicant's relationships, habits, and activities.

For the neighborhood canvas, current and past residences are important as we should not discount the possibility of developing information of value simply because an applicant has relocated several times in their life or, in many cases, how long ago the applicant may have resided in the area. Developing information from neighborhood residents is but one method to use. Several creative methods should also be employed to gain the most complete and accurate information available. For example, a search of police calls for service at the location may reveal information about activities, police investigations, or even crimes that may have been reported from or associated with the residence. Homes may be located in High Intensity Drug Trafficking Areas (HIDTA) where police intelligence reports may reveal activities or involvement of the location in the illicit drug trade. While the use and abuse of 911 call systems has been a problem for several decades, a more recent issue is the practice of making prank calls, false alarms, and "SWATing" to illegally summon a police response as a sick and frequently dangerous joke.[803] Satellite imaging through the various Internet search engines is also gaining popularity with investigators, being used by both the federal, state, and local agencies as well as various intelligence groups.[804] Simple searches using Internet-based web mapping services may reveal information through aerial and street-level photographs of the condition of the residence, vehicles, and the like.[805]

Next is visiting the residence. Other industries are recommending home visits to determine applicant fit for the position through direct observation of home life, family acceptance, and other important factors related to the position.[806] This provides an opportunity to interview family members or the significant other, roommates, other residents, and any persons who are acquaintances or who have knowledge of the applicant's character or behaviors. Other relevant information may include plain view observations of the condition of the home, lifestyle, criminal or code violations, vehicles, weapons, and information that may not be voluntarily revealed by the applicant. The home visit should be both scheduled and unscheduled to maximize the ability to develop new information.

Home ownership as well as if the location is rented should be established. Also establish if the applicant has any other interests in real property that may include other homes, businesses, rental units, and so forth in order to search for any issues, code violations, back taxes, and the like which may be a problem. Afford the applicant the opportunity to respond to any issues disclosed or discovered.

ELECTRONIC SOURCES: PROSPERING IN THE INFORMATION AGE

In the information age we live in, virtually nothing cannot be found. Ushering in the Age of Aquarius has brought with it a plethora of new and accessible ways to find information on practically any and every subject, including our applicants. Cyberspace has changed the entire face of information dissemination affording virtually unrestricted access to the general public that was unheard of in times past.[807] The electronic media maelstrom is also overshadowed by the social networking sites, blogs, and countless information sources available through the normal channels and legal use of the Internet. Search engines abound, and information can be pieced together like a puzzle from the unlimited connections made by simply typing in a name and hitting the "Enter" key! This is likely the most prolific resource available to the contemporary background investigator. Most organizational leaders seem to agree with this concept as the research has revealed that 75% of the U.S. organizations surveyed have formal policies in place that mandate online searches for information on job applicants.[808] Even the lay person who is not techno savvy would be forced to agree when faced with the evidence that use of the Internet is mandatory in this day and age. The list of examples of information availability is proverbially endless. Here are some excellent examples from schools, businesses, the military, and the political arena that will give this discussion some very profound meaning:

1. Pictures of students drinking alcohol in dorms are posted on a photo website, and they are charged with violating school rules of conduct.[809]
2. A nursing student posting a picture of herself with a human placenta on a social networking site is suspended from the program.[810]
3. A coach's picture posted on a photo sharing website of him drinking alcohol with students as well as being perceived as condoning hazing is fired.[811]
4. A teacher blogs negative comments about students that leads to her suspension.[812]
5. A professor was caught in an embarrassing situation by posting her use of a non-credible source of literature for use in her college class.[813]
6. A school teacher who published her sex worker escapades of stripping and prostitution through the use of an online commercial advertising network resigns.[814]
7. A high school teacher was subsequently fired for posting racy photographs of herself on the Internet.[815]
8. A restaurant had its liquor license revoked for pictures of allowing underage drinking in the establishment.[816]
9. A video of a navy captain involved in sexually suggestive acts and innuendo as well as the offensive nature of the content of the video leads to his removal from command.[817]
10. An Israeli soldier posted compromising pictures of humiliating and immoral actions on the part of the soldier.[818]

11. Teens sexting each other leading to criminal charges.[819]
12. One state attorney general's investigation revealed over 3500 sex offenders were using social networking sites.[820]
13. Other types of posts on the Internet (e.g., a personal diary) are leading to criminal charges.[821]
14. Several social networking sites where pictures have been posted have been used in criminal trials to show the character flaws of defendants and reveal new evidence.[822]
15. A professional cheerleader posts pictures to her social networking webpage of writing vulgar and anti-Semitic comments with a marker on a friend who was unconscious.[823]
16. A Canadian woman on long-term sick leave loses her insurance benefits after her agent found photos of her on her social network page in which she was attending a party and not appearing to suffer from her compensated affliction.[824]
17. Teens were discovered posting nude pictures of themselves on a social networking site.[825]
18. Text messages were a key piece of evidence in a sex scandal involving the former mayor of Detroit and his aide.[826]
19. A married state-level lawmaker allegedly answers advertisements to have sex with other males through the use of an online commercial advertising network.[827]
20. A married U.S. congressman attempting to solicit an adulterous relationship through the use of an online commercial advertising network resigns.[828]
21. A married U.S. congressman lying about soliciting sex chats and posting lewd pictures of himself on his social networking site as well as through e-mails and telephone conversations also resigns.[829]

The law enforcement and public safety officers of the country have also demonstrated these types of behaviors as evidenced in the following examples:

1. An officer was fired for the posting of pictures of criminal evidence and inappropriate behavior on a social networking site.[830]
2. A video sharing website featured a video of an intoxicated Pennsylvania police officer engaging in inappropriate behavior and conduct at a neighborhood bar.[831]
3. A deputy sheriff's pictures were posted of her feigning the smoking of marijuana, having possession of a liquor bottle, and having her gun in mouth while in uniform in her police car.[832]
4. A New Jersey SWAT team's posed pictures in uniform with a racy restaurant's waitresses were posted to the Internet.[833]
5. An official of a youth detention facility who had not been effectively screened in his previous corrections position was subsequently convicted of numerous crimes involving inappropriate and criminal conduct with teenage detainees at his facility was also an avid user of social networking sites.[834]
6. A police department blog was found to have hundreds of racist comments entered.[835]
7. A police officer posted information to a social networking site about his ulterior persona and controversial beliefs led to court challenge and ultimately irreparable damage to his reputation.[836]
8. A video sharing website video was used as evidence to convict an officer of untruthfulness.[837]

9. There have been numerous high-profile incidents where officers have been called to task for their social networking information posts that have forced police departments to examine the online conduct of both new applicants as well as in-service police officers.[838]

This subsection discusses the areas of (1) the Internet and digital information sources, (2) the social networking phenomenon, and (3) commercial and online networked communities.

Internet and Digital Information Sources

Digital information that can be retrieved from these sources includes both files and photographs. Information and images are stored on personal computers, laptops, smart phones, and digital cameras. The digital information stream is one that is difficult to wrap our heads around because of two issues, the magnitude of the information and the naivety of those who believe that posting the most personal aspects of their lives in this online forum will somehow forever remain a secret. Far too often, users of these modes of information capture, storage, retrieval, and dissemination fail to grasp the damage that can be done until it is too late to even moderately repair any subsequent loss of reputation as well as the impending embarrassment. Dismissed by most as information that is casually shared with no concern over the lack of security of the content or context of the message, these types of messages and images continue to be uploaded to the Internet at astounding rates.[839] Textbook examples of this are the images from Abu Ghraib wherein several spontaneous photographs of alleged acts of humiliating and torturing prisoners were subsequently uploaded to the Internet and went viral, and the soldiers involved have incurred consequences of criminal convictions as well as the ominous notoriety that continues to follow them years after the incident.[840] Interestingly, this notoriety has also negatively affected employment prospects for some involved.

Personal/Business Computers

First on the list are computers. Most American households possess some type of computer. Many people also have laptops and other types of computer compatible systems. Computers themselves are used to commit a wide array of crimes from fraud and cyber stalking, to hacking, to the retrieval and storage of child pornography.[841] Systems can be open access, password protected, or have sophisticated encryption codes that prevent anyone except the primary user access. The science of steganography is the method of decoding these types of computer file protections.[842] In as much of a wealth of incriminating information a person's computer can prove to be, they are also susceptible to immediate damage and destruction. For criminal investigations, information access may be accomplished by permission of the owner or user as well as the use of a search warrant. The search warrant will cover the retrieval of the actual computer as well as allow the search for files contained on the drive. Many suspects are computer savvy and will place protections in place to prevent access to their illegal files. These security measures may require access to specific passwords or codes in order to view the information. One court has ruled in a child pornography case that there is no right against self-incrimination in refusing to reveal the code to a password-protected hard drive.[843]

An applicant's personal computer may have information that may be central to their fitness for duty. Requesting an applicant's permission to view their personal computer files may not be practical as well as subject to immediate alteration or deletion of files if the applicant is aware ahead of time of the request. As discussed in the next section, this type of information collection and review may be wholly dependent on information culled from an analysis of the applicant's ISP records. A work computer owned by the employer, however, is another story. These types of systems can be accessed with the employer's consent. In addition, the employee may have been or currently be under investigation for improper use of their business computer. Accessing pornography at work has been the subject of numerous studies wherein the results have concluded that the majority of these illicit photographs are downloaded at a person's workplace. One of these studies revealed that over two-thirds of all pornography is downloaded at a person's place of employment.[844] This includes legal pornography that is equated to a violation of organizational policies for computer use. Child pornography being accessed through work-based computer systems, as similarly discussed in the military, also represents a problem that must be considered.[845] During the employment review, these may be worthwhile inquiries on the part of the background investigator.

Internet

The Internet or World Wide Web (WWW) as previously mentioned has opened so many avenues of inquiry that we cannot fully comprehend the ultimate investigative power of this electronic source.[846] Internet connections open the privacy of an applicant's home to the entire world of information, temptation, and opportunity. Users also falsely believe in a high level of privacy in these types of communications through digital downloads. Make no mistake about it, Big Brother is watching and recording! Each time a search is done and files viewed or downloaded, a digital fingerprint is left behind in the form of records maintained by the ISP. By law, these records are rendered confidential by the mandates of the *Electronic Communications Privacy Act of 1986*, which protects the privacy of an Internet customer's personal information from disclosure by the ISP.[847] However, records can be released by use of a subpoena for the Internet Protocol (IP) and the ISP.[848] In these types of administrative investigations, a subpoena may not be feasible; however, some information may be released by the ISP without the customers' or subscribers' permission. For example, in cases of exigent circumstances or the inadvertent discovery of a crime by the ISP,[849] an applicant can also give permission to the background investigator to obtain these types of records. Federal law provides the customer or subscriber the right to knowingly and voluntarily waive their right to privacy in ISP logs.[850] As in most of the tools in the investigator's toolbox, this type of waiver may not need to be exercised depending on the applicant's response to the request. Applicant reluctance to volunteer the permission as well as an applicant who may decide to voluntarily withdraw from the hiring process may be strong indicators of some type of wrongdoing. The applicant may also admit to wrongdoing just by the background investigator making the request and pursuing any indicators that the applicant may be involved in activities that would preclude them from being hired. The department can also implement consistent policy on this and mandate an applicant volunteer the records of a predetermined time frame such as 1 or 2 years of ISP logs. If the applicant voluntarily signs the waiver, the records can be retrieved and reviewed for activities that would preclude their candidacy. If the applicant refuses, the department could then remove the applicant from the process for failure to meet processing requirements. This method may prove very helpful to the investigative process. Web trails may also have some perishability though as several experts recommend personal searches of such info and eradicating as much information as possible in light of cleansing a job applicant's virtual reputation.[851] Be aware that the applicant may have considered this and conducted such a search and destroy mission prior to entering the processing stages for the position.

OSINT, as discussed earlier in this chapter, is also an excellent method of discovering information on an applicant. Internet search engines, news articles, social networking sites, blogs, video sharing sites, photo sharing sites, and public databases all have great potential at providing information on an applicant that may be relevant to their candidacy. Anything reported in the public domain is likely usable in the background investigation as long as the information is accurate, truthful, and does not violate any of the existing purging requirements at the federal and state levels.[852]

In as much as the Internet is a prolific source of information, all information garnered must be verified.[853] Verification should take place through the source of the information as well as follow-up interviews with the applicant. One of the first issues to examine is exclusivity of legal access to the Internet address in question. The site or computer may have multiple users in a household or business. Another task is to establish the method used to connect to the Internet so that the information can be tracked back to the system used.[854] This will help verify if the applicant is the actual subject of the illegal or inappropriate computer activities. Hacking sites has also become very popular, and the information posted may be false and erroneous, but implicating the customer or subscriber.[855] The background investigator must also consider that the information discovered may be the product of some illegal activity or hacking on the part of a third party and not the doing of the applicant. Websites and individual computers are often the target of cyber criminals who use unsuspecting customers' and subscribers' ISPs and computer systems to commit their own crimes.[856] Yet another problem is the use of pools of IP addresses assigned at random.[857] This may falsely implicate a customer or subscriber in some type of wrongdoing. Great care must be taken in analyzing these records and assigning blame to the right person.

Cellular Phones

The popularity of cellular phones has reached unprecedented levels in our society. Once a luxury, cellular phones have risen to the level of necessity in our highly mobile and digitally communicative networks. Most every cellular phone has a camera, and they are being used to capture real-time images and videos and send them through the airwaves. As previously discussed though, they are also being used to capture and send as well as receive images and videos that may be inappropriate as well as criminal in nature. Child pornography, criminal acts, drug use and paraphernalia, and inappropriate and intoxicated behaviors all seem to be the vanguard for those who want to memorialize their escapades. These unwitting acts on the part of the applicant may provide a fruitful investigative opportunity for the background investigator.

As in any cell phone communications, the same rules would apply insofar as mandating review through a search warrant. Likened to ISPs and computers though, the applicant can give voluntary permission for the background investigator to review the photographs and videos on their personal cellular telephone. This can also be made a part of policy as was previously mentioned. If this investigative tactic is used, wait until the applicant arrives for their official interview and ask them to produce their cellular telephone. When they do, either ask permission to review the photographs and videos or provide them with a formal waiver to examine the telephone as a part of the hiring and background investigation process. If they refuse, they can be removed for failure to meet processing requirements. If this is not policy, and the organizational administration will allow a verbal request to view the cellular phone files, the background investigator should ask and gauge the response of the applicant. If they do not voluntarily provide the background investigator with permission, then at the very least, may warrant additional investigation into the applicant's habits.

E-Mails

Electronic mail is a part of our everyday lives. One of the primary sources of communication in both our personal and professional lives, we find that it is hard to imagine what life was like before the e-mail revolution. E-mails are equally a consistent cause for concern and embarrassment for many. In some cases, the tocsin for bad acts to come. For example, the Major Hasan e-mails prior to the Fort Hood massacre revealed his extremist and terrorist beliefs.[858] Cyber stalking has also entered the mainstream wherein electronic means are used to harass or threaten another.[859] More often, even when no criminal act is involved, the mere nature and characterization of e-mails of questionable content that are made public are also creating barriers for those seeking positions of trust.[860] This may also be an avenue of investigation pursued by the background investigator.

Personal e-mails would be difficult to access, but employer e-mail systems are likely the domain of the employer and open to review if given permission by the employer. The applicant may have a history of creating or forwarding inappropriate e-mails that could have been investigated or addressed by the employer and documented in the personnel file. There also may be incidents that have not come to the attention of the employer and hence not investigated at the point of the background investigation, but may come to light if this type of inquiry is suggested. In criminal investigations, some cases allow for voluntary disclosure of e-mails.[861] However, employer e-mail systems are often fair game and open for inspection and use in disciplinary matters as well as for the background investigator to examine if the employer is willing to allow such access.

Social Networking Phenomenon

The uninhibited social networking phenomenon seems to be analogous to a powerful intoxicant wherein users lose all sense of control and common sense when they first sign into their online account. A virtual high is somehow experienced from the gases emitted from the computer that causes this blind euphoria. And, while devoid of the ensuing hunger pains, the hangover can be quite devastating. With feelings of loneliness coupled with exhibitionism and masked by a notion of quasi-secrecy of communication, people are emboldened to share their most intimate and embarrassing secrets and images with the cyber world, ironically a place that was created so that there would be no secrets. It is impossible to explain by anyone other than a trained psychologist how we freely lose our inhibitions locked away in the comfort of our homes with only the computer as our friend. People seem to love the unfettered opportunity to digitally document their escapades and broadcast them to the entire World Wide Web.

Not only the refuge of countless souls but also used by criminal enterprises as gangs sometimes post information and photographs that assist investigators in identifying criminal associates and details of offenses and activities and in learning information about their various organizations.[862] Extremist and vigilante groups are flocking to these social networking sites by the thousands to express right wing beliefs and spew hate laced prose to like-minded radicals in attempts to rally support for criminal acts all in the name of some lunatic of the day who has access to the Internet.[863] The use of these social networking sites is even at the center of some high-profile political scandals.[864] When will we ever learn?

Consequently, the use of social networking sites as an investigative resource is a highly recommended practice for the background investigator.[865] Numerous organizations use social networking sites in support of developing unabridged information on their prospective charges. Colleges and universities are routinely using social networking sites to screen freshman applicants.[866] Higher education institutions are also using social networking sites after students are admitted as well through the development of evidence of violations of campus policies such as violations of the restrictions on drinking and other transgressions.[867]

The business sector follows close behind. Many company recruiters are using social networking sites to ascertain how applicants project themselves in their pictures and postings which may indicate that they are unfit for the role applied for.[868] Applicants are also called to task when social networking information conflicts with resume and job application assertions.[869] One independent survey revealed that in excess of 40% of employers search social networking sites for information concerning their applicants.[870] Some of the information revealed through posts and photographs can demonstrate excessive alcohol use, illegal drug use, videos and photographs depicting the applicant in compromising and at times, illegal positions, postings on their work relationships and issues with former or current employers, as well as other character-based assessments have all been found on these types of sites. Some opponents though believe the use of this information may cross the legal boundaries developed through the *Fair Credit Reporting Act* and EEOC guidelines.[871] As a rule of thumb, if an applicant has put the information out in this open forum, then the information is legal to obtain and use in adverse employment actions.

For the background investigator, a threefold approach should be followed: (1) Internet name searches, (2) bait accounts, and (3) forced disclosure of the applicant.

Internet Name Searches

Often a simple search will reveal an array of the applicant's accounts in the current social networking sites. Some allow full access, while most require an online invitation. Checking the preliminary information as well as the information and pictures that are immediately accessible at this point as well as saving any information located to the background investigator's files should be accomplished.

Bait Accounts

Because of the restrictions applicants can place on their accounts, the background investigator should consider developing bait accounts. These can be accomplished by using volunteer serving police officers for photographs and using fictitious names and monikers. This activity is legal in the criminal investigations realm for identifying and tracking offenders who are active child predators and pornographers. This practice is also recommended in the background investigation process. Sending a bait request to the applicant may provide an opportunity for access to their posts and pictures that may lead to some very valuable investigative information.

Forced Disclosure of the Applicant

After conducting the online searches to establish if the applicant has any social networking accounts, and if the bait account technique is used to garner any additional information, upon formal interview of the applicant, they should be made to access all social networking accounts in the presence of the background investigator. The applicant should be advised that failure to fully disclose all sites or comply at that time would be grounds for removal from the hiring process. Once the applicant accesses the site or sites, then a comparison to the known information can be made as well as a review of the content. This information can be very valuable when accounts have posts and pictures of activities that are unfavorable to the applicant's character. More importantly, this type of evidence can be downloaded before the applicant has had the chance to eradicate the files. Information of this nature can be used in the current investigation, any follow-up activities, and even shared with the psychologist if the information is relevant to this type of assessment.

Commercial and Online Networked Communities

Lastly, there has been an onslaught of commercial and online networked communities. One very high-profile site offered an erotic services section that was determined to have numerous prostitutes selling their wares from the web.[872] These types of sites may also provide information on the applicant. Consumer-to-consumer sites offering products, merchandise, and conducting online auctions may provide information on an applicant's possible criminal activities. Commercial sites offering the applicant's name, merchandise, or business information may also be helpful in cross-referencing to the applicant's disclosures in their applicant materials. Some sites aggregate consumer opinions and reviews of service companies and contractors and make them available to those seeking the same types of services.[873] Applicants may be referred to by name or business affiliation and may provide both positive and negative information that may be followed up or at least addressed with the applicant to establish their account of the incidents revealed.

PROCESSES OF DEALING WITH THE CANDIDATE

Once the entire investigation is completed, the candidate can be scheduled for their final interview and any subsequent closing processes. This section addresses those processes as (1) the issue of applicant integrity, (2) the concepts of employment interviews, (3) interview types and techniques, (4) statement analysis (SA), and (5) truth detection methods and devices.

Issue of Applicant Integrity

The highest priority in the entire process of screening law enforcement and public safety officers is establishing to a reasonable certainty, the applicant's integrity. In fact, the predominant purpose of the entire pre-employment investigation is to establish the candor and integrity of the applicant.[874] This requirement extends to all written and oral disclosures and admissions by the applicant.[875] Records searches, personal and professional references, and interviews of independently developed sources will never provide the depth, breadth, and quality of information that will need to come from the applicant personally. Research has revealed that substantial portions of job applicants will offer untruths regarding their qualifications for a specific role in order to make themselves more competitive against the pool of applicants they see as their competition.[876] Being dishonest during the pre-employment interview process has been deemed the most patent breach of trust possible.[877] Ultimately, the applicant's capacity and willingness to disclose truthful statements in the process will often drive the level of investigation that must be expended in the screening process. The more an applicant lies, the more difficult the investigation may become. The immense consternation that this will cause the background investigator, as well as the needless waste of limited investigative resources, aggravated by the applicant's intention to circumvent the process warrants a severe consequence for the applicant. The applicant has, for all intents and purposes, knowingly and intentionally attempted to outwit the system to present themselves as qualified candidates for the most trusted of roles with the full awareness that they are in fact not qualified. Otherwise, why would they lie in the first place? In many instances, the issue is not the indiscretion the applicant is trying to conceal, rather the attempt to conceal the information from the background investigator and organization. Widely accepted in most circles, the cover-up of an incident is considered far worse than the incident itself.[878] This level of deceit requires the severest of consequences. To many this may seem to be a draconian level of punishment. In reality, if an applicant is willing to take this type of chance in the initial screening and is successful, they are emboldened to repeat this behavior in their careers. From this timeless prophecy, the punishment fully fits the crime!

The background investigation often helps reasonably establish an applicant's patterns of honesty and trustworthiness.[879] As tried and true as the background investigation process is though, the process may never fully reveal the certainty of the veracity of an applicant's capacity for high levels of integrity.[880] Scaffolded processes that include multiple layers of internal, external, and professional review give us the opportunity to obtain the best picture possible of an applicant given the potential for missing information, information that is not available, nor disclosed during the normal course of the investigation. Another impediment we face in the search for integrity is a natural truth bias.[881] We often believe that people applying to the field are, in general, very honest and forthright. This orientation frequently taints our ability to examine the applicant and information independently and objectively to form the most appropriate assessment.

In holding the line to such a standard, much discussion has been offered in the requirement of business necessity. Law enforcement and public safety positions must be held to the highest standards of integrity, far beyond those required of the average citizen.[882] Consequently, we have a bona fide qualification that integrity is the highest regarded trait among those who enter the public safety and law enforcement fields. The legal precedents for preserving these high levels of integrity among law enforcement officers are insurmountable. The foundational discovery motion case can be traced back to the decision in *Brady v. Maryland* (1963).[883] In this decision, the court mandated any exculpatory information must be disclosed to the defense in a case. This decision underscores the ability of the defense to obtain derogatory information against the government witness and use that information to impeach the credibility of any subsequent testimony offered in the proceeding.[884] The disclosure of officer misconduct, inappropriate actions, and the concealment of evidence are all included in the requirements of this decision. Several companion cases were also decided, including *United States v. Agurs* (1976), *United States v. Bagley* (1985), and *Kyles v. Whitley* (1995), which all follow similar themes of disclosing exculpatory information.[885] As a result of these decisions, there is a move to standardize organizational policies in how these *Brady* requests are handled as inconsistency and lack of policy have led to serious legal problems for departments and prosecutors, resulting in the losses of numerous criminal cases.[886] A similar discovery case was decided in New York State just prior to the *Brady* decision. In the decision of *People v. Rosario* (1961), all documentation, including the officer's handwritten notes, is discoverable by the defense.[887] The most damaging of court decisions can be found in the case of *Giglio v. United States* (1972).[888] In this case, a central theme is the credibility of government witnesses and the impact on their ability to testify in criminal proceedings. Prosecutors are held to severely high standards for disclosure in the criminal cases commenced necessitating very strict procedures be codified and followed.[889] Public defenders are also developing sophisticated databases that can track public records of officer issues, complaints, and transgressions that can later be used to attack their credibility in criminal trials.[890] Credibility, both prehire and posthire, is critical to the effectiveness of the officer and agency alike. When we fail to meet this standard, then a pall is cast over the entire discipline as a whole. Also emphasized as the ultimate priority of the courts, the concern of officer truthfulness and integrity is eloquently stated in the decision of *Grabinger v. Conlisk* (1972):

> We must note that a law enforcement officer is in a peculiar and unusual position of public trust and responsibility, and by virtue thereof, the public body has an important interest in expecting the officer to give frank and honest replies to questions relevant to his fitness to hold public office.[891]

As is also affirmed in the decisions of *City of Canton v. Harris* (1989) and *Huemiller v. Ogden Civil Service Commission* (2004), honesty is paramount to an officer's performance of sworn duties.[892] The court decisions supporting the right of a municipality to hold their police officers to strict levels of integrity are pervasive and extensive.[893] The varied court decisions have become so scrutinizing of officer honesty that in the decision of *Brogan v. United States* (1998), an officer under investigation was charged with a felony for lying to a federal agent by simply offering an exculpatory "no" to the questioning.[894] The landmark decision of *Garrity v. New Jersey* (1967) sets the foundation for the ability to force an officer to tell the truth under penalty of discipline and discharge that vitiates an officer's *Fifth Amendment* rights against compulsory self-incrimination.[895] In essence, the officer has no constitutional right to lie to or withhold information from their employer. The courts feel so strongly about this topic that federal case law requires truthfulness from employees even when the question may be deemed improper.[896] However, there may be ethical, procedural, and civil implications of how the question is asked, so understanding these boundaries is an acute concern in the pre-employment screening process.

More recent cases have directly applied to the hiring process of police officers. For example, in the decision of *Village of Oak Lawn v. Illinois Human Rights Commission* (1985), a police officer applicant's untruthfulness in the application process served as grounds to render the applicant unfit to serve as a police officer.[897] In another pre-employment-related court decision, *City of Cambridge v. Civil Service Commission* (1997), a department was allowed to bypass a candidate who was untruthful to a judge.[898] In the latest decision in *NASA v. Nelson* (2011), the U.S. Supreme Court affirmed right of government to screen applicants for honesty and trustworthiness through the use of reference interviews.[899] A review of the relevant state-level laws will also reveal these types of requirements to be truthful in all communications. An example found under the *Florida Law* mandates the following in the processing of law enforcement applicants:

> Not have been convicted of any felony or of a misdemeanor involving perjury or a false statement, or have received a dishonorable discharge from any of the Armed Forces of the United States. Any person who, after July 1, 1981, pleads guilty or nolo contendere to or is found guilty of any felony or of a misdemeanor involving perjury or a false statement is not eligible for employment or appointment as an officer, notwithstanding suspension of sentence or withholding of adjudication. Notwithstanding this subsection, any person who has pled nolo contendere to a misdemeanor involving a false statement, prior to December 1, 1985, and has had such record sealed or expunged shall not be deemed ineligible for employment or appointment as an officer.[900]

The *New York State Correction Law* mirrors a similar requirement in the language addressing the issue of untruthfulness specifically as follows:

> Nothing in this article shall be construed to affect any right an employer may have with respect to an intentional misrepresentation in connection with an application for employment made by a prospective employee or previously made by a current employee.[901]

Some will argue that this qualification may cause adverse impact in the selection of protected classes of applicants. Irregardless of all protected classes, as well as unprotected classes, truthfulness is both color and gender blind. We must realize that truthfulness must come in all colors, genders, and religions. Most importantly, race, color, national origin, religion, sex, age, disability, veteran status, or other protected class should not be a conveniently excusable trait or human characteristic to offer deception in any setting, especially the pre-employment investigation process. Such was the case in the decision of *Mister v. Illinois C.G.R.R.* (1987), wherein a district court struck down an applicant's claim of racial discrimination as the basis for adverse action as the applicant had lied on the employment application concerning a previous termination from another job.[902] More importantly, the court affirmed that the defendant company would have rejected all applicants, regardless of race, if an applicant was untruthful in the manner revealed.[903] Aligned with this issue, one research study examined the rates of truthfulness of applicants who had been processed by a large law enforcement agency. The average rate of untruthfulness for the entire applicant population revealed that while 40% was the average rate at which applicants had lied in the applications, race classifications presented a different picture. A stratified analysis revealed that while some protected populations were untruthful at a rate of 30% of the applications, other protected populations had an untruthfulness rate of over 71% of the applications.[904] However, in all race classes, the standard is the same, to simply tell the truth.

Some may also argue that information which the applicant omits may not be intentional, may be through the lack of understanding of the process, misperception, or lack of clarity in the directions or requests. For the overwhelming majority of these incidents of failure to disclose, upon discovery, applicants will experience an epiphany of "delayed" integrity in an effort to rationalize the omission and innocently continue in the process.[905] However, if there is credibility to this theory in the screening process used, then the process must be changed to reflect the highest levels of transparency and lucidity. Once the process is sound, then the sanction for untruthfulness must be unmitigated and severe. Having an enforceable sanction is meaningless unless you actually enforce the sanction both consistently and fairly. Policy must be clear and unequivocal that any false statement made by an applicant will result in not only removal from the process but also later discharge if discovered after employment.[906] The language of the admonition must be unwavering in direction and purpose. For example, the statement the applicant will swear to should include this type of wording: "I understand that any false and/or deliberate misrepresentations, whether by omission or commission, will result in my application being automatically and irrevocably rejected from further consideration."[907] Passive voice and ambiguous language will lead to applicant's searching for loopholes and administrators vacillating in their decisions to reject applicants based upon feigned misunderstandings.

A classic case to review can be found in the findings of *Sindermann v. Civil Service* (1995), wherein a police applicant failed to disclose material facts of a previous termination and was later discharged from employment with the police department after these facts were uncovered based on an anonymous tip.[908] Department administrators should also consider policy that precludes the applicant from any future processing with the agency if they return later on down the line. This should also be clear in the application process so that the applicant understands if they lie, they are subjected to lifetime exclusion from further processing with the agency. The applicant should be presented with a form that advises them of this provision and have them attest to the form either by signing in the witness of the background investigator or authorized staff member, or by use of a notarized statement. Any untruth penned or uttered by the applicant must be acted upon appropriately by the background investigator and administrator alike.[909]

This point is so critical that the issue cannot be adequately emphasized to the level of importance represented to the process itself. Spinning the old motto of the three "L"s of success in real estate that translates to location, location, location, applicants will visualize success in the process through three distinctly different "L"s: Lies, Lies, Lies! The mendacities of law enforcement applicants will never cease to astonish even the most seasoned of background investigators. For the most part, politicians are the absolute worst in conveying any semblance of the truth to the American public. Throughout time, politicians have demonstrated from the very astute to the extremely poor, skills at lying to their constituents.[910] In one particularly shocking case, a federal judge was impeached for lying to the Senate and FBI during the appointment and confirmation process.[911] The American businessman is certainly not far behind. However, the difference between businessmen and our politicians is that our politicians are selected by a democratic process to hold positions of trust in our government. There is much astonishment and wonder in the dichotomy presented though as these same politicians, who are the leaders at the local, state, and federal levels who require absolute honesty and integrity for all those who work for them, are frequently devoid of any ability to simply tell the truth themselves. As utterly frustrating and disgusting as their behaviors are though, public safety and law enforcement have always been the first, last, and only line of defense of the American system of truth, order, and justice. From this precept, we must always hold the line, raise the standard, and defend the need to maintain the highest levels of professionalism in the ranks. The charge goes to the responsibility of the leadership of the organization to develop and enforce clear and unequivocal rules of truthfulness for the law enforcement organization as a whole.[912]

The examples are pervasive and numerous of police officers and supervisors who have been caught lying to cover up illegal acts, violations of policy, falsifying and tampering with official reports, computer records, falsifying and planting incriminating evidence, excessive force, lying during court testimony, and witness tampering.[913] Some departments have publicly claimed that officers in their ranks have lied and will never be called to testify in a case.[914] Law enforcement personnel who are involved in criminal acts also frequently lose their credibility and are stripped of the ability to testify in court proceedings.[915] Lying on an application for a law enforcement position can be extremely problematic for an applicant.[916] Hiring an applicant who has been discovered lying on an application can be even more problematic for the applicant and the hiring agency.[917] We also must constantly deal with the timeless perception and issue of the *Code of Silence* causing internal and external problems in agencies across the country.[918] The mystical *Thin Blue Line* that separates the police from the public is perception entwined with reality rather than being an absolute. To address these issues, department administrators are galvanizing complete truthfulness policies, which must be reinforced in the pre-employment screening process.[919] However, cases emerging across the country where officers are being disciplined and terminated for minor transgressions such as calling in sick when not legitimately ill must also be tempered given the amount of damage they can cause in the long term.[920] If this is a practice of the agency, then the same policies must transcend the hiring assessment if an applicant has engaged in this type of behavior in their previous employments. If these character flaws are discovered in the pre-employment investigation, the applicant must be removed with extreme prejudice from the process in order to prevent any future issues or claims. Terminating police officers who lie is an argument not only for organizational policy but also, more importantly, for public policy.[921] This dialogue must be ongoing and drive positive and progressive change in the process of in-service as well as pre-employment screening (see below).

The Effects of Compromised Officer Integrity[922]

Three Baltimore City Police Department Officers Convicted in Civil Rights Case

Department of Justice
Office of Public Affairs
For Immediate Release
Friday, June 11, 2010

WASHINGTON—A federal jury yesterday convicted a Baltimore Police Department (BPD) officer, Gregory Mussmacher, on civil rights and obstruction charges related to his physical abuse in 2004 of a then 17 year old arrestee whom Mussmacher assaulted with a baton while the teen was handcuffed, shackled, and temporarily blinded by pepper-spray. A second former BPD officer, Guy Gerstel, pleaded guilty on the first day of trial to lying to the FBI, and admitted that he too had assaulted the teenager while he was restrained. A third former officer, Sergeant Wayne Thompson, also pleaded guilty, admitting that he engaged in obstruction of justice to help cover up the assaults.

At trial, Gerstel and Thompson testified against their former colleague, defendant Mussmacher. They and other government witnesses established that Mussmacher had gotten into a verbal argument with the teenager at the scene of his arrest. In response to verbal taunting from the teen, Mussmacher took off his badge and gun, removed the teen's handcuffs, and challenged him to a fight. After the arrestee refused to fight the officer, Mussmacher pepper-sprayed him in the face. A short time later, when Mussmacher had him alone in a room at the police station, he used his police baton to slam the fully-restrained teenager in the face, breaking his orbital bone and fracturing his jaw in two places. The evidence established that Mussmacher then submitted false and misleading police reports to cover up what had happened.

"Law enforcement officers who use their badges as an excuse to commit egregious acts of violence are an affront to the rule of law," said Thomas E. Perez, Assistant Attorney General for the Civil Rights Division. "The Civil Rights Division will continue to aggressively prosecute officers who abuse their power in this manner."

"Most law enforcement officers earn our confidence by performing their duties with honor and integrity," said U.S. Attorney Rod J. Rosenstein of the District of Maryland. "Police officers who abuse suspects, write false reports and obstruct justice must be held accountable so that citizens can have confidence in law enforcement agencies."

Sentencing is scheduled for September 23, 2010, and Mussmacher faces a maximum sentence of 30 years in prison.

This case was investigated by the Baltimore Division of the FBI, and was prosecuted by Trial Attorneys Forrest Christian and Kevonne Small, and Special Litigation Counsel Jeffrey Blumberg, with support from the Baltimore U.S. Attorney's Office (United States Department of Justice Office of Public Affairs, 2010).

The Strict Reliance on Applicant Honesty in Pre-Employment Disclosures[923]

Busy Investigators Often Forced to Rely on Honesty of Applicants (Dash, 1990)

Leon Dash of *The Washington Post*

Every year, the Department of Corrections selects between 900 and 1000 recruits, sends them off for 6 weeks of training, and hopes they make it so that they can be assigned to the D.C. jail or one of the department's seven prisons at Lorton.

The qualifications are few. They must be at least 21 years old. They should have a high school diploma or equivalency degree, although that is not a rigid requirement. They cannot be drug users and they cannot have a felony conviction.

But the department's handful of background investigators have too many applications to do extensive checking, officials say. They send fingerprints to the FBI, run a computer check for criminal records and mail form letters to previous employers. Beyond that, they depend on the truthfulness of the applicants.

Sometimes the applicants lie.

Roger Dawson, for example. When he filled out D.C. personnel form 171 in October, noting that he wanted to become a correctional officer, he omitted any mention of three convictions since 1987—having sex with a minor and two theft offenses—and his continuing probation.

Dawson, 31, said he did list two convictions under the old Federal Youth Corrections Act, knowing they could not be held against him; as permitted under this law on crimes committed by young adults, the convictions were expunged after Dawson completed 4 years in prison in 1981.

On February 26, along with a host of other recruits, Dawson was sworn in as a probationary officer in the Department of Corrections and enrolled at the department's training academy. A month later, on March 27, Dawson was arrested again, this time on a felony charge of having sex with an 8 year old girl. Now awaiting trial, he is being held at the Modular Facility in Lorton, where he trained during his month as a probationary officer. He has pleaded not guilty.

Department officials said they did not know why Dawson's record did not turn up during the background check. Benny O. Hodges, the department's associate director for administration, said he was certain that Dawson's name was run through the National Crime Information Computer. "I would say that is something that wouldn't happen again in 50 years. NCIC is the best system available," Hodges said.

Hodges said no real harm was done because Dawson "never made it out of the training academy. See, you're not employed until you go through the whole probationary process, and that's one year." He said the department was still doing some checking on Dawson at the time of his arrest.

Seeking out improvements

Corrections officials also have rejected some people whose criminal records were picked up. Nonetheless, they said in interviews they believe the system needs improvement. Right now, the department has no central registry to determine whether an applicant has applied before, was previously rejected or was fired from a Corrections job.

Walter B. Ridley, Hodges's boss and the director of Corrections, said the department is developing a cross-reference file to keep tabs on such things. "We're the first to admit that there are a lot of things that haven't been brought on line at Corrections," Ridley said. "We're moving as rapidly as we can to bring them on line."

The Dawson case is one illustration of how the hiring process sometimes goes awry. There are other examples, according to officers interviewed:

A former probationary officer at the jail, fired last year for coming to work "incoherent," was allowed to return to the department last month and is enrolled at the training academy.

A former officer at the D.C. jail, forced to resign because of suspected drug dealing with an inmate, reapplied and was rehired last year. In April, during his probationary employment period, he was fired in a second drug-related incident.

A former jail officer, in her reapplication, omitted any mention of being arrested on drug charges. When she came before the Department of Corrections' interview panel in March, three officers from the jail were serving on the panel that week. They recognized her and alerted a background investigator. Subsequently, she was rejected.

Asked about some of these examples, Hodges disputed the notion that the system has serious flaws. "If only three slip by, I think we did an excellent job," he said.

Until 8 months ago, when Ridley and Hodges set up a formal recruiting office, background checks were left to the department's five-member warrant squad—which had to squeeze in the checks while serving warrants and picking up parole violators.

But the new office also is overwhelmed. The background investigators find it impossible to do a thorough job on the 150 applications that come to the office every 2 months, officials say.

If they had time, the background investigators would have a lot of information to look at. They have the applicant's 171 form from the D.C. personnel office, which includes basic information; a medical examination form; a urinalysis questionnaire; an authorization allowing the department to request any criminal records; and a 20-page personal history statement, which asks about previous employment, drug use, and criminal involvement.

Roger Dawson was working as a security guard when he applied to the D.C. government for three different jobs in October. The ambulance corps rejected his application. The police department interviewed him for a crossing guard post but never contacted him further. In November, the Department of Corrections invited him to come to its Grimke headquarters at 1923 Vermont Ave. NW.

Among other things, he filled out the personal history statement, lying about his criminal record. He also had to submit a urine sample, which did not concern him because he had never used drugs. It was negative. A month later, he received his letter of acceptance.

We Want to Be Perfect

Dawson reported to the department's training academy on March 5. After 2 weeks of classes, he and seven classmates were sent to the Maximum Security Facility at Lorton for a firsthand look. Almost immediately, he ran into a lieutenant who recognized him from Dawson's days as an inmate at Lorton's Youth Center.

The lieutenant led Dawson to a captain's office. "The lieutenant here tells me you were in the Youth Center," Dawson remembers the captain saying. "Tell me about that."

Dawson said, "I was there. I served my time under the Federal Youth Corrections Act. I did my time."

But the matter did not end there. On March 22, he was ordered to meet a recruitment officer, who wanted to know about the Youth Act convictions. Dawson explained that his record had been expunged. The officer wanted proof; Dawson obtained a computer printout from Superior Court showing the deletion. The officer was satisfied, Dawson said.

Five days later, Dawson was arrested on the new sex charge. That night, he was in a cell at the D.C. jail. After Corrections officials became aware of his arrest, they fired him. As a probationary officer, Dawson had no right of appeal. He received his last check while incarcerated.

Corrections officials consider the Dawson case a fluke.

"We want to be perfect," Hodges said. "We're working toward perfection. We are going to be perfect, but right now we're 99.9 percent.... Come back in a year and we'll be perfect."

Concepts of Employment Interviews

The concepts of employment interviews may seem analogous to criminal interviews to the aspiring or fledgling background investigator. In many respects, they seek the same outcomes to establish the truth of the matter being investigated. They are quite different in many aspects though. Criminal interviews and interrogations seek to establish culpability in a crime for the most part. There are few rules other than when the person of interest becomes a target and custody occurs, only then do their constitutional rights against compulsory self-incrimination attach. Tactics can be of deception and even characterized as harsh at times. The goal is to clear the crime, arrest the offender, and assist in the court prosecution.

Rules of engagement are quite different in an employment interview than they are in a criminal interview. In the pre-employment interview, many questions concerning protected information may result in severe legal consequences.[924] A haphazard approach to selection and deselection as well as a mistake in hiring can cost an organization millions of dollars to repair.[925] No amount of money thrown at the problem can repair the media humiliation and loss of public trust though. The pre-employment interview seeks to primarily establish one aspect, the applicant's fit to the human resource needs of the organization.[926] The selection interview targets questions and techniques that establish the best suited applicants as opposed to those who are only interested in employment.[927] Consequently, hiring new employees is the most important function performed by the leaders of an organization.[928]

The employment interview allows for the review of sought after characteristics, behaviors, and capacity of the applicant as matched to the role applied for. Experience, training, attitude, decision-making skills, capacity for adapting to new and challenging roles, and many other topics can be discussed and assessed during the interview process. Information to be gleaned from the employment interview includes the ability to predict future performance and behavior of the applicant based upon their past history and how they reveal and explain their past conduct.[929] Some argue that the interview may not necessarily be the most valid predictor of future performance.[930] The interview can reveal many insights into the applicant's characteristics, social skills, personality, and attitudes toward the job.[931] The employment interview can also probe social cognition through asserted attitudes and responses toward social responsibility and social justice. Research by the U.S. Border Patrol revealed a set of criteria that can be used in developing interview questions that can screen for counter productivity; the criteria were listed as follows:

1. Conscientiousness
2. Cooperativeness
3. Emotional maturity
4. Initiative
5. Integrity/honesty
6. Judgment
7. Sensitivity to the needs of others
8. Use of force[932]

Questions formed around a solid set of criteria will provide an opportunity to gauge verbal responses as well as classical bodily clues that indicate if an applicant is sincere in their assertions. These responses can then be compared to the applicant's past history to confirm or refute historical patterns and trends in behaviors. Other areas that can be explored deal with controversial issues of police discretion and acceptance of the dangers the person will face once they enter the profession. Police discretion embraces a mindset of fair and consistent enforcement of the laws. Frequent enforcement of the law in lieu of more discretionary approaches to resolve conflicts and issues encountered by the officer is constructively impossible in the diverse environments and cultures they will be exposed to on a daily basis.[933] Therefore, discretionary powers are an inescapable prerequisite of the police officer's responsibilities.[934] Police discretion is a critical element to establish with the applicant. Take, for example, a traffic officer who stops a couple who were speeding to get to a veterinarian's office as their dog was choking to death. The officer unilaterally and callously decided that the couple could get another dog as he delayed them further by issuing a traffic ticket. This incident not only garnered national news headlines and television reports for the insensitive manner in which the officer acted but also spawned an online protest site that as of last count had 3500 signatures belying the officer's, chief's, and mayor's actions.[935] Or a U.S. Department of Fish and Wildlife agent who issued a summons to a mother whose daughter had saved a federally protected bird from being killed by a cat, only to have the summons rescinded and in the process, draw an embarrassing level of media attention and public discord.[936] Clearly apparent in these examples is that the police are more often called to task not on the actions taken, but rather the method in which they were taken.[937] Incidents such as these force the agenda of exploring these strong mindsets in the pre-employment process and weeding applicants who fail to understand the need for prudent discretion in dealing with the American public in the role of a law enforcement officer. Interviews should fully explore a candidate's beliefs on discretionary powers of law enforcement officers and the variability the applicant is willing to demonstrate to bring a balance to their sworn duties. Strong beliefs may also indicate the lack of maturity in an applicant, one of the most important aspects to establish concerning an applicant's personality.[938]

Another area to establish is that the applicant understands as well as accepts the frequent dangers of the role. Police officers experience the highest rates of workplace violent crime compared to all other professions.[939] This may come as a complete shock to the applicant, but it is not TV cops and robbers! The background investigator must establish to the best of their ability with the applicant the understanding that the job is growing ever more dangerous with increasing numbers of police and corrections officers being killed in car accidents, violent assaults, gun battles, and assassinations in a society that is becoming more crime ridden and ever more recalcitrant, antigovernment, and specifically antipolice.[940] Too many have been hired who enjoy the notion or idea of being a police officer until that dream becomes a reality. They then spend an entire career avoiding the dangerous situations, the toughest shifts, and busy patrol assignments, and forever bury themselves in safe administrative assignments in order to ride out their career in relative safety. Lastly, the background investigator must establish if the applicant is willing to use justified deadly force if necessary during the course of their duties. Some applicants just are not prepared to take the life of another even if justified and in the defense of themselves or innocent third parties.

One misnomer of the entry level employment interview process is that the applicant must be specifically questioned or tested on job responsibilities. These types of KSA will be trained after the applicant is hired.[941] The employment interview establishes if the applicant has the capacity to learn, adapt, and grow if hired into the position. Yet another misnomer is that the interview alone can determine if an applicant is fit or unfit for the role. Employment interviews are only one narrow component of the overall evaluation process used for final selection of an applicant.

Interview Types and Techniques

The employment interview process can be broken down into two broad categories: interview types and interview techniques. This section defines the various models of interviewing that can be used during the employment process. Additionally, this subsection also serves as a reminder of the varied and effective techniques of the interview process that can be employed when dealing with the range of applicants who will be interviewed.

Interview Types

There are three main interview types of styles used in the law enforcement field: (1) accusatory, (2) information gathering, and (3) behavior analysis.[942] The type of interview will depend wholly on the relevant aspects of the job function that the organization's leadership and policy makers decide to explore. As previously discussed, the major job responsibilities (MJR) are subjected to a job task analysis (JTA) in order to establish the required knowledge, skills, and abilities (KSAs) to perform the role effectively.[943] KSAs are then translated into qualification standards that define the basic eligibility requirements for a specific occupation or occupational grouping.[944]

Once these qualifying standards are developed, then the type of interview process that will best assess the applicant's abilities to fill the role is designed. Part of the testing process can then be delivered by the use of specific interviewing models. For all intents and purposes, the selection interview is anticipated to provide the organization's management with the level of job qualifications met by the applicant, so the best fit can be obtained in making the final selection of an individual applicant.[945] Selection model constructs include the assessment of an applicant's (1) conceptual knowledge, (2) capacity for analytical thinking, (3) their understanding of the practice of the skill, and (4) their application of the skill.[946] These types of models provide a conceptual framework for which we can proceed in the development of the specific interview model or models that will be used.

Interviews can be structured or unstructured, successive and sequential with lateral or hierarchical layers, and panel situations that address key questions or scenarios. For example, in situational interviews, the applicant is provided with a hypothetical scenario or situation and asked what they would do if faced with such an incident or dilemma. The quantification is also subject to challenge as the assessment parameters would be extremely difficult to define in such an unstructured interview. Because of the lack of structure, the lack of equity can be demonstrated, and there is also limited predictive validity to the method. Validated interview processes are researched based upon job requirements and provide a formative level of structural rigidity. Interviews should be highly structured in order to be fair and comprehensive. For example, support for the use of cognitive interviewing (CI) in the selection process has been raised.[947] CI involves methods of inquiry that require the applicant to recall the event in different order, for example, in free recall, cued recall, or serialized recall in order to test the memory as well as the veracity of the account. Other types of employment interview methods that increase structure to the process and afford more accuracy and interrater reliability include frame of reference (FOR) interviews and descriptively anchored ratings (DAR) which when combined provide for a more accurate analysis process.[948] FOR interviews are a shared understanding of defined performance standards leading to the reduction of subjectivity of the rating while increasing the reliability of the rating. Another recommended method is the chronological in-depth structured (CIDS) interview that explores an applicant's entire history including equal discussion of successes and failures, in order to establish specific patterns and trends demonstrated by the applicant in all of their previous employments.[949] This process is also entitled behaviorally based or behavioral description interviews (BDI) as the responses reinforce the concept of past behaviors being a valid predictor of future performance expectations.[950] An excellent example of the component process of behaviorally based interviewing includes the following:

1. Link the interview questions to four to six key competencies of the job.
2. Make the questions challenging but not too difficult or lengthy.
3. Ensure everyone involved in interviewing knows the responses and key points.
4. Ask every candidate the same questions in the same order.
5. Reserve a portion of the interview for a review of the candidate's education, experience, and job history.
6. Probe so the example can be visualized: "What were you thinking? Why did you approach it that way? What was the result?"
7. Look for "STAR" answers—descriptions of the situation, task, action, and result.
8. Ask overlapping questions that confirm more than one competency.
9. Ask candidates if they would like the question repeated.
10. Rate each response as it is given.[951]

This process of comprehensive interviewing should be augmented with a crediting plan that allows for the measurement of the applicant's qualifications that include the factors of education, experience, and training to receive credit and add to final rank on an eligibility list.[952] This process must leave room for additional exploratory questions though as there will never be the opportunity to include every possible question in a standardized format. The background investigator must be given the ability to probe issues and information that is developed beyond the scope of the regimented process.

Other examples include job simulation questions or in-box exercises, much like those used in assessment center testing methodology.[953] The applicant is provided with a modified version of the full assessment center scenario process so that the interviewer can assess basic decision-making skills and responses to a series of prepared questions. Case studies would also be a useful technique to measure an applicant's reactions to specific incidents and how they would respond or handle the situation if involved or in control of the incident.

The interview process must also be measured in an unbiased and validated manner. Much like the behaviorally anchored rating system (BARS) used in performance assessment, responses and behaviors must be categorized into unacceptable, acceptable, and superior behaviors so that the interviewer can not only numerically rate the applicant for their responses but also more importantly articulate how the response either meets or does not meet the required standard based upon the results of the JTA. This can be accomplished through the use of a ranking interview wherein the applicant is scored according to the objective standard and then is ranked among the pool of applicants in order to develop a list of potential candidates.[954]

In the absence of a scaling or quantified rating system, the background investigator should utilize other validated methods of applicant interview assessment. There are three generally accepted constructs in rating applicant interviews: (1) job-related interview content (e.g., job knowledge), (2) interviewee performance (e.g., impression management tactics), and (3) personal/demographic characteristics (e.g., candidate attractiveness).[955] The applicant can often be assessed in each one of these categories and accurately compared to other applicants in the process in order to make the best hiring decision from the group. A second recommended method involves accepted practices in assessing responses to questions regarding their required KSA of the role applied for. A range of models to consider in the assessment of an applicant's responses include the following:

1. SAR (situation, action, results)
2. STAR (situation, task, action, results)
3. CCAR (context, challenge, action, results)[956]

The background investigator should always use an accepted and validated model to conduct any and all assessments. This practice will ensure the validity of the process and equity to the individual candidates as opposed to an arbitrary method designed by the background investigator and subject to intense scrutiny by those in oversight positions.

Interview Techniques

Interview techniques in the employment interview process have many parallels to the criminal investigation process. However, there are equally as many differences as there are similarities. For the purposes of this discussion, highlights of the process are included along with comparisons and contrasts.

Preparation is likely the most fundamental need of the interview process. Failing to devote the proper time, attention, and resources to an employment interview that results in a poor hire can be one of the costliest mistakes made in an organization.[957] Therefore, careful planning is essential to all pre-employment interviews.[958] Preparation includes not only the completion of all of the investigative steps of the background investigator but also a full review of all of the supporting documentation for the case. The background investigator should have an intimate knowledge of the facts included on every shred of paper associated with the case.

The next consideration is the setting of the applicant interview. There are generally two separate environments used: the police station and the applicant's residence. The applicant's workplace should be avoided so as not to place the applicant in an untenable situation with their current employer. The interview is always done with the highest levels of respect and professionalism in deference to the applicant.[959] This is necessary in order to maintain every contact with the applicant is always the most positive interaction possible. We are making the best effort to welcome the qualified applicant to the ranks of our agencies, and until we know otherwise, they must all be treated as though they may be hired. Only the evidence discovered at the time of the interview can dictate our assumptions of an applicant's acceptability for hire, facts that would lead us to believe they are unfit for the role, or if the evidence is fairly indistinctive or nondescript.[960] All interviews should be face-to-face whenever possible. Telephone interviews should be strictly limited to simple verifications, notifies, and fairly inconsequential, but needed investigative information. For all substantive interviews, the applicant should appear in person, so the background investigator can use the range of options, abilities, and responsive behaviors to assess the applicant's truthfulness.

Foundationally, there are five elements that should be considered when planning for and administering the interview. These elements include (1) establishing rapport, (2) introducing the topic of concern, (3) eliciting narrative detail, (4) clarification of specific questions, and (5) closure.[961] With respect to rapport building, the concept may be the most crucial element. As a fundamental component of neurolinguistic programming and the neurolinguistic interviewing process, the development of rapport with the interviewee to establish the relationship on a common set of beliefs or grounds is essential to the success of the interview.[962] Rapport building encourages a willingness in the interviewee to voluntarily cooperate with the inquiry.[963] Development of the proper rapport usually brings with it the feelings or perception of a relationship between interviewer and interviewee. Information tends to flow much more freely when this relationship is developed or, at the very least, perceived to be developed by the applicant. This is a crucial perception on behalf of the applicant as the background investigator will encounter the similar range of personalities in the pre-employment investigation process as they do in the criminal investigation process. From the introvert to the narcissist, from the buff to the disinterested, from the honest to the corrupt, no shortage of personalities will be had. Adapting to this range of personalities prevents the background investigator from appearing disingenuous and developing concomitant barriers to the rapport building process. In fact, rapport building is a key element in overcoming an interviewee's propensity to present untruths that paint themselves in a favorable light to the background investigator.[964] The subject being interviewed will usually provide information when they believe it will afford them some advantage over the interviewer or in the situation at hand.[965]

Another tactic in the pre-employment interview process is the early or preliminary interview. In part, this interview is fact-finding and probative. In addition, an early interview may be perceived by the applicant as no investigation has been conducted at this point. Consequently, they may be more comfortable in speaking and apt to offer false statements that can say much about the applicant's character.[966] This method is only recommended in the rare cases where the background investigator's experience and training would lead them to believe there are issues to explore with the applicant prior to the full investigation being completed. Fully document the circumstances and statements in order to be able to accurately recall and either confirm or refute later developments in the investigation when the timing is appropriate.

In the employment interview, proper and appropriate question development is of real concern. An interview involves far more than just asking questions.[967] Remember the balancing act that we must face in probing the applicant's past, weeding out the unqualified, and, in the process, not disenfranchising the qualified applicant. The background investigator must avoid the risk of contaminating the interview by selecting the proper environment as well as avoiding negative behaviors that would distance or create communication barriers with an interviewee.[968]

This all occurs under the mantle of protecting the applicant's employment law entitlements and civil rights. The valid and comprehensive job description should not only be the guide but also more importantly the driver of the questions asked.[969] Prepared and focused questions can be used to develop a candidate comparison platform.[970] That platform should then be used for the interview of all applicants in the process in order to demonstrate the levels of equity to any oversight body. The types of questions asked are only part of the issue as while any question can conceivably be asked of an applicant, the matter falls to what type of adverse action was taken based upon the responses.[971] Inappropriate or illegal questions may at a minimum buy us significant liability and, at a maximum, force the organization into a position to hire an otherwise unqualified or unfit candidate.

The employment interview is primarily designed to cull and evaluate information for the selection process that includes the applicant's past experiences and training that relate to the job sought.[972] Applicant behavioral domains that should be explored during the employment interview include socials skills, interpersonal and communication skills, motivation, situational problem solving, dependability and trustworthiness, and attitudes toward appearance. The applicant interview process can be strengthened by providing structure through previously designed questions and consistency in order to validate the process and produce better predictive results.[973] Questions should be designed around fulfilling organizational principles, edicts, mission, and vision in order to assess the applicant's ability to fulfill these organizational precepts.[974] Questions designed to assess job knowledge and behaviors must have input from all levels in the organization, including managers in order to be appropriate measures to predict future successes.[975] Questions must also be designed to capture characteristics that are desired of those who will take the agency into the future. Highly sought after characteristics for the future public safety officers should include their ability to be innovative and creative in the workplace with work processes, work environment, and the products of their efforts.[976]

Background investigators should use cognitive interview techniques, by asking open-ended questions and allowing the interviewee to recall as much information as they can about the situation being explored.[977] Open-ended questions that are tailored to the applicant's background can also lead to very revealing information specific to the applicant's qualifications, motivations, and behavior patterns. Facts developed from the interview should drive the process, not intuition or emotional connection to the applicant or process itself.[978] Another method that can be employed is the use of reverse-order interviewing wherein the applicant is asked to recall a specific event in reverse order than the original chronology.[979] Research has revealed that this method results in higher levels of detection of those who are being untruthful about an event or incident. The background investigator should adhere to the guidelines in order to avoid any discriminatory practices while also controlling and guiding the interview toward establishing the truth.

Classic behavioral cues and body language emerge from the criminal side of the street. The very basic and advanced principles can be employed in the pre-employment realm as well. Just as in a criminal case, the background investigator's ability to read behaviors and traits, along with knowledge of the background of the case as well as the subject, all work to the background investigator's benefit in the interview process.[980] One of the most revealing traits is eye movement during questioning. Eye movement is a long proven method to detect deception in interviewees.[981] However, while the value of nonverbal cues is relevant to the employment interview process, care must be taken in developing an over reliance on these observations which may lead to an unwarranted negative influence on the final assessment.[982] In addition, some research has also led to the theory that ethnicity and gender may have an impact on the investigator's ability to accurately read clues in eye movements that would indicate deceptive practices or statements.[983] Body language, shifting, fidgeting, sweating, nervous ticks, labored speech, delayed responses, and many other responses that would be inconsistent or uncharacteristic to the setting may all be signs of deception. Once deception is detected, the background investigator should practice the proper methods of confronting the applicant wherein the ultimate disclosure may be dependent upon tapping the proper emotion or rationale the subject will use to open up.[984]

The background investigator should continuously evaluate what is being said during the interview and continuously develop and refine the strategy of the interview in a real-time manner.[985] Strategy refinement can also emerge from other scientific interview principles that induce cooperation and connection from an interviewee. Kinesics or kinesthetic interviewing (e.g., matching the interviewee's body language and gestures) as well as paralanguage (e.g., matching an interviewee's voice characteristics in rate, tone, inflection, and pitch) are proven methods of developing the connection needed to allow for the free flow of information in the interview.[986] Another advanced method used in organizational settings to detect dishonesty is the concept of signal detection theory (SDT).[987] SDT, in part, theorizes that recollections and judgments of memory of an event are stronger than recollections of the familiarity of acquired knowledge.[988] SDT can also measure the confidence levels of the memories.[989] The theory rests on a series of principles: (1) separating verbal signals or cues from noise, (2) the recognition of how biases may influence the ambiguity of the response, and (3) the presence vs. the absence of certain verbal signals.[990] Companion research emphasizes the recognition of deceptive signals as well as the manner in which an interviewee relates their account of the incident as opposed to the inconsistencies found in the account of the incident.[991] The background investigator should continually experiment with new and advanced methods in order to become fluent in varied methods as well as have a range of options when assessing an applicant's responses to interview questions.

The process of dealing with applicant admissions is the next step. The overwhelming majority of an applicant's disclosures will be exculpatory in nature. The background investigator will also find the need to effectively manage and properly dispose of inculpatory assertions. Candidates should be made to understand that they need to be completely honest in all written and verbal disclosures. Criminal history does not necessarily equate to legal actions, and candidates may fear admission may lead to arrest rather than just exclusion from employment prospects. An admission, depending on departmental policies and state laws, may also not prove to be grounds to exclude an applicant from further processing and ultimate hire. Obtaining an initial admission though may not be sufficient in and of itself for the investigation. Any inculpatory admission requires a deeper exploration and further development of the facts surrounding the act disclosed.[992] The next decision is the most perplexing though. The processing agency's administrators must decide how to properly handle serious admissions of a criminal nature. First and foremost, the admission will be used for job suitability. We can all agree to that is the foundational precept of the employment interview. But should the application of the information disclosed to reject the applicant be the only use for the information? Other considerations are if the admission is of a severe enough level to report to the current employer in work-related matters or external and private matters that would negatively impact the applicant's current position.

Lastly, will the admission lead to a full criminal investigation and criminal actions? The implications are latent in the criminal, civil, and ethical arenas. In the criminal realm, the seriousness of the admission must dictate a criminal investigation. The background investigator would need to end the administrative or employment interview once sufficient information or details were provided that would lead them to believe the exclusionary crime or act had been committed. The admission would be sufficient evidence to remove an applicant from the process even in the absence of independent evidence or witnesses to corroborate the information. The timeline to consider is when an admission reaches the point to ensure removal of the applicant from the process without damaging any subsequent criminal inquiry and prosecution. The applicant's rights against compulsory self-incrimination under the decision of *Miranda v. Arizona* (1966) would directly apply in these cases.[993] The applicant would then be turned over to the agency's criminal investigators if jurisdiction applied or to the appropriate jurisdiction that would be responsible for the investigation.

There are also issues of potential civil litigation when the applicant is not dealt with appropriately to end any potential future conduct. Employee thefts are but one example of this; however, admissions will run the gamut. Failing to report these situations may incur civil liability on the part of the processing agency as well as the current employer may be found liable for any subsequent negligent hiring or retention claims. There is also an ethical question as to if the applicant's serious admissions should be reported to the employer or other relevant party. All of these questions must be addressed ahead of time, and the processing agency's administration must develop a departmental policy that specifically provides guidance for these issues as they arise because they will.

The final consideration is the documentation needs. The fact that this is an administrative interview should make the importance of documentation no less important than if this were a criminal investigation. In fact, clear and accurate documentation of the statement is a critical step in providing the proper foundation to support and defend adverse employment actions.[994] The interview of the applicant should include some type of recording process to capture the accuracy in the best available form possible.[995] The applicant's statement can be given orally and synopsized in writing by the background investigator, typed out or written out and signed by the applicant, audiotaped, videotaped, or taken through stenographic transcription. The statement should then be added to the original final investigative package and preserved in the manner required of the *Best Evidence Rule*.[996]

Statement Analysis

Advances in science and technology have been an evolving concept since the earliest days of policing. Burning up shoe leather has not been replaced but rather augmented by scientific discoveries and the application to the analysis of physical and biological evidence. As discussed later, the application of the earliest technology in truth verification included the polygraph examination. Further developments have led to the introduction of the voice stress analysis (VSA). Some of the most interesting and contemporary advancements have been enjoyed in the area of linguistics and the interpretation of the written and spoken word. While these innovations have been primarily focused on the criminal investigation realm, their application to the pre-employment investigation process cannot be overlooked.

There is a bifurcated purpose to establishing an applicant's capacity to communicate with the written word. First, we must establish the basics of the applicant's writing acumen, methods of expression, tone of response, and demonstration of their educational level. Language and writing skills should be tested at the outset of a process in order to establish an applicant's ability to communicate at the level required for the position of public safety and law enforcement officer. How an applicant writes as well as practices basic language skills is often used as an early disqualifier for the job applied for.[997] Capacity should reveal the applicant's functional communication ability as well as level of mastery of the English language. Lexical diversity is defined as the range of the interviewee's vocabulary and is an important measure of an applicant's ability to effectively communicate at all required levels.

The second purpose is to establish a foundation for the follow-up investigation and all of the requisite applicant interviews. Foundational research in linguistic relativity has led to the theory that the content and structure of a person's language patterns is a driver to shape social cognition and the accompanying philosophical views of values, ethics, and social norms. Neurolinguistics has built upon this notion to understand how the human brain processes information relative to our capacity for the use, intent of the message, and inferences that can be drawn from the specific language used. The emerging science of SA may prove quite helpful in the latter. Known by several variations in terminology, to wit, SA, statement validity analysis (SVA), and response analysis (RA), is an emerging science that may prove to be a very valuable tool to employ in job applicant assessment. The theory centers on the ability to detect truth or deception based upon the interpretation of overt behavioral indicators that are consistent with credibility or the lack thereof.[998] These types of behavioral indicators are postulated to be apparent in a subject's memorialization and recall of a specific event or incident. The human brain develops a set of internalized grammatical rules, and those rules drive thoughts, ideas, and motivation.[999] Analysis of these thoughts can lead to keen insight into the applicant's drivers and possible deceptive practices. The applicant's words would be used to detect deception independent of the facts of the incident.[1000] The analysis involves structure and form as well as the interpretation of semantics used by the subject.[1001] In addition, as in the analysis of any statement, omissions of key information are also the proverbial red flags to deception, and an effort must be made to establish the reason this information was omitted. SVA is a process of review that includes (1) the amount of detail reported in the writing, (2) coherence of the writing, and (3) admissions of the lack of memory.[1002] Areas of analysis include the (1) specific parts of the speech or writing (e.g., nouns, pronouns, and verbs), (2) extraneous information, (3) lack of conviction, and (4) the balance of the statement.[1003] SVA involves three separate components: (1) the structured interview, (2) a criteria-based content analysis (CBCA), and (3) a final examination of the validity of the process (validity checklist).[1004]

CBCA is the preeminent method of assessing veracity and detecting truth or deception in the recall and reporting of events.[1005] CBCA was primarily designed for use with the interviews of child sexual abuse victims but has been expanded to use with adults based upon the successes. In fact, one field study revealed very high confidence and reliability levels of the CBCA process in detecting the truthful nature of statements given by child sexual abuse victims.[1006] CBCA research is also somewhat incongruent in that others have found there are limits to the effectiveness of the concept in practice.[1007] One issue that can be problematic in the use of CBCA as a procedure of SVA is the lack of consistency between raters or interrater reliability.[1008] Interrater reliability can be increased though through proper training methods.[1009]

Reality monitoring (RM) is yet another technique showing promise in the application to interviewing subjects in the investigative process. RM is the process of distinguishing between the origins of one's memory through determining if the memory derives from an external source (e.g., acquisition of the memory through a perceptual process) or an internal source (e.g., development from the processes of reasoning, imagination, and thoughts).[1010] One research study revealed RM to be more accurate than CBCA at establishing the difference between truthful and deceptive interviewees.[1011]

In SA, the applicant writes out their own narrative or account of the incident or event, and then through analysis of the subject's word choices, phrases, tense, an assessment of the applicant's thoughts, motivations, and candor can be had. The language used is then transformed into a tool to query the subject's statement for direct and ancillary information that may be included in order to deceive the background investigator.[1012] A simple method to put this theory into practice would be for a department's pre-employment screening process to include a written statement of the applicant. The analysis can then be conducted by an SA expert and dissected for the cues that would lead to an applicant profile and additional lines of questioning that could be used on the applicant in subsequent interviews.

Many argue that due to the proliferation of electronic methods and the use of the Internet to plagiarize personal history statements as well as the availability of those in the field who professionally write such statements that the practice of submission should be abandoned.[1013] With this possibility in mind, the applicant should be required to write the statement on-site rather than be allowed to complete the statement out of the investigator's presence. The statement must be written in the controlled environment of the police headquarters or office in order to ensure the statement is that of the applicant's.

If an SA expert is not available, there are also some simple online resources that the background investigator can utilize as guidelines for evaluating personal statements to measure if the original question has been answered, specificity, tests of knowledge, and how much extraneous information is included that distracts from the original purpose of the statement.[1014] Granted, there are some methods that may be considered voodoo science and should be avoided. The methods of SA have shown promise and fundamental successes that may have direct application and relevance to the pre-employment screening process. If anything, they can be considered yet another tool the background investigator can use in their continuing quest for the truth.

Truth Detection Methods and Devices

Interestingly, research has revealed that contrary to a common belief, the majority of job applicants support the use of integrity tests in the employment process with the levels of support being found in direct correlation to the analyzed scores of the test takers. Those applicants who supported the use of integrity testing often had the highest ratings of integrity in the pool of test takers.[1015] This section delineates the various methods of truth detection that augment the scope of the conventions of the investigative process. Interviews, references checking, and records searches are often inadequate to establish an applicant's veracity. Several additional methods can also be employed as long as they are consistent with relevant state and federal level employment laws. This section discusses (1) integrity tests, (2) polygraph examinations, and (3) voice stress analysis.

Integrity Tests

Discussed in previous chapters as personality testing, integrity tests are designed to use a paper and pencil approach to establish if an applicant demonstrates patterns of untruthfulness, propensities for criminal behavior, and counterproductive habits that would theoretically predict poor performance issues. These types of tests are used across the country in varying forms in a very wide range of employment roles. The courts have supported the use of these types of instruments in general.[1016] The individual states are also authorizing the use of these types of tests in pre-employment screening laws with the requirement that the test in and of itself is not the primary basis for the adverse employment decision.[1017] However, one case established that the use of a pre-employment screening instrument that focused on character and work attitudes unlawfully discriminated against applicants who may have had certain political views or affiliations and lenient attitudes toward drug use or highly liberal beliefs as decided in *Thompson v. Borg-Warner Protective Services* (1996).[1018] Contradictory evidence exists though both in support of and rejection of the ability of this type of testing process to accurately forecast a prospective employee's potential for counterproductive behaviors, discipline problems, absenteeism, and congruence with future supervisory performance evaluations.[1019] If an agency decides to use these types of tools, much research into test history, validity, and legal challenge must be reviewed before selecting an examination that will meet the needs of the specific agency.

These must also be used in concert with the remainder of the selection process and not used as a stand-alone screening tool.

Polygraph Examinations

In a perfect world, we would not need polygraph machines and examiners. But in the perfect world, we would not need the police either! In plain fact, applicants will choose to conceal information from the background investigator necessitating the use of truth verification methods such as the polygraph.[1020] Absent the polygraph, or other instrument, as a truth detection device, we are severely limited in our ability to paint the best picture of the applicant with the available, limited, and sometimes flawed information we discover. The polygraph provides the background investigator with an unparalleled opportunity to discover unknown information of past events that can only be disclosed by the person being interviewed.[1021]

There are numerous legal issues that impact the use of the polygraph test in the pre-employment screening process. In the criminal and civil arenas, the science of polygraphy and admissibility into evidence are controlled by two legal precedents, *Frye v. United States* (1923) and the more recent *Daubert v. Merrell Dow Chemicals, Inc.* (1993).[1022] Some courts have accepted the value of the polygraph and the probative value afforded as research has indicated higher-quality information gains when used in forensic settings.[1023] Case decisions are mixed though, indicating a reluctance on behalf of the courts to fully accept through consensus that polygraph is a true science.[1024] The U.S. Supreme Court in *United States v. Scheffer* (1998) noted the potential for the polygraph to unduly influence a jury using this language:

> Such jurisdictions may legitimately determine that the aura of infallibility attending polygraph evidence can lead jurors to abandon their duty to assess credibility and guilt. Those jurisdictions may also take into account the fact that a judge cannot determine, when ruling on a motion to admit polygraph evidence, whether a particular polygraph expert is likely to influence the jury unduly.[1025]

The debate in the criminal courts will likely carry on long after we are gone. In the application of the polygraph examination to the employment law arena, two bodies of legislation prevail: the *Employee Polygraph Protection Act of 1988* and the *Americans with Disabilities Act of 1990*.[1026] The *Employee Polygraph Protection Act of 1988* was implemented to prevent the denial of employment opportunities by prohibiting the use of lie detectors by employers involved in or affecting interstate commerce.[1027] Exemptions in the *Employee Polygraph Protection Act of 1988* include federal, state, and local government bodies; however, the Act does not circumvent any provision of any state or local law or of any negotiated collective bargaining agreement that prohibits lie detector tests or is more restrictive with respect to lie detector tests than any provision of the act.[1028] The *Employee Polygraph Protection Act of 1988* defines the polygraph as follows:

> An instrument that records continuously, visually, permanently, and simultaneously changes in cardiovascular, respiratory, and electrodermal patterns and minimum instrumentation standards; and is used, or the results of which are used, for the purpose of rendering a diagnostic opinion regarding the honesty or dishonesty of an individual.[1029]

Much case law has also been decided with respect to the use of polygraph examinations in the pre-employment screening process. For example, the polygraph can be used to establish an applicant's financial status, illegal drug use and abuse, health status, and criminal history as decided in.[1030] Numerous other cases support the use of polygraph examinations in the employment law realm with respect to pre-employment screening of law enforcement and corrections personnel.[1031] Polygraph examinations can also be extended for use in departmental promotional processes as decided in *Brown v. State of Tennessee* (1982).[1032] The proviso though is that the polygraph for promotions must be authorized through an established policy and sanctioned by civil service and municipal regulations as decided in *Hatfield Township v. Stanley* (1988).[1033] The Federal EEOC has also taken the position that the use of polygraph tests is not injurious to protected classes of persons. The tests are nonbiased in nature and do not adversely impact an applicant's candidacy solely on the basis of race, gender, age, or national origin.[1034] The individual states have also adapted legislation to meet the needs of the federal regulations. State legislatures have chosen to both allow and deny the use of polygraph for public safety positions. For example, under the *Connecticut Code*, a polygraph is defined as "Any mechanical or electrical instrument or device of any type used or allegedly used to examine, test or question individuals for the purpose of determining truthfulness."[1035] The *Connecticut Code* also allows the use of polygraphs for police and corrections personnel employment screening.[1036] In contrast, the *Rhode Island General Law* expressly prohibits the use of a pre-employment polygraph examination as a condition of employment.[1037] Included in the law is an additional prohibition of using an out-of-state entity to conduct a polygraph of an applicant for in state employment.[1038] Each individual state's laws should be consulted for the legal parameters allowed.

Timing of the examination is influenced in the legal sense by the type of questions that will be asked and topic areas explored. Under the provisions of ADA, the use of a polygraph to physiologically measure if an applicant is offering truthful responses to questions is legal. The ADA does not consider the polygraph test a medical examination even though the process does measure physiological responses. The responses are a measure to assess an applicant's veracity and not physical or psychological conditions. In the pre-COE stage, the applicant can be asked any questions that are not medical or psychological in nature or designed to elicit such a response. Once the COE has been issued, then a limited and controlled line of questioning with respect to medical and psychological information may proceed. The restrictions on the interrogatory include prohibitions on requesting information related to addictions and treatment or rehabilitation programs. In addition, the examiner cannot ask prohibited disability-related questions as part of the test.[1039] The polygrapher should avoid these questions from the perspective of not only to protect the applicant's rights but also to limit and avoid fabricated claims of dependencies that would allow certain disability-related protections included in the ADA. In addition, if an applicant chooses to self-declare their dependencies, these protections would attach. However, if the applicant chooses not to self-declare on their own, there is no obligation or reason to explore these protected areas. Any and all information developed in the medical and psychological areas must be treated as strictly confidential and limited in review to only those persons with the authority to review, assess, and make decisions on the information discovered. Ultimately, the organizational leaders and managers must accept the responsibility for ensuring the legal and ethical use of any and all information and disclosures made during the conduct of the polygraph examination.[1040]

The American Polygraph Association asserts in their Statement of Purpose that the polygraph is the most accurate scientific means of establishing if a test subject has been truthful.[1041] Polygraph examinations are very helpful tools to assist in determining any prior undisclosed and undetected information related to crimes, serious transgressions and misconduct, drug use, and other required information from an applicant's past. Agencies will post the parameters of the polygraph examination in the job announcement so that the applicant knows ahead of time what areas will be explored. For example, the Missouri State Highway Patrol posts these standards for review:

1. Employment history
2. Traffic record
3. Financial history
4. Current illegal drug usage
5. Record of criminal convictions
6. Basic honesty[1042]

The polygraph is also an excellent tool at discovering false statements and omissions made by the applicant during the application process. In addition to the aforementioned list, polygraph questionnaires and examiners should also explore the numerous contemporary areas brought to the surface in this textbook, including involvement in random acts of violence, mob violence, a deeper probing into crimes that may have been conducted through the use of the Internet, and many others so that a thorough and effective use of the tool can be accomplished. A review of the text and comparison to existing questionnaires should raise several new areas of review that the polygrapher should consider in their examinations of new applicants.

The use of polygraph is allowed in federal, state, and local government for public safety, corrections, and school systems employment screening. Exemptions are also included for the private sector commercial businesses for specified federal contractors, armored car personnel, high security or safety risk positions as in pharmaceutical companies, nuclear power plants, public works departments, and toxic waste handlers. Highly regarded as a valid investigative tool, numerous federal agencies including the FBI, Central Intelligence Agency, National Security Agency, Defense Department, Treasury Department, and most of the largest police agencies in the nation also depend heavily on the use of the polygraph for both pre-employment as well as in posthire investigations that transpire during continued employment.[1043] One study revealed that approximately half of the subjects polygraphed led to the disclosure of varying degrees of probative information of direct and indirect value.[1044] tool to predict future misconduct and criminal behavior by providing the opportunity to more fully examine an applicant's past.[1045] The most optimistic of these views is that the polygraph serves as a far better deterrent to untruthfulness rather than as a postincident method of detection.[1046] The merits cannot be ignored.

The process of the examination is a very regimented method to ensure that all interviewees are treated consistently and fairly during the examination. Long before the applicant is scheduled for the test, the background investigation should be completed so that the polygraph examiner can become versed in the details of the applicant's known past in order to better prepare for the examination.[1047] The forensic psychophysiologist or polygrapher (polygraph examiner) conducts the psychophysiological detection of deception (PDD) or polygraph testing. Just prior to the examination, the applicant is advised of the test protocol and given a period of time to adjust to thought of the impending examination. Usually two questionnaires are used, the personal history statement and a separate polygraph questionnaire, standardized or modified/designed by the polygrapher, which will include upwards of a 100 or more questions. The primary target areas of the questions are criminal activities, illegal drug use, thefts, and sex crimes. Some argue that the polygraph is an accurate method of establishing past illegal drug use in the absence of other more conventional methods such as arrests records, witnesses, and other conventional means.[1048] The examination involves the use of standard analog-type instruments that simultaneously record a series of multiple physiological responses. The analysis includes measurements of changes in cardiovascular activity (e.g., heart rate, pulse, and blood pressure), electrodermal activity (e.g., sweat-gland activity and changes in the electrical conductivity in the skin demonstrating stress or emotional responses), and respiratory activity (e.g., measured changes in the thoracic and abdominal areas). A range of tests can be employed including (1) relevant–irrelevant test, (2) comparison question test, (3) guilty knowledge test, and (4) concealed information test.

Tests will result in the examiner concluding that the examinee's responses fall into one of three categories: truthful, deceptive, or, in some cases, inconclusive. Alternate conclusions that are possible are false-positive errors (false positive), wherein the examinee was truthful, but the results of the test led the examiner to conclude that the examinee was deceptive. In contrast, the examiner could conclude with a finding of false-negative errors (false negative) wherein a deceptive applicant was believed to be truthful during the test.

The training, experience, and skill of the examiner will have the most significant impact on the validity of the examination. The examiner's question development and powers of observation used with a cooperative and lucid examinee will greatly enhance the confidence levels of the test.

Variations in outcomes are often attributable to the applicant's physical and emotional condition at the time of the examination as well as their willingness to circumvent the science by any means they see as necessary. For example, applicants often use information from Internet websites that purport the use of methods, tactics, and tricks in an attempt to alter the results and conceal their untruths.[1049] Other extremes include using illegal drugs, prescribed medications, and over-the-counter medications in an attempt to change their physical condition and defeat the test. If the applicant is discovered attempting to alter the conditions of the examination by these and other dubious means, then they can be removed from the process for their fraudulent practices and dishonesty as well as failing to meet the pre-employment processing requirements. The examiner should copiously document observations and discovered attempts at deception or alteration of the process.

Infrequently cases will arise where the applicant believes they have failed the process for any number of legitimate reasons. In these circumstances, the results of an examination may be disputed by the applicant. Consultation with the examiner is the first step to determine the circumstances and decide on a course of action. Applicant claims can be rejected by the agency or acted upon in the form of allowing for a second examination or use of an independent examiner (usually chosen by the processing agency from another agency or hired as an independent contractor by the hiring agency). Care must be exercised in these situations as the potential for examiner bias may exist depending on which party has engaged the alternate polygrapher's services and subsequent expert opinions.[1050] If an applicant is allowed to hire their own examiner, the processing agency should mandate that the agency's polygraph examiner oversee the test and have access to all reports, printouts, and notes of the contract examiner.

In spite of the century-old history of the inception and evolution of the science of polygraphy, there is never a loss enjoyed of cynics who will challenge the science for various personal, political, and legal reasons.[1051] Sadly, polygraphs have also failed in some very high profile cases of pre-employment screening.[1052] For these reasons, the polygraph should never be used to supplant the full background investigation.[1053] Just as required in the use of integrity tests, the results of the polygraph examination should not be the sole deciding factor in the screening process but rather provide a decision-support tool to augment the final selection or deselection process.[1054] This is supported by case law in the decision of *Anderson v. City of Philadelphia* (1988) wherein the polygraph must not encapsulate the entire basis to deny employment to police applicants.[1055]

Voice Stress Analysis

The last whistle-stop on the rails to discover the truth is the concept of VSA. VSA has been introduced into the field of investigations as an alternative to the traditional polygraph examination. The theory of VSA is that under stress, psychophysiological responses will be manifested in voice patterns that are indicative of untruthfulness and can be recorded and analyzed through computer enhancement. Law enforcement and corrections agencies across the country and internationally have bought into this concept purchasing the equipment and training staff in operation and analysis.

There are federal- and state-level legal considerations to research prior to use in the pre-employment investigation process. As a fledgling method of truth verification, the method of VSA has not avoided regulation by both federal- and state-level legislation. For example, the *Employee Polygraph Protection Act of 1988* includes the "VSA" in the definition of "lie detector."[1056] This definition brings the method under the control of the state legislatures as well that tend to severely restrict the use of truth detection instruments included in the scope of the polygraph. Several states have legislation that allows the use of the VSA in pre-employment investigations such as Nevada, Florida, and Colorado, to name a few.[1057]

More important than legalization is the banning of the use of the VSA in many other states.[1058] New York State provides an excellent comparison to others. In locals such as Nevada, Florida, and Colorado, the use of the VSA is legal under state laws. In states such as Rhode Island, the use of the VSA in pre-employment screening is illegal. New York State presents a dichotomy of thought processes as the use of polygraph is legal; however, the use of the VSA is banned from any use in the pre-employment screening process. The *New York Labor Law* defines the *Psychological Stress Evaluator* as "Any mechanical device or instrument which purports to determine the truth or falsity of statements made by an employee or prospective employee on the basis of vocal fluctuations or vocal stress."[1059] This same body of law prohibits the use of the VSA in the pre-employment screening process.[1060] Conspicuously excluding the VSA while allowing the polygraph speaks volumes to the opinions cast by votes of the New York legislature concerning confidence levels in the method and technology.

VSA is being used in many agencies across the country to screen new applicants in lieu of the traditional polygraph examination. The VSA is also being used in screening corrections officer candidates.[1061] If anything can be said about the method, VSA is certainly gaining popularity in the country. The method brings a high level of controversy when compared to the polygraph. Considered a pseudoscience or junk science by polygraphers, the issue has polarized those who are believers in their personal use and attachment to each methodology of truth verification. The existing research on the VSA is not without significant controversy as to the validity of findings, but more importantly, valid research has revealed marginal validity in the use of VSA at detecting untruthfulness.[1062] This has caused volley fire from both sides that has not developed solutions and credible validation methods but created more problems. What gets lost in the arguments over technology and science are the real issues that both ideological processes, for good or ill, are highly dependent on the investigative acumen and interview skills of the examiner as opposed to the science and technology. Overcoming an applicant's subterfuge rests in the investigator's knowledge, skills, abilities, and experiences, not at the end of a probe or at the head of the microphone. Metaphorically speaking, the impetus for the belief system is in lie detection and those who advocate for polygraph as well as those who advocate for VSA both practice the same belief in the same church, only praying at different pews as it were. At best, the methods will someday be validated and accepted at comparative levels in the eyes of practitioners and legal scholars. At worst, even if believed to be junk science, the VSA is still another reputed tool, prop, or gaff to entice the applicant into telling the truth. And if you do not know the right answer, never trust the salesman's advice!

Oral Boards and Assessment Centers

The final options for employment interview processes include oral boards/panel interviews and assessment centers.

Oral Boards/Panel Interviews

Oral boards and panel interviews are commonly used in the public safety officer selection process. Proponents of the process assert that the structure and makeup of the panel process lends itself to accurate assessments and predictors of applicant quality and fit to the position applied for.[1063] Panel interviews and oral boards are for the most part extremely subjective interview processes. They can be unfairly and illegally influenced by any number of nefarious reasons including dirty politics, personal agendas, biases, inequity in panel member status (e.g., rank, position, political influence), and panel inconsistency (e.g., alternating or rotating members or multiple panels). One example includes a field test experiment of police promotional candidates, an analysis of controlled, criteria-based assessments of interviews. During this research, two issues emerged: a natural bias toward candidates and assessors of the same race and that proportionately African American assessors rated African American candidates higher than proportionate numbers of White assessors against White applicants.[1064] Female applicants also suffer undue biases in the law enforcement and frequently male-dominated culture. Poorly developed or politically driven oral boards can cause far more harm than good in the selection process.

There are several considerations that must be assessed when developing these types of exercises. Panel members must be screened for attitudes or conduct that manifests gender bias as in the case of sexual harassment and hostile work environment behaviors, comments, or patterns of these types of complaints that are revealed must lead to rejection of the panel member.[1065] Panel and oral board interviews should also never be a purported validation tool for the administrator's or reigning politician's preconceived selections or rejections for the position. Few other hiring process components will lead to quicker discovery, embarrassment, and liability. Lastly, applicants can usually beat the process by the use of stock answers, inside information from previous interviewees, and simply preparing well for the interview. Panel interviews rarely involve creativity and probing standardized questions that can adequately test an applicant's fit for the position. How many times can you ask, "*Why do you want to be a police officer*?" And suffer through the same droning response from every applicant, "*To protect and serve the community, Sir!*" These types of questions have only slightly higher value than the stock or mindless answers the applicant is truly forced to provide. These situations usually debilitate to a pro forma pass that creates the potential for long-term and irreparable damage. In contrast, they may also lead to rejection of a qualified applicant because they did not make a connection to the panel, may not share the same values as the panel, or may present themselves in a manner that personally influences the panel regardless of their qualifications.

If a panel process is used, then strict guidelines, training, monitoring, and sanctions for failure to adhere to the legitimacy of a fair selection process must be maintained. Questions and rating methods must be statistically validated and assessors trained in not only the methodology but also, most importantly, the issues of rater bias addressed from the outset. A standardized and anchored interview format must be used to ensure consistency in delivery and assessment techniques.[1066] Diverse board members coupled with a range of assessment model questions such as general questions, situational questions, and others will assist in providing enough diversity and opportunity for the applicant to compete fairly against all others in the pool.[1067]

Assessment Centers

Assessment center methodology carries with it a slightly higher level of credibility and predictive value. Assessment center methodology carries much of the same in the way of consistency of process, validation of standards, and many other problematic issues associated with oral boards and panel interviews. Some hold the opinion that assessment centers have provided opportunities for agencies to reduce the ubiquitous adverse impact issues facing organizations.[1068] Implementation though has caused much controversy and challenge in the methods of assessment and selection as well as undue influences on assessors to improperly interpret codified standards to match demonstrated characteristics to desired hiring quotas. Even the best of processes is called into question once an eligibility list is published. When the process is flawed, incompetent, or corrupt, the problem for the agency grows geometrically in diminished morale, promotion of unqualified personnel, public image, and legal defense costs. To avoid these issues, the process must include parameters of valid behavioral and knowledge standards to properly assess an applicant's capacity to function in the role.[1069] The process should also include multiple assessors who are properly trained to avoid bias in the assessment of all types of applicants, as well as a cadre of assessment techniques to provide successful opportunities to all who compete for the vacant positions.[1070] An exacting and independent oversight body and process should also be in place to monitor and ensure that these standards are consistently being met.

Final Interview

The last stage of the interview process is conducting the final interview with the applicant. At the very close of all of the investigative processes wherein all reference interviews have been completed, all supporting documentation collected, professional assessments such as the medical and psychological examinations concluded, and all identified investigative follow-up steps have been exhausted, the applicant should then be scheduled for a final interview. Prior to the interview, a full review of all documentation, interviews, notes, and ancillary information should take place and then a meeting scheduled with the supervisor or manager in order to discuss the interview strategy and the need to emphasize, explore, and address any critical areas that have surfaced in the investigation.

The purpose of this interview is to review the full results of the background investigation with the applicant, clarify any issues or discrepancies that have arisen, afford the applicant an opportunity to offer an explanation for any of these discrepancies, and ascertain if the applicant is still interested in being hired or has decided to withdraw from the process. The interview should be conducted between the background investigator and applicant alone. During the entire process, the background investigator will develop a relationship with the applicant that will influence rapport and comfort levels for the communication. If the final supervisory meeting and case review indicate that the applicant interview may be overly complex or if the applicant will be recommended for rejection, then an additional interviewer should be present. The level and severity of the issues may also dictate the need for the background investigation supervisor or manager to be present as well.

Lastly, never forget that the interrogatory is founded in the concepts of an employment interview. No matter what information is discovered, the purpose of the interview is focused on establishing the parameters to either recommend acceptance or rejection for the position. On the positive side, our work should be geared toward the approach of as welcoming an orientation as possible as many applicants may meet the qualifications and be offered a position within our organizations. This is our time to demonstrate the quality and integrity of our organization to the incoming guard. On the negative side, applicant rejections are for the majority of cases, a fact of life. We must resist the temptation to treat the rejected applicant in any manner less than the most professional standards demanded of our vocation. The bottom line is that the liars will be rejected, and the criminals may end up atoning for their evil ways when passed over to a criminal investigator for follow-up of newly discovered criminal activities. Our objective is simple, to keep these candidates from slipping through the system to enter the ranks, not to prove a point to anyone, least of all, the applicant.

FINAL REVIEWS AND RECOMMENDATIONS

The culmination of the entire process is the final case reviews through the hierarchy of the organization along with the recommendation for acceptance or rejection. The final investigative package will include the final investigative report or summary of the background investigator. This report includes only the factual information as compared to the categories investigated. The background investigator can compare conduct to standards and in incidents of clear violations where there is no room for interpretation, bring this information to light in the report. For example, a felony conviction or recent exclusionary illegal drug use would qualify for this type of entry. Failure to meet the minimum qualifications would also be appropriate, for example, if the applicant did not have a valid driver's license or did not fall within mandatory age limit guidelines. The background investigator should include a closing section that delineates (1) disqualifying information; (2) positive characteristics, behaviors, and traits; and (3) negative characteristics, behaviors, and traits.

If this is not the case, then the final review would be the vehicle to decide if the applicant is not only qualified, but will be chosen, then that recommendation must come from the supervisory or command ranks of the organization. The final investigative report or summary of the background investigator should not include a recommendation for approval for hire or decertification and rejection of the applicant. There are divergent opinions to this; however, this is the soundest practice in the hiring realm. Unlike criminal investigations where most often the criminal investigator can decide to make a criminal arrest based upon the facts of a case, in the hiring realm, there are countless issues that may very well impact the final decision to hire or reject an applicant. This information is usually evolving as well, so a preliminary decision by the background investigator to reject or hire may very well be positively or negatively impacted literally to the point that the person receives their notification of the decision. Legal, operational, and, sadly, political influences will all come to bear in a process that will resemble a neoclassical tragedy wherein only sometimes do the affairs of state have a happy ending—in this case, the hiring of enough qualified applicants to fill the vacancies. Consider the rationale for such a policy as follows:

1. *Investigator connection to the applicant*: Background investigators often develop a close relationship with applicant as they may share many common beliefs about the profession. This may tend to unduly influence a background investigator's opinions seeing an applicant's dreams for the role, their family, friends, and the like. The background investigator should not have to assume the responsibility of conceivably taking this opportunity away from the applicant.
2. *Investigator follow-up questions from the applicant*: Applicants will desire information as quickly as possible about their candidacy. The background investigator is usually the primary and frequently sole point-of-contact for the organization. The background investigator is often placed in difficult positions when an applicant asks if they will be hired or not, and the background investigator must be able to maintain their distance as well as keep the information on the final decision confidential. If the background investigator does not make the final recommendation, they can maintain these relationships with the applicant until the process is completed and the administration has made their final call.
3. *Applicants are usually connected to someone in the organization or some outside influential entity*: This may cause political pressure; contacts from internal entities such as command officers and external entities such as politicians or persons of influence will reach out to the background investigator "informally" expecting inside information and decisions on hiring. The background investigator should not have to assume this burden. By removing them from the decision-making process, they can be honest in their dealings with others when these contacts are made.
4. *The final decision rests with the hiring authority*: Background investigators need to save face as many times they will reject an applicant and for any number of reasons, the applicant may be hired, in contrast to the background investigator's recommendations. Since there are no secrets in policing, this will eventually filter back to the applicant and consequently cause problems down the line when there must be a working relationship between the two, especially in smaller agencies where this is inevitable.

5. *Confidentiality of the process*: The entire hiring process must remain strictly confidential in order to protect the interests of all involved, organization and applicant alike. If the background investigator believes they have influenced the hiring decision or is aware of the status, they may inadvertently disclose this information to the applicant or a third party which may compromise the investigation. An extreme example involves that of a supervisor who prematurely released an applicant's tentative hire date without the chief's approval which resulted in the supervisor's termination.[1071]

There are other considerations to be sure, but the bottom line in all of this is that the background investigator in this process is, as in criminal investigations, a finder of fact. Facts of a positive, neutral, and negative nature are brought forward by the background investigator to the hiring authority (e.g., usually the chief or sheriff). In a discrimination lawsuit (e.g., adverse impact claims), the hiring authority is the only person who can be the instrument of demise and must be able to answer for the legal and justifiable reasons why an applicant was rejected. In conjunction, for any of the negligence claims (e.g., hiring, retention, supervision), the person who "hired" the candidate is the person who will ultimately need to answer for the decision to appoint and retain. As the chief or sheriff, you will be directly and personally named and not part of the nameless or unidentified "et al." reference that is so prominent in every lawsuit.

A background investigator recommendation can either help or haunt, depending on the level of agreement or contradiction found. And trying to unduly influence the background investigator's report can result in grave and dire circumstances for the organization as a whole.[1072] The safest practice is to have one person, the hiring authority (or a supervisor/manager, acting as an agent of the hiring authority), not the background investigator, make these types of recommendations. This should be a separate and distinct report in the package included as a cover to the entire investigation. Some may question this wisdom in the absence of being challenged by a plaintiff's attorney or judicial review. But as the classic Latin axiom "*Caveat Emptor*" deftly warns us, let the buyer beware! Everything we say in the pre-employment realm, whether qualified or unqualified, we will invariably own. Do not succumb to the allure and fallacy of "Off-The-Record" remarks as they do not exist. Like temptresses or the Sirens of Homer's *Odyssey*, heading in that uncharted direction will lead to ruin. More importantly, if these comments are not documented, they are subject to memory failures, self-serving recollections, and maligned and twisted interpretations. Qualified, articulable, and evidence-based information can be elicited from the background investigator as they were the closest to the investigation, but there is minimal room for "opinions" in this process. Opinions are, for the most part, damaging, rather than elucidating and productive contributions.

The final recommendations summary should be completed by the designee of the hiring authority. This report should be factually based and include (1) the categories of all of the organization's qualifying/disqualifying categories, (2) a definition of the qualifying/disqualifying factors of the category, and (3) a summary in each section of how the applicant either meets the standards or has failed to meet the standards. This categorical outline should be a mirror image of the background investigator's categorical outline so that consistency is maintained, referencing from one document to the other is made easy, and assures that nothing is missed in the development of the final review for recommendations. The final investigative package should be placed in a three-ring binder and divided into two major sections: (1) organizational information and (2) general information. This delineation ensures that the categories of information included are compartmentalized, so no breach of confidentiality will occur. The following is an example of the distinctions:

Part I—Organizational Information

Final Recommendations Summary of the Hiring Authority Designee that includes all information on medical, psychological, polygraph (if applicable), the categorical analysis of qualifying and disqualifying factors, and the final recommendation for rejection or hire:

1. All applicant waivers and releases of liability
2. The COE
3. Results and report of the psychological examination and all related questionnaires
4. Results and report of the medical examination and all related questionnaires
5. Results and report of the polygraph examination and all related questionnaires
6. Results and report of the physical agility test and all related questionnaires
7. Recommendations for certification or decertification

Part II—General Information

Background investigator summary that includes all aspects of the investigation:

1. Criminal liability history
2. Civil liability history
3. Credit history
4. Educational and training history
5. Military service
6. Employment history
7. Personal and professional references
8. Final applicant interview results
9. Qualifying characteristics
10. Disqualifying characteristics
11. Neutral characteristics
12. A sworn statement of the background investigator to provide the opportunity for admission into evidence in a civil or administrative hearing as hearsay evidence in the event that the background investigator is unable to appear to testify

Appendices

1. Interview forms
2. Investigator notes
3. Applicant photographs
4. Applicant fingerprints
5. Copies of all records collected (e.g., educational records, records checks, credit reports, professional licenses, employment records, driver's license, Social Security Card, passport)
6. Any and all relevant supporting information, documentation, and materials *that are not protected or included in the organizational information list* earlier (e.g., policy and procedures, lists of disqualifying characteristics, law and code violation sections)

From the delineation included earlier, the processing agency can ensure that the proper protections are in place for organization and candidate alike. Some additional words of caution though. In the final case review, the designee of the hiring authority must comb through the package to find and remove information that violates these rules. Part I may include all protected information that is allowed to be used in the hiring decision concerning psychological, medical, and related information. Part II and the appendices include all general information that can be used for applicant processing. In reviewing Part II and the appendices, all protected information that is approved for use in the process must be moved to Part I. For example, a consumer or credit report that contains medical information should be either redacted and left in the appendix or relocated in Part I to ensure the information is not inadvertently released in some future request.

A crossover report and supportive documentation include the results of the polygraph and any companion questionnaires. The release of the polygraph to another agency is one of organizational policy and must be decided up front, so there is no confusion to the release or refusal to release this information. If the organizational policy allows release of this information, then a codicil should attach. If the polygraph examination includes questions that can be interpreted of a medical or psychological nature, then they should be redacted before release to another agency presenting a waiver for release of liability perfected by the applicant. This information should be redacted from all documents including the polygraph report and any and all related documents and questionnaires. The polygraph is a test of integrity, not a psychological or medical examination per se. However, this type of protected information is explored during the process for the purpose of testing integrity. An applicant's failure or success in the examination can be reported as well as admissions the applicant has made during the preinterview, actual examination, and postinterview processes related to the polygraph, however, to protect the applicant and processing agency from litigation, areas such as psychological and medical information should not be shared with other agencies.

In addition, other considerations should be used when releasing information. Often times applicant references speak on the condition of some level of anonymity in order to protect their own interests. Absent a legal requirement or judicial order to release this type of information as well as the identities of those involved, this information should also be redacted from the package.

The final consideration is that when soliciting opinions, there is a genuine desire to allow input from others and to bring quality to the organizational process in question. This is a validated and widely recognized approach to building quality into organizational systems. There is also a negative side to this. To put it bluntly, do not ask questions you do not want to hear the answers to! If at the outset, as the hiring authority, you intend on disregarding the recommendations of your staff and command or if they conflict with yours, then do not ask the question. The results will also haunt you. They will always be revealed at some point, internally and through the rumor mill, or externally in the courts of jurisprudence and public embarrassment. There are several high-profile examples of how staff opinions were sought in the hiring process and when disregarded, only intensified the problems created in the poor hiring decision.[1073] Your best course of action is to make the decision based upon the facts of the investigation rather than trying to later justify your actions based upon the opinions and advice you received that was unqualified or worse yet, qualified. To avoid these problems and in order to effectively manage the risks associated with the hiring process, the final review and command reports must all be consistent with the evidence of the investigation and with proper protocols (see below).[1074]

Case Study

These are the actual case highlights from a police department's investigation into a police applicant. Only the summary of the rejection based information has been included for review:

1. *Drug use*: Applicant admitted to marijuana use within the previous year to application to the agency. Applicant used marijuana no less than 15 times during an 8 month period. The applicant has also admitted to using marijuana between the time he took the entrance exam and the time he was placed on the decertification list, not the conduct of a viable candidate for police officer. The town believes it would not be in the public interest to appoint the applicant to the position of police officer for the town due to his use of an illegal drug in the recent past. The town believes that the use of marijuana 15 times far exceeds the often used phrase of "experimentation." The applicant also listed cocaine use on an application for another department, failing to list such use on the application being reviewed in the current department. Applicant's response was that this was an "oversight."
2. *Employment history*: During the course of the background investigation and interview, the following facts were learned about the applicant: In the past 12 years, the applicant has worked at 38 jobs, he has quit 16 times, resigned 6 times, and been fired 6 times.
3. *Military service*: The applicant was involuntarily discharged from the U.S. military for personality disorder in 1996. The applicant told the interviewers he deceived the military psychologist about his feelings to convince the psychologist he was not fit to serve.
4. *Financial background*: The applicant is past due on four accounts for a total of $8514.00. The applicant has a very poor credit rating, a nine, which is the worst credit rating by the credit bureaus. He has been the subject of an eviction process for continuously late rental payments. He is on a payment plan with the Internal Revenue Service for payment of back taxes. He has been the subject of five letters to the Registry of Motor Vehicles from the town for delinquent excise tax payments since 1999. He failed to list outstanding credit debt on his application to the police department. The applicant does not accept responsibility for his financial condition but places that responsibility on his wife.
5. *Child support obligations*: The applicant told the interviewers that he quit a job because of the cost of a health insurance plan. The applicant was under court order to provide health insurance for his daughter. The mother of the child did not live with the applicant. The applicant quit the job, and the child was without health insurance until the mother became employed and received the benefit.
6. *Residences*: The investigator found that the applicant had completed applications for employment with several other police departments and that there are serious discrepancies in our being able to determine where the applicant has resided in particular for the year prior to application.

7. *General information*: The opinion of the investigator, a sergeant with 21 years' experience, 9 as a detective trained in interviewing and interrogation methods, that the applicant was deceptive when he answered questions regarding the omission of credit information. The opinion of the investigator is that the applicant lacks the integrity, responsibility, truthfulness, and integrity to be a police officer.

POSTINVESTIGATION CHANGES TO THE FINAL INVESTIGATIVE PACKAGE

Infrequently, changes and updates to the final investigative package may be required. Depending on the delay in time between the completion of the investigation and the actual hire date, additional follow-up activities may need to be completed in the way of updated record checks, new information that has been brought to the attention of the background investigation unit, and applicant disclosures of incidents or conduct that have transpired after the investigation has been completed. Some applicants, by mistake or design, will be involved either directly or peripherally, in conduct or incidents that often negatively affect their candidacy. A common example is a violation of the vehicle and traffic law. Other examples are far more serious encompassing felony charges.[1075] A monitoring process should be in place for those who are approved but have not been hired by the agency. A minimum of an updated records and wants check should be completed just prior to the notification of the applicant for their hire. For those who were not hired, or decertified, any and all correspondence, formal appeals, and litigation materials must also be added to the final investigative package.

RELEASING INFORMATION TO OTHER EMPLOYERS

Applicants to the public safety professions frequently submit multiple applications to a wide range of agencies in hopes of gaining their dream job. Jurisdictional boundaries are crossed at the municipal, state, and federal levels where applicants will make the cut to be processed fully by several agencies either at various times or contemporaneously to each other. Agencies who process will make as well as receive requests for information on cross-agency applicants. The decision to release is a balance between liability, policy, approval of house counsel, and interagency cooperation. In this day and age of controverting priorities that unduly drive the investigative process wherein the thirst for information is only quenched by the dripping budget faucet, alternative methods must be employed. Sharing information on cross-applicants is a method that is cost-effective for all agencies who decide to participate. Territorial rights and ignorance need to give way to the letter and spirit of interagency cooperation in this process. We are all looking for the same outcome, quality applicants. Sharing information is a proven method to achieve these humble goals. Varying legal opinions are influenced by the changes in the negligent referral statutes that are in place or being considered in many states. From a relationship perspective, the foundation cannot be sustained on a "Get, but not give" attitude. If we want cooperation, we must be willing to go well beyond expectations to give cooperation.

As discussed earlier, once the package is divided into three major components, then the release of information to other agencies by use of the waiver is simplified. Only the information in Part II and the appendices should then be released, and all protected information can be controlled by the agency in Part I. Again, redacting medical, psychological, and protected information included in Part II and the appendices would be the only concern for releasing information to another employer. Ensure to include the waiver and release of liability with each request as well as the contact person who the information was released to in a log kept with each package.

A few closing considerations are the need to allow photocopying of information if needed by the agency to assist in their processes. Hopefully other agencies will respond in kind when you need information. Allow the release of as much information as authorized by department and legal authority. Lastly, a policy decision must be made on allowing access to the background investigator for any follow-up questions that may need to be asked. As a general rule, this should not be necessary if the investigation is complete. If this request is made, there may be concerns with not only the inadvertent release of protected information but also how the interview is recorded and the solicitation of "opinions" or off-the-record comments from the background investigator. These should only be allowed in unusual circumstances and where the ground rules have been set for the parameters of the interview. The best practice would also include the hiring authority designee be present to monitor the interview and interject when the interview crosses these types of mutually agreed upon boundaries.

DEFENDING THE FINAL DECISION

The last component to the process is defending the final decision to certify and hire or decertify and reject. Each will be subject to formal and informal review and scrutiny. The administrator's lot may leave much to be desired at this point. From the certification and hiring standpoint, the defense of the decision will include claims of nepotism, cronyism, possible negligence in hiring and retention claims, and general resistance and false assertions from those who were not hired or connected to those in the organization who, from their myopic exposure, believe they have a world vista and perceived qualifications to comment intelligently on the process. Recalcitrant and unqualified applicants can also be added to this category who will add unnecessary layers to the process that must be defended in an environment where what they allege in the public earshot cannot be defended adequately in the same arena due the privacy protections afforded them in the process.[1076]

From the applicant's perspective, an issue that is often presented is how negative information is used. All negative information, unless of such a nature as to be an automatic disqualifier, must be evaluated based upon a nexus between type of crime, offense, or event, the removal in time from the incident, and any rehabilitation or restitution efforts. Under many circumstances, the applicant has the right to challenge any negative findings of the background and present contradictory evidence in order to clear their name.[1077] The burden of proof for us is high in this process. Some state-level mandates also require applicant notification of the reasons for rejection. For example, in New York State, "No applicant shall be disqualified unless given a written statement of the reasons for the disqualification, and afforded an opportunity to make an explanation and to submit facts in opposition to such disqualification."[1078] If we cannot properly articulate the reason for rejection, then why are we rejecting the applicant?

Organizational goals and vision for the hiring process may also conflict with political influences, candidate pools, attrition rates, budgets, legal issues, federal oversight and consent decrees, community outcry, and many other issues that may force the hiring agenda. The issues are overwhelming. The focus, however, should be the most critical defense lines that must be adhered to in spite of all of these other influences. The first is defending the decision through the organization's chain of command, and the second is defense in the judicial system. From the organizational perspective, the use of the investigative process to reveal the applicant's fitness for the role must compare the findings to the organizational and legal standards required to meet the threshold of decertification. If this threshold cannot be met, then the applicant would constructively meet the minimum standards for hire. The New York State Department of Civil Service builds on this by recommending "Objective and well documented reasons for all decisions to qualify or disqualify applicants will minimize problems and facilitate response to challenges."[1079]

From a legal perspective, the facts of the case are not created by the law; rather they exist independently of the law as they are discovered by the investigator.[1080] The law acts as a filter to ensure the proper legal and procedural rules are followed in order to ensure the concept of procedural justice is adhered to. Investigative significance of the information developed is then balanced against the probative significance for the reviewer of fact. Central to the defense will be the validity of the codified criteria used to disqualify and qualify applicants in general as compared to the plaintiff's background.[1081]

In the organization and in the courts, the background investigator will be the subject of the same scrutiny as the applicants themselves as the case is argued.[1082] One clear consideration for defense of the hiring decision is compliance with the rules of etiquette and protocol for the environment the decision will be defended in.[1083] In order to bring evidence forward in this type of setting, the background investigator must study the facts of the case, have an immense level of credibility in the organization, and be able to effectively translate the case to terms that fit the environment where presented, whether at internal proceedings through the chain of command and human resources personnel or through the civil court process.[1084] The only way to do this is to fully understand what constitutes evidence. Evidence can be classified into three categories: (1) direct evidence, (2) circumstantial evidence, and (3) real evidence.[1085] Evidence must also be considered from the perspective of admissibility in order to be useful and must meet three requirements: (1) relevancy, (2) materiality, and (3) competency.[1086] Court is different than the organizational chain of command. And both are certainly different than defending the decision to the applicant, politicians, and public. What may be created are the conditions for the perfect storm analogy of applicant ire, political and public pressure, and patent violations of an applicant's employment rights. Add the ambiguity of appointments that are made in spite of internal review and recommendations from senior administrators to the contrary, and the results can be cataclysmic.[1087] However, the tastiest fodder for the plaintiff's attorney comes from the practice of revisionist history or negationism in the hiring process. After all this analysis, the person of average intelligence and reason will be required to make a decision as to whether or not the process was fair and equitable. Think we have a snowball's chance in hell in that scenario? Bottom line is just do it right from the start. Our processes should be technically adept and transparent enough to protect the privacy rights of those who apply as well as the ability to ensure accountability through proper oversight (see the following Case Example).

Case Example of Ambiguous Rules and Actions in the Background Investigation Process[1088]

SAPD Bent the Hiring Rules

San Antonio Express News

In 1994, aspiring police officer Joseph Anthony Evans finally got his lucky break with a big city department. For several years, his cadet applications ended up in the rejection baskets of police departments in Austin, Dallas, Fort Worth and San Antonio.

Background investigators found he had a drunken driving conviction. They also concluded Evans tried to hide a criminal trespass arrest, a hit-and-run conviction and an internal investigation of sexual misconduct at a corrections officer job.

Beyond his past, San Antonio also denied Evans a badge because polygraphs showed deceptive or inconclusive answers to questions ranging from illegal drug use to stealing from employers.

"Joseph Evans is not San Antonio Police Department officer material," investigator Ignacio Cantu wrote in a 1992 memo recommending rejection for Cadet Applicant No. 233.

But a second try with the SAPD 2 years later had a happier outcome for Evans, even though employment screeners once again recommended he not be hired for all the old reasons.

Then-Deputy Chief Gilbert Sandoval overrode the recommendations and ordered the 30 year old Army veteran onto the force, according to records the San Antonio Express-News obtained from Evans' personnel file.

That decision, it turns out, would be one the department would regret.

Some 12 years into his career, in 2006, Evans' own colleagues in the narcotics and SWAT units swooped in to arrest him on what would become federal charges of allowing methamphetamine trafficking out of his Churchill Estates house.

Stripped of his badge, gun and the public's trust, Evans is scheduled Wednesday for sentencing to up to 3 years in prison.

Whether the hiring override was an isolated incident or part of a broader pattern that ushered other problem officers onto the force is unknown because of an exception in public records laws.

Since 2000, some 30 of the department's roughly 1975 sworn officers have been fired under criminal indictment. Dozens more have been fired for serious non-criminal infractions and several currently are under investigation for claims of sexual misconduct.

Two officials involved in the hiring of Evans, who is black, say other applicants recommended for rejection during the administration of Chief William O. Gibson also were let onto the police force when the department was under pressure to meet affirmative action goals.

But verifying which officers had backgrounds dotted with red flags like Evans' remains difficult. Powerful police unions, among them San Antonio's, quietly pushed through a state law in 1987 that keeps similarly revealing records behind a wall of secrecy.

The Express-News was able to throw open a rare window on how Evans was hired by obtaining a set of personnel records the city keeps strictly off limits.

In addition to understanding the past, knowing how today's department filters recruits has implications for the present and future. The Police Department is preparing to mount one of the most ambitious hiring campaigns in years, while also grappling with a spate of police misconduct allegations.

Sandoval, who retired in 1997 and works now as a private security consultant, said he overrode other rejections from applicant screeners amid political pressure from City Hall to hire more black and female officers.

"It was pretty common, to overturn recommendations" when a candidate was a tossup—sometimes for Anglos, said Sandoval, who served in his position over the employment section for several years. "That was from City Hall. They wanted more minorities. It was more like, 'You know we just need more minorities. We need more blacks. We need more females.' "

City records show that, in fiscal year 1993, before Evans was let in, 90 of SAPD's 1485 sworn officers were women, 88 were black, and 581 were Hispanic. By fiscal 1995, after Evans was on board, the force had increased to 1617 officers. Of those, 95 were black, 622 were Hispanic and 98 were female.

Sandoval said he didn't remember the Evans case and was emphatic that he would "never, ever" have issued an exception for a disqualifying DWI, a previous department rejection and deceptive polygraph test results.

But when told of records showing he did just that, he said, "I'm hoping that if my name is on that then I just plumb screwed up. It's not something that I would have done but maybe I did. I'm not perfect."

Capt. Larry Birney, who served directly under Sandoval as police academy commander in 1994, issued a signed memo to the city manager's office recommending that Evans be rejected. But 48 h later, Sandoval signed his name over Birney's signature line on a different memo. It reversed Birney's initial rejection. The only explanation this memo offered was, "additional information has been obtained."

The same day, Sandoval signed another memo, this one on Chief Gibson's signature line, opening the doors to the future felon. Sandoval offered no elaboration beyond, "I am satisfied that he is good material for pre-police training."

Birney said he remembers none of the episode. But he did recall that Evans was not the only rejected minority applicant whom Sandoval hired over his objections. He said the two men sometimes quarreled bitterly over these hires.

"I wouldn't say it was common but it wasn't uncommon, either," Birney said. "I can tell you horror stories."

But he declined to talk further on the record, saying the issue was still too sensitive.

Hiding drug deals

Evans' downfall came when police colleagues began surveillance of his live-in girlfriend, who reportedly was dealing methamphetamine from his home in early 2006. According to investigative records, police learned he not only knew about her illegal business and allowed drugs in his house, but he also used his police officer position to help her out.

Evans allegedly tried using his position to get his girlfriend off the hook by offering her as a police informant, purged a police criminal file and once even deflected her arrest.

In that instance, Evans had gone to a downtown hotel where his girlfriend allegedly was dealing drugs. Evans, who was off duty, met the responding patrol officers and convinced them the call was false, the reports allege. Later, a witness told investigators that after the officers left Evans stuffed "the dope" in his pants and took it home.

In another instance shortly after the investigation of his girlfriend began, Evans tried to get her accepted as an informant. The reports show that when the detectives refused on grounds that she was under investigation, Evans replied: "I know, that's why I called you. In case something happens, I'm covered."

In October, Evans cut a deal with prosecutors to avoid trial. He pleaded guilty to a reduced charge of not telling other officers about the drug dealing. Drug-trafficking conspiracy charges, as well as a state marijuana charge against him, were dismissed.

In a brief interview, Evans initially declined comment but then denied getting special consideration. He also disputed being rejected at other departments and questioned the documentation showing so.

"I wasn't hired for other than what my credentials were," he said. "I was qualified."

When asked if his hiring was related to affirmative action goals, he said, "That allegation is false."

The revelation that top department brass intervened to hire a rejected officer candidate, and that Sandoval and Birney say others recommended for rejection gained admittance as well, comes as the Police Department weathers scrutiny over accusations of brutality, sexual misconduct and improper strip searches.

To help assuage criticism last year, police officials hired the nonprofit Police Executive Research Forum to sort out some of those allegations. Its analysis of the allegations continues.

Birney and Sandoval said they couldn't remember details about other questioned applicants let onto the SAPD.

Records withheld

When the Express-News requested personnel records of dozens of fired and indicted cops, city officials were quick to cite the 1987 law that effectively exempts their hiring records from the Texas Public Information Act.

Those records include background investigation results, employment committee evaluations and field training performance scores. Such material may reveal whether others got special consideration.

The newspaper obtained Evans' hiring file after it became public during his prosecution.

The override then raises questions about current police hiring practices at a time when the department is faced with a mandate to hire a large number of new officers amid some pressure to hire more black and female officers.

The city will hire nearly 160 officers—half of whom will replace retirees—to fill a shortage already painfully felt amid soaring homicide rates.

In Dallas, in Washington, DC, and in San Antonio, similar pressurized conditions led to lowered standards and the hiring of unqualified cops who later committed crimes or brought discredit to their departments.

Chief William McManus, while deploring the Evans hiring when told of it recently, said he knows of no instance since he joined the department 2 years ago when his office let an obviously disqualified officer onto the force.

He said personal experience motivates him to make sure the department, through the checks and balances his own office provides, holds all applicants to high standards.

As a young lieutenant in the Washington police department, McManus recounted, he witnessed a hiring scandal that damaged public trust in that institution for years.

According to Washington Post reports, hiring standards were virtually thrown out in 1989 when Congress required the city to quickly hire 500 officers. In the ensuing years, nearly 200 of the new hires allowed in with little screening and scant training wound up accused of crimes or fired for offenses ranging from drug dealing and theft to rape and murder. Among the hires were known drug dealers, gang members and felons.

"That's not going to happen," McManus said. "I go over every folder myself. You have to put the appropriate hiring policies in place, then you have to stick to them. If you don't people will wind up getting fired and indicted and the department gets a black eye."

McManus acknowledged his office is under some pressure from City Hall to hire more women and black officers this year, in part because their numbers fall below goals in the city's affirmative action plan.

Only two cadets of the police academy's current class of 89 are black and 20 are women, according to statistics provided by the department. Most of the department's 1975 sworn officers are Hispanic. But only 108, or about 5%, are black. Women account for 8%.

McManus said the emphasis to attain higher numbers will be on recruitment and retaining those officers once they make the force, rather than bending hiring rules.

"We're way low on our numbers in terms of women and black officers, yeah," McManus said. "But you've got to look at some other method of retention, as opposed to lowering standards."

Under public scrutiny

Still, there is no current way to independently verify official assurances to uphold rules. Only when department vetting and training practices became publicly known did Washington shore them up. It also was public scrutiny that led Dallas leaders to twice fix a similar problem—in 1993 and again in 2004.

Ben Click, Dallas police chief from 1993 to 1999, arrived in the midst of a spate of officer indictments and misconduct scandals.

The first thing he did was commission an internal audit of new employee hiring and training processes. It showed that during a rush to hire hundreds of Dallas officers in 1989, under an affirmative action ordinance, dozens of cadets could not shoot, failed lie detector and psychological tests and had criminal backgrounds. Others were caught robbing immigrants, pawning property room evidence and abusing drugs, he said.

"They were filling the positions, alright, but they made some exceptions that were unbelievable. One of the deputy chiefs was signing off on the exceptions," Click recalled. "It was outrageous. The danger is you lose the public's trust and support. And it's a real threat to public safety too."

Click's successor in 1999, former Dallas Police Chief Terrell Bolton, weakened hiring standards again for black, Hispanic and female recruits. By 2003, dozens of them were being fired and indicted on charges of corruption, abuse and malfeasance. The Dallas City Council pressed the department to tighten the standards again in 2004 in response to media disclosures showing the chief or his top deputies personally intervened to get them hired.

In San Antonio, pressure to diversify the department in the 1980s and 1990s was on too.

In 1985, now-deceased Sgt. Horace Neaves, who was in charge of applicant processing, went public with allegations that SAPD brass had relaxed admission standards to hire less-qualified black applicants over better-qualified Anglo and Hispanic ones. Neaves was demoted and transferred to night duty as a jailer.

He won a lawsuit against the city over the transfer, according to news reports at the time. But there is no information the city or media ever investigated his root claims.

Several current and former San Antonio officers who have overseen or been involved in the hiring process said they were unaware of any overrides of rejected officers in the years since Evans was hired.

"They're very strict over there; in fact they've been criticized for being too strict," said retired police Capt. Larry Carnot, who commanded the police academy from 2000 to 2002 and now does applicant screening for the Bexar County Sheriff's Office. "A DWI? You're out right there. If you're caught deceptive on the polygraph, you're gone."

He and several others acknowledged they might not have been in the loop or processed so many hundreds of applicants some might have slipped through without their knowledge. In Evans' case, Sandoval signed on behalf of Chief Gibson, who could not be located for comment in the past few weeks.

"We had trouble recruiting minorities and losing to the private sector, which offered more money," said former Police Chief Albert Ortiz, who served from 2002 to 2006. "But in terms of bending the rules and regulations, no. I mean, if you passed, you passed, and if you didn't, you didn't."

Birney, who served another stint last year overseeing the police academy, insisted there was no repeat of what he experienced in 1994.

"The whole affirmative action culture has changed. Everything's changed," Birney said. "This time around, as far as I know, it was straight as an arrow."

CONCLUSION

This chapter represents a holistic approach to the entire investigative process. The previous chapters have addressed philosophical, social, organizational, and legal requirements as the foundation for the pre-employment investigation process. This chapter has used the components of the actual process to develop the investigative framework and supportive structure that allows for complete investigation and the culmination into the proper development of the final investigative package. Among the character examinations that will occur include criminal, credit, employment, and military history, as well as the applicant's capacity for high levels of integrity as verified through myriad truth detection methods. Finally, this chapter closes with the postinvestigation processes of case review and recommendations for certification or decertification of the applicant.

DISCUSSION QUESTIONS AND EXERCISES

1. Discuss in detail how your department's background investigation process compares to the various stages presented in this chapter. Analyze the areas that the department could improve and develop a series of recommendations for change.
2. Review your department's policies on automatic disqualifiers for applicants. Evaluate how they compare to the example department policies presented. Based

on this comparison, would you recommend changes to your department's categories for automatic excluders for applicants? Justify your responses.

3. Conduct a 5-year analysis of the reasons and categories for which applicants have been disqualified for. Determine if any patterns are consistent in the attrition rates. Should these types of patterns be discovered, what recommendations would you make based upon the review of the issues and policies presented in this chapter that could improve investigative processes?
4. Research your department's policy and procedures on how the applicant's final investigative package is reviewed. Determine if any improvement could be made and what recommendations do you have for change.
5. Research your department's policy and procedures on how applicants are vetted for their candor in the process. Determine if any improvement could be made and what recommendations you have for change.

6 The Past Predicting the Future of Pre-Employment Investigations

LEARNING OBJECTIVES

- To develop an appreciation of the projected future trends in the process of the pre-employment investigations for public safety organizations
- To develop an appreciation for the projected challenges of recruiting qualified applicants to enter the ranks of public safety organizations
- To develop an understanding of the potential for technological advances to enhance the screening of the applicant in the pre-employment investigation process
- To develop a full appreciation for the critical need of public safety organizations to wholly commit to provide the appropriate personnel and resources to conduct the pre-employment investigation process in an effective, efficient, and unbiased manner

KEY TERMS AND CONCEPTS

- The negative influences of organizational culture
- Future recruiting challenges
- Connecting prehire predictors to posthire behavior
- Specialized training and certification of background investigators
- DNA as a future pre-employment screening tool

INTRODUCTION

We have come to the point where knowledge and ideology translate into practice. The previous chapters have provided the fundamental and advanced principles of pre-employment investigations as well as a framework and structure to develop the investigation upon. This chapter briefly examines the past and current issues and attempts to forecast future issues and trends in the process. Also included are some recommendations for long-term strategic change to the process in order to improve the quality of investigations that translates into the quality of our new hires and, consequently, the quality of our organizations.

WHAT DOES THE FUTURE HOLD IN STORE?

Much effort was put forth in the first few chapters of this book to develop the understanding of the multitude of issues facing the screening process for public safety applicants and the organizations that are confronting the challenges of replacing those who are leaving the ranks in droves. This chapter postulates several issues and predictions of the future of the pre-employment screening process for public safety organizations. Included in this chapter are (1) Recruits: The Rhetorical Key to Our Future, (2) Pension Alarm Has Been Sounded, (3) Connecting Pre-employment Investigations to Future Performance Predictors, (4) Federalism May Not Be a Bad Idea after All, (5) Specialized Training and Certification as a Background Investigator, (6) Increased Use of Technology in Screening Applicants, and (7) Posthire and Expanded Roles of Screening.

Recruits: The Rhetorical Key to Our Future

We have somehow miraculously survived centuries of this type of rhetoric. Every class in every department in every part of the country receives the same charge: "You are the future of law enforcement!" Puerile in the charge, we convince the incoming peacekeepers that they are the architects of the future of our organizations, the model for the profession, the change agents, and the protectors of all that is right. We then force them into the ranks and do everything we can to destroy their drive and passion, stifle innovation and creativity, expect unachievable standards, and then offer them up as sacrifices to the gods of politics as soon as we can use them to make a name for ourselves. And we do not waste any time doing it. We then sit back as administrators, politicians, and community members and feign an unparalleled level of amazement at the monsters we have created: negationism in the finest state of perfection. We then cry laziness, misconduct, and corruption when the culture has once again perpetuated itself and has yet another generation that will be with us until they can retire. This is the perpetual cycle of law enforcement.

The overwhelming majority of officers do not begin their careers searching for ways to hide behind buildings, abuse over time, and count the days until they can be elevated to the level of second-class citizen when they retire. They start out believing in a cause and the ideology of justice, believing they can make a difference, and believing in the profession. Until we change the way we do business, no amount of pre-employment investigation, screening for pathologies, or taking one more urine sample will change the current state of, or future of, the profession. We insanely waste an inordinate amount of time and resources in search of the perfect candidate that we can work to ruin as quickly as organizationally and culturally possible. This is also not the "Royal We" as we do this as an institution, as a society, and as managers on a 24/7 basis. This has been a repetitive cycle of absurdity that the field has been known for, yet no one person or organization makes any attempt to change. As line officers, there is a clarity of the problems of the administration that is suddenly clouded and transferred back to the line when we become administrators. We simply just blame the cop for everything we as a profession and society have done to create him (or her). And no matter how hard we work or how many we hire, these fledglings will never be able to change this: the consummate definition of insanity.

Pension Alarm Has Been Sounded

Public sector employment has found itself in the middle of great controversy. While public safety and law enforcement officers for the previous sesquicentennial were often underpaid and undercompensated for the level of danger and responsibility embodied in the role, the public rarely, unless an officer was killed in the line of duty, paid much attention other than to provide an empty platitude of sympathy. The American industrial and manufacturing complex provided most jobs that paid 200%–400% higher wages than law enforcement, wages collected without having to put their life on the line on a daily basis. As those jobs have disappeared over the years, public sector positions began to reach parity with their formerly dominant private sector counterparts for pay and benefits. Those who have lost their jobs have decided to conveniently blame the officer on the street, not the greedy mismanagement of the American businessman for today's lack of dominant pay structures and reaching levels of parity. Those who chose high-paying private sector manufacturing, sales, and investment jobs also had the opportunity to take competitive examinations for public safety positions, but, as with the greed that is rife in the business world, chose money over a life of public service at the risk of life and family. A quick search of the Internet does not reveal a monument to any discipline including investment bankers, line autoworkers, or manufacturing workers that bears the names of 19,000 employees who have been killed in the line of duty. The same people who protected those same investment bankers, line autoworkers, and manufacturing workers every day they donned a uniform and carried a gun.

Enter the politician who is now championing the rights of the downtrodden American people, coincidentally the voting public. On the surface, their words are altruistic in nature, with a sole desire to serve the American taxpayer. The same people who have double-dipped and raised their girth in proportion to height now stand fast to protect the American people from the protectors; the irony! The contemporary politicians have now metaphorically taken the place of Paul Revere, riding the countryside and crying, "The pensions are coming, the pensions are coming!" This vitriolic rhetoric concerning pensions is reverberating through the public safety arena, sweeping the country, and has led many state legislatures to significantly alter and suggest total abolition of pensions, benefits, and collective bargaining rights. These sentiments are being supported by the bile of public safety administrators desperately selling out their organizations and entire profession in a feeble attempt to temporarily protect their fiefdoms.

This shortsightedness and ruthless effort to use shock value to garner the support of an unwitting public was developed with no thought of the long-term damage that will equate to the diminished safety of their respective communities. This tocsin will have many devastating consequences to the entire field of public safety. Among them is the fact that there was a reason for 20 year pensions in law enforcement, fire service, corrections, parole, probation, and other public safety positions—there is only so long the average person can physically and emotionally handle the rigors and dangers of the role. Images of a 64 year old police officer running to a shooting or bank robbery are only eclipsed by the images of 64 year old fireman trying to drag an unconscious person from a raging fire. Is this our future?

Turnover will likely be much higher as public safety officers, energized by the first time they can wear the uniform, will quickly come to the stark conclusion that they cannot work 35 or 40 years as a law enforcement officer or firefighter. The knowledge drain and exodus of institutional knowledge are on a cyclical pattern of 20–25 years in the law enforcement field. As those who enter the field realize that they will not be able to endure the long haul, they will spend around 5 years to get vested and then leave while they are young enough and marketable enough to pursue other safer and more lucrative careers. Recruitment, hiring, training, equipment, promotions, and the level of service will all suffer greatly under the burden of employment cycles that are 5–10 years, not 20–25 years. The savings in pensions will only be washed away in increased recruitment, training, and liability costs with the lack of experiential or tacit knowledge in law enforcement organizations as a detriment to productivity, efficiency, and effectiveness. That's the good news. Those who are marginal and cannot find other employment will trudge along for 40 years as unproductive employees robbing the organization of the opportunity to eventually replace these problematic employees. But, this is the typical uninformed and knee-jerk reactions so prominent in the American people today. This may very well be the classic self-fulfilling prophecy. Whose head will we want on a spear then?

Connecting Pre-Employment Investigations to Future Performance Predictors

Much has been bantered about over the past half century about developing models to predict future performance behaviors. Predictive models in the law enforcement field are usually a reactive anecdote rather than a validated model. This can be explained by understanding the difference between the Monday morning quarterback vs. the use of a crystal ball. In some miraculous and mystical way, we somehow always "knew that was going to happen!" However, these extrapolations come at a time well after the conduct has occurred.

The future may require the study of the etiology (causes) of candidate misconduct or developing recruiting methods with long-term goals in mind (grade school or middle school recruitment and mentoring) to better systems to focus on recruiting lower risk groups and populations for candidacy in the law enforcement field. This changing paradigm of profiling applicants may be a method of targeting groups that have higher probabilities of success in the role that will ultimately equate to better efficiencies in the process of recruiting, screening, hiring, and retention. This would require significant in-depth study of an applicant's background and development of measurement tools to conduct longitudinal analyses that are more accurate predictors of performance and behaviors than the conventional models we have used in parochial processing methods.

While we realize that the most valid predictor of future performance is past behaviors, we do not develop measurement systems that capture characteristics, behaviors, experiences, age at hire, marital status, credit record, and other validated variables that lead to predictive abilities. An example is using a predictive model to measure the comparisons to future performance found in performance ratings, complaints, civil litigations, general internal affairs records, frequency of discipline, and separation from service. This feedback loop, as previously mentioned in Chapter 1, could provide a level of predictor analysis not yet realized in the field, but carrying great value to the pre-employment screening process of the future.

Federalism May Not Be a Bad Idea after All

This country is lauded for the ability to effectively separate the priorities of local, state, and federal jurisdictions in order to balance the needs of the respective groups. Considering a federalism concept for the pre-employment investigation process would make sense from an investigative and resource management mindset. The future may hold the use of a fundamental national standard for the public safety officer pre-employment screening process as well as the ability to access a national database and network to technological advances that can provide historical searches of past applications for those applicants who submit applications at the local, state, and federal levels for employment.

A national background investigation standard and protocol: We see these types of protocols developed for numerous areas that include crime rates, violent crimes, intelligence information development, vehicle thefts, sex offender registries, and other investigative resources that enhance the criminal investigator's ability to track and solve crime. What if in the future a national standard and protocol for the basic components of a public safety officer background investigation could be developed? A model would enhance the ability of ensuring more thorough and complete investigations that could be compared from jurisdiction to jurisdiction. Information development would form under a common structure and could be shared easily. Best practices could also be a continuous improvement and benchmark of quality for such a system.

A national background investigation database: Upon application to any agency, the physical application and all related materials could be entered into the common database and accessed by any local, state, or federal agency processing the applicant. Think of the benefits of such a system. The current system is that the specific agency responsible for the processing of an applicant conducts the entire investigation, collects records from a wide array of entities, and maintains the entire record under lock-and-key at an agency-based in-house repository. Consequently, information, records, and investigative findings are far too dispersed, not available, or at mercy of the applicant to disclose where they have applied. A national database could go far to resolve these issues. The basic pre-employment investigation has information that is common in the range of applications from a national security clearance to the smallest of police agencies. Each agency would be responsible to redact or exclude any information that was protected from consideration in the selection process.

State-level systems would also be very effective as an alternative measure. Each local and state agency already develops the investigative information and records related to the background investigation and within a specific state will have to meet the state-level legal and civil service commission requirements. Redundant searches for many of the records we seek in background investigations such as criminal records, traffic records, fingerprints, reference checking, employment records, and other required information could save countless resources for agencies that have limited means. A state-level clearinghouse for all investigations of local and state agencies would also go far to reduce duplication of efforts for investigators who have completed tasks that can be used perpetually in the process. The only difference would be the redaction of psychological and medical records as each agency should be responsible for their own professional evaluations. As an aside, this concept could extend to psychological and medical screening where a state standard could be developed, authorized professionals could competitively bid for state-level contracts, and user agencies would have a statewide defendable standard as well as avail themselves of economies of scale in the fee structures. Technology would need to be adaptable to both administrative scalability (e.g., facilitated information sharing from a single system accessed by multiple public safety agencies) and functional scalability (e.g., providing system upgrades and enhancements with minimal expenditure, disruption, and effort).

A similar concept was the experimentation with certified resumes in the private sector. Private human resource and investigative firms would develop a certified investigation of an applicant along with a resume that included the historical record of criminal and reference checks of the applicant.[1] A national- or state-level database could provide a similar product with a certified information chain useful for public safety officer applications.

Specialized Training and Certification as a Background Investigator

With the move for more specializations in the criminal justice field, there is a level of common sense in considering the pre-employment investigation as such a specialized area of investigation that should include a requirement for a minimum amount of specialized training, testing, certification, and quite possibly, accreditation of the discipline. This refers to certification and accreditation beyond the basic scope of accreditation of agencies as discussed in Chapter 2.

As has been brought forth in this book, the discipline is extremely complex and replete with requirements that will certainly confuse the average officer, investigator, supervisor, and administrator. The level of functional comprehension required can be a daunting task to even the most skilled and knowledgeable of background investigators. Consequently, there will be no room for the faint of heart as this field grows even more complex as time passes, litigation expands, and requirements for pre-employment investigative processes propagate. The days of a basic records check and calling a few references that are stapled to a psych report have long since passed. We have slowly seen this evolution of required training for numerous positions in law enforcement organizations as a requirement for certification and licensure and as a requirement for state- and federal-level department accreditation. Position accreditation similar to that in polygraph examiners, crash management experts, financial crime analysts, and forensic investigations are all akin to the level of specialized knowledge required in the conduct of the pre-employment investigation. Requiring specialized training, certification, and discipline-specific accreditation can do nothing but benefit the field.

Increased Use of Technology in Screening Applicants

As discussed in Chapter 5, the use of technology in the investigative process is growing in acceptance and application. The polygraph was the preeminent technological advancement in this field for decades. In some jurisdictions, polygraph has given way to the use of the voice stress analysis (VSA) as a means to mirror the theory of using technology to advance the methods of truth detection.

Ink-and-roll cards have been replaced in many locations with live scans. Live scans of fingerprints are used to capture an electronic image of the impression. With the onset of automated fingerprint identification searches (AFIS), an applicant's fingerprints can be compared against unsolved crimes at the local, state, and federal levels. Biometric technology, besides the use of automated fingerprint systems, can also include the use of eye scans and voice recognition and may prove to be very useful tools for the background investigator of the future.[2] As this technology advances and becomes more accessible, the applications to the pre-employment screening process may increase as this type of identifying information is collected and adapted to the investigative process on a national level.

Facial recognition is also growing in popularity. Essentially, facial recognition involves the capture of a subject's image, conversion to a biometric signature of the individual, and then computer technology screens other normalized signatures for matching features.[3] Facial recognition software is being used in jurisdictions in Florida and Nevada with successes in identifying subjects, and there may be applications to the background investigation process as that technology evolves and database access becomes more available.[4] With the increase of cameras and CCTV throughout the country, imagine the possibilities of being able to search accessible digital databases for images of an applicant anywhere they may have been captured on camera. The possibilities are continually growing for this field.

While advanced biometrics and facial recognition are on the horizon, one advance is within our collective reach. DNA analysis, also as discussed in Chapter 5, may be the next logical step in ascertaining if an applicant has been involved in any outstanding major crimes where biological evidence has been collected and preserved. The potential for clearing an applicant of any unsolved crimes of this nature is likely the most remarkable advance in technology that is currently available for use as pre-employment screeners.

Posthire and Expanded Roles of Screening

Another trend that has potential for full integration into the future of the pre-employment screening process is the use of screening for promotional examinations as well as consistent monitoring of current employees for acts that are criminal in nature or violate organizational policies.

Research has revealed an increase in screening for promotional and lateral internal transfers due to redefined and increased liability for the potential for supervisory harassment of employees where the organization need not have active or direct knowledge of the harassment to be liable.[5] Current employees in the public and private sectors are also being reinvestigated at predetermined intervals in order to monitor their credibility. Some private sector organizations are using automated continuous screening models to actively discover posthire issues that develop.[6] Currently, federal probation officers must undergo a pre-employment investigation as well as reinvestigations every 5 years they are employed.[7]

Role definition and usage is also growing. Public safety positions are defined as law enforcement, corrections, firefighters, and emergency dispatchers. Municipalities are also adding many other nontraditional positions to the ranks of the background investigation process. From the lowest to the highest levels in organizations, even city managers are being investigated prior to appointment.[8] Because of heightened awareness and increasing liability issues related to bad hires, this trend will continue into the future.

CONCLUSION

This final chapter brings together the concepts of the past as a method of predicting the future and how these future trends will significantly impact the entire discipline: from developing an understanding of the timeless flaws we have in our organizational systems and culture, to the looming issues of budgetary constraints that will drive compensation structures and create the greatest challenges to recruit qualified personnel in our history, to how we must creatively rethink making connections from the positive and negative characteristics that are manifested in our seasoned officers and reverse engineer the problem from a behavioral and past history perspective in order to develop profiles of those applicants who will have the best chances of being successful in our organizations. Other predictions draw some distinct benefits from the propensity of the federal government to nationalize processes and systems; adding the notion of a federally managed database for pre-employment investigations of public safety positions has merit. Other future trends will likely include a move toward specialization, certification, and possibly accreditation of this type of investigation as the private sector has already moved in this direction in order to bring credibility to their processes.[9] Technology use will also grow in the field as reduced cost and increased accessibility will give way to enhancing the investigative process, increasing efficiency and effectiveness. And the scope of positions eligible for extensive background investigations will widen considerably as organizations struggle to prevent bad hire situations that create serious and lasting problems. The future of pre-employment investigations in the public sector will present some of the greatest challenges as well as opportunities as we travel the road ahead.

The grandest of efforts has been put forth in convincing you that the pre-employment investigation is the most important investigation that an organization will undertake. This book has presented an evidence-based approach to the contemporary concepts, issues, and practices, arguing for the complete overhaul of processes and the commitment of organizational administrators to support the efforts of their investigative units in the selection of the best and brightest who will fill the ranks for the generations to come. Positions of trust in the public safety realm strictly require the thorough evaluation and screening of all applications for employment.[10] Of all the scientific advances in behavioral science, testing methodologies, and technological advances in the field, the pre-employment investigation remains the only proven component of the process that best affords the opportunity to predict behavior and select the best-fit applicant for the job.[11] This requires the tenacity of the sage and indefatigable background investigator who desires to be an integral part of the future of their organization by finding the best candidates through the only true method, the search for the truth of an applicant's past. This also requires organizations to adhere to the legal and moral responsibilities in selecting applicants who will be responsible for the protection of our society.[12]

The contemporary job applicant in all fields is being examined with much scrutiny in light of the serious problems created by hiring unqualified, unfit, and untruthful persons for the roles they are being considered for.[13] Conducting the background investigation will likely abate the proverbially painful, embarrassing, and litigious situations that an unfit applicant can cause the agency.[14] Faulty performance and disciplinary problems are the sequela of faulty hiring practices. Political scandals of failing to properly screen appointees are rampant in our history.[15] We often suffer from the normalcy bias, continually telling ourselves, "That can't or will never happen here!" This level of denial and failure to change the process creates the harbinger of what's to come. History tells us that we cannot escape the fact that it is incumbent upon the hiring agency to conduct the most complete investigation possible prior to hiring.[16] The system is fraught with politics and special interest groups all having competing interests that unduly influence the process. As an aside, we will always be haunted by the question, "Did political correctness play a contributing role in the deaths of numerous innocent people at the Fort Hood military base?"[17] As a direct correlation, we must never ascribe to the fallacy that making necessary compromises to further a greater good or notion of achieving social justice will not come without the higher price of diminishing or wholly sacrificing public safety; not quite what we bargained for when we made the trade! The law enforcement field is no different when we allow hiring decisions to be influenced by those who have no business or expertise offering opinions in the hiring process. Society's remedy for poor hiring practices is the impending threat and reality of litigation against the organization and its administrators.[18] The *Doctrine of Infallibility* or *Papal Infallibility* unfortunately does not extend to Chief Joe or Sheriff Bubba when the lawsuit is filed. And the same administrators who are held accountable can reminisce of the old times telling stories that all begin with "When I was King…!"

Worse yet is the concept of Chaos Theory, which postulates that minor changes in a system can have long-term negative effects and cause irreparable damage. Also known as the *Butterfly Effect*, one bad hire in any size agency can have devastating effects on the organization, community, and criminal justice system as a whole depending on the egregious nature of the transgression. Did Abner Loiuma and Rampart teach us anything? One thing we do learn is not to belabor the question, "Is there a point of diminishing returns in the background investigation process?"

To prevent the cause célèbre and to prevent having the blood on our own hands, we must accept that complete and thorough investigations are a necessity, certainly not a luxury and never a burden. We must also become disenthralled by the trappings of political influence as the primary driver of hiring processes. Political influence affords an ability to engage in a form of disenfranchised morality that rationalizes marginal to corrupt decisions and actions in the pre-employment hiring process. And if you have trouble managing and controlling the hiring process of your organization, you will most certainly *Inherit the Wind*.

DISCUSSION QUESTIONS AND EXERCISES

1. Discuss in detail how your department's changing benefits and compensation structures will impact the quality of future applicants to the department as the issues have been discussed in this chapter. Analyze the areas that the department could improve and develop a series of recommendations for change.
2. Review your department's processes, if any, that compare the performance of current officers against the information found in their background investigations. Evaluate if there are any correlations to past behavior that may have been predictors of current performance. Based on this comparison, would you recommend changes to the department's selection process for new applicants?
3. Analyze what training has been offered by your agency specifically for background investigators. Determine how many have had training and the recency and quality of that training. Based upon this analysis, develop a series of recommendations that will address any training needs identified from your analysis.
4. Research your department's access and use of technology in aiding in the background investigation process. Determine if any improvement could be made and what recommendations do you have for change.
5. Research your department's position on expanded use of the background investigation process for other positions in the organization and larger governmental entity. Determine if any expansion of the job categories for in-depth investigations could be made and what recommendations you have for change.

Appendix A: Santa Barbara Application

Police Officer: Academy Graduate*
$2233–$2714 Biweekly
$58,070–$70,584 Yearly
(Candidate may be eligible for POST pay $396/month, specialty pay 2%–6% of salary, and uniform allowance $1038/year.)

The position:
Under general supervision, a police officer performs law enforcement and crime prevention work for the protection of life and property; patrols assigned area in police car, on motorcycle, or on foot, enforcing federal, state, and municipal laws and ordinances; issues warnings and citations for violations; responds to a variety of calls for public service; maintains constant radio contact with communications center; conducts preliminary investigations; testifies in court; apprehends, arrests, and books suspects; and does other work as required.

Special pay: Officers may qualify for a variety of special pays in addition to the salary listed above including bilingual pay, educational pay for intermediate and advanced post certificates, and bonus pay for special assignments such as detective, investigator, canine handler, F.T.O., DARE, beat coordinator, D.D.T., community relations, training officer, traffic officer, school resource officer, and a variety of grant-funded assignments.

Employment standards:

Eligibility: To be eligible as a police officer academy graduate candidate, applicant must be currently enrolled in or have passed a P.O.S.T. approved academy. Out-of-state applicants may also be eligible for hire as an academy graduate candidate by successful completion of the "Basic Course Waiver Process" administered by P.O.S.T.

Knowledge of: Oral and written communication skills required for report writing, verbal explanations of the law, and court testimony; Basic Peace Officer Standards of Conduct and public relations.

Skill in: Using and maintaining firearms and police-related equipment.

Ability to: Think and act quickly in emergency situations, assess the situation accurately, and apply police training and proper conduct in stressful situations; make accurate observations, document and communicate details, and recognize hazards, potential hazards, and crime problems; understand and follow written and oral directions and established police procedures; deal tactfully and effectively with members of the community and explain laws, rules, and regulations; accurately communicate details of a situation in courtroom testimony; learn procedures and techniques involved in specialized police work such as

* Santa Barbara Police Department (n.d.).

crime scene investigations, traffic investigations, and detective work; learn and enforce the applicable federal, state, and municipal codes and motor vehicle codes, including laws of arrest, search, and seizure. *Ability to speak Spanish is highly desirable.*

License requirement: Applicant must possess a valid California driver's license at the time of appointment. Traffic positions may require possession or acquisition of a Class "M" California driver's license to operate motorcycles.

Age: Applicants must be at least 21 years of age at the time of appointment.

Physical: Weight proportionate to height, normal hearing, and color vision; at least 20/100 vision, correctable to 20/25 (20/200 correctable to 20/25 with *soft* contact lenses); excellent health. Must also meet physical and psychological standards required to perform police officer duties.

Selection process:
The selection process may consist of the following:

1. Oral exam
2. Polygraph
3. Background investigation
4. Psychological evaluation
5. Medical examination and controlled substances screening

Candidates must successfully complete each phase of the selection process in order to be scheduled for subsequent phases.

Filing deadline:
City applications and attached acknowledgment of reasons for rejection are being accepted on a continuous basis until further notice. Also, you must submit a copy of your P.O.S.T. basic police academy certificate.

Acknowledgment of police officer applicant standards/reasons for rejection:
According to the Commission of Peace Officers Standards and Training Manuals, and the City of Santa Barbara Municipal Code, the following list identifies some of the more common potential reasons for rejection. Please read the list carefully. It is designed to assist you in understanding and assessing the requirements for the position. You may call the Human Resources office at (805) 564-5316, if you have any questions.

Peace officer citizenship requirement: *Please check the box that applies to you.*

I am a citizen of the United States.

I am a permanent resident alien who has applied for and will obtain U.S. citizenship within 3 years of the filing of this application.

Reasons for rejection are the following:

1. Conviction of any felony.
2. Conviction of any sex crime.
3. Conviction of larceny (Section 484 PC).

4. Conviction of or involvement in any other crime, whether adult or juvenile, the nature and seriousness of which would relate to the sensitivity and exposure characterized by this job classification.
5. Use of marijuana, narcotics, or other habit-forming drugs (other than prescribed) within the last year will disqualify. Any prior use or abuse of previously listed substances may disqualify. Failure to reveal prior use will disqualify.
6. Failure to possess a valid operator's license issued by the State of California; willful disregard of traffic rules and regulations; any grounds for which an operator's license might be refused.
7. A bad employment record; discourteous; disloyal; indecisive; undependable; uncooperative; lacking in capacity to work; insubordinate; disobedient; lacking in force, initiative, and judgment; lacking proper work habits and industry; emotionally unstable; unable to accept responsibility; unable to get along well with others; and intemperance.
8. Does not have well-balanced credit.
9. Poor community and neighborhood reputation.
10. Falsification of any required application or report.
11. Failure to have a high school diploma, GED certificate, or equivalent.
12. Personality disorders.
13. Does not meet physical standards.
14. Failure to pass controlled substances screening.

References

California Commission on Peace Officers Standards and Training (POST)—Background Investigation Manual.

P.O.S.T. Administration Manual.

City of Santa Barbara Municipal Code.

Acknowledgment: *Read the following statements and sign below:*

I understand that as part of the qualifying process for police officer, I will have a polygraph examination, psychological evaluation, a physical examination including controlled substances screening, and a thorough background investigation. I will also be required to complete a detailed personal history statement. Any falsification of information or failure to meet the standards listed above will result in my disqualification.

I acknowledge that I have read and understand the Applicant Standards/Reasons for Rejection listed above.

Please type your name here. ____

Appendix B: Alaska Department of Corrections

Alaska Department of Corrections Recruitment*

Definitions

Conditional job offer:
Chosen applicants are given a job offer that is conditional upon successful completion of all phases of the recruitment/selection process. Candidates must successfully complete all phases of the process or his/her conditional job offer will be rescinded. Detailed directions are provided to the applicant at the conditional job offer stage of the recruitment/selection process. Candidates who successfully complete and pass each examination will become eligible for appointment as a correctional officer.

Controlled substance:
Controlled substance means a drug, substance, or immediate precursor included in the schedules set out in AS 11.71.140–11.71.190.

Conviction:
Conviction is when a person is found guilty of a crime. This includes modification of sentence from whatever authority including suspended imposition of sentences, set-aside, expunged of record, withheld, executive clemency, or pardon.

Duration:

1. The probationary period for correctional officer I/II who are hired without a current Alaska Police Standards Council (APSC) certification shall be the length of time required to receive APSC certification.
2. The probationary period for correctional officers at the II level who have a current APSC certification upon promotion or appointment to the correctional officer II classification shall be 6 months.

Good moral character [lack of]:
The absence of acts or conduct that would cause a reasonable person to have substantial doubts about an individual's honesty, fairness, and respect for the rights of others and for the laws of the state and the nation; for purposes of this standard, a determination of lack of "good moral character" is not restricted to acts that reflect moral turpitude, but may be based upon a consideration of all aspects of a person's character; the following are indicators of a lack of good moral character:

* Alaska Department of Corrections Recruitment (n.d.).

1. Illegal conduct; conduct involving moral turpitude, including dishonesty, fraud, deceit, or misrepresentation.
2. Intentional deception or fraud, or attempted deception or fraud in an application, examination, or other document for securing employment, eligibility, or certification.
3. Conduct that adversely reflects on a person's fitness to perform as a probation, parole, or correctional, such as
   a. Intoxication while on duty
   b. Unauthorized absences from duty not involving extenuating circumstances
   c. History of personal habits off the job which could affect the officer's performance on the job, such as excessive use of alcohol
4. Undue familiarity with inmates, probationers, or parolees is the conduct that adversely reflects on a person's fitness to perform as a probation, parole, or correctional officer.
5. Illegal purchase, use, possession, transportation, distribution, cultivation, manufacture, or sale of any controlled substance, any imitation controlled substance, or alcohol in an area that has adopted a local option under AS 04.11.490–04.11.500.

Misdemeanor:

1. Crime classified as a misdemeanor in Alaska at the time the crime was committed.
2. Crime committed in another jurisdiction for which there was a conviction in that jurisdiction by a civilian or military court is a misdemeanor conviction if the crime has elements similar to those of a misdemeanor under Alaska law at the time the offense was committed.
3. For purposes of determining whether, under this paragraph, a crime is to be considered a misdemeanor or whether a conviction is to be considered a misdemeanor conviction, an offense punishable as a misdemeanor in Alaska or under the law of another jurisdiction that results in a completed suspended imposition of sentence, expungement of record, or a pardon is a misdemeanor conviction unless the offense was committed by the person before the age of 21.

Misdemeanor crime of domestic violence:
Any offense that

1. Is a misdemeanor under federal or state law; and
2. Has, as an element, the "use or attempted use of physical force, or the threatened use of a deadly weapon," committed by a current or former spouse, parent, or guardian of the victim; [or] by a person with whom the victim shares a child in common; [or] by a person who is cohabiting with or has cohabited with the victim as a spouse, parent, or guardian; [or] by a person similarly situated to a spouse, parent, or guardian of the victim; or
3. As otherwise defined by other state or territory of the United States or by military court, and which the applicant has been convicted.

Moral turpitude:
An act of baseness, vileness, or depravity in the private and social duties which a man owes to his fellow men or to society in general, contrary to accepted and customary rule of right and duty between man and man.

Pre-certification:
Prior to December 31, 2004, applicants were required to obtain pre-certification prior to applying for correctional officer I vacancies. The pre-certification process consisted of successfully completing and passing a comprehensive background investigation. Candidates who were successful in this process received a "pre-certification" card that allowed them to apply for correctional officer vacancies.

Probationary period:
The probationary period shall be regarded as part of the examination process that shall be utilized for closely observing the employee's work and adjustment to the position. Employees who, in the judgment of the employer, have satisfactorily passed the probationary period shall be retained and given permanent status in the job class at the end of the probationary period. Employees who, in the judgment of the employer, have not satisfactorily passed or will not satisfactorily pass the probationary period shall not be retained in the job class.

Appendix C: Seattle Police Officer Qualifications

Seattle Police Department—Hiring Process—Qualifications*

Qualifications:

The following standards apply to all candidates for police officer:

Minimum standards

- Applicants must be at least 20.5 years of age at the time of taking the exam to be hired.
- U.S. citizenship is required.
- Proof of high school diploma or a certified GED.
- A valid Washington State driver's license is required prior to being hired.
- Military discharge under honorable conditions (fair employment laws apply).

Drug use:

- Have *not* used marijuana within the 3 years prior to the date of this Acknowledgment of Minimum Standards Regarding Illegal Drug Use
- Have *not* used marijuana more than 25 times within the 10 years prior to the date of this Acknowledgment of Minimum Standards Regarding Illegal Drug Use
- Have *not* used cocaine or crack within the 10 years prior to the date of this Acknowledgment of Minimum Standards Regarding Illegal Drug Use
- Have *not* used club drugs, such as, but not limited to, ketamine, GHB, rohypnol, or MDMA (ecstasy), within the 5 years prior to the date of this Acknowledgment of Minimum Standards Regarding Illegal Drug Use
- Have *not* used any hallucinogens, LSD, mushrooms, or psilocybin within the 10 years prior to the date of this Acknowledgment of Minimum Standards Regarding Illegal Drug Use
- Have *not* used PCP, angel dust, wet, or phencyclidine within the 10 years prior to the date of this Acknowledgment or Minimum Standards Regarding Illegal Drug Use
- Have *not* used opium, morphine, or heroin within the 10 years prior to the date of this Acknowledgment of Minimum Standards Regarding Illegal Drug Use
- Have *not* used methamphetamine, crank, crystal, ice, speed, glass, or amphetamine within the 10 years prior to the date of this Acknowledgment of Minimum Standards Regarding Illegal Drug Use
- Have *not* inhaled aerosols, sometimes referred to as huffing (paint) or whippets (nitrous oxide), or used kat within the 5 years prior to the date of this Acknowledgment of Minimum Standards Regarding Illegal Drug Use

* Seattle Police Department (1995–2011).

- Have *not* used four or more controlled substances within the 10 years prior to the date of this Acknowledgment of Minimum Standards Regarding Illegal Drug Use
- Have *not* used any illegal drug(s) or illegally used pharmaceuticals more than 25 times within the 10 years prior to the date of this Acknowledgment of Minimum Standards Regarding Illegal Drug Use
- Have *not* used any illegal drug(s) while employed in a criminal justice and/or law enforcement capacity
- Have *not* manufactured or cultivated illegal drug(s) for the purpose of the sales/marketing of the drug(s)

Please note that use of illegal drugs and the illegal use of prescription drugs, referred to in this acknowledgment, mean the use of one or more drugs, the possession or distribution of which is unlawful under the *Uniform Controlled Substances Act.*

Traffic record:
An applicant's driving record will be thoroughly assessed and may be a factor for disqualification. Examples of infractions/traffic crimes that may be disqualifying:

- Driving while intoxicated (DWI), reckless driving, or hit and run driving.
- Suspension of your driver's license within 5 years of the date of application.
- Three or more moving violations (speeding, negligent driving, etc.) in the past 5 years of the date of application will be carefully reviewed.
- Two or more accidents within 5 years of the date of application, wherein applicant was judged to be at fault and/or charged with a moving violation.

Criminal record:
An applicant's criminal record, including all arrests, prosecutions, deferred prosecutions, "Alford" pleas, and nonconviction information, will be thoroughly assessed and may be grounds for disqualification. The following will be disqualifying:

- Any adult felony conviction
- Any misdemeanor or felony conviction while employed in a criminal justice and/or law enforcement capacity
- Any domestic violence conviction

Employment record:
An applicant's employment history, including any terminations, or leaving an employer in lieu of termination, will be thoroughly assessed and may be grounds for disqualification.

Financial record:
An applicant's credit history, including excessive credit card debt or unresolved accounts in collection, will be thoroughly assessed and may be grounds for disqualification. The following will be disqualifying:

- Failure to pay income tax or child support

Appendix D: Sample Policy

Policy Orders
Auburn Police Department
Standard Operating Procedure

	Effective Date **05-01-07**	Number **32**
Subject **Selection of sworn personnel**		
Distribution **All sworn personnel**	Rescinds **32 dated 05-01-04**	
Review Date **May 2009**	Associated with **31, 35**	

I. Purpose

The purpose of this policy is to establish procedures for selecting police officers and to ensure that the process is efficiently and fairly administered and is nondiscriminatory. The process shall be designed to select the persons who possess the skills, knowledge, and abilities necessary to meet the challenges of present-day law enforcement and community service.

II. Policy

It shall be the policy of the Auburn Police Department to select the highest caliber candidate available in full compliance with all federal and state laws.

III. Administrative practices and procedures

A. Responsibility for the selection process:
1. Selection responsibility shall be the sole responsibility of the Auburn Police Department with recommendation made to the Auburn City manager.
2. The City Human Resources Department shall have the responsibility of administering the entry-level test (written component and physical fitness/agility test) for police applicants (phase I).
3. The Police Department shall have the responsibility of administering the Department's Hiring Process (phase II) which consists of the following:
    a. Oral board interview
    b. Background investigation
    c. Job suitability assessment
    d. Polygraph examination
    e. Physical examination with a contracted health-care facility
4. Final authority and responsibility for administering the role of the Auburn Police Department in the selection process shall be vested in the chief of police.
5. The Human Resources director shall have final authority and responsibility for administering the role of the City of Auburn Human Resources Department in the selection process.

6. The deputy chief shall be responsible for working closely with the Human Resources Department in the selection process.
7. All selection of Auburn Police Department Police Officers shall be conducted in accordance with City of Auburn City Charter.
8. Phase 1 shall be waived for any police applicants for original appointment who are full-time sworn officers at the time of application and are certifiable by the Maine Criminal Justice Academy.

B. Adverse impact

The City of Auburn Human Resources Department Affirmative Action Officer and the deputy chief shall monitor the selection process to ensure that any bias or unfairness is eliminated from the system. If adverse impact is found in any segment of the selection process, steps shall be taken immediately to minimize or eliminate the discriminatory impact upon affected candidates.

C. Reliability and validity

1. All written testing administered by the City of Auburn Human Resources Department to applicants for employment with the Auburn Police Department shall be documented as having validity and reliability.
2. All other testing administered by the City of Auburn Human Resources Department shall be of practical value and appropriate in determining predictions about a candidate's future job performance. Rating criteria or minimum qualifications for all elements of the selection process shall be job related and nondiscriminatory.
3. Validity of the selection process shall be determined by one of the following methods:
   a. Criterion-related validation
   b. Construct validation
   c. Content validation
4. Should the City of Auburn Human Resources Department elect to contract with a private sector organization or vendor, all selection process testing shall meet the professional and legal requirements of utility, validity, and minimum adverse impact.

D. Selection process scoring

1. All elements of the selection process shall be administered and coordinated by the Police Department's deputy chief who shall be sufficiently trained in carrying out the selection functions.
2. All scoring, evaluation, and interpretations shall be done in a uniform manner. All candidates shall be treated the same in regard to the operational elements of the hiring process. Time limits, oral instructions, practice problems, answer sheets, and scoring formulas shall be identified for all candidates. Reasonable accommodations may be implemented for any candidate with a bona fide disability.

E. Storage and disposal of selection material

1. Selection material shall be the responsibility of the City of Auburn Human Resources Department and Police Department. Materials shall be stored in a locked file cabinet in a secure location within the Human Resources Department when not in use. Access to said materials shall be limited

to the chief of police or his designee and Human Resources Department staff. Persons with access to selection material shall ensure that the information contained therein is kept confidential and is not unnecessarily disseminated.

2. Selection materials shall be disposed of in a manner that prevents disclosure of the information therein. No selection material will be disposed of without the approval of the Human Resources director. Once the approval is given, the materials will be shredded prior to disposal. Burning is also an acceptable means of disposal.

F. Reapplication, retesting, and reevaluation
   1. An applicant who fails phase I testing, and does not become eligible for phase II, shall be encouraged to reapply at any time in the future and participate in the next testing procedure.
   2. An applicant who has failed phase I testing shall be offered the opportunity to make an appointment with the Human Resources Department to better understand the identified weaknesses and learn how he might strengthen his ability to be successful in the testing procedure on another occasion. Inquiries shall be made within 30 days.
   3. Any applicant who has failed
      a. A polygraph test or mental examination shall not be eligible for any portion of the selection process for a period of 2 years.
      b. An applicant who fails to appear or complete the hiring requirements shall be disqualified as a candidate and may reapply for any succeeding examination.

G. Ineligible candidate notification
   1. Those candidates who are determined to be ineligible shall be informed, in writing, within 30 calendar days of such a decision.
   2. Candidates who are not eligible as a result of a single test, examination, interview, or investigation shall be advised of the specific reason, in writing, within 30 days.
   3. The City of Auburn Human Resources Department and the Auburn Police Department shall maintain selection data for a period of not less than 5 years. The results of medical examinations shall be maintained indefinitely in a secure location within the Human Resources Department and shall not be destroyed. The results of psychological and polygraph testing shall be maintained indefinitely within a secure location of the Police Department's Administrative Division and shall not be destroyed.
   4. A copy of the written notice sent by the Police Department for individuals found to be ineligible in phase II shall be provided to the City of Auburn Human Resources Department.

IV. Applications/selection

A. Initial contact
   1. All individuals expressing an interest in employment with the Auburn Police Department shall be referred either to the City of Auburn Human Resources Department or the Auburn Police Department.

2. If the individual is inquiring from a location outside the Auburn area, he will be advised of the website, phone number, or address for the City's Human Resources Department or the Auburn Police Department. The individual shall be advised that a personal appearance is not necessary to initiate the process.
3. An information packet and application shall be mailed to any individual who expresses an interest in employment.
4. Individuals who may lack necessary information or who omit information that can be corrected prior to the testing process shall not be rejected.
5. During the selection process, contact shall be maintained with the applicant. He shall be periodically informed of the status of his application and of any anticipated employment date if the individual is selected as a probationary officer.

B. Testing eligibility and scheduling
1. All candidates shall be notified as to the date and location of the written, physical, and oral examination in sufficient time to allow for necessary travel and employment arrangements.
2. All candidates shall furnish the City's Human Resources Department with copies of the following documents prior to testing:
   a. A copy of his driver's license.
   b. A copy of a high school diploma or GED certificate.
   c. Any military information.
3. All applicants at the time of their formal application shall be provided with the following information:
   a. A detailed list of all components of the selection process.
   b. The expected duration of the selection process.
   c. Complete information on retesting, reapplication, and reevaluation.
   d. A list of areas in which polygraph questions will be drawn.

C. Written examination
1. The written examination shall be the first of the examinations that police applicants must successfully pass to be considered eligible for employment with the Auburn Police Department.
2. Applicants must achieve a predetermined passing score to be eligible for further testing.
3. The written examination shall meet the standards of utility, validity, and adverse impact, as described in Section III of this document.
4. Applicants who fail the examination shall be informed accordingly within 30 calendar days of taking the examination.
5. The written examination shall be given at a location other than the Police Department.
6. All candidates who pass the written examination shall be notified, and their application will be referred to the Police Department for evaluation.

D. Eligibility list
1. At the conclusion of the written examination, the City's Human Resources Department shall compile an eligibility list. When a vacancy is created, the chief of police will request names from the eligibility list.
2. The eligibility list shall be in effect for 2 years.

E. Physical agility testing
   1. The Auburn Police Department shall use the Physical Fitness Training Standards set forth by the Maine Criminal Justice Academy.
   2. Applicants shall be provided with an outline of the physical agility requirements prior to the testing to allow them to prepare for the examination.

F. Oral interview
   1. The oral board shall include, but not be limited to, the following representatives:
      a. Deputy chief
      b. A patrol/detective representative
      c. A command unit representative
      d. A member of the community
   2. Oral board examinations shall be as consistent and objective as possible and use a standardized rating scale for recording performance results.

G. Condition offer of employment

V. An applicant shall be given a conditional offer of employment prior to a full background investigation. A conditional offer of employment *does not* guarantee employment with the City of Auburn.

A. Background investigation
   1. A complete and thorough background investigation shall be completed on all candidates prior to appointment to probationary status.
   2. An Auburn Police candidate's background investigation shall be conducted by the support services commander or the CID commander.
   3. The applicant will receive a background investigation questioner. The applicant will return the completed questioner to the chief of police in a sealed envelope. Any false statements or omissions will subject the applicant to disqualification or dismissal from the process.
   4. The background investigation shall include, but not be limited to, examination, verification, or an interview in the following areas:
      a. Qualified credentials.
      b. Educational references.
      c. Military records.
      d. Prior employment.
      e. Medical references.
      f. Social and character references (minimum 3).
      g. Criminal records check (FBI, NCIC, SBI, Auburn Police records, town of residence).
      h. Neighborhood check.
      i. If involved in a relationship, interview with the significant other.
      j. Credit history.
   5. The background investigator will prepare a written report to be submitted to the chief of police. The report will cover all areas outlined in the previous section.
   6. A record of each candidate's background investigation shall be retained for 5 years.
   7. Background investigators shall receive proper training in collecting background information.

B. Photograph and fingerprints
   1. During the hiring process, each applicant will complete three fingerprint cards. One card shall be sent to the FBI for Criminal Record History Information, another to the State Bureau of Identification. The third shall become a permanent part of the candidate's file.
   2. During the background investigation, each candidate shall be photographed for identification purposes.
C. Administrative review
   1. At this point in the selection process, the chief of police, deputy chief of police, CID commander, and support services commander will meet to discuss the candidates' background investigation and oral board evaluation.
   2. After review and discussion, a determination will be made as to whether to continue the background investigations beyond this point.
D. Job suitability assessment and evaluation
   1. Prior to offer of hire, candidates shall undergo a psychological screening and evaluation.
   2. Only qualified professionals shall be used to assess the emotional stability and psychological fitness of candidates.
   3. The job suitability assessment test battery shall consist of the following:
      a. Preference index.
      b. Analytical judgment.
      c. Verbal comprehension.
      d. 16PF.
      e. Vocational preference inventory.
      f. Guilford–Zimmerman temperament survey.
      g. Personal interview.
      h. Sentence completion test.
E. Pre-employment polygraph examination
   1. The pre-employment polygraph examination shall be used as an investigative aid to determine truthfulness of an applicant relating to the information provided during the pretest interview and on the application.
   2. The polygraph shall be the only authorized deception detection device utilized by the Auburn Police Department.
   3. Prior to the polygraph examination, candidates shall be provided with a pre-polygraph questionnaire from which the polygraph questions will be drawn.
   4. Pre-employment polygraph examinations shall follow the recognized standards in the polygraph field.
   5. The administration of all polygraph examinations and the evaluation of the subsequent results shall be conducted only by an approved professionally trained polygraph examiner holding credentials from a recognized training program.
   6. The results of the polygraph shall not be the sole determinant of employment status, but an admission during the pretest, test, or posttest, together with other information, may be sufficient to support a determination of ineligibility.

F. Medical examination
   1. Prior to appointment as a probationary officer, candidates shall be scheduled for a comprehensive medical examination.
   2. The examination is designed to reveal any medical problems that may inhibit work performance or contribute to work-related disabilities.
   3. Only a licensed physician, as determined and selected by the City of Auburn Human Resources director, shall be used to determine the general health of candidates.
   4. The medical examination consists of the following components:
      a. Occupational and medical history.
      b. Physician physical examination.
      c. Lab studies (lipid profile II, CBC with differential, urinalysis, complete chemistry profile).
      d. EKG with interpretation.
      e. Vision test.
      f. Hearing test.
      g. Purified protein derivative injection (TB) with follow-up.
      h. EKG stress test.
      i. Tetanus/diphtheria injection.
      j. Functional component.

G. Final review

Upon completion and receipt of all pertinent material, the police chief shall make a final review of the candidate's complete background file and shall determine if the candidate is to be hired as a probationary officer.

H. Probationary period
   1. One of the most important components of the selection process is the probationary period of employment, during which the probationary officer's training and work performance may be evaluated and a decision made in regard to his permanent status.
   2. Probationary officers upon being hired shall complete an employment probationary period that lasts for at least 1 year after graduation from the MCJA or the date the MCJA Board of Trustees waives the basic training requirement.
   3. Probationary officers shall be evaluated in compliance with SOP 35.
   4. Probationary officers shall follow the same procedures for contesting performance reports during their probationary period, as outlined in SOP 35.
   5. The work performance of each probationary employee is evaluated using valid, useful, and nondiscriminatory procedures, as outlined in Section III of this document.

Per order of: Phillip Crowell Jr.

Chief Phillip L. Crowell Jr.

Appendix E: Sample Conditional Offers of Employment

Auburn Police Department

Phillip L. Crowell
Chief of Police

Jason D. Moen
Deputy Chief

Rita P. Beaudry
Office Manager

Offer of Conditional Employment

I. Purpose: The purpose of this agreement is to extend to the applicant an *offer of conditional employment.* The applicant must meet the following listed terms and conditions before being hired by the Auburn Police Department. All applicants for the listed position of *patrol officer* are required to successfully comply with these same conditions.

II. Parties: This is an agreement between the Auburn Police Department and

________________________ ________________________

(Printed name of applicant) (Social security #)

III. Terms and conditions: An applicant must meet the following terms and conditions:

A. Minimum employment standards for a Maine law enforcement officer
B. Minimum required training entrance standards to the MCJA, as mandated by the state
C. *Sufficient physical condition, as determined by a medical history and examination*, necessary to perform the essential functions of the aforementioned position
D. Any additional requirements specified by the Auburn Police Department, which may include the following:

_√_ Background investigation _√_ Medical physical
_√_ Polygraph examination _√_ Psychological test(s)

IV. Length of agreement: This *offer of conditional employment* shall remain valid and in effect for 1 year from the effective date of this agreement, provided, however, this offer shall be immediately withdrawn upon the applicant's failure to meet satisfactorily any one of the aforementioned terms and conditions. The applicant will receive an offer of probationary employment subject to a probationary period and other conditions, after all the conditions have been satisfied in this agreement. The effective date of this agreement is __________________.

V. Acknowledgment: Successful compliance with these job-related and necessary conditions of employment is required to carry out the essential functions of the aforementioned position. I have read and understood the terms of this *offer of conditional employment* and agree by these terms.

________________________________ ________________________________

(Chief of police) (Date) (Applicant signature) (Date)

Conditional offer of employment

Applicant:

Position:

Social Security Number:

Date:

Your application for the position of police officer with the Irondequoit Police Department has been processed, and we tender to you a *conditional* offer of employment in the aforementioned position, upon availability. ____________________ *(Applicant's initials)*

This offer of employment is conditional upon your successfully completing the following as determined in the standards cited in the written job description for the position and all applicable federal, state, and county statutes and administrative regulations (check all that apply):

_______ A comprehensive medical examination by a licensed physician employed by the Town of Irondequoit for this purpose, to be administered according to guidelines set forth by the Town of Irondequoit for its Police Department employees

_______ Successful completion of a psychological examination, which is to be administered by a licensed psychologist, employed by the Town of Irondequoit for this purpose

_______ Successful completion of all testing, screening, and evaluations as required by the Monroe County Civil Service Commission

_______ A background investigation conducted according to guidelines set forth by the Town of Irondequoit for its Police Department employees

_______ Successful completion of all civil service requirements relating to transfer of civil service status from another police agency

_______ Successful completion of any compulsory minimum training standards for Town of Irondequoit Police Department officers as required by regulations established in accordance with the New York State Bureau for Municipal Police

_______ Successful completion of a probationary period of up to 26 weeks during which time you will be given additional training and evaluated as to your abilities

Should you fail to complete any of the aforementioned requirements with the exception of those required by state law or regulation, the Police Department will investigate the circumstances to determine whether a responsible accommodation may be made that will permit you to perform the essential job functions required of the position without undue hardship or disruption to the employer. If such accommodation is not possible or practicable, or if you fail any requirement imposed by state or federal law or regulation, this offer of employment will be withdrawn.

<u>Do not terminate your present employment</u>; this is merely a <u>conditional</u> offer of employment which will be exercised upon position availability.

__________ (Applicant's initials)

You will be notified when and where to appear to complete the process outlined earlier.

I have read and understand this correspondence.

Police officer

Candidate signature: ________________________ **Date:** ______________________

Witness signature: __________________________ **Date:** ______________________

Appendix F: Sample Personal History Statement (IPD)

Irondequoit Police Department
Background Investigation Questionnaire

Richard J. Boyan
Chief of Police

Personal history of: ____

Last name | **First name** | **Middle name**

____

Address

______________________ ______________________

Date of birth (MM/DD/YYYY) **Social security number**

Date questionnaire issued: ______________ [*for completion only by the investigator*]

Date questionnaire completed: ______________ [*for completion only by the investigator*]

Background investigator: ______________________________

(All information contained in this questionnaire is confidential.)

Dear Applicant,

Your application for the position of police officer has reached the stage of the background investigation—a critical portion of the selection process. So that the Irondequoit Police Department will be able to conduct an investigation of your character and fitness for the position, you will be required to supply certain information.

You are responsible for personally delivering to the Irondequoit Police Department Background Investigator copies of the following documents, which are to be returned with the questionnaire. (NOTE: Civil service may also require copies—these are additional.)

1. Birth certificate
2. Marriage certificate
3. Divorce and separation decrees
4. High school transcripts and diploma
5. College transcripts and diploma if applicable
6. Degree and transcripts from all educational institutions attended
7. Armed forces discharge and separation certificates (include DD form 214 if applicable)
8. "3 in 1" credit history report
9. Letter of naturalization (if applicable)
10. Pistol permit
11. Passport (to include all pages of transactions)
12. All public safety–related educational and training certificates
13. New York state driver's license
14. All vehicle registrations owned by you and your spouse
15. All authorization and consent releases which apply to you as supplied by the Irondequoit Police Department. (Note these must be signed and notarized PRIOR to being returned.) These include the following:
    - Authorization for release of personal information form
    - AFFIDAVIT for background investigation questionnaire
    - AFFIDAVIT for waiver of rights
    - HIPAA release for all medical and psychological records

Failure to submit any of the aforementioned applicable documents may disqualify you from further consideration.

The alteration of any submitted document will result in your immediate disqualification.

Instructions

Read all instructions carefully before completing this personal history questionnaire.

This personal history questionnaire is intended for the use of the Irondequoit Police Department. You must answer all questions truthfully and completely. According to civil service law, a candidate may be rejected if he/she has intentionally made a false statement of material fact, or has practiced or attempted to practice any deception or fraud in his/her application. Omitting information or giving false information may result in the immediate rejection of your application and the removal of your name from further consideration for appointment. All information contained herein may be subject to verification, that is, source documentation, polygraph, and screening procedures. Information contained herein will be considered to be strictly confidential and will not be disclosed to any unauthorized person(s). The information contained herein, and the results of this background investigation, may be released with proper authorization for other law enforcement background investigations.

The answers to the questions contained in this personal history questionnaire MUST BE HAND PRINTED in your own handwriting, legibly in BLACK INK only. Each individual question must be answered. DO NOT leave any questions blank. If a question does not apply to your particular circumstance, insert "N/A" (not applicable) in that field. If the answer to a question is unknown, write "UNKNOWN" in that field. When answering questions that require dates, you must insert both month and year. You must provide complete address information when requested. All addresses must include street addresses with house/apartment numbers, city, state, and zip code. Partial address responses are unacceptable. If additional space is needed to explain your answers, use the back of the page in which the question is asked, and be sure to include the reference letter and number of the item being explained to the left of the answer.

Be aware that your spelling, grammar, and neatness will be considered as part of the selection process. Your attire, speech, and manner will also be evaluated during all segments of the background investigation process and will be considered in the final selection.

You may be required to take a polygraph examination to determine the authenticity of the information given by you. Questions asked during this examination will be derived from the following categories: past criminal activity, sexual offenses, drug and alcohol use/involvement, activities that might prove embarrassing to the Irondequoit Police Department, and those areas that the examiner deems necessary, given the responses of the candidate to these questions.

Warning

Candidates are cautioned to answer every question truthfully and without evasion. Failure to provide accurate information, or deliberately providing false *or incomplete* information, is the ground for rejection for appointment and/or discharge after appointment.

Have you read and understood all of the aforementioned instructions?

☐ **Yes** ☐ **No**

____________________ ____________________

Signature of candidate **Date**

Section A: Personal Data

1. Name: ____________________

Last First Middle

2. Residence: ____________________

____________________ (include zip)

3. County: ____________________

4. Telephone: (H) ____________________

(C) ____________________

(W) ____________________

5. D.O.B. __________ Present age: __________

6. Place of birth: ____________________

7. Sex: ______ Hgt: ______ Wgt: ______ Hair color: ______ Weight: ______

8. Social security no.: ____________________

9. __________ ____________________

__________ ____________________

__________ ____________________

__________ ____________________

10. Citizen of the Unites States? ____________________

11. If other than native born, please give details: ____________________

____

12. Have you ever been known by another name? [ ] Yes [ ] No. If yes, give the names and reasons for using them:

____

____

13. May we contact your current employer? ____________________

14. May we contact you at work? ____________________

15. Hours available? Home: ____________________

Work: ____________________

16. Present

Marital status: ____________________ Spouse name: __________

Date married: __________ Location: __________

17. *Family members*—Incl. parents, brothers, sisters, children, and all "step" variations of such, spouses and ex-spouses (incl. their maiden names), and in-laws.

Name	Address	Telephone (w/Area Code)	DOB (If Known)	Relationship
	______	______		
	______	______		
	______	______		
	______	______		
	______	______		
	______	______		
	______	______		
	______	______		
	______	______		
	______	______		
	______	______		
	______	______		
	______	______		
	______	______		
	______	______		
	______	______		
	______	______		
	______	______		
	______	______		
	______	______		
	______	______		
	______	______		
	______	______		
	______	______		
	______	______		
	______	______		

18. *Others who you have ever resided with*
(do not include those already mentioned in *FAMILY MEMBERS* section).

Name	Address	Telephone (w/Area Code)	DOB (If Known)	Relationship

19. *Children's school information* (incl. biological, step, and any other children ever residing with you).

Child's Name	Grade	School Name, Address, and Telephone No.

20. *All residences*—List all locations where you have ever resided starting at birth to present.

Dates From	To	Location	Own/Rent/Other—Describe Circumstances—If Rented, List Landlord Name/Address/Telephone No.

21. *Dating relationships*—List all persons with whom you have ever dated or otherwise had a dating relationship. (Begin with most recent and work backward. Use additional paper if necessary.)

Dates: From – To	Name	Age (Prior)	Address (Prior)	Current Address (If Known)

Section B: Judicial Proceedings

Criminal

1. Have you *ever* been arrested, detained, questioned, or the subject of any violation, misdemeanor, or felony in any jurisdiction in any country?
(must include any juvenile delinquency and youthful offender adjudications)
[ ] Yes (If yes, describe the details in the following table) [ ] No

Date	Violation(s) Charged	Disposition	Law Enforcement Agency	Court of Jurisdiction	Coconspirators? Yes/No
	________	________			
	________	________			
	________	________			
	________	________			
	________	________			
	________	________			
	________	________			
	________	________			

Provide circumstances of each arrest in the following table referencing by date of violation (use additional paper if needed).

Traffic

2. Have you *ever* been arrested for any traffic violation, misdemeanor, or felony in any jurisdiction?
(Must include any juvenile delinquency and youthful offender adjudications. List even if found not guilty.)
[ ] Yes (if yes, describe the details in the following table) [ ] No

Date	Violation(s) Charged	Disposition	Law Enforcement Agency	Court of Jurisdiction

Provide circumstances of each arrest in the following table referencing by date of violation (use additional paper if needed).

Civil

3. Have you ever been called, summoned, or subpoenaed to appear as a witness or in any other capacity before a grand jury, legislative committee, hearing board, referee, or administrative agency in any jurisdiction? (Transfer officers should disregard listing any actions you were involved in as a witness for the People of the State of New York that occurred as part of their routine job duties.)

[ ] Yes [ ] No If yes, give details: ____________________

____

____

____

____

4. Have you ever been involved in any capacity in any civil proceedings (i.e., family court, Supreme Court, small-claims court, etc.) in any court in this state or in any other jurisdiction? (Transfer officers should disregard listing any actions you were involved in as a witness for the People of the State of New York that occurred as part of your routine job duties.)

[ ] Yes [ ] No If yes, give details in the following table:

Date	Court	Plaintiff, Defendant, Witness	Describe	Disposition

Section C: D.M.V. Information

1. List all states in which you have, or have ever had, a driver's license.

State	Operator's License No./Client I.D. No.	Class	Date Issued	Date of Expiration	License Ever Suspended or Revoked? (Yes/No). If Yes, Describe

2. List all vehicles registered to you and other members of your household and indicate who they are registered to.

State	Reg. No.	Year	Make	Model	Type	Color	Exp.	Registered to

3. Have you ever received any traffic citations for which you cannot remember the date, location, or offense?

[ ] Yes [ ] No If yes, give details: ____________________

____

____

4. Has your driver's license ever been suspended or revoked?

[ ] Yes [ ] No If yes, give details: give details: ____________________

____

____

5. Are there any proceedings or charges involving any violations of law, or any fines or penalties, now pending against you that have not been paid?

[ ] Yes [ ] No If yes, give details: ______________________________

____

____

6. List all motor vehicle accidents you have been involved in as a driver, passenger, or pedestrian.

Date	Location	Injury? Yes/No	Report? Yes/No	Investigation Agency	Driver, Passenger, Pedestrian	Describe Cause
	________					________
	________					________
	________					________
	________					________
	________					________
	________					________
	________					________
	________					________
	________					________
	________					________
	________					________

Section D: Employment and Experience History

1. Start with most recent and go backward.

Dates From/To	Employer Name and Address	Telephone	Position(s) Held	Immediate Supervisor	Reason for Leaving

2. Were you ever fired, terminated, discharged, or asked to resign from any position or organization?

Yes ____________ No ____________ If yes, give details: ____________________________

3. Have you ever been the subject of any disciplinary action or received any memorandum, suspensions, etc., that are not mentioned earlier?

Yes ____________ No ____________ If yes, give details: ____________________________

4. Have you ever as a condition of appointment to, or retention of, a position been required to submit to a lie detector (polygraph) test or any other electronic test designed to test your truthfulness?

Yes ____________ No ____________ If yes, give details: ____________________________

5. Have you ever subverted or attempted to subvert any type of lie detector (polygraph) test or any other electronic test designed to test your truthfulness or been accused of doing such?

Yes ____________ No ____________ If yes, give details: ____________________________

6. Has any employer or agency ever conducted an inquiry, background, or character investigation concerning your fitness for a position?

Yes ____________ No ____________ If yes, give details: ____________________________

7. Do you have or have you ever held any professional license, permit, or certificate authorizing you to practice any occupation, profession, or calling?
Yes ____________ No ____________ If yes, give details: ____________________________

8. Have you ever applied for a civil service position other than this one?
Yes ____________ No ____________ If yes, give details:

Date	Location	Position	Results

9. Has any such application ever been rejected?
Yes ____________ No ____________ If yes, give details: ____________________________

10. Have you ever received or are you now receiving benefits under the law concerning unemployment, disability, worker's compensation, social security, welfare, or social assistance of any kind?
Yes ____________ No ____________ If yes, give details:

From	To	Type of Assistance	Agency	Reason

11. Has any such application ever been rejected?
Yes ____________ No ____________ If yes, give details: ____________________________

12. Have you ever made any statement or assertion on an application for such benefit which you knew to be false or deceptive?
Yes ____________ No ____________ If yes, give details: ____________________________

13. Have you ever been a notary public or commissioner of deeds?
Yes ____________ No ____________ If yes, give details: ____________________________
____
____
____

14. Do you hold or have you ever held any interest as an officer, partner, or shareholder in any business, partnership, or venture?
Yes ____________ No ____________ If yes, give details: ____________________________
____
____
____

15. Has anyone ever suggested to you that you submit drug, alcohol, or mental health testing or evaluation?
Yes ____________ No ____________ If yes, give details: ____________________________
____
____
____
____

16. Have you ever subverted or attempted to subvert a drug, alcohol, or mental health testing or evaluation?
Yes ____________ No ____________ If yes, give details: ____________________________
____
____
____
____

17. Have you ever violated an employer's fitness-for-duty policy?
Yes ____________ No ____________ If yes, give details: ____________________________
____
____
____
____

18. Have you ever fallen asleep while working or been accused of doing such?
Yes____________ No____________ If yes, give details: ____________________________
____
____
____

19. Have you ever undergone any type of anger management counseling or training or has it been suggested you do such?
Yes____________ No____________ If yes, give details: ____________________________
____
____
____
____

Section E: Educational Qualifications

1. Complete the following concerning all schools, colleges, and universities which you attended in receding order:

From/To	Name of Educational Institution, Address, and Telephone No.	Grades Attended	Graduated Yes/No	Type of Degree/ Diploma	Date Received
________	________ ________ ________ Tel. no. ________				
________	________ ________ ________ Tel. no. ________				
________	________ ________ ________ Tel. no. ________				
________	________ ________ ________ Tel. no. ________				
________	________ ________ ________ Tel. no. ________				
________	________ ________ ________ Tel. no. ________				
________	________ ________ ________ Tel. no. ________				

2. Do you possess a high school equivalency or G.E.D. diploma?
Yes ____________ No ____________ If yes, give details:

Date	Number	Issuing Agency	Location of Classes (If Applicable)

3. Complete the following concerning teachers, counselors, deans, instructors, or other persons who have knowledge of your educational qualifications or character:

Name	School/Company	Title	Telephone No.

4. Were you ever involved, in any way, in any disciplinary investigation, action, or proceeding at any educational institution that you attended?
Yes ___________ No ___________ If yes, give details: ___________________________

____

____

____

____

5. Are you fluent in any foreign language?
Yes ___________ No ___________ If yes, give details:

Language	Spell (Check If Appropriate)	Read (Check If Appropriate)	Write (Check If Appropriate)

6. List any other skills or training that are not listed in this section concerning employment. Include hobbies or other interests. (Attach copies or relevant certificates, diplomas, etc.)

Section F: Medical History

1. Complete the following concerning any *medical* examination or treatment you have had or requested for illnesses, injuries, physical defects, or other ailments.

Date	Physician's Name, Address, and Telephone No.	Reason for Examination	Diagnosis/Treatment
	____ ____ ____ Tel. no. ____	____ ____ ____ ____	____ ____ ____ ____
	____ ____ ____ Tel. no. ____	____ ____ ____ ____	____ ____ ____ ____
	____ ____ ____ Tel. no. ____	____ ____ ____ ____	____ ____ ____ ____
	____ ____ ____ Tel. no. ____	____ ____ ____ ____	____ ____ ____ ____
	____ ____ ____ Tel. no. ____	____ ____ ____ ____	____ ____ ____ ____
	____ ____ ____ Tel. no. ____	____ ____ ____ ____	____ ____ ____ ____
	____ ____ ____ Tel. no. ____	____ ____ ____ ____	____ ____ ____ ____
	____ ____ ____ Tel. no. ____	____ ____ ____ ____	____ ____ ____ ____

Date	Physician's Name, Address, and Telephone No.	Reason for Examination	Diagnosis/Treatment
	____ ____ ____ Tel. no. ____	____ ____ ____ ____	____ ____ ____ ____
	____ ____ ____ Tel. no. ____	____ ____ ____ ____	____ ____ ____ ____
	____ ____ ____ Tel. no. ____	____ ____ ____ ____	____ ____ ____ ____
	____ ____ ____ Tel. no. ____	____ ____ ____ ____	____ ____ ____ ____
	____ ____ ____ Tel. no. ____	____ ____ ____ ____	____ ____ ____ ____
	____ ____ ____ Tel. no. ____	____ ____ ____ ____	____ ____ ____ ____
	____ ____ ____ Tel. no. ____	____ ____ ____ ____	____ ____ ____ ____
	____ ____ ____ Tel. no. ____	____ ____ ____ ____	____ ____ ____ ____
	____ ____ ____ Tel. no. ____	____ ____ ____ ____	____ ____ ____ ____

2. Read each item carefully. Check "Yes" if you have ever had the noted condition or "No" if you have not.

Yes	No	Condition		Yes	No	Condition
		Asthma				Defective color perception
		Hay fever				Eye glasses/contact lenses
		Other allergies				Other eye condition
		Anemia				Ulcers
		Enlarged spleen				Gall bladder condition
		Bleeding from nose				Hepatitis or jaundice
		Bleeding from lung				Undescended testicle
		Bleeding in urine				Varicocele or hydrocele
		Bleeding in stool				Urethritis
		Back injury or condition				Hospitalized for any reason
		Amputation				Any surgery
		Fracture or sprain				Malaria
		Any joint conditions				Rheumatic fever
		Cartilage injury				Venereal disease
		Arthritis or bursitis				Any psychiatric counseling or exam
		Foot trouble				Frequent headaches
		Other bone condition				Fainting spells
		Abnormal blood pressure				Head injury
		Heart murmur or condition				Epilepsy or seizures
		Varicose veins				Convulsive seizures
		Perforated eardrum				Blackouts
		Mastoid				Hemorrhoids or hernia
		Other ear condition				Albumin/sugar in urine
		Bed-wetting beyond age 16				Any kidney condition
		Sleep disorder or sleep walking				Any gland condition
		Alcoholism				Any nose condition
		Nervousness				Any speech defect
		Use of a narcotic drug				V.A. medical claim
		Any mental disorder				Received disability pay
		Family mental disorder				Any liver condition
		Sinusitis				Infantile paralysis
		Tuberculosis				Other infection
		Chronic bronchitis				Tetanus immunization

Yes	No	Condition		Yes	No	Condition
		Pneumonia/pleurisy				Any skin disorder
		Diabetes				Currently taking medication
		Cysts/tumors				Rejection on any medical examination
		Selective service 1 Y or 4 Y classification				Anxiety

3. Have you ever had any physical or emotional/psychiatric condition which has impaired your abilities?
Yes ____________ No ____________ If yes, give details and describe if it has ever affected your ability to function in any employment or educational setting? __________________

4. Has there been any history of emotional or psychiatric disorder in your immediate family?
Yes ____________ No ____________ If yes, give details: __________________

5. Complete the following concerning any drugs you are using or you have ever used, given away, or sold. Place the *total number of instances* in the boxes where appropriate:

Item	Never Used	Have Used	Date of Last Use	Frequency of Use—Minimum and Maximum Times Used in 1 Week	Given Away	Have Sold	Date of Last Sale
Marijuana							
Hash							
Hash oil							
LSD							
PCP							
Cocaine/crack							
Heroin							
Amphetamines							
Inhalants							
Steroids							

(*continued*)

Item	Never Used	Have Used	Date of Last Use	Frequency of Use—Minimum and Maximum Times Used in 1 Week	Given Away	Have Sold	Date of Last Sale
Barbiturates							
Mushrooms							
Peyote							
GHB (ecstasy)							
Tranquilizers							
Growth-enhancing substances							
Performance-enhancing substances							
Anxiety, stress, mood altering substances							
Other drugs in abusing manner							

If you answered that you have ever used or sold any of the aforementioned drugs, describe the dates and circumstances of each use and the identities of who else was involved with you. If you have possessed any of the aforementioned but not used them, also describe the date and circumstances surrounding each such possession.

6. Have you ever shared drugs with anyone?
Yes ____________ No ____________ If yes, give details: ____________________________
____
____
____

7. Have you ever been addicted to the use of alcoholic beverages?
Yes ____________ No ____________ If yes, give details: ____________________________
____
____
____

8. Complete the following concerning any examination, treatment, or counseling you have had, requested, or have been referred by medical personnel to seek for any *psychiatric, anxiety, stress, anger management, or emotional condition.*

Date	Physician's Name, Address, and Telephone No.	Reason for Examination	Diagnosis/Treatment
	________ ________ ________ Tel. no. ________	________ ________ ________ ________	________ ________ ________ ________
	________ ________ ________ Tel. no. ________	________ ________ ________ ________	________ ________ ________ ________
	________ ________ ________ Tel. no. ________	________ ________ ________ ________	________ ________ ________ ________
	________ ________ ________ Tel. no. ________	________ ________ ________ ________	________ ________ ________ ________
	________ ________ ________ Tel. no. ________	________ ________ ________ ________	________ ________ ________ ________
	________ ________ ________ Tel. no. ________	________ ________ ________ ________	________ ________ ________ ________

(*continued*)

Date	Physician's Name, Address, and Telephone No.	Reason for Examination	Diagnosis/Treatment
	____________ ____________ ____________ Tel. no. ________	____________ ____________ ____________ ____________	____________ ____________ ____________ ____________
	____________ ____________ ____________ Tel. no. ________	____________ ____________ ____________ ____________	____________ ____________ ____________ ____________
	____________ ____________ ____________ Tel. no. ________	____________ ____________ ____________ ____________	____________ ____________ ____________ ____________

9. Have you ever seen/spoken with any physician, physician assistant, nurse, nurse practitioner, therapist, psychotherapist, or *any* other medical professional, paraprofessional, or other person for the purpose of receiving, or being referred to receive, treatment, advice, referral, counseling, or any other service that is not already listed by you in this section?
Yes __________ No __________ If yes, give details: ______________________
____
____
____
____
____
____
____
____
____
____

Section G: Military Service

1. Do you have or have you ever had any selective service classification?
Yes ___________ No ___________ If yes, give details:

Date	Classification	Issuing Authority

2. Are you now or have you ever been a conscientious objector or otherwise been opposed to the use of firearms for any reason?
Yes ___________ No ___________ If yes, give details: ___________

3. Have you ever served in the armed forces of the United States?

From	To	Branch	Serial Number	Type of Discharge

4. If you had military experience, what was the highest rank you attained? ___________

5. What was your last rank? ___________

6. Have you ever received a discharge or separation for military service which was less than honorable?
Yes ___________ No ___________ If yes, give details: ___________

7. If you received a discharge that was less than honorable, have you ever made an application for upgrading your discharge?
Yes ___________ No ___________ If yes, give details: ___________

8. Did you ever receive medical, psychiatric, psychoanalytic, or psychological treatment for any injury or illness while in the military service?

Date	Type of Treatment	Location

9. Are you now or have you ever been in any Reserve National Guard unit?
Yes ____________ No ____________ If yes, give details:

From	To	Name of Unit	Location

10. Did you receive any commendations, awards, or medals in connection with your military service?
Yes ____________ No ____________ If yes, give details:

Date	Name of Award	Conduct	Awarding Agency

11. Were you ever subject to any discipline proceedings during your military service to include court martial? (summary proceedings or article 15 actions)
Yes ____________ No ____________ If yes, give details:

Date	Charge	Location	Disposition

12. What types of specialized training or education did you complete during your military service?
Yes ____________ No ____________ If yes, give details:

From	To	Type of Training	Location

13. Do you receive or have you ever received any benefits related to your military service to include those administered by the Veteran's Administration?
Yes ____________ No ____________ If yes, give details:

From	To	Type of Benefit	Agency Granting Benefit

14. Have you ever been the subject of any character or background investigation with regard to any appointment, employment, or military service you performed?
Yes ____________ No ____________ If yes, give details:

Date	Type and Reason for Investigation	Employer/Agency

Section H: Credit History and Civil Proceedings

Loans

1. List the details in the following table about all loans you have had in which you or your spouse is/was a principal debtor, mortgagor, cosigner, guarantor, or surety (mortgage, car loans, personal loans, etc.)

Creditor Name and Address	Account No.	Purpose of Loan (House, Car, etc.)	Amount Borrowed	Current Balance	Paid as Agreed? Y/N
______ ______ ______					
______ ______ ______					
______ ______ ______					
______ ______ ______					
______ ______ ______					
______ ______ ______					
______ ______ ______					
______ ______ ______					
______ ______ ______					

Credit cards

2. List the details in the following table about all credit cards you have had in which you or your spouse is/was a principal card holder.

Creditor Name and Address	Account No.	Purpose of Loan (House, Car, etc.)	Amount Borrowed	Current Balance	Paid as Agreed? Y/N

Judgments/bad debts, etc.

3. List in the following table all information concerning any judgments, bad debts, arrearage, fines, or penalties ever filed against you or your spouse or any partnership or corporation in which you or your spouse has a principal interest.

Creditor Name and Address	Account No.	Purpose of Loan (House, Credit Card, Car, etc.)	Amount Borrowed	Amount of Default
______ ______ ______				
______ ______ ______				
______ ______ ______				
______ ______ ______				
______ ______ ______				
______ ______ ______				

4. Have you or any partnership or corporation in which you have a principal interest ever been adjudicated either voluntarily or involuntarily?

Yes ____________ No ____________ If yes, give details: ____________________________

____

____

Section I: References

Personal

1.

Name and Address	Employer and Address
______ ______ ______ Telephone:	______ ______ ______ Telephone:
Relationship to reference: ______	

Name and Address	Employer and Address
______ ______ ______ Telephone:	______ ______ ______ Telephone:
Relationship to reference: ______	

Name and Address	Employer and Address
______ ______ ______ Telephone:	______ ______ ______ Telephone:
Relationship to reference: ______	

Business

2.

Name and Address	Employer and Address
______ ______ ______ Telephone:	______ ______ ______ Telephone:
Relationship to reference: ______	

Name and Address	Employer and Address
______ ______ ______ Telephone:	______ ______ ______ Telephone:
Relationship to reference: ______	

Name and Address	Employer and Address
______ ______ ______ Telephone:	______ ______ ______ Telephone:
Relationship to reference: ______	

Section J: Miscellaneous

1. Have you ever been supported, financially or otherwise, by any organization which advocates, advises, or supports the overthrow of the government of the United States or any political entity or subdivision, by the use of violence, force, or any other unlawful means?
Yes ___________ No ___________ If yes, give details: ___________________________

____

____

2. Were you ever, or are you now, a member or supporter of any social, labor professional, or fraternal organizations? (i.e., VFW, Elks, Moose, Rotary, Urban League, etc.)
Yes ___________ No ___________ If yes, give details: ___________________________

____

____

3. Do you now own or have you ever owned any firearms?
Yes ___________ No ___________ If yes, give details:

From	To	Make	Type	Serial No.

4. Do you now hold or have you ever held a pistol permit or any similar authorization to carry a firearm in this state or any other?
Yes ___________ No ___________ If yes, give details:

Date Issued	Issuing Authority	Certificate/Permit No.

5. Has any such application by you for such a permit ever been denied?
Yes ___________ No ___________ If yes, give details: ___________________________

____

____

6. List any recreational activities, hobbies, and activities in which you engage and any affiliated clubs or organizations in which you are now or ever were involved with (i.e., YMCA, Scouting, etc.).

____

____

____

____

7. Do you have any knowledge or information of any circumstances, conditions, or qualifications other than what has been in the foregoing questions which may be relevant, directly or indirectly, to an assessment of your character, maturity, integrity, temperament, fitness, qualification, or eligibility for appointment to the position of police officer?

Yes ___________ No ___________ If yes, give details: ___________________________

____

____

____

____

____

8. Briefly state your reasons for wanting to become a police officer (100 words or less).

In your own handwriting, copy the following paragraph in the space provided. Sign the form in the appropriate place, *having your signature witnessed by a NOTARY PUBLIC.* Your signature affixed in the indicated location is an endorsement of your agreement with the contents of your handwritten paragraph.

AFFIDAVIT

Background investigation questionnaire—Certification of truthfulness

"I ______________________ hereby acknowledge that I have read the instructions contained in the foregoing application and have completed the application in accordance with the instructions. I affirm that I had adequate time to complete the application fully, truthfully, and to the best of my knowledge. I am aware that any omission, deception, or any attempt to deceive by me in the completion of this application or in the subsequent character investigation to be conducted by the Irondequoit Police Department may result in a rejection of my application from consideration for the position of police officer."

____

____

____

____

____

____

____

____

____

____

____

____

____

____

____

____

____

____

____

____

____

____

____

____

Notice: False statements made herein are punishable as a class A Misdemeanor pursuant to section 210.45 of the New York State Penal Law.

Dated__________________________ Applicant's signature________________________

Sworn to before me, this _________day of _________20_________

____

Notary public

In your own handwriting, copy the following paragraph in the space provided. Sign the form in the appropriate place, *having your signature witnessed by a NOTARY PUBLIC.* Your signature affixed in the indicated location is an endorsement of your agreement with the contents of your handwritten paragraph

AFFIDAVIT

Waiver of right to access or challenge background investigation

"I ____________________ hereby waive any and all rights that I may have under the laws of the United States and the laws of the state of New York, concerning access to documents and information developed and obtained by members of the Irondequoit Police Department in their investigation of my character and fitness for the position of police officer. This waiver includes, but is not limited to, any rights of learning the identity of any person, organization, or business from which any type of information is received from as well as any written oral statements made by any person interviewed by said members of the Irondequoit Police Department. In the event I do not receive the position applied for, I also agree to waive any right to any recourse or challenge of such decision not to hire me."

Notice: False statements made herein are punishable as a class A Misdemeanor pursuant to section 210.45 of the New York State Penal Law.

Dated______________________ Applicant's signature____________________

Sworn to before me, this ________day of ________20________

____

Notary public

Appendix G: Sample Application Materials (APD)

City of Auburn, Maine
Hiring procedures for police officers

Effective July 1, 2006, the City of Auburn implemented a new city charter. The new charter permits the Police Department to promulgate hiring and promotion procedures in lieu of the Civil Service Commission and Civil Service Ordinances, which were eliminated from the new charter.

The following hiring procedures are intended to set minimum standards for hiring while, at the same time, allowing for maximum flexibility in hiring qualified officers throughout the year. Candidates who have fulfilled these requirements will be placed on an eligibility list for consideration for future hire.

Please note that there are two separate hiring procedures. One is for the candidates who have not graduated from the Maine Criminal Justice Academy's Basic Law Enforcement Program (or from another comparable program from another state).

The second is for candidates who have graduated from the Maine Criminal Justice Academy's Basic Law Enforcement Program (or from another comparable program from another state) and who have been employed as a law enforcement officer in another municipality, county, and state agency.

Hiring procedure for candidates not currently certified by the Maine Criminal Justice Academy:

Step 1: Applications may be picked up at the Human Resource Department, Fourth floor, 60 Court Street, Auburn, ME 04210. Application packets may also be obtained by e-mailing the human resource office at dgrimmig@ci.auburn.me.us or cmumau@ci.auburn.me.us. Applications may also be downloaded from the City of Auburn's website: www.auburnmaine.org. Please call the human resource office at 207-333-6601 ext 1416 or 1414 for application packets or if you have difficulties downloading the packets from the website.

Step 2: Applicants must have attained the age of 21 and be high school graduates or have passed a high school equivalency exam. Applicants must also possess a valid driver's license and, if a nonresident, be able to obtain a Maine driver's license within 6 months.

Step 3: All applicants must pass the ALERT test. The ALERT test is a literacy test required for admission by the Maine Criminal Justice Academy. The ALERT test is administered by the MCJA in Waterville. Please call the academy at (208) 877-8000 for the dates and times that the test is administered and to register for the test. The test is also administered at the Southern Maine Technical College (207-799-9564).

There is a fee for this exam. Applicants may find out the cost of the exam when they call or register. You will receive a letter from the MCJA advising you if you passed or failed the

ALERT test. A minimum score of (*45*) is required for consideration. Please attach a copy of the letter with your completed application.

Step 4: All applicants are required to take the physical agility test (PAT) administered by the MCJA. This PAT is required for entrance to the MCJA and is adjusted for the candidate's age and gender. A copy is provided in the application packet and is on the city's website. As is the case with the ALERT test, candidates must call the academy for the dates and times that the PAT is administered and register for the PAT. A letter from the MCJA stating that you have passed the PAT must accompany your completed application.

Step 5: Return the following information to the Human Resource Department:

Completed application
Letter from the MCJA regarding ALERT score
Letter from MCJA regarding pass/fail of PAT
High school diploma or certificate from equivalency exam
DD214 if served in military
Copies of certificates or licenses such as EMT or other specialized trainings
College transcript (if applicable, must be sent directly to the City of Auburn Human Resources Department)

Step 6: The Human Resources Department will maintain a bank of completed applications until there is an opening at the Police Department. At that time, the Human Resources Department will forward the completed application packets to the police chief.

Step 7: The chief or his designee will review the application packets and will contact the most qualified candidates for an initial screening interview.

Step 8: The police chief will conduct a background check on those candidates who have passed the initial screening. An applicant will be given a conditional offer of employment prior to the background check.

Step 9: The applicant will receive a background investigation questionnaire from the chief of police. The applicant will return the completed questionnaire to the chief of police in a sealed envelope.

Step 10: Upon a conditional offer of employment, successful candidates will take a polygraph exam and a psychological exam. The police chief reserves the right to administer other assessments to determine the candidate's suitability for work as a police officer.

Step 11: Upon a conditional offer of employment, the candidate will take a medical exam and a substance abuse test. The candidate must pass these two exams in order to be eligible for hire.

Step 12: The successful candidate will be hired and then scheduled to attend the MCJA, which is an 18 weeks course held in Vassalboro. The new hire must successfully complete the MCJA program in order to become a certified police officer and to continue employment with the City of Auburn.

Hiring procedures for candidates currently certified as police officers

The City of Auburn will waive the requirements to take the ALERT test and the physical agility for those candidates who have received certification from the Municipal/County/State Law Enforcement Program. In the case of an out-of-state candidate, the police chief will determine if the program is comparable to the MCJA program.

The applicant with current certifications will provide the following information to the human resources office:

Completed application
Copy of certification from MCJA or similar program
High school diploma or certificate from equivalency exam
DD214 if served in military
College transcript (if applicable, must be sent directly to the City of Auburn Human Resources Department)

Candidates with current law enforcement certifications will follow Steps 6 through 11 mentioned earlier. Applicants may be invited to do a ride-along program with a field-training officer as part of the applicant screening process. Successful candidates will not be required to attend the MCJA; however, out-of-state candidates *will* be required to take a course on the State of Maine laws.

Job application

City of Auburn Police:______________
Human Resource Department,
60 Court Street,
Auburn, Maine 04210 (207)333-6601 ext 1414 or 1416

Date:______________

Name:____________________________________Social Security #:______________
Last First MI
Present
Address:____Tel. #:______________
Street:
___________________________________How long there?______________
City, State, Zip Code
E-mail address:____

Date of birth:______________ Place of birth:______________________________
Can you perform the job for which you have applied with or without reasonable accommodation?
Yes_____ No _____

Have you ever served on any Police/Fire department? Yes____ No____
Volunteer _____ Full time _____
Date served: _____________________ Location: _____________________
Length of service: ____________ Reason for leaving: __________________________

List any relatives working for the City of Auburn:
Name: *Relationship:*

____

____

Have you ever been convicted of any criminal action or motor vehicle violations such as speeding or operating under the influence? ______________________________

____

____

____

Do you have a valid driver's license? Yes ___ No ____ State: _____ License no.: _____

Military service: Active duty ( ) Reserve duty ( ) None ( )

Branch:_____________Date of entry: __________ Date of discharge: __________

Type of discharge: ______________________ Highest rank: ______________________

Present reserve status: Active ( ) Inactive ( ) None ( )

Note: A photo static copy of your discharge, DD214, is required with this application.

Education

High school: ____________________ *Year graduated*: ____________
Address: ____
Business or technical school: __________________ *Year graduated*: ____________
Address: ____
College: ____________________ *Major*: __________ *Degree*: __________
Address: ______________________ Minor: ______________________

Account for all employment since high school (list last position first)

From/to: ___ Name/address of *Former employer*: ___ *Salary*: ___ *Position*: ___ *Supervisor*: ___ Reason for *Leaving*: ___

____

____

____

Work-related references

Name: __________ *Address*: ____________________ *Tel.#*: ____ *Occupation*: _____

____

____

____

I certify that all statements made on this application are true and complete to the best of my knowledge. I understand that any false statements or omissions will subject me to disqualification or dismissal.

__________ ______________________________

Date: *Signature*:

City of Auburn, Maine
Information release

I hereby authorize the release of the following information to representatives of the City of Auburn, including but not limited to the personnel office and the Auburn Police Department:

1. Complete transcript of all secondary and postsecondary scholastic records
2. Complete record of all credit information
3. Complete record of all past and present employment information
4. A security clearance check
5. Military service records

I also realize that persons other than those listed as references may be contacted for job-related and personal character references and I authorize that as well. I hereby authorize and release any individual, company, or corporation to release any verbal or written information requested by a representative from the Auburn Police Department.

I also agree to sign any other release forms required to obtain any of the above records.

Date: ____________ *Signature*: ________________________________

A substance abuse test(s) and/or a job-related medical exam(s)/physical(s) will be required after a conditional offer of employment has been made.

City of Auburn, Maine
Applicant background investigation questionnaire

1. *Drug/alcohol use*
   a. Have you ever used illegal drugs? If so, what and when?

   ____

   ____

   b. Have you ever used steroids? If so, what and when?

   ____

   ____

   c. Have you ever sold drugs? If so, what and when?

   ____

   ____

   d. Have you ever been in an environment where illegal drugs were being used? If so, explain the situation. What did you do?

   ____

   ____

   e. Do you drink alcohol? If so, how often and how much?

   ____

   ____

   f. Have you abused prescription drugs? If so, what and when?

   ____

   ____

   g. Do you smoke or use tobacco products?

   ____

   ____

   h. Have you ever been intoxicated? If so, when?

   ____

   ____

i. Have you ever driven while intoxicated? If so, how many times and when?

____

____

j. Have you ever awoken and been unable to recall the events of the night before? If so, when? Explain the circumstances.

____

____

2. *Past criminal behavior/police contact*

a. Have you ever been stopped for a traffic violation? If so, when and for what reason? Did you receive any traffic tickets? List municipality and year ticket(s) received.

____

____

b. Have the police ever responded to your residence? If so, when and for what reason?

____

____

c. Have you ever called the police? If so, when and for what reason?

____

____

d. Have you ever been convicted of a crime? If so, explain.

____

e. Have you ever been arrested? If so, explain.

____

____

f. Have you ever been a suspect in a crime? If so, explain.

____

____

g. Have you ever been questioned about a crime? If so, explain.

h. Have you ever been handcuffed? If so, where, when, and why?

i. Have you ever been detained by police? If so where, when, and why?

j. Have you ever been fingerprinted by police? If so where, when, and why?

k. Have you ever been summoned to appear in court? If so, where, when, and why?

l. Have you ever had anything expunged from your record? If so, what and where?

m. Have you ever stolen anything in your lifetime? If so, what, where, when, and why?

n. What other law enforcement agencies have you applied to?

o. Have you ever applied for a restraining order, a protection order or any other type of court order? If so, where, when, and why?

p. Have you ever been subjected to a restraining order, a protective order, or any other type of court order? If so, where, when, and why?

____

____

3. *Employment history*

a. Where are you currently employed? How long employed? What are your current job assignments?

____

b. The Auburn Police Department provides protection and service to the community 24 hours a day, 365 days a year. Is there anything that prevents you from working certain hours of the day or days during the week?

Yes ____________________ No ____________________

If you answered yes, please explain why. ____________________

____

c. List all other places of employment during your lifetime. What were your reasons for leaving each job?

____

____

____

____

____

____

____

____

d. Have you ever been injured at work? If so, have you ever been on work compensation? What was the nature of the injury?

____

e. Have you ever been suspended or reprimanded at work? If so, when, where, by whom, and for what reason?

____

____

f. Have you ever had a dispute with a coworker? If so, explain.

g. What is your attendance record of work?

h. Have you ever been accused of sexual harassment? If so, when, where, by whom, and what was the accusation?

i. Have you ever fired from a job or asked to leave? If so, when, where, by whom, and for what reason?

j. Have you ever had any issues with any former employees or coworkers? If so, explain.

4. *Aggression*

a. Describe something that annoys you. Does this make you angry?

b. Do you get angry often? If so, how often?

c. Has anyone ever recommended that you seek anger management classes? If so, who, when, and why?

d. Have you ever been enrolled in anger management classes? If so, where, when, and why?

e. Have you ever been in a physical fight as an adult? If so, where, when, and why? Explain the circumstances.

____

____

5. *Mental health history*

a. Do you have, or have you ever had, a psychiatric illness or disorder? If so, when and what type of illness or disorder?

____

____

b. Have you ever been admitted to a psychiatric institution? If so, when, where, and for what reason?

____

____

c. Have you ever been treated for a psychiatric illness or disorder? If so, when, where, and for what reason?

____

____

d. Name of physician(s) and/or councilors(s) treating and or prescribing medication.

____

____

e. Have you ever submitted to a psychological evaluation of any kind? If so, when, where, and for what reason?

____

____

6. *Education/college history*

a. Do you have a high school diploma? List high school and date of graduation.

____

____

b. Have you attended college? If so, list all the colleges of enrollment and dates of attendance.

____

____

c. Do you have a college degree? If so, list the name of institution and date of graduation.

____

____

d. Were you subject to any disciplinary actions while attending college? If so, explain.

____

____

e. Did you have any contact with the campus security or campus police while attending college? If so, explain.

____

____

7. *Driving history*

a. Have you ever been in a motor vehicle accident? If so, when and where? Explain what happened.

____

____

b. Has your license ever been suspended or revoked in any state? If so, when, where, and for what reason?

____

____

c. Have you had a driver's license in any other state? If so, where and why?

____

____

d. Has your registration ever been suspended or revoked? If so, where, when, and for what reason?

____

____

e. Have you ever been stopped for a traffic violation? If so, where, when, and for what reason?

____

____

8. *Firearms*

a. Do you own a firearm? If so, what type of weapon? What is the weapon used for?

____

____

b. Have you ever shot a firearm? If so, when and why?

____

____

c. Have you ever held or possessed a firearm? If so, when and why?

____

9. *Financial issues*

a. Do you have any financial issues? If so, explain.

____

____

b. How is your credit?

____

____

c. Have you ever declared bankruptcy? If so, when, where, and why?

____

____

10. *Civil matters/lawsuits*

a. Have you ever been a litigant in a civil suit? If so, when and where?

____

____

Explain the facts of the case.

b. Have you ever used the legal system to recover damage for a loss resulting from the acts or omissions of another person, a company or corporation, or a government? If so, when and where?

Explain the facts of the case.

c. Have you ever used the legal system to seek injunctive relief of any kind? If so, when and where?

Explain the facts of the case.

11. *Gambling*

a. Do you gamble? If so, where and how often?

b. Do you have, or have you applied for, casino rewards card (e.g., Foxwoods "Wampum" card)?

c. Do you have, or have you ever had, a gambling problem?

12. *Military*
    a. Have you ever been in the military? If so, which branch of military and what rank did you achieve? What type of discharge did you receive? Were you ever disciplined while in the military? If so, explain.

    ____

    ____

    ____

    ____

    ____

13. *Personal information/family/friends/neighbors*
    a. Have you ever been known by any other name? If so, what is the name(s) and what was the reason for the change?

    ____

    ____

    b. What other addresses have you lived at during the last 10 years?

    ____

    ____

    ____

    ____

    ____

    ____

    c. Do you have any children? If so, name and ages?

    ____

    ____

    d. Do you have a spouse or significant other? List name, DOB, addresses, and phone number(s).

    ____

    ____

e. Do you have an ex-spouse? List name, DOB, address, and phone number(s).

____

____

f. Has any member of your immediate family ever been arrested or convicted of any crime? If so, who and what was the charge(s)?

____

____

g. Do you have any issues with any neighbors (past or present)? If so, explain.

____

____

h. Do you have any issues with any friend or former friends? If so, explain.

____

i. Name three of your closest friends and provide their contact information.

____

____

____

14. *Miscellaneous*

a. Have you ever gone to a pawn shop? If so, when, where, and why?

____

____

____

b. What are your hobbies?

____

____

____

____

Appendix H: Sample Information Release and Liability Waivers

CITY OF AUBURN, MAINE

INFORMATION RELEASE

I hereby authorize the release of the following information to representatives of the City of Auburn, including but not limited to the personnel office and the Auburn Police Department:

1. Complete transcript of all secondary and post-secondary scholastic records
2. Complete record of all credit information
3. Complete record of all past and present employment information
4. A security clearance check
5. Military service records

I also realize that persons other than those listed as references may be contacted for job-related and personal character references, and I authorize that as well. I hereby authorize and release any individual, company, or corporation to release any verbal or written information requested by a representative from the Auburn Police Department.

I also agree to sign any other release forms required to obtain any of the aforementioned records.

________________ ____

Date: **Signature:**

A substance abuse test(s) and/or a job-related medical exam(s)/physical(s) will be required after a conditional offer of employment has been made.

Insert picture of applicant here.

IRONDEQUOIT POLICE DEPARTMENT
AUTHORIZATION
FOR RELEASE OF PERSONAL INFORMATION

To Whom It May Concern:

I, ____________________________, release, review, and fully disclose all records, or any part thereof, concerning myself to any duly authorized agent of the Irondequoit Police Department, whether the said records are of a public, private, or confidential nature.

The purpose of this authorization is to give my consent for full and complete disclosure of any and all records of the following:

- Educational institutions
- Public utility companies
- Rental and/or tenant records for any apartment, house, townhouse, dormitory, or duplex
- Armed Forces of the United States or any other country or territory, or Reserve Forces or National Guard
- Financial or credit institutions, including records of any depository, savings, checking, or mortgage accounts, and also the records of commercial or retail credit agencies (including credit reports and/or ratings)
- Employment and pre-employment records and/or files, including salary records, backgrounds reports, polygraph test questions, answers and reports, pre-employment and promotional examination results, efficiency ratings, disciplinary ratings, disciplinary actions, complaints or grievances filed by or against me, and Internal Affairs investigations
- Real and personal property tax statements and records and other financial statements and records wherever filed
- Records of complaint, arrest, trial, and/or convictions for alleged or actual violations of law, including criminal and/or traffic records including those cases in which there was a finding of not guilty
- Records of complaints of any criminal or civil nature made by or against me, where so ever located, including the records and recollections of any attorneys at law or other counsel, whether representing me or another person in any criminal or civil case in which I have ever been a party or had an interest
- Medical, psychological, and psychiatric reports of consultation, treatment, and evaluation at or by any hospital, clinic, private practitioner, and/or the U.S. Department of Veteran's Administration

Health Insurance Portability and Accountability Act of 1996 (HIPAA) Compliance authorization

1. By my granting the release of such records, I am knowingly waiving any and all rights to privacy that I have under the HIPAA.
2. This authorization is for any and all medical, psychological, and psychiatric reports of consultation, treatment, and evaluation at or by any hospital, clinic, private practitioner, and/or the U.S. Department of Veteran's Administration for the purpose of employment with the Irondequoit Police Department, and shall remain in effect for 1 year from the below indicated date of authorization.
3. I may cancel this authorization at anytime by submitting a written request to any such care provider who is covered by this authorization.
4. I understand that such cancellation will not apply to any information that was already released in response to this authorization.
5. Because the person and agency that this information is being released to is not a health-care or medical insurance provider covered by privacy regulations, this information could be redisclosed by the recipient and no longer protected under this rule.

It is my specific intent to provide access to personal information and to release copies and abstracts, however personal or confidential they may appear to be. The sources of information specifically enumerated herein are for illustrative purposes only, and such enumeration shall not be used to deny access to any records not specifically identified herein. The reason for this authorization is to provide full and free access to the background and history of my personal life for the specific purpose of conducting a background investigation which may provide pertinent data for the Irondequoit Police Department to consider in determining my suitability for employment by that department.

Whether my application is approved or disapproved, the sources of any confidential information will not be revealed to me. I agree to indemnify and hold harmless the organization and person to whom this request is presented, as well as their employers, employees, and agents from and against all claims, damages, losses, and expenses, including reasonable attorney's fees arising out of or by reason of complying with this request.

This release form, and any copy of this release form, even though the said photocopy does not contain original writing of my original signature, will be valid and should be honored for a period of one (1) year from the date of my signature.

I do hereby affirm by affixing my signature hereto that I fully understand and agree to the contents of this authorization for release of personal information.

Name: ____________________________

SS #: ____________________________

DOB: ____________________________

Signature: ____________________________ Dated: ____________________________

Sworn to before me this ____________ day of ______________ 20 _____

____

Notary Public / Commissioner of Deeds

Endnotes

CHAPTER 1

[1] Hall, 1997
[2] Kane & White, 2009
[3] Hall, 1997, p. ix
[4] New York State Division of Criminal Justice Services Office of Public Safety, 2010
[5] *Omnibus Crime Control and Safe Streets Act of 1968*
[6] Bonne, 2004
[7] Cronkhite, 2008, p. 250
[8] Muraskin & Roberts, 2009, p. 329
[9] Oliver, 2002, p. 67
[10] Richardson, 1980
[11] Orrick, 2010
[12] United States Department of Justice Bureau of Justice Statistics, 2004
[13] Hickman & Reaves, 2006, p. 5
[14] Wallman, 2009
[15] Richardson, 1980
[16] Benson, 1978
[17] Struckhoff, 1994
[18] Struckhoff, 1994
[19] Hall, 1997, p. ix
[20] Coffey, 1990, p. 129
[21] San Antonio Express-News, 2008
[22] Raab, 1985
[23] Braibanti, 1962
[24] Amendola, Hawkins, Nicoletti, Scrivner, & Maltarese, 2008
[25] Newburn & Webb, 1999
[26] Lynch, 1998, p. 132
[27] Braswell, McCarthy, & McCarthy, 2002, p. 59
[28] *The Police Executive*, 2003, p. 2
[29] Sheridan, 2008
[30] San Antonio Express-News, 2008
[31] Braswell, McCarthy, & McCarthy, 2002, p. 61
[32] Conklin, 2003, p. 3
[33] Weizel, 2008a
[34] Burns & Somaiya, 2010; Eichler, 2010; George Washington University, 2001; Muir & Hopper, 2010; Hosenball, 2011; Tandon, 2010
[35] Lundstrom & Stanton, 2009, B1
[36] Jones, 1994
[37] Watson, 2010
[38] Peterson, 1999
[39] Amendola, Weber, & Mercer, 1999, p. 1
[40] Eiserer, 2006b
[41] Parks, 2001, p. 9
[42] Benson, 1978
[43] International Association of Chiefs of Police, 1989, p. 1
[44] Goodwin, 2010

[45] Gaines, Kappeler, & Vaughn, 1999, p. 123
[46] United States Merit Systems Protection Board, 2005, p. 4
[47] Slowik, 2001, p. 78
[48] United States Courts, n.d.a
[49] Carson, 2011; Earley, n.d.; Willing & Watson, 2001; Wise, 1995
[50] Bell, 2011; Dunlap & Kovaleski, 2007; Gatton, 2008; Ripley, 2007
[51] Coffey, 1990, p. 12
[52] Berger, 1995; Comstock, 2008; Fire Science Colleges, 2010; McKay, 2009; O'Neil, 1995; Thomas, 2007
[53] Ahlers, 2004
[54] Massad, 2006
[55] *New York Times*, 2010
[56] Gold, 2004
[57] Vaas, 2009
[58] Sonnenberg, 1994, p. 202
[59] Nelson, 2000, p. 87
[60] Van Maanen as cited in Culbertson & Weisheit, 2002, p. 67
[61] United States General Accounting Office, 1998, p. 16
[62] Goodman, 1998
[63] Grabell, 2008
[64] United States Department of Justice, 2007b
[65] Reaves & Hickman, 2004, p. xiii
[66] Hickman & Reaves, 2006, p. 8
[67] Goldstein, 2010c
[68] Givens & Friery, 2006
[69] Drucker, 1985, p. 309
[70] Spina, 2011
[71] Parks, 2001, p. 9
[72] Vann, 1999
[73] Dunham & Alpert, 2001, p. 205
[74] Robinson, 2008
[75] *Public Personnel Management*, 1998
[76] Sanz, 1995
[77] Associated Press, 2006a
[78] Palmiotto, 2001
[79] Goodman, 1998
[80] *Wikipedia*, 2007
[81] Dilanian, 2010
[82] *Violent Crime Control and Law Enforcement Act of 1994*
[83] Craig, 2009a; Craig, 2009c
[84] Weizel, 2008c
[85] Patterson, 2007
[86] Powell, 2007
[87] Gallup, Inc., 2008
[88] Harris Interactive, 2008, p. 10
[89] Miller & Hess, 1994, p. 72
[90] Scrivner, 2006, p. 1
[91] Hanna, 2011; MyFoxBoston.com, 2011; Reagle, 2009; Ryan, 2009
[92] *California Government Code* Section 1031 (d); Also see *Florida Law* Section 943.13(7)
[93] Goodman, 1998
[94] Biddle and Associates, Inc., 1978
[95] Taylor, Moersch, & McClure Franklin, 2003, p. 367

96 Walker, 1999, p. 304
97 Independent Commission on the Los Angeles Police Department, 1991, xvi
98 Independent Commission on the Los Angeles Police Department, 1991, xvi
99 Albanese, 2006, p. 80
100 Bolman & Deal, 1997, p. 123
101 Rostow, Davis, Levy, & Brecknock, 2001, p. 36
102 Skeel, 2006
103 Colaprete, 2005b, p. 160
104 Dantzker, 2003, p. 306
105 *Wikipedia*, 2009
106 Craig, 2009b
107 Trautman, 2009
108 Cooper, 2007
109 Souryal, 2003, p. 331
110 Eiserer, 2006a
111 Massad, 2006
112 Associated Press, 2004e; Daemmrich, 1993, Gottfredson, 1997; WOAI.com, 2010
113 United States Merit Systems Protection Board, 2005, p. 4
114 Chaiken & Cohen, 1972; Also see Aamodt & Flink, 2001 as cited in Aamodt, 2004, p. 7 and Abbatiello, 1969 as cited in Aamodt, 2004, p. 12
115 Kane & White, 2009
116 Parks, 2001, p. 10
117 Roberg, Kuykendall, & Novak, 2002, p. 128
118 Alpert & Dunham, 1997, p. 43
119 Vostock, 2009
120 Pfeiffer, 2009
121 Sinha, 2009
122 Isidore, 2010
123 Brosseau, 2008
124 Skeel, 2006
125 Colaprete, 2005b, p. 157
126 Ritch, 1997
127 Siegel, 2006, p. 19
128 Delattre, 1989, p. 121
129 Fyfe, Greene, Walsh, Wilson, & McLaren, 1997, p. 275
130 *Staffing Industry Review Magazine*, 2010
131 Brosseau, 2008
132 Sinha, 2009
133 de Geus, 1997, p. 112
134 Carlson, 2002, p. 116
135 Banks, 2004, p. 36
136 Time.Com, 1994
137 Hogarty, 2008
138 Taylor, Kubu, Fridell, Rees, Jordan, & Cheney, 2005
139 *Law and Order*, 2000a
140 Futty, 2007
141 Grant, 2007
142 Jelinek, 2011
143 Skeel, 2006
144 Narramore & Stephen, 1998
145 Dixon, 2008
146 Hogarty, 2008

[147] Forman, 2008
[148] Walton, 1986, p. 248
[149] Drucker, 1985, p. 310
[150] United States General Accounting Office, 1998, p. 16
[151] Moore & Stephens, 1991, p. 83
[152] Orrick, 2008
[153] Sinha, 2009
[154] Sanow, 2001
[155] Susan L. Sayles & James S. Albritton as cited in Sewell, 1999, pp. 154–171
[156] Williams, 2002, p. 86
[157] Elliot, 2010
[158] Tansey & Riordan, 1991
[159] Langworthy & Travis, 1994, p. 215
[160] Colaprete & Hardwich, 2007, p. 13
[161] Jurkiewicz, 2000
[162] Orrick, 2002, p. 100
[163] Delattre, 1989, p. 121
[164] Hogarty, 2008
[165] Colaprete, 2008
[166] Colaprete, 2006
[167] Schein, 1980, p. 21
[168] Wren, Clark, & Deriso, 2006; Also see, *Hanks v. Hubbard Broadcasting, Inc.* (1992); *Navaretta v. Group Health, Inc.* (1993); *Pearson v. Simmonds Precision Products, Inc.* (1993); *Stewart v. Jackson & Nash* (1992); *Toscano v. Greene Music* (2004)
[169] Barlow, 1993
[170] McKinney, 2004, p. 223
[171] *Cunningham v. Gates* (1997); Kay, 2004; Martinelli & Pollock, 2000
[172] Marion & Oliver. 2006, p. 333
[173] See *Tennessee v. Garner* (1985); *Graham v. Connor* (1989)
[174] McKinney, 2004, p. 223
[175] Schloss & Lahr, 2008, p. 50; Also see *Murdock v. Dinsmoor* (1989)
[176] Lynch, 1998, p. 193
[177] Dempsey & Forst, 2005, p. 99
[178] Ross, 2003, p. 95
[179] Smith, 2004
[180] Grant & Kemme, 1993b; Weizel, 2008f
[181] City of Auburn, Georgia Police Department, n.d., p. 9
[182] Sanow, 2001, p. 4
[183] Kappeler, 1995, p. 102
[184] Orrick, 2009, p. 46
[185] Muraskin & Roberts, 2009, p. 331
[186] Stamatis, 1996, p. 9
[187] Hammer, 1996, p. 240
[188] de Geus, 1997, p. 113
[189] Gilbert, 2001, p. 43

CHAPTER 2

[1] Peat, 2004, p. 20
[2] *Fraternal Order of Police v. Freeman* (1978)
[3] Hogg & Wilson, 1995, p. 5
[4] Koper, Maguire, & Moore, 2001, p. 42

[5] Taylor, Kubu, Fridell, Rees, Jordan, & Cheney, 2005
[6] Hulsey & Goodwin, 2001, p. 6
[7] United States Department of the Interior, 1998g
[8] Bing, Davison, & Arvey, 2009, p. 12
[9] Thomas, 2009
[10] Cascio, 2006, p. 236
[11] Milakovich & Gordon, 2007, p. 318
[12] Milakovich & Gordon, 2007, p. 318
[13] Geller, 1985, p. 395
[14] United States Department of the Interior, 1998g
[15] United States Department of the Interior, 1998g
[16] *Swearer v. Karoleski* (1989)
[17] *Law and Order*, 2000b
[18] Rafilson, 1999, p. 85
[19] Oliver, 2002, p. 68
[20] Strecher, 1997, p. 104
[21] Ohio Office of Criminal Justice Services, 2003
[22] Trattner, 1982, p. 384
[23] Phillips, 2005
[24] Bing, Davison, & Arvey, 2009, p. 13
[25] Rafilson, 1999
[26] Gendar, 2005
[27] Parks, 2001, p. 9
[28] *Buffalo News*, 1998
[29] Krause, 2010b
[30] Forman, 2008
[31] Trautman, 2009
[32] Gottfredson, 1997
[33] ABC.DaytonNewsSource.com, 2011; FoxNews.com, 2011a; FoxNews.com, 2011b; Sullivan, 2011a
[34] Axelrod, 2010; Baker, 2010; Fertoli, 2010; Marzulli, 2010b; NBCNewYork.com, 2010; Schmidt, 2010; *Washington Times*, 2011
[35] United States General Accounting Office, 1998, p. 16
[36] Bryant, 2010; Spielman & Main, 2010
[37] Bacque, 2010
[38] Gendar & Parascandola, 2011
[39] *Code of Federal Regulations* (2001a), Part 108, Sec. 108.33(b)(2) Quoted: "The investigation the criminal records check must not disclose that the individual has been convicted or found not guilty by reason of insanity, in any jurisdiction, during the 10 years ending on the date of such investigation, of any of the crimes listed below (See relevant section for specific crimes including, but not limited to murder, felony assault, kidnapping, rape, etc.)
[40] Whisenand & Ferguson, 2005, p. 217
[41] Purpura, 2001, p. 294
[42] *Davis v. City of Dallas* (1985)
[43] Cordner & Sheehan, 1999, p. 432
[44] Taylor, Kubu, Fridell, Rees, Jordan, & Cheney, 2005
[45] Farrell, 1998
[46] Nelson, 1999
[47] *McCarthy v. Philadelphia Civil Service Commission* (1976); Also see *Boston School Committee*, 3 MLC 1603 (1977), *Town of Lee,* 11 MLC 1274 (1984), and *City of Worcester*, 5 MLC 1414 (1978) for additional information regarding residency requirements
[48] Fyfe, Greene, Walsh, Wilson, & McLaren, 1997, p. 27

[49] California Commission on Peace Officer Standards and Training, 2009
[50] Tennessee Department of Commerce and Insurance, 2009
[51] Alabama Peace Officers Standards and Training Commission, 2009
[52] Wyoming Peace Officer Standards and Training, 2009
[53] Missouri Peace Officer Standards and Training, 2009
[54] Nevada Commission on Peace Officers' Standards and Training, 2009
[55] Texas Commission on Law Enforcement Officer Standards and Education, 2009a
[56] Oklahoma Council on Law Enforcement Education and Training, 2009
[57] Washington State Criminal Justice Training Commission, 2009
[58] New York State Department of Civil Service, 2006, p. 10
[59] New York State Department of Civil Service, 2006, p. 10
[60] Lundstrom & Stanton, 2009, B1
[61] Associated Press, 2003
[62] City of Auburn, Georgia Police Department, n.d.
[63] United States Department of Homeland Security Customs and Border Patrol, 2008
[64] *Code of Federal Regulations*
[65] *Code of Federal Regulations,* 2009
[66] *Code of Federal Regulations,* 2009
[67] *Code of Federal Regulations,* 2009
[68] Fishman & Brazytis, 2008, p. 3
[69] Washington State Patrol, n.d.a
[70] McCartney, 2005, p. 2
[71] Federal Bureau of Investigation, 2009a
[72] Federal Bureau of Investigation, 2009b
[73] South Carolina Highway Patrol, 2009
[74] Washoe County Sheriff's Office, 2009
[75] New Hampshire Department of Safety Division of State Police, 2010b
[76] Weldon, 2003
[77] Farley & Allotta, 1984
[78] Bradway, 1935, p. 6
[79] *The Aniston Star*, 2008
[80] *United States Department of State Foreign Affairs Manual* Volume 9—Visas, 9 FAM 40.21(a) N2.2 Defining "Moral Turpitude" (CT: VISA-753; 06-29-2005) p. 2
[81] *Itani v. Ashcroft* (2002); Also see *United States v. Gloria,* 494 F.2d 477, 481 (5th Cir.1974) (quoting *United States v. Smith,* 420 F.2d 428, 431 (5th Cir.1970) and *Black's Law Dictionary* 1160 (4th ed.1957).
[82] See *Matter of Ajami*, 22 I. & N. Dec. 949, 950 (BIA 1999)
[83] *Kellerman v. Holder* (2009)
[84] *Itani v. Ashcroft* (2002); Also see *Rodriguez-Herrera v. INS,* 52 F.3d 238, 239–40 (9th Cir.1995)
[85] Aspen, Mora, Goff, & Sweig, 1958, p. 148
[86] Kelly, 1991
[87] Chapman, 1970, p. 125
[88] Holt, 1993, p. 370
[89] Geller & Stephens, 2003, p. 362
[90] Biddle and Associates, Inc., 1978
[91] Bennett & Hess, 2004, p. 200
[92] United States Equal Employment Opportunity Commission (2010)
[93] Griffin, 1996, p. 391
[94] Bolman & Deal, 1997, p. 123
[95] Sanow, 2001, p. 4
[96] Decicco, 2000, p. 2
[97] Cohen, 1993, p. 222

98 Schein, 1980, p. 5
99 Wolf, 1999
100 Sharp, 2003, p. 83
101 Slowik, 2002
102 LaGrange, 1993, p. 249
103 Sacramento Police Department, n.d.
104 Moore & Stephens, 1991, p. 83
105 Robbins, 1995, p. 209
106 Walker, 1999, p. 306
107 Chaiken & Cohen, 1972
108 Oliver, 2002
109 Banks, 2004, p. 28
110 *Davis v. City of Dallas* (1985)
111 *Davis v. City of Dallas* (1985)
112 Janik, 1994
113 Taylor, Moersch, & McClure Franklin, 2003, p. 367
114 Lail & Kale, 2005
115 *Leonel v. American Airlines, Inc.* (2005)
116 Coutts, 1990
117 United States Equal Employment Opportunity Commission, 1978
118 Taylor, Kubu, Fridell, Rees, Jordan, & Cheney, 2005
119 American Psychological Association, 2009
120 Uniform Guidelines.com, n.d.
121 Sayles & Strauss, 1981, p. 185
122 Klein, n.d.
123 *Washington v. Davis* (1976), Footnote 13
124 *Watson v. Fort Worth Bank and Trust* (1988)
125 Trattner, 1982, p. 383
126 Associated Press, 2011k; Mayko, 2009
127 Strausberg, 2002
128 Aksamit. 2002
129 Washington State Patrol, n.d.c
130 Greenhouse, 2009
131 U. S. Newswire, 2005
132 Estes, 2004
133 Mills-Senn, 2007
134 Klein, n.d.
135 Katunich, 2005, p. 4
136 Logsdon, 2009
137 HR-Guide.com, 2001
138 Scroggins, Thomas, & Morris, 2008
139 Aamodt, 1997a
140 *Jordan v. City of New London* (1999)
141 Rachlin, 1997
142 Brandon & Lippman, 2000
143 Collingwood, Thomas, Means, & Hoffman, 2000, p. 164
144 Doyle, n.d.
145 Reintzell, 1997
146 O'Leary, 1976
147 Forsythe, 2004
148 Boynton Beach Police Department, n.d.
149 Siuru, 1999

[150] Rafilson, 2000
[151] Gotay, 2010, p. 33
[152] Washington State Patrol, n.d.b
[153] Timmins, 2005
[154] *Powell v. Reno* (1997)
[155] *Peanick v. Reno* (1995)
[156] *Lanning v. South Eastern Pennsylvania Transit Authority—SEPTA* (2002)
[157] Horne, 1999
[158] Carless, 2006
[159] *Americans with Disabilities Act of 1990*
[160] Ivancevich, 2007, p. 221
[161] New York State Department of Civil Service, 2006, p. 10
[162] Cappitelli, 2009, p. 16
[163] Kirksey & Smith, 1998, p. 65
[164] South Carolina Highway Patrol, 2009
[165] New Hampshire Department of Safety Division of State Police, 2010b
[166] Dempsey & Forst, 2005, p. 91
[167] South Carolina Highway Patrol, 2009
[168] New Hampshire Department of Safety Division of State Police, 2010b
[169] Peat, 2004, p. 20
[170] Brantner-Smith, 2009
[171] *Brown v. Benton* (1978)
[172] *Americans with Disabilities Act of 1990*
[173] *Americans with Disabilities Act of 1990*
[174] United States Department of Homeland Security Customs and Border Patrol, 2008
[175] Bennett & Hess, 2004, p. 202
[176] Cohen, 1993, p. 222
[177] Schein, 1980, p. 21
[178] Sokolove & Field, 2002, p. 55
[179] Griffin, 1996, p. 391
[180] Bennett & Hess, 2007, p. 51
[181] Becker, 2000, p. 197
[182] Geller & Stephens, 2003, p. 358
[183] Maheshwari, 1993
[184] Tersine & Jones, 1973
[185] Kast & Rosensweig, 1972
[186] Maheshwari, 1993
[187] Temponi, Bryant, & Fernandez, 2009
[188] Cusins, 1994
[189] Weizel, 2008e
[190] *Privacy Act of 1974*
[191] Hoffman, 2001, p. 191; Also see the *Privacy Act of 1974*, Sections (b)(7) and (b)(8)
[192] *Computer Security Law of 1987*
[193] *Federal Information Security Management Act of 2002*
[194] *Freedom of Information Law*
[195] McClain, 1978
[196] *Code of Federal Regulations*, 2009
[197] Title 5 of the *United States Code* [U.S.C.], Section 552
[198] United States Department of State, 2008, p. 3
[199] *Freedom of Information Law*
[200] New York State Department of State, 2009

[201] Stein, 1998
[202] *New York State Civil Rights Law* Section 50a—Right of Privacy
[203] *Quill*, 1999
[204] *Suppan v. Kratzer* (1995)
[205] *Quill*, 1995
[206] Scott, 2006b
[207] Weizel, 2008c
[208] United States Securities and Exchange Commission, 2007
[209] Weizel, 2008d
[210] King, 2007
[211] *Gold v. City of College Station* (2001)
[212] George, 2006
[213] Meeks, 2005
[214] United States Equal Employment Opportunity Commission, 1991, p. 7
[215] Scott, 2008
[216] *U. S. v. Virginia* (1998)
[217] Federal Acquisitions Regulations System, 2003
[218] *U. S. v. Virginia* (1998)
[219] Terhune, 2008
[220] Sullivan, 2006
[221] Burns, 2004
[222] Goliath, 2008
[223] Counts, 2010
[224] Anderson, 1991
[225] Herzog, 2001, p. 441
[226] United States Office of Personnel Management, n.d.
[227] Barney, 1997, p. 255
[228] Geller & Stephens, 2003, p. 361
[229] Barney, 1997, p. 383
[230] Drucker, 1985, p. 568
[231] Stamatis, 1996, p. 26
[232] Hersey, & Blanchard, 1988, p. 156
[233] Peters & Austin, 1985, p. 249
[234] Giuliani, 2002, p. 107
[235] United States Merit Systems Protection Board, 2005, p. 4
[236] Biggs, 2001, p. 2
[237] Peak, Evans, & Adams, 1998, p. 165
[238] International Association of Chiefs of Police, 1989, p. 5
[239] Lyman, 2002, p. 15
[240] Hess & Hess Orthmann, 2010, p. 9
[241] Danaher, 2003, p. 133
[242] Craig, 2009a; Craig, 2009c
[243] Peak, Evans, & Adams, 1998, p. 165
[244] 42 U.S. Code Section 12111(d) and 29 C.F.R. Section 1630.13(a); *Downs v. Massachusetts Bay Transportation Authority* (1998); *Evans v. Department of Homeland Security* (2007)
[245] Knox, 2010
[246] Harrington, n.d., p. 72
[247] Reilly, 2009; Also see *Nazir v. United Airlines, Inc.* (2009)
[248] *Carrisales v. Department of Corrections* (1998)
[249] Grant & Terry, 2005, p. 361
[250] Cohen & Chaiken, 1987, p. 2

251 Dantzker, 2003, p. 306
252 Lesce, 1998, p. 175
253 Garmire, 1982, p. 160
254 Grant & Terry, 2008, p. 355
255 *Civil Rights Act of 1964*; *United States Code*
256 Callahan, 1990
257 Independent Commission on the Los Angeles Police Department, 1991, xvi
258 Danaher, 2003, p. 134
259 Cawley, Miron, Araujo, Wasserman, Mannello, & Huffman, 1976, MM 95
260 Lyman, 2002, p. 14
261 Johnson, 2004
262 Colaprete, 2007
263 Marcum, 2005
264 Gove, 2004
265 Becker, 2000, p. 197
266 San Antonio Express-News, 2008
267 Moore, 2005
268 Kirksey & Smith, 1998, p. 66
269 Moore & Stephens, 1991, p. 67
270 Colaprete, 2002a
271 Cawley, Miron, Araujo, Wasserman, Mannello, & Huffman, 1976, MM 94
272 Galetta & Colaprete, 2010
273 Turner, 2000, p. 50
274 Geberth, 1998, p. 194
275 Holden, 2005, p. 652
276 Schneider & Somers, 2005
277 Lichtenstein & Plowman, 2009
278 Uhl-Bien, Marion, & McKelvey, 2007
279 Giuliani, 2002, p. 100
280 Howell & Costley, 2006, p. 3
281 Engel & Worden, 2003
282 Kotter, 1996, p. 6
283 Pritchett, 1992, p. 5
284 Erwin, 2009
285 Courtright & Smuddle, 2009
286 Goleman, Boyatzis, & McKee, 2002, p. 148
287 10News.com, 2010; Armon, 2010; Barboza & Winton, 2010; Collins, 2010; Fiedler, 2011; Liu, 2010; Queally & Friedman, 2010; Kmitch, 2010; Putney, 2011; Silver & McNulty, 2003; Wong, 2011; WoodTV.com, 2009; Zaniewski, 2010
288 Covey, 1992, p. 186
289 Orrick, 2008
290 Sutton, 2007
291 Hersey & Blanchard, 1988, p. 353
292 Oldham, 2003
293 Strauss, Tetroe, & Graham, 2009
294 Fahey & Burbridge, 2008
295 Templeton, Schmidt, & Taylor, 2009
296 Uhl-Bien, Marion, & McKelvey, 2007
297 Colaprete, 2004b
298 Drucker, 1985, p. 5
299 Dearing, 2009
300 Dearing, 2009

[301] Purpura, 2001, p. 94
[302] Ritch, 1997
[303] Sayles & Strauss, 1981, p. 175
[304] Peters & Austin, 1985, p. 115
[305] Zappe, 2009
[306] Barker, Hunter, & Rush, 1994, p. 289
[307] Barker, Hunter, & Rush, 1994, p. 289
[308] Hulsey & Goodwin, 2001, p. 6
[309] Bratton & Gold, 1999, p. 167
[310] Bratton & Gold, 1999, p. 166
[311] Holt, 1993, p. 374
[312] Holt, 1993, p. 377
[313] Bennett & Hess, 2004, p. 202
[314] Hesselbein & Cohen, 1999, p. 277
[315] Covey, 1992, p. 178
[316] Archbold, 2006, p. 61
[317] McMartin, 1981
[318] McMartin, 1981
[319] Archbold, 2006, p. 65
[320] Laudenslager, 1974
[321] Danning, 1999
[322] Laudenslager, 1974
[323] Thibault, Lynch, & McBride, 2004, p. 315
[324] Walker, 1998, p. 63
[325] Hersey & Blanchard, 1988, p. 156
[326] Volet, Vauras, & Salonen, 2009
[327] De Fruyt, Bockstaele, Taris, & Van Heil, 2006, p. 582
[328] Independent Commission on the Los Angeles Police Department, 1991, xvi
[329] Fuss & Snowden, 2004, p. 60
[330] Snowden & Fuss, 2000
[331] Colaprete, 2005a, p. 119
[332] *City of Canton v. Harris*. 489 US 378, 390 (1989)
[333] Dees, 1998, p. 14
[334] Colaprete, 2002b
[335] Singh & Abraham, 2008
[336] Howard, 1991
[337] Colaprete, 2003, p. 16
[338] Colaprete, 2004c
[339] Hundersmarck, 2009
[340] Pitts, Glensor, & Peak, 2007
[341] Massoni, 2009
[342] Matteucci, 2005
[343] Goodman, 1998
[344] Colaprete, 2004a
[345] McDonnell & Colaprete, 2010, p. 77
[346] Colaprete, 2009b
[347] Society for Human Resource Management Weblink: http://www.shrm.org/Pages/default.aspx
[348] Mid-Atlantic Personnel Assessment Consortium (MAPAC) Weblink: http://www.ipacweb.org/mapac/index.htm.
[349] National Association of Professional Background Screeners (NAPBS) Weblink: http://www.napbs.com/i4a/pages/index.cfm?pageid=1.

[350] Association of Certified Background Investigators (ACBI) Weblink: http://www.acbi.net/.
[351] California Background Investigators Association (CBIA) Weblink: http://www.scbia.com/.
[352] Bermes, 2008
[353] Gladis, 2007
[354] Tracy, 2007
[355] McCue & McNulty, 2003, p. 34
[356] Welsh & Harris, 2004, p. 5
[357] Cordner & Sheehan, 1999, p. 218
[358] Garmire, 1982, p. 40
[359] Soto, 1998a
[360] United States Department of Justice, 2001, p. 18
[361] Kappeler, 2001, p. 189
[362] Pollock, 2004, p. 369
[363] Zappe, 2009
[364] Anonymous, 2008b
[365] Lichtenstein & Plowman, 2009
[366] Kirksey & Smith, 1998, p. 66
[367] Hedeen, 2009
[368] Harrington, n.d., p. 73
[369] *Rhode Island General Law* Section 28-6.1-1
[370] McCartney, 2005, p. 7
[371] Kappeler, 2001, p. 192
[372] Commission on Accreditation for Law Enforcement Agencies, 2009a
[373] Oklahoma State Bureau of Investigation, 2009
[374] Commission on Accreditation for Law Enforcement Agencies, 2009b
[375] Virginia Law Enforcement Professional Standards Commission, 2008, p. 35
[376] Commission for Florida Law Enforcement Accreditation, Inc., 2009
[377] New York State Division of Criminal Justice Services Officer of Public Safety, 2002, p. 38
[378] Pennsylvania Law Enforcement Accreditation Commission, 2009, p. 15
[379] *Polygraph Protection Act of 1988*
[380] Washington Association of Sheriffs and Police Chiefs, 2007, p. 10
[381] *Rhode Island General Law* 28-6.1-1
[382] New York State Division of Criminal Justice Services Officer of Public Safety, 2002, p. 40
[383] Virginia Law Enforcement Professional Standards Commission, 2008, p. 35
[384] United States Equal Employment Opportunity Commission, 1991, p. 7
[385] Washington Association of Sheriffs and Police Chiefs, 2007, p. 10
[386] Commission for Florida Law Enforcement Accreditation, Inc., 2009
[387] Virginia Law Enforcement Professional Standards Commission, 2008, p. 35
[388] New York State Division of Criminal Justice Services Officer of Public Safety, 2002, p. 38
[389] Dees, 1998, p. 14
[390] Eiserer, 2009a
[391] Fuss & Snowden, 2004, p. 62
[392] Snowden & Fuss, 2000
[393] Scott, 2008
[394] van Buskirk, 2009
[395] Slahor, 2010, p. 10
[396] Stohr & Collins, 2009, p. 182
[397] Sonnenberg, 1994, p. 11
[398] Bolman & Deal, 1997, p. 117
[399] Orrick, 2008
[400] Thibault, Lynch, & McBride, 2004, p. 315

CHAPTER 3

[1] Kappeler, 2002, p. 7
[2] See *United States Bill of Rights* and *Fourteenth Amendment to the United States Constitution*
[3] Rostow, Davis, Levy, & Brecknock, 2001, p. 36
[4] *Enterprise Wire Company and Enterprise Independent Union* (1966)
[5] *Cleveland Board of Education v. Loudermill* (1985)
[6] Anonymous, 2009a; Sharp, 2009; Watson, 2011
[7] Ellington, 2006
[8] Bourne, 2006; *Tye v. Cincinnati* (1992)
[9] Wetterich, 2007
[10] Richter, 2007
[11] Viser, 2005
[12] Anonymous, 2005
[13] *Civil Rights Act of 1871*
[14] *Civil Rights Act of 1964*
[15] *Civil Rights Act of 1964*
[16] United States Equal Employment Opportunity Commission, n.d., Sections 703(d) and (e)
[17] United States Equal Employment Opportunity Commission, 2009a
[18] *Equal Employment Opportunity Act of 1972*
[19] *Crime Control Act of 1973*
[20] *Civil Rights Act of 1991*
[21] United States Department of Justice, 2008b
[22] *Pregnancy Discrimination Act*
[23] United States Equal Employment Opportunity Commission, 2009a
[24] United States Census Bureau (2008) Race data collection categories include: (a) White, (b) American Indian or Alaska Native, (c) Asian, (d) Hispanic or Latino, (e) Black or African American, (f) Native Hawaiian or Other Pacific Islander, and (g) Some Other Race.
[25] United States Equal Employment Opportunity Commission, 2009c
[26] *Fraternal Order of Police Newark Lodge 12 v. City of Newark* (1997)
[27] *Equal Pay Act of 1963*
[28] United States Equal Employment Opportunity Commission, 2009a
[29] *Griggs v. Duke Power* (1971)
[30] *Albemarle Paper v. Moody* (1975); Also see *Wards Cove Packing v. Antonio* (1989); *Civil Rights Act of 1991; EEOC v. Ford Motor Co. and United Automobile Workers of America* (2005)
[31] *EEOC v. Dial Corporation* (2006)
[32] *EEOC v. Daimler Chrysler Corporation* (2005)
[33] *Robinson v. Lorillard Corporation* (1971)
[34] *Commonwealth of Pennsylvania v. O'Neill* (1972)
[35] *Vanguard Justice Society v. Hughes* (1979)
[36] *Age Discrimination in Employment Act of 1967*; Also see *Reed v. Signode Corporation* (1986)
[37] United States Equal Employment Opportunity Commission, 2009a
[38] *Code of Federal Regulations* (2001b), Title 29, Sec. 1607.3
[39] *Code of Federal Regulations* (2001b), Title 29, Sec. 1607.11
[40] *Crawford v. Department of Homeland Security* (2007)
[41] *Drayton v. St. Petersburg* (1979)
[42] *Drayton v. St. Petersburg* (1979)
[43] Kansas University Medical Center, 2009
[44] Souryal, 2003, p. 267
[45] Scuro, 2004, p. 26

[46] Sherman, 2009; See *Ricci v. Destefano* (2009)
[47] Kinnard, 2009
[48] Chronicle of Higher Education, 2009
[49] Stohr & Collins, 2009, p. 226
[50] *Americans with Disabilities Act of 1990*
[51] Associated Press, 2000
[52] *The Employment Law Post*, 2010
[53] Klein, 2010
[54] Aamodt, 1997b
[55] *United States Code*
[56] *Title 42* of the *United States Code Section 1983*
[57] *Monroe v. Pape* (1961)
[58] *Monell v. New York City Department of Social Services* (1978); Also see *Allen v. Muskogee* (1997)
[59] *Cunningham v. Gates* (1997)
[60] Martinelli & Pollock, 2000
[61] *Owen v. City of Independence, Missouri* (1980)
[62] *Immigration Reform Control Act of 1986*
[63] *Homeland Security Act (HSA) of 2002*
[64] Janik, 1994
[65] Cornell University Law School Legal Information Institute Labor and Employment Laws Weblink: http://topics.law.cornell.edu/wex/table_labor.
[66] *New York State Civil Service Law* Article 58
[67] *Rhode Island General Law* Section 42-112-1
[68] *Rhode Island General Law* Section 28-5-3 and 28-5-5
[69] New York State Division of Human Rights, 2007
[70] New York State Division of Human Rights, 2007
[71] *New York State Human Rights Law* Section 296 1(a)
[72] Gatling, 2005
[73] Morris, 2008; Also see *SeaRiver Maritime, Inc. v. Industrial Medical Services, Inc.* (1989)
[74] Smith, 2004
[75] Payne, 2002, p. 6
[76] HR Briefing, 2001
[77] *Brown v. Youth Services of South Dakota, Inc.* (2000)
[78] Ingber, 1993
[79] Bach, 2006
[80] *Benson v. Northwest Airlines, Inc.* (1997); *Marquay v. Eno* (1995)
[81] *Ponticas v. K.M.S. Investments* (1983)
[82] *Hines v. Aandahl Construction Co. L.L.C.* (2006)
[83] Anonymous, 2006c
[84] McCord, 1999
[85] Sack, 1995
[86] Trial, 2003
[87] Levin, 2009
[88] Adler & Peirce, 1996; Mulligan, 1995; Novack, 1995
[89] Rosen, 2007, p. 4
[90] Alpert, 1989
[91] Dunham & Alpert, 2001, p. 191
[92] Miller & Fenton, 1991, p. 187
[93] *Stokes v. Bullins* (1988)
[94] Ferguson, 2003
[95] Martenegara & Kleiner, 2003; Meese & Ortmeier, 2004, p. 214

[96] Dorris & Kleiner, 2003
[97] O'Connor & Starks, 1999
[98] Hughes, 2000; Also see *Oakley v. Flor-Shin* (1998)
[99] Woska, 1991
[100] *City of Canton v. Harris* (1989)
[101] *Scott v. Blanchet High School* (1987)
[102] Sinclair-Bernadino, 2006
[103] Douris, 2006, p. 55
[104] Stokes, 2000
[105] Kamerick, 2010
[106] Besnoff & Cohen, 2007
[107] *Matt v. Pressley* (2006)
[108] Anonymous, 2006a; Anonymous, 2006c; Note: Also see *Boyd v. Fulton Terrace Associates. L.L.C.* (2006)
[109] Friel, 2009; Hand, 2011; Hedeen, 2009
[110] *McLean v. Kirby Co.* (1992); *Read v. The Scott Fertilizer Co.* (1998)
[111] Douris, 2006, p. 55
[112] McCord, 1999, p. 5
[113] Davies, 2003; Sinclair-Bernadino, 2006
[114] Besnoff & Cohen, 2007
[115] Grant & Kemme, 1993a
[116] Associated Press, 2011d
[117] *Parker v. Williams* (1988)
[118] Whisenand & Ferguson, 2005, p. 218
[119] Anonymous, 2004: See *Saine v. Comcast Cablevision of Arkansas Inc.* (2003)
[120] Barada, n.d.
[121] Means, 2007, p. 33
[122] *Aguillard v. McGowen* (2000); *Benavides v. County of Wilson* (1992); *Bohmfalk v. City of New Orleans* (1993); *Johnson v. Mers* (1996); *Kelly v. City of New York* (2005); *Longin v. Kelly* (1995); *Wassum v. City of Bellaire, Texas* (1988); *Young v. City of Dimmitt* (1989)
[123] *Texas Skaggs, Inc. v. Joannides* (1979); *Watson v. City of Hialeah* (1989); *Yunker v. Honeywell, Inc.* (1993)
[124] *Ahern v. Odyssey Re (London) Ltd.* (2001)
[125] *Allen v. City of Los Angeles* (1976); *Anderson Trucking Service, Inc. v. Gibson* (2004); *Board of County Commissioners of Bryan County, Oklahoma v. Brown* (1997); *Bonsignore v. City of New York* (1982); *Brittany v. Heather* (1989); *City of Canton v. Harris* (1989); *Gaines v. Monsanto* (1983); *Geidel v. Bradenton Beach* (1999); *Gurkin v. The Nurse Connection, Inc.* (2002); *J. v. Victory Tabernacle Baptist Church* (1988); *Lewis v. Goodie* (1992); *Monell v. New York City Department of Social Services* (1978); *Moon v. Winfield* (1974); *Owen v. City of Independence, Missouri* (1980); *Petrik v. New Hampshire Ins. Co.* (1979); *Phillips v. Edwin P. Stimpson Co., Inc.* (1991); *Southeastern Apartments Management, Inc. v. Jackman* (1999); *Thompson v. Chapel* (1997)
[126] *Abbott v. Payne* (1984); *Basel v. McFarland* (1999); *Carlsen v. Wackenhut Corporation* (1994); *Easley v. Apollo Detective Agency, Inc.* (1979); *Garcia v. Duffy* (1986); *Hardy v. Town of Hayneville* (1999); *Peters v. Bellinger* (1959); *Ponticas v. K.M.S. Investments* (1983); *Tallahassee Furniture Co., Inc. v. Harrison* (1991); *Welsh Manufacturing v. Pinkerton's, Inc.* (1984)
[127] Sinclair-Bernadino, 2006
[128] Goodz, 1999
[129] *Florida Statute* 768.096
[130] The Florida Senate, 2009; Jones, 2004
[131] Bowes & Kapsidelis, 2009
[132] *Parker v. District of Columbia* (1988)

[133] Kuzmits, Thacker, & Osbourn, 1991, p. 207; Also see *Alva Cape Alva Steamship Company v. City of New York* (1968); *Curley v. General Valet Service* (1973); *Williams v. Feather Sound, Inc.* (1980)
[134] *Battista v. Cannon* (1996)
[135] *Johnson v. Cannon* (1996)
[136] *Colon v. City of Newark* (2006)
[137] *McCrink v. City of New York* (1947)
[138] *Peck v. Siau* (1992)
[139] *Kenneth R. v. Roman Catholic Diocese* (1997)
[140] Barron, 2010
[141] Sager, 2010
[142] McCall, 2010
[143] *Ponticas v. K.M.S. Investments* (1983)
[144] *Ponticas v. K.M.S. Investments* (1983); Also see *Borden v. Capital District Transportation Authority* (2003) & *Detone v. Bullitt Courier Service, Inc.* (1988)
[145] *Alaska Employment Letter*, 2010
[146] Fenton, Kelley, Ruud, & Bulloch, 1997
[147] Duhart, 2001, p. 1
[148] *Occupational Safety and Health Act of 1970* Section 5, Duties, (a) (1)
[149] Schloss & Lahr, 2008, p. 49
[150] Ruud, 1997
[151] Title 42 Section 1983 of the *United States Code Section* 1983
[152] Hughes, 2000
[153] *Kitchen v. K-Mart Corporation* (1997), Section 390, Chattel for Use by Person Known to be Incompetent
[154] Anonymous, 2008a
[155] HR Briefing, 2001
[156] Weizel, 2009
[157] Mateja, 2004
[158] Rosner, Halcrow, & Levins, 2011
[159] USLegal.com, 2011b
[160] *Arnold v. City of San Antonio* (2009); *Battista v. Cannon* (1996); *Board of County Commissioners of Bryan County, Oklahoma v. Brown* (1997); *Johnson v. Cannon* (1996); *Williams v. Santana* (2009)
[161] *Aguillard v. McGowen* (2000); *Bohmfalk v. City of New Orleans* (1993); *Johnson v. Mers* (1996); *Longin v. Kelly* (1995); *Wassum v. City of Bellaire, Texas* (1988); *Young v. City of Dimmitt* (1989)
[162] Rosner, Halcrow, & Levins, 2011
[163] Winston, 2005, p. 4
[164] *Bardin v. Lockheed Aeronautical Systems Company* (1999)
[165] *Jensen v. Prudential Financial* (2005)
[166] *Ramos v. Equiserve* (2005)
[167] *Mahan v. Am-Gard, Inc.* (2003); *Mueller by Math v. Community Consolidated School District 54* (1989)
[168] *Cox v. Nasche* (1996)
[169] *McCleskey v. Vericon Resources, Inc.* (2003)
[170] *NASA v. Nelson* (2011)
[171] Givens & Friery, 2005
[172] *Young v. Providence* (2005)
[173] *Board of County Commissioners of Bryan County, Oklahoma v. Brown* (1997)
[174] *Harrington v. County of Suffolk* (2009)
[175] *Giglio v. United States* (1972)

[176] *Silva v. Lucky Stores* (1998)
[177] Weissberg, 1999; Also see *Allen v. Muskogee* (1997); *Leite v. Providence* (1978); *Monell v. New York City Department of Social Services* (1978); *Sewell v. Town of Lake Hamilton* (1998); *Walker v. New York* (1993); *Whitney v. Warden*
[178] *Simpson v. Western Graphics Corporation* (1982)
[179] *Casenas v. Fujisawa* (1997)
[180] Newbold, 2001; Spector, 1998; Also see *United States v. Agurs* (1976) and *Kyles v. Whitley* (1995)
[181] *Casenas v. Fujisawa* (1997); *Cotran v. Rollins Hudig Hall International, Inc.* (1998)

CHAPTER 4

[1] *Americans with Disabilities Act of 1990*
[2] *Americans with Disabilities Act of 1990*
[3] Litchford, 1993
[4] Woodford & Woodford, 2006
[5] United States Equal Employment Opportunity Commission, 2002
[6] United States Equal Employment Opportunity Commission, 2002
[7] United States Equal Employment Opportunity Commission, 2002
[8] United States Equal Employment Opportunity Commission, 2002
[9] United States Equal Employment Opportunity Commission, 1991, p. 2
[10] United States Equal Employment Opportunity Commission, 1991, p. 1
[11] United States Equal Employment Opportunity Commission, 2009a
[12] *Americans with Disabilities Act of 1990*
[13] *Rehabilitation Act of 1973*
[14] United States Department of Justice, 1997
[15] United States Department of Justice, 1997
[16] United States Department of Justice, 1997
[17] United States Equal Employment Opportunity Commission, 1991, p. 2
[18] United States Equal Employment Opportunity Commission, 1991, p. 14
[19] Bagley, 1995, p. 422
[20] Mook, 2002
[21] Barnes, Cleaveland, & Florencio, 2003
[22] United States Department of Justice Civil Rights Division Disability Rights Section, n.d.
[23] United States Equal Employment Opportunity Commission, 1997
[24] United States Department of Justice Civil Rights Division Disability Rights Section, n.d.
[25] Bruyere, 2002; Findlaw.com, 1999
[26] Kilberg, 2002
[27] *School Board of Nassau County, Florida v. Arline* (1987)
[28] United States Equal Employment Opportunity Commission, 1990, SEC. 12211. [Section 512]
[29] LePere, 2002
[30] Kochakian, 2008
[31] Colbridge, 2000, p. 15
[32] Levy, 1997b
[33] United States Equal Employment Opportunity Commission, 2002
[34] *Miller v. City of Springfield* (1999)
[35] United States Equal Employment Opportunity Commission, 2008; Also see *Americans with Disabilities Act Amendments Act of 2008*
[36] *Sutton v. United Airlines* (1999)
[37] *Murphy v. United Parcel Service, Inc.* (1999)
[38] *U.S. Airways v. Barnett* (2002)

[39] United States Equal Employment Opportunity Commission, 2008
[40] United States Equal Employment Opportunity Commission, 2008
[41] Kochakian, 2008
[42] Sherwyn, Eigen, & Klausner, 2000
[43] Hofmann, 2008
[44] Scuro, 2002, p. 16
[45] Tolle, 2007
[46] *Baltimore Business Journal*, 1997
[47] Levy, 1997a
[48] Perkins, 2003
[49] Litchford, 1993
[50] Fletcher, 1997
[51] United States Courts, n.d.c
[52] *Health Insurance Portability and Accountability Act of 1996*
[53] Kohn, 2004
[54] *Health Information Technology for Economic and Clinical Health Act*
[55] Covered Entities: A Justice Department ruling in 2005 severely limited the use of prosecutions for violating medical privacy laws to primarily include "covered entities." Consequently, those in other categories have been released from the criminal liability involved in records releases that do not fall within this category of care giver or records retention repository or system. Pear, 2005
[56] United States Department of Health and Human Services, 2009
[57] Tribble, 2001
[58] *Code of Federal Regulations* (2010). *Title 42: Chapter I—Public Health Service, Department of Health and Human Services, Subchapter A—General Provisions, Part 2—Confidentiality of Alcohol and Drug Abuse Patient Records, Subpart B-2.13, Confidentiality Restrictions, and Subpart C-2.31 Form of Written Consent and 2.33 Disclosures Permitted With Written Consent*
[59] *Information Management Journal*, 2009
[60] *Americans with Disabilities Act of 1990*
[61] *United States Code* Title 42 Chapter 126 Section 12101
[62] National Registry of Workers Compensation Specialists, n.d.b
[63] Rosen, 2010
[64] Rosen, 2010
[65] National Registry of Workers Compensation Specialists, n.d.b
[66] National Registry of Workers Compensation Specialists, n.d.a
[67] Also see *Bahr v. Council Bluffs C.S.C.* (1996)
[68] United States Equal Employment Opportunity Commission, 1991, p. 6
[69] Collins, 2003, Section 2: Hiring and Creating New Positions
[70] Mayer, 2009, p. 14
[71] Cochrane, Tett, & Vandecreek, 2003, p. 529; Also see *Barnes v. Cochran* (1996); *Barnes v. Broward County Sheriff's Office* (1999)
[72] Cappitelli, 2009, p. 16
[73] United States Department of Justice, 1997
[74] American Polygraph Association, 2009, Sections 3.4.1 and 3.4.2, p. 3
[75] American Polygraph Association, 2009, Section 3.4.3, p. 3
[76] Bryant, 2007
[77] Cawthorn, 2006
[78] Hulsey & Goodwin, 2001, p. 6
[79] *Leonel v. American Airlines, Inc.* (2005)
[80] Lail & Kale, 2005
[81] *Bragdon v. Abbott* (1998)

[82] Heinzl, 2001
[83] *Leonel v. American Airlines, Inc.* (2005)
[84] Colbridge, 2000, p. 19; United States Equal Employment Opportunity Commission, 1991, p. 6
[85] Joyce, 2007
[86] Collins, 2003, Section 2: Hiring and Creating New Positions; Also see *Allied Chemical Workers v. Pittsburgh Plate and Glass Co.* (1971)
[87] United States Equal Employment Opportunity Commission, 2000
[88] Slowik, 2005
[89] *Florida Law* Section 943.13(6)
[90] Robinson, Fisbone, & Daley, 1982
[91] Higginbotham, 1995
[92] Perry, 1994, p. 89
[93] Weizel, 2009
[94] United States Courts, n.d.b
[95] United States Equal Employment Opportunity Commission, 2000
[96] United States Equal Employment Opportunity Commission, 2000
[97] United States Equal Employment Opportunity Commission, 2000
[98] United States Equal Employment Opportunity Commission, 2000
[99] *Cremer v. Macomb* (1996)
[100] Zachary, 2001
[101] Washington State Patrol, n.d.c
[102] United States Department of Labor, 2000
[103] *Norman-Bloodsaw v. Lawrence Berkeley Laboratory* (1998)
[104] Benton, 2007
[105] *Genetic Information Nondiscrimination Act of 2008*
[106] Lopez, 1995
[107] Birch & Chisholm, 2008
[108] Carmean, 1998
[109] Owens, 1995
[110] Ruggles, 1998
[111] *DFEH v. City of Merced Police Department* (1988)
[112] *DFEH v. City of Merced Police Department* (1988)
[113] Woestendiek, 1993
[114] Goodman, 1993
[115] Lounsberry, 1992
[116] Medick, 1997
[117] Codispoti, 2005
[118] Owens, 1995
[119] Med-Tox Health Services, 1999
[120] Carmean, 1998
[121] Washoe County Sheriff's Office, 2009
[122] Washoe County Sheriff's Office, 2009
[123] Perry, 1994, p. 86
[124] Fletcher, 1997
[125] *Gensbauer v. The May Department Stores* (1999)
[126] National Methamphetamine Training and Technical Assistance Center, 2009
[127] Hananel, 2010
[128] Maer, 2010
[129] Roberg, Kuykendall, & Novak, 2002, p. 129
[130] Sharp, 2003, p. 83
[131] Esler, 2007; Kovaleski, 2008; Zeleny, 2007
[132] Paybarah, 2008

[133] Messner, 1981
[134] Linskey, 2010
[135] Hakim & Rashbaum, 2008
[136] Gonzales, 2008
[137] *The New York Times*, 2009
[138] Pew Research Center for the People and the Press, 1998
[139] Braibanti, 1962
[140] Grant, 2007
[141] Hewett, 2004
[142] Rives, 2001
[143] Osterloh & Becker, 1990
[144] Young, 2000
[145] Hodes, 1990
[146] Drummer, Gerostamoulos, Chu, Swann, Boorman, & Cairns, 2007
[147] Hagan, 2001
[148] National Institute of Health, n.d.a
[149] National Institute of Health, n.d.b
[150] Carraher, 1991
[151] *Drug-Free Workplace Act* of *1988*
[152] Deming, 1990
[153] Young, 2000
[154] United States Department of Transportation, 2009
[155] Hagan, 2001
[156] Sharp, 2004
[157] Roberg, Novak, & Cordner, 2005, p. 189
[158] Schmalleger, 2007, p. 297
[159] Lehman, Farabee, Holcom, & Simpson, 1995
[160] Fendrich & Kim, 2002
[161] Osterloh & Becker, 1990
[162] United States Department Drug Enforcement Administration, n.d.; Also see *Controlled Substances Act of 1970*
[163] Wefing, 2000
[164] United States Equal Employment Opportunity Commission, 1991, p. 7; United States Equal Employment Opportunity Commission (2000
[165] Disability and Technical Business Assistance Centers, 1992, Section 8.3
[166] United States Department of Justice, 1997
[167] United States Department of Justice, 1997
[168] United States Equal Employment Opportunity Commission, 2002
[169] *Skinner v. Railway Labor Executives Association* (1989); Also see: *National Treasury Employees Union v. Von Raab* (1989) & *Gonzales v. Metropolitan Transportation Authority E* (1999)
[170] *Buckley v. Consolidated Edison of New York, Inc.* (1998); Colbridge, 2000, p. 19
[171] *NASA v. Nelson* (2011)
[172] *Shield Club v. City of Cleveland* (1986)
[173] Murphy & Barlow, 1994
[174] *Willis v. Roche Biomedical Laboratories, Inc.* (1995)
[175] *Ishikawa v. Delta Airlines* (2003)
[176] Slowik, 2002
[177] United States Department of Justice, 1997
[178] United States Department of Justice, 1997
[179] United States Coast Guard, 2010
[180] TestCountry.org, 2011

[181] Kuntz, n.d.
[182] CollegeGrad.com, 2009—Provided by QuinStreet, Inc.
[183] Dolan, 2011; ESPN.com, 2004; Williams, 2011
[184] Brennan, Kanayama, Hudson, & Pope, 2011
[185] Buckley, Yesalis, Friedl, Anderson, Streit, & Wright, 1988; Livingstone, 2005; MSNBC.com, 2008; NPR.org. 2007; Weaver, 2005
[186] National Drug Intelligence Center, 2005
[187] Denham, 2009
[188] *Anabolic Steroids Control Act of 1990*; *Controlled Substances Act of 1970*
[189] United States Department of Justice Drug Enforcement Administration Office of Diversion Control, 2004
[190] National Drug Intelligence Center, 2005; Also see the *Anabolic Steroids Control Act of 2004*
[191] United States Department of Justice Drug Enforcement Administration Office of Diversion Control, 2004
[192] Kraska, Bussard, & Brent, 2010, p. 177
[193] Beam & Leach, 2005
[194] Brittain & Mueller, 2010; Cramer, 2009a; Dwyer, 2009
[195] Erdely, 2005
[196] Gillis, 2008
[197] Baker, 2008
[198] Parascandola, 2007; Parascandola, 2010a
[199] 13wham.com, 2011; Ali, 2011; Cassi, 2010; LaDuca, 2010; Morgan, 2005; Potts, 2010
[200] Dailey & Erdely, 2005
[201] Poe, 2005
[202] Papacosta & Nassis, 2011
[203] McDevitt, 2007
[204] Beam & Leach, 2005
[205] Colaprete, 2005b
[206] Hamid, Deren, Beardsley, & Tortu, 1999
[207] Magura, Sung-Yeon, & Shapiro, 1995
[208] Mieczkowski, 1995
[209] American Journal of Trial Advocacy, 1988
[210] Ozminkowski, Mark, Goetzel, Blank, Walsh, & Cangianelli, 2003
[211] Riley, Lu, & Taylor, 2000
[212] Gibson & Manley, 1991
[213] Mieczkowski, Newel, & Wraight, 1998
[214] Wong, Tran, & Tung, 2005
[215] Drummer, 2006
[216] Cone, 1993
[217] Cholakis & Bruce, 2007, p. 34
[218] Cholakis & Bruce, 2007, p. 33
[219] Dyer & Wilkinson, 2008
[220] Bosker & Huestis, 2009; Jenkins, Oyler, & Cone, 1995
[221] Townsend, Fanning, & O'Kennedy, 2008
[222] Lillsunde, 2008
[223] Kintz & Samyn, 2002
[224] Klinzig, Vinner, Brassart, Houdain, Humbert, & Lhermitte, 2007
[225] Lewis, 2005b; Psychemedics Corporation, 2007
[226] Mieczkowski, 1995
[227] Srogi, 2006
[228] Mieczkowski, 1997
[229] Baker, 2009; Rouen, & Kimber, 2004

[230] Mieczkowski, Newel, & Wraight, 1998
[231] Magura, Sung-Yeon, & Shapiro, 1995
[232] Mieczkowski, 1997
[233] Lewis, 2005b
[234] Mieczkowski & Newel, 1993b
[235] Mieczkowski, Lersch, & Kruger, 2002
[236] Polla, Stramesi, Pichini, Palmi, Vignali, & Dall'Olio, 2009
[237] NorthCountryGazette.org, 2007
[238] Baker, 2009
[239] Inciardi & Cicero, 2009
[240] Byrne, Lander, & Ferris, 2009
[241] Wartell & La Vigne, 2004, p. 1
[242] Schneider, Bailey, Cicero, Dart, Inciardi, Parrino, & Munoz, 2009
[243] Tetrault, Desai, Becker, Fiellin, Concato, & Sullivan, 2008
[244] McCabe, Cranford, & West, 2008
[245] McCabe, 2008
[246] Office of National Drug Control Policy, 2007; Manchikanti, 2007
[247] Havens, Ocer, Leukefeld, Webster, Martin, O'Connell, Surratt, & Inciardi, 2007
[248] Riggs, 2008
[249] Ford & Schroeder, 2009
[250] Hamilton, 2009
[251] Butler, Fernandez, Chang, Benoit, Morey, Black, & Katz, 2010; Office of National Drug Control Policy, 2007
[252] Lessenger & Feinberg, 2008; Mendelson, Flower, Pletcher, & Galloway, 2008
[253] McCabe, 2007
[254] Ford, 2008; Harrell & Broman, 2009
[255] Tetrault, Desai, Becker, Fiellin, Concato, & Sullivan, 2008
[256] Green, Grimes, Licari, Budman, & Butler, 2009; Office of National Drug Control Policy, 2007
[257] Lessenger & Feinberg, 2008
[258] Goldsworthy, Schwartz, & Mayhorn, 2008
[259] *Roe v. Cheyenne Mountain Conference Resort, Inc.* (1997)
[260] *Krocka v. Branfield* (1997)
[261] Mieczkowski & Newel, 1993a
[262] CollegeGrad.com, 2009—Provided by QuinStreet, Inc.
[263] O'Keefe, 1987
[264] Miller, 2007
[265] Crawford, 2004
[266] Biermann, Schwarze, Zedler, & Betz, 2004
[267] Brown University, 2007
[268] CollegeGrad.com, 2009—Provided by QuinStreet, Inc.
[269] Barnum & Gleason, 1994
[270] *American Journal of Trial Advocacy*, 1988
[271] *Cutler v. Quality Terminal Services, LLC* (2008); Tanner, 2010
[272] Osterloh & Becker, 1990
[273] Mason, 1998
[274] Biermann, Schwarze, Zedler, & Betz, 2004
[275] Crawford & Haberfield, 2005
[276] Drury & Masci, 1999
[277] Cholakis & Bruce, 2007, p. 32; Jaffee, Trucco, Levy, & Weiss, 2007; Poe, 2005
[278] Rives, 2001
[279] Brown University, 2007
[280] Wu, Bristol, Sexton, Cassella-McLane, Holtman, & Hill, 1999

[281] Dasgupta, Wahed, & Wells, 2002
[282] Dasgupta, 2003
[283] Dasgupta, Wahed, & Wells, 2002
[284] Johnston, Michaud, & Warner, 2009
[285] Lewis, 2005b
[286] Miller, 2007
[287] Sagall, 2005
[288] Murphy & Barlow, 1994
[289] Munsey, 2002
[290] Anderson, 2005
[291] Dolan, Rouen, & Kimber, 2004
[292] Montagna, Stramesi, Vignali, Groppi, & Polettini, 2000
[293] Millhorn, Monaghan, Montero, Reyes, Roman, Tollasken, & Walls, 2009
[294] Saunders, 2009
[295] Hall & Degenhardt, 2003
[296] McGreevy, 2010; Smith, 2010b
[297] Manderson, 1999
[298] Welchand & Leinwand, 2010
[299] Schaper, 2006; Sulzberger & Medina, 2011
[300] Scherwell, 2010
[301] Brown, 2010
[302] *Wikipedia*, 2011c
[303] Kershaw & Cathcart, 2009
[304] Taylor, 1998
[305] United States Food and Drug Administration, 2006
[306] United States Food and Drug Administration, 2006
[307] United States Food and Drug Administration, 2006
[308] Cohen, 2009
[309] DuPont, 1999
[310] Young, 2011a
[311] *United States v. Lopez* (1995); *United States v. Morrison* (2000)
[312] *Gonzales v. Raich* (2005)
[313] Hertzberg, 2005
[314] Newbern, 2000; Also see *Controlled Substances Act of 1970*
[315] Christenson, 2004; Szalavitz, 2011
[316] Pacula, Chriqui, Reichmann, & Terry-McElrath, 2002
[317] Martinez, 2011; *New York Times*, 2011; ProCon.org, 2010
[318] Associated Press, 2011j
[319] Freeman, 2011; Martinez, 2011c
[320] O'Connell & Bou-Mattar, 2007
[321] *California Health and Safety Code, HS 11362.5*
[322] *Compassionate Use Act of 1996*
[323] *California Health and Safety Code, HS 11362.5 (A)*
[324] O'Connell & Bou-Mattar, 2007
[325] *California Health and Safety Code, HS 11362.5 (B)*
[326] Johnson, 2011b
[327] Urie & Meltzer, 2011
[328] Welchand & Leinwand, 2010
[329] Leff & Wohlsen, 2010
[330] *California Health and Safety Code, HS 11362.5 (2)*
[331] *The Police Chief Magazine*, 2009
[332] *Davis v. City of Dallas* (1985)

[333] *City of Canton v. Harris* (1989)
[334] *Ross v. RagingWire Telecommunications, Inc.* (2008)
[335] *Ross v. RagingWire Telecommunications, Inc.* (2008)
[336] *Ross v. RagingWire Telecommunications, Inc.* (2008); *Compassionate Use Act of 1996*
[337] Koppel, 2011
[338] Agar, 2011
[339] Tahmincioglu, 2010
[340] Tahmincioglu, 2010
[341] Sharp, 2003, p. 84
[342] Sharp, 2003, p. 82
[343] Sharp, 2003, p. 81
[344] Kohn, 2003
[345] Bouchard & Bacque Dion, 2006
[346] Gail, 2009
[347] Buckhalter, 2008
[348] Grimm, 2008
[349] Seef, 2011b
[350] Man, Stoeber, & Walus, 2009
[351] Maxwell & Rutkowski, 2008
[352] Lineberry & Bostwick, 2006
[353] Washington State law proscribes the selling of a counterfeit controlled substance and the charge is a C Felony under the statute. Washington State Legislature RCW 69.50.410
[354] Michigan Courts (2010) Offense Variables for Crimes Involving a Controlled Substance; *Nebraska Code* Chapter 28-Crimes and Punishment Section 28-416-Prohibited Acts; Violations; Penalties; Onecle (2006, November 21). *Florida Crimes Code Section 831.31—Forgery And Counterfeiting—Counterfeit Controlled Substance; Sale, Manufacture, Delivery, or Possession with Intent to Sell, Manufacture, or Deliver*; *Unconsolidated Pennsylvania Statutes* Title 35: Health and Safety Drugs, Poisons, And Dangerous Substances Controlled Substance, Drug, Device, and Cosmetic Act Section 780-113
[355] Lutter, 2005
[356] Gaines, Kappeler, & Vaughn, 1999, p. 125
[357] *National Prohibition Act of 1920* (*Volstead Act*)
[358] *Americans with Disabilities Act of 1990*
[359] United States Department of Justice, 1997
[360] Disability and Technical Business Assistance Centers, 1992
[361] United States Equal Employment Opportunity Commission, 2002
[362] *Bailey v. Georgia Pacific Corporation* (2002)
[363] Tetrault, Desai, Becker, Fiellin, Concato, & Sullivan, 2008
[364] Osofsky, Dralle, & Greenleaf, 2001, p. 42
[365] Scuro, 2001, p. 22
[366] Bercaw, 2002, p. 135
[367] Holusha, 2007
[368] Williams, 2002, p. 87
[369] Fitch, 2011, p. 24
[370] Irving, Ponsi, Hardesty, Salazar, Carpenter, Welborn, & Jolly, 2011
[371] Associated Press, 2009c
[372] Keyes, 2011
[373] Reaume, 2009, p. 20
[374] Associated Press, 2004a
[375] Grabell, 2008
[376] Times Online, 2007
[377] Cochrane, Tett, & Vandecreek, 2003

[378] Jones, Hyams, & Wessely, 2003
[379] Mills-Senn, 2007
[380] Janik, 1994
[381] OurAlheimer's.com, 2006
[382] Grant & Terry, 2005, p. 362
[383] Wambaugh, 2002, pp. 23–29
[384] *Diagnostic and Statistical Manual of Mental Disorders* (DSM-IV) (1994)
[385] Herrmann, Durante, & Ford, 2001
[386] Eber, 2004
[387] Holzman & Kirschner, 2003 p. 87
[388] Wolf, 1999
[389] Scrivner, 1994
[390] Holzman & Kirschner, 2003 p. 85
[391] Langworthy & Travis, 1994, p. 230
[392] Claussen-Rogers & Arrigo, 2005, p. 4
[393] Lee, 2006
[394] Curran, 1998, p. 92
[395] Black, 1994; Doyle, n.d.; Tawney, 2008, p. 34
[396] Goldman, 2009; Lewis, 2005a; Mello, 1995
[397] Birkman-Fink, 2009; Doyle, n.d.; Krajewski & Goffin, 2009
[398] Purpura, 2001, p. 95
[399] Detrick & Chibnall, 2002
[400] Hargrave & Hiatt, 1989
[401] Arnold & Thiemann, 1992
[402] United States Equal Employment Opportunity Commission, 2000
[403] United States Department of Justice, 2001, p. 19
[404] *Hayden v. County of Nassau* (1998)
[405] Ryan, Ployhart, & Friedel, 1998
[406] Coutts, 1990; Blinkhorn & Johnson, 1990; Epstein, 2008
[407] Miller & Barrett, 2008
[408] Harland, Rauzi, & Biasotto, 1995; Rosse, Ringer, & Miller, 1996
[409] Dietz, 1995; Katunich, 2005, p. 4
[410] United States Equal Employment Opportunity Commission, 2000
[411] MacKay, 2009
[412] Hood, 2009; Smith, McCarthy, & Zapolski, 2009,
[413] Black, 2000 as cited in Aamodt, 2004, p. 37
[414] *Wikipedia*, 2010a
[415] Super, 2006
[416] Inwald, 1988
[417] Hustmyre, 2002, p. 81
[418] Curran, 1998
[419] Janik, 1995
[420] Clark, Olson, Porter, & Leichner, 2001, p. 31
[421] Lee, 2006
[422] Osofsky, Dralle, & Greenleaf, 2001, p. 42
[423] Janik, 1995
[424] Inwald, 1988
[425] *Denhof, et al. v. City of Grand Rapids* (2005); Also see *City of New York v. New York Division of Human Rights* (1997)
[426] *Coleman v. N.Y.* (2007)
[427] *Bennett v. County of Suffolk* (1998)
[428] *Karraker v. Rent-A-Center* (2005); Lewis, 2005a; Also see *Staples v. Rent-A-Center* (2000)

[429] See *Bryan v. City of Des Moines* (1978); *Patch v. Civil Service Commission of Des Moines* (1980)
[430] *Police Benevolent Association Local 319 v. Township of Plainsboro* (1998)
[431] *Herman v. Commonwealth Department of General Services* (1984)
[432] *City of Boston v. Boston Police Patrolmen's Association* (1979)
[433] *Kraft v. Police Commissioner of Boston* (1995)
[434] *Burge v. City of Dover, Kent County Chan. Ct.* (1993)
[435] *Tingler v. City of Tampa* (1981)
[436] *Joseph v. Salt Lake City* (2003)
[437] *Wertz v. Wilson* (1997)
[438] *Sienkiewicz v. County of Santa Cruz* (1987)
[439] *Redmond v. City of Overland Park* (1987)
[440] *Wilson v. City of Baton Rouge* (2009)
[441] *Benningfield v. City of Houston* (1998)
[442] *Benningfield v. City of Houston* (1998)
[443] *Dodd v. Septa* (2007)
[444] *Air Force, 437 Wing and AFGE L-1869* (2000); *Conte v. Horcher* (1977); *Flynn v. Sandahl* (1995); *Haynes v. Police Board of Chicago* (1997); *Kansas City Kansas Police and FOP Lodge 4* (1988)
[445] *City of Overland Park* (1987); *Haynes v. Police Board of Chicago* (1997); *Thomas v. Corwin* (2007)
[446] *Merillat v. Michigan State University* (1995)
[447] *Caver et al. v. City of Trenton* (2005)
[448] *Galas v. Ward* (1990)
[449] *Reynolds v. Arizona* (1993)
[450] United States Equal Employment Opportunity Commission, 1997
[451] See *Albury v. New York City Civil Service Commission* (1969); *Anastasia Vey, In re* (1994); *Daley v. Koch* (1989); *Going v. Kennedy* (1958); *Greenberg v. New York Department of Correctional Services* (1997); *Howard v. City of Southfield* (1996); *Jachyra v. City of Southfield* (1996); *Jones v. Wittenberg University* (1976); *Klotsche v. City of New York* (1985); *McCabe v. Hoberman* (1969); *Nilsson v. City of Mesa* (2007); *Stearns v. Gilchrist* (1976); *Strauss v. Hannig* (1939); *Thomasson v. Valentine* (1942)
[452] *McKenna v. Fargo* (1978)
[453] *Bonsignore v. City of New York* (1982); Also see *Bell v. City of Miami* (1990)
[454] Parks, 2001, p. 311
[455] *Neumerski v. Califano* (1981); *Nolan v. Police Commissioner of Boston* (1981); *Shirsat v. Mutual Pharmaceutical* (1996)
[456] See *Jaffee v. Redmond* (1996); *Koch v. Cox* (2007); *Koch v. Stanard* (1992); *Mason v. Stock* (1994); *Valentin v. Bootes* (1998); *Williams v. District of Columbia* (1997)
[457] See *Childs v. Williams, Ph.D.* (1992); *Cremer v. Macomb Board of Fire and Police Commissioners* (1994); *Greenawalt v. Indiana Department of Corrections* (2005); *J.N. v. Bellingham School District* (1994); *Miller v. Pancucci* (1992); *Ring v. Fox* (1977); *Seigfried v. City of Easton* (1992)
[458] Bercaw, 2002, p. 132
[459] Carl Hawkins as cited in Amendola, Hawkins, Nicoletti, Scrivner, & Maltarese, 2008
[460] *Bopp v. Institute for Forensic Psychology* (1997)
[461] *Federal Rules of Evidence* Section 702
[462] *Frye v. United States* (1923)
[463] *Daubert v. Merrell Dow Chemicals, Inc.* (1993)
[464] *Kumho Tire Co. v. Carmichael* (1999)
[465] *General Electric Co. v. Joiner* (1997)
[466] *Federal Rules of Evidence*

[467] *Matter of Murray v. County of Nassau Civil Service Commission* (2007)
[468] Craig & McDermott, 2010; Doorley, 2010
[469] Lee, 2006
[470] Craig & McDermott, 2010
[471] See *Americans with Disabilities Act of 1990*; *Health Insurance Portability and Accountability Act of 1996*; *Health Information Technology for Economic and Clinical Health Act* (HITECH Act); Wilson, 2009; Also, refer to your own state laws of medical and psychological records privacy
[472] Wilson, 2010b
[473] *Americans with Disabilities Act of 1990*
[474] *City of Haverhill,* 16 MLC 1077 (1989)
[475] *The City of New York et al., v. The Patrolmen's Benevolent Association of the City of New York, Inc. et al., and The Sergeants' Benevolent Association of the City of York et al.* (2009)

CHAPTER 5

[1] New York State Division of Criminal Justice Services Bureau for Municipal Police, 1991, p. 4.1.2
[2] Osterburg & Ward, 2004, p. 5
[3] O'Hara & O'Hara, 1981, p. 5
[4] Adams, Caddell, & Krutsinger, 2004, p. 5
[5] Gilbert, 2001, p. 38
[6] 13wham.com, 2009
[7] Biggs, 2001, p. 3
[8] New York State Division of Criminal Justice Services, 1991, p. 18
[9] Osterburg & Ward, 2004
[10] Mauriello, 2003, p. 1-1
[11] Cohen & Chaiken, 1987, p. 1
[12] Mauriello, 2003, p. 1-1
[13] Gilbert, 2001, p. 36
[14] Bartlett, 2005
[15] Beagrie, 2004
[16] Bezemer & Kress, 2008
[17] Crainer & Dearlove, 2004
[18] Gillan, 2010
[19] Crawford, 2009
[20] Ottesen, 2008
[21] Brecher, 2010
[22] Kedem, 2005
[23] Collins, 2005
[24] Miller & Lehr, 2007
[25] Landale, 2006
[26] Capelluti, 2004
[27] Marken, 2006
[28] Shepherd & Kori, 2005
[29] O'Hara & O'Hara, 1981, p. 31; Szczesny, 2002, p. 126
[30] Kabel & Frost, 2008
[31] Ashton, 2004
[32] Dreyfack, 2004
[33] Hess & Hess Orthmann, 2010, p. 72
[34] Mulkeen, 2008
[35] Zuk, 2009

[36] O'Quinn, 2004
[37] Mulkeen, 2008
[38] Baron, 2007
[39] Smith, 2009b
[40] Osterburg & Ward, 2004, p. 155
[41] Missouri State Highway Patrol Human Resources Division, 2009
[42] For guidance see *Federal Rules of Evidence*: Rule 802. Hearsay Rule; Rule 803. Hearsay Exceptions: Availability of Declarant Immaterial; Rule 804. Hearsay Exceptions; Declarant Unavailable; Rule 805. Hearsay Within Hearsay; Rule 901. Requirement of Authentication or Identification Rule 902. Self-Authentication; Article; X. Contents of Writings, Recordings, and Photographs, Rule 1001. Definitions; Rule 1002. Requirement of Original; Rule 1003. Admissibility of Duplicates; Rule 1004. Admissibility of Other Evidence of Contents; Rule 1005. Public Records; Rule 1006. Summaries; Rule 1007. Testimony or Written Admission of Party; Also see for an example the *California Evidence Code* Sections 1520–1523
[43] Givens & Friery, 2005
[44] Snyder, 1996
[45] Allen, 2007
[46] O'Callahan, 2006; Parrish, 2007; Villano, 2006
[47] Kamerick, 2010
[48] Burden, 2010; CareerExcuse.com, 2009–2010; FakeResume.com, n.d.; Winter, 2010a
[49] Brain, 2011; Guthrie, 2009; Sabatini, 2006; Tuna & Weinstein, 2008; Venugopal, 2009
[50] Patel, 2009
[51] Katzanek, 2010; Marquet International Ltd., 2006–2011; UND.com, 2001; Weiss, 2011
[52] Shulman, 2009
[53] Marquet & Peterson, n.d.
[54] Bliss, 2008
[55] Zeidner, 2007
[56] HumanResourcesCompany.net, 2009
[57] Bliss, 2008; McMullen, 2008; Katzanek, 2010
[58] Walzer, 2007
[59] Shumaker, 2003
[60] See *Angelopoulos v. New York Civil Service Commission* (1991); *Aubuchon v. Knauf* (2004); *Bi-State Development Agency and Amalgamated Transit Union* (2008); *Brennan v. Kaluczky* (1996); *Christopher v. Department of the Army* (2008); *Crawford Rehabilitation v. Weisman* (1997); *Gaston v. State of New Jersey* (2008); *Gray v. Department of Personnel* (1994); *Kosan v. Utah Department of Corrections* (2008); *Milligan-Jensen v. Michigan Technological University* (1992); *Philbrick v. County of Volusia* (1996); *Puckett v. City of San Francisco* (1962); *Purdy v. Cole* (1975); *Smart v. Geren* (2008); *Wolfbauer v. Office of Personnel Management* (2008)
[61] See *Falls Church Construction v. Laidler (1997); FitzGerald v. Department of Homeland Security (2008); Kristufek v. Hussman Foodservice Company (1993); Perez v. U.S. Postal Service (1993); Thomlinson v. Omaha (1995)*
[62] *Cameron v. Department of Justice* (2004)
[63] *Code of Federal Regulations*, 2009
[64] *Digital Signature Act of 1999*
[65] PR Web, 2009
[66] Ellingsen, 2009; Also see the *Immigration Reform and Control Act of 1986*
[67] *Intelligence Report and Terrorism Prevention Act of 2004*; *Payroll Practitioner's Monthly*, 2006
[68] *The Federal Register*, 2009
[69] Sharon, 2007
[70] *Payroll Manager's Letter*, 2005b

71 Anonymous, 2009c
72 *Payroll Manager's Letter*, 2005a
73 Swartz, 2005; Also see the *Immigration and Nationality Act*
74 Anonymous, 2008d
75 Anonymous, 2008c
76 Krause, 2010a
77 Klein, 2010; Smith, 2009a
78 Reed, 2009
79 United States Citizenship and Immigration Services, 2009
80 *Illegal Immigration Reform and Immigrant Responsibility Act of 1996; Payroll Manager's Report*, 2008; *Payroll Manager's Letter*, 2009
81 Adams, 2009
82 Truesdell, 2009
83 *The Federal Register*, 2008; Nitz, 2009
84 Wilson, 2009
85 Decicco, 2000, p. 3
86 Harlan & Mueller, 1992; Kohls & Luke, 1977
87 Fuss, McSheehy, & Snowden, 1998, p. 172; Nelson, 2000, p. 85
88 Dash, 1990
89 City of Auburn, Maine Police Department, 2009; Town of Irondequoit, New York Police Department, 2011
90 Dash, 1990
91 Dudley, 1974
92 Wollack, Waibel, & Guenther, Inc., 1977
93 Adams, 2000
94 *McCleskey v. Vericon Resources, Inc.* (2003)
95 *Cox v. Nasche* (1996)
96 City of Auburn, Georgia Police Department, n.d., p. 9
97 Boyer, 2011a; Henry, 2010
98 Missouri State Highway Patrol, 2007b
99 Federal Bureau of Investigation, 2010b
100 Federal Bureau of Investigation, 2010c
101 Fingerprint Technologies, 2009; New Hampshire Department of Safety Division of State Police, 2010a; New York Fingerprinting Service, 2008–2009; Office of the Attorney General of the State of California, 2010
102 United States Department of Justice Bureau of Justice Statistics, 2009
103 Estimates are that the use of palm print searches collected from crime scenes can increase clearance rates as high as 35 percent: Horiba Scientific, 1996–2010
104 Federal Bureau of Investigation, 2010a
105 Federal Bureau of Investigation, 2009d; Irwin, 1987
106 Missouri State Highway Patrol, 2007a
107 Geoghegan, 2008
108 Ho, 2011
109 *National Firearms Act* (1934)
110 *Gun Control Act of 1968; National Firearms Act* (1934)
111 *Brady Handgun Violence Prevention Act* (1993)
112 Federal Bureau of Investigation, 2008b
113 Bowling & Hickman, 2006
114 Federal Bureau of Investigation, 2010k; *18 U.S.C. Section 922*
115 See *United States Code* Title 18, Part I, Chapter 44, Section 925A
116 Bureau of Alcohol, Tobacco, Firearms, and Explosives, 2010
117 *Federal Gun Free School Zone Act of 1995*

[118] *Wikipedia*, 2010b
[119] New York State Division of State Police, 2010
[120] *District of Columbia v. Heller* (2008); *McDonald v. Chicago* (2010); *Robertson v. Baldwin* (1897)
[121] *Law Enforcement Officers Safety Act* (LEOSA) (2004)
[122] *Ord v. District of Columbia* (2009); *People v. Rodriguez* (2006)
[123] *Federal Gun Free School Zone Act of 1995*; *Law Enforcement Officers Safety Act* (LEOSA) (2004)
[124] *Code of Federal Regulations*, 2009
[125] New York State Department of Civil Service, 2006, p. 18
[126] Harrington, n.d., p. 72
[127] Craig, 2010a; YNN Staff, 2010
[128] Sager, 2010
[129] Example found in the *New York State Correction Law*, Chapter 43 of the Consolidated Laws, Article 23-A Licensure and Employment of Persons Previously Convicted of One or More Criminal Offenses, Section 752: Unfair Discrimination Against Persons Previously Convicted of One or More Criminal Offenses Prohibited
[130] *New York State Correction Law*, Chapter 43 of the Consolidated Laws, Article 23-A Licensure and Employment of Persons Previously Convicted of One or More Criminal Offenses, Section 750: Definitions, Subdivision 5: "Employment" means any occupation, vocation or employment, or any form of vocational or educational training. Provided, however, that "employment" shall not, for the purposes of this article, include membership in any law enforcement agency.
[131] Basch, 2007
[132] Boerger, 2001
[133] Ramker, 2006, p. 1
[134] Baker, 2008c; Beebe, 2010; Wall, 2009
[135] Mulick, 2006; Sisak, 2011
[136] Chang, 2010
[137] Marzulli, 2010a; Mooney, 2010; NorthCountryGazette.org, 2007; *The Vancouver Sun,* 2010; United States Department of Justice, 2008a
[138] Marzulli, Shiffrel, & Gendar, 2008; Trahan, 2009
[139] Kelley, 2007; Six, 2008
[140] Eiserer, 2010a
[141] Peterson, 2010
[142] Hawkins, 2009; Marzulli & McShane, 2009
[143] O'Hara, 2007
[144] Thibault, Lynch, & McBride, 2004, p. 316
[145] Rodriguez, 2011; Schott, 2011; Waller, 2008
[146] Hayes, 2010; Kotz, 2010; Tuohy, 2010
[147] Clarke, 2003, p. 1
[148] Bahls, 1999
[149] National Archive of Criminal Justice Data, n.d.
[150] Federal Bureau of Investigation, 2010d
[151] Rashbaum, 2005
[152] Branch, 2010
[153] Winston, 2005, p. 12
[154] Waller, 2008
[155] Juliano, 2011
[156] Zetter, 2005
[157] Hatch, 2003
[158] Associated Press, 2010a; Henson, 2010
[159] *Socorro v. IMI Data Search, Inc.* (2003)

[160] *CHRI Rules and Regulations* Section 10 Subdivision 3 prohibits the use of NYSPIN to conduct pre-employment record checks.
[161] Friel, 2009
[162] Associated Press, 2010d; Lyons, 2010; Mills, 2010; Nocera, Gendar, & McShane, 2009; Robinson, 2009b; Ross, 2010; Whigham, 2010
[163] *New York State Correction Law*, Chapter 43 of the Consolidated Laws, Article 23-A Licensure and Employment of Persons Previously Convicted of One or More Criminal Offenses, Section 753: Factors to be Considered Concerning a Previous Criminal Conviction, Presumption
[164] *Soto v New York State Office of Mental Retardation and Developmental Disabilities* (2010)
[165] Waller, 2008
[166] *Douglas El. v. Southeastern Pennsylvania Transportation Authority* (SEPTA) (2007)
[167] *Douglas El. v. Southeastern Pennsylvania Transportation Authority* (SEPTA) (2007)
[168] *Silvera v. Orange County School Board* (2001)
[169] *Silvera v. Orange County School Board* (2001)
[170] *Commonwealth of Pennsylvania Department of Corrections v. Krempowsky* (1997)
[171] *United States v. Baer* (2003)
[172] *National Crime Prevention and Privacy Compact of 1998*
[173] *Crime Identification Technology Act of 1998*
[174] United States Department of Justice Bureau of Justice Statistics, 2009
[175] United States Department of Justice Bureau of Justice Statistics, 2009
[176] *National Child Abuse Protection Act of 1993*
[177] *Volunteers for Children Act of 1998: Public Law 105-251*
[178] *Volunteers for Children Act of 1998: Public Law 105-251*
[179] *Volunteers for Children Act of 1998: Public Law 105-251*
[180] United States Department of Justice Bureau of Justice Statistics, 2009
[181] Federal Bureau of Investigation, 2010e
[182] Wisconsin Department of Justice, n.d.
[183] See New York State Police Information Network (NYSPIN) Policy and Procedure, Section 10—CHRI Rules and Regulations, Subdivision 3 which prohibits the use of NYSPIN to conduct pre-employment records checks
[184] Hatch, 2003
[185] *New York State Correction Law*, Chapter 43 of the Consolidated Laws, Article 23-A Licensure and Employment of Persons Previously Convicted of One or More Criminal Offenses, Section 754: Written Statement Upon Denial of License or Employment
[186] Surk, 2010
[187] Baker, 2008b; Boston.com, 2009; CNN World, 2009
[188] Cambanis, 2007
[189] Constitution.org, n.d.; Also see the provisions of *Chapter 47. Uniform Code of Military Justice: Subsection X Punitive Articles, 77 through 134*
[190] Johnson, 2008
[191] New York State Office of Mental Health, 2009; Reference *New York State Mental Hygiene Law*
[192] *New York State Correction Law*, Chapter 43 of the Consolidated Laws, Article 23-A Licensure and Employment of Persons Previously Convicted of One or More Criminal Offenses, Section 750: Definitions, Subdivision (3) Direct Relationship
[193] United States Equal Employment Opportunity Commission, 2006; Also see *Green v. Missouri Pacific Railroad Company* (1975)
[194] United States Equal Employment Opportunity Commission, 2006; Also see *Green v. Missouri Pacific Railroad Company* (1975)
[195] South Carolina Highway Patrol, 2009
[196] Siegel, 2006, p. 19
[197] WPTV, 2010
[198] Carter, 2009, p. 10

[199] Roach, 2007
[200] Brown, 2007
[201] Carter, 2009, p. 11
[202] Ratcliffe, 2007
[203] Ratcliffe, 2007
[204] Gottschalk, 2009
[205] White, 2008
[206] Keane & Kleiven, 2009
[207] Deukmedjian & de Lint, 2007
[208] Bibel & Faggiani, 2006
[209] Dowty, 2010; New York State Division of Criminal Justice Services, 2010; Maryland Governor's Office of Crime Control and Prevention, 2008; North Carolina Department of Crime Control and Public Safety, 2009; Willon, 2009
[210] Gomez, 2003
[211] Diaz, 1999, p. 50
[212] Federal Bureau of Investigation, 2010f
[213] Federal Bureau of Investigation, 2010g
[214] National Counterterrorism Center, 2009; United States Department of Homeland Security, 2009
[215] *Wikipedia*, 2011e
[216] Kelley & Abrials, 2003, p. 24
[217] Pfaelzer & Berson, 1975
[218] Baker & Moynihan, 2010; Beja, 2010; Rivera & Baker, 2010a
[219] Smith & Farole, 2009, p. 1
[220] Sampson, 2007, p. 1
[221] Rennison & Welchans, 2000, p. 1
[222] United States Department of Justice Office of Justice Programs, 1998, p. v
[223] Durose, Harlow, Langan, Motivans, Rantala, & Smith, 2005, p. 2
[224] Anderson & Aviles, 2006
[225] Alhabib, Nur, & Jones, 2010
[226] Bueno, 2009
[227] Sampson, 2007, p. 5
[228] Smith & Farole, 2009, p. 1
[229] United States Department of Justice Office of Justice Programs, 1998, p. v
[230] Graves, 2002, p. 137
[231] Sampson, 2007, p. 7
[232] ABCNews.Go.com, 2008a; CBSAtlanta.Com, 2010; Celona, Doyle, & Roberts, 2007; KTVB.com, 2010; Lukachick, 2010; Martinez, 2009; NorthCountryGazette.org, 2010; Prieto, 2010; Rizzo, 2010; Zick, 2010
[233] Aamodt, Brewster, & Raynes, 1998
[234] Carretta, 2008
[235] Blau, Cunningham, & Nelson, 2011
[236] Stuart, 2003, p. 44
[237] *Violence Against Women Act of 1994*
[238] Center for Problem-Oriented Policing, 2010; Also see The Duluth Model from Domestic Abuse Intervention Programs, 2008
[239] National Center for Victims of Crime, 2004, p. 3
[240] National Center for Victims of Crime, 2004, p. 1
[241] Associated Press, 2004d; Associated Press, 2011a; Associated Press, 2011f; Barron, 2011; CBSNews.Com, 2011; CNN Wire Staff, 2011c; Fairbanks, 2010; FoxNews.com, 2007; Johnston, 2010; Martin, 2011; Mgbatogu, 2010; Patterson, 2011; Rivera & Baker, 2010b; Ryan Evans, 2011; Shea, 2008b; Sherman, 2010b; Siemaszko, 2011; Turner, 2011; VinZant, 2011; Yaniv, 2011; YNN Staff, 2011b; Zick & Dunning, 2010

[242] Bazelon, 2011; National Center on Shaken Baby Syndrome, n.d.
[243] Draper, Pfaff, Pirkis, Snowdon, Lautenschlager, Wilson, & Almeida, 2008
[244] Lepisto, Astedt-Kurki, Joronen, Luukkaala, & Paavilainen, 2010
[245] Hunter, Nixon, & Parr, 2010
[246] *National Child Abuse Protection Act of 1993*
[247] Johnson, 1998, p. 77
[248] Craig, 2011c
[249] Sisak, 2011
[250] Smith & Farole, 2009, p. 1
[251] Graves, 2002, p. 137
[252] Ramker, 2006, p. 4
[253] See *Domestic Violence Offender Gun Ban* and *Lautenberg Amendment* (1997); *Fraternal Order of Police v. United States* (1998); *Fraternal Order of Police v. United States* (1999)
[254] Bryan, 2010
[255] Nathan, 2000
[256] Spector, 2010b
[257] Adams, 2002
[258] Brean, 2010; Gay, 2010b; Gryta, 2011b; Lohr, n.d.; Montaldo, 2007; Tokasz & Warner, 2010
[259] Weisel, 2005, p. 4
[260] McCue, Smith, Diehl, Dabbs, McDonough, & Ferrara, 2001
[261] *Kansas v. Hendricks* (1997); Liptak, 2010; Megerian, 2010; *United States v. Comstock* (2010)
[262] Freeman, Sandler, & Socia, 2009
[263] KTLA.com, 2010
[264] Cuniff, 2010; Johnson, 2006; TMZ.com, 2007
[265] New York State Assembly, n.d.
[266] Kreytak, 2010; Scuro, 2001, p. 24
[267] McNiff, 2010b
[268] Grace, 2010a
[269] Pulkkinen, 2010b
[270] Andreatta, 2010; FoxNews.com, 2010; Harris & Tanglao, 2011; Schouten, 2011; Sullivan, 2009; Thompson, 2011; Zremski, 2011
[271] *Drug-Induced Rape Prevention and Punishment Act of 1996*; Also see *Controlled Substances Act of 1970*
[272] Grace, 2010b; Hewett, 2004
[273] DePresca, 2003b
[274] National Drug Intelligence Center and the Sexual Assault Services Office of George Mason University, 2003
[275] Ayres, 2006; Kates, 2009; Leung, 2004a
[276] Casey, 2008; CNN Wire Staff, 2011b; Note: See the definition of Pedophilia, Encyclopedia of Mental Disorders, 2011
[277] *Adam Walsh Child Protection and Safety Act* (2006); *Jacob Wetterling Crimes Against Children and Sexually Violent Offender Registration* Act (1994); *Megan's Law* (the State's Sex Offenders Registry System); *Pam Lychner Sexual Offender Tracking and Identification Act of 1996*; *Violent Crime Control and Law Enforcement Act of 1994*
[278] United States Department of Justice, 2011
[279] The390.com, n.d.; United States Department of Justice, 2010
[280] United States Department of Health and Human Services, 2010
[281] Hartenstein, 2010; Hartenstein, 2011a; Kreytak, 2009; Kreytak, 2010; Nelson, 2010; *Orlando Sentinel*, 1989; Weiss & Baker, 2011; Zehnder, 2010
[282] Andreatta, 2011; Bailey, 2011b; Cline, 2010; FoxNews.com, 2007; Friedman, 2010; Gryta, 2011a; O'Connor, 2011; Shahid, 2011a

[283] Tanner, 2005, p. 44
[284] McGlone, 2011
[285] Alfano, 2010; Freile, 2011b; Leonard, 2011
[286] CNN Wire Staff, 2011d; CNN Wire Staff, 2011e
[287] Goldman, 2011
[288] Collins, 2007
[289] Associated Press, 2004b; Branch, 2010; CNN.com, 2005; Friedlander, 2009; Ingold, 2007; Kenney, 2011a; Kenney, 2011b; Mandell, 2010; Martinez, 2010b; Sanchez, 2010; Van Horn, 2010; Sheridan, 2011b; Sheridan, 2011c; Sheridan, 2011d; Sullivan, 2011b; Van Timmeren, 2010; WMUR.com, 2010; Wong, 2010; WorldNetDaily.com, 2005
[290] BuffaloNews.com, 2011a; Federal Bureau of Investigation, 2010h; Namuo, 2010; Warner, 2011; Wood, 2011b; YNN Staff, 2011
[291] Associated Press, 2011h; Craig, 2011b; WHEC.com. 2010
[292] Gilman, 2010
[293] Gay, 2010a; NassauCountyNY.gov, 2010
[294] United States Department of Justice United States Attorney Eastern District of Pennsylvania, 2009; Wood, 2011b
[295] Marshall, 2010
[296] Martinez, 2001a
[297] Finkelhor & Ormrod, 2004, p. 4
[298] Wortley & Smallbone, 2006, p. 7
[299] Callinan, 2004: Fagundes, 2009; Federal Bureau of Investigation, 2008a; Ryan, 2008; Traynor, 1998
[300] Fantino, 2003, p. 28; Quan, 2010
[301] Jolly, 2011; Pileggi, 2010; Smith, 2010b; Winter, 2010b
[302] Associated Press, 2010f; Maready, 2008; Perez, 2010
[303] Chou, 2010; Federal Bureau of Investigation, 2009c; Zubak-Skees, 2010
[304] Associated Press, 2010f; Grieco, 2009
[305] Gowan, 2010
[306] Pulkkinen, 2010a
[307] ABCLOCAL.GO.com, 2010; Bigelow, 2009; Brennan, 2010; Buffalonews.com, 2011b; Contreras, 2010; Egelko, 2008; Emery, 2010; Maslanik, 2011; McGlone, 2011; O'Hare, 2010
[308] *United States v. Knox* (1993)
[309] Wortley & Smallbone, 2006, p. 6
[310] Nakashima, 2008; Schmidt, 2010
[311] Davenport, 2009
[312] Cook, 2010b; Fagundes, 2009; Simon, 2011; Zeigler, 2011b
[313] McCullagh, 2008
[314] Associated Press, 2009f
[315] Ahmed, 2009; Brunker, 2009; CBS/AP, 2009; *Messenger Post Newspaper*, 2011; Mangan, 2010; Moskowitz, 2010; Richmond, 2009; Sheridan, 2011a; Stone, 2009
[316] Inbar, 2009
[317] Hill, 2009
[318] Koch, 2010; Missouri General Assembly, 2009; National Criminal Justice Resource Center, 2001; Rowe, 2008
[319] McCurley & Snyder, 2004
[320] Snyder, 2003, p. 1
[321] Associated Press, 2007c
[322] Jones, 2007
[323] Eschholz & Vaughn, 2001
[324] Rowe, 2009

[325] Associated Press, 2009d; Associated Press, 2010c; ClickOrlando.com, 2009; Dulaney, 2010; Kelly, 2008; KVUE News, 2008; NewsChannel5.com, 2010; Osorio, 2010; Prohaska, 2011; Regneir, 2010; WIBW.com, 2010
[326] Elly, 2010
[327] United States Equal Employment Opportunity Commission, n.d.
[328] Bellows & Kleiner, 2001
[329] Hoppe, 2009; Roberts, 2009; UPI.com, 2011; Whaley, 2009
[330] Associated Press, 2006b
[331] Cavanaugh, 2006; Loudon, 2011
[332] Chase, 2011
[333] Gomez-Preston & Trescott, 1990; Lee, 2009; Rose, 2009; Thissen, 2009; Thissen, 2010
[334] Hayden, 2008
[335] Associated Press, 2007a; WHEC.Com, 2009a
[336] CBSAtlanta.Com, 2009; *City of Ontario v. Quon* (2010); Elly, 2010; Sherman, 2010a; WHIOTV.com, 2010
[337] Kitzmiller, 2010
[338] WFTV.com, 2010a
[339] Caulfield, 2011; Encyclopedia of Mental Disorders, 2011; Eiserer, 2009d; Malinowski, 2010a; Malinowski, 2010b; NewsAdvance.com, 2009; Parsons, 2008
[340] Eiserer, 2007; Varnum, 2009
[341] Borland, 2008
[342] Armon, 2003; Associated Press, 2010d; Keeshan, 2004; Keeshan, 2008; KnoxNews.com, 2008; Mann, 2001; O'Connor & Starks, 1999
[343] Lucio, 2009; McDermott, 2009; Nicholson, 2010
[344] Alanez, 2009; Alanez & Ortega, 2009; Associated Press, 2011b; Esquivel, 2010; Gryta, 2005; JustNews.com, 2007; JustNews.com, 2009; King & Shirek, 2007; Krause & Crawford, 2010; WFTV.com, 2010b
[345] Alvarez, 2009; Brown, 2004; Contreras, 2005; Francis, 2009; Hamacher, 2009a; Holley, 2010; Hoye, 2011; O'Connor, 2011; United States Department of Justice, 2007a
[346] Bohn, 2009; Gendar & Boyle, 2009; Grace, Croghan, & Siemaszko, 2011: Lorenz, 2009; McBride, 2010; WSBTV.com, 2009
[347] Cramer, 2009b; Pagliery, 2009
[348] Freile, 2010; Grace, 2011a; Hughes, 2002; NassauCountyNY.gov, 2008; Peltz, 2011; Prohaska, 2011; *The Record*, 2003; Seef, 2010; WMCTV.com, 2011
[349] *Prison Rape Elimination Act of 2003* (PREA)
[350] Levine & Griffith, 2011;
[351] AltoonaMirror.com, 2008; Bowes & Kapsidelis, 2009; Federal Bureau of Investigation, 2010h; Nielsen, 2010; Ross, 2007
[352] Associated Press, 2005; Bakersfield.com, 2009; Bender, 2010; Emison, 2009; Hedgpeth, 2010; Hofeditz & Acosta, 2009; Kennedy, 2011; Morrell, 2004; Ross, 2007; Sacramento Metro News, 2009; United Press International, 2010
[353] Associated Press, 2008d; Barker, 2010a; Barker, 2010b; Freile, 2011a; Gamblin, 2010; LATimes.com, 2006; Maclachlan, 2010; Mursch, 2008; O'Connor, 2010; Pagliery, 2009; *People v. Gainey* (2001); Raclin & Asbury, 2006; Schapiro, 2011
[354] Associated Press, 2004c; Balassone, 2008; Balmert, 2009; Chattanoogan.com, 2006; DiPaola, 1992; KCBA.com, 2010; Kenney, 2004; LATimes.com, 1987; McGreevy, n.d.; Mendoza, 2003; Miller, 2008b; OrlandoSentinel.com, 2007; Perez, 1993; PoliceOne.com, 2000; Shea, 2008a; Stirgus, 2000; Tran, 2002; Walker & Irlbeck, 2003; Zash & Quesinberry, 2010
[355] San Antonio Express-News, 2008
[356] Schogol, 2005
[357] United States General Accountability Office, 2006
[358] MedicineNet.Com, 2011

[359] Altman, 1986
[360] McCue, Smith, Diehl, Dabbs, McDonough, & Ferrara, 2001, p. 94
[361] Associated Press, 2011c; Dolak, 2011; Graham, Wood, & Moran, 2011; Hartenstein, 2011b; Koppelman, 2011; Ramde, 2011; Rossi, 2010; Sullivan, 2010; Wesh.com, 2010; White, 2011; Willing, 2011; Wyman, 2010
[362] Tavernise, 2010
[363] DNA.gov, n.d.; *Justice for All Act of 2004*
[364] 9WYSR.com, 2011; Associated Press, 2011g; ENewsPF.com, 2011; NY.Gov, 2010; Phucas, 2011
[365] *Daubert v. Merrell Dow Chemicals, Inc.* (1993); Sanow, 2002, p. 4
[366] USLegal.com, 2011a
[367] Federal Bureau of Investigation, 2011a
[368] Associated Press, 2011b; Coker, 2011; Deutsch, 2009; Gregory, 2011; Hoye, 2011; MySanAntonio.com, 2007
[369] Corr, 2002, p. 38
[370] Martin, 2002
[371] Robertson, 1999, p. 24
[372] Baum, 2006
[373] Lodge, 2010
[374] Langton & Planty, 2010; Newman, 2003, p. 3
[375] Alpert, 2007
[376] Smith, 2000, p. 102
[377] Newman, 2003, p. 3
[378] *Fair and Accurate Credit Transactions Act of 2003*
[379] Newman, 2003, p. 8
[380] WCAX.com, 2009
[381] Wartell & La Vigne, 2004, p. 1
[382] Ho, 2011; Richert, 2011; Wartell & La Vigne, 2004, p. 2; WGRZ.com, 2011
[383] O'Hara, 2010
[384] Cox, 2000, p. 39
[385] Schram & Greene, 2010; Watkins, 2011
[386] *Bank Secrecy Act of 1970; Federal Bank Act of 1970; The Hobbs Act* (1951); *The Identity Theft and Assumption Deterrence Act of 1998; Money Laundering Act of 1986; Racketeer Influenced and Corrupt Organizations Act* (RICO); Scuro, 2003, p. 10; *Title 18, U.S. Code 1028. Fraud and Related Activity in Connection with Identification Documents, Authentication Features, and Information*
[387] Davidsen, 2010; Rochesterathome.com, 2008
[388] The IndyChannel.com, 2009
[389] Dow, 2009; Manley, 2009
[390] Associated Press, 2010b; Burch, 2009; McLaughlin, 2010
[391] King Greenwood, 2007
[392] Dolnick, 2009; *New York Times,* 1999; Rankin, 1998; Seef, 2011a; Walsh, 2008
[393] Federal Bureau of Investigation, 2010j; Valot, 2010
[394] Murray, 2009; Porter, 2009
[395] Vick, 2008
[396] Bailey, 2011a; Leung, 1996
[397] Associated Press, 1995; *The Standard,* 1999
[398] Herbeck, 1998
[399] Anonymous, 2010
[400] Federal Bureau of Investigation, 2010i
[401] Bykowicz & Linskey, 2009
[402] Snowden & Fuss, 2000

[403] Bellah, 2001, p. 222
[404] National White Collar Crime Center (NW3C), 2011
[405] Internet Crime Complaint Center (IC3), 2011
[406] International Association of Financial Crimes Investigators, 2010
[407] National Insurance Crime Bureau, 2011
[408] Association of Certified Fraud Examiners, 2011; Society of Financial Examiners, 2011
[409] *Crime Control Act of 1990; Federal Youth Corrections Act*
[410] United States Department of Justice Bureau of Justice Statistics, 2009
[411] *New York State Criminal Procedure Law*; *New York State Family Court Act; New York State Penal Law*
[412] *Juvenile Corrections Act* (n.d.)
[413] Leung, 2004b
[414] Jewell & Prohaska, 2010
[415] Snyder, 2003, p. 1
[416] Associated Press, 2011i
[417] McCurley & Snyder, 2004, p. 1
[418] CNN Wire Staff, 2011g; McCarren, 2011
[419] Boyer, 2011b; CBSChicago.Com, 2011; FoxNews.com, 2011d; FoxNews.com, 2011e; Jonsson, 2011; Newall, 2011; Vaughan, 2011
[420] FoxNews.com, 2011f
[421] Halverstadt & Marks, 2011
[422] Sampson, 2002a, p. 1
[423] Sampson, 2002a, p. 2
[424] Young, 2011b
[425] Dale, 2011
[426] Federal Bureau of Investigation, 2011b
[427] Privacy Rights Clearing House, 2006
[428] Federal Bureau of Investigation, 2011b
[429] Larson, 2003; Minnesota Judicial Branch Self Help Center, n.d.
[430] Hendricks, 2009
[431] Federal Bureau of Investigation, 2011b
[432] Electronic Privacy Information Center, n.d.; Also see the Findlaw (Findlaw.com, 2011b) dedicated website of state specific information on expungement laws at http://criminal.findlaw.com/crimes/expungement/expungement-state-info.html
[433] *California Code of Regulations*, n.d., p. 33; Also refer to fair employment practices in other states through State and Local Government on the Net (1995–2010) at http://www.statelocalgov.net/50states-jobs.cfm
[434] Maryland Department of Public Safety and Correctional Services, 2011
[435] Ortiz, 2007
[436] Minnesota Judicial Branch Self Help Center, n.d.
[437] Minnesota Judicial Branch Self Help Center, n.d.
[438] Minnesota Judicial Branch Self Help Center, n.d.
[439] *United States v. Flowers* (2004)
[440] Privacy Rights Clearing House, 2006
[441] Gregg, 2009
[442] Pitsch, 2009
[443] Brady-Lunny, 2009; Delazio, 2009; Ku & Musgrave, 2006; Olson & McEnroe, 2006
[444] *Rhode Island General Law* Title 12 Criminal Procedure Section 12-1.3-4
[445] *New York State Human Rights Law* Section 296—16: Allows the use of sealed record information in the consideration of police candidates covered under NYS CPL 160.50-2 application for employment as a police officer or peace officer as those terms are defined in subdivisions thirty-three and thirty-four of section 1.20 of the criminal procedure law; provided further

that the provisions of this subdivision shall not apply to an application for employment or membership in any law enforcement agency with respect to any arrest or criminal accusation which was followed by a youthful offender adjudication, as defined in subdivision one of section 720.35 of the criminal procedure law, or by a conviction for a violation sealed pursuant to section 160.55 of the criminal procedure law, or by a conviction which is sealed pursuant to section 160.58 of the criminal procedure law.

446 Electronic Privacy Information Center, n.d.

447 Minnesota Judicial Branch Self Help Center, n.d.

448 *Information Management Journal,* 2007; Liptak, 2006

449 California Courts Self Help Center, 2010

450 Scott, 2004

451 Scott, 2004, p. 6

452 Grace, 2011b

453 Amsden, 2010; Associated Press, 2010d; Michel, 1996; Moorhead, 2008; Palotas, 2008

454 Isaacson, 2009; WCAX.com, 2009

455 *City of Canton v. Harris* (1989); *NASA v. Nelson* (2011); *The Shield Club v. City of Cleveland* (1986)

456 Federal Bureau of Investigation, 2009b

457 Federal Bureau of Investigation, 2009b

458 Federal Bureau of Investigation, 2009b

459 Martinez, 2011b; Seelye, 2006

460 Nebehay, 2011

461 Gryta, 2011c; Michel, 1997; Nagle, 2008

462 Bolger, 2011; Campbell, 2010b

463 Government Printing Office, 2004

464 *Intelligence Reform and Terrorism Prevention Act of 2004; Patriot Act* (2001)

465 Federal Bureau of Investigation, 2011c

466 *Life*, 2002; Purdy & Bergman, 2003

467 Calabresi, 2010; Candiotti, Cratty, Meserve, Ahlers, & Jamjoom, 2010; Dao, 2009; Johnson & Robbins, 2010; Kates, 2010; McNiff, 2010a; Simon, 2010

468 Grier, 2010

469 CNN U.S., 2001; Gellner, 2010

470 Candiotti, Cratty, Meserve, Ahlers, & Jamjoom, 2010; CBS/AP, 2010; Kates, 2010; Mulvihill, 2010

471 MacIntosh, 2007

472 Hoffer, 2011

473 Whitelaw, 2009

474 United States Department of Justice, Office of Justice Programs, Office of Juvenile Justice and Delinquency Programs, 1999

475 Associated Press, 2011e

476 United States Department of Justice, Office of Justice Programs, Office of Juvenile Justice and Delinquency Programs, 1999

477 *Wikipedia*, 2011a

478 Robson, 2006

479 Harvey & Ward, 1996

480 Harlow, 2005, p. 1

481 Strom, 2001

482 CNN Wire Staff, 2011f; FoxNews.co, 2011c; Investors.com, 2011; WTMJ, 2011; Yusko, 2010

483 *Hate Crime Statistics Act of 1990* (P. L. 101-275)

484 ClearLead Inc., n.d.

485 MyAddiction.com, 2011

486 Selekman, 2008

[487] Brown University, 2005
[488] Griffiths, 2003
[489] Associated Press, 2006c; Fry, 2005; Gibson, 2001; Guerriero, 2007; Hoffman, 2003; Lehman, 2011; Lynem, 1999; Malone, 2010; McGregor, 2011; Miller, 2010; Pederson, 2009; Rae, 2008; Schmidt, 2008
[490] Baldo, Cristofoletti, Majori, Cibin, Peron, Dal Zotto, Zampieri, Sala, & Trivello, 2006
[491] Wexler & Wexler, 1992
[492] *Americans with Disabilities Act of 1990*
[493] ADA.gov, n.d.; Boston University Center for Psychiatric Rehabilitation, n.d.; United States Equal Employment Opportunity Commission, 2009b
[494] For example, the *New York State Civil Practice Law and Rules*
[495] Barnum, 2011; Gurman, 2011; Johnson, 2011a; Targeted News Service, 2011a
[496] Dunn, 2002
[497] *Bradley Amendment* (1986)
[498] Arkansas Department of Finance and Administration; Florida Department of Revenue; Idaho Department of Health and Welfare; New York State Department of Taxation and Finance
[499] McGonigle, 2011
[500] Scott, Emerson, Antonacci, & Plant, 2006, p. 6
[501] Scott, Emerson, Antonacci, & Plant, 2006, p. 4
[502] United States Department of Transportation National Highway Traffic Safety Administration, 2010, p. 3, Table 3: Drug Test Results for Fatally Injured Drivers, by State, 2009
[503] Dilan, 2009
[504] Canfield, 2010; Lovett, 2010; Martinez, 2010a; Passalugo, 2010; Robinson, 2009a
[505] New York State Department of Motor Vehicles, 2011a
[506] *Tennessee v. Garner* (1985)
[507] *Graham v. Connor* (1989)
[508] *Scott v. Harris* (2007)
[509] *County of Sacramento v. Lewis* (1998)
[510] *City of Canton v. Harris* (1989)
[511] Brennan, 2009; CBC News, 2008; ClickOrlando.com, 2008; Craig, 2011c; KRQE.com, 2010; *Messenger Post Newspaper*, 2009; MyFoxOrlando.com, 2009; WCAX.com, 2009; Williams & Macenka, 2009
[512] *Driver's Privacy Protection Act of 1994*; *United States Code* Title 18, Chapter 123, Section 2721, Subsections (a), (b), (d), and (e): Prohibition on the Release and Use of Certain Personal Information from State Motor Vehicle Records
[513] Louisiana Department of Public Safety Office of Motor Vehicles, 2011; New York State Department of Motor Vehicles, 2011b
[514] Cooper, 2011; Murray & Light, 2010; Svaldi, 2011
[515] Goodman, 2010
[516] Kaufman & Butler, 2010; Singletary, 2010; Tucker, 2010
[517] Leslie & Garner, 2010
[518] See Fair Employment Agencies in the 50 States: Craig Pratt and Associates, Inc., n.d.
[519] Tucker, 2010
[520] Brain, 2011
[521] Hsu, 2009
[522] Bell, 2010
[523] Waller, 2010
[524] Bell, 2010
[525] Hsu, 2009
[526] Vaas, 2009
[527] *Fair Credit Reporting Act*; *United States Code* Title 15, Chapter 41 Consumer Credit Protection
[528] *Fair and Accurate Credit Transactions Act of 2003* Section 312

[529] Cassady & Mierzwinski, 2004, p. 4; Douris, 2006, p. 56; Pierce & Ackerman, 2005, p. 1
[530] *Smith v. Hireright Solutions, Inc.* (2009)
[531] *United States Code* Title 15, Chapter 41, Subchapter III, Section 1681a Definitions; Rules of Construction, (h) The term "employment purposes" when used in connection with a consumer report means a report used for the purpose of evaluating a consumer for employment, promotion, reassignment or retention as an employee; Also see *Fair Credit Reporting Act* Section 603(h) which limits the use of employee background checks to employment purposes: "The term 'employment purposes' when used in connection with a consumer report means a report used for the purpose of evaluating a consumer for employment, promotion, reassignment or retention as an employee."
[532] Sixel, 2010; Tucker, 2010
[533] *Robinson v. City of Dallas* (1975)
[534] Federal Trade Commission, 1999 *United States Code* Title 15, Chapter 41: Consumer Credit Protection, Subchapter III, Section 1681a Definitions; Rules of Construction, (k) Adverse Action (1) (B) (ii) "A denial of employment or any other decision for employment purposes that adversely affects any current or prospective employee."
[535] *United States v. Imperial Palace Inc.* (2004); *United States v. Quality Terminal Services, LLC* (2009); Federal Trade Commission, 2004; Federal Trade Commission, 2009
[536] *Bakker v. McKinnon* (1998); *Cousin v. Trans Union Corporation* (2001);
[537] *Fair Credit Reporting Act* Section 605 (b) (3)
[538] *Fair Credit Reporting Act* Section 603(f)
[539] *United States Code* Title 15, Chapter 41, Subchapter III, Section 1681a Definitions; Rules of Construction, (j) (1) Overdue Child Support
[540] Kane, 1998
[541] Haynes, 1998
[542] *United States Code* Title 15, Chapter 41, Subchapter III, Section 1681a Definitions; Rules of Construction, (d) (1) (B)
[543] *United States Code* Title 15, Chapter 41, Subchapter III, Section 1681a Definitions; Rules of Construction (e)
[544] *United States Code* Title 15, Chapter 41, Subchapter III, Section 1681a
[545] *Fair Credit Reporting Act*
[546] *United States Code* Title 11: Bankruptcy, Chapter 5, Subchapter II, Section 525 Protection Against Discriminatroy Treatment
[547] Haynes, 1998
[548] *Philbin v. Trans Union Corporation* (2001); Also see *Dalton v. Capital Associated Indus., Inc.* (2001)
[549] *Wilson v. Prudential Financial* (2009)
[550] *Dalton v. Capital Associated Indus., Inc.* (2001)
[551] Privacy Rights Clearing House, 2006; Also see *Obabueki v. International Business Machines Corporation* (2002)
[552] *Obabueki v. Choicepoint, Inc.* (2002); Also see *Obabueki v. International Business Machines Corporation* (2002)
[553] Haynes, 1998
[554] *Fair Credit Reporting Act*
[555] *Fair Credit Reporting Act*
[556] Cohen, 1998, p. 104
[557] Brinckerhoff, 1998; Juliano, 2011; Winston, 2005, p. 4
[558] Brinckerhoff, 1998
[559] Livshits, MacGee, & Tertilt, 2006, p. 2
[560] *Bankruptcy Act of 1978*
[561] *Bankruptcy Abuse Prevention and Consumer Protection Act of 2005*

[562] *United States Code* Title 11: Bankruptcy, Chapter 5, Subchapter II, Section 525 Protection Against Discriminatory Treatment
[563] Indiana Department of Financial Institutions, n.d.
[564] *White v. Kentuckiana Livestock Market, Inc.* (2005)
[565] Pedone & Patil, 2011; Also see *Rea v. Federated Investors* (2010)
[566] *Marshall v. District of Columbia Government* (1977)
[567] *Detz v. Hoover* (1982)
[568] Schloss & Lahr, 2008, p. 24
[569] Consumer Federation of America, 2002, p. 34
[570] *Americans with Disabilities Act of 1990*
[571] *United States Code* Title 15, Chapter 41, Subchapter III, Section 1681a Definitions; Rules of Construction, (d) Consumer Report (3) (A) (B) (C)
[572] *United States Code* Title 15, Chapter 41, Subchapter III, Section 1681a Definitions; Rules of Construction, (i) Medical Information
[573] *Fair Credit Reporting Act*
[574] Craig Pratt and Associates, Inc., n.d.
[575] Broady, 2010; Leslie & Garner, 2010; Sixel, 2010
[576] Federal Trade Commission, 1999
[577] Federal Trade Commission, 1999
[578] Federal Trade Commission, 1999
[579] Lieber, 2010
[580] Federal Bureau of Investigation, 2009a
[581] South Carolina Highway Patrol, 2009
[582] South Carolina Highway Patrol, 2009
[583] South Carolina Highway Patrol, 2009
[584] *Family Educational Rights and Privacy Act* (1974)
[585] *Family Educational Rights and Privacy Act* (1974)
[586] United States Department of Education, 2010; Also see State specific examples like the *New York State Education Law* Article 1 Section 2-A Release of Directory Information
[587] Lankes, 2011
[588] Austin, Skager, Bailey, & Bates, 2007; Cratty, 2011
[589] American Academy of Child and Adolescent Psychiatry, 2010
[590] National Center for Chronic Disease Prevention and Health Promotion, 2010
[591] National Center for Chronic Disease Prevention and Health Promotion, 2010
[592] National Center for Children Exposed to Violence, 2006
[593] MSNBC.com, 2011; Toppo, 2009
[594] Center for Disease Control and Prevention, 2011
[595] Center for Disease Control and Prevention, 2011
[596] Dale, 2011
[597] Porter, 2011; TheAustralian.com, 2011
[598] Aamodt, 1997a
[599] Manis, Archbold, & Hassell, 2008
[600] Schulte, 2010
[601] Post Wire Services, 2011
[602] Hauser & O'Connor, 2007; WHEC.Com, 2011
[603] *The Jeanne Clery Disclosure of Campus Security Policy and Campus Crime Statistics Act* (1990)
[604] Electronic Code of Federal Regulations, 2011
[605] CrimeVictimServices.org, n.d.; *Higher Education Amendment Act* (1998)
[606] Beckwith & Burke, 2000, p. 109
[607] Yusko, 2010

[608] Associated Press, 2007d; Goldman, 2007; Mandell, 2010; McCurley Bierlien, 2008; Ossad, 2011; Schorn, 2007; SecurityOnCampus.net, 2007
[609] Ward, 2009
[610] Tapper & Miller, 2007
[611] Contreras & Gollin, 2009; Ezell, 2009; Lagorio, 2006; Lederman, 2006; Millar, 2007; Morlin, 2006
[612] Cramer, 2004
[613] Foster, 2001
[614] Moore, 2009
[615] Thompson, 2006
[616] Pina, 2010
[617] Lumadue, 2006
[618] Geeser, n.d.; Honeycutt Spears, 2006; Saltzman, 2007
[619] Associated Press, 2006d; Associated Press, 2007e; Carter & Kelleher, 2005; Chan, 2007; *Columbian*, 2005; NBC-2.com, 2006a; NBC-2.com, 2006b; Poinski, 2006; Swift, 2006; Tims, 2010a; Tims, 2010b
[620] Schemo, 2008
[621] Cramer, 2004
[622] Weber & Horvath, 2008
[623] Contreras & Gollin, 2009; Capriccioso, 2006
[624] Kapsidelis & Martz, 2009
[625] Martz & Kapsidelis, 2008
[626] Virginia Commonwealth University, 2008
[627] Maine.gov, 2008; Oregon Student Assistance Commission Office of Degree Authorization, n.d.; Texas Higher Education Coordinating Board, 2011; Washington Higher Education Coordinating Board, n.d.
[628] Massachusetts Office of Student Financial Assistance, n.d.
[629] Stratton, 2002; WHDH.com, 2003
[630] Committee on Governmental Affairs, 2004
[631] Pulkkinen, 2010c; Stepankowsky, 2009; Sullivan, 2008
[632] Fox News, 2011; The Smoking Gun, 2011a
[633] Associated Press, 2008a; Jaschik, 2008
[634] BBC News, 2007
[635] Washington State Legislature, 2011
[636] Tims, 2010a
[637] *Gilty v. Village of Oak Park* (1990)
[638] *Gilty v. Village of Oak Park* (1990)
[639] AmericanRhetoric.com, 1962
[640] Brown & Graczyk, 2010
[641] Department of the Navy, n.d.; Office of Naval Intelligence, n.d.
[642] Department of the Navy, n.d.; Office of Naval Intelligence, n.d.
[643] Hoch, 2010; Morgan, 2010
[644] Auerbach, 1999
[645] Robbins, 2010
[646] Alvarez, 2007; Maze, 2007; Schor, 2008
[647] Kifner, 2006; Klatell, 2009; Kouri, 2006; Robson, 2006; United States Department of Justice Bureau of Alcohol, Tobacco, Firearms, and Explosives, 2010; Webster, 2009
[648] Wood, 2011a
[649] Graham, 1998; Reuters, 1998; White, 2007
[650] McGovern, 2008
[651] Gerhart, 2010; Salit & Milkovits, 2010; Somerville, 2009
[652] Martin, Gibbs, Johnson, & Sullivan, 2010

653 *Gun Control Act* (1968; *Lautenberg Amendment* (1997)
654 *Army Lawyer*, 1997
655 DD Form 2760—Qualification to Possess Firearms or Ammunition (2002) can be found at http://www.dia.mil/careers/pre-employment/Fire%20Arms%20Forms%20_DD%20Form%202760%20.pdf
656 Somerville, 2009
657 Radefeld, 2005
658 Hoffman, 2010; Johnson, 2008; Nolan, 2010; Stengle, 2011; Suhr, 2011; The Smoking Gun, 2011c
659 Associated Press, 2008c; Maugh, 2008
660 Coker, 2007
661 Fitzpatrick, 2010, p. 44
662 Wilson, 2010c
663 Hefling, 2011a
664 Associated Press Worldstream, 2000
665 Bender, 2011; McGlone, 2011; Quan, 2010; United States Department of Defense, 2009b
666 Cook, 2010a
667 Scahill, 2009
668 Hornick, 2009
669 Hindery, 2011
670 Blatt, 2011; KEZI.com, 2011; Levine, 2011; Schapiro, 2011; Shahid, 2011b
671 Ivie & Garland, 2011
672 Holmes, 2010
673 Smith, Segal, & Segal, 2008
674 Smith, Segal, & Segal, 2008
675 Alvarez, 2008; Associated Press, 2008b; Chong & Maugh, 2006; Ikin, Sim, Creamer, Forbes, McKenzie, Kelsall, Glass, McFarlane, Abramson, Ittak, Dwyer, Blizzard, Delaney, Horsley, Harrex, & Schwarz, 2004
676 Fitzpatrick, 2010, p. 44
677 Cable News Network, 2007
678 Elbogen, Wagner, Fuller, & Calhoun, 2010
679 Holmes, 2010
680 Gerhart, 2010; Grossman & Siddle, 2000; Hefling, 2011b; Salit & Milkovits, 2010; Wallis, 2007
681 Larson, Hammer, Conway, & Schmied, 2011
682 Flaherty, 2010; Goldstein, 2010a; Goldstein, 2010b
683 *Americans with Disabilities Act of 1990*
684 *Freedom of Information Act*; *Privacy Act of 1974*—5 USC Section 552a
685 National Archives, 2010; National Archives, n.d.a; National Archives, n.d.b
686 *Uniform Code of Military Justice*
687 Headquarters Department of the Army, 2010; *Wikipedia*, 2011b
688 Headquarters Department of the Army, 2006; United States Department of Defense, 2009a
689 Military.com, 2011
690 Selective Service System, 2009a; Selective Service System, 2009b
691 Nelson, 2000
692 Cascio, 2006, p. 240
693 Woolnough, 2004
694 Cleary, Hunt, Walter, & Robertson, 2009; Hauge, Skogstad, & Einarsen, 2009; Lajoie, 2010; Simons & Mawn, 2010
695 Anonymous, 2011a; Darrow, 2011; Johnson & Indvik, 1994; Magin, May, McElduff, & Goode, 2011
696 Anonymous, 2011b

697 Anonymous, 2011c; Harrell, 2011
698 Anonymous, 1996; Kedjidjian, 1996
699 Anonymous, 1998; Johnston, 1997
700 Kreimer, 2004
701 Bach, 2006
702 Sonnenberg, 1994, p. 165
703 Slowik, 2003, p. 98
704 *Charleston Gazette*, 2010
705 WHEC.Com, 2009a; WHEC.Com, 2009b
706 Eiserer, 2010b; Eiserer, 2010c; Nielsen, 2010
707 Jackson, 2009; Ludwig, 2009; WHEC.Com, 2009a
708 Murphy, 2006
709 Goodson, 2007; Nielsen, 2010; Romer, 2009
710 Kesseli, 2006
711 Craig, 2011a
712 Jones, 1994; Timms & Krause, 2010a; Timms & Krause, 2010b
713 Timms & Krause, 2010c
714 Slack, 2006
715 *California Government Code* Section 1031 (d)
716 *Texas Occupations Code* Section 1701.451(a)(1)
717 Texas Commission on Law Enforcement Officer Standards and Education, 2009b
718 *Farr v. State Civil Service Commission (Department of Corrections)* (2008)
719 *Athens Daily Review*, 2007; Harki, 2009; McNary, 2009
720 McNary, 2009
721 Abshire, 2007; Grace, 2003; Young, 2007
722 Eiserer, 2010b
723 Edwards, 2002; Korte, 2002
724 Stokes, 2000
725 United States Merit Systems Protection Board, 2005, p. 4
726 Harshman & Chachere, 2000, p. 30
727 Associated Press, 2007f; Reicher, 1996
728 Kleiman & White, 1991, p. 90
729 Kleiman & White, 1991, p. 84
730 Cronkhite, 2008, p. 250; Danaher, 2003, p. 133
731 Beaudette, 1999
732 United States Merit Systems Protection Board, 2005, p. i
733 Repa, 1999
734 McConnell, 2000
735 Craig, 2010c
736 Buettner, 2011
737 Cabot, 2005
738 *Scott v. Blanchet High School* (1987)
739 Martz & Kapsidelis, 2008
740 Craig, 2010b
741 Beckwith & Burke, 2000, p. 109; Soto, 1998b, p. 93
742 Hadley & Ware, 2007, as cited in Career Directors International, 2007, p. 21
743 Cabot, 2005
744 McConnell, 2007
745 Barada, n.d.
746 Woolnough, 2004
747 Verherke, 1998, p. 117
748 Harshman & Chachere, 2000, p. 34

[749] *Valdez v. Warner*, (1987)
[750] *Davis v. The Board of County Commissioners of Dona Ana County* (1999)
[751] *Jerner v. Allstate Insurance Company* (1995)
[752] *Jerner v. Allstate Insurance Company* (1995)
[753] *Jerner v. Allstate Insurance Company* (1995)
[754] *Richland School District v. Mabton School District* (2002)
[755] *Richland School District v. Mabton School District* (2002)
[756] *Richland School District v. Mabton School District* (2002)
[757] *Randi W. v. Muroc Joint Unified School District* (1997)
[758] *Randi W. v. Muroc Joint Unified School District* (1997)
[759] Collins, 1998
[760] Matteucci, 2009
[761] Ballam, 2002, p. 448
[762] Reuben, 1994, p. 32
[763] Verherke, 1998
[764] O'Hara, 2009b
[765] FindLaw.com, 2011a
[766] Carrico, 2000; *True v. Ladner* (1986)
[767] *Hett v. Ploetz* (1963); *Manguso v. Oceanside Unified School District* (1984); *Zerr v. Johnson* (1995)
[768] *Gibson v. Overnight Transport Company* (2003); *Gibson v. Philip Morris, Inc.* (1997); *Robinson v. Shell Oil Co.* (1997)
[769] Leonard, 1995; Martucci & Boatright, 1995; *Indiana Code* Title 22. Labor and Safety, Article 5. Unlawful Labor Practices Chapter. 3 Blacklisting; *Maine Revised Statute* Title 17, Chapter 17: Blacklisting; *North Carolina General Statutes* Section 14-355: Blacklisting Employees
[770] *Indiana Code* Title 22. Labor and Safety, Article 5. Unlawful Labor Practices Chapter. 3 Blacklisting IC 22-5-3-1 Disclosure of Information After Employee's Discharge Section 1. (a)
[771] *Doe v. U.S. Civil Service Commission* (1980)
[772] *Garcia v. Walder Electronics, Inc.* (1990)
[773] *Ostrowe v. Lee* (1931)
[774] *Gibson v. Phillip Morris, Inc.* (1997)
[775] Bagley, 1995, p. 387
[776] Klein, Pappas, & Kim, 2004
[777] *J. Crew Group, Inc. v. Griffin* (1990); *Lewis v. Equitable Life Assurance Society of the United States* (1986); *Van-Go Transport Co., Inc. v. New York City Board of Education* (1997); *White v. Blue Cross and Blue Shield of Massachusetts Inc.* (2004); *Wieder v. Chemical Bank* (1994); *Wright v. Guarinello* (1995)
[778] Repa, 1999
[779] Schwartz, 2009
[780] *Kestenbaum v. Pennzoil, Co.* (1988)
[781] *Pittard v. Four Seasons Motor Inn, Inc.* (1984)
[782] Adler & Peirce, 1996
[783] Open-Oregon.com, 1999; *Hurlbut v. Gulf Atlantic Life Insurance Company* (1987)
[784] *Bardin v. Lockheed Aeronautical Systems Company* (1999); *Garcia v. Walder Electronics, Inc.* (1990); *O'Shea v. General Telephone Company* (1987)
[785] Schwartz, 2009; *Kuwik v. Starmark Star Marketing and Administration, Inc.* (1993)
[786] Collins, 1998, p. 12; Eggert, 2006
[787] McConnell, 2000
[788] Hobbs Fry, n.d., p. 3 A
[789] Rumberger.com, 2008
[790] *Bals v. Verduzco* (1992)

[791] *Butler v. Central Bank and Trust Company* (1970); *Duncantell v. Universal Life Insurance Company* (1969); *Houston v. Grocers Supply Company* (1981); *Moore and Associates v. Metropolitan Insurance Company* (1980); *Zuniga v. Sears, Roebuck, & Co.* (1983)

[792] Daigle, 2008

[793] Bahls, 1999; Ballam, 2002, p. 455; *California Civil Code* Section 47(c); Carrico, 2000; Daigle, 2008; *Florida Statute* Section 768.095; *Hawaii Revised Statute* Section 663-1.95 Employers' Job Reference Immunity; Hobbs Fry, n.d., p. 5; *Illinois Code* Chapter 745 *Civil Immunities Employment Record Disclosure Act*; *Louisiana Revised Statutes* Section 23:291 Disclosure of Employment Related Information; Presumptions; Causes of Action; Definitions; New York State Senate, 2003; Novack, 1995; Spector, 2002, p. 10

[794] *Bishop v. Wood* (1976); *Garcia v. Walder Electronics, Inc.* (1990); *Johnson v. Martin* (1991); *Ratliff v. City of Milwaukee* (1986); *Susan M. Miron v. University of New Haven Police Department, et al.* (2007)

[795] *Introini v. Richland County* (1993)

[796] *Wells v. Minor* (1991)

[797] *Duncantell v. Universal Life Insurance Company* (1969); *Gengler v. Phelps* (1978); *Litman v. Massachusetts Mutual Life Insurance Company* (1984); *Lyle v. Waddle* (1945); *Mayfield v. Gleichert* (1969); *McDermott v. Hughly* (1989); *Patane v. Broadmoor Hotel, Inc.* (1985); *Renfro Drug Company v. Lawson* (1942); *Wilks v. DeBolt* (1948)

[798] *Smith v. Holley* (1992)

[799] *McQuirk v. Donnelley* (2000)

[800] Collins, 1998, p. 12; *Siegert v. Gilley* (1991)

[801] *Resnick v. Blue Cross and Blue Shield of Missouri* (1995)

[802] *Nadeau v. County of Ramsey* (1979)

[803] 911Dispatch.com, 2008; Adams, 2010; Frampton, 2010; Kavilanz, 2009; KPCC Wire Services, 2010; Kroskob, 2010; Nolin, 2010; Sampson, 2002b; The Smoking Gun, 2011b; Van Denburg, 2011; Weathersbee, 2008

[804] Eltman, Dai, & Sambriski, 2010

[805] Hartley, 2009

[806] Kwicien, 2010

[807] Tinsley, 2008

[808] Cross-Tab, 2010

[809] Reilly, 2004

[810] Babcock, 2011; Campbell, 2010a

[811] Read, 2006

[812] Phillips-Sandy, 2011

[813] Young, 2009

[814] CBSNews.Com, 2010b; Dwoskin, 2011; Fasick & Gonen, 2010; Hutchinson, 2010

[815] Gavish, 2009

[816] Miles, 2008

[817] Jaffe, 2011

[818] Hadid, 2010

[819] CBSNews.Com, 2010a; Lutz, 2010

[820] Matthews, 2009

[821] Sina Corporation, 2010

[822] Associated Press, 2007b; Evans, 2007; Lovett, 2009; McCullagh, 2009b; Perez, 2007; Tucker, 2008

[823] Fee & Raposa, 2008

[824] Associated Press, 2009b

[825] O'Crowley, 2009

[826] Bunkley, 2008

[827] LoBianco, 2011

828 Jaffee, 2011
829 Hernandez, 2011; Howard, 2011; Malcolm, 2011; McCullagh, 2011; Olshan & Sheehy, 2011
830 WHIOTV.com, 2007
831 ABCLOCAL.GO.com, 2009; WBZTV.com, 2009
832 Elly, 2010
833 Miller, 2008a
834 Mustian, 2010; Ward, 2007
835 Walters, 2009
836 Dwyer, 2009
837 Peltz & Long, 2010
838 Daigle, 2010, p. 13
839 Holson, 2009
840 Associated Press, 2009a; Gourevitch & Morris, 2008; Lagorio, 2005
841 Martin, 2003, p. 52; Schmidt, 1998, p. 39
842 Sheetz, 2003, p. 47
843 McCullagh, 2009a
844 Wright, 2010
845 Zeigler, 2011a
846 Rachlin, 2000; Saltzman, Cramer, & Ellement, 2009
847 *Electronic Communications Privacy Act of 1986*; Littlejohn Shinder, 2003, p. 44
848 Donofrio, 2001a, p. 103
849 United States Department of Justice Computer Crime and Intellectual Property Section Criminal Division, 2009, p. 136
850 Strang, 2001; United States Department of Justice Computer Crime and Intellectual Property Section Criminal Division, 2009, p. 137
851 ExecuNet.com, 2005; The Ladders, n.d.
852 Vaas, 2009
853 Strandberg, 2000, p. 17
854 Donofrio, 2001b, p. 82
855 Kiesler & Gendar 2011; Levy, 2008
856 Meyer & Short, 1998, p. 28
857 Donofrio, 2001a, p. 104
858 Ross & Schwartz, 2009
859 Hitchcock, 2003, p. 18
860 Dedman, 2010; Grimaldi & Vick, 2008; Kleiss, 2009; MonroeRising.com, 2010; Spector, 2010a
861 United States Department of Justice Computer Crime and Intellectual Property Section Criminal Division, 2009, p. 135
862 Watkins, 2010a
863 Davies, 2009; Dodds, 2011
864 Gendar, 2011
865 Dees, 2009; Reeger, 2009; Wortham, 2009; Zeidner, 2007
866 Caputo, 2007; Long, 2007
867 Chalfant, 2005; Higginbotham, 2008; Knight, 2007; Reilly, 2004; Vallee, 2006
868 Bennett, 2008; *Staffing Industry Review Magazine*, 2010
869 Joyce, 2010
870 Greenfield, 2011
871 Fishman & Brazytis, 2008, p. 2
872 Duke, 2009; Connecticut Attorney General, 2009; Green, 2006; KIROTV.com, 2010; Mikkelsen, 2010; MSNBC.com, 2009
873 *Wikipedia*, 2011d
874 Scaramella, Cox, & McCamey, 2011, p. 43

[875] *Sindermann v. Civil Service* (1995)
[876] Delp, 2002
[877] Immem, 2011
[878] Ackman, 2002
[879] Juliano, 2011
[880] Trautman, 2005, p. 123
[881] Amos, 2008
[882] Schofield, 1998
[883] *Brady v. Maryland* (1963)
[884] Judge, 2005
[885] *Kyles v. Whitley* (1995); *United States v. Agurs* (1976); *United States v. Bagley* (1985)
[886] Lisko, 2011; Van Derbeken, 2010
[887] *People v. Rosario* (1961)
[888] *Giglio v. United States* (1972)
[889] Justice.gov, 2008
[890] Moran, 2000
[891] *Grabinger v. Conlisk* (1972)
[892] *City of Canton v. Harris* (1989); *Huemiller v. Ogden Civil Service Commission* (2004)
[893] *Brickman v. New Orleans Aviation Board* (1959); *City of Tampa and Hillsborough County Police Benevolent Association* (1997); *County of Los Angeles Sheriff's Department and Association of Los Angeles Deputies* (1997); *Demauro v. Loren-Maltese* (2001); *Garner v. Civil Service Commission of Metropolitan Government of Nashville* (2009); *John Carter v. Township of Bordentown* (2007); *Leggett v. Northwest State College* (1962); *Rodriguez v. Board of Commissioners Port of New Orleans* (1977)
[894] *Brogan v. United States* (1998)
[895] *Garrity v. New Jersey* (1967)
[896] *Bryson v. United States* (1969); *Lachance v. Erickson* (1998)
[897] *Village of Oak Lawn v. Illinois Human Rights Commission* (1985)
[898] *City of Cambridge v. Civil Service Commission* (1997)
[899] *NASA v. Nelson* (2011)
[900] *Florida Law* Section 943.13(4)
[901] *New York State Correction Law*, Chapter 43 of the Consolidated Laws, Article 23-A Licensure and Employment of Persons Previously Convicted of One or More Criminal Offenses, Section 751: Applicability
[902] *Mister v. Illinois C.G.R.R.* (1987)
[903] *Mister v. Illinois C.G.R.R.* (1987)
[904] Colaprete, 2005b
[905] Shapiro, 2004
[906] Sheridan, 2008
[907] San Bernadino County Sheriff's Department, n.d.
[908] *Sindermann v. Civil Service* (1995)
[909] Hustmyre, 2002, p. 79
[910] CNN.com, 1998; Cuomo, Vlasto, & Dwyer, 2011; Epstein, 2011; Gendar, Lauinger, & Kennedy, 2011; Memoli & Susman, 2011; TMZ.com, 2011
[911] Memoli, 2010
[912] Serpas & Hagar, 2010, p. 120
[913] Anderson, 2010; Basu, 2010; Bowers & Washington, 2008; Brown, 2009; Cerota, 2010; Click2Houston.com, 2010; DiPrizio, 2008; Eiserer, 2006a; Eiserer, 2009d; Eiserer, 2010c; Eligon, 2009; Emily, 2009; *Ithaca Journal*, 2009a; *Ithaca Journal*, 2009b; Lemire, 2011; Levin & Goldsmith, 2011; McGregor, 2009; *New York Times*, 1995; Nisperos, 2008; O'Hara, 2009a; Parascandola, 2010b; Pignataro, 2010; Pinkerton, 2010; Santana, 2009; Steinberg, 1993; Vick, 2008; WDSU.com, 2009; WLWT.com, 2009; Wright, 2009; Yaniv & Shapiro, 2011

914 Van Derbeken, 2010
915 Hamacher, 2009b
916 Associated Press, 2007e
917 Brady-Lunny, 2008
918 Goffard, 2009
919 Ellement, 2010; Fargen & Gelzinis, 2009
920 Eiserer, 2008; KPCC Wire Services, 2009; Wilonsky, 2010
921 Spector, 2008
922 United States Department of Justice Office of Public Affairs, 2010
923 Dash, 1990
924 *Law and Order*, 2003, p. 42
925 Ramsey, 2011
926 Bovee & Thill, 1989, p. 340
927 Cheatham & Erickson, 1984, p. 32
928 Ramsey, 2011
929 Moyer & Dunphy, 2007
930 Roberg, Kuykendall, & Novak, 2002, p. 133
931 Cheatham & Erickson, 1984, p. 32
932 Leamon, 1999, p. 70
933 Miller & Hess, 1994, p. 71
934 Hoover, 1975, p. 11
935 ABCNews.Go.com, 2008b; Canning, Doherty, & Ibanga, 2008; ThePetitionSite.com, 2011
936 WUSA9.com, 2011a; WUSA9.com, 2011b
937 Albanese, 2008, p. 199
938 Cordner & Sheehan, 1999, p. 193
939 Duhart, 2001, p. 1
940 ABCNews.Go.com, 2009; ABCNews.Go.com, 2011a; ABCNews.Go.com, 2011b; ABCNews.Go.com, 2011c; Associated Press, 2009e; Associated Press, 2010e; Babwin, 2010; Bartley, 2011; CBS8.com, 2011; Chiesi, 2010; CNN Wire Staff, 2011a; Corcoran, 2011; Elfrink, 2011a; Elfrink, 2011b; Gast, 2011; Hope, 2007; Johnson, 2009; Koopmans, 2011; LATimes.com, 1988; Lush & Stacy, 2011; Mann, 2011; Moore, 2011; Neiwert, 2010; Olson, 2011; Potter, James, Esposito, & Martinez, 2010; Perez-Pena & Schweber, 2011; Preuitt, 2009; Raby, 2011; Schabner, 2011; Sewell, 2011; Verbano, 2011; Watkins, 2010b; Welsh-Huggins, 2011; Williams, 2010; Wilson, 2011
941 Cordner & Sheehan, 1999, p. 194
942 Vrij, Mann, Kristen, & Fisher, 2007
943 United States Department of the Interior, 1998c
944 United States Department of the Interior, 1998d
945 United States Department of the Interior, 1998f
946 Kleiman & Benek-Rivera. 2010
947 Hess & Ortmann, p. 182; Memon & Bull, 1991, p. 14
948 Melchers, Lienhardt, Von Aarburg, & Kleinmann, 2011
949 Colvin, 1999
950 Ivancevich, 2007, p. 224
951 Dunn, 2010
952 United States Department of the Interior, 1998a
953 Ivancevich, 2007, p. 224
954 United States Department of the Interior, 1998e
955 Huffcutt, 2011
956 Dortch, 2010; Whitacre, 2007
957 Scully, 2011
958 Alexander Hamilton Institute, 1991, H1; Burg, 1999, p. 38; Perkins, 2003; Rabon, 1992, p. 69

[959] *Law and Order*, 2003, p. 42
[960] Inbau, Reid, Buckley, & Jayne, 2001, p. 68
[961] Read, Powell, Kebbell, & Milne, 2009
[962] Garrett, 2010
[963] Rabon, 1992, p. 6
[964] Burke, 2001; Kidwell, 2009
[965] Napier, 2002
[966] Burg, 1999, p. 38
[967] Inbau, Reid, Buckley, & Jayne, 2001, p. 66
[968] Sandoval, 2003
[969] Alexander Hamilton Institute, 1991, H11
[970] Scully, 2011
[971] Bible, 1998
[972] United States Department of the Interior, 1998b
[973] Griffin, 1996, p. 392
[974] Roman, 2010
[975] Kaspar & Mosley, 2008
[976] Malakate, Andriopoulos, & Gotsi, 2007
[977] Bennett & Hess, 2007, p. 168
[978] Moyer & Dunphy, 2007
[979] Vrij, Mann, Fisher, Leal, Milne, & Bull, 2007
[980] Napier, 2002
[981] Wilson, 2010a, p. 44
[982] DeGroot & Gooty, 2009
[983] Wilson, 2010a, p. 46
[984] Zulawski & Wicklander, 1998, p. 83
[985] Szczesny, 2002, p. 128
[986] Sandoval & Adams, 2001
[987] Scott, 2006a
[988] Wixted & Mickes, 2010
[989] Pleskac & Busemeyer, 2011
[990] Scott, 2006a
[991] Matsumoto, Hwang, Skinner, & Frank, 2011
[992] Zulawski & Wicklander, 1998, p. 85
[993] *Miranda v. Arizona* (1966)
[994] Burke, 2001
[995] Reece, 2003, p. 67
[996] *Federal Rules of Evidence*: Rule 1001 and 1008
[997] Gillan, 2010
[998] Sabourin, 2007
[999] Matsumoto, Hwang, Skinner, & Frank, 2011
[1000] Adams, 1996
[1001] Rabon, 1994, p. 34
[1002] Porter & Yuille, 1996
[1003] Adams, 1996
[1004] Sabourin, 2007
[1005] Anonymous, 2009b
[1006] Akehurst, Manton, & Quandte, 2011
[1007] Blandon-Gitlin, Pezdek, Lindsay, & Hagen, 2009
[1008] Anson, Golding, & Gully, 1993
[1009] Godert, Gamer, Rill, & Vossel, 2005

1010 Johnson & Raye, 1981, p. 67
1011 Vrij, Mann, Kristen, & Fisher, 2007
1012 Rabon, 1994, p. 29
1013 Papadakis & Wofsky, 2010
1014 Doran & Brizee, 2010
1015 Jones & Joy, 1989
1016 *Pluskota v. Roadrunner Freight* (1994); *State of Minnesota By Spannaus v. Century Camera, Inc.* (1981)
1017 *Rhode Island General Law* 28-6.1-1(b)
1018 *Thompson v. Borg-Warner Protective Services* (1996)
1019 Ivancevich, 2007, p. 232; United States Congress, Office of Technology Assessment, 1990
1020 Gordon, 2008, p. 70
1021 Warner, 2005
1022 *Daubert v. Merrell Dow Chemicals, Inc.* (1993); *Frye v. United States* (1923)
1023 Honts & Schweinle, 2009
1024 *United States v. Henderson* (2005); *United States v. Scheffer* (1998)
1025 *United States v. Scheffer* (1998)
1026 *Americans with Disabilities Act of 1990*; *Employee Polygraph Protection Act of 1988*
1027 United States Government Printing Office, 1988
1028 United States Government Printing Office, 1988
1029 United States Government Printing Office, 1988
1030 *Croddy v. Federal Bureau of Investigation* (2006)
1031 *Anderson v. City of Philadelphia* (1988); *Fraternal Order of Police v. Freeman* (1978); *Hall v. United Parcel Service* (1989); *Mullen v. County of Suffolk* (2007); *O'Hartigan v. Department of Personnel* (1991); *Porto v. Town of Harrison* (1984); *Stone v. Chelan County Sheriff's Department* (1988); *Truesdale v. University of North Carolina* (1988); *Woodland v. City of Houston* (1991)
1032 *Brown v. State of Tennessee* (1982)
1033 *Hatfield Township v. Stanley* (1988)
1034 United States Equal Employment Opportunity Commission, 1987
1035 *Connecticut Code*—Sec. 31-51g (a) Use of polygraph prohibited. Penalty. Exceptions.
1036 *Connecticut Code*—Sec. 31-51g. (d) (1) and (2) Use of polygraph prohibited. Penalty. Exceptions.
1037 *Rhode Island General Law* 28-6.1-1
1038 *Rhode Island General Law* 28-6.1-1(c)
1039 *The Police Chief*, 1997, p. 25; United States Department of Justice, 1997; United States Equal Employment Opportunity Commission, 2000
1040 Stohr & Collins, 2009, p. 187
1041 American Polygraph Association, 2009, p. 1
1042 Missouri State Highway Patrol Human Resources Division, 2009
1043 Archibold & Becker, 2008; Eggen & Vedantam, 2006; Johnson, 1999
1044 Warner, 2005
1045 San Antonio Express-News, 2008
1046 Bennett & Hess, 2004, p. 197
1047 Slowik, 2008
1048 Weizel, 2008a
1049 Machado, 2007
1050 Handler & Barrera, 2007
1051 Miller, 2000
1052 Warrick & Eggen, 2007
1053 Roberg, Kuykendall, & Novak, 2002, p. 128

[1054] Handler, Honts, Krapohl, Nelson, & Griffin, 2009
[1055] *Anderson v. City of Philadelphia* (1988)
[1056] United States Government Printing Office, 1988
[1057] Sharp, 2003, p. 83; Targeted News Service, 2011b; Washoe County Sheriff's Office, 2009
[1058] *Law and Order*, 2002
[1059] *New York Labor Law* Article 20-B Section 733 Definitions.
[1060] *New York Labor Law* Article 20-B Section 734 Practitioner Limitations.
[1061] Baines, 2011a
[1062] Baines, 2011a; Baines, 2011b; Damphousse, Pointon, Upchurch, & Moore, 2007
[1063] Grant & Terry, 2005, p. 362; Narramore & Stephen, 1998; Trautman, 2005, p. 123
[1064] Buckley, Jackson, Bolino, Veres, & Feild, 2007
[1065] Horne, 1999
[1066] Horne, 1999
[1067] Clark, Olson, Porter, & Leichner, 2001, p. 30
[1068] Griffin, 1996, p. 393
[1069] Alpert & Dunham, 1997, p. 56
[1070] Hale, 2005, p. 24
[1071] Bernstein, 2011
[1072] 13wham.com, 2009; Craig, 2010c
[1073] Craig, 2011c; Jones, 1994; Powell, 2007
[1074] Craig, 2010d
[1075] Mills, 2007; Redmond, 2007
[1076] Runyon, 2010
[1077] *HR Management*, n.d.
[1078] New York State Department of Civil Service, 2006, p. 10
[1079] New York State Department of Civil Service, 2006, p. 10
[1080] Abimbola, 2002, p. 534
[1081] Wolf, 1999
[1082] DePresca, 2003a, p. 165
[1083] Gunderson, 2003
[1084] Hess & Hess Orthmann, 2010, p. 662
[1085] Gould Publications, 2000, p. 2-4-13
[1086] Gould Publications, 2000, p. 2-4-14
[1087] Cooper, 2007; Jones, 1994
[1088] Bensman & Contreras, 2008

CHAPTER 6

[1] Anonymous, 1987
[2] Todd, 2001, p. 34
[3] Grinnell & Burke, 2001, p. 36
[4] Todd, 2001, p. 32
[5] Rankin, 1999
[6] McGregor, 2006
[7] United States Courts, n.d.a
[8] Bumstead, 2009; Scott, 2006b
[9] National Association of Professional Background Screeners, 2011
[10] Collins, 2003
[11] Whisenand & Ferguson, 2005, p. 218
[12] Nelson, 1999, p. 42
[13] Privacy Rights Clearing House, 2010

[14] Ortmeier & Davis, 2012, p. 198
[15] Stewart & Craig, 2011; Suderman, 2011
[16] McNary, 2009
[17] Thompson, 2009
[18] Fuss, McSheehy, & Snowden, 1998, p. 172

Bibliography

9WSYR.com (2011, January 11). Schumer, Fitzpatrick call for mandatory DNA fingerprinting. Retrieved on April 17, 2011 from http://www.9wsyr.com/news/local/story/Schumer-Fitzpatrick-call-for-mandatory-DNA/iA2FQYS6jkGp5n2Hf3q0qQ.cspx.

911Dispatch.com (2008, March 28). 911 Prankster sentenced to 3 years in jail. Retrieved on April 30, 2011 from http://www.911dispatch.com/2008/03/911-prankster-sentenced-to-3-years-in-jail/.

10News.com (2010, September 23). Budget woes force Chula Vista Police layoffs: Thirty-three police officers laid off. Retrieved on February 14, 2011 from http://www.10news.com/news/25138140/detail.html.

13wham.com (2009, July 13). Trowbridge allegedly falsified info on Gary Pignato. Retrieved on October 13, 2010 from http://www.13wham.com/news/local/story/Trowbridge-Allegedly-Falsified-Info-on-Gary/JU6b9sIYvkSbZI9nsNyEfw.cspx.

13wham.com (2011, March 18). Batavia detention officers indicted in anabolic steroid case. Retrieved on March 19, 2011 from http://www.13wham.com/news/local/story/anabolic-steroids-batavia-detention-facility/RWYl9_jxBkKb-D6cP_2X3g.cspx?rss=509.

Aamodt, M. G. (1997a). *What We Know about Law Enforcement Selection in 1997*. Baltimore, MD: Mid-Atlantic Personnel Assessment Consortium.

Aamodt, M. G. (1997b). *Legal Issues in Selecting Law Enforcement Personnel*. Baltimore, MD: Mid-Atlantic Personnel Assessment Consortium.

Aamodt, M. G. (2004). *Law Enforcement Selection: Research Summaries*. Washington, DC: Police Executive Research Forum.

Aamodt, M. G., Brewster, J. A., & Raynes, B. L. (1998, September 16). Is the "police personality" predisposed to domestic violence? Quantico, VA: Paper Presented at the FBI Conference on Domestic Violence by Police Officers.

Abbott v. Payne (1984).

Abclocal.go.com (2009, April 16). Erie PA, cop caught on YouTube. Retrieved on October 18, 2010 from http://abclocal.go.com/wtvg/story?section=news/national_world&id=6764346.

Abclocal.go.com (2010, September 23). Madigan: Suspect had 1,600 child porn images. Retrieved on January 18, 2011 from http://abclocal.go.com/wls/story?section=news/local&id=7685874.

AbcNews.go.com (2008a, February 27). Jury snares ex-cop who killed pregnant girlfriend. Retrieved on October 29, 2010 from http://abcnews.go.com/TheLaw/story?id=4355338&page=1.

AbcNews.go.com (2008b, August 18). Traffic cop to blame for dog's death? Pet owners were stopped for speeding while rushing dying pet to vet. Retrieved on June 5, 2011 from http://abcnews.go.com/video/playerIndex?id=5601495.

AbcNews.go.com (2009, August 26). Cop killed by elderly driver: 79-year-old has been charged with homicide by negligent operation. Retrieved on February 20, 2011 from http://abcnews.go.com/video/video?id=8411053.

AbcNews.go.com (2011a, January 20). 2 Miami cops killed in shootout. Retrieved on February 20, 2011 from http://abcnews.go.com/US/video/miami-cops-killed-shootout-12722968.

AbcNews.go.com (2011b, January 24). Suspected Florida cop killer dead: St. Petersburg Police found 39-year-old Hydra Lacy Jr. dead in his home. Retrieved on February 20, 2011 from http://abcnews.go.com/US/video/suspected-florida-cop-killer-dead-12750750.

AbcNews.go.com (2011c, January 25). Manhunt for suspected Oregon cop shooter: Police say avid Durham is armed and traveling with his dog Huckleberry. Retrieved on February 20, 2011 from http://abcnews.go.com/US/video/manhunt-for-suspected-oregon-cop-shooter-david-durham-12759531.

ABC.Daytonnewssource.com (2011, March 11). Top stories—Civil Service Board announces police recruit scores. Retrieved on April 14, 2011 from http://abc.daytonsnewssource.com/shared/newsroom/top_stories/videos/wkef_vid_6103.shtml.

Abimbola, K. (2002, December). Questions and answers: The logic of preliminary fact investigation. *Journal of Law and Society*, *29*(4), 533–559.

Abshire, R. (2007, September 16). Sheriff: No staff leniency, Kaufmann, he faults agencies that let officers become 'Gypsy Cops.' Retrieved on November 6, 2009 from http://proquest.umi.com.library.keuka.edu/pqdweb?did=1336599481&sid=1&Fmt=3&clientId=3663&RQT=309&VName=PQD.

Ackman, D. (2002, January 25). Crime and cover-up. Retrieved on April 1, 2011 from http://www.forbes.com/2002/01/25/0125topnews.html.

Adam Walsh Child Protection and Safety Act (2006).

Adams, A. (2009, September). Employees and fraud: Work eligibility. Retrieved on March 16, 2010 from http://proquest.umi.com.library.keuka.edu/pqdweb?did=1865399731&sid=1&Fmt=2&clientId=3663&RQT=309&VName=PQD.

Adams, D. B. (2002, March). *Summary of State Sex Offender Registries, 2001*. Washington, DC: United States Department of Justice, Office of Justice Programs, Bureau of Justice Statistics.

Adams, J. (2010, August 30). "SWATing" becomes growing problem for authorities: Untraceable cellphones used in pranks on 911 operators. Retrieved on April 30, 2011 from http://www.nbclosangeles.com/news/local/SWATing-Becomes-Growing-Problem-for-Authorities-101759483.html.

Adams, P. (2000, August). City job applicants must waive privacy act rights Auburn requirement: Some question need for such a wide-ranging release form. Retrieved on September 13, 2010 from http://proquest.umi.com.library.keuka.edu/pqdweb?index=27&did=59046925&SrchMode=1&sid=5&Fmt=3&VInst=PROD&VType=PQD&RQT=309&VName=PQD&TS=1284425035&clientId=3663.

Adams, S. H. (1996). Statement analysis: What do suspects' words really reveal? Retrieved on July 24, 2011 from http://web.ebscohost.com.library.keuka.edu/ehost/detail?vid=5&hid=110&sid=e3273d33-5fa7-4328-bcbc-0764c45e691c%40sessionmgr110&bdata=JnNpdGU9ZWhvc3QtbGl2ZQ%3d%3d#db=sih&AN=SM167485.

Adams, T. F., Caddell, A. G., & Krutsinger, J. L. (2004). *Crime Scene Investigation* (2nd edn.). Upper Saddle River, NJ: Prentice Hall Publishing.

ADA.gov (n.d.). *The Americans with Disabilities Act. Title II Technical Assistance Manual Covering State and Local Government Programs and Services*. Retrieved on February 13, 2011 from http://www.ada.gov/taman2.html.

Adler, R. S. & Peirce, E. R. (1996). Encouraging employers to abandon their "no comment" policies regarding job references: A reform proposal. *Washington and Lee Law Review*, *53*(4), 1381–1469.

Advanced Research (2006, September 26). Beware of negligent entrustment when employees change departments. Retrieved on March 30, 2009 from http://www.arsbackgrounds.com/negligent_entrustment.html.

Agar, J. (2011, February 11). Judge upholds Walmart's firing of Michigan medical marijuana user. Retrieved on June 1, 2011 from http://www.mlive.com/news/grand-rapids/index.ssf/2011/02/judge_upholds_walmarts_firing.html.

Age Discrimination in Employment Act (1967).

Aguillard v. McGowen (2000).

Ahern v. Odyssey Re (London) Ltd (2001).

Ahlers, M. M. (2004, February 5). Report: Felons hired in rush to fill screener jobs. Retrieved on February 8, 2010 from http://www.cnn.com/2004/US/02/05/tsa.felons.screeners/index.html.

Ahmed, M. (2009, January 14). Teen 'sexting' craze leading to child porn arrests in US. Retrieved on October 14, 2010 from http://technology.timesonline.co.uk/tol/news/tech_and_web/article5516511.ece.

Air Force, 437 Wing and AFGE L-1869 (2000).

Akehurst, L., Manton, S., & Quandte, S. (2011, March/April). Careful calculation or a leap of faith? A field study of the translation of CBCA ratings to final credibility judgments. Retrieved on July 24, 2011 from http://proquest.umi.com.library.keuka.edu/pqdweb?did=2308169021&sid=5&Fmt=2&clientId=3663&RQT=309&VName=PQD.

Alaska Department of Corrections Recruitment (n.d.). Alaska Department of Corrections recruitment. Retrieved on February 7, 2010 from http://www.correct.state.ak.us/corrections/co_recruitment/materials/definitions.jsf.

Aksamit, N. (2002, March 18). Affirmative action clash is looming: The police and firefighter unions disagree with minority groups over the importance of test scores in city promotions. What's next affirmative action at a glance. Retrieved on October 26, 2009 from http://proquest.umi.com.library.keuka.edu/pqdweb?did=110607574&sid=2&Fmt=3&clientId=3663&RQT=309&VName=PQD.

Alabama Peace Officers Standards and Training Commission (2009). ePOST. Retrieved on October 20, 2009 from http://www.apostc.state.al.us/.

Alanez, T. (2009, June 23). Complaints from strippers, hog-tied dui suspect force Broward County deputy to resign. Retrieved on October 20, 2009 from http://www.palmbeachpost.com/state/content/state/epaper/2009/06/23/0623deputy.html.

Alanez, T. & Ortega, J. (2009, September 1). Tally of charges against BSO deputy accused of sex abuse rises to 27. Retrieved on September 21, 2009 from www.chicagotribune.com/topic/sfl-bleiweiss-deputy-arrest-b090109,0,7147113.story.

Alaska Employment Letter (2010, February 18). Workplace violence and the ADA. Retrieved on February 20, 2010 from http://hrhero.com/hl/articles/2010/02/18/workplace-violence-and-the-ada/?HLW.

Albanese, J. S. (2006). *Professional Ethics in Criminal Justice: Being Ethical When No One is Looking*. Boston, MA: Pearson Education, Inc.

Albanese, J. S. (2008). *Criminal Justice* (4th edn.). Boston, MA: Pearson Education, Inc.

Albemarle Paper v. Moody (1975).

Albury v. New York City Civil Service Commission (1969).

Alexander Hamilton Institute (1991). *Effective Interviews for Every Situation*. Maywood, NJ: Modern Business Reports—Alexander Hamilton Institute, Inc.

Alfano, S. (2010, December 31). Mother and daughter accused of molesting teen boy for three years, police say. Retrieved on January 19, 2011 from http://www.nydailynews.com/news/national/2010/12/31/2010-12-31_mother_and_daughter_accused_of_molesting_teen_boy_for_three_years_police_say.html?obref=obinsite.

Alhabib, S., Nur, U., & Jones, R. (2010, May). Domestic violence against women: Systematic review of prevalence studies. Retrieved on October 11, 2010 from http://web.ebscohost.com.library.keuka.edu/ehost/detail?vid=20&hid=15&sid=c11a669b-e675-487a-9271-e6576c348b8e%40sessionmgr12&bdata=JnNpdGU9ZWhvc3QtbGl2ZQ%3d%3d#db=cin20&AN=2010588375.

Ali, A. (2011, January 10). New Jersey moves to curb steroid use by police. Retrieved on March 19, 2011 from http://www.reuters.com/article/2011/01/11/us-newjersey-steroids-idUSTRE7096A820110111.

Allen, A. (2007, May 21). Commentary: Dishonest resumes poison an already flawed system. Retrieved on February 22, 2011 from http://proquest.umi.com.library.keuka.edu/pqdweb?did=1275246751&sid=3&Fmt=3&clientId=3663&RQT=309&VName=PQD.

Allen v. City of Los Angeles (1976).

Allen v. Muskogee (1997).

Allied Chemical Workers v. Pittsburgh Plate and Glass Co (1971).

Alpert, G. P. (1989, September–October). Law enforcement: City of Canton v. Harris and the deliberate indifference standard. Retrieved on October 24, 2009 from http://search.ebscohost.com.library.keuka.edu/login.aspx?direct=true&db=sih&AN=SM120094&site=ehost-live.

Alpert, G. P. & Dunham, R. G. (1997). *Policing Urban America* (3rd edn.). Prospect Heights, IL: Waveland Press, Inc.

Alpert, L. I. (2007, January 8). ID theft 101: Beauty cons her way onto Ivys' rolls as an Ed. ringer. Retrieved on February 11, 2011 from http://www.nypost.com/p/news/regional/ringer_theft_beauty_cons_her_way_uzNMfKVkXRVCWu4YjmkEDM.

Altman, L. K. (1986, February 4). New DNA test offers biological 'fingerprints' for crime fight. Retrieved on January 18, 2011 from http://www.nytimes.com/1986/02/04/science/new-dna-test-offers-biological-fingerprints-for-crime-fight.html.

AltoonaMirror.com (2008, August 5). Altoona police officer charged in teen sex case. Retrieved on December 6, 2010 from http://www.altoonamirror.com/page/content.detail/id/509805.html.

Alva Cape Alva Steamship Company v. City of New York. (1968). Retrieved on November 15, 2009 from http://openjurist.org/405/f2d/962/alva-cape-alva-steamship-co-v-city-of-new-york-a.

Alvarez, A. (2009, August 6). What the Jonathan Bleiweiss case reveals about fetishizing Latino immigrants. Retrieved on October 28, 2010 from http://guanabee.com/2009/08/jonathan-bleiweiss-gay-latino-fetish.

Alvarez, L. (2007, February 14). Army giving more waivers in recruiting. Retrieved on August 7, 2011 from http://www.nytimes.com/2007/02/14/us/14military.html.

Alvarez, L. (2008, April 18). Nearly a fifth of war Veterans report mental disorders, a private study finds. Retrieved on August 15, 2010 from http://www.nytimes.com/2008/04/18/us/18vets.html.

Amendola, K. L., Hawkins, C., Nicoletti, J., Scrivner, E., & Maltarese, L. (2008, April 30). Cutting-edge recruitment and selection: Current perspectives and future challenges. Retrieved on November 23, 2009 from http://www.cops.usdoj.gov/Default.asp?Item=1621.

Amendola, K. L., Weber, R. W., & Mercer, B. S. (1998, March/April). Minimizing the risks: Personnel selection strategies. Retrieved on September 19, 1999 from www.communitypolicing.org/exchange/e19_98/e19amend.htm.

American Academy of Child and Adolescent Psychiatry (2010). Teens: Alcohol and other drugs. Retrieved on March 19, 2011 from http://aacap.org/page.ww?name=Teens:+Alcohol+and+Other+Drugs&section=Facts+for+Families.

American Journal of Trial Advocacy (1988, Spring). Urinalysis drug tests: Do they make the grade? Retrieved on January 24, 2010 from http://search.ebscohost.com.library.keuka.edu/login.aspx?direct=true&db=sih&AN=SM121402&site=ehost-live.

American Psychiatric Association (1994). *Diagnostic and Statistical Manual of Mental Disorders* (DSM-IV). Washington, DC: American Psychiatric Association.

American Polygraph Association (2009, March 31). By-laws and standards of practice. Retrieved on November 22, 2009 from http://www.polygraph.org/section/about-us/laws-and-standards-practice.

American Psychological Association (2009). Rights and responsibilities of test takers: Guidelines and expectations. Retrieved on October 20, 2009 from http://www.apa.org/science/ttrr.html.

AmericanRhetoric.com (1962, May 12). General Douglas Macarthur: Sylvanus Thayer award acceptance address—"Duty, Honor, Country." Retrieved on April 15, 2011 from http://www.americanrhetoric.com/speeches/douglasmacarthurthayeraward.html.

Americans with Disabilities Act (1990).

Americans with Disabilities Act Amendments Act (2008).

Amos, O. (2008, June 24). The truth game. Retrieved on July 26, 2011 from http://proquest.umi.com.library.keuka.edu/pqdweb?did=1499497711&sid=6&Fmt=3&clientId=3663&RQT=309&VName=PQD.

Amsden, R. (2010, October 22). Former police commissioner gets 8 years. Retrieved on October 22, 2010 from http://www.unionleader.com/article.aspx?headline=Former+police+commissioner+gets+8+years&articleId=4d05d16f-68c2-4137-9555-086fe4dbe819.

Anabolic Steroids Control Act (1990).

Anabolic Steroids Control Act (2004).

Anastasia Vey, In re. (1994).
Anderson, C. (2005, December). Presumptive and confirmatory drug tests. Retrieved on January 24, 2010 from http://search.ebscohost.com.library.keuka.edu/login.aspx?direct=true&db=aph&N=19048180&site=ehost-live.
Anderson, J. (2010, June 11). City police officer convicted on a 2004 charge in beating of teen: Officer faces up to 30 years in prison. Retrieved on October 28, 2010 from http://articles.baltimoresun.com/2010-06-11/news/bs-md-ci-bpd-civil-rights-case-convic20100611_1_misdemeanor-assault-and-misconduct-officer-gregory-m-mussmacher-police-officer.
Anderson, J. R. (1991, December 9). No one cares if it's true' background checks have little limit. Retrieved on September 13, 2010 from http://proquest.umi.com.library.keuka.edu/pqdweb?index=38&did=102842746&SrchMode=1&sid=5&Fmt=3&VInst=PROD&VType=PQD&RQT=309&VName=PQD&TS=1284425368&clientId=3663.
Anderson, T. R. & Aviles, A. M. (2006, Fall). Diverse faces of domestic violence. Retrieved on October 11, 2010 from http://web.ebscohost.com.library.keuka.edu/ehost/detail?vid=21&hid=-15&sid=c11a669b-e675-487a-9271-e6576c348b8e%40sessionmgr12&bdata=JnNpdGU9ZWhvc3QtbGl2ZQ%3d%3d#db=c8h&AN=2009341099.
Anderson Trucking Service, Inc. v. Gibson (2004).
Anderson v. City of Philadelphia (1988).
Andreatta, D. (2010, February 23). Webster official's alleged indelicate e-mails cited. Retrieved on February 23, 2010 from http://www.democratandchronicle.com/article/20100223/NEWS01/100223020/1002/NEWS.
Andreatta, D. (2011, February 23). Carlos Cardenas pleads not guilty in Albion homicide. Retrieved on February 25, 2011 from http://www.democratandchronicle.com/article/20110225/NEWS01/102250331/Carlos-Cardenas-pleads-not-guilty-Albion-homicide?odyssey=mod|newswell|text|Home|s.
Anonymous (1987, June). Certified resumes eliminate hiring fears. Retrieved on September 13, 2010 from http://proquest.umi.com.library.keuka.edu/pqdweb?index=42&did=1041477&SrchMode=1&sid=5&Fmt=2&VInst=PROD&VType=PQD&RQT=309&VName=PQD&TS=1284426038&clientId=3663.
Anonymous (1996, September). Workplace violence profiled in latest BLS survey. Retrieved on April 19, 2011 from http://proquest.umi.com.library.keuka.edu/pqdweb?index=30&did=11080095&SrchMode=1&sid=5&Fmt=6&VInst=PROD&VType=PQD&RQT=309&VName=PQD&TS=1303228322&clientId=3663.
Anonymous (1998, March). More than 60 million working women tracked in new federal health report. Retrieved on April 19, 2011 from http://proquest.umi.com.library.keuka.edu/pqdweb?did=28318958&sid=5&Fmt=3&clientId=3663&RQT=309&VName=PQD.
Anonymous (2004, January). Employer faces liability for customer's assault by worker. Retrieved on February 16, 2010 from http://proquest.umi.com.library.keuka.edu/pqdweb?did=552072991&sid=1&Fmt=2&clientId=3663&RQT=309&VName=PQD.
Anonymous (2005, January). Affirmative action plan no longer allowed. Retrieved on November 6, 2009 from http://proquest.umi.com.library.keuka.edu/pqdweb?did=788304751&sid=2&Fmt=3&clientId=3663&RQT=309&VName=PQD.
Anonymous (2006a, July). Employer not liable for former employee's assault on patient. Retrieved on February 15, 2010 from http://proquest.umi.com.library.keuka.edu/pqdweb?did=1103359031&sid=1&Fmt=2&clientId=3663&RQT=309&VName=PQD.
Anonymous (2006b, July). Employer of guard who assaulted third party may be liable for negligent hiring. Retrieved on February 15, 2010 from http://proquest.umi.com.library.keuka.edu/pqdweb?did=1103359011&sid=1&Fmt=2&clientId=3663&RQT=309&VName=PQD.
Anonymous (2006c, October). Employer liable for foreseeable burglary of customers by employee. Retrieved on February 15, 2010 from http://proquest.umi.com.library.keuka.edu/pqdweb?did=1179895971&sid=1&Fmt=2&clientId=3663&RQT=309&VName=PQD.

Anonymous (2008a, March). Negligent entrustment. Retrieved on November 15, 2009 from http://proquest.umi.com.library.keuka.edu/pqdweb?did=1456110151&sid=1&Fmt=3&clientId=3663&RQT=309&VName=PQD.

Anonymous (2008b, May 13). Nepotism statutes sadly necessary. Retrieved on October 13, 2009 from http://proquest.umi.com.library.keuka.edu/pqdweb?index=59&did=1477861171&SrchMode=1&sid=2&Fmt=3&VInst=PROD&VType=PQD&RQT=309&VName=PQD&TS=1255433071&clientId=3663.

Anonymous (2008c, June 20). How to verify an employee's eligibility. Retrieved on March 16, 2010 from http://proquest.umi.com.library.keuka.edu/pqdweb?did=1498393681&sid=1&Fmt=3&clientId=3663&RQT=309&VName=PQD.

Anonymous (2008d, September). Employers hit the name-SSN verification trifecta. Retrieved on March 16, 2010 from http://proquest.umi.com.library.keuka.edu/pqdweb?did=1540361491&sid=1&Fmt=3&clientId=3663&RQT=309&VName=PQD.

Anonymous (2009a, July 28). Minority hiring timeline for Danbury Police Department. Retrieved on November 6, 2009 from http://proquest.umi.com.library.keuka.edu/pqdweb?did=1807158841&sid=2&Fmt=3&clientId=3663&RQT=309&VName=PQD.

Anonymous (2009b, November 7). Cognitive psychology; data on cognitive psychology reported by researchers at California State University. Retrieved on July 24, 2011 from http://proquest.umi.com.library.keuka.edu/pqdweb?did=1888887011&sid=5&Fmt=3&clientId=3663&RQT=309&VName=PQD.

Anonymous (2009c, November 23). A better way to hire: Incentives to use 'e-verify' are welcome. Retrieved on March 16, 2010 from http://proquest.umi.com.library.keuka.edu/pqdweb?did=1926239611&sid=1&Fmt=3&clientId=3663&RQT=309&VName=PQD.

Anonymous (2010, June 19). U. S. Department of Justice; former police officer charged with $889,000 ponzi scheme. Retrieved on February 20, 2011 from http://proquest.umi.com.library.keuka.edu/pqdweb?did=2053642901&sid=1&Fmt=3&clientId=3663&RQT=309&VName=PQD.

Anonymous (2011a, March). Rise in workplace violence but fewer victims. Retrieved on April 19, 2011 from http://proquest.umi.com.library.keuka.edu/pqdweb?did=2301714871&sid=2&Fmt=3&clientId=3663&RQT=309&VName=PQD.

Anonymous (2011b, March). Top security threats and management issues facing corporate America. Retrieved on April 19, 2011 from http://proquest.umi.com.library.keuka.edu/pqdweb?did=2314402151&sid=2&Fmt=2&clientId=3663&RQT=309&VName=PQD.

Anonymous (2011c, March 29). Homicide and nonfatal violent crimes in the workplace declined. Retrieved on April 19, 2011 from http://proquest.umi.com.library.keuka.edu/pqdweb?did=2304638841&sid=2&Fmt=3&clientId=3663&RQT=309&VName=PQD.

Anonymous v. Dobbs Ferry Union Free School District (2002).

Anson, D. A., Golding, S. L., & Gully, K. J. (1993, June). Child sexual abuse investigations. Retrieved on July 24, 2011 from http://web.ebscohost.com.library.keuka.edu/ehost/detail?vid=5&hid=110&sid=e3273d33-5fa7-4328-bcbc-0764c45e691c%40sessionmgr110&bdata=JnNpdGU9ZWhvc3QtbGl2ZQ%3d%3d#db=sih&AN=SM142805.

Archbold, C. A. (2006, March). Police legal advisors in the USA: Past, present, and future. *Police Practice and Research*, *7*(1), 61–76.

Archibold, R. C. & Becker, A. (2008, May 27). Border agents, lured by the other side. Retrieved on March 30, 2009 from http://www.nytimes.com/2008/05/27/us/27border.html?_r=1.

Arkansas Department of Finance and Administration Retrieved from http://www.arkansas.gov/dfa.

Armon, R. (2003, July 3). Ex-cop, a convicted molester, blames training, may sue city. Rochester, NY: Democrat and Chronicle.

Armon, R. (2010, September 12). Police layoffs to start tonight: Akron and union fail to meet for last-minute negotiations, blame each other for the stalemate police/union official wants a trained mediator. Retrieved on February 14, 2011 http://www.ohio.com/news/102717489.html.

Army Lawyer (1997, August). Criminal law note. Retrieved on April 16, 2011 http://web.ebscohost.com.library.keuka.edu/ehost/detail?vid=8&hid=111&sid=b3f5dc62-a935-427d-9ab9-e87305912346%40sessionmgr110&bdata=JnNpdGU9ZWhvc3QtbGl2ZQ%3d%3d#db=mth&AN=9710162551.

Arnold, D. W. & Thiemann, A. J. (1992). To test or not to test: The status of psychological testing under ADA. Retrieved on November 21, 2009 from http://search.ebscohost.com.library.keuka.edu/login.aspx?direct=true&db=eric&AN=ED374575&site=ehost-live.

Arnold v. City of San Antonio (2009).

Ashton, R. (2004, February 5). Sell the message. Retrieved on March 16, 2010 from http://proquest.umi.com.library.keuka.edu/pqdweb?did=578824011&sid=3&Fmt=4&clientId=3663&RQT=309&VName=PQD.

Aspen, M., Mora, R., Goff, B., & Sweig, H. (1958). The role of common law concepts in modern criminal jurisprudence (a symposium). *Criminal Law Case Notes and Comments, 49*, 145–151.

Associated Press (1995, November 30). Former Chattanooga officer on trial for fraud. Retrieved on February 20, 2011 from http://proquest.umi.com.library.keuka.edu/pqdweb?did=19364505&sid=1&Fmt=3&clientId=3663&RQT=309&VName=PQD.

Associated Press (2000, January 17). Job discrimination suits tripled in '90s. Rochester, NY: Democrat and Chronicle.

Associated Press (2003, August 26). Dallas police chief fired after 'An Accumulation of Issues.' Retrieved on October 9, 2009 from http://www.usatoday.com/news/nation/2003-08-26-dallas-police_x.htm.

Associated Press (2004a, June 18). City of Tacoma releases David Brame's lost psych test. Retrieved on October 4, 2009 from http://community.seattletimes.nwsource.com/archive/?date=20040618&slug=webbrame18.

Associated Press (2004b, August 3). Mary Kay Letourneau released from prison. Retrieved on October 12, 2010 from http://www.usatoday.com/news/nation/2004-08-03-teacher-released_x.htm.

Associated Press (2004c, July 26). Cape coral officer faces sex charges involving two teens. Retrieved on December 6, 2010 from http://staugustine.com/stories/072604/sta_2471395.shtml.

Associated Press (2004d, October 23). A decade after Susan Smith case, South Carolina city still trying to heal. Retrieved on December 11, 2010 from http://www.usatoday.com/news/nation/2004-10-23-susan-smith_x.htm/.

Associated Press (2004e, December 2). 18 N.C. officers could face suspension of police certification in cheating case. Retrieved on August 4, 2011 from http://www.policeone.com/investigations/articles/94173-18-N-C-Officers-Could-Face-Suspension-of-Police-Certification-in-Cheating-Case/.

Associated Press (2005, September 16). Ex-detective pleads guilty to child porn. Retrieved on October 29, 2010 from http://lubbockonline.com/stories/091605/sta_091605097.shtml.

Associated Press (2006a, July 13). Dallas rebuilding scandalized police department to better tackle crime. Retrieved on October 9, 2009 from http://origin.foxnews.com/story/0,2933,203303,00.html?sPage=fnc/politics/lawenforcement.

Associated Press (2006b, December 15). LAPD probing claim ex-deputy chief traded promotions for sex. Retrieved on November 3, 2010 from http://abclocal.go.com/kabc/story?section=news/local&id=4854675.

Associated Press (2006c, August 25). Despite ban, gambling abounds in Hawaii. Retrieved on February 8, 2011 from http://www.msnbc.msn.com/id/14509349/ns/us_news-life/.

Associated Press (2006d, September 9). Juvenile center appointee loses job over degree flap. Retrieved on April 13, 2011 from http://proquest.umi.com.library.keuka.edu/pqdweb?did=1126362911&sid=6&Fmt=3&clientId=3663&RQT=309&VName=PQD.

Associated Press (2007a, August 31). Texas police chief accused of sexually assaulting male employees. Retrieved on September 27, 2010 from http://www.foxnews.com/story/0,2933,295355,00.html.

Associated Press (2007b, September 16). Authorities turn to social networking sites to make cases. Retrieved on March 13, 2010 from http://www.lexisnexis.com.library.keuka.edu/us/lnacademic/results/docview/docview.do?docLinkInd=true&risb=21_T8805007784&format=GNBFI&sort=RELEVANCE&startDocNo=1&resultsUrlKey=29_T8805007788&cisb=22_T8805007787&treeMax=true&treeWidth=0&csi=304481&docNo=1.

Associated Press (2007c, June 9). Sex offenders getting younger, more violent. Retrieved on October 13, 2010 from http://www.msnbc.msn.com/id/19143411/.

Associated Press (2007d). University chief fired after student rape, slaying: Two eastern Michigan officials also lose jobs; cover-up alleged. Retrieved on April 1, 2011 from http://www.msnbc.msn.com/id/19790500/ns/us_news-education/.

Associated Press (2007e, March 1). Dog with college degree may appear in court: Attorney says police chief, canine earned degrees from same online school. Retrieved on April 13, 2011 from http://www.msnbc.msn.com/id/17398521/ns/us_news-weird_news/.

Associated Press (2007f, February 1). Employers can be sued for leaving bad stuff out of references. Retrieved on April 25, 2011 from http://chronicle.augusta.com/stories/1997/02/01/biz_203447.shtml.

Associated Press (2008a, October 21). Virginia legislators seek review of police chief's degree. Retrieved on August 15, 2010 from http://www.charlotteobserver.com/2008/10/21/267138/virginia-legislators-seek-review.html.

Associated Press (2008b, November 29). Bases brace for surge in stress-related disorders. Retrieved on August 15, 2010 from http://www.msnbc.msn.com/id/27968227/.

Associated Press (2008c, March 14). Pentagon releases sexual harassment data: Survey finds more women feeling harassed, but fewer reports filed. Retrieved on October 9, 2010 from http://www.msnbc.msn.com/id/23636487/.

Associated Press (2008d, September 26). News anchor Darlene Rodriguez's husband, a New York policeman, admits sexual contact with teen. Retrieved on October 28, 2010 from http://www.nydailynews.com/news/ny_crime/2008/09/26/2008-09-26_news_anchor_darlene_rodriguezs_husband_a.html.

Associated Press (2009a, June 29). Abu Ghraib scandal haunts US soldier who appeared in photos. Retrieved on August 17, 2010 from http://www.mlive.com/news/us-world/index.ssf/2009/06/abu_ghraib_scandal_haunts_us_s.html.

Associated Press (2009b, November 23). Woman loses benefits over Facebook photo: Canadian, who was on sick leave, shown having fun at Chippendales, on trip. Retrieved on May 30, 2011 from http://www.msnbc.msn.com/id/34089972/ns/technology_and_science-tech_and_gadgets/t/woman-loses-benefits-over-facebook-photos/.

Associated Press (2009c, July 7). Detective at Rodney King trial kills self: Woman who testified in beating trial of LAPD officers commits suicide in station house. Retrieved on August 20, 2009 from http://www.cbsnews.com/stories/2009/07/07/national/main5140688.shtml.

Associated Press (2009d, December 8). Jailer gets jail for having sex in jail. Retrieved on November 1, 2010 from http://www.katu.com/news/weird/78806867.html.

Associated Press (2009e, April 4). Shooter wearing bulletproof vest guns down 3 Pittsburgh officers, upset over losing job. Retrieved on December 6, 2010 from http://www.foxnews.com/story/0,2933,512560,00.html.

Associated Press (2009f, October 5). Child porn arrests: 'Shooting Fish in a Barrel'—Arresting child-porn suspects is 'Like Shooting Fish in a Barrel' if police have the will. Retrieved on January 18, 2011 from http://www.cbsnews.com/stories/2009/10/05/ap/national/main5364768.shtml.

Associated Press (2010a, July 11). New York woman, Sylvie Nelson, stopped over and over over ID mix-up with Georgia crime suspect. Retrieved on August 18, 2010 from http://www.nydailynews.com/news/2010/07/11/2010-07-11_new_york_woman_sylvie_nelson_stopped_over_and_over_over_id_mixup_with_georgia_cr.html.

Associated Press (2010b, October 20). Former Sheriff's employees guilty of theft. Retrieved on October 22, 2010 from http://www.miamiherald.com/2010/10/20/1881953/former-sheriffs-employees-guilty.html.

Associated Press (2010c, February 12). Jail deputy facing inmate sex charges. Retrieved on November 1, 2010 from http://www.news10.net/news/national/story.aspx?storyid=75241.

Associated Press (2010d, December 22). Ex-Niagara falls, NY cop jailed for drugs, grope. Retrieved on December 24, 2010 from http://www.syracuse.com/newsflash/index.ssf/story/ex-niagara-falls-ny-cop-jailed-for-drugs-grope/ba9e151006c74cb79b84226c39e2284c.

Associated Press (2010e, December 31). Police: Man fires rounds into Ohio police dept. Retrieved on January 1, 2011 from http://www.daytondailynews.com/news/ohio-news/police-man-fires-rounds-into-ohio-police-dept–1042633.html.

Associated Press (2010f, July 30). Child porn charge for SC pastor, wife. Retrieved on January 18, 2011 from http://chronicle.augusta.com/latest-news/2010-07-30/child-porn-charge-sc-pastor-wife?v=1280477147.

Associated Press (2011a, January 1). Deputies: Fla. dad stabs 6-year-old son 20 times. Retrieved on January 1, 2011 from http://www.kltv.com/Global/story.asp?S=13768310.

Associated Press (2011b, January 10). Serial elderly rape suspect Billy Joe Harris caught. Retrieved on January 10, 2011 from http://www.myfoxdfw.com/dpp/news/011011-Serial-Elderly-Rape-Suspect-Billy-Joe-Harris-Caught.

Associated Press (2011c, January 17). Philly police announce arrest in stranglings case. Retrieved on January 18, 2011 from http://www.google.com/hostednews/ap/article/ALeqM5jfUeZmOw RXT5S5PSMp7SkIKUaWVg?docId=981942952476495eb9374e75f78c6b65.

Associated Press (2011d, February 12). Los Angeles priest removed for affair 40 years ago. Retrieved on February 12, 2011 from http://news.yahoo.com/s/ap/us_priest_removed.

Associated Press (2011e, March 1). Feds: 700 Gang members with drug ties arrested. Retrieved on March 3, 2011 from http://news.yahoo.com/video/us-15749625/feds-700-gang-members-with-drug-ties-arrested-24378088#video=24398863.

Associated Press (2011f, April 4). Toddler dies after beating in NYC foster home. Retrieved on April 7, 2011 from http://online.wsj.com/article/AP99278e13acfb448eb933ca1816e3d440.html.

Associated Press (2011g, March 25). House approves bill to broaden DNA database. Retrieved on April 16, 2011 from http://www.ktvb.com/news/politics/House-approves-bill-to-broaden-DNA-database-118688519.html.

Associated Press (2011h, April 26). Lawyer Robbie Levin suspended over webcam flashing incident. Retrieved on April 26, 2011 from http://www.gadailynews.com/news/66031-lawyer-robbie-levin-suspended-over-webcam-flashing-incident.html.

Associated Press (2011i, April 30). Pa. girl, 10 charged with murder in death of baby. Retrieved on May 1, 2011 from http://news.yahoo.com/s/ap/us_young_girl_murder_charge.

Associated Press (2011j, July 20). 5 Men indicted in medical marijuana crackdown: Five men have been indicted on federal charges that arose from a crackdown on medical marijuana dispensaries in Spokane earlier this year. Retrieved on July 20, 2011 from http://seattletimes.nwsource.com/html/localnews/2015674977_apwamarijuanaindictments.html.

Associated Press (2011k, July 28). New Haven firefighters settle claims of racial bias. Retrieved on August 4, 2011 from http://www.nytimes.com/2011/07/29/nyregion/new-haven-firefighters-settle-race-discrimination-claims.html?_r=2&scp=1&sq=new%20haven%20&st=cse.

Associated Press Worldstream (2000, October 19). Sex tourism trial opens in France. Retrieved on March 13, 2010 from http://www.lexisnexis.com.library.keuka.edu/us/lnacademic/results/docview/docview.do?docLinkInd=true&risb=21_T8805082670&format=GNBFI&sort=REL EVANCE&startDocNo=1&resultsUrlKey=29_T8805082675&cisb=22_T8805082674&tree Max=true&treeWidth=0&csi=138211&docNo=1.

Association of Certified Background Investigators (ACBI). Weblink: http://www.acbi.net/.

Association of Certified Fraud Examiners (ACFE). (2011). Weblink: http://www.acfe.com/.

Athens Daily Review (2007, January 27). Exclusive web content: TCLEOSE reprimand letters for Michael Meissner. Retrieved on September 26, 2010 from http://www.athensreview.com/local/x212225215/EXCLUSIVE-WEB-CONTENT-TCLEOSE-reprimand-letters-for-Michael-Meissner.

Aubuchon v. Knauf (2004).

Auerbach, J. G. (1999, April 29). Chief of IBM's lotus gets plenty of mileage out of past as a marine. Retrieved on May 18, 2010 from http://search.ebscohost.com.library.keuka.edu/login.aspx?direct=true&db=aph&AN=1781816&site=ehost-live.

Austin, G., Skager, R., Bailey, J., & Bates, S. (2007, Winter). Biennial heavy alcohol and drug use among high school students. Retrieved on March 19, 2011 from http://webcache.googleusercontent.com/search?q=cache:HQF0I31v8iIJ:www.adp.ca.gov/prevention/pdf/10th_CSS_Heavy_Substance_Use_Report.pdf+alcohol+and+drug+use+in+schools&cd=6&hl=en&ct=clnk&gl=us&client=firefox-a&source=www.google.com.

Axelrod, J. (2010, August 2). NYC says FDNY test not discriminatory: Federal judge appoints special master to ensure diversification; city says it will appeal court's decision. Retrieved on April 14, 2011 from http://www.cbsnews.com/stories/2010/08/02/eveningnews/main6737773.shtml.

Ayres, C. (2006, March 10). Sheriff's son guilty of gang rape he recorded on video. Retrieved on February 11, 2011 from http://www.timesonline.co.uk/tol/news/world/us_and_americas/article739536.ece.

Babcock, K. (2011, January 4). Facebook photo with placenta leads to JCCC student dismissal, lawsuit. Retrieved on January 6, 2011 from http://sunpublications.com/201101045561/news/facebook-photo-with-placenta-leads-to-jccc-student-dismissal-lawsuit.html.

Babwin, D. (2010, December 4). Chicago police see spike in cop killings, assaults. Retrieved on December 6, 2010 from http://www.timesunion.com/news/article/Chicago-police-see-spike-in-cop-killings-assaults-860241.php.

Bach, P. (2006, January 17). Background checks worth effort. Retrieved on February 16, 2010 from http://proquest.umi.com.library.keuka.edu/pqdweb?did=970661891&sid=1&Fmt=3&clientId=3663&RQT=309&VName=PQD.

Bacque, P. (2010, February 4). TSA orders Richmond airport to give security clearance to a felon. Retrieved on February 8, 2010 from http://www2.wsls.com/sls/news/state_regional/article/tsa_orders_richmond_airport_to_give_security_clearance_to_felon/79015/.

Bagley, C. F. (1995). *Managers and the Legal Environment: Strategies for the 21st Century* (2nd edn.). St. Paul, MN: West Publishing Company.

Bahls, J. E. (1999, January). Available upon request. Retrieved on October 6, 2009 from http://findarticles.com/p/articles/mi_m3495/is_1_44/ai_53889125/?tag=content;col1.

Bahr v. Council Bluffs C.S.C. (1996).

Bailey, P. (2011a, February 14). Former police officer, school district employee, pleads guilty to larceny. Retrieved on February 21, 2011 from http://www.wktv.com/news/crime-reports/rome/Former-Rome-Police-officer-school-district-employee-pleads-guilty-to-grand-larceny-116165774.html.

Bailey, P. (2011b, February 14). Man sentenced for taping sexual act with autistic child. Retrieved on February 21, 2011 from http://www.wktv.com/news/crime-reports/rome/Man-sentenced-for-taping-sexual-act-with-autistic-child-116166014.html.

Bailey v. Georgia Pacific Corporation (2002).

Baines, D. (2011a, March 15). 'Father' of voice stress analysis received Phd after six hours of bible study at strip mall. Retrieved on July 26, 2011 from http://proquest.umi.com.library.keuka.edu/pqdweb?did=2295214451&sid=2&Fmt=3&clientId=3663&RQT=309&VName=PQD.

Baines, D. (2011b, March 16). B.C. corrections using 'Truth Verification' device to screen job applicants. Retrieved on July 26, 2011 from http://proquest.umi.com.library.keuka.edu/pqdweb?did=2296172291&sid=2&Fmt=3&clientId=3663&RQT=309&VName=PQD.

Baker, A. (2008a, April 10). Police department to start routinely testing officers for steroid use. Retrieved on January 18, 2010 from http://search.ebscohost.com.library.keuka.edu/login.aspx?direct=true&db=aph&AN=31594067&site=ehost-live.

Baker, A. (2008b, August 17). Afghanistan's epidemic of child rape. Retrieved on October 9, 2010 from http://www.time.com/time/world/article/0,8599,1833517,00.html.

Baker, A. (2008c, December 9). Assault inquiry brings charges for 3 officers. Retrieved on October 18, 2010 from http://www.nytimes.com/2008/12/10/nyregion/10mineo.html.

Baker, A. (2009, December 17). Court backs police commissioner on drug testing of officers. Retrieved on January 18, 2010 from http://cityroom.blogs.nytimes.com/2009/12/17/court-upholds-police-commissioners-authority-on-discipline/.

Baker, A. (2010, January 13). Judge cites discrimination in N.Y. fire dept. Retrieved on April 14, 2011 from http://www.nytimes.com/2010/01/14/nyregion/14fire.html.

Baker, A. & Moynihan, C. (2010, July 16). Paterson signs bill limiting stop-and-frisk data. Retrieved on October 10, 2010 from http://cityroom.blogs.nytimes.com/2010/07/16/paterson-signs-bill-limiting-street-stop-data/.

Bakersfield.com (2009, October 8). Former deputy sentenced to 57 months for possessing child porn. Retrieved on September 5, 2010 from http://people.bakersfield.com/home/Blog/BreakingNewsTeam/50397.

Bakker v. McKinnon (1998).

Balassone, M. (2008, August 19). Ex-turlock officer pleads no contest over sex with teen girl. Retrieved on December 6, 2010 from http://www.modbee.com/2008/08/19/398216/ex-turlock-officer-pleads-no-contest.html.

Baldo, V., Cristofoletti, M., Majori, S., Cibin, M., Peron, C., Dal Zotto, A., Zampieri, N., Sala, M., & Trivello, R. (2006, March–April). Relationship between pathological gambling, alcoholism, and drug addiction. Retrieved on February 13, 2011 from http://web.ebscohost.com.library.keuka.edu/ehost/detail?hid=9&sid=c2c9c9fd-604a-40aa-8504-95895203904c%40sessionmgr114&vid=5&bdata=JnNpdGU9ZWhvc3QtbGl2ZQ%3d%3d#db=cmedm&AN=16649512.

Ballam, D. A. (2002, Spring). Employment references—Speak no evil, hear no evil: A proposal for meaningful reform. *American Business Law Journal, 39*(3), 445–466.

Balmert, J. (2009, February 19). Athens police officer requests courts remove 2 misdemeanors. Retrieved on December 6, 2010 from http://thepost.ohiou.edu/Main.asp?SectionID=1&SubSectionID=1&ArticleID=27173.

Bals v. Verduzco (1992).

Baltimore Business Journal (1997, August 15). Clear job descriptions key to hiring disabled. Retrieved on November 18, 2009 from http://proquest.umi.com.library.keuka.edu/pqdweb?did=13522926&sid=1&Fmt=2&clientId=3663&RQT=309&VName=PQD.

Banks, C. (2004). *Criminal Justice Ethics: Theory and Practice* (2nd edn.). Thousand Oaks, CA: Sage Publications, Inc.

Bank Secrecy Act (1970).

Bankruptcy Abuse Prevention and Consumer Protection Act. (2005).

Bankruptcy Act (1978).

Barada, P. W. (n.d.). What's negligent hiring? Retrieved on July 6, 2009 from http://www.workplaceviolence911.com/docs/20041130.htm.

Barboza, T. & Winton, R. (2010, September 8). Long beach faces possible police layoffs: As the city faces $18.5 million in budget cuts, some officers who patrol the streets could be laid off if the city and the police union can't come to agreement. Retrieved on February 14, 2011 from http://articles.latimes.com/2010/sep/08/local/la-me-0908-lb-police-20100908.

Bardin v. Lockheed Aeronautical Systems Company (1999).

Barker, J. (2010a, May 7). Deputy charged with child sex crimes fired: John Mitchell Tomlinson faces six counts of sexual battery. Retrieved on May 28, 2010 from http://dailyme.com/story/2010050700003606/deputy-charged-child-sex-crimes-fired-.html.

Barker, J. (2010b, November 12). Former deputy convicted of child sex battery, faces 90 years. Retrieved on November 19, 2010 from http://www.nwfdailynews.com/news/deputy-34833-faces-former.html.

Barker, T., Hunter, R. D., & Rush, J. P. (1994). *Police Systems and Practices: An Introduction*. Englewood Cliffs, NJ: Prentice-Hall Career and Technology, Prentice-Hall, Inc.

Barlow, D. (1993, April). The evolution of risk management. Retrieved on October 14, 2009 from http://web.ebscohost.com.library.keuka.edu/ehost/detail?vid=4&hid=6&sid=c7e73d38-ddac-4a22-95ec-a3d0ae178d36%40sessionmgr10&bdata=JnNpdGU9ZWhvc3QtbGl2ZQ%3d%3d#db=buh&AN=14415294.

Barnes, M., Cleaveland, K. A., & Florencio, P. S. (2003, April). *Chevron v. Echazabal*: Public health issues raised by "Threat-to-Self" defense to adverse employment actions. Retrieved on November 25, 2009 from http://web.ebscohost.com.library.keuka.edu/ehost/detail?vid=4&hid=6&sid=c7e73d38-ddac-4a22-95ec-a3d0ae178d36%40sessionmgr10&bdata=JnNpdGU9ZWhvc3QtbGl2ZQ%3d%3d#db=buh&AN=14415294.

Baron, D. (2007, February/March). Do your writing skills let you down? Retrieved on March 16, 2010 from http://proquest.umi.com.library.keuka.edu/pqdweb?did=1221836251&sid=3&Fmt=4&clientId=3663&RQT=309&VName=PQD.

Barnes v. Broward County Sheriff's Office (1999).

Barnes v. Cochran (1996).

Barney, J. B. (1997). *Gaining and Sustaining Competitive Advantage*. Reading, MA: Addison-Wesley Publishing Company.

Barnum, A. (2011, February 15). Dupage officials seek arrest of 42 parents. Retrieved on February 20, 2011 from http://proquest.umi.com.library.keuka.edu/pqdweb?did=2266220151&sid=2&Fmt=3&clientId=3663&RQT=309&VName=PQD.

Barnum, D. T. & Gleason, J. M. (1994, July). The credibility of drug tests: A multi-stage Bayesian analysis. Retrieved on January 24, 2010 from http://search.ebscohost.com.library.keuka.edu/login.aspx?direct=true&db=sih&AN=9408152514&site=ehost-live.

Barron, J. (2010, April 8). Woman assaulted by priest settles suit against Newark diocese. Retrieved on April 9, 2010 from http://www.nytimes.com/2010/04/09/nyregion/09abuse.html?src=me&ref=nyregion.

Barron, J. (2011, July 13). 7 Blocks to walk, Brooklyn boy never got home. Retrieved on July 23, 2011 from http://www.nytimes.com/2011/07/14/nyregion/arrest-made-in-brooklyn-killing-of-leiby-kletzky.html?pagewanted=all.

Bartlett, S. (2005, February). Put it in writing. Retrieved on March 16, 2010 from http://proquest.umi.com.library.keuka.edu/pqdweb?did=821989851&sid=3&Fmt=2&clientId=3663&RQT=309&VName=PQD.

Bartley, N. (2011, February 1). Suspect in corrections officer's death had scratches, bites, bloody clothes. Retrieved on February 1, 2011 from http://seattletimes.nwsource.com/html/localnews/2014101552_monroe02m.html.

Basch, A. J. (2007, April 30). Workplace violence and background checks. Retrieved on November 8, 2009 from http://search.ebscohost.com.library.keuka.edu/login.aspx?direct=true&db=bwh&AN=24955987&site=ehost-live.

Basel v. McFarland (1999).

Basu, K. (2010, November 1). Frank Carter trial may begin within a month. Retrieved on November 1, 2010 from http://www.floridatoday.com/article/20101101/NEWS01/11010313/1086/Frank+Carter+trial+may+begin+this+month+in+Melbourne.

Battista v. Cannon (1996).

Baum, K. (2006, April). *Identity Theft, 2004*. Washington, DC: United States Department of Justice, Office of Justice Programs, Bureau of Justice Statistics.

BBC News. (2007, February 22). Fraudulent forensic expert jailed: A bogus forensic psychologist who supplied evidence in hundreds of court cases has been jailed for five years. Retrieved on April 13, 2011 from http://news.bbc.co.uk/2/hi/uk_news/england/manchester/6386069.stm.

Bazelon, E. (2011, February 2). Shaken-baby syndrome faces new questions in court. Retrieved on March 24, 2011 from http://www.nytimes.com/2011/02/06/magazine/06baby-t.html?_r=1&pagewanted=1.

Beagrie, S. (2004, November 30). How to… produce powerful business writing. Retrieved on March 16, 2010 from http://proquest.umi.com.library.keuka.edu/pqdweb?did=781652531&sid=3&Fmt=4&clientId=3663&RQT=309&VName=PQD.

Beam, A. & Leach, L. (2005, September 22). Myrtle beach, S.C., police officer got steroids from Shortt. Retrieved on January 18, 2010 from http://search.ebscohost.com.library.keuka.edu/login.aspx?direct=true&db=nfh&AN=2W61197721937&site=ehost-live.

Beaudette, J. (1999, September). The truth is out there. Retrieved on June 7, 2011 from http://www.lexisnexis.com.library.keuka.edu/us/lnacademic/results/docview/docview.do?docLinkInd=true&risb=21_T7577964092&format=GNBFI&sort=RELEVANCE&startDocNo=1&resultsUrlKey=29_T7577964098&cisb=22_T7577964097&treeMax=true&treeWidth=0&csi=210628&docNo=16.

Becker, R. F. (2000). *Criminal Investigation*. Gaithersburg, MD: Aspen Publishers, Inc.

Beckwith, R. J. & Burke, T. W. (2000, August). Using informants: Who can be trusted? *Law and Order Magazine*, *48*(8), 109–110.

Beebe, M. (2010, August 21). Officer pleads guilty in assault. Retrieved on September 5, 2010 from http://www.buffalonews.com/city/article44606.ece.

Beja, M. (2010, July 17). Gov. David Paterson signs law ending stop-and-frisk database. Retrieved on October 10, 2010 from http://www.democratandchronicle.com/article/20100717/NEWS01/7170319/1002/NEWS.

Bell, R. (2010, November 15). More companies conduct screening of new employees. Retrieved on February 26, 2011 from http://proquest.umi.com.library.keuka.edu/pqdweb?did=2230673831&sid=1&Fmt=3&clientId=3663&RQT=309&VName=PQD.

Bell, R. (2011). Skywayman: The story of Frank W. Abagnale Jr. Retrieved on February 11, 2011 from http://www.trutv.com/library/crime/criminal_mind/scams/frank_abagnale/index.html.

Bell v. City of Miami (1990).

Bellah, J. (2001, October). Identity theft: Ruining credit and creating criminal records. *Law and Order Magazine*, *49*(10), 222–226.

Bellows, R. & Kleiner, B. H. (2001). Sexual harassment in government. Retrieved on July 26, 2011 from http://proquest.umi.com.library.keuka.edu/pqdweb?did=281035471&sid=2&Fmt=3&clientId=3663&RQT=309&VName=PQD.

Benavides v. County of Wilson (1992).

Bender, B. (2010, July 23). Pentagon workers tied to child porn. Retrieved on August 17, 2010 from http://www.boston.com/news/nation/washington/articles/2010/07/23/pentagon_workers_tied_to_child_porn/.

Bender, B. (2011, January 8). Pentagon vows action on porn cases; inspector general says investigators will vet 1,700 files. Retrieved on April 16, 2011 from http://proquest.umi.com.library.keuka.edu/pqdweb?did=2232445591&sid=1&Fmt=3&clientId=3663&RQT=309&VName=PQD.

Bensman, T. & Contreras, G. (2008, January 27). SAPD bent hiring rules. Retrieved on August 13, 2011 from http://proquest.umi.com.library.keuka.edu/pqdweb?did=1419232081&sid=1&Fmt=3&clientId=3663&RQT=309&VName=PQD.

Bennett, R. (2008, February 4). Keeping a cool profile on myspace could just cost you your next post. Retrieved on March 13, 2010 from http://technology.timesonline.co.uk/tol/news/tech_and_web/the_web/article3300531.ece.

Bennett, W. M. & Hess, K. M. (2004). *Management and Supervision in Law Enforcement* (4th edn.). Belmont, CA: Thomson Wadsworth.

Bennett, W. M. & Hess, K. M. (2007). *Criminal Investigation* (8th edn.). Belmont, CA: Thomson Wadsworth.

Bennett v. County of Suffolk (1998).

Benningfield v. City of Houston (1998).

Benson, G. C. S. (1978). Political corruption in America. Retrieved on November 26, 2009 from http://search.ebscohost.com.library.keuka.edu/login.aspx?direct=true&db=sih&AN=SM066086&site=ehost-live.

Benson v. Northwest Airlines, Inc. (1997).

Benton, J. A. (2007, Winter). Are your genes protected? Federal legislation and genetic discrimination. Retrieved on November 17, 2009 from http://proquest.umi.com.library.keuka.edu/pqdweb?did=1408601731&sid=1&Fmt=4&clientId=3663&RQT=309&VName=PQD.

Bercaw, G. H. (2002, July). Psychological assessment. *Law and Order Magazine*, *50*(7), 132–136.

Berger, L. (1995, January 5). Former fire official denies new charges: Courts: John Orr, an ex-glendale investigator imprisoned for arson, is accused of setting 1984 blaze that killed four. Retrieved on July 30, 2011 from http://articles.latimes.com/1995-01-05/local/me-16567_1_arson-investigator.

Bermes, E. O. (2008, March). Coaching vs. consulting: Which is which and what to look for. Retrieved on October 31, 2009 from http://proquest.umi.com.library.keuka.edu/pqdweb?did=1458467781&sid=1&Fmt=3&clientId=3663&RQT=309&VName=PQD.

Bernadette Brown v. the City of New York, et al. (1998).

Bernstein, H. (2011, April 5). Brookline board fires police sergeant. Retrieved on April 29, 2011 from http://www.nashuatelegraph.com/news/914716-196/brookline-police-sergeant-fired.html.

Besnoff, L. & Cohen, A. J. (2007, April 1). Hazardous hires. Retrieved on March 30, 2009 from http://wasteage.com/mag/waste_hazardous_hires/.

Bezemer, J. & Kress, G. (2008, April). Writing in multimodal texts. Retrieved on March 16, 2010 from http://proquest.umi.com.library.keuka.edu/pqdweb?did=1446306081&sid=3&Fmt=2&clientId=3663&RQT=309&VName=PQD.

Bi-State Development Agency and Amalgamated Transit Union (2008).

Bibel, D. & Faggiani, D. (2006). Intelligence and information sharing in policing: Observations on and pitfalls in developing regional data consortia. Retrieved on October 10, 2010 from http://web.ebscohost.com.library.keuka.edu/ehost/detail?vid=12&hid=11&sid=4c672b52-8d14-4332-a8cb-b1ff63c84f64%40sessionmgr11&bdata=JnNpdGU9ZWhvc3QtbGl2ZQ%3d%3d#db=sih&AN=26955079.

Bible, J. (1998, May 15). Hiring without opening yourself up to lawsuits. Retrieved on November 17, 2009 from http://proquest.umi.com.library.keuka.edu/pqdweb?did=29483764&sid=1&Fmt=2&clientId=3663&RQT=309&VName=PQD.

Biddle and Associates, Inc. (1978). Background investigation guide. Retrieved on September 13, 2010 from http://web.ebscohost.com.library.keuka.edu/ehost/detail?vid=4&hid=105&sid=322c9a61-9e8d-40c3-96a0-ada73d8258bf%40sessionmgr113&bdata=JnNpdGU9ZWhvc3QtbGl2ZQ%3d%3d#db=sih&AN=SM048464.

Biermann, T., Schwarze, B., Zedler, B., & Betz, P. (2004, June). On-site testing of illicit drugs: The use of the drug testing device toxiquick. Retrieved on January 24, 2010 from http://search.ebscohost.com.library.keuka.edu/login.aspx?direct=true&db=aph&AN=13291065&site=ehost-live.

Bigelow, B. (2009, August 7). Man blames cat for child pornography found on his computer. Retrieved on October 24, 2010 from http://latimesblogs.latimes.com/unleashed/2009/08/man-blames-cat-child-pornography.html.

Biggs, M. (2001). *Just the Facts: Investigative Report Writing*. Upper Saddle River, NJ: Prentice Hall Publishing.

Bing, M. N., Davison, H. K., & Arvey, R. (2009, Spring). Using a repeated-measures approach to validating personality tests in small samples: A feasibility study with implications for small businesses. *Journal of Managerial Issues*, *21*(1), 11–35.

Birch, J. & Chisholm, C. M. (2008, November). Occupational colour vision requirements for police officers. Retrieved on November 25, 2009 from http://search.ebscohost.com.library.keuka.edu/login.aspx?direct=true&db=cmedm&AN=19076554&site=ehost-live.

Birkman-Fink, S. (2009, July). Personality testing: The hidden sustainability weapon. Retrieved on October 21, 2009 from http://proquest.umi.com.library.keuka.edu/pqdweb?did=1811139681&sid=3&Fmt=2&clientId=3663&RQT=309&VName=PQD.

Bishop v. Wood (1976).

Black, K. R. (1994). Personality screening in employment. Retrieved on October 22, 2009 from http://search.ebscohost.com.library.keuka.edu/login.aspx?direct=true&db=buh&AN=9412141065&site=ehost-live.

Blandon-Gitlin, I., Pezdek, K., Lindsay, D. S., & Hagen, L. (2009, October). Criteria-based content analysis of true and suggested events. Retrieved on July 24, 2011 from http://proquest.umi.com.library.keuka.edu/pqdweb?did=1844703441&sid=5&Fmt=2&clientId=3663&RQT=309&VName=PQD.

Blatt, R. (2011, June 29). Marines dismiss Yonathan Melaku. Retrieved on June 29, 2011 from http://wamu.org/news/11/06/29/marines_dismiss_yonathan_melaku.php.

Blau, R., Cunningham, J. H., & Nelson, K. (2011, September 4). Mayor Bloomberg: I'm not sorry for keeping quiet on arrest of Stephen Goldsmith's leaving office. Retrieved on September 4, 2011 from http://www.nydailynews.com/ny_local/2011/09/04/2011-09-04_mayor_bloomberg_im_not_sorry_for_hiding_arrest_behind_stephen_goldsmiths_leaving.html.

Bliss, G. (2008, April 25). Commentary: Be wary of resume fraud and diploma mills. Retrieved on February 22, 2011 from http://proquest.umi.com.library.keuka.edu/pqdweb?did=1492908581&sid=3&Fmt=3&clientId=3663&RQT=309&VName=PQD.

Blinkhorn, S. & Johnson, C. (1990, December). The insignificance of personality testing. Retrieved on October 22, 2009 from http://search.ebscohost.com.library.keuka.edu/login.aspx?direct=true&db=ulh&AN=9101141205&site=ehost-live.

Board of County Commissioners of Bryan County, Oklahoma v. Brown (1997).

Boerger, D. (2001, December). Use caution in checking for criminal histories. Retrieved on July 7, 2009 from http://columbus.bizjournals.com/columbus/stories/2001/12/17/smallb2.html.

Bohmfalk v. City of New Orleans (1993).

Bohn, K. (2009, January 28). Former CIA station chief target of rape inquiry. Retrieved on October 28, 2010 from http://articles.cnn.com/2009-01-28/world/cia.rape.allegations_1_justice-department-covert-officers-cia-spokesman-mark-mansfield?_s=PM:WORLD.

Bolger, T. (2011, July 11). Commack man charged under social host law. Retrieved on July 12, 2011 from http://www.longislandpress.com/2011/07/11/commack-man-charged-under-social-host-law/.

Bolman, L. G. & Deal, T. E. (1997). *Reframing Organizations: Artistry, Choice, and Leadership* (2nd edn.). San Francisco, CA: Jossey-Bass.

Bonne, J. (2004, January 21). Most firms now use background checks. Retrieved on August 18, 2010 from http://today.msnbc.msn.com/id/4018280.

Bonsignore v. City of New York (1982).

Bopp v. Institute for Forensic Psychology (1997).

Borden v. Capital District Transportation Authority (2003).

Borland, S. (2008, October 8). Police officer faces jail after having sex with a woman he met attending a 999 call. Retrieved on December 6, 2010 from http://www.dailymail.co.uk/news/article-1071730/Police-officer-faces-jail-having-sex-woman-met-attending-999-call.html.

Bosker, W. M. & Huestis, M. A. (2009, November). Oral fluid testing for drugs of abuse. Retrieved on January 18, 2010 from http://search.ebscohost.com.library.keuka.edu/login.aspx?direct=true&db=cmedm&AN=19745062&site=ehost-live.

Boston School Committee, 3 MLC 1603 (1977).

Boston.com (2009, April 20). Legalized rape in Afghanistan. Retrieved on October 9, 2010 from http://www.boston.com/bostonglobe/editorial_opinion/editorials/articles/2009/04/20/legalized_rape_in_afghanistan/.

Boston University Center for Psychiatric Rehabilitation (n.d.). The Americans with Disabilities Act (ADA). Retrieved on October 9, 2010 from http://www.bu.edu/cpr/reasaccom/whatlaws-adaact.html.

Bouchard, M. & Bacque Dion, C. (2006). Growers and facilitators: Monitoring trends in innovations in the marijuana cultivation industry. Retrieved on February 9, 2010 from http://search.ebscohost.com.library.keuka.edu/login.aspx?direct=true&db=sih&AN=26954977&site=ehost-live.

Bourne, D. (2006, July 25). Judge oks beach police department's settlement over exam. Retrieved on November 6, 2009 from http://proquest.umi.com.library.keuka.edu/pqdweb?did=1082717881&sid=2&Fmt=3&clientId=3663&RQT=309&VName=PQD.

Bovee, C. L. & Thill, J. T. (1989). *Business Communication Today* (2nd edn.). New York: Random House, Inc.

Bowers, M. & Washington, M. (2008, December 4). Active, ex-Norfolk police officers indicted on felony charges. Retrieved on October 28, 2010 from http://hamptonroads.com/2008/12/active-exnorfolk-police-officers-indicted-felony-charges.

Bowes, M. & Kapsidelis, K. (2009, January 29). VCU police chief arrested in undercover solicitation sting. Retrieved on August 15, 2010 from http://www2.timesdispatch.com/news/2009/jan/29/vcuugat29_20090129-101608-ar-91398/.

Bowling, M. & Hickman, M. J. (2006, November). Background checks for firearm transfers, 2005. Washington, DC: United States Department of Justice, Office of Justice Programs, Bureau of Justice Statistics.

Boyd v. Fulton Terrace Associates. L.L.C. (2006).

Boyer, B. (2011a, August 13). Sex offender gets 3 years for conning census bureau. Retrieved on August 13, 2011 from http://www.philly.com/philly/news/new_jersey/20110813_Sex_offender_gets_3_years_for_conning_Census_Bureau.html.

Boyer, D. (2011b, August 8). Philadelphia mayor talks tough to black teenagers after 'Flash Mobs.' Retrieved on August 13, 2011 from http://www.washingtontimes.com/news/2011/aug/8/mayor-talks-tough-to-black-teens-after-flash-mobs/.

Boynton Beach Police Department (n.d.). Employment. Retrieved on October 24, 2009 from http://www.bbpd.org/employment.htm#What%20does%20the%20employment%20process%20consist%20of%20for%20Police%20Officer.

Bradford, D. (1998, Winter). Police officer candidate background investigation: Law enforcement management's most effective tool for employing the most qualified candidate. *Public Personnel Management*, *27*(4), 423–445.

Bradley Amendment (1986).

Bradway, J. S. (1935, November). Moral turpitude as the criterion of offenses that justify disbarment. *California Law Review*, *24*(1), 9–27.

Brady Handgun Violence Prevention Act (1993).

Brady-Lunny, E. (2008, January 27). Probe closed of officer's undisclosed DUI arrest. Retrieved on October 13, 2009 from http://proquest.umi.com.library.keuka.edu/pqdweb?index=75&did=1419816931&SrchMode=1&sid=2&Fmt=3&VInst=PROD&VType=PQD&RQT=309&VName=PQD&TS=1255434330&clientId=3663.

Brady-Lunny, E. (2009, May 5). Murder conviction expunged from Beaman's record; some bond money returned. Retrieved on February 5, 2011 from http://web.ebscohost.com.library.keuka.edu/ehost/detail?hid=13&sid=83ac1063-0972-4530-a77b-7200704592ca%40sessionmgr14&vid=8&bdata=JnNpdGU9ZWhvc3QtbGl2ZQ%3d%3d#db=nfh&AN=2W62896338045.

Brady v. Maryland (1963).

Bragdon v. Abbott (1998).

Braibanti, R. (1962, Winter). Reflections on bureaucratic corruption. Retrieved on November 26, 2009 from http://search.ebscohost.com.library.keuka.edu/login.aspx?direct=true&db=sih&AN=SM064606&site=ehost-live.

Brain, M. (2011, January 31). How stuff works: Be aware of more screenings when job searching. Retrieved on February 22, 2011 from http://proquest.umi.com.library.keuka.edu/pqdweb?did=2254652491&sid=2&Fmt=3&clientId=3663&RQT=309&VName=PQD.

Branch, A. (2010, August 2). Not all sex offenders the same, advocates of changing Texas list say. Retrieved on October 9, 2010 from http://www.star-telegram.com/2010/08/01/2376305/not-all-sex-offenders-the-same.html.

Brandon, H. & Lippman, B. (2000, November). Surfing for success: Using the web to improve recruitment. *The Police Chief Magazine*, *67*(11), 37–41.

Brantner-Smith, B. (2009). Surviving the police background investigation. Retrieved on November 6, 2009 from http://policelink.monster.com/education/articles/105301-surviving-the-police-background-investigation.

Braswell, M. C., McCarthy, B. R., & McCarthy, B. J. (2002). *Justice and Crime Ethics* (4th edn.). Cincinnati, OH: Anderson Publishing Company.

Bratton, J. & Gold, J. (1999). *Human Resource Management: Theory and Practice* (2nd edn.). Mahwah, NJ: Lawrence Erlbaum Associates, Inc., Publishers.

Brean, B. (2010, September 2). Penfield Popeye's attack victim: "I had a horrible experience." Retrieved on March 24, 2011 from http://www.whec.com/news/stories/s1726311.shtml.

Brecher, N. D. (2010, January/February). Words speak louder than actions. Retrieved on March 16, 2010 from http://proquest.umi.com.library.keuka.edu/pqdweb?did=1974312201&sid=3&Fmt=3&clientId=3663&RQT=309&VName=PQD.

Brennan, G. (2009, October 30). Probe: Officer was drinking day of crash. Retrieved on November 20, 2009 from http://proquest.umi.com.library.keuka.edu/pqdweb?did=1889457591&sid=1&Fmt=3&cl ientId=3663&RQT=309&VName=PQD.

Brennan, T. (2010, October 8). Prosecutor: Child porn suspect had thousands of images on his computer. Retrieved on January 18, 2011 from http://www.ktvb.com/news/crime/Boise-man-charged-with-10-counts-of-possessing-child-porn-104589474.html.

Brennan v. Kaluczky (1996).

Brennan, B. P., Kanayama, G., Hudson, J. I., & Pope, H. G. (2011, January 20). Human growth hormone abuse in male weightlifters. Retrieved on April 13, 2011 from http://www.ncbi.nlm.nih.gov/pubmed/21175915.

Brickman v. New Orleans Aviation Board (1959).

Brinckerhoff, C. W. (1998, July 10). FTC staff opinion letter: Fair Credit Reporting Act Sections 603(f), 604(b), 606, 615(a). Retrieved on February 25, 2011 from http://library.findlaw.com/1998/Jul/10/130759.html.

Brittain, A. & Mueller, M. (2010, December 12). N.J. doctor supplied steroids to hundreds of law enforcement officers, firefighters. Retrieved on March 19, 2011 from http://www.nj.com/news/index.ssf/2010/12/hundreds_of_nj_police_firefigh.html.

Brittany v. Heather (1989).

Broady, A. (2010, November 5). Credit report can affect your job search. Retrieved on February 26, 2011 from http://proquest.umi.com.library.keuka.edu/pqdweb?did=2181330291&sid=1&Fmt=3&clientId=3663&RQT=309&VName=PQD.

Brogan v. United States. (1998).

Brosseau, C. (2008, October 28). Tucson Police Department struggles to find qualified recruits. Retrieved on October 12, 2009 from http://www.tucsoncitizen.com/altss/printstory/local/100898.

Brown, A. M. (2010, March 4). Why are people taking plant fertiliser for fun? The Murky world of 'Party Drugs.' Retrieved on June 1, 2011 from http://blogs.telegraph.co.uk/news/andrewmcfbrown/100028413/why-are-people-taking-plant-fertiliser-for-fun-inside-the-murky-world-of-legal-highs/.

Brown, A. K. & Graczyk, M. (2010, October 15). Witnesses say Fort Hood gunman kept firing outside. Retrieved on October 15, 2010 from http://news.yahoo.com/s/ap/20101015/ap_on_re_us/us_fort_hood_shooting.

Brown, B. (2004, July 1). Magana guilty on 41 counts. Retrieved on October 29, 2010 from http://www.dailyemerald.com/2.2358/magana-guilty-on-41-counts-1.212507.

Brown, R. (2009, May 20). Tape of beating leads to firing of 5 officers. Retrieved on October 28, 2010 from http://www.nytimes.com/2009/05/21/us/21birmingham.html.

Brown, S. D. (2007, Winter). The meaning of criminal intelligence. Retrieved on October 10, 2010 from http://web.ebscohost.com.library.keuka.edu/ehost/detail?vid=8&hid=11&sid=4c672b52-8d14-4332-a8cb-b1ff63c84f64%40sessionmgr11&bdata=JnNpdGU9ZWhvc3QtbGl2ZQ%3d%3d#db=aph&AN=27949197.

Brown University (2005, September). Problem gambling in youth—A hidden addiction. Retrieved on February 13, 2011 from http://web.ebscohost.com.library.keuka.edu/ehost/detail?hid=9&sid=c2c9c9fd-604a-40aa-8504-95895203904c%40sessionmgr114&vid=5&bdata=JnNpdGU9ZWhvc3QtbGl2ZQ%3d%3d#db=aph&AN=18577214.

Brown University (2007, June). False positives in youth drug tests. *Brown University Child and Adolescent Behavior Letter, 23*(6), 2–3.

Brown v. Benton (1978).

Brown v. State of Tennessee (1982).

Brown v. Youth Services of South Dakota, Inc. (2000).

Brunker, M. (2009, January 15). 'Sexting' surprise: Teens face child porn charges. Retrieved on October 14, 2010 from http://www.msnbc.msn.com/id/28679588/.

Bruyere, S. M. (2002, June). Occupational safety and health disability nondiscrimination in the workplace: Complying with dual requirements. Retrieved on August 7, 2011 from http://www.ilr.cornell.edu/edi/hr_tips/article_1.cfm?b_id=34&h_id=7&view=true.

Bryan v. City of Des Moines (1978).

Bryan, S. (2010, April 29). Warrant issued for Davie officer who skips second trial. Retrieved on October 28, 2010 from http://articles.sun-sentinel.com/2010-04-29/news/fl-davie-cop-fugitive-20100428_1_second-trial-new-jury-vally-getejanc.

Bryant, A. (2007, May 16). Wilton board oks hiring another cop. Retrieved on November 21, 2009 from http://proquest.umi.com.library.keuka.edu/pqdweb?did=1271994051&sid=1&Fmt=3&clientId=3663&RQT=309&VName=PQD.

Bryant, S. (2010, January 7). Chicago PD comes up with fool proof plan to hire more minorities and keep federal government off their back? Retrieved on May 5, 2011 from http://pafop38.com/2010/01/07/chicago-pd-comes-up-with-fool-proof-plan-to-hire-more-minorities-and-keep-the-federal-government-off-their-back/.

Bryson v. United States (1969).

Buckhalter, D. (2008, May 29). Jackson County authorities find sophisticated hydroponic marijuana greenhouse. Retrieved on February 9, 2010 from http://search.ebscohost.com.library.keuka.edu/login.aspx?direct=true&db=nfh&AN=2W62W63675122717&site=ehost-live.

Buckley, M. R., Jackson, K. A., Bolino, M. C., Veres, J. G., & Feild, H. S. (2007, Autumn). The influence of relational demography on panel interview ratings: A field experiment. Retrieved on July 27, 2011 from http://proquest.umi.com.library.keuka.edu/pqdweb?did=1366458951&sid=4&Fmt=4&clientId=3663&RQT=309&VName=PQD.

Buckley, W. E., Yesalis, C. E., Friedl, K. E., Anderson, W. A., Streit, A. L., & Wright, J. E. (1988, December 16). Estimated prevalence of anabolic steroid use among male high school seniors. Retrieved on April 13, 2011 from http://jama.ama-assn.org/content/260/23/3441.abstract.

Buckley v. Consolidated Edison of New York, Inc. (1998).

Bueno, J. (2009, November). Responding to domestic violence. Retrieved on October 11, 2010 from http://web.ebscohost.com.library.keuka.edu/ehost/detail?vid=20&hid=15&sid=c11a669b-e675-487a-9271-e6576c348b8e%40sessionmgr12&bdata=JnNpdGU9ZWhvc3QtbGl2ZQ%3d%3d#db=c8h&AN=2010494966.

Buettner, J. (2011, February 24). Fox news chief, Roger Ailes, urged employee to lie, records show. Retrieved on April 16, 2011 from http://www.nytimes.com/2011/02/25/nyregion/25roger-ailes.html?_r=1&ref=bernardbkerik.

Buffalo News (1998, October 1). Upgrade the requirements for new cops. Retrieved on April 15, 2011 from http://proquest.umi.com.library.keuka.edu/pqdweb?did=34761859&sid=1&Fmt=3&clientId=3663&RQT=309&VName=PQD.

Buffalonews.com (2011a, February 7). Two charged in rape of East Aurora girl: Police say men met 12-year-old on web. Retrieved on February 8, 2011 from http://www.buffalonews.com/city/police-courts/police-blotter/article334338.ece.

Buffalonews.com (2011b, April 6). Key evidence hearing set in child porn case. Retrieved on April 9, 2011 from http://www.buffalonews.com/city/police-courts/police-blotter/article385831.ece.

Bumstead, B. (2009, May 30). Wagner, Rendell push House Dems to let police do background checks. Retrieved on October 13, 2009 from http://proquest.umi.com.library.keuka.edu/pqdweb?index=18&did=1735835161&SrchMode=2&sid=2&Fmt=3&VInst=PROD&VType=PQD&RQT=309&VName=PQD&TS=1255430937&clientId=3663.

Bunkley, N. (2008, December 2). Aide to former Detroit mayor pleads guilty in sex scandal. Retrieved on March 13, 2010 from http://infoweb.newsbank.com.library.keuka.edu/iw-search/we/InfoWeb?p_product=NewsBank&p_theme=aggregated5&p_action=doc&p_docid=124D4392E707C2A0&p_docnum=29&p_queryname=3.

Burch, J. (2009, February 27). Okaloosa County Sheriff arrested on federal charges. Retrieved on October 22, 2010 from http://www.wkrg.com/florida/article/arrest_warrant_issued_for_sheriffs_arrest/24000/Feb-27-2009_1-00-pm/.

Burden, A. (2010, February 9). Special report: Online company offers to fake resumes. Retrieved on March 18, 2011 from http://www.kgw.com/news/special-reports/Fake-References-83867287.html.

Bureau of Alcohol, Tobacco, Firearms, and Explosives (2010). How to become a Federal Firearms Licensee (FFL). Retrieved on September 22, 2010 from http://www.atf.gov/firearms/how-to/become-an-ffl.html.

Burg, T. E. (1999, October). Timing critical when interviewing white collar subjects. *Law and Order Magazine*, *47*(10), 37–39.

Burge v. City of Dover, Kent County Chan. Ct. (1993).

Burke, T. T. (2001, Fall). Documenting and reporting a confession with a signed statement: A guide for law enforcement. *FBI Law Enforcement Bulletin*, *70*(2), 17–22.

Burns, G. (2004, April 27). Screening firms often don't catch criminals. Retrieved on February 16, 2010 from http://proquest.umi.com.library.keuka.edu/pqdweb?did=624323101&sid=1&Fmt=3&clientId=3663&RQT=309&VName=PQD.

Burns, J. F. & Somaiya, R. (2010, October 23). Wikileaks founder on the run, trailed by notoriety. Retrieved on October 24, 2010 from http://www.nytimes.com/2010/10/24/world/24assange.html?_r=1.

van Buskirk, L. A. (2009, June 19). Cost-cutting can wind up being expensive. Retrieved on March 16, 2010 from http://search.ebscohost.com.library.keuka.edu/login.aspx?direct=true&db=bwh&AN=42203809&site=ehost-live.

Butler, S. F., Fernandez, K. C., Chang, A., Benoit, C., Morey, L. C., Black, R., & Katz, N. (2010, January). Measuring attractiveness for abuse of prescription opioids. Retrieved on January 20, 2010 from http://search.ebscohost.com.library.keuka.edu/login.aspx?direct=true&db=aph&AN=47481604&site=ehost-live.

Butler v. Central Bank and Trust Company (1970).

Bykowicz, J. & Linskey, A. (2009, December 2). Baltimore mayor convicted of one count of fraud: Dixon is acquitted of three charges but could be forced to leave office. Retrieved on October 28, 2010 from http://www.washingtonpost.com/wp-dyn/content/article/2009/12/01/AR2009120101925.html.

Byrne, M. H., Lander, L., & Ferris, M. (2009, February). The changing face of opioid addiction: Prescription pain pill dependence and treatment. Retrieved on January 20, 2010 from http://search.ebscohost.com.library.keuka.edu/login.aspx?direct=true&db=aph&AN=36988009&site=ehost-live.

Cable News Network (2007, March 13). Study: Thousands of veterans return with mental illness. Retrieved on August 15, 2010 from http://www.cnn.com/2007/US/03/13/stress.troops/.

Cabot, S. J. (2005, July 1). Avoiding negligent hiring lawsuits: What you don't know about applicants can hurt you. Retrieved on April 25, 2011 from http://www.hr.com/en/communities/staffing_and_recruitment/avoiding-negligent-hiring-lawsuits–what-you-don_eacu2jd3.html.

Calabresi, M. (2010, March 11). Why the Jihad Jane case is a win for the Patriot Act. Retrieved on March 13, 2010 from http://www.time.com/time/nation/article/0,8599,1971245,00.html.

California Background Investigators Association (CBIA). Weblink: http://www.scbia.com/.

California Civil Code

California Code of Regulations (n.d.). Title 2. Administration: Division 4. Fair employment and housing commission. Retrieved on February 6, 2011 from http://www.fehc.ca.gov/act/pdf/code_regulations.pdf.

California Commission on Peace Officer Standards and Training (2009). What is POST? Retrieved on October 20, 2009 from http://www.post.ca.gov/About_Us/What_is_POST.asp.

California Courts Self Help Center (2010, January 4). Clean up your criminal record. Retrieved on February 6, 2011 from http://www.courtinfo.ca.gov/selfhelp/other/crimlawclean.htm#top.

California Evidence Code

California Government Code

California Health and Safety Code

Callahan, M. (1990, October). Deliberate indifference: The standard for municipal and supervisory liability. Retrieved on October 25, 2009 from http://proquest.umi.com.library.keuka.edu/pqdweb?did=6112088&sid=2&Fmt=2&clientId=3663&RQT=309&VName=PQD.

Callinan, R. (2004, November 22). Caught in their own web: Time looks inside the police investigation into internet child pornography that has led to hundreds of arrests in Australia. Retrieved on March 14, 2010 from http://proquest.umi.com.library.keuka.edu/pqdweb?did=935695861&sid=1&Fmt=2&clientId=3663&RQT=309&VName=PQD.

Cambanis, T. (2007, October 31). Dubai and rape: French youth tells his story. Retrieved on October 9, 2010 from http://www.nytimes.com/2007/10/31/world/africa/31iht-dubai.4.8133097.html.

Cameron v. Department of Justice (2004).

Campbell, M. (2010a, December 31). Nursing students dismissed for Facebook photo. Retrieved on January 6, 2011 from http://www.kansascity.com/2010/12/30/2551869/nursing-student-expelled-for-posting.html.

Campbell, R. P. (2010b). State law. Retrieved on July 12, 2011 from http://www.socialhostliability.org/law/.

Candiotti, S., Cratty, C., Meserve, J., Ahlers, M. M., & Jamjoom, M. (2010, March 13). Al Qaeda suspect's work at nuclear sites prompts call for probe. Retrieved on March 13, 2010 from http://www.cnn.com/2010/CRIME/03/13/new.jersey.terror.probe/.

Canfield, D. (2010, July 6). Troy woman charged under Leandra's law. Retrieved on July 18, 2010 from http://www.troyrecord.com/articles/2010/07/06/news/doc4c32b0d5ae61b834149042.txt.

Canning, A., Doherty, P., & Ibanga, I. (2008, August 17). Dog's death dogs traffic cop. Retrieved on June 5, 2011 from http://abcnews.go.com/GMA/story?id=5598075t.

Capelluti, J. (2004, February). Speak no evil. Retrieved on March 16, 2010 from http://proquest.umi.com.library.keuka.edu/pqdweb?did=547906771&sid=3&Fmt=4&clientId=3663&RQT=309&VName=PQD.

Cappitelli, P. A. (2009, September). Post script to the chief's counsel column. *The Police Chief Magazine*, *76*(9), 16.

Capriccioso, R. (2006, May 24). Unwanted export? Retrieved on April 14, 2011 from http://www.insidehighered.com/news/2006/05/24/diulus.

Caputo, A. (2007, October 21). Someone's always watching: Colleges checking networking web pages of prospective students. Retrieved on March 14, 2010 from http://infoweb.newsbank.com.library.keuka.edu/iw-search/we/InfoWeb?p_product=NewsBank&p_theme=aggregated5&p_action=doc&p_docid=11CC5A170ECEAE10&p_docnum=66&p_queryname=3.

Career Directors International (2007). *2006–2007 Research Study Career Industry Mega Trends: What You and Your Clients Need to Know*. Melbourne, FL: Author.

CareerExcuse.com (2009–2010). Home page. Retrieved on March 18, 2011 from http://careerexcuse.com/.

Carless, S. A. (2006, April). Applicant reactions to multiple selection procedures for the police force. Retrieved on October 23, 2009 from http://proquest.umi.com.library.keuka.edu/pqdweb?did=995218511&sid=2&Fmt=2&clientId=3663&RQT=309&VName=PQD.

Carlsen v. Wackenhut Corporation (1994).

Carlson, D. P. (2002). *When Cultures Clash: The Divisive Nature of Police-Community Relations and Suggestions for Improvement*. Upper Saddle River, NJ: Pearson Education, Inc.

Carmean, G. (1998, February). Vision screening for police officers. *Law and Order Magazine*, *46*(2), 86–93.

Carraher, J. (1991, October). Progress report: Drug tests. Retrieved on November 25, 2009 from http://proquest.umi.com.library.keuka.edu/pqdweb?did=1318887&sid=1&Fmt=2&clientId=3663&RQT=309&VName=PQD.

Carretta, C. M. (2008, March). Domestic violence: A worldwide exploration. Retrieved on October 11, 2010 from http://web.ebscohost.com.library.keuka.edu/ehost/detail?vid=20&hid=6&sid=c11a669b-e675-487a-9271-e6576c348b8e%40sessionmgr12&bdata=JnNpdGU9ZWhvc3QtbGl2ZQ%3d%3d#db=c8h&AN=2009854563.

Carrico, M. (2000, March 1). References and the defamation trap. Retrieved on April 21, 2011 from http://www.modrall.com/0926071190840405.art.

Carson, T. (2011, January 18). Imprisoned spy gets 8 more years for contacting Russia. Retrieved on January 18, 2011 from http://news.yahoo.com/s/nm/us_spy_sentence.

Carter, D. L. (2009, June). *Law Enforcement Intelligence: A Guide for State, Local, and Tribal Law Enforcement Agencies* (2nd edn.). Washington, DC: United States Department of Justice Office of Community Oriented Policing Services.

Carter, M. & Kelleher, S. (2005, September 10). Local FEMA chief had little disaster experience; his degree came from alleged "Diploma Mill." Retrieved on April 14, 2011 from http://proquest.umi.com.library.keuka.edu/pqdweb?did=894467031&sid=1&Fmt=2&clientId=3663&RQT=309&VName=PQD.

Carrisales v. Department of Corrections (1998).

Cascio, W. F. (2006). *Managing Human Resources: Productivity, Quality of Work Life, Profits* (7th edn.). Boston, MA: McGraw-Hill Irwin.

Casenas v. Fujisawa (1997).

Casey, M. (2008, March 11). Pedophile suspect stands trial in Thailand—Canadian arrested after interpol appeal Germans unscrambled incriminating photos. Retrieved on March 14, 2010 from http://infoweb.newsbank.com.library.keuka.edu/iw-search/we/InfoWeb?p_product=NewsBank&p_theme=aggregated5&p_action=doc&p_docid=11F5DF25415E20D0&p_docnum=60&p_queryname=3.

Cassady, A. & Mierzwinski, E. (2004, June). Mistakes do happen: A look at errors in consumer credit reports. Washington, DC: National Association of State PIRGs.

Cassi, S. (2010, September 29). Northampton County corrections officer fired in wake of steroid charges. Retrieved on March 19, 2011 from http://www.lehighvalleylive.com/northampton-county/index.ssf/2010/09/northampton_county_corrections_2.html.

Caulfield, P. (2011, September 4). New Mexico state police officer caught having sex on hood of car while in uniform is fired. Retrieved on September 4, 2011 from http://www.nydailynews.com/news/national/2011/09/04/2011-09-04_frisky_new_mexico_police_officer_caught_having_sex_on_hood_of_car_is_fired.html.

Cavanaugh, K. (2006, December 30). 11 LAPD officers accuse Berkow (IA chief) of sex, racial bias. Retrieved on November 3, 2010 from http://www.freerepublic.com/focus/f-news/1760354/posts.

Caver et al. v. City of Trenton (2005).

Cawley, D. F., Miron, H. J., Araujo, W. J., Wasserman, R., Mannello, T., & Huffman, Y. (1976). *Managing Criminal Investigations Manual*. Washington, DC: University Research Corporation.

Cawthorn, G. (2006, September 16). City police look for more than just a few good men. Retrieved on November 21, 2009 from http://proquest.umi.com.library.keuka.edu/pqdweb?did=1129161611&sid=1&Fmt=3&clientId=3663&RQT=309&VName=PQD.

CBC News (2008, November 17). 3rd Metro Vancouver officer facing charge of impaired driving. Retrieved on May 1, 2011 from http://www.cbc.ca/news/canada/british-columbia/story/2008/11/17/bc-third-vancouver-police-officer-impaired-driving.html.

CBS8.com (2011, August 6). Police chief calls shooting death of SDPD officer an 'assassination.' Retrieved on August 18, 2011 from http://www.cbs8.com/story/15222889/police-chief-calls-shooting-death-of-sdpd-officer-an-assassination.

CBS/AP (2009, January 15). "Sexting" shockingly common among teens: Latest case involves three teen girls in Pa. who sent nude pics to three boys. Retrieved on October 14, 2010 from http://www.cbsnews.com/stories/2009/01/15/national/main4723161.shtml.

CBS/AP (2010, March 12). U.S. knew of Sharif Mobley, officials say. Retrieved on March 13, 2010 from http://www.cbsnews.com/stories/2010/03/12/national/main6293288.shtml.

CBSAtlanta.Com (2009, October 15). Bond set for officer who allegedly exposed himself: Steven Turner also sent picture of privates to woman, police say. Retrieved on November 1, 2010 from http://www.cbsatlanta.com/news/21308151/detail.html.

CBSAtlanta.Com (2010, October 22). Atlanta police officer charged with hitting girlfriend: Same officer fired after body slamming woman at airport. Retrieved on November 1, 2010 from http://www.cbsatlanta.com/news/25484559/detail.html.

CBSChicago.Com (2011, June 6). 5 Teens charged in Streeterville mob attacks. Retrieved on August 13, 2011 from http://chicago.cbslocal.com/2011/06/06/6-teens-charged-in-streeterville-mob-attacks/.

CBSNews.Com (2010a, June 5). "Sexting" leads to child porn charges for teens. Retrieved on October 24, 2010 from http://www.cbsnews.com/stories/2010/06/05/eveningnews/main6552438.shtml.

CBSNews.Com (2010b, September 27). Melissa Petro (pictures): NYC elementary teacher admits being Craigslist prostitute. Retrieved on September 27, 2010 from http://www.cbsnews.com/8301-504083_162-20017689-504083.html.

CBSNews.Com (2011, July 14). NYC boy spent hours with suspect before murder. Retrieved on July 23, 2011 from http://www.cbsnews.com/stories/2011/07/14/national/main20079404.shtml.

Celona, L., Doyle, J., & Roberts, G. (2007, February 11). Cop-shoot hubby's NYPD wife busted: She tried to dump gunman's car: Police. Retrieved on October 29, 2010 from http://www.nypost.com/p/news/regional/item_i1zXybeIsNKPevQ5sTZdcJ.

Center for Disease Control and Prevention (2011, March 11). Injury prevention and control: Violence prevention—About school violence. Retrieved on March 19, 2011 from http://www.cdc.gov/ViolencePrevention/youthviolence/schoolviolence/index.html.

Center for Problem-Oriented Policing (2010). Related POP projects. Retrieved on October 11, 2010 from http://www.popcenter.org/problems/domestic_violence/related.

Cerota, A. (2010, May 19). HPD officers accused of beating teen testify in court. Retrieved on October 28, 2010 from http://abclocal.go.com/ktrk/story?section=news/local&id=7450018.

Chaiken, B. & Cohen, J. M. (1972). Police background characteristics and performance: Summary. Retrieved on October 11, 2009 from http://www.rand.org/pubs/reports/R999.1/.

Chalfant, D. (2005, November 2). Facebook postings, photos incriminate dorm party-goers: University students caught in compromising situation through online group. Retrieved on March 13, 2010 from http://www.thenortherner.com/2.9399/facebook-postings-photos-incriminate-dorm-party-goers-1.1281445.

Chan, S. (2007, February 1). Report says 14 in fire dept. used fake degrees. Retrieved on April 9, 2011 from http://www.nytimes.com/2007/02/01/nyregion/01fire.html?_r=1&ex=1170997200&en=c9cc64865a9f26d7&ei=5070.

Chang, D. (2010, October 6). Two cops accused of robbing undercover officer. Retrieved on November 1, 2010 from http://www.nbcphiladelphia.com/news/breaking/Two-Cops-Accused-of-Robbing-an-Undercover-Officer.html?dr.

Chapman, S. G. (1970). *Police Patrol Readings* (2nd edn.). Springfield, MA: Charles C. Thomas, Publisher.

Charleston Gazette (2010, December 30). Police; oversight needed. Retrieved on April 19, 2011 from http://proquest.umi.com.library.keuka.edu/pqdweb?did=2225507621&sid=2&Fmt=3&clientId=3663&RQT=309&VName=PQD.

Chase, C. (2011, January 4). ESPN fires announcer for calling female colleague 'sweet baby.' Retrieved on January 4, 2011 from http://sports.yahoo.com/blogs/post/ESPN-pulls-announcer-for-calling-female-colleagu?urn=top-303299.

Chattanoogan.com (2006, December 5). Prosecutors to retry former East Ridge police officer. Retrieved on December 6, 2010 from http://www.chattanoogan.com/articles/article_97762.asp.

Cheatham, T. R. & Erickson, K. V. (1984). *The Police Officer's Guide to Better Communication.* Glenview, IL: Scott, Foresman and Company.

Chevron v. Echazabal (2002).

Chiesi, V. R. (2010, December 6). Trial of alleged cop shooter begins. Retrieved on December 6, 2010 from http://rochester.ynn.com/content/top_stories/525966/trial-of-alleged-cop-shooter-begins/.

Childs v. Williams, Ph.D. (1992).

Cholakis, P. N. & Bruce, R. (2007, July). Drug testing in the workplace: A look at oral fluid-based testing. *Professional Safety*, *52*(7), 31–36.

Chong, J. R. & Maugh, T. H. (2006, March 1). Study details mental health of war veterans: More than one-third sought psychological help in the year after their return from Iraq. Retrieved on August 15, 2010 from http://www.commondreams.org/headlines06/0301-06.htm.

Chou, R. (2010, February 26). U.K. tip leads to Cary child porn arrest. Retrieved on April 1, 2011 from http://www.wral.com/news/local/story/7127536/.

Christopher v. Department of the Army (2008).

Chronicle of Higher Education (2009, April 9). Historically black college sued for discriminating against white instructors. Retrieved on April 9, 2009 from http://chronicle.com/jobs/blogs/onhiring/994.

Christenson, V. (2004, Spring). Courts protect ninth circuit doctors who recommend medical marijuana use. Retrieved on January 28, 2010 from http://search.ebscohost.com.library.keuka.edu/login.aspx?direct=true&db=aph&AN=14040302&site=ehost-live.

City of Auburn, Georgia Police Department (n.d). Applicant for POST certified position. Auburn, GA: Author.

City of Auburn, Maine Police Department (2009). City of Auburn, Maine Police Department applicant background investigation questionnaire. Auburn, ME: Author.

City of Boston v. Boston Police Patrolmen's Association (1979).

City of Canton v. Harris (1989).

City of Haverhill, 16 MLC 1077 (1989).

City of New York v. New York Division of Human Rights (1997).

City of Ontario v. Quon (2010).

City of Overland Park (1987).

City of Tampa and Hillsborough County Police Benevolent Association (1997).

City of Worcester, 5 MLC 1414 (1978).

Civil Rights Act (1871).

Civil Rights Act (1964).

Civil Rights Act (1991).

Clark, D. W., Olson, J. W., Porter, L. M., & Leichner, R. M. (2001, December). The human resource roundtable: A recruitment and risk management tool. *The Police Chief Magazine*, *68*(12), 29–35.

Clarke, R. V. (2003, September). Shoplifting. Washington, DC: United States Department of Justice Office of Community Oriented Policing Services.

Claussen-Rogers, N. L. & Arrigo, B. A. (2005). *Police Corruption and Psychological Testing: A Strategy for Pre-Employment Screening*. Durham, NC: Carolina Academic Press.

Cleary, M., Hunt, G. E., Walter, G., & Robertson, M. (2009, December). Dealing with bullying in the workplace: Toward zero tolerance. Retrieved on February 5, 2011 from http://web.ebscohost.com.library.keuka.edu/ehost/detail?hid=13&sid=83ac1063-0972-4530-a77b-7200704592ca%40sessionmgr14&vid=4&bdata=JnNpdGU9ZWhvc3QtbGl2ZQ%3d%3d#db=c8h&AN=2010509028.

ClearLead Inc. (n.d.). Gambling addiction—Gambling addiction statistics. Retrieved on February 13, 2011 from http://www.clearleadinc.com/site/gambling-addiction.html.

Click2Houston.com (2010, March 30). Teen who claims HPD beating goes to trial: Alleged beating caught on camera. Retrieved on October 28, 2010 from http://www.msnbc.msn.com/id/39833690/ns/local_news-houston_tx/.

ClickOrlando.com (2008, December 1). Report: Police officer involved in crash has history of unsafe driving: 2 Critically injured in crash. Retrieved on November 1, 2010 from http://www.clickorlando.com/news/18180560/detail.html.

ClickOrlando.com (2009, December 22). Police: Officer fondled female inmates: Michael Coombs, 53, faces battery charges. Retrieved on November 1, 2010 from http://www.clickorlando.com/news/22041669/detail.html.

Cline, J. (2010, March 2). Carroll charged with six counts of second-degree sexual exploitation of a minor: International investigation concludes as Carroll charged with six counts of child pornography. Retrieved on April 2, 2011 from http://www.technicianonline.com/news/carroll-charged-with-six-counts-of-second-degree-sexual-exploitation-of-a-minor-1.2175232.

CNN.com (1998, September 26). A chronology key moments in the Clinton. Retrieved on October 12, 2010 from http://edition.cnn.com/2005/LAW/11/22/teacher.sex/index.html.

CNN.com (2005, November 23). Guilty of sex with student, teacher avoids prison. Retrieved on October 12, 2010 from http://edition.cnn.com/2005/LAW/11/22/teacher.sex/index.html.

CNN U.S. (2001, March 29). Special forces—Timothy Mcveigh. Retrieved on February 8, 2011 from http://articles.cnn.com/2001-03-29/us/profile.mcveigh_1_timothy-mcveigh-oklahoma-city-bombing-religion-basic-training-fort-bragg?_s=PM:US.

CNN Wire Staff (2011a, January 28). Detroit police release dramatic video of precinct shootings. Retrieved on February 1, 2011 from http://articles.cnn.com/2011-01-28/justice/michigan.shooting.video_1_detroit-police-officers-shooting?_s=PM:CRIME.

CNN Wire Staff (2011b, January 31). Organizer of child sex ring in Thailand sentenced to 25 years. Retrieved on February 1, 2011 from http://articles.cnn.com/2011-01-31/justice/new.jersey.sex.ring_1_child-pornography-thailand-young-boys?_s=PM:CRIME.

CNN Wire Staff (2011c, March 2). Police: Father stabs baby to death; deputies kill dad. Retrieved on March 18, 2011 from http://articles.cnn.com/2011-03-02/justice/california.baby.stabbed_1_second-deputy-involved-shooting-deputies-baby-son?_s=PM:CRIME.

CNN Wire Staff (2011d, March 8). At least 18 charged in alleged sexual assault of Texas girl. Retrieved on March 18, 2011 from http://www.cnn.com/2011/CRIME/03/07/texas.rape.arrests/index.html?iref=obinsite.

CNN Wire Staff (2011e, March 14). Alleged gang rape of girl 11, ignites firestorm in Texas community. Retrieved on March 18, 2011 from http://www.cnn.com/2011/CRIME/03/14/texas.alleged.rape/index.html.

CNN Wire Staff (2011f, May 16). McDonald's attack suspects face hate crime charges. Retrieved on August 16, 2011 from http://www.cnn.com/2011/CRIME/05/16/maryland.mcdonalds.beating/index.html?iref=obinsite.

CNN Wire Staff (2011g, August 16). 'Flash Mob' robs Maryland 7-eleven in less than a minute, police say. Retrieved on August 16, 2011 from http://www.cnn.com/2011/CRIME/08/16/maryland.flash.mob/index.html?eref=rss_topstories&utm_source=feedburner&utm_medium=feed&utm_campaign=Feed%3A+rss%2Fcnn_topstories+%28RSS%3A+Top+Stories%29.

CNN World. (2009, March 6). Report: More young girls face rape in Afghanistan. Retrieved on October 9, 2010 from http://articles.cnn.com/2009-03-06/world/afghan.women_1_taliban-human-rights-nato?_s=PM:WORLD.

Cochrane, R. E., Tett, R. P., & Vandecreek, L. (2003, October). Psychological testing and the selection of police officers. *Criminal Justice and Behavior*, *30*(5), 511–537.

Code of Federal Regulations (2001a, January 1). Title 14: Labor. Retrieved on February 8, 2010 from http://frwebgate.access.gpo.gov/cgi-bin/get-cfr.cgi?TITLE=14&PART=108&SECTION=33&YEAR=2001&TYPE=TEXT.

Code of Federal Regulations (2001b, July 1). Title 29: Labor. Washington, DC: U.S. Government Printing Office.

Code of Federal Regulations (2004, July 23). Title 28: Chapter I—Department of Justice part 25.10 department of justice information systems, the national instant criminal background check system, 25.10 correction of erroneous system information. Retrieved on August 17, 2010 from http://ecfr.gpoaccess.gov/cgi/t/text/text-idx?c=ecfr&sid=2801d6039f3b5ad5c98b648l6eb5d8ae&rgn=div8&view=text&node=28:1.0.1.1.26.1.4.10&idno=28.

Code of Federal Regulations (2009, October). Title 5 administrative personnel. Retrieved on October 7, 2009 from http://ecfr.gpoaccess.gov/cgi/t/text/text-idx?c=ecfr&tpl=/ecfrbrowse/Title05/5cfr731_main_02.tpl.

Code of Federal Regulations (2010, August 17). Title 42: Chapter I—Public Health Service, Department of Health and Human Services, subchapter a—General provisions, part 2—Confidentiality of alcohol and drug abuse patient records. Retrieved on August 19, 2010 from http://ecfr.gpoaccess.gov/cgi/t/text/text-idx?c=ecfr&tpl=/ecfrbrowse/Title42/42cfr2_main_02.tpl.

Code of Virginia

Codispoti, A. (2005, March 30). Injury from war keeping soldier off force: He can't be a police officer, but Peoria may consider for alternate job. Retrieved on November 25, 2009 from http://proquest.umi.com.library.keuka.edu/pqdweb?did=817414191&sid=1&Fmt=3&clientId=3663&RQT=309&VName=PQD.

Coffey, A. R. (1990). *Law Enforcement: A Human Relations Approach*. Englewood Cliffs, NJ: Prentice-Hall, Inc.

Cohen, A. R. (1993). *The Portable MBA in Management*. New York: John Wiley & Sons, Inc.

Cohen, D. (1998, March). Giving notification where it's due. *Security Management*, 103–105.

Cohen, P. J. (2009). Medical marijuana: The conflict between scientific evidence and political ideology. Part one of two. Retrieved on January 28, 2010 from http://search.ebscohost.com.library.keuka.edu/login.aspx?direct=true&db=cmedm&AN=19296351&site=ehost-live.

Cohen, B. & Chaiken, J. (1987, September). Investigators who perform well. Washington, DC: United States Department of Justice National Institute of Justice Office of Communication and Research Utilization.

Coker, M. (2007, November 11). Tailhook scandal sinks into history: Today's navy has more than 4,600 women serving in combat roles, most of them in Iraq's theater of operations. Retrieved on April 16, 2011 from http://proquest.umi.com.library.keuka.edu/pqdweb?did=1380866241&sid=2&Fmt=3&clientId=3663&RQT=309&VName=PQD.

Coker, M. (2011, April 1). Miguel Lerma Jr., border patrol officer, held in sexual assaults of women in garden grove and long beach. Retrieved on April 2, 2011 from http://blogs.ocweekly.com/navelgazing/2011/04/miguel_lerma_jr_sex_assault.php.

Colaprete, F. A. (2002a, October). Managing change in the investigative process: A process-centered approach to professional development and change management. Retrieved on October 25, 2009 from http://proquest.umi.com.library.keuka.edu/pqdweb?did=293673331&sid=3&Fmt=2&clientId=3663&RQT=309&VName=PQD.

Colaprete, F. A. (2002b, November). Andragogy and technology: Tools in the contemporary police training process. *The Law Enforcement Executive Forum Journal*, *2*(4), 1–16. The Illinois Law Enforcement Executive Institute.

Colaprete, F. A. (2003, November/December). Eclecticism: Blending the best adult education philosophies in law enforcement training. *The Law Enforcement Trainer*, *18*(6), 12–17.

Colaprete, F. A. (2004a, October). The case for investigator mentoring: The Rochester experience. Retrieved on October 25, 2009 from http://proquest.umi.com.library.keuka.edu/pqdweb?did=743160041&sid=3&Fmt=2&clientId=3663&RQT=309&VName=PQD.

Colaprete, F. A. (2004b, October). Knowledge management. Retrieved on October 25, 2009 from http://proquest.umi.com.library.keuka.edu/pqdweb?did=737569961&sid=3&Fmt=4&clientId=3663&RQT=309&VName=PQD.

Colaprete, F. A. (2004c, November). Training internal investigators: A study in hybrid instructional program development. *Law Enforcement Executive Forum*, *4*(7), 19–27.

Colaprete, F. A. (2005a, July). Criminal investigator training: A stratified analysis of preferred didactic strategies. *Law Enforcement Executive Forum*, *5*(4), 109–125.

Colaprete, F. A. (2005b, August). Police hiring standards: A comparative analysis of police applicant attrition rates. *Law Enforcement Executive Forum*, *5*(5), 143–162.

Colaprete, F. A. (2006, March). Generation x and y in law enforcement: A comparative analysis of generational cohorts. Paper presentation. *The Academy of Criminal Justice Sciences 43rd Annual Meeting*, Baltimore, MD.

Colaprete, F. A. (2007, July/August). Performance evaluations in jails: Missed opportunities for training and professional development. Retrieved on October 25, 2009 from http://proquest.umi.com.library.keuka.edu/pqdweb?did=1327326901&sid=3&Fmt=2&clientId=3663&RQT=309&VName=PQD.

Colaprete, F. A. (2008, September). Generations: Leading the organization's human resources to greatness. Retrieved on September 2, 2009 from http://grad.norwich.edu/mja/directorscorner/08_28_08/index.html.

Colaprete, F. A. (2009a). *Background Investigations: Contemporary Concepts, Issues, and Practices*. Rochester, NY: Justice Systems Solutions, LLC.

Colaprete, F. A. (2009b). *Mentoring in the Criminal Justice Professions: Conveyance of the Craft*. Springfield, MA: Charles C. Thomas, Publisher.

Colaprete, F. A. & Hardwich, J. (2007, March). Officer safety and community policing: An examination of officer opinions of compromised safety. *The Law Enforcement Executive Forum Journal*, *7*(3), 1–16. The Illinois Law Enforcement Executive Institute.

Colbridge, T. D. (2000, December). Prohibited discrimination under the Americans with Disabilities Act. *FBI Law Enforcement Bulletin*, *69*(12), 14–21.

Coleman v. N.Y. (2007).

CollegeGrad.com (2009). Drug testing and other possible conditions of employment. Provided by QuinStreet, Inc. Retrieved on January 24, 2010 from http://www.collegegrad.com/jobsearch/New-Job-Preparation/Drug-Testing-And-Other-Possible-Conditions-Of-Employment/.

Collingwood, T., Thomas, R., Means, R., & Hoffman, R. (2000, June). Personnel testing. *Law and Order Magazine*, *48*(6), 164.

Collins, J. M. (1998, September). Liability issues and the furnishing of employment references. *The Police Chief Magazine*, *65*(9), 12–15.

Collins, J. M. (2003). The chief's guide to labor relations. Retrieved on October 29, 2010 from http://www.aele.org/2003macp-labor.html.

Collins, K. D. (2005, Spring). The use of plain-language principles in Texas litigation formbooks. Retrieved on March 16, 2010 from http://proquest.umi.com.library.keuka.edu/pqdweb?did=848162401&sid=3&Fmt=4&clientId=3663&RQT=309&VName=PQD.

Collins, M. K. (2007, March). Child pornography: A closer look. Retrieved on October 24, 2010 from http://www.policechiefmagazine.org/magazine/index.cfm?fuseaction=display&article_id=1139&issue_id=32007.

Collins, T. (2010, July 17). Police layoffs hit Oakland, one of the nation's most crime-ridden cities: Police layoffs leave the city of Oakland with almost 10 percent fewer cops despite last minute negotiations. Retrieved on February 14, 2011 from http://www.csmonitor.com/From-the-news-wires/2010/0717/Police-layoffs-hit-Oakland-one-of-the-nation-s-most-crime-ridden-cities.

Colvin, G. (1999, June 21). Looking to hire the very best? Ask the right questions. Lots of them. Retrieved on July 17, 2011 from http://money.cnn.com/magazines/fortune/fortune_archive/1999/06/21/261735/index.htm.

Columbian (2005, September 11). Region's FEMA chief defends background. Retrieved on April 14, 2011 from http://proquest.umi.com.library.keuka.edu/pqdweb?did=895957071&sid=1&Fmt=3&clientId=3663&RQT=309&VName=PQD.

Commission for Florida Law Enforcement Accreditation, Inc. (2009, July). *Standards Manual Edition 4.0*. Orlando, FL: Author.

Commission on Accreditation for Law Enforcement Agencies. (2009a, January 15). Law enforcement accreditation standards. Retrieved on October 20, 2009 from http://www.calea.org/Online/CALEAPrograms/LawEnforcement/lawenfprogram.htm.

Commission on Accreditation for Law Enforcement Agencies. (2009b, September 1). Police accreditation coalitions (PACS). Retrieved on November 3, 2009 from http://www.calea.org/online/Clients/PACList.htm.

Committee on Governmental Affairs (2004, May 11 and 12). Bogus degrees and unmet expectations: Are taxpayer dollars subsidizing diploma mills? Retrieved on March 19, 2011 from http://www.credentialwatch.org/reports/mills.pdf.

Commonwealth of Pennsylvania Department of Corrections v. Krempowsky (1997).

Commonwealth of Pennsylvania v. O'Neill (1972).

Compassionate Use Act (1996).

Computer Security Law (1987).

Comstock, D. C. (2008, April). Background checks. Retrieved on February 15, 2010 from http://proquest.umi.com.library.keuka.edu/pqdweb?did=1468582831&sid=1&Fmt=2&clientId=3663&RQT=309&VName=PQD.

Cone, E. J. (1993, September). Saliva testing for drugs of abuse. Retrieved on January 18, 2010 from http://search.ebscohost.com.library.keuka.edu/login.aspx?direct=true&db=cmedm&AN=8215090&site=ehost-live.

Conklin, J. E. (2003). *Why Crime Rates Fell*. Boston, MA: Pearson Education—Allyn & Bacon.

Connecticut Attorney General (2009, May 12). Attorney general says craigslist erotic services section inadequate. Retrieved on September 5, 2010 from http://www.ct.gov/ag/cwp/view.asp?A=2341&Q=439912.

Connecticut Code

Constitution.org (n.d.). Chapter 47. Uniform code of military justice. Retrieved on October 9, 2010 from http://www.constitution.org/mil/ucmj19970615.htm.

Consumer Federation of America (2002, December 17). Credit score accuracy and implications for consumers. Retrieved on August 18, 2010 from www.ncrainc.org/.../CFA%20NCRA%20**Credit**%20**Score**%20Report.pdf.

Conte v. Horcher (1977).

Contreras, A. & Gollin, G. (2009, March/April). The real and the fake degree and diploma mills. Retrieved on April 7, 2011 from http://web.ebscohost.com.library.keuka.edu/ehost/detail?vid=7&hid=111&sid=8b68f380-de5e-409e-8eed-e2a570345a70%40sessionmgr113&bdata=JnNpdGU9ZWhvc3QtbGl2ZQ%3d%3d#db=aph&AN=36984690.

Contreras, G. (2005, July 5). SAPD officer charged with sexual assault on transsexual. Retrieved on October 18, 2010 from http://www.ksat.com/news/4686888/detail.html.

Contreras, G. (2010, June 29). Child porn verdict: Guilty. Retrieved on October 24, 2010 from http://www.mysanantonio.com/news/local_news/child_porn_verdict_guilty_97411149.html.

Controlled Substances Act of 1970. (2010, February 10). Retrieved on December 1, 2009 from http://www.justice.gov/dea/pubs/csa.html.

Cook, J. (2010a, September 3). Pentagon declined to investigate hundreds of purchases of child pornography. Retrieved on April 16, 2011 from http://news.yahoo.com/s/yblog_upshot/20100903/us_yblog_upshot/pentagon-declined-to-investigate-hundreds-of-purchases-of-child-pornography.

Cook, R. (2010b, January 12). 44 Suspects arrested in Georgia computer child porn sweep; more expected. Retrieved on January 18, 2011 from http://www.ajc.com/news/44-suspects-arrested-in-273098.html.

Cooper, M. (2007, November 6). Giuliani says successes surpass Kerik's mistakes. Retrieved on April 16, 2011 from http://www.nytimes.com/2007/11/06/us/politics/06giuliani.html?ref=bernardbkerik.

Cooper, M. (2011, February 14). Recession blamed for rise in bankruptcies: Filings have gone up by as much as 35 percent a year since the law was made more stringent in 2005. Retrieved on February 22, 2011 from http://proquest.umi.com.library.keuka.edu/pqdweb?did=2266590411&sid=2&Fmt=3&clientId=3663&RQT=309&VName=PQD.

Corcoran, R. (2011, February 15). 1 US immigration agent dead, 1 injured in Mexico. Retrieved on February 15, 2011 from http://news.yahoo.com/s/ap/20110216/ap_on_re_la_am_ca/lt_mexico_ice_agents_shot.

Cordner, G. W. & Sheehan, R. (1999). *Police Administration* (4th edn.). Cincinnati, OH: Anderson Publishing Company.

Cornell University Law School Legal Information Institute Labor and Employment Laws Weblink: http://topics.law.cornell.edu/wex/table_labor.

Corr, K. (2002, May). Internet fraud complaint center. *Law and Order Magazine*, *50*(5), 38–43.

Cotran v. Rollins Hudig Hall International, Inc. (1998).

Council on Law Enforcement Education and Training (2009). Council on law enforcement education and training. Retrieved on October 20, 2009 from http://www.ok.gov/cleet/.

Counts, G. (2010, January 13). Source: Private company missed infractions on officer's background. Retrieved on January 25, 2010 from http://www.charlotteobserver.com/topstories/story/1178074.html.

County of Los Angeles Sheriff's Department and Association of Los Angeles Deputies (1997).

County of Sacramento v. Lewis. (1998).

Courtright, J. L. & Smuddle, P. M. (2009, Fall). Leveraging organizational innovation for strategic reputation management. Retrieved on August 27, 2009 from http://proquest.umi.com.library.keuka.edu/pqdweb?did=1883874191&sid=1&Fmt=2&clientId=3663&RQT=309&VName=PQD.

Cousin v. Trans Union Corporation (2001).

Coutts, L. M. (1990). Police hiring and promotion: Methods and outcomes. Retrieved on November 23, 2009 from http://www.ncjrs.gov/app/publications/abstract.aspx?ID=125378.

Covey, S. R. (1992). *Principle-Centered Leadership*. New York: Fireside—Simon & Schuster.

Cox, B. D. (2000, November). False reports: When things aren't what they seem. *Law and Order Magazine*, *48*(11), 39–43.

Cox v. Nasche (1996).

Craig, G. (2009a, August 20). Greece police chief Rahn indictment related to hiring. Retrieved on August 20, 2009 from http://www.democratandchronicle.com/article/20090820/NEWS01/908200330/Greece+Police+Chief+Rahn+indictment+related+to+hiring&referrer=NEWSFRONTCAROUSEL.

Craig, G. (2009b, July 16). Greece police department's hiring of Joseph scrutinized. Retrieved on July 17, 2009 from http://www.democratandchronicle.com/apps/pbcs.dll/article?AID=2009907160337.

Craig, G. (2009c, October 7). Greece police chief denies fabricating, falsifying records. Retrieved on October 9, 2009 from http://www.democratandchronicle.com/apps/pbcs.dll/article?AID=2009910070345.

Craig, G. (2010a, March 24). DA seeks to disqualify Rahn's lawyer. Retrieved on March 24, 2010 from http://www.democratandchronicle.com/article/20100324/NEWS01/100324024/1002/NEWS.

Craig, G. (2010b, April 9). Merritt Rahn's trial shifts focus to hiring of Gary Pignato. Retrieved on April 9, 2010 from http://www.democratandchronicle.com/article/20100409/NEWS01/4090335/1002/NEWS.

Craig, G. (2010c, April 13). Merritt Rahn told me to falsify background documents, Trowbridge says. Retrieved on April 15, 2010 from http://www.democratandchronicle.com/article/20100413/NEWS01/4130331.

Craig, G. (2010d, April 15). Merritt Rahn's memo on Gary Pignato's background report called unusual. Retrieved on April 15, 2010 from http://www.democratandchronicle.com/article/20100415/NEWS01/4150349.

Craig, G. (2011a, February 8). Chad Rahn Case Will Be Decided by Judge, Not Jury. Retrieved on February 8, 2011 from http://www.democratandchronicle.com/article/20110208/NEWS01/102080325/1002/NEWS.

Craig, G. (2011b, April 1). Judge sentences 'sexual predator' to 20 years in prison. Retrieved on April 1, 2011 from http://www.democratandchronicle.com/article/20110401/NEWS01/110401016/1002/NEWS/Judge-sentences-sexual-predator-20-years-prison?odyssey=mod_sectionstories.

Craig, G. (2011c, April 17). Chad Rahn's police career dotted with iffy incidents. Retrieved on April 18, 2011 from http://www.democratandchronicle.com/article/20110417/NEWS01/104170358/1002/NEWS.

Craig, G. & McDermott, M. (2010, March 28). More Merritt Rahn misdeeds alleged ahead of trial. Reprinted with permission from the Democrat and Chronicle Media Group http://www.democratandchronicle.com/. Retrieved on March 28, 2010 from http://www.democratandchronicle.com/article/20100328/NEWS01/3280370/More-Merritt-Rahn-misdeeds-alleged-ahead-of-trial&referrer=NEWSFRONTCAROUSEL.

Craig Pratt & Associates, Inc. (n.d.). Fair employment agencies in the 50 states. Retrieved on February 22, 2011 from http://www.amyopp.com/pdf/Fair_Employment_Practices_Agencies_in_the_50_States.pdf.

Crainer, S. & Dearlove, D. (2004, Winter). The write stuff. Retrieved on March 16, 2010 from http://proquest.umi.com.library.keuka.edu/pqdweb?did=872128981&sid=3&Fmt=2&clientId=3663&RQT=309&VName=PQD.

Cramer, M. (2009a, July 5). Police officers in Boston disciplined for steroid use. Retrieved on March 19, 2011 from http://www.hardsweat.com/2154-police-officers-in-boston-disciplined-for-steroid-use/.

Cramer, M. (2009b, October 2). Details of alleged rape told in court: Female officer seeks to extend restraining order. Retrieved on December 14, 2009 from http://www.boston.com/news/local/massachusetts/articles/2009/10/02/court_hears_female_officer_detail_alleged_rape_by_colleague/.

Cramer, R. (2004). Diploma mills: Diploma mills are easily created and some have issued bogus degrees to federal employees at government expense. Gao-04-1096t. Retrieved on April 7, 2011 from http://web.ebscohost.com.library.keuka.edu/ehost/detail?vid=7&hid=111&sid=8b68f380-de5e-409e-8eed-e2a570345a70%40sessionmgr113&bdata=JnNpdGU9ZWhvc3QtbG12ZQ%3d%3d#db=eric&AN=ED483250.

Cratty, C. (2011, March 18). D.C. elementary school student allegedly brought cocaine to school. Retrieved on March 18, 2011 from http://www.cnn.com/2011/CRIME/03/18/dc.school.cocaine/.

Crawford, C. (2004, December 26). Tablets may lead to drug test grief. Retrieved on January 24, 2010 from http://search.ebscohost.com.library.keuka.edu/login.aspx?direct=true&db=nfh&AN=200412261015657721&site=ehost-live.

Crawford, C. & Haberfield, I. (2005, November 27). New doubts on drug tests. Retrieved on January 24, 2010 from http://search.ebscohost.com.library.keuka.edu/login.aspx?direct=true&db=nfh&AN=200511271021520812&site=ehost-live.

Crawford Rehabilitation v. Weisman (1997).

Crawford, W. (2009, May/June). Writing for obscurity. Retrieved on March 16, 2010 from http://proquest.umi.com.library.keuka.edu/pqdweb?did=1729109781&sid=3&Fmt=3&clientId=3663&RQT=309&VName=PQD.

Crawford v. Department of Homeland Security (2007).

Cremer v. Macomb Board of Fire and Police Commissioners (1994).

Cremer v. Macomb (1996).

Crete v. City of Lowell. (2005). Retrieved on March 30, 2009 from http://www.ca1.uscourts.gov/cgi-bin/getopn.pl?OPINION=04-1891.01A.

Crime Control Act (1973).

Crime Control Act (1990).

Crime Identification Technology Act. (1998). Retrieved on October 9, 2010 from http://frwebgate.access.gpo.gov/cgi-bin/getdoc.cgi?dbname=105_cong_public_laws&docid=f:publ251.105.

CrimeVictimServices.org (n.d.). Relevant laws re: Campus safety and school responsibility to victims. Retrieved on April 1, 2011 from http://www.crimevictimservices.org/page/victimsrights/46.

Croddy v. Federal Bureau of Investigation (2006).

Cronkhite, C. L. (2008). *Criminal Justice Administration: Strategies for the 21st Century*. Sudbury, MA: Jones & Bartlett Publishers.

Cross-Tab (2010, January). *Online Reputation in a Connected World*. Bellevue, WA: Author.

Culbertson, R. G. & Weisheit, R. A. (2002). *Order Under Law* (6th edn.). Prospect Heights, IL: Waveland Press, Inc.

Cuniff, M. (2010, May 4). Suspect not on registry: Man accused of rape is sex offender. Retrieved on October 9, 2010 from http://web.ebscohost.com.library.keuka.edu/ehost/detail?vid=4&hid=8&sid=872c83a2-eb3e-4e76-9e3d-c3666d69edad%40sessionmgr13&bdata=JnNpdGU9ZWhvc3QtbGl2ZQ%3d%3d#db=nfh&AN=2W64247457608.

Cunningham v. Gates (1997).

Cuomo, C., Vlasto, C., & Dwyer, D. (2011, June 6). Rep. Anthony Weiner: 'The picture was of me and I sent it.' Retrieved on June 8, 2011 from http://abcnews.go.com/Politics/rep-anthony-weiner-picture/story?id=13774605.

Curley v. General Valet Service (1973).

Curran, S. F. (1998, October). Pre-employment psychological evaluation of law enforcement applicants. *The Police Chief Magazine*, *65*(10), 88–95.

Cusins, P. (1994). Understanding quality through systems thinking. Retrieved on October 24, 2009 from http://proquest.umi.com.library.keuka.edu/pqdweb?did=843060&sid=2&Fmt=3&clientId=3663&RQT=309&VName=PQD.

Cutler v. Quality Terminal Services, LLC. (2008).

Daemmrich, J. (1993, February 10). 28 Mids risking expulsion stolen exam mires Academy in cheating scandal. Retrieved on August 4, 2011 from http://articles.baltimoresun.com/1993-02-10/news/1993041090_1_naval-academy-cheating-exam.

Daigle, E. P. (2008, December). The application of qualified privilege in background investigations. Retrieved on April 25, 2011 from http://www.halloran-sage.com/Knowledge/articleDetail.aspx?storyid=4448.

Daigle, E. P. (2010, May). Social networking policies: Just another policy? *The Police Chief Magazine*, *77*(5), 12–13.

Dailey, K. & Erdely, S. R. (2005, October). To catch a cop. Retrieved on January 18, 2010 from http://search.ebscohost.com.library.keuka.edu/login.aspx?direct=true&db=hch&AN=18302356&site=ehost-live.

Dale, M. C. (2011, January 18). NJ Cyberbully forwarded lewd photos, gets 45 days. Retrieved on January 18, 2011 from http://news.yahoo.com/s/ap/us_lewd_photos_cyberbullying;_ylt=Auvy_48VEWwJ2VOSCk_9HOkXIr0F;_ylu=X3oDMTNhYW45bzJpBGFzc2V0Ay9zL2FwL3VzX2xld2RfcGhvdG9zX2N5YmVyYnVsbHlpbmcEY2NvZGUDbXBfZWNfOF8xMARjcG9zAzYEcG9zAzYEc2VjA3luX3RvcF9zdG9yaWVzBHNsawNuamN5YmVyYnVsbHk-.

Daley v. Koch (1989).

Dalton v. Capital Associated Indus., Inc. (2001).

Damphousse, K. R., Pointon, L., Upchurch, D., & Moore, R. K. (2007, June). Assessing the validity of voice stress analysis tools in a jail setting. Retrieved on July 26, 2011 from https://www.ncjrs.gov/pdffiles1/nij/grants/219031.pdf.

Danaher, L. (2003, June). The investigative paradigm. *Law and Order Magazine*, *51*(6), 133–134.

Danning, J. J. (1999, December). Experienced pros make top legal advisors. Retrieved on October 30, 2009 from http://search.ebscohost.com.library.keuka.edu/login.aspx?direct=true&db=hch&AN=2668826&site=ehost-live.

Dantzker, M. L. (2003). *Understanding Today's Police* (3rd edn.). Upper Saddle River, NJ: Pearson Education, Inc.

Dao, J. (2009, November 5). Suspect was 'Mortified' about deployment. Retrieved on March 13, 2010 from http://www.nytimes.com/2009/11/06/us/06suspect.html.

Darrow, D. (2011, January 16). Workplace violence. Retrieved on April 19, 2011 from http://proquest.umi.com.library.keuka.edu/pqdweb?did=2239255931&sid=2&Fmt=3&clientId=3663&RQT=309&VName=PQD.

Dasgupta, A. (2003, February). Urinary adulterants and drugs-of-abuse testing. Retrieved on January 24, 2010 from http://search.ebscohost.com.library.keuka.edu/login.aspx?direct=true&db=c8h&AN=2003156746&site=ehost-live.

Dasgupta, A., Wahed, A., & Wells, A. (2002, February). Rapid spot tests for detecting the presence of adulterants in urine specimens submitted for drug testing. Retrieved on January 24, 2010 from http://search.ebscohost.com.library.keuka.edu/login.aspx?direct=true&db=cmedm&AN=11863230&site=ehost-live.

Dash, L. (1990, June 13). Busy investigators often forced to rely on honesty of applicants. Retrieved on September 13, 2010 from http://proquest.umi.com.library.keuka.edu/pqdweb?index=40&did=72596325&SrchMode=1&sid=5&Fmt=3&VInst=PROD&VType=PQD&RQT=309&VName=PQD&TS=1284426038&clientId=3663.

Daubert v. Merrell Dow Chemicals, Inc. (1993).

Davenport, J. (2009, October). Child porn police use spy software to arrest 200. Retrieved on January 18, 2011 from http://www.thisislondon.co.uk/standard/article-23754576-child-porn-police-use-spy-software-to-arrest-200-suspects.do.

Davidsen, B. (2010, October 8). I-team 10 investigation: Suspended Greece police sergeant resigns. Retrieved on October 9, 2010 from http://www.whec.com/news/stories/S1782461.shtml?cat=566.

Davies, C. J. (2009, October 9). Policing the Facebook extremists. Retrieved on August 2, 2011 from http://www.wired.co.uk/magazine/archive/2009/11/start/policing-the-facebook-extremists.

Davies, K. R. (2003, November). Finessing the facts. Retrieved on February 16, 2010 from http://proquest.umi.com.library.keuka.edu/pqdweb?did=465900891&sid=1&Fmt=4&clientId=3663&RQT=309&VName=PQD.

Davis v. City of Dallas (1985).

Davis v. The Board of County Commissioners of Dona Ana County (1999).

Dearing, J. W. (2009, September). Applying diffusion of innovation theory to intervention development. Retrieved on October 27, 2009 from http://proquest.umi.com.library.keuka.edu/pqdweb?did=1844690701&sid=2&Fmt=2&clientId=3663&RQT=309&VName=PQD.

Decicco, D. (2000, December). Police officer candidate assessment and selection. *FBI Law Enforcement Bulletin*, *69*(12), 1–6.

Dedman, B. (2010, June 29). Palin e-mails reveal a powerful 'First Dude': In Sarah Palin Administration, her spouse was active in state business. Retrieved on November 1, 2010 from http://www.msnbc.msn.com/id/35238034/.

Dees, T. (1998, February). We don't get those kinds of cases. *Law and Order Magazine*, *46*(2), 14–16.

Dees, T. (2009, November). Social networks for better policing: Facebook, Twitter, blogs, and Google voice. *Law and Order Magazine*, *57*(11), 32–36.

DeGroot, T. & Gooty, J. (2009, February 25). Can nonverbal; cues be used to make meaningful personality attributions in employment interviews. Retrieved on July 27, 2011 from http://proquest.umi.com.library.keuka.edu/pqdweb?index=13&did=1736413751&SrchMode=1&sid=4&Fmt=6&VInst=PROD&VType=PQD&RQT=309&VName=PQD&TS=1311769157&clientId=3663.

De Fruyt, F., Bockstaele, M., Taris, R., & Van Heil, A. (2006). Police interview competencies: Assessment and associated traits. *European Journal of Personality*, *20*, 567–584.

Delattre, E. J. (1989). *Character and Cops: Ethics in Policing*. Washington, DC: American Enterprise Institute for Public Policy Research.

Delazio, S. (2009, November 18). Expunged record lessens penalty in death: With juvenile record erased, Gardner gets lighter sentence for manslaughter, drug count. Retrieved on February 5, 2011 from http://web.ebscohost.com.library.keuka.edu/ehost/detail?hid=13&sid=83ac1063-0972-4530-a77b-7200704592ca%40sessionmgr14&vid=8&bdata=JnNpdGU9ZWhvc3QtbGl2ZQ%3d%3d#db=nfh&AN=2W63361177256.

Delp, M. (2002, December 16). The many benefits of a pre-employment screening process. Retrieved on October 21, 2009 from http://www.asashop.org/autoinc/nov2002/manage.htm.

Demauro v. Loren-Maltese (2001).

Deming, J. (1990, April). Drug-free workplace is good business. Retrieved on November 25, 2009 from http://proquest.umi.com.library.keuka.edu/pqdweb?did=706324&sid=1&Fmt=2&clientId=3663&RQT=309&VName=PQD.

Dempsey, J. S. & Forst, L. S. (2005). *An Introduction to Policing*. Belmont, CA: Thomson Wadsworth.

Denham, B. E. (2009). Association between narcotic use and anabolic-androgenic steroid use among American adolescents. Retrieved on April 13, 2011 from http://www.ncbi.nlm.nih.gov/pubmed/20001694.

Denhof et al. v. City of Grand Rapids (2005).

Department of the Navy (n.d.). Department of the Navy core values charter. Retrieved on April 16, 2011 from http://ethics.navy.mil/content/corevaluescharter.aspx.

DePresca, J. (2003a, October). Courtroom testimony. *Law and Order Magazine*, *51*(10), 165–168.

DePresca, J. (2003b, October). Date rape drugs. *Law and Order Magazine*, *51*(10), 210–213.

Detone v. Bullitt Courier Service, Inc. (1988).

Detrick, P. & Chibnall, J. T. (2002, Fall). Prediction of police officer performance with the Inwald Personality Inventory. Retrieved on November 21, 2009 from http://search.ebscohost.com.library.keuka.edu/login.aspx?direct=true&db=sih&AN=SM197790&site=ehost-live.

Detz v. Hoover (1982).

Deukmedjian, J. E. & de Lint, W. (2007, September). Community into intelligence: Resolving information uptake in the RCMP. Retrieved on October 10, 2010 from http://web.ebscohost.com.library.keuka.edu/ehost/detail?vid=6&hid=110&sid=4c672b52-8d14-4332-a8cb-b1ff63c84f64%40sessionmgr11&bdata=JnNpdGU9ZWhvc3QtbGl2ZQ%3d%3d#db=aph&AN=26447293.

Deutsch, L. (2009, June 9). Veteran LAPD detective faces 1986 murder charge. Retrieved on June 21, 2009 from http://news.yahoo.com/s/ap/20090609/ap_on_re_us/us_detective_killing.

DFEH v. City of Merced Police Department (1988).

Diaz, T. (1999, September). Computer-enhanced investigations. *The Police Chief Magazine*, *66*(9), 50–56.

Dietz, N. (1999, January). Recruiters weigh personality testing. Retrieved on October 22, 2009 from http://search.ebscohost.com.library.keuka.edu/login.aspx?direct=true&db=f5h&AN=1492308&site=ehost-live.

Digital Signature Act (1999).

Dilan, M. M. (2009, November 18). "Leandra's Law" passes in the senate, strengthening penalties on drunk drivers carrying child passengers. Retrieved on February 21, 2011 from http://www.nysenate.gov/press-release/leandra-s-law-passes-senate-strengthening-penalties-drunk-drivers-carrying-child-passe.

Dilanian, K. (2010, September 7). Border patrol is grappling with misconduct cases in its ranks: In the last 18 months, five border patrol agents have been accused or convicted of sex crimes or assaults. The latest case involved the alleged assault of a suspected drug smuggler. Retrieved on May 5, 2011 from http://articles.latimes.com/2010/sep/07/nation/la-na-border-patrol-20100908.

DiPaola, J. (1992, September 17). Officer charged with molesting teen. Retrieved on December 6, 2010 from http://articles.sun-sentinel.com/1992-09-17/news/9201220004_1_police-explorers-police-officers-victim.

DiPrizio, J. (2008, December 29). Memphis police officer fired, accused of beating transgender suspect. Retrieved on October 28, 2010 from http://www.myeyewitnessnews.com/news/local/story/Memphis-Police-Officer-Fired-Accused-of-Beating/p92mTont1U6Me_gGJjZ6WQ.cspx.

Disability and Technical Business Assistance Centers (1992, January). Employment provisions (Title I) technical assistance manual. Retrieved on November 22, 2009 from http://www.adata.org/adaportal/Employment/Browse_TAM_I/Browse_TOC.html.

District of Columbia v. Heller (2008).

Dixon, D. (2008, March 23). Police have to work much harder to draw fraction of applicants they once attracted. Retrieved on October 31, 2009 from http://proquest.umi.com.library.keuka.edu/pqdweb?did=1449949621&sid=1&Fmt=3&clientId=3663&RQT=309&VName=PQD.

DNA.gov (n.d.). Federal legislation on forensic DNA. Retrieved on January 18, 2011 from http://www.dna.gov/statutes-caselaw/federal-legislation/.

Dodd v. SEPTA. (2007).

Dodds, P. (2011, July 31). Extremists flock to Facebook for recruits. *Democrat and Chronicle*, 19A–20A.

Doe v. U.S. Civil Service Commission (1980).

Dolak, K. (2011, March 5). 'East Coast Rapist' captured in Connecticut: The man accused of terrorizing women with sexual assaults for over 12 years arrested. Retrieved on April 16, 2011 from http://abcnews.go.com/US/east-coast-rapist-aaron-thomas-captured-dna-matched/story?id=13064889.

Dolan, M. (2011, March 21). Barry Bonds steroid case goes to trial: The former giants slugger is accused of lying when he denied using performance-enhancing drugs. Retrieved on April 13, 2011 from http://articles.latimes.com/2011/mar/21/local/me-bonds-trial-opener-20110321-1.

Dolan, K., Rouen, D., & Kimber, J. (2004, June). An overview of the use of urine, hair, sweat, and saliva to detect drug use. Retrieved on January 18, 2010 from http://search.ebscohost.com.library.keuka.edu/login.aspx?direct=true&db=aph&AN=13572214&site=ehost-live.

Dolnick, S. (2009, November 5). Kerik confesses to cheating I.R.S. and telling lies. Retrieved on October 18, 2010 from http://www.nytimes.com/2009/11/06/nyregion/06kerik.html?_r=1&partner=rss&emc=rss.

Domestic Abuse Intervention Programs (2008). The Duluth model—History. Retrieved on October 11, 2010 from http://www.theduluthmodel.org/history.php.

Domestic Violence Offender Gun Ban (1997).

Donofrio, A. (2001a, July). Part I—Subpoena power: An understanding of internet protocol addresses can bring investigators closer to a suspect. *Law Enforcement Technology*, 102–106.

Donofrio, A. (2001b, August). Part II—Subpoena power: Knowing what information may be available and what information internet service providers keep can help investigations of computer-related crime. *Law Enforcement Technology*, 76–82.

Doorley, S. (2010, March 24). *New York v. Merritt Rahn: Molineux/Ventimiglia Application*. Ind. # 2009/0724 & 0871.

Doran, J. & Brizee, A. (2010, September 7). Writing the personal statement. Retrieved on September 13, 2010 from http://owl.english.purdue.edu/owl/resource/642/01/.

Dorris, M. J. & Kleiner, B. H. (2003). New developments concerning negligent hiring in public schools. Retrieved on February 16, 2010 from http://proquest.umi.com.library.keuka.edu/pqdweb?did=344699931&sid=1&Fmt=3&clientId=3663&RQT=309&VName=PQD.

Dortch, D. T. (2010, November 11). Don't forget those KSA answers just yet. Retrieved on July 17, 2011 from http://proquest.umi.com.library.keuka.edu/pqdweb?did=2185608881&sid=1&Fmt=3&clientId=3663&RQT=309&VName=PQD.

Douglas El. v. Southeastern Pennsylvania Transportation Authority (SEPTA) (2007).

Douris, S. (2006, December). Negligent hiring… passing around the bad apple. *Law and Order Magazine*, *54*(12), 55–58.

Dow, H. (2009, June 26). Police under fire: Were crime scenes tainted? Retrieved on August 23, 2009 from http://www.cbsnews.com/stories/2000/06/26/48hours/main209573.shtml.

Downs v. Massachusetts Bay Transportation Authority (1998).

Dowty, D. (2010, February 1). Onondaga crime analysis center shares success stories during open house. Retrieved on October 11, 2010 from http://www.syracuse.com/news/index.ssf/2010/02/onondaga_crime_analysis_center_1.html.

Doyle, A. (n.d.). Employment tests. Retrieved on October 24, 2009 from http://jobsearch.about.com/od/careertests/a/employmenttests.htm.

Draper, B., Pfaff, J. J., Pirkis, J., Snowdon, J., Lautenschlager, N. T., Wilson, I., & Almeida, O. P. (2008, February). Long-term effects of childhood abuse on the quality of life and health of older people: Results from the depressions and early prevention of suicide in general practice project. Retrieved on October 11, 2010 from http://web.ebscohost.com.library.keuka.edu/ehost/detail?vid=24&hid=13&sid=c11a669b-e675-487a-9271-e6576c348b8e%40sessionmgr12&bdata=JnNpdGU9ZWhvc3QtbGl2ZQ%3d%3d#db=c8h&AN=2009778919.

Drayton v. St. Petersburg (1979).

Dreyfack, R. (2004, April). The write way to jump start your career. Retrieved on March 16, 2010 from http://proquest.umi.com.library.keuka.edu/pqdweb?did=603423871&sid=3&Fmt=3&clientId=3663&RQT=309&VName=PQD.

Driver's Privacy Protection Act (1994).

Drucker, P. F. (1985). *Management Tasks, Responsibilities, Practices*. New York: Harper & Row, Publishers, Inc.

Drug-Free Workplace Act of *1988*. Retrieved on November 26, 2009 from http://frwebgate.access.gpo.gov/cgi-bin/getdoc.cgi?dbname=browse_usc&docid=Cite:+41USC701.

Drug-Induced Rape Prevention and Punishment Act of 1996 (Public Law 104-305).

Drummer, O. H. (2006, August). Drug testing oral fluid. Retrieved on January 18, 2010 from http://search.ebscohost.com.library.keuka.edu/login.aspx?direct=true&db=cmedm&AN=17268583&site=ehost-live.

Drummer, O. H., Gerostamoulos, D., Chu, M., Swann, P., Boorman, M., & Cairns, I. (2007, August). Drugs in oral fluid in randomly selected drivers. Retrieved on January 24, 2010 from http://search.ebscohost.com.library.keuka.edu/login.aspx?direct=true&db=aph&AN=25935935&site=ehost-live.

Drury, D. L. & Masci, V. (1999, August). Urine drug screening: Can counterfeit urine samples pass inspection? Retrieved on January 24, 2010 from http://search.ebscohost.com.library.keuka.edu/login.aspx?direct=true&db=sih&AN=2204438&site=ehost-live.

Dudley, W. E. (1974, May). Reviewing the personal history statement. Retrieved on September 13, 2010 from http://web.ebscohost.com.library.keuka.edu/ehost/detail?vid=4&hid=105&sid=322c9a61-9e8d-40c3-96a0-ada73d8258bf%40sessionmgr113&bdata=JnNpdGU9ZWhvc3QtbGl2ZQ%3d%3d#db=sih&AN=SM013692.

Duhart, D. T. (2001, December). *Violence in the Workplace, 1993–1999*. Washington, DC: United States Department of Justice, Office of Justice Programs, Bureau of Justice Statistics.

Duke, A. (2009, May 13). Official: Craigslist to replace 'Blatant Internet Brothel.' Retrieved on September 5, 2010 from http://www.cnn.com/2009/TECH/05/13/craigslist.sex.ads/.

Dulaney, J. (2010, July 24). Stormy affair led to cop sex scandal. Retrieved on September 5, 2010 from http://www.allbusiness.com/crime-law-enforcement-corrections/law-police-forces/14845972-1.html.

Duncantell v. Universal Life Insurance Company (1969).

Dunham, R. G. & Alpert, G. P. (2001). *Critical Issues in Policing: Contemporary Readings* (4th edn.). Prospect Heights, IL: Waveland Press, Inc.

Dunlap, D. W. & Kovaleski, S. F. (2007, September 27). In a 9/11 survival tale, the pieces just don't fit. Retrieved on February 14, 2011 from http://www.nytimes.com/2007/09/27/nyregion/27survivor.html.

Dunn, H. (2010, July 12). Behavioural interviews deserve accolades. Retrieved on July 27, 2011 from http://proquest.umi.com.library.keuka.edu/pqdweb?did=2095451001&sid=4&Fmt=3&clientId=3663&RQT=309&VName=PQD.

Dunn, M. (2002, May 29). Man wants $30,000 child support back; not my son, so pay up. Retrieved on February 20, 2011 from http://web.ebscohost.com.library.keuka.edu/ehost/detail?hid=7&sid=ad66db90-f8fb-43a0-b3a0-a26957b3a8c0%40sessionmgr104&vid=5&bdata=JnNpdGU9ZWhvc3QtbGl2ZQ%3d%3d#db=nfh&AN=2002052910036946l5.

DuPont, R. L. (1999, March-April). Examining the debate on the use of medical marijuana. Retrieved on January 28, 2010 from http://search.ebscohost.com.library.keuka.edu/login.aspx?direct=true&db=cmedm&AN=10220812&site=ehost-live.

Durose, M. R., Harlow, C. W., Langan, P. A., Motivans, M., Rantala, R. R., & Smith, E. L. (2005, June). *Family Violence Statistics: Including Statistics on Strangers and Acquaintances*. Washington, DC: United States Department of Justice, Office of Justice Programs, Bureau of Justice Statistics.

Dwoskin, E. (2011, February 10). Melissa Petro gives up her fight to be a teacher after prostitution revelation. Retrieved on May 30, 2011 from http://blogs.villagevoice.com/runninscared/2011/02/melissa_petro_g.php.

Dwyer, J. (2009, March 10). The officer who posted too much on MySpace. Retrieved on October 1, 2009 from http://www.nytimes.com/2009/03/11/nyregion/11about.html.

Dyer, K. R. & Wilkinson, C. (2008, January). The detection of illicit drugs in oral fluid: Another potential strategy to reduce illicit drug-related harm. Retrieved on January 18, 2010 from http://search.ebscohost.com.library.keuka.edu/login.aspx?direct=true&db=aph&AN=27601371&site=ehost-live.

Earley, P. (n.d.). Family of spies: The John Walker Jr. spy case. Retrieved on February 6, 2011 from http://www.trutv.com/library/crime/terrorists_spies/spies/walker/1.html.

Easley v. Apollo Detective Agency, Inc. (1979).

Eber, H. W. (2004, December). An ADA-compliant psychological assessment procedure. Retrieved on November 17, 2009 from http://proquest.umi.com.library.keuka.edu/pqdweb?did=778496101&sid=1&Fmt=3&clientId=3663&RQT=309&VName=PQD.

Edwards, J. (2002, March 20). Evandale leaders shrug at report. Retrieved on April 20, 2011 from http://www.enquirer.com/editions/2002/03/20/loc_evendale_leaders.html.

EEOC v. Daimler Chrysler Corporation (2005).

EEOC v. Dial Corporation (2006).

EEOC v. Ford Motor Co. and United Automobile Workers of America. (2005).

Egelko, B. (2008, May 9). Bernie Ward admits to child porn in plea deal. Retrieved on October 24, 2010 from http://articles.sfgate.com/2008-05-09/news/17154156_1_child-pornography-child-porn-charge-plea-deal.

Eggan, D. & Vedantam, S. (2006, May 1). Polygraph results often in question; CIA, FBI defend test's use in probes. Retrieved on October 13, 2009 from http://proquest.umi.com.library.keuka.edu/pqdweb?index=5&did=1029503141&SrchMode=1&sid=4&Fmt=3&VInst=PROD&VType=PQD&RQT=309&VName=PQD&TS=1255437023&clientId=3663.

Eggert, D. B. (2006, March 23). Let's get "Personnel": Giving and receiving employer references. Retrieved on April 27, 2011 from http://www.wadleighlaw.com/employerreference.pdf.

Eichler, A. (2010, October 24). The impact of the Wikileaks war logs. Retrieved on October 24, 2010 from http://www.theatlanticwire.com/opinions/view/opinion/The-Impact-of-the-WikiLeaks-War-Logs-5509/.

Eiserer, T. (2006a, February 5). Dallas police struggle to recruit officers. Retrieved on October 9, 2009 from http://www.dallasnews.com/sharedcontent/dws/news/localnews/stories/020506dnmetrecruiting.29dcc6c.html.

Eiserer, T. (2006b, February 7). Police recruiting: Dallas' thinning blue line. Retrieved on October 9, 2009 from http://www.policeone.com/police-recruiting/articles/123054-Police-recruiting-Dallas-thinning-blue-line/.

Eiserer, T. (2007, September 8). 'Dallas SWAT' officer fired for having sex with prostitute. Retrieved on December 6, 2010 from http://www.dallasnews.com/sharedcontent/dws/news/localnews/stories/080107dnmetfirings.39a237e.html.

Eiserer, T. (2008, October 8). Document shows officer admitted to turning in fake notes. Retrieved on September 27, 2010 from http://crimeblog.dallasnews.com/archives/2008/10/documents-show-officer-admitte.html.

Eiserer, T. (2009a, March 3). Dallas police officer resigns after lying about military record. Retrieved on September 26, 2010 from http://crimeblog.dallasnews.com/archives/2009/03/-a-dallas-police-officer.html.

Eiserer, T. (2009b, October 13). Judge upholds firing of Dallas police officer repeatedly accused of improper advances. Retrieved on September 26, 2010 from http://crimeblog.dallasnews.com/archives/2009/10/judge-upholds-firing-of-dallas.html.

Eiserer, T. (2009c, October 14). Dallas police officer resigns after accusation in prostitution incident. Retrieved on September 26, 2010 from http://crimeblog.dallasnews.com/archives/police-misconduct/.

Eiserer, T. (2009d, December 16). Dallas officer accused of faking burglary story to hide sex act in squad car. Retrieved on September 26, 2010 from http://www.dallasnews.com/sharedcontent/dws/news/localnews/stories/DN-officersex_16met.ART.State.Edition1.4bfddfc.html.

Eiserer, T. (2010a, January 14). Dallas police chief David Kunkle fires officer accused of sending sexually explicit images. Retrieved on September 26, 2010 from http://crimeblog.dallasnews.com/archives/2010/01/dallas-police-chief-david-kunk-6.html.

Eiserer, T. (2010b, March 18). State law allows some police departments to hide alleged misconduct from public view. Retrieved on September 26, 2010 from http://crimeblog.dallasnews.com/archives/2010/03/about-eight-months-ago-i.html.

Eiserer, T. (2010c, June 2). Dallas police officer indicted on oppression charge maintains innocence. Retrieved on September 26, 2010 from http://www.dallasnews.com/sharedcontent/dws/dn/latestnews/stories/060310dnmetcopindict.1bfe6af.html.

Elbogen, E. B., Wagner, H. R., Fuller, S. R., & Calhoun, P. S. (2010, September). Correlates of anger and hostility in Iraq and Afghanistan war veterans. Retrieved on April 17, 2011 from http://proquest.umi.com.library.keuka.edu/pqdweb?did=2138474161&sid=1&Fmt=2&clientId=3663&RQT=309&VName=PQD.

Electronic Code of Federal Regulations (2011, March 17). Title 34: Education Section 668.46 institutional security policies and crime statistics. Retrieved on March 19, 2011 from http://ecfr.gpoaccess.gov/cgi/t/text/text-idx?c=ecfr&sid=de61811d1a772c82e986ef8ee7cb117e&rgn=div8&view=text&node=34:3.1.3.1.34.4.39.6&idno=34.

Electronic Communications Privacy Act (1986).

Electronic Privacy Information Center (n.d.). Expungement. Retrieved on February 6, 2011 from http://epic.org/privacy/expungement/.

Elfrink, T. (2011a, January 20). Two Miami-Dade cops killed in Liberty city shootout, several others wounded (update). Retrieved on May 1, 2011 from http://blogs.miaminewtimes.com/riptide/2011/01/miami-dade_cop_shot_and_killed.php.

Elfrink, T. (2011b, January 21). Johnny Sims, the suspect who killed two cops, had long record, nasty tats. Retrieved on May 1, 2011 from http://blogs.miaminewtimes.com/riptide/2011/01/johnny_sims_the_suspect_who_ki.php.

Eligon, J. (2009, February 12). An officer is accused of beating a suspect. Retrieved on October 28, 2010 from http://www.nytimes.com/2009/02/12/nyregion/12cop.html.

Ellement, J. R. (2010, January 21). Officers who lie will face dismissal. Retrieved on September 27, 2010 from http://www.boston.com/news/local/massachusetts/articles/2010/01/21/officers_who_lie_will_face_dismissal/.

Ellingsen, C. (2009, October). Who do you know? Retrieved on March 16, 2010 from http://search.ebscohost.com.library.keuka.edu/login.aspx?direct=true&db=buh&AN=44882158&site=ehost-live.

Ellington, M. J. (2006, April 27). Reynolds consent decree won't end contempt cases. Retrieved on November 6, 2009 from http://proquest.umi.com.library.keuka.edu/pqdweb?did=1027712581&sid=2&Fmt=3&clientId=3663&RQT=309&VName=PQD.

Elliot, J. (2010, April 13). Justice department moves to reform notorious New Orleans Police Department. Retrieved on September 5, 2010 from http://tpmmuckraker.talkingpointsmemo.com/2010/04/thomas_perez_on_the_danziger_bridge_shootings.php?ref=mp.

Elly, W. (2010, October 22). Hillsborough deputy under investigation over Facebook pictures. Retrieved on May 1, 2011 from http://www.myfoxtampabay.com/dpp/news/local/hillsborough/facebook-photos-deputy-investigation-102210.

Eltman, F., Dai, S., & Sambriski, B. (2010, August 14). Smile! Aerial images being used to enforce laws. Retrieved on August 15, 2010 from http://news.yahoo.com/s/ap/20100814/ap_on_hi_te/us_eyes_in_the_sky;_ylt=AhYk2jYksDWg4DhtIo9yhFOl24cA;_ylu=X3oDMTM3NXI5OXRxBGFzc2V0A2FwLzIwMTAwODE0L3VzX2V5ZXNfaW5fdGhlX3NreQRjY29kZQNtb3N0cG9wdWxhcgRjcG9zAzUEcG9zAzUEc2VjA3luX3RvcF9zdG9yaWVzBHNsawNzbWlsZWFlcmlhbGk-.

Emery, S. (2010, October 13). Man suspected in child porn case charged with molestation. Retrieved on October 24, 2010 from http://www.ocregister.com/articles/child-270862-badgett-pornography.html.

Emily, J. R. (2009, March 31). Fourth former Dallas officer in fake-drug scandal gets one-year probation. Retrieved on October 18, 2010 from http://www.dallasnews.com/sharedcontent/dws/dn/latestnews/stories/033109dnmetfakedrugs.37653f9.html.

Emison, C. (2009, September 17). Ex-Hawley chief arrested on child porn charges. Retrieved on September 26, 2010 from http://www.reporternews.com/news/2009/sep/17/ex-hawley-chief-arrested-child-porn-charges/.

Employee Polygraph Protection Act (EPPA) (1998).

Encyclopedia of Mental Disorders. (2011). Paraphilias. Retrieved on January 12, 2011 from http://www.minddisorders.com/Ob-Ps/Paraphilias.html#ixzz0TOKOcGTp.

ENewsPF.com (2011, April 8). IL house passes amendment to strengthen Illinois' DNA database. Retrieved on April 16, 2011 from http://www.enewspf.com/latest-news/latest-local/23349-il-house-passes-amendment-to-strengthen-illinois-dna-database.html.

Engel, R. S. & Worden, R. E. (2003, February). Police officers' attitudes, behavior, and supervisory influences: An analysis of problem solving. Retrieved on October 25, 2009 from http://proquest.umi.com.library.keuka.edu/pqdweb?did=379168581&sid=2&Fmt=4&clientId=3663&RQT=309&VName=PQD.

Enterprise Wire Company and Enterprise Independent Union. (1966).

Epstein, J. (2011, June 7). Report: Anthony Weiner coached woman to lie. Retrieved on June 7, 2011 from http://www.politico.com/news/stories/0611/56395.html.

Equal Employment Opportunity Act (1972).

Equal Pay Act (1963).

Erdely, S. R. (2005, October). Juicers in blue. Retrieved on January 18, 2010 from http://search.ebscohost.com.library.keuka.edu/login.aspx?direct=true&db=aph&AN=18302354&site=ehost-live.

Erwin, D. (2009, Summer). Changing organizational performance: Examining the change process. Retrieved on October 27, 2009 from http://proquest.umi.com.library.keuka.edu/pqdweb?did=1731939091&sid=2&Fmt=3&clientId=3663&RQT=309&VName=PQD.

Eschholz, S. & Vaughn, M. S. (2001). Police sexual violence and rape myths: Civil liability under Section 1983. *Journal of Criminal Justice*, *29*(5), 389–405.

Esler, G. (2007, February 17). Barack Obama is the dream presidential candidate, alas, in U.S., elections, fairytales seldom come true. Retrieved on November 25, 2009 from http://search.ebscohost.com.library.keuka.edu/login.aspx?direct=true&db=nfh&AN=24110557&site=ehost-live.

ESPN.com (2004, December 2). Admissions before BALCO grand jury detailed. Retrieved on April 13, 2011 from http://sports.espn.go.com/espn/news/story?id=1936592.

Esquivel, P. (2010, April 6). Westminster police officer and corrections officer held in kidnap, rape of woman: Police say det. Anthony Orban is being held in the alleged attack at gunpoint of a woman at Ontario mills mall. Jeff Thomas Jelinek, the corrections officer, is accused of being an accessory. Retrieved on October 29, 2010 from http://articles.latimes.com/2010/apr/06/local/la-me-officers-arrested6-2010apr06.

Estes, A. (2004, September 17). Suit seeks end to police hiring quotas. Retrieved on October 26, 2009 from http://proquest.umi.com.library.keuka.edu/pqdweb?did=694455951&sid=2&Fmt=3&clientId=3663&RQT=309&VName=PQD.

Evans, M. (2007, April 14). Internet plays key role in vehicular manslaughter sentence. Retrieved on March 13, 2010 from http://www.santabarbaranewsroom.com/news/crime–justice/internet-plays-key-role-in-vehicular-manslaughter-sentence.html.

Evans v. Department of Homeland Security (2007).

ExecuNet.com (2005). Dealing with your digital dirt. Retrieved on June 5, 2011 from http://www.abilitiesenhanced.com/digital-dirt.pdf.

Ezell, A. (2009, Fall). Recent developments with degree mills: Accreditation mills and counterfeit diploma and transcript operations. Retrieved on February 22, 2011 from http://proquest.umi.com.library.keuka.edu/pqdweb?did=1920976461&sid=3&Fmt=3&clientId=3663&RQT=309&VName=PQD.

Fagundes, P. (2009, September). Fighting internet child pornography—The Brazilian experience. Retrieved on January 18, 2011 from http://www.policechiefmagazine.org/magazine/index.cfm?fuseaction=display_arch&article_id=1892&issue_id=92009.

Fahey, D. F. & Burbridge, G. (2008, Spring). Application of diffusion of innovations models in hospital knowledge management systems: Lessons to be learned in complex organizations. Retrieved on October 26, 2009 from http://search.ebscohost.com.library.keuka.edu/login.aspx?direct=true&db=f5h&AN=31857840&site=ehost-live.

Fair and Accurate Credit Transactions Act (2003).

Fair Credit Reporting Act. (As amended 2010, July 21). Retrieved on February 22, 2011 from http://www.ftc.gov/bcp/edu/pubs/consumer/credit/cre30.pdf.

Fairbanks, S. (2010, December 4). Man charged under new choking law. Retrieved on December 4, 2010 from http://rochester.ynn.com/content/top_stories/525874/man-charged-under-new-choking-law/.

FakeResume.com (n.d.). Fake resume: The Machiavellian guide to getting a job. Retrieved on March 18, 2011 from http://www.fakeresume.com/.

Falls Church Construction v. Laidler (1997).

Family Educational Rights and Privacy Act (1974).

Fantino, J. (2003, December). Child pornography on the internet: New challenges require new ideas. *The Police Chief Magazine*, *70*(12), 28–30.

Fargen, J. & Gelzinis, P. (2009, September 28). Mass. officers caught lying on duty will be fired. Retrieved on September 27, 2010 from http://www.policeone.com/chiefs-sheriffs/articles/1915693-Boston-officers-caught-lying-on-duty-will-be-fired/.

Farley, L. D. & Allotta, J. J. (1984, July). Standards of proof in discharge arbitration: A practitioner's view. Retrieved on February 7, 2010 from http://search.ebscohost.com.library.keuka.edu/login.aspx?direct=true&db=sih&AN=5870578&site=ehost-live.

Farr v. State Civil Service Commission (Department of Corrections) (2008).

Fasick, K. & Gonan, Y. (2010, September 27). Bronx teacher admits: I'm an ex-hooker. Retrieved on September 27, 2010 from http://www.nypost.com/p/news/local/bronx/bx_teach_admits_an_ex_hooker_HAs5wQMrW8KdcAfpgrK3WP.

Federal Acquisitions Regulations System. (2003, October 1). Title 48 chapter 1 federal acquisition regulation. Retrieved on November 16, 2009 from http://www.access.gpo.gov/nara/cfr/waisidx_03/48cfrv1_03.html.

Federal Bank Act (1970).

Federal Bureau of Investigation (2008a, March 6). Major child porn ring busted. Retrieved on October 24, 2010 from http://www.fbi.gov/news/stories/2008/march/innocent_images030608.

Federal Bureau of Investigation (2008b). NICS: National instant criminal background check system. Retrieved on November 23, 2009 from http://www.fbi.gov/hq/cjisd/nics.htm.

Federal Bureau of Investigation (2009a). Background investigation: Employment disqualifiers. Retrieved on March 30, 2009 from http://www.fbijobs.gov/51.asp.

Federal Bureau of Investigation (2009b). Employment drug policy. Retrieved on March 30, 2009 from http://www.fbijobs.gov/52.asp.

Federal Bureau of Investigation (2009c, October 27). RIT graduate student pleads guilty to receipt of child pornography. Retrieved on February 17, 2010 from http://buffalo.fbi.gov/dojpressrel/pressrel09/bffo102709.htm.

Federal Bureau of Investigation (2009d, May 8). 30-Year-old murder solved by the 'Hit-of-the-Year.' Retrieved on September 20, 2010 from http://www.fbi.gov/page2/may09/iafis_050809.html.

Federal Bureau of Investigation (2010a). Integrated automated fingerprint identification system (IAFIS). Retrieved on September 20, 2010 from http://www.fbi.gov/hq/cjisd/iafis.htm.

Federal Bureau of Investigation (2010b). Ordering of fingerprint cards and training AIDS. Retrieved on September 20, 2010 from http://www.fbi.gov/hq/cjisd/forms/orderingfps.htm.

Federal Bureau of Investigation (2010c). Recording legible fingerprints. Retrieved on September 7, 2010 from http://www.fbi.gov/hq/cjisd/takingfps.html.

Federal Bureau of Investigation (2010d). Uniform crime reports. Retrieved on October 8, 2010 from http://www.fbi.gov/about-us/cjis/ucr/ucr.

Federal Bureau of Investigation (2010e). National incident based reporting system. Retrieved on October 9, 2010 from http://www.fbi.gov/about-us/cjis/ucr/ucr#nibrs.

Federal Bureau of Investigation (2010f). N-dex: Law enforcement national data exchange. Retrieved on October 11, 2010 from http://www.fbi.gov/about-us/cjis/n-dex/n-dex.

Federal Bureau of Investigation (2010g). Critical incident response group. Retrieved on October 11, 2010 from http://www.fbi.gov/about-us/cirg/investigations-and-operations-support/investigations-operations-support.

Federal Bureau of Investigation (2010h, August 10). Former New York state parole board member and state assemblymen sentenced for online enticement of minors. Retrieved on October 13, 2010 from http://albany.fbi.gov/dojpressrel/pressrel10/alfo081010.htm.

Federal Bureau of Investigation (2010i, September 29). City of Miami officer sentenced in civil rights and identity theft cases. Retrieved on November 1, 2010 from http://miami.fbi.gov/dojpressrel/pressrel10/mm092910.htm.

Federal Bureau of Investigation (2010j, January 14). Guilty pleas in Union County corruption probe former Sheriff Howard Wells, former county tax assessor Willie E. Randall, Jr., and union county residents Farr and Beacham entered guilty pleas today. Retrieved on January 19, 2011 from http://columbia.fbi.gov/dojpressrel/pressrel10/co011410.htm.

Federal Bureau of Investigation (2010k, January). Brady handgun violence prevention act of 1993. Retrieved on February 7, 2011 from http://www.fbi.gov/about-us/cjis/nics/general-information/nics-overview.

Federal Bureau of Investigation (2011a). Combined DNA index system (CODIS). Retrieved on January 18, 2011 from http://www.fbi.gov/about-us/lab/codis.

Federal Bureau of Investigation (2011b). Arrest disposition submission. Retrieved on February 6, 2011 from http://www.fbi.gov/about-us/cjis/fingerprints_biometrics/arrest-disposition-submission.

Federal Bureau of Investigation (2011c). Terrorist screening center. Retrieved on February 8, 2011 from http://www.fbi.gov/about-us/nsb/tsc/tsc_faqs.

Federal Civil Service Reform Act (1978).

Federal Food, Drug, and Cosmetic Act (1938).

Federal Gun Free School Zone Act (1995).

Federal Information Security Management Act (2002).

Federal Rules of Evidence

Federal Trade Commission (1999, March). Using consumer reports: What employers need to know. Retrieved on February 22, 2011 from http://business.ftc.gov/documents/bus08-using-consumer-reports-what-employers-need-know.

Federal Trade Commission (2004, July 14). Job applicants not informed of their rights under federal credit law, FTC alleges: Bad credit lowered consumers' odds for casino jobs. Retrieved on February 22, 2011 from http://www.ftc.gov/opa/2004/07/imperial.shtm.

Federal Trade Commission (2009, August 11). Two companies pay civil penalties to settle FTC charges; failed to give required notices to fired workers and rejected job applicants. Retrieved on February 22, 2011 from http://www.ftc.gov/opa/2009/08/qts.shtm.

Federal Youth Corrections Act (1950).

Fee, G. & Raposa, L. (2008, November 5). Caitlin Davis' life is not so cheery now. Retrieved on May 30, 2011 from http://news.bostonherald.com/track/inside_track/view/2008_11_05_Caitlin_Davis_booted_from_Patriots__cheering_squad/srvc=home&position=also.

Fendrich, M. & Kim, J. Y. S. (2002, Winter). The experience and acceptability of drug testing: Poll trends. Retrieved on January 19, 2010 from http://search.ebscohost.com.library.keuka.edu/login.aspx?direct=true&db=aph&AN=6583099&site=ehost-live.

Fenton, J. W., Kelley, D. E., Ruud, W. N., & Bulloch, J. A. (1997, September). Employer legal liability for employee workplace violence. *SAM Advanced Management Journal*, *62*, 44–48.

Ferguson, J. (2003, February). Negligent hiring, retention, and supervision. Retrieved on February 16, 2010 from http://proquest.umi.com.library.keuka.edu/pqdweb?did=287794751&sid=1&Fmt=2&clientId=3663&RQT=309&VName=PQD.

Fertoli, A. (2010, September 17). City rejects judge's alternative hiring proposals for FDNY. Retrieved on April 14, 2011 from http://www.wnyc.org/articles/wnyc-news/2010/sep/17/city-rejects-judges-alternative-hiring-proposals-fdny/.

Fiedler, E. (2011, January 17). Camden, N. J., braces for police, firefighter layoffs. Retrieved on February 14, 2011 from http://www.npr.org/2011/01/17/132929677/camden-n-j-braces-for-police-firefighter-layoffs.

Findlaw.com (1999). The direct threat exception to the ADA: Avoiding a Hobson's choice. Retrieved on August 7, 2011 from http://library.findlaw.com/1999/Apr/1/130829.html.

Findlaw.com (2011a). Elements of libel and slander. Retrieved on April 30, 2011 from http://injury.findlaw.com/defamation-libel-slander/elements-of-libel-and-slander.html.

Findlaw.com (2011b). Expungement and criminal records: State specific information. Retrieved on February 6, 2011 from http://criminal.findlaw.com/crimes/expungement/expungement-state-info.html.

Fingerprint Technologies (2009). Welcome to fingerprint technologies. Retrieved on September 7, 2010 from http://fingerprints4all.com/default.htm.

Finkelhor, D. & Ormrod, R. (2004, December). Child pornography: Patterns from NIBRS. Juvenile Justice Bulletin, United States Department of Justice, Office of Justice Programs, Office of Juvenile Justice and Delinquency Programs, pp. 1–7.

Fire Science Colleges (2010, June 9). 10 Most famous arsonists and why. Retrieved on July 30, 2011 from http://www.firesciencecolleges.com/blog/2010/10-famous-arsonists-and-why/.

Fishman, N. & Brazytis, J. (2008, June 22). Employeescreeniq unveils list of 2009 background screening trends. Retrieved on March 16, 2010 from http://www.prweb.com/releases/2009/03/prweb2247434.htm. (Note: This is a PDF News memo attached to the Webpage URL)

Fitch, B. D. (2011, January). Understanding the psychology of police misconduct. *The Police Chief Magazine*, *78*(1), 24–27.

FitzGerald v. Department of Homeland Security (2008).

Fitzpatrick, L. (2010, July 12). How we fail our female vets. *Time*, 42–45.

Flaherty, A. (2010, August 15). Hundreds of PTSD soldiers likely misdiagnosed. Retrieved on August 15, 2010 from http://news.yahoo.com/s/ap/20100815/ap_on_go_ca_st_pe/us_soldiers_wrongly_discharged.

Fletcher, M. (1997, November 10). Making pre-employment screening work. Retrieved on November 25, 2009 from http://proquest.umi.com.library.keuka.edu/pqdweb?did=22393153&sid=1&Fmt=2&clientId=3663&RQT=309&VName=PQD.

Florida Department of Revenue. Retrieved from http://www.myflorida.com/dor.

Florida Law

Florida Statute

Flynn v. Sandahl (1995).

Ford, J. A. (2008, Spring). Nonmedical prescription drug use and delinquency: An analysis with a national sample. Retrieved on January 20, 2010 from http://search.ebscohost.com.library.keuka.edu/login.aspx?direct=true&db=aph&AN=33295622&site=ehost-live.

Ford, J. A. & Schroeder, R. D. (2009, January). Academic strain and non-medical use of prescription stimulants among college students. Retrieved on January 28, 2010 from http://search.ebscohost.com.library.keuka.edu/login.aspx?direct=true&db=sih&AN=35651077&site=ehost-live.

Forman, M. (2008, May 30). Detroit police would promote 400 officers, but who will replace them. Retrieved on October 12, 2009 from http://michiganmessenger.com/1320/detroit-police-would-promote-400-officers-but-who-will-replace-them.

Forsythe, C. (2004, January). The future of simulation technology for law enforcement. Retrieved on October 22, 2009 from http://proquest.umi.com.library.keuka.edu/pqdweb?did=538351751&sid=3&Fmt=4&clientId=3663&RQT=309&VName=PQD.

Foster, A. L. (2001, March 23). Some professors are surprised to be on a university's roster. Retrieved on April 13, 2011 from http://chronicle.com/article/Some-Professors-Are-Surprised/18341.

Fox News (2011). Report: DHS official targeted in phony degree investigation. Retrieved on April 3, 2011 from http://us.foxnews.mobi/quickPage.html?page=26048&content=49927944&pageNum=-1.

FoxNews.com (2007, August 24). Judge sentences John Couey to death for murdering Jessica Lunsford. Retrieved on July 30, 2011 from http://www.foxnews.com/story/0,2933,294371,00.html.

FoxNews.com (2010, March 10). Massa: Yeah, I groped male staff but not sexually. Retrieved on August 11, 2011 from http://www.foxnews.com/politics/2010/03/09/massa-groped-sexually/.

FoxNews.com (2011a, March 19). Public safety workers blast Ohio city's decision to lower police recruit standard. Retrieved on April 14, 2011 from http://www.foxnews.com/us/2011/03/19/public-safety-workers-blast-decision-lower-police-recruit-test-scores-ohio/.

FoxNews.com (2011b, March 16). DOJ forces Dayton police dept to lower test standards. Retrieved on April 14, 2011 from http://video.foxnews.com/v/4588921/doj-forces-dayton-police-dept-to-lower-test-standards?playlist_id=86858.

FoxNews.com (2011c, August 6). Hundreds rampage through neighborhoods surrounding Wisconsin state fair. Retrieved on August 8, 2011 from http://www.foxnews.com/us/2011/08/06/hundreds-rampage-through-neighborhoods-surrounding-wisconsin-state-fair/.

FoxNews.com (2011d, August 10). Questions arise over whether 'Flash Mob' attacks in U.S. cities motivated by race. Retrieved on August 13, 2011 from http://www.foxnews.com/us/2011/08/10/flashmob-attacks-in-us-cities-raise-questions-over-possible-race-motivation/.

FoxNews.com (2011e, August 11). 911 Calls from Wisconsin fair reportedly show some 'Flash Mob' attacks were racially motivated. Retrieved on August 13, 2011 from http://www.foxnews.com/us/2011/08/11/11-calls-from-wisconsin-fair-reportedly-show-some-flash-mob-attacks-were/?test=latestnews.

FoxNews.com (2011f, September 1). Melee breaks out in Florida at teen football game. Retrieved on September 6, 2011 from http://www.foxnews.com/sports/2011/09/01/melee-breaks-out-in-florida-at-teen-football-game/.

Frampton, N. (2010, August 23). Dispatchers: Many 911 calls not emergencies. Retrieved on April 30, 2011 from http://proquest.umi.com.library.keuka.edu/pqdweb?did=2116889621&sid=1&Fmt=3&clientId=3663&RQT=309&VName=PQD.

Francis, T. (2009, August 3). Broward deputy charged with sex crimes. Retrieved on October 28, 2010 from http://blogs.browardpalmbeach.com/juice/2009/08/sex_crimes_broward_sheriffs_deputy.php.

Fraternal Order of Police Newark Lodge 12 v. City of Newark (1997).

Fraternal Order of Police v. Freeman (1978).

Fraternal Order of Police v. United States (1998).

Fraternal Order of Police v. United States (1999).

Freedom of Information Act (1982).

Freedom of Information Law

Freeman, D. (2011, February 25). "Wal-Mart of Weed" set to open: Should medical marijuana go mainstream? Retrieved on June 1, 2011 from http://www.cbsnews.com/8301-504763_162-20036512-10391704.html.

Freeman, N. J., Sandler, J. C., & Socia, K. M. (2009, June). Time-series analysis on the impact of sex offender registration and community notification laws on plea bargaining rates. Retrieved on October 9, 2010 from http://www.ncjrs.gov/App/publications/Abstract.aspx?id=249921.

Freile, V. E. (2009, December 4). City employee pleads not guilty to rape charge. Retrieved on December 4, 2009 from http://www.democratandchronicle.com/article/20091204/NEWS01/912040327/City-employee-pleads-not-guilty-to-rape-charge.

Freile, V. E. (2010, November 18). Monroe County Sheriff's captain facing rape charge. Retrieved on November 18, 2010 from http://www.democratandchronicle.com/article/20101118/NEWS01/101118018/Monroe-County-Sheriff-s-captain-facing-rape-charge&referrer=NEWSFRONTCAROUSEL.

Freile, V. E. (2011a, February 10). Park police sergeant accused of sexually abusing teen girl. Retrieved on February 11, 2011 from http://www.democratandchronicle.com/article/20110210/NEWS01/110210007/Park-police-sergeant-accused-sexually-abusing-teen-girl?odyssey=mod|mostview.

Freile, V. E. (2011b, April 7). Rochester man accused of sex misconduct with 2 young girls. Retrieved on April 8, 2011 from http://www.democratandchronicle.com/article/20110407/NEWS01/110407009/Rochester-man-accused-sex-misconduct-2-young-girls?odyssey=mod|mostview.

Friedlander, W. S. (2009, March). Teacher-student sexual abuse: Wrongs, rights, and remedies. Retrieved on July 25, 2011 from http://www.plaintiffmagazine.com/Mar09/Friedlander_Teacher-student%20sexual%20abuse%20-%20wrongs%20rights%20and%20remedies_Plaintiff%20magazine.pdf.

Friedman, E. (2010, March 3). U.K. teen reports babysitter's 'Disturbing' messages about raping N.C. child: Student is charged with six counts of second degree sexual exploitation of a minor. Retrieved on April 2, 2011 from http://abcnews.go.com/US/british-teen-tips-cops-off-potential-child-rape/story?id=9991207.

Fry, S. (2005, September 17). Former officer gets jail time: Prosecutor says Pfortmiller stole drug-buy money. Retrieved on February 8, 2011 from http://cjonline.com/stories/091705/loc_pfort miller.shtml.

Frye v. United States (1923).

Fuss, T., McSheehy, B., & Snowden, L. (1998, April). Under investigation: Importance of background investigations in North Carolina. *The Police Chief Magazine*, *65*(4), 58–63.

Fuss, T. & Snowden, L. (2004, March). Importance of background investigations. *Law and Order Magazine*, *52*(3), 58–63.

Futty, J. (2007, July 15). Ratio of black officers declining: Force has trouble recruiting from minority groups. Retrieved on October 12, 2009 from http://www.accessmylibrary.com/coms2/summary_0286-31892418_ITM.

Fyfe, J. J., Greene, J. R., Walsh, W. F., Wilson, O. W., & McLaren, R. C. (1997). *Police Administration* (5th edn.). Boston, MA: McGraw-Hill Irwin.

Gaines v. Monsanto (1983).

Gaines, L. K., Kappeler, V. E., & Vaughn, J. B. (1999). *Policing in America* (3rd edn.). Cincinnati, OH: Anderson Publishing Co.

Galas v. Ward (1990).

Galetta, G. A. & Colaprete, F. A. (2010, March). Preliminary and continued criminal investigation effectiveness: A study of investigative processes. *Law Enforcement Executive Forum*, *10*(1), 125–143.

Gallup, Inc. (2008, November). Honesty/ethics in professions. Retrieved on October 9, 2009 from http://www.gallup.com/poll/1654/honesty-ethics-professions.aspx.

Gamblin, B. (2010, March 12). Sheriff's lieutenant faces additional sexual battery charges (arrest report). Retrieved on November 19, 2010 from http://www.nwfdailynews.com/articles/sheriff-26781-lieutenant-additional.html.

Garcia v. Duffy (1986).

Garcia v. Walder Electronics, Inc. (1990).

Garmire, B. L. (1982). Local government police management (2nd edn.). Washington, DC: International City/County Management Association.

Garner v. Civil Service Commission of Metropolitan Government of Nashville (2009).

Garrett, A. (2010, January). How to clear those interview hurdles. Retrieved on July 24, 2011 from http://proquest.umi.com.library.keuka.edu/pqdweb?did=1961779221&sid=4&Fmt=3&client Id=3663&RQT=309&VName=PQD.

Garrity v. New Jersey (1967).

Gast, P. (2011, March 23). Reward grows in killing of Georgia police officer. Retrieved on March 24, 2011 from http://www.cnn.com/2011/CRIME/03/23/georgia.athens.officer/.

Gaston v. State of New Jersey (2008).

Gatling, P. L. (2005, April 21). City human rights commission fights discrimination. Retrieved on November 7, 2009 from http://search.ebscohost.com.library.keuka.edu/login.aspx?direct=true&db=ulh&AN=16867428&site=ehost-live.

Gatton, A. (2008, September 12). The fantacist of 9/11: The story of Tania Head's escape from the twin towers captivated America and made her a heroine among survivors... just one problem—She wasn't even there that day. Retrieved on February 14, 2011 from http://www.dailymail.co.uk/femail/article-1054790/The-fantasist-9-11-The-story-Tania-Heads-escape-Twin-Towers-captivated-America-heroine-survivors–Just-problem–wasnt-day.html.

Gavin, R. (2009, July 9). Pot ring nets 13 suspects: Feds say international gang fueled network with hydroponic marijuana. Retrieved on February 9, 2010 from http://search.ebscohost.com.library.keuka.edu/login.aspx?direct=true&db=nfh&AN=2W639018435&site=ehost-live.

Gavish, E. (2009, August 31). Bikini-Clad teacher Tiffany Shepherd turns to porn after being fired from Florida high school. Retrieved on October 12, 2010 from http://www.nydailynews.com/news/national/2009/08/31/2009-08-31_bikiniclad_teacher_tiffany_shepherd_turns_to_porn_after_being_fired_from_florida.html.

Gay, M. (2010a, September 14). Pediatrician in child porn case flees house arrest. Retrieved on October 24, 2010 from http://www.aolnews.com/crime/article/pediatrician-indicted-for-child-porn-flees-house-arrest/19633551.

Gay, M. (2010b, October 20). Diary of co-defendant grabs spotlight in Conn. murder trial. Retrieved on March 23, 2011 from http://www.aolnews.com/2010/10/20/co-defendants-diary-grabs-spotlight-in-conn-murder-trial/.

Geberth, V. J. (1998, October). Detective rotation: An enigma. *Law and Order Magazine*, *46*(10), 194–196.

Geeser, M. (n.d.). Dr. Fake: Making up your resume. Retrieved on March 18, 2011 from http://www.8newsnow.com/story/1881494/dr-fake-making-up-your-resume?redirected=true.

Geidel v. Bradenton Beach (1999).

Geller, W. A. (Ed.). (1985). Police leadership in America: Crisis and opportunity. Chicago, IL: American Bar Foundation.

Geller, W. A. & Stephens, D. W. (2003). *Local Government Police Management* (4th edn.). Washington, DC: International City/County Management Association.

Gellner, R. (2010, March 29). Christian Militia terrorists in U.S. charged in plot against police officers. Retrieved on February 8, 2011 from http://www.examiner.com/world-news-in-national/christian-militia-terrorists-u-s-charged-plot-against-police-officers.

Gendar, A. (2005, March 3). They've been arrested, been fired, and now they're... black marks in blue: Brass signs off on Rogue's gallery of hires. Retrieved on July 7, 2009 from http://www.nydailynews.com/archives/news/2005/03/03/2005-03-03_they_ve_been_arrested__been_.html.

Gendar, A. (2011, June 5). Anthony Weiner's stimulating week: How a lewd Twitter photo may have derailed politician's future. Retrieved on June 5, 2011 from http://www.nydailynews.com/news/politics/2011/06/05/2011-06-05_how_weiner_burned_anatomy_of_tough_week_dicey_future.html?r=news.

Gendar, A. & Boyle, C. (2009, April 28). NYPD cops accused of raping drunk woman are expected in court. Retrieved on April 28, 2009 from http://www.nydailynews.com/news/ny_crime/2009/04/28/2009-04-28_raperap_cops_are_expected_in_court.html.

Gendar, A., Lauinger, J., & Kennedy, H. (2011, June 6). Teary Rep. Anthony Weiner admits he sexted, tweeted crotch pic; will not step down amid scandal. Retrieved on June 6, 2011 from http://www.nydailynews.com/ny_local/2011/06/06/2011-06-06_rep_anthony_weiner_admits_he_tweeted_crotch_photo_says_he_will_not_step_down_ami.html?r=news.

Gendar, A. & Parascandola, R. (2011, February 16). Two TSA agents arrested at JFK airport for stealing $39k from passenger's bag. Retrieved on February 20, 2011 from http://www.nydailynews.com/news/ny_crime/2011/02/16/2011-02-16_two_tsa_agents_arrested_at_jfk_airport_for_stealing_39k_from_passengers_bag.html.

General Electric Co. v. Joiner (1997).

Genetic Information Nondiscrimination Act (2008).

Gensbauer v. The May Department Stores (1999).

Gengler v. Phelps (1978).

Geoghegan, S. (2008, June). The latest in mobile AFIS. Retrieved on September 21, 2010 from http://www.hendonpub.com/resources/articlearchive/details.aspx?ID=206887.

George, C. (2006, June 1). Whistle-Blowers' safety net trimmed. Retrieved on October 24, 2009 from http://search.ebscohost.com.library.keuka.edu/login.aspx?direct=true&db=nfh&AN=2W62W63922080815&site=ehost-live.

Gerhart, A. (2010, October 1). Suicides of four soldiers in a week stun Fort Hood. Retrieved on April 16, 2011 from http://proquest.umi.com.library.keuka.edu/pqdweb?did=2151163251&sid=3&Fmt=3&clientId=3663&RQT=309&VName=PQD.

George Washington University (2001, June 29). The Pentagon papers: Secrets, lies, and audiotapes. Retrieved on January 15, 2011 from http://www.gwu.edu/~nsarchiv/NSAEBB/NSAEBB48/.

de Geus, A. (1997). *The Living Company*. Boston, MA: Harvard Business School Press.

Gibson, G. (2001, March 3). Ex-city police officer gets 14 years for bank robberies: He stole $250,000, lost much of it gambling. Retrieved on February 8, 2011 from http://articles.baltimoresun.com/2001-03-03/news/0103030087_1_snow-motz-gambling.

Gibson, G. S. & Manley, S. (1991). Alternative approaches to urinalysis in the detection of drugs. Retrieved on January 18, 2010 from http://search.ebscohost.com.library.keuka.edu/login.aspx?direct=true&db=aph&AN=12966737&site=ehost-live.

Gibson v. Overnight Transport Company (2003).

Gibson v. Philip Morris, Inc. (1997).

Giglio v. United States (1972).

Gilbert, J. N. (2001). *Criminal Investigation* (5th edn.). Upper Saddle River, NJ: Prentice Hall.

Gillan, R. (2010, January). Viewpoint. Retrieved on March 16, 2010 from http://proquest.umi.com.library.keuka.edu/pqdweb?did=1941228721&sid=3&Fmt=3&clientId=3663&RQT=309&VName=PQD.

Gillis, C. (2008, June 16). When the police are on the juice. Retrieved on January 18, 2010 from http://search.ebscohost.com.library.keuka.edu/login.aspx?direct=true&db=aph&AN=32567324&site=ehost-live.

Gilman, B. (2010, October 7). Tewksbury man charged with statutory rape faces life sentence. Retrieved on October 28, 2010 from http://fwix.com/boston/share/7f48815952/tewksbury_man_charged_with_statutory_rape_faces_life_sentence.

Gilty v. Village of Oak Park (1990). Retrieved on April 13, 2011 from http://ftp.resource.org/courts.gov/c/F2/919/919.F2d.1247.89-2764.html.

Giuliani, R. W. (2002). *Leadership*. New York: Miramax Books.

Givens, B. & Friery, T. (2005, August 5). Groups warn of privacy risks in employment screening. Retrieved on August 18, 2010 from http://www.privacyrights.org/ar/DOJbackgrd.htm.

Givens, B. & Friery, T. (2006, May 22). Comments on the FTC on accuracy in background checks and insurance reports. Retrieved on March 29, 2010 from http://www.privacyrights.org/ar/FTC-BGChks.htm.

Gladis, S. (2007, December). Executive coaching builds steam in organizations. Retrieved on October 31, 2009 from http://proquest.umi.com.library.keuka.edu/pqdweb?did=1420647811&sid=1&Fmt=3&clientId=3663&RQT=309&VName=PQD.

Godert, H. W., Gamer, M., Rill, H. G., & Vossel, G. (2005, September). Statement validity assessment: Inter-reliability of criteria-based content analysis in the mock-crime paradigm. Retrieved on July 24, 2011 from http://proquest.umi.com.library.keuka.edu/pqdweb?did=914355271&sid=5&Fmt=4&clientId=3663&RQT=309&VName=PQD.

Goffard, C. (2009, April 23). 'Code of Silence' marks rift between Calif. agencies. Retrieved on October 28, 2010 from http://www.policeone.com/chiefs-sheriffs/articles/1814016-Code-of-silence-marks-rift-between-Calif-agencies/.

Going v. Kennedy (1958).

Gold v. City of College Station (2001).

Gold, L. E. (2004, October). No background check for guard becomes key in lawsuit. Retrieved on February 15, 2010 from http://search.ebscohost.com.library.keuka.edu/login.aspx?direct=true&db=buh&AN=14687798&site=ehost-live.

Goldman, R. (2007, June 20). School accused of covering up student's murder: Woman's parents say university misled them about murder on campus. Retrieved on April 1, 2011 from http://abcnews.go.com/US/story?id=3296170&page=1.

Goldman, R. (2009, September). Personality testing. Retrieved on October 21, 2009 from http://proquest.umi.com.library.keuka.edu/pqdweb?did=1861878621&sid=3&Fmt=4&clientId=3663&RQT=309&VName=PQD.

Goldman, R. (2011, March 29). Girl, 11, allegedly raped by eight teen gang members in park restroom: Gang members used older girl to lure alleged victim to scene of the crime. Retrieved on April 1, 2011 from http://abcnews.go.com/US/middle-schooler-raped-teens-park-restroom/story?id=13248297.

Goldstein, A. M. & Epstein, S. D. (2008, Fall). Personality testing in employment: Useful business tool or civil rights violation? Retrieved on October 21, 2009 from http://proquest.umi.com.library.keuka.edu/pqdweb?did=1652735191&sid=3&Fmt=3&clientId=3663&RQT=309&VName=PQD.

Goldstein, D. (2010a, October 20). Sen. Bond: Troops with combat stress discharged, not treated. Retrieved on April 17, 2011 from http://proquest.umi.com.library.keuka.edu/pqdweb?did=2169506281&sid=1&Fmt=3&clientId=3663&RQT=309&VName=PQD.

Goldstein, D. (2010b, October 21). Senator: Stressed troops get boot instead of care; Shington. Retrieved on April 17, 2011 from http://proquest.umi.com.library.keuka.edu/pqdweb?did=2169506281&sid=1&Fmt=3&clientId=3663&RQT=309&VName=PQD.

Goldstein, S. (2010c, September 24). Dallas police chief fires 6 more officers. Retrieved on September 26, 2010 from http://www.dallasnews.com/sharedcontent/dws/news/localnews/stories/DN-firings_24met.ART.State.Edition2.3335c2a.html.

Goldsworthy, R. C., Schwartz, N. C., & Mayhorn, C. B. (2008, June). Beyond abuse and exposure: Framing the impact of prescription-medication sharing. Retrieved on January 20, 2010 from http://search.ebscohost.com.library.keuka.edu/login.aspx?direct=true&db=aph&AN=32544177&site=ehost-live.

Goleman, D., Boyatzis, R., & McKee, A. (2002). *Primal Leadership: Realizing the Power of Emotional Intelligence*. Boston, MA: Harvard Business School Publishing.

Goliath. (2008, July 1). Does your background checker put you in jeopardy? A case for best practices and due diligence. Retrieved on March 29, 2010 from http://goliath.ecnext.com/coms2/gi_0198-532836/Does-your-background-checker-put.html.

Gomez, H. (2003, March). Linking intelligence information. Retrieved on October 10, 2010 from http://web.ebscohost.com.library.keuka.edu/ehost/detail?vid=20&hid=109&sid=4c672b52-8d14-4332-a8cb-b1ff63c84f64%40sessionmgr11&bdata=JnNpdGU9ZWhvc3QtbGl2ZQ%3d%3d#db=sih&AN=SN082139.

Gomez-Preston, C. & Trescott, J. (1990, March). Over the edge. Retrieved on August 28, 2011 from http://web.ebscohost.com.library.keuka.edu/ehost/detail?vid=4&hid=105&sid=278523e6-9a69-40a9-89ec-67f4e073451d%40sessionmgr115&bdata=JnNpdGU9ZWhvc3QtbGl2ZQ%3d%3d#db=aph&AN=9005210609.

Gonzales v. Metropolitan Transportation Authority E (1999).

Gonzales v. Raich (2005).

Gonzales, J. (2008, March 18). Governor Paterson admits to sex with other women for years. Retrieved on February 9, 2010 from http://www.nydailynews.com/news/2008/03/17/2008-03-17_gov_paterson_admits_to_sex_with_other_wo.html.

Goodman, H. (1993, December 22). City settles lawsuit on firefighters: Three men who sued after rejection based on their vision will be in the next fire academy class. Retrieved on November 25, 2009 from http://proquest.umi.com.library.keuka.edu/pqdweb?did=1365052341&sid=10&Fmt=3&clientId=3663&RQT=309&VName=PQD.

Goodman, H. (1998, September 14). Screening of police is called lax in Philadelphia: The department's anti-corruption office found "minimal, if any, standards" for hiring. Retrieved on September 6, 2011 from http://articles.philly.com/1998-09-14/news/25756000_1_police-officers-39th-police-district-police-force.

Goodman, P. S. (2003, June 18). The new poor: Peddling relief, firms put debtors in deeper hole. Retrieved on February 22, 2011 from http://www.nytimes.com/2010/06/19/business/economy/19debt.html.

Goodson, J. (2007, March 19). NS mayor suspends hiring of police chief. Retrieved on September 26, 2010 from http://jacksonvilleprogress.com/local/x154937506/NS-mayor-suspends-hiring-of-police-chief.

Goodwin, L. (2010, July 9). Oakland cop apologizes for killing transit rider. Retrieved on July 9, 2010 from http://news.yahoo.com/s/yblog_upshot/oakland-cop-apologizes-for-killing-transit-rider;_ylt=Ap1ZaoovnLZCb09bioPmJSBH2ocA;_ylu=X3oDMTRmYThrdms3BGFzc2V0A3libG9nX3Vwc2hvdC8yMDEwMDcwOS9vYWtsYW5kLWNvcC1hcG9sb2dpemVzLWZvci1raWxsaW5nLXRyYW5zaXQtcmlkZXIEY2NvZGUDbW9zdHBvcHVsYXIEY3BvcwM2BHBvcwM2BHNlYwN5bl90b3Bfc3RvcmllcwRzbGsDb2FrbGFuZGNvcGFw.

Goodz, J. M. (1999, January). Recently enacted statute gives employer favorable presumption against claims of negligence. Retrieved on November 15, 2009 from http://library.findlaw.com/1999/Jan/1/126347.html.

Gordon, N. J. (2008, November). Today's instruments for truth testing. *The Police Chief Magazine*, *75*(9), 70–78.

Gotay, A. (2010, February). Predictive models for police physical tests. *Law and Order Magazine*, *58*(2), 32–35.

Gottfredson, L. S. (1997, February 6). Racially gerrymandering the content of police tests to satisfy U.S. Justice Department: A case study. Retrieved on August 4, 2011 from http://www.ipacweb.org/files/nassau/gottfredson3.html.

Gottschalk, P. (2009, June). Information sources in police intelligence. Retrieved on October 10, 2010 from http://web.ebscohost.com.library.keuka.edu/ehost/detail?vid=4&hid=12&sid=4c672b52-8d14-4332-a8cb-b1ff63c84f64%40sessionmgr11&bdata=JnNpdGU9ZWhvc3QtbGl2ZQ%3d%3d#db=cja&AN=44269171.

Gould Publications. (2000). *Manual for Police in the State of New York*. Binghamton, NY: Author.

Gourevitch, P. & Morris, E. (2008, March 24). Annals of war: Exposure, the woman behind the camera at Abu Ghraib. Retrieved on August 17, 2010 from http://www.newyorker.com/reporting/2008/03/24/080324fa_fact_gourevitch.

Gove, T. (2004, November). Unique challenges to the new supervisor. Retrieved on October 25, 2009 from http://proquest.umi.com.library.keuka.edu/pqdweb?did=768185891&sid=2&Fmt=4&clientId=3663&RQT=309&VName=PQD.

Government Printing Office (2004). The 9/11 commission report: Final report of the national commission on terrorist attacks upon the united states official government addition. Washington, DC: Author.

Gowan, C. (2010, September 14). Guilty plea in child porn case. Retrieved on October 29, 2010 from http://www.timesunion.com/local/article/Guilty-plea-in-child-porn-case-657117.php.

Grabell, M. (2008, November 12). Crimes by air marshals raise questions about hiring. Retrieved on March 30, 2009 from http://www.usatoday.com/news/washington/2008-11-12-air-marshals_N.htm.

Grabinger v. Conlisk (1972).

Grace, F. (2003, April 2). 38 Drug cases thrown into question. Retrieved on September 26, 2010 from http://www.cbsnews.com/stories/2003/04/03/eveningnews/main547479.shtml.

Grace, M. (2010a, January 29). Fashion designer and serial rapist Anand Jon Alexander pleads not guilty to raping underage models. Retrieved on February 20, 2011 from http://www.nydailynews.com/news/ny_crime/2010/01/29/2010-01-29_fashion_designer_and_serial_rapist_anand_jon_alexander_to_face_rape_charges_in_n.html.

Grace, M. (2010b, August 14). Prosecutors to expand search for date-rape victims of alleged rapist Hugues Akassy to Washington, DC. Retrieved on February 20, 2011 from http://www.nydailynews.com/news/2010/08/14/2010-08-14_rapesuspect_hunt_widens_to_dc.html.

Grace, M. (2011a, January 7). Accused sicko youth counselor has sex with 13-year-old girl in courthouse bathroom: Prosecutors. Retrieved on February 20, 2011 from http://www.nydailynews.com/news/ny_crime/2011/01/07/2011-01-07_accused_sicko_youth_counselor_has_sex_with_13yearold_girl_in_courthouse_bathroom.html?obref=obinsite.

Grace, M. (2011b, January 18). Harrison David, accused ringleader in alleged Columbia drug ring, to live with correction officer. Retrieved on January 19, 2011 from http://www.nydailynews.com/news/ny_crime/2011/01/18/2011-01-18_harrison_david_accused_ringleader_in_alleged_columbia_drug_ring_to_live_with_cor.html.

Grace, M., Croghan, L., & Siemaszko, C. (2011, May 27). NYPD cops found not guilty of rape: 'The Prosecution Really Failed to Prove Their Case,' Juror says. Retrieved on May 27, 2011 from http://www.nydailynews.com/news/ny_crime/2011/05/27/2011-05-27_no_rape_raps_because_the_prosecution.html.

Graham, C. R. (1998, July). Don't trade on the uniform. Retrieved on April 15, 2011 from http://proquest.umi.com.library.keuka.edu/pqdweb?did=31989293&sid=1&Fmt=3&clientId=3663&RQT=309&VName=PQD.

Graham, T., Wood, S., & Moran, R. (2011, January 18). Kensington slaying suspect arrested. Retrieved on April 16, 2011 from http://articles.philly.com/2011-01-18/news/27034691_1_dna-sample-second-dna-test-state-police.

Graham v. Connor (1989).

Grant, D. A. & Kemme, J. (1993a, March). Employment lawyers rethink advice. Retrieved on October 23, 2003 from http://0-proquest.umi.com.novacat.nova.edu/pqdweb?index=25&did=000000001232755.

Grant, D. A. & Kemme, J. (1993b, March). How to conduct security checks on prospective employees. Retrieved on October 23, 2003 from http://0-proquest.umi.com.novacat.nova.edu/pqdweb?index=25&did=000000001232755.

Grant, H. & Terry, K. J. (2005). *Law Enforcement in the 21st Century*. Boston, MA: Pearson Education, Inc.

Grant, H. & Terry, K. J. (2008). *Law Enforcement in the 21st Century* (2nd edn.). Boston, MA: Pearson Education, Inc.

Grant, S. (2007, March 6). Need police chicks? How to recruit a female officer. Retrieved on October 12, 2009 from http://www.officer.com/web/online/Operations-and-Tactics/Need-Police-Chicks/3$35169.

Graves, A. J. (2002, July). Child abuse and domestic violence. *Law and Order Magazine*, *50*(7), 137–142.

Gray v. Department of Personnel (1994).

Green, S. J. (2006, November 16). Prostitution sting leads to 104 arrests. Retrieved on September 5, 2010 from http://seattletimes.nwsource.com/html/localnews/2003432936_craigslist16m.html.

Green, T. C., Grimes, S. J. M., Licari, A., Budman, S. H., & Butler, S. F. (2009, July 1). Women who abuse prescription opioids: Findings from the addiction severity index-multimedia version connect prescription opioid database. Retrieved on January 20, 2010 from http://search.ebscohost.com.library.keuka.edu/login.aspx?direct=true&db=cmedm&AN=19409735&site=ehost-live.

Green v. Missouri Pacific Railroad Company (1975).

Greenberg v. New York Department of Correctional Services (1997).

Greenfield, S. (2011, January 4). Understanding employment background checks. Retrieved on February 21, 2011 from http://www.nvdaily.com/vec/2011/01/understanding-employment-background-checks.php.

Greenhouse, S. (2009, June 30). For employers, ruling offers little guidance on how to make their hiring fair. Retrieved on October 26, 2009 from http://proquest.umi.com.library.keuka.edu/pqdweb?did=1768718181&sid=2&Fmt=3&clientId=3663&RQT=309&VName=PQD.

Greenawalt v. Indiana Department of Corrections (2005).

Gregg, K. (2009, March 25). Supporters urge speedier erasure of criminal records. *The Providence Journal*, A6.

Gregory, J. (2011, April 1). US customs officer accused of raping 2 women. Retrieved on April 2, 2011 from http://abclocal.go.com/kabc/story?section=news/local/orange_county&id=8047057.

Grieco, L. (2009, July 29). Female child porn suspect pleads guilty. Retrieved on January 18, 2011 from http://www.daytondailynews.com/blogs/content/shared-gen/blogs/dayton/daytoncourts/entries/2009/07/29/a_30yearold_miamisburg_woman_w.html.

Grier, P. (2010, March 10). Jihad Jane: How does Al Qaeda recruit US-born women? Retrieved on March 13, 2010 from http://www.csmonitor.com/USA/2010/0310/Jihad-Jane-How-does-Al-Qaeda-recruit-US-born-women.

Griffin, R. W. (1996). *Management* (5th edn.). Boston, MA: Houghton Mifflin Company.

Griffiths, M. (2003, December). Internet gambling: Issues, concerns, and recommendations. Retrieved on February 13, 2011 from http://web.ebscohost.com.library.keuka.edu/ehost/detail?hid=9&sid=c2c9c9fd-604a-40aa-8504-95895203904c%40sessionmgr114&vid=5&bdata=JnNpdGU9ZWhvc3QtbGl2ZQ%3d%3d#db=aph&AN=12063496.

Griggs v. Duke Power (1971).

Grimaldi, J. V. & Vick, K. (2008, September 4). Palin e-mails show intense interest in trooper's penalty. Retrieved on November 1, 2010 from http://www.washingtonpost.com/wp-dyn/content/article/2008/09/03/AR2008090303210.html.

Grimm, F. (2008, May 4). Tougher marijuana laws are bad economics. Retrieved on February 9, 2010 from http://search.ebscohost.com.library.keuka.edu/login.aspx?direct=true&db=nfh&AN=2W62W63188422025&site=ehost-live.

Grinnell, M. & Burke, T. W. (2001, November). Face recognition technology. *Law and Order Magazine*, *49*(11), 36–40.

Grossman, D. & Siddle, B. K. (2000). Psychological effects of combat. Retrieved on April 15, 2011 from http://www.killology.com/print/print_psychological.htm.

Gryta, M. (2005, January 25). Suspended officer pleads guilty in sex abuse cases. Retrieved on November 3, 2010 from http://proquest.umi.com.library.keuka.edu/pqdweb?did=784708301&sid=1&Fmt=3&clientId=3663&RQT=309&VName=PQD.

Gryta, M. (2011a, February 17). Rapist sentenced to 17 years in jail: Fled Buffalo after repeatedly assaulting and impregnating 11-year-old victim. *The Buffalo News,* C1–C2.

Gryta, M. (2011b, April 7). Jury selection begins in trial of Cummings' half brother. Retrieved on April 9, 2011 from http://www.buffalonews.com/city/police-courts/courts/article386952.ece.

Gryta, M. (2011c, April 7). Ex-cop gets jail for assaulting city officer. Retrieved on April 9, 2011 from http://www.buffalonews.com/city/police-courts/courts/article386224.ece.

Guerriero, J. (2007, August 12). Compulsive gamblers can lose more than money. Retrieved on February 13, 2011 from http://web.ebscohost.com.library.keuka.edu/ehost/detail?hid=9&sid=c2c9c9fd-604a-40aa-8504-95895203904c%40sessionmgr114&vid=6&bdata=JnNpdGU9ZWhvc3QtbGl2ZQ%3d%3d#db=nfh&AN=2W62W61866529065.

Gun Control Act (1968).

Gunderson, M. P. (2003, July). Five tips for testifying in court. *Law and Order Magazine*, *51*(7), 110–113.

Gurkin v. The Nurse Connection, Inc. (2002).

Gurman, S. (2011, February 16). Man who owes $82,000 in child support captured. Retrieved on February 20, 2011 from http://proquest.umi.com.library.keuka.edu/pqdweb?did=2270810511&sid=1&Fmt=3&clientId=3663&RQT=309&VName=PQD.

Guthrie, J. (2009, March 5). Beware the risky business of resume fraud. Retrieved on February 22, 2011 from http://proquest.umi.com.library.keuka.edu/pqdweb?did=1656118401&sid=3&Fmt=3&clientId=3663&RQT=309&VName=PQD.

Hadid, D. (2010, August 16). On Facebook: Israeli soldier posed with bound Arab. Retrieved on August 17, 2010 from http://news.yahoo.com/s/ap/20100816/ap_on_re_mi_ea/ml_israel_palestinians_facebook.

Hagan, P. (2001, April). The testing imperative. Retrieved on November 25, 2009 from http://proquest.umi.com.library.keuka.edu/pqdweb?did=71542480&sid=1&Fmt=3&clientId=3663&RQT=309&VName=PQD.

Hakim, D. & Rashbaum, W. K. (2008, March 10). Spitzer is linked to prostitution ring. Retrieved on February 9, 2010 from http://www.nytimes.com/2008/03/10/nyregion/10cnd-spitzer.html.

Hale, C. (2005, September). Assessment centers: Part I. *Law and Order Magazine*, *53*(2), 22–24.

Hall, J. E. (2008, October). Legal briefings. Retrieved on November 17, 2009 from http://proquest.umi.com.library.keuka.edu/pqdweb?did=1590058331&sid=1&Fmt=3&clientId=3663&RQT=309&VName=PQD.

Hall, K. (Ed.). (1997). *Records of the Wickersham Commission on Law Observance and Enforcement*. Bethesda, MD: University Publications of America.

Hall, W. & Degenhardt, L. (2003). Medical marijuana initiatives: Are they justified? How successful are they likely to be? Retrieved on January 28, 2010 from http://search.ebscohost.com.library.keuka.edu/login.aspx?direct=true&db=aph&AN=10342419&site=ehost-live.

Hall v. United Parcel Service (1989).

Halverstadt, L. & Marks, S. (2011, April 7). 2 Arrested in death of Glendale Teen. Retrieved on April 8, 2011 from http://www.azcentral.com/arizonarepublic/local/articles/2011/04/07/20110407wvmunoz0407.html.

Hamacher, B. (2009a, August 26). More charges for deputy accused of molesting immigrants: Deputy kept records of nearly 30 men, added notes according to court documents. Retrieved on October 28, 2010 from http://www.nbcmiami.com/news/local-beat/More-Charges-for-Deputy-Accused-of-Molesting-Immigrants-54985057.html.

Hamacher, B. (2009b, September 14). Deputy accused of assault dropped from murder trials: BSO deputy won't be called to testify in three murder cases. Retrieved on October 28, 2010 from http://www.nbcmiami.com/news/local-beat/Deputy-Accused-of-Assualt-Dropped-From-Murder-Trials-59221582.html.

Hamid, R., Deren, S., Beardsley, M., & Tortu, S. (1999, September). Agreement between urinalysis and self-reported drug use. Retrieved on January 18, 2010 from http://search.ebscohost.com.library.keuka.edu/login.aspx?direct=true&db=cmedm&AN=10468109&site=ehost-live.

Hamilton, G. J. (2009, November). Prescription drug abuse. Retrieved on January 20, 2010 from http://search.ebscohost.com.library.keuka.edu/login.aspx?direct=true&db=eric&AN=EJ860976&site=ehost-live.

Hammer, M. (1996). *Beyond Reengineering: How the Process-Centered Organization is Changing Our Work and Our Lives*. New York: HarperCollins Publishers.

Hananel, S. (2010, September 15). Report: Illegal drug use up sharply last year. Retrieved on October 8, 2010 from http://www.google.com/hostednews/ap/article/ALeqM5jTk5T17CTJnewt3AsnnhDh7RFRuAD9I8O58G0.

Hand, J. (2011, January 2). Sexual assault victim files suit against city. Retrieved on January 2, 2011 from http://www.democratandchronicle.com/article/20110102/NEWS01/110102007/1003/Sexual-assault-victim-files-suit-against-city.

Handler, M. D. & Barrera, R. (2007). A case study in PDD cooperation. Retrieved on July 26, 2011 from http://proquest.umi.com.library.keuka.edu/pqdweb?did=1444314311&sid=6&Fmt=2&clientId=3663&RQT=309&VName=PQD.

Handler, M., Honts, C. R., Krapohl, D. J., Nelson, R., & Griffin, S. (2009, January 2). Integration of pre-employment polygraph screening into the police selection process. Retrieved on July 24, 2011 from http://truth.boisestate.edu/eyesonly/HontsPublications/HandlerEtAlPreprint.pdf.

Hanks v. Hubbard Broadcasting, Inc. (1992).
Hanna, C. (2011, May 27). Former Massachusetts K9 cop sentenced to prison for starving his own dog. Retrieved on June 5, 2011 from http://dogpostdaily.com/2011/05/former-massachusetts-k9-cop-sentenced-to-prison-for-starving-his-own-dog/.
Hardy v. Town of Hayneville (1999).
Hargrave, G. E. & Hiatt, D. (1989, Summer). Use of the California Psychological Inventory in law enforcement officer selection. Retrieved on October 13, 2009 from http://web.ebscohost.com.library.keuka.edu/ehost/detail?vid=14&hid=8&sid=d30bed09-3932-47cc-9ef4-6811f3bac285%40sessionmgr4&bdata=JnNpdGU9ZWhvc3QtbGl2ZQ%3d%3d#db=buh&AN=6390930.
Harki, G. A. (2009, December 27). Still in uniform: Problem police rarely lose certification in W.Va. Retrieved on April 19, 2011 from http://proquest.umi.com.library.keuka.edu/pqdweb?did=1929168711&sid=2&Fmt=3&clientId=3663&RQT=309&VName=PQD.
Harlan, J. P. & Mueller, P. A. (1992, January–February). Legal issues in detention officer applicant investigations. Retrieved on September 13, 2010 from http://web.ebscohost.com.library.keuka.edu/ehost/detail?vid=4&hid=105&sid=322c9a61-9e8d-40c3-96a0-ada73d8258bf%40sessionmgr113&bdata=JnNpdGU9ZWhvc3QtbGl2ZQ%3d%3d#db=sih&AN=SM134847.
Harland, L. K., Rauzi, T., & Biasotto, M. M. (2008, January 27). Perceived fairness of personality tests and the impact of explanations for their use. Retrieved on October 22, 2009 from http://search.ebscohost.com.library.keuka.edu/login.aspx?direct=true&db=buh&AN=9509256436&site=ehost-live.
Harlow, C. W. (2005, November). *Hate Crime Reported by Victims and Police*. Washington, DC: United States Department of Justice, Office of Justice Programs, Bureau of Justice Statistics.
Harrell, E. (2011, March). *Workplace Violence, 1993–2009*. Washington, DC: United States Department of Justice Program Bureau of Justice Statistics.
Harrell, Z. A. T. & Broman, C. L. (2009, October). Racial/ethnic differences in correlates of prescription drug misuse among young adults. Retrieved on January 20, 2010 from http://search.ebscohost.com.library.keuka.edu/login.aspx?direct=true&db=aph&AN=43768262&site=ehost-live.
Harrington, P. (n.d.). *Recruiting and Retaining Women: A Self-Assessment Guide for Law Enforcement*. Los Angeles, CA: National Center for Women and Policing.
Harrington v. County of Suffolk (2009).
Harris, D., & Tanglao, L. (2011, February 11). Woman behind congressman Chris Lee's Craigslist fallout speaks out. Retrieved on February 11, 2011 http://abcnews.go.com/Politics/congressman-christopher-lees-craigslist-woman-yesha-callahan-speaks/story?id=12890665.
Harris Interactive (2008). *A Study about Air Marshals*. New York: Author.
Harshman, E. F. & Chachere, D. R. (2000, January). Employee references: Between the legal devil and ethical deep blue sea. *Journal of Business Ethics*, *23*(1), 29–39.
Hartenstein, M. (2010, October 5). Man sentenced to life in prison for brutal pornography-inspired rape, murder of 12-year-old niece. Retrieved on February 20, 2011 http://www.nydailynews.com/news/world/2010/10/05/2010-10-05_man_sentenced_to_life_in_prison_for_brutal_pornographyinspired_rape_murder_of_12.html?obref=obinsite.
Hartenstein, M. (2011a, July 3). HIV-positive father charged with raping 6-month old son knowing he had the disease. Retrieved on July 4, 2011 http://www.nydailynews.com/news/national/2011/07/03/2011-07-03_hivpositive_father_charged_with_raping_6month_old_son_knowing_he_had_the_disease.html.
Hartenstein, M. (2011b, August 28). 'Austin Powers' actor faces life in prison over abduction, torture, rape of 20-year-old. Retrieved on September 4, 2011 http://www.nydailynews.com/gossip/2011/08/28/2011-08-28_austin_powers_actor_faces_life_in_prison_over_abduction_torture_rape_of_20yearol.html.
Hartley, D. (2009, June 22). Google street view catches Dutch muggers. Retrieved on March 13, 2010 http://www.geek.com/articles/google/google-street-view-catches-dutch-muggers-20090622/.

Harvey, B. & Ward, T. (1996, April). Starting off on the right foot. Retrieved on February 15, 2010 http://search.ebscohost.com.library.keuka.edu/login.aspx?direct=true&db=sih&AN=9605050335&site=ehost-live.

Hatch, D. (2003, September). Erroneous background checking leads to liability. Retrieved on March 29, 2010 from http://findarticles.com/p/articles/mi_m0FXS/is_9_82/ai_107835616/.

Hate Crime Statistics Act (1990). (P. L. 101-275).

Hatfield Township v. Stanley (1988).

Hauge, L. J., Skogstad, A., & Einarsen, S. (2009, October–December). Individual and situational predictors of workplace bullying: Why do perpetrators engage in the bullying of others? Retrieved on February 5, 2011 from http://web.ebscohost.com.library.keuka.edu/ehost/detail?hid=13&sid=83ac1063-0972-4530-a77b-7200704592ca%40sessionmgr14&vid=4&bdata=JnNpdGU9ZWhvc3QtbGl2ZQ%3d%3d#db=c8h&AN=2010509099.

Hauser, C. & O'Connor, A. (2007, April 16). Virginia Tech shooting leaves 33 dead. Retrieved on April 13, 2011 from http://www.nytimes.com/2007/04/16/us/16cnd-shooting.html.

Havens, J. R., Ocer, C. B., Leukefeld, C. G., Webster, J. M., Martin, S. S., O'Connell, D. J., Surratt, H. L., & Inciardi, J. A. (2007). Differences in prevalence of prescription opiate misuse among rural and urban probationers. Retrieved on January 20, 2010 from http://search.ebscohost.com.library.keuka.edu/login.aspx?direct=true&db=aph&AN=25084710&site=ehost-live.

Hawaii Revised Statute

Hawkins, K. (2009, May 8). Illinois ex-cop indicted in death of 3rd wife. Retrieved on May 8, 2009 from http://news.yahoo.com/s/ap/20090508/ap_on_re_us/us_police_officer_s_wife.

Hayden, J. (2008, December 30). DPD supervisor investigated for alleged taped sex with subordinates. Retrieved on April 8, 2009 from http://www.kdvr.com/kdvr-dpdsupervisorinvestigatedfo-8162122,0,2902187.story.

Hayden v. County of Nassau (1998).

Hayes, K. (2010, November 9). Kimberly Cates murder: Guilty verdict for Steven Spader in N.H. Home invasion death. Retrieved on March 23, 2011 from http://www.cbsnews.com/8301-504083_162-20022275-504083.html.

Haynes v. Police Board of Chicago (1997).

Haynes, W. (1998, December 10). Section 605(a) of the Fair Credit Reporting Act. Retrieved on February 21, 2011 from http://www.ftc.gov/os/statutes/fcra/nadell.shtm.

Headquarters Department of the Army (2006, May 15). Separation program designator (SPD) codes. Retrieved on April 18, 2011 from http://veterancourtcodes.com/vccpdf/SPD%20Codes.pdf.

Headquarters Department of the Army (2010, April 27). Personnel separations: Active duty enlisted administrative separations. Retrieved on April 18, 2011 from http://www.apd.army.mil/pdffiles/r635_200.pdf.

Health Information Technology for Economic and Clinical Health Act

Health Insurance Portability and Accountability Act (HIPAA). (1996).

Hedeen, M. (2009, December 3). City employee jailed on rape charges. Retrieved on December 4, 2009 from http://rochester.ynn.com/all-regions-news-2134-content/top_stories/489381/city-employee-jailed-on-rape-charges/?ap=1&MP4.

Hedgpeth, D. (2010, July 23). Probe links 20 defense workers to online child pornography. Retrieved on January 20, 2010 from http://www.washingtonpost.com/wp-dyn/content/article/2010/07/23/AR2010072305182.html.

Hefling, K. (2011a, February 15). AP newsbreak: Veterans say rape cases mishandled. Retrieved on February 15, 2011 from http://news.yahoo.com/s/ap/20110215/ap_on_go_ot/us_military_sexual_abuse.

Hefling, K. (2011b, April 15). Veterans advocate kills self after war tours. Retrieved on April 16, 2011 from http://news.yahoo.com/s/ap/us_popular_veteran_suicide.

Heinzl, T. (2001, March 16). New York man with HIV sues American airlines, alleges bias in hiring. Retrieved on November 21, 2009 from http://search.ebscohost.com.library.keuka.edu/login.aspx?direct=true&db=nfh&AN=2W61385821674&site=ehost-live.

Hendricks, D. (2009, May 5). Former officer's convictions to be expunged. Retrieved on December 6, 2010 from http://thepost.ohiou.edu/main.asp?Search=1&ArticleID=28213&SectionID=1&SubSectionID=3&S=1.

Henry, D. (2010, May 21). Agents raid of sex offender census worker. Retrieved on August 13, 2011 from http://abclocal.go.com/wpvi/story?section=news/crime&id=7454726.

Henson, M. (2010, July 6). Same name Vexes N.Y. woman at border. Retrieved on August 18, 2010 from http://www.wcax.com/Global/story.asp?S=12763201.

Herbeck, D. (1998, October 6). 4 City police officers, fire lieutenant go to trial in $265,000 loan-fraud case. Retrieved on February 20, 2011 from http://proquest.umi.com.library.keuka.edu/pqdweb?did=34934154&sid=1&Fmt=3&clientId=3663&RQT=309&VName=PQD.

Herman v. Commonwealth Department of General Services (1984).

Hernandez, R. (2011, June 16). Weiner resigns in chaotic final scene. Retrieved on June 28, 2011 from http://www.nytimes.com/2011/06/17/nyregion/anthony-d-weiner-tells-friends-he-will-resign.html.

Herrmann, D. S., Durante, M. K., & Ford, R. (2001, Fall). An experimental validation study of the SASSI: Predicting alcohol related behavior in law enforcement applicants. Retrieved on October 13, 2009 from http://proquest.umi.com.library.keuka.edu/pqdweb?did=98651942&sid=4&Fmt=2&clientId=3663&RQT=309&VName=PQD.

Hersey, P. & Blanchard, K. H. (1988). *Management of Organizational Behavior: Utilizing Human Resources* (5th edn.). Englewood Cliffs, NJ: Prentice-Hall, Inc.

Hertzberg, H. (2005, June 27). Watched pot. Retrieved on January 28, 2010 from http://search.ebscohost.com.library.keuka.edu/login.aspx?direct=true&db=lfh&AN=17405868&site=ehost-live.

Herzog, S. (2001, October). Suspect police officers investigated by former police officers: Good idea, bad idea? *Law and Policy*, *23*(4), 441–467.

Hess, K. M. & Hess Orthmann, C. H. (2010). *Criminal Investigation* (9th edn.). Clifton Park, NY: Delmar Cengage Learning.

Hesselbein, F. & Cohen, P. M. (1999). *Leader to Leader*. New York: Jossey-Bass.

Hett v. Ploetz (1963).

Hewett, R. (2004, April). Drugs of abuse testing. Retrieved on January 24, 2010 from http://search.ebscohost.com.library.keuka.edu/login.aspx?direct=true&db=cin20&AN=2004205989&site=ehost-live.

Hickman, M. J. & Reaves, B. A. (2006, May). Law enforcement and administrative statistics, 2003: Data for individual and local agencies. Washington, DC: United States Department of Justice, Office of Justice Programs, Bureau of Justice Statistics.

Higginbotham, D. (2008, December 2). Wanted: Incriminating Facebook photos. Retrieved on March 13, 2010 from http://media.www.msureporter.com/media/storage/paper937/news/2008/12/02/CampusNews/Wanted.Incriminating.Facebook.Photos-3565390.shtml.

Higginbotham, J. (1995, March). Medical hiring standards and the ADA. Retrieved on November 23, 2009 from http://search.ebscohost.com.library.keuka.edu/login.aspx?direct=true&db=sih&AN=9504072887&site=ehost-live.

Higher Education Amendment Act (1998).

Hill, C. (2009, October 20). Father poses as young boy to lure young girls into child porn. Retrieved on February 20, 2011 from http://www.nydailynews.com/money/2009/10/20/2009-10-20_father_poses_as_young_boy_to_lure_young_girls_into_child_porn.html.

Hindery, R. (2011, March 24). US soldier gets 24 years for murders of 3 Afghans. Retrieved on March 24, 2011 from http://news.yahoo.com/s/ap/us_afghan_probe.

Hines v. Aandahl Construction Co. L.L.C. (2006).

Hitchcock, J. A. (2003, December). Cyberstalking and law enforcement. *The Police Chief Magazine*, *70*(12), 16–27.

Ho, V. (2011, February 1). Former UW doctor gives up license after drugs-for-sex charge. Retrieved on February 1, 2011 from http://www.seattlepi.com/local/434487_doctor.html?source=mypi.

The Hobbs Act (1951).

Hobbs Fry, E. (2000, June). Providing employee references: The risks, the defenses, the future. Retrieved on July 6, 2009 from http://sbaer.uca.edu/research/asbe/1997/PDF/12.pdf.

Hoch, M. (2010, July 14). The struggle over rules of engagement in Afghanistan. Retrieved on April 16, 2011 from http://www.pbs.org/newshour/rundown/2010/07/the-struggle-over-rules-of-engagement-in-afghanistan.html.

Hodes, N. L. (1990, March). Drugs in the workplace: New York State is meeting the challenge. Retrieved on November 25, 2009 from http://proquest.umi.com.library.keuka.edu/pqdweb?did=1061864&sid=1&Fmt=2&clientId=3663&RQT=309&VName=PQD.

Hofeditz, J. & Acosta, S. (2009, September 15). Former police chief accused of possession of child porn. Retrieved on April 19, 2011 from http://proquest.umi.com.library.keuka.edu/pqdweb?did=1859577381&sid=1&Fmt=3&clientId=3663&RQT=309&VName=PQD.

Hoffer, S. (2011, February 24). Khalid-Ali M Aldawsari: What we know so far about the Saudi terror suspect in Texas. Retrieved on February 25, 2011 from http://www.aolnews.com/2011/02/24/khalid-ali-m-aldawsari-what-we-know-so-far-about-the-saudi-terr/.

Hoffman, D. (2001, October). Privacy Act and criminal investigations. *Law and Order Magazine*, *49*(10), 191–192.

Hoffman, L. (2003, May 25). Detective's violent death tied to gambling addiction: New Mexico woman turns to robbery, apparently to pay debts. Cornered, she forces police to shoot her. Retrieved on February 8, 2011 from http://articles.latimes.com/2003/may/25/news/adna-detective25.

Hoffman, M. (2010, March 12). Former materiel command chief faces article 32. Retrieved on January 25, 2011 from http://www.airforcetimes.com/news/2010/03/airforce_sex_scandal_031210w/.

Hofmann, M. A. (2008, October 6). ADA changes spark concerns over employment practices. Retrieved on November 18, 2009 from http://proquest.umi.com.library.keuka.edu/pqdweb?did=1582594151&sid=5&Fmt=3&clientId=3663&RQT=309&VName=PQD.

Hogarty, D. (2008, February 17). More NYPD recruiting trouble as exam takers decline. Retrieved on October 12, 2009 from http://gothamist.com/2008/02/17/more_nypd_recru.php.

Hogg, A. & Wilson, C. (1995). Is the psychological screening of police applicants a realistic goal? The successes and failures of psychological screening. Payneham, SA: National Police Research Unit.

Holden, L. M. (2005). Complex adaptive systems: Concept analysis. *Journal of Advanced Nursing*, *52*(6), 651–657.

Holley, P. J. (2010, February 27). SAPD cop accused of raping transgendered woman. Retrieved on November 1, 2010 from http://www.mysanantonio.com/news/local_news/SAPD_officer_accused_of_sexually_assaulting_man.html.

Holmes, L. (2010, June 2). The psychological effects of trauma. Retrieved on August 15, 2010 from http://mentalhealth.about.com/cs/traumaptsd/a/trauma.htm.

Holson, L. (2009, December 9). Text messages: Digital lipstick on the collar. Retrieved on March 13, 2010 from http://www.lexisnexis.com.library.keuka.edu/us/lnacademic/results/docview/docview.do?docLinkInd=true&risb=21_T8805082670&format=GNBFI&sort=RELEVANCE&startDocNo=1&resultsUrlKey=29_T8805082675&cisb=22_T8805082674&treeMax=true&treeWidth=0&csi=6742&docNo=8.

Holt, D. H. (1993). *Management Principles and Practices* (3rd edn.). Englewood Cliffs, NJ: Prentice-Hall Career and Technology, Prentice-Hall, Inc.

Holusha, J. (2007, October 8). Dispute is cited in Wisconsin shooting. Retrieved on February 24, 2010 from http://www.nytimes.com/2007/10/08/us/08cnd-shoot.html?_r=1&hp.

Holzman, A. & Kirschner, M. (2003, September). Pre-employment psychological evaluations. *Law and Order Magazine*, *51*(9), 85–87.

Homeland Security Act (HSA) (2002).

Honeycutt Spears, V. (2006, October 3). Guilty of peddling fear, hope; backed by Phony degrees, Curran claimed he could cure the dying. Retrieved on April 13, 2011 from http://proquest.umi.com.library.keuka.edu/pqdweb?did=1139239871&sid=5&Fmt=3&clientId=3663&RQT=309&VName=PQD.

Honts, C. R. & Schweinle, W. (2009, July 16). Information gain of psychophysiological detection of deception in forensic and screening settings. Retrieved on July 26, 2011 from http://proquest.umi.com.library.keuka.edu/pqdweb?index=6&did=1831331891&SrchMode=2&sid=6&Fmt=6&VInst=PROD&VType=PQD&RQT=309&VName=PQD&TS=1311679393&clientId=3663.

Hood, S. B. (2009, August). Validity in psychological testing and scientific realism. Retrieved on October 21, 2009 from http://proquest.umi.com.library.keuka.edu/pqdweb?index=4&did=1869936941&SrchMode=2&sid=1&Fmt=2&VInst=PROD&VType=PQD&RQT=309&VName=PQD&TS=1256130613&clientId=3663.

Hoover, L. T. (1975, July). *Police Educational Characteristics and Curricula*. Washington, DC: United States Department of Justice, Law Enforcement Assistance Administration National Institute of Law Enforcement and Criminal Justice.

Hope, B. (2007, March 15). Two auxiliary police officers killed in Greenwich village. Retrieved on September 27, 2010 from http://www.nysun.com/new-york/two-auxiliary-police-officers-killed-in-greenwich/50486/.

Hoppe, C. (2009, May 5). DPS director resigns after allegations of sexual harassment. Retrieved on September 27, 2010 from http://www.dallasnews.com/sharedcontent/dws/dn/latestnews/stories/050409dnmetdpshead.1cb342f2.html.

Horiba Scientific (1996–2010). PrintQuest. Retrieved on September 27, 2010 from http://www.horiba.com/us/en/scientific/products/forensics/afis-apis/details/printquest-174//?Ovly=1.

Horne, P. (1999, November). Policewomen: 2000 A.D. redux. *Law and Order Magazine*, *47*(11), 52–62.

Hornick, E. (2009, May 13). Obama reverses course on alleged prison abuse photos. Retrieved on March 13, 2010 from http://www.cnn.com/2009/POLITICS/05/12/prisoner.photos/.

Hosenball, M. (2011, January 28, 2011). Exclusive: The next generation of Wikileaks. Retrieved on January 28, 2011 from http://news.yahoo.com/s/nm/20110128/tc_nm/us_wikileaks;_ylt=AlvgWcstaRPCxmz4qCvch5tkWRIF;_ylu=X3oDMTM5NjBiZ3QwBGFzc2V0Ay9zL25tLzIwMTEwMTI4L3RjX25tL3VzX3dpa2lsZWFrcwRjY29kZQNtcF9lY184XzEwBGNwb3MDNARwb3MDNARzZWMDeW5fdG9wX3N0b3JpZXMEc2xrA2V4Y2x1c2l2ZXRoZQ–.

Houston v. Grocers Supply Company (1981).

Howard, D. (2011, June 6). Weiner used Jewish sexual stereotype to Facebook sexting partner. Retrieved on June 6, 2011 from http://www.radaronline.com/exclusives/2011/06/weiner-used-jewish-sexual-stereotype-facebook-sexting-partner.

Howard, L. S. (1991, June 17). Police liability worries seen rising. Retrieved on October 25, 2009 from http://proquest.umi.com.library.keuka.edu/pqdweb?did=1248169&sid=2&Fmt=2&clientId=3663&RQT=309&VName=PQD.

Howard v. City of Southfield (1996).

Howell, J. P. & Costley, D. L. (2006). *Understanding Behaviors for Effective Leadership* (2nd edn.). Upper Saddle River, NJ: Pearson Education, Inc.

Hoye, S. (2011, September 2). Philadelphia cop charged with rape. Retrieved on September 6, 2011 from http://www.cnn.com/2011/CRIME/08/31/pennsylvania.officer.rape/index.html?siref=obinsite.

HR Briefing (2001, March 1). *Negligent Entrustment: Employee Drivers Raise Your Liability*. Frederick, MD: Aspen Publishers, Inc., ISSN 1080-1847, pp. 2–3.

HR-Guide.com (2001). HR guide to the internet: Personnel selection methods cognitive ability measures. Retrieved on October 20, 2009 from http://www.hr-guide.com/data/G314.htm.

HR Management (n.d.). Passing the screen test. Retrieved on March 29, 2010 from http://www.hrmreport.com/article/Passing-the-screen-test/.

Hsu, T. (2009, June 7). Trapped: It's hard to get a job if your credit is bad. Retrieved on February 21, 2011 from http://articles.latimes.com/2009/jun/07/business/fi-cover-badcredit7.

Huemiller v. Ogden Civil Service Commission (2004).

Huffcutt, A. I. (2011, March). An empirical review of the employment interview construct literature. Retrieved on July 17, 2011 from http://proquest.umi.com.library.keuka.edu/pqdweb?did=2266734541&sid=1&Fmt=2&clientId=3663&RQT=309&VName=PQD.

Hughes, J. V. (2002, January 25). Ex-parole officer indicted on sexual assault charge. Retrieved on October 18, 2010 from http://www.highbeam.com/doc/1P1-49795552.html.

Hughes, T. (2000, June). Board of the county commissioners of Bryan County, Oklahoma, v. Jill Brown: Municipal liability and police hiring decisions. *The Justice Professional, 13*(2), 143–162.

Hulsey, F. S. & Goodwin, M. (2001, June). Fast track application process speeds hiring. *FBI Law Enforcement Bulletin, 70*(6), 5–8.

HumanResourcesCompany.net. (2009, November 24). The rise of fake resume and degree companies: How this complicates background checks. Retrieved on March 18, 2011 from http://humanresourcescompany.net/2009/11/the-rise-of-fake-resume-and-degree-companies-how-this-complicates-background-checks/.

Hundersmarck, S. (2009, August). Police recruit training: Facilitating learning between the academy and field training. Retrieved on October 31, 2009 from http://proquest.umi.com.library.keuka.edu/pqdweb?did=1823157541&sid=1&Fmt=3&clientId=3663&RQT=309&VName=PQD.

Hunter, C., Nixon, J., & Parr, S. (2010). Mother abuse: A matter of youth justice, child welfare, or domestic violence? Retrieved on October 11, 2010 from http://web.ebscohost.com.library.keuka.edu/ehost/detail?vid=20&hid=113&sid=c11a669b-e675-487a-9271-e6576c348b8e%40sessionmgr12&bdata=JnNpdGU9ZWhvc3QtbG12ZQ%3d%3d#db=cmedm&AN=20726145.

Hurlbut v. Gulf Atlantic Life Insurance Company (1987).

Hustmyre, C. (2002, December). Applicant screening. *Law and Order Magazine, 50*(12), 76–81.

Hutchinson, B. (2010, September 28). Bronx art teacher Melissa Petro blabs about sex exploits as stripper, hooker at open-mic events. Retrieved on September 28, 2010 from http://www.nydailynews.com/ny_local/2010/09/28/2010-09-28_bronx_hooker_teacher_blabs_on_about_past.html.

Idaho Department of Health and Welfare. Retrieved from http://www.healthandwelfare.idaho.gov.

The Identity Theft and Assumption Deterrence Act (1998).

Ikin, J. F., Sim, M. R., Creamer, M. C., Forbes, A. B., McKenzie, D. P., Kelsall, H. L., Glass, D. C., McFarlane, A. C., Abramson, M. J., Ittak, P., Dwyer, T., Blizzard, L., Delaney, K. R., Horsley, K. W. A., Harrex, W. K., & Schwarz, H. (2004, Winter). War-related psychological stressors and risk of psychological disorders in Australian veterans of the 1991 Gulf war. Retrieved on August 15, 2010 from http://bjp.rcpsych.org/cgi/content/full/185/2/116.

Illinois Code

Illegal Immigration Reform and Immigrant Responsibility Act (1996).

Immem, W. (2011, July 16). A brief guide on how not to get that job. Retrieved on July 17, 2011 from http://proquest.umi.com.library.keuka.edu/pqdweb?did=2399729451&sid=3&Fmt=2&clientId=3663&RQT=309&VName=PQD.

Immigration and Nationality Act

Immigration Reform and Control Act (1986).

Inbar, M. (2009, December 2). 'Sexting' bullying cited in teen's suicide: 13-year old Hope Whitsell hanged herself after topless photos circulated. Retrieved on January 12, 2011 from http://today.msnbc.msn.com/id/34236377/ns/today-today_people/.

Inbau, F. E., Reid, J. E., Buckley, J. P., & Jayne, B. C. (2001). *Criminal Interrogation and Confessions* (4th edn.). Gaithersburg, MD: Aspen Publishers, Inc.

Inciardi, J. A. & Cicero, T. J. (2009, Winter). Black beauties, gorilla pills, footballs, and hillbilly heroin: Some reflections on prescription drug abuse and diversion research. Retrieved on January 20, 2010 from http://search.ebscohost.com.library.keuka.edu/login.aspx?direct=true&db=aph&AN=42635510&site=ehost-live.

Independent Commission on the Los Angeles Police Department (1991). *Report of the Independent Commission on the Los Angeles Police Department*. Los Angeles, CA: Author.

Indiana Code.

Indiana Department of Financial Institutions (n.d.). Bankruptcy—Fresh start or big mistake? Retrieved on March 9, 2011 from http://docs.google.com/viewer?a=v&q=cache:W9FjYCYZy70J:www.in.gov/dfi/BANKRUPTCY.doc+bankruptcy&hl=en&gl=us&pid=bl&srcid=ADGEEShXXX-Emh_5FgxNX4f2u1wIZswzSZUk7aHm5tcneLIfcw_XpOx8df21dYsShl2hTAcIhHu1gm1f2bNYvXgdC5x8gLcpcwZ-v1j_hRKIf37ZZZpqKlWoSyYo4MQin-nKpKU-CqG4&sig=AHIEtbSEQDYAHNlG85mUbKdaGAnicd_iJw.

Information Management Journal (2007, January/February). E-records live forever. Retrieved on February 5, 2011 from http://web.ebscohost.com.library.keuka.edu/ehost/detail?hid=11&sid=83ac1063-0972-4530-a77b-7200704592ca%40sessionmgr14&vid=8&bdata=JnNpdGU9ZWhvc3QtbGl2ZQ%3d%3d#db=aph&AN=24289381.

Information Management Journal (2009, March/April). Nationwide E-health records by 2014. Retrieved on November 20, 2009 from http://search.ebscohost.com.library.keuka.edu/login.aspx?direct=true&db=lxh&AN=39885791&site=ehost-live.

Ingber, C. J. (1993, December). Duty to protect. Retrieved on February 15, 2010 from http://search.ebscohost.com.library.keuka.edu/login.aspx?direct=true&db=sih&AN=SM146030&site=ehost-live.

Ingold, J. (1993, December). Ex-Brighton teacher offered plea deal in sex case. Retrieved on October 12, 2010 from http://www.denverpost.com/ci_5062026.

Intelligence Reform and Terrorism Prevention Act of 2004. (2004, December 7). Retrieved on August 18, 2010 from http://www.gpoaccess.gov/serialset/creports/pdf/108-796/108-796_intel_reform.html.

International Association of Chiefs of Police (1989). Criminal investigation. Arlington, VA: Author.

International Association of Financial Crimes Investigators. (2010). Welcome. Retrieved on January 19, 2011 from http://www.iafci.org/web/Home/AM/ContentManagerNet/HomePages/IAFCI_1501_20080611T073612HomePage.aspx?Section=Home.

Internet Crime Complaint Center (IC3) (2011). Welcome to IC3. Retrieved on January 19, 2011 from http://www.ic3.gov/default.aspx.

Introini v. Richland County (1993).

Investors.com (2011, August 12). Concealing black hate crimes. Retrieved on August 16, 2011 from http://www.investors.com/NewsAndAnalysis/Article.aspx?id=581399&obref=outbrain&p=2.

Inwald, R. E. (1988, November). Five-year follow-up study of departmental terminations as predicted by 16 pre-employment psychological indicators. Retrieved on October 13, 2009 from http://proquest.umi.com.library.keuka.edu/pqdweb?did=570587&sid=4&Fmt=2&clientId=3663&RQT=309&VName=PQD.

Irving, D., Ponsi, L., Hardesty, G., Salazar, D., Carpenter, E., Welborn, L., & Jolly, V. (2011, September 22). Officer charged in Kelly Thomas death isolated. Retrieved on September 22, 2011 from http://www.ocregister.com/articles/thomas-318392-ramos-officer.html.

Irwin, D. (1987, May 4). Study cites automated fingerprint identification systems computer technology reportedly cutting crime rate. Retrieved on September 21, 2010 from http://articles.latimes.com/1987-05-04/news/mn-4788_1.

Isidore, C. (2010, June 17). Out-of-work job applicants told unemployed need not apply. Retrieved on October 13, 2009 from http://finance.yahoo.com/news/Outofwork-job-applicants-told-cnnm-3498252371.html?x=0.

Ishikawa v. Delta Airlines (2003).

Isaacson, R. (2009, April 27). Two former Glasgow police dept. majors plead guilty. Retrieved on October 31, 2009 from http://www.justice.gov/dea/pubs/states/newsrel/2009/detroit042709.html.

Itani v. Ashcroft (2002). Retrieved on February 7, 2010 from http://openjurist.org/298/f3d/1213.

Ithaca Journal (2009a, April 28). Kinge seeks $850K from state. Retrieved on April 21, 2011 from http://pqasb.pqarchiver.com/ithacajournal/access/1692566891.html?FMT=ABS&date=Apr+28%2C+2009.

Ithaca Journal (2009b, July 22). Kinge timeline. Retrieved on April 21, 2011 from http://pqasb.pqarchiver.com/ithacajournal/access/1799640291.html?FMT=ABS&date=Jul+22%2C+2009.

Ivancevich, J. M. (2007). *Human Resource Management* (10th edn.). Boston, MA: McGraw-Hill Irwin.

Ivie, D. & Garland, B. (2011, April 27). Stress and burnout in policing: Does military experience matter? Retrieved on April 16, 2011 from http://proquest.umi.com.library.keuka.edu/pqdweb?did=2296494491&sid=1&Fmt=2&clientId=3663&RQT=309&VName=PQD.

J. v. Victory Tabernacle Baptist Church (1988).

J. Crew Group, Inc. v. Griffin (1990).

Jachyra v. City of Southfield (1996).

Jackson, M. (2009, February 23). Police chief Bolton fired. Retrieved on November 1, 2010 from http://crossroadsnews.com/view/full_story/1986540/article-Police-Chief-Bolton-fired.

Jacob Wetterling Crimes Against Children and Sexually Violent Offender Registration Act (1994).

Jaffe, G. (2011, January 4). Navy fires capt. Owen Honors over raunchy videos. Retrieved on January 4, 2011 from http://www.washingtonpost.com/wp-dyn/content/article/2011/01/04/AR2011010405432.html.

Jaffee, M. (2011, February 9). Congressman Chris Lee resigns after shirtless photo posted on internet. Retrieved on May 30, 2011 from http://abcnews.go.com/Politics/congressman-chris-lee-resigns-shirtless-photo-posted-internet/story?id=12878937.

Jaffee, W. B., Trucco, E., Levy, S., & Weiss, R. D. (2007, July). Is the urine really negative? A systematic review of tampering methods is urine drug screening and testing. Retrieved on January 24, 2010 from http://search.ebscohost.com.library.keuka.edu/login.aspx?direct=true&db=cmedm&AN=17588487&site=ehost-live.

Jaffee v. Redmond (1996).

Janik, J. (1994, October). Why psychological screening of police candidates is necessary: The history and rationale. Retrieved on February 15, 2010 from http://search.ebscohost.com.library.keuka.edu/login.aspx?direct=true&db=sih&AN=SM152475&site=ehost-live.

Janik, J. (1995, September). Considerations for conducting psychological pre-employment interviews of law enforcement officer applicants. *Journal of Police and Criminal Psychology*, *10*(3), 44.

Jaschik, S. (2008, September 8). VCU releases details on improper degree. Retrieved on August 15, 2010 from http://www.insidehighered.com/news/2008/09/08/vcu.

The Jeanne Clery Disclosure of Campus Security Policy and Campus Crime Statistics Act (1990).

Jelinek, P. (2011, March 7). Report says too many whites, men leading the military. Retrieved on March 8, 2011 from http://news.yahoo.com/s/ap/20110308/ap_on_re_us/us_military_diversity.

Jenkins, A. J., Oyler, J. H., & Cone, E. J. (1995, October). Comparison of heroin and cocaine concentrations in blood and plasma. Retrieved on January 18, 2010 from http://search.ebscohost.com.library.keuka.edu/login.aspx?direct=true&db=cmedm&AN=8926729&site=ehost-live.

Jensen v. Prudential Financial (2005).

Jerner v. Allstate Insurance Company. (1995).

Jewell, D. & Prohaska, T. J. (2010, August 20). Slain employee planned to quit group home job over safety fears. Retrieved on February 20, 2011 from http://www.buffalonews.com/incoming/article158784.ece.

John Carter v. Township of Bordentown (2007).

Johnson v. Cannon. (1996).

Johnson v. Mers (1996).

Johnson v. Martin (1991).

Johnson, C. (2008, March 5). The 'Rape' of Okinawa. Retrieved on October 9, 2010 from http://www.atimes.com/atimes/Japan/JC05Dh01.html.

Johnson, D. (2011a, February 18). Lee County Sheriff's office heads child support roundup. Retrieved on February 20, 2011 from http://proquest.umi.com.library.keuka.edu/pqdweb?did=2269772791&sid=1&Fmt=3&clientId=3663&RQT=309&VName=PQD.

Johnson, G. (2009, November 29). Four Washington police officers murdered in coffee shop. Retrieved on December 6, 2010 from http://www.myfox8.com/wghp-washington-police-murdered-091129,0,6835383.story.

Johnson, K. (1999, April 5). Government agencies see truth in polygraphs: Courts still call lie detectors 'Junk Science.' Retrieved on October 13, 2009 from http://proquest.umi.com.library.keuka.edu/pqdweb?index=15&did=40305511&SrchMode=1&sid=4&Fmt=3&VInst=PROD&VType=PQD&RQT=309&VName=PQD&TS=1255437023&clientId=3663.

Johnson, K. (2011b, February 10). In Montana, a bid to end medical use of Marijuana. Retrieved on June 1, 2011 from http://www.nytimes.com/2011/02/11/us/11marijuana.html?_r=1&partner=rss&emc=rss.

Johnson, M. K. & Raye, C. L. (1981). Reality monitoring. *Psychological Review*, *88*(1), 67–85.

Johnson, P. & Indvik, J. (1994). Workplace violence: An issue of the nineties. Retrieved on April 21, 2011 from http://www.questia.com/googleScholar.qst?docId=5001710880.

Johnson, R. (2006, October 10). AG Stenehjem criticized for not complying with national sex offender registry. Retrieved on October 9, 2010 from http://web.ebscohost.com.library.keuka.edu/ehost/detail?vid=4&hid=8&sid=872c83a2-eb3e-4e76-9e3d-c3666d69edad%40sessionmgr13&bdata=JnNpdGU9ZWhvc3QtbGl2ZQ%3d%3d#db=nfh&AN=2W6912056309.

Johnson, R. R. (1998, April). A patrol officer's guide to identifying child abuse. *Law and Order Magazine*, *46*(4), 77–79.

Johnson, R. R. (2004, July). Motivating senior officers. Retrieved on October 25, 2009 from http://proquest.umi.com.library.keuka.edu/pqdweb?did=673964521&sid=2&Fmt=4&clientId=3663&RQT=309&VName=PQD.

Johnston, F. E. (1997, September). No safe haven: Male violence against women at home, at work, and in the community. Retrieved on April 19, 2011 from http://proquest.umi.com.library.keuka.edu/pqdweb?did=23075076&sid=5&Fmt=2&clientId=3663&RQT=309&VName=PQD.

Johnston, G. (2010, December 9). Woman's death appears self-inflicted. Retrieved on December 9, 2010 from http://rochester.ynn.com/content/top_stories/526347/woman-s-death-appears-self-inflicted/.

Johnston, R. G., Michaud, E. C., & Warner, J. S. (2009, March). The (In) security of drug testing. Retrieved on January 24, 2010 from http://search.ebscohost.com.library.keuka.edu/login.aspx?direct=true&db=buh&AN=37018485&site=ehost-live.

Jolly, K. (2011, June 8). Former substitute teacher arrested for child pornography. Retrieved on June 8, 2011 from http://rochester.ynn.com/content/all_news/546135/former-substitute-teacher-arrested-for-child-pornography-possession/.

Jones, E., Hyams, K. C., & Wessely, S. (2003, March 22). Screening for vulnerability to psychological disorders in the military: An historical survey. Retrieved on August 15, 2010 from http://www.accessmylibrary.com/article-1G1-102340349/screening-vulnerability-psychological-disorders.html.

Jones, H. J. (1994, November 24). Deputy promotion creates an uproar. Retrieved on October 26, 2009 from http://proquest.umi.com.library.keuka.edu/pqdweb?did=1245314061&sid=1&Fmt=3&clientId=3663&RQT=309&VName=PQD.

Jones, J. W. (2004). My employee did what? What Florida employers can do to prevent and defend negligent hiring claims. Retrieved on April 25, 2011 from http://www.thehumanequation.com/en/news_rss/articles/2004/what_florida_employers_can_do_to_prevent_and_defend_negligent_hire_claims.aspx.

Jones, J. W. & Joy, D. (1989, August 31). Empirical investigation of job applicants' reactions to taking a pre-employment honesty test. Retrieved on March 10, 2010 from http://www.eric.ed.gov/ERICWebPortal/Home.portal?_nfpb=true&ERICExtSearch_

SearchValue_0=pre+employment+investigation&searchtype=basic&ERICExtSearch_SearchType_0=kw&_pageLabel=RecordDetails&objectId=0900019b801171a7&accno=ED315679&_nfls=false.

Jones, M. (2007, July 22). How can you distinguish a budding pedophile from a kid with real boundary problems. Retrieved on October 13, 2010 from http://www.nytimes.com/2007/07/22/magazine/22juvenile-t.html.

Jones v. Wittenberg University (1976).

Jonsson, P. (2011, July 22). Flash mob attacks: Rising concern over black teen involvement—from Milwaukee to Philadelphia to Chicago, officials are enforcing curfews and requiring chaperones for teens, after several flash mob attacks allegedly involving black youths. Retrieved on August 13, 2011 from http://www.csmonitor.com/USA/2011/0809/Flash-mob-attacks-Rising-concern-over-black-teen-involvement.

Jordan v. City of New London (1999).

Joseph v. Salt Lake City (2003).

Joyce, A. (2007, February 18). Should you tell? For people with mental illness, there's no easy answer. Retrieved on November 21, 2009 from http://proquest.umi.com.library.keuka.edu/pqdweb?did=1218347331&sid=1&Fmt=3&clientId=3663&RQT=309&VName=PQD.

Joyce, E. (2010, April 7). 6 Career-killing Facebook mistakes. Retrieved on April 11, 2010 from http://finance.yahoo.com/career-work/article/109267/6-career-killing-facebook-mistakes.

Judge, L. A. (2005, November). Disclosing officer untruthfulness to the defense: Is a liars squad coming to your town? Retrieved on July 17, 2011 from http://policechiefmagazine.org/magazine/index.cfm?fuseaction=display_arch&article_id=744&issue_id=112005.

Juliano, M. C. (2011, February 26). More firms performing background checks. Retrieved on February 26, 2011 from http://proquest.umi.com.library.keuka.edu/pqdweb?did=2276874651&sid=1&Fmt=3&clientId=3663&RQT=309&VName=PQD.

Jurkiewicz, C. L. (2000, Spring). Generation x and the public employee. Retrieved on March 26, 2005 from http://www.findarticles.com/p/articles/mi_qa3779/is_200004/ai_n8892977/.

Justice for All Act (2004).

Justice.gov (2008, October). Criminal resource manual: Issues related to trials and other court proceedings. Retrieved on July 16, 2011 from http://www.justice.gov/usao/eousa/foia_reading_room/usam/title9/5mcrm.htm#9-5.100.

JustNews.com (2007, March 20). Miami police officer charged with rape, kidnapping: Miami beach man may have been targeting illegal immigrants police say. Retrieved on October 29, 2010 from http://www.justnews.com/news/11307538/detail.html.

JustNews.com (2009, April 2). Deputy facing battery charges resigns: Officer accused of 'inappropriate contact.' Retrieved on October 28, 2010 from http://www.justnews.com/news/19079666/detail.html.

Juvenile Corrections Act. (n.d.). Retrieved on February 5, 2011 from http://www.the3rdjudicialdistrict.com/jca.htm.

J.N. v. Bellingham School District (1994).

Kabel, K. & Frost, L. (2008, Spring). Curiosity is a very aggressive thing: A conversation between Peer Hultberg and Niels Frank. Retrieved on March 16, 2010 from http://proquest.umi.com.library.keuka.edu/pqdweb?did=1494219971&sid=3&Fmt=3&clientId=3663&RQT=309&VName=PQD.

Kamerick, M. (2010, April 1). Some experts say resume fraud is up in recession: Great hire or costly mistake? Retrieved on March 18, 2011 from http://www.bizjournals.com/albuquerque/stories/2010/04/05/focus1.html.

Kane, R. & White, M. D. (2009, November). Bad cops. Retrieved on March 28, 2010 from http://search.ebscohost.com.library.keuka.edu/login.aspx?direct=true&db=aph&AN=45270038&site=ehost-live.

Kane, T. E. (1998, October 27). Solomon letter. Retrieved on February 22, 2011 from http://www.ftc.gov/os/statutes/fcra/solomon.shtm.

Kansas City Kansas Police and FOP Lodge 4 (1988).
Kansas University Medical Center (2009). Affirmative action/equal opportunity/disability glossary. Retrieved on July 7, 2009 from http://kumc.edu/eoo/glossary.html.
Kansas v. Hendricks (1997).
Kappeler, V. E. (1995). *Policing and Society: Touchstone Readings*. Prospect Heights, IL: Waveland Press, Inc.
Kappeler, V. E. (2001). *Critical Issues in Police Civil Liability* (3rd edn.). Prospect Heights, IL: Waveland Press, Inc.
Kappeler, V. E. (2002). *Police Civil Liability: Supreme Court Cases and Materials*. Prospect Heights, IL: Waveland Press, Inc.
Kapsidelis, K. & Martz, M. (2009, January 31). Another twist for VCU. Retrieved on August 15, 2010 from http://www2.timesdispatch.com/news/2009/jan/31/chef31_20090130-221814-ar-89490/.
Karraker v. Rent-A-Center (2005).
Kaspar, W. A. & Mosley, P. A. (2008, Summer). Making the good hire. Retrieved on July 27, 2011 from http://proquest.umi.com.library.keuka.edu/pqdweb?did=1499657701&sid=4&Fmt=3&clientId=3663&RQT=309&VName=PQD.
Kast, F. E. & Rosenzweig, J. E. (1972, December). General systems theory, applications for organization and management. Retrieved on October 24, 2009 from http://proquest.umi.com.library.keuka.edu/pqdweb?did=940966&sid=2&Fmt=2&clientId=3663&RQT=309&VName=PQD.
Kates, B. (2009, October 27). Richmond high school gang rape: Cops arrest 2 in attack on Calif. Teen girl: Bystanders did nothing. Retrieved on February 20, 2011 from http://www.nydailynews.com/news/national/2009/10/27/2009-10-27_richmond_high_school_gang_rape_cops_arrest_2_in_attack_on_calif_teen_girl_bystan.html.
Kates, B. (2010, March 12). Al Qaeda-linked New Jersey man Sharif Mobley, arrested in Yemen, worked in nuclear power plants. Retrieved on March 13, 2010 from http://www.nydailynews.com/news/world/2010/03/12/2010-03-12_al_qaedalinked_new_jersey_man_sharif_mobley_arrested_in_yemen_worked_in_nuclear_.html.
Katunich, L. J. (2005, August). Pre-employment psychological and personality testing. *Fair Employment Practice Guidelines*, (603), 1–4.
Katzanek, J. (2010, March 21). Resume fraud getting more tempting. Retrieved on February 22, 2011 from http://proquest.umi.com.library.keuka.edu/pqdweb?did=1989014721&sid=3&Fmt=3&clientId=3663&RQT=309&VName=PQD.
Kaufman, D. A. & Butler, C. M. (2010, August 27). Illinois employers can no longer use credit checks in employment decisions under most circumstances. Retrieved on February 22, 2011 from http://www.natlawreview.com/article/illinois-employers-can-no-longer-use-credit-checks-employment-decisions-under-most-circumsta.
Kavilanz, P. B. (2009, September 8). 911 Abuse: Calling with the sniffles—chronic abuse of 911 for non-emergency issues is wasting billions of dollars every year and overwhelming the safety net of health care. And taxpayers are left with the tab. Retrieved on April 30, 2011 from http://money.cnn.com/2009/08/24/news/economy/healthcare_911_abuse/index.htm.
Kay, J. (2004, March 1). Ethical dilemmas. Retrieved on April 15, 2011 from http://proquest.umi.com.library.keuka.edu/pqdweb?did=573590791&sid=4&Fmt=3&clientId=3663&RQT=309&VName=PQD.
KCBA.com (2010, October 7). Salinas police employee arrested for sex with minor. Retrieved on December 6, 2010 from http://www.kcba.com/Global/story.asp?S=13288736.
Kedjidjian, C. B. (1996, March). Work can be murder for women. Retrieved on April 19, 2011 from http://proquest.umi.com.library.keuka.edu/pqdweb?did=10132922&sid=5&Fmt=2&clientId=3663&RQT=309&VName=PQD.
Keane, N. & Kleiven, M. E. (2009, Autumn). Risky intelligence. Retrieved on October 10, 2010 from http://web.ebscohost.com.library.keuka.edu/ehost/detail?vid=10&hid=11&sid=4c672b52-8d14-4332-a8cb-b1ff63c84f64%40sessionmgr11&bdata=JnNpdGU9ZWhvc3QtbGl2ZQ%3d%3d#db=aph&AN=43202159.

Keeshan, C. (2004, February 11). Ex-police officer starts serving jail sentence: Holiday hills patrolman convicted of using badge to obtain sexual favors. Retrieved on November 1, 2010 from http://proquest.umi.com.library.keuka.edu/pqdweb?did=544442471&sid=1&Fmt=3&clientId=3663&RQT=309&VName=PQD.

Keeshan, C. (2008, June 20). Ex-cop faces battery charges. Retrieved on November 1, 2010 from http://proquest.umi.com.library.keuka.edu/pqdweb?did=1583671481&sid=1&Fmt=3&clientId=3663&RQT=309&VName=PQD.

Kedem, A. (2005, March/April). It's all in the delivery. Retrieved on March 16, 2010 from http://proquest.umi.com.library.keuka.edu/pqdweb?did=803105451&sid=3&Fmt=4&clientId=3663&RQT=309&VName=PQD.

Kellerman v. Holder (2009). Retrieved on February 7, 2010 from http://74.125.47.132/search?q=cache%3AQzFmu2dheh4J%3Acaselaw.lp.findlaw.com%2Fdata2%2Fcircs%2F6th%2F083927p.pdf+Sosa-Martinez+v.+United+States+AG&hl=en&gl=us.

Kelley, J. & Abrials, D. (2003, November). Overcoming information sharing obstacles. *The Police Chief Magazine, 70*(11), 24–28.

Kelley, T. (2007, March 23). Metro briefing New Jersey: Camden: Police officer indicted. Retrieved on October 28, 2010 from http://query.nytimes.com/gst/fullpage.html?res=9E02EFDC1530F930A15750C0A9619C8B63.

Kelly v. City of New York (2005).

Kelly, J. P. (2008, November 26). Quincy corrections officer accused of raping female inmate. Retrieved on December 14, 2009 from http://www.patriotledger.com/news/cops_and_courts/x1514658755/Quincy-corrections-officer-accused-of-raping-female-inmate.

Kelly, R. M. (1991, December). Burden of proof in criminal offenses or moral turpitude cases. Retrieved on February 7, 2010 from http://search.ebscohost.com.library.keuka.edu/login.aspx?direct=true&db=sih&AN=SM136245&site=ehost-live.

Kenneth R. v. Roman Catholic Diocese (1997).

Kennedy, H. (2011, April 12). Federal agent in Florida who crusaded against child pornography probed for possession of kiddie porn. Retrieved on May 27, 2011 from http://www.nydailynews.com/news/national/2011/04/12/2011-04-12_federal_agent_in_florida_who_crusaded_against_child_pornography_probed_for_posse.html.

Kenney, D. (2004, December 10). Coleman makes initial court appearance. Retrieved on December 6, 2010 from http://www.wlbt.com/Global/story.asp?S=2678564&nav=2CSfU53u.

Kenney, N. (2011a, May 11). Memphis teacher arrested for sex with teen. Retrieved on June 28, 2011 from http://www.wmctv.com/story/14628069/memphis-teacher-arrested-for-sex-with-teen.

Kenney, N. (2011b, June 27). Memphis teacher charged with sex with boy. Retrieved on June 28, 2011 from http://www.wmctv.com/story/14981072/memphis-teacher-charged-with-sex-with-boy.

Kershaw, S. & Cathcart, R. A. (2009, July 17). Marijuana is gateway drug for two debates. Retrieved on October 8, 2010 from http://www.nytimes.com/2009/07/19/fashion/19pot.html.

Kesseli, D. (2006, October 21). Former Bangor police officer focus of criminal investigation. Retrieved on October 13, 2009 from http://web.ebscohost.com.library.keuka.edu/ehost/detail?vid=12&hid=8&sid=d30bed09-3932-47cc-9ef4-6811f3bac285%40sessionmgr4&bdata=JnNpdGU9ZWhvc3QtbGl2ZQ%3d%3d#db=nfh&AN=2W62W6609370914.

Kestenbaum v. Pennzoil, Co. (1988).

Keyes, C. (2011, January 19). Army to implement new mental health screening procedures. Retrieved on January 23, 2011 from http://articles.cnn.com/2011-01-19/us/military.mental.health_1_suicidal-ideation-predeployment-screening-process-combat-stress?_s=PM:US.

KEZI.com (2011, July 4). Man on the run for 54 years in custody. Retrieved on July 4, 2011 from http://kezi.com/news/local/216943.

Kidwell, M. (2009, January). What happened? An epistemics of before and after in "at-the-scene" police questioning. Retrieved on March 28, 2010 from http://search.ebscohost.com/login.aspx?direct=true&db=sih&AN=36606658&site=ehost-live.

Kiesler, S. & Gendar, A. (2011, May 29). Student who got lewd picture from rep. Anthony Weiner's Twitter account denies she's his mistress. Retrieved on June 1, 2011 from http://www.nydailynews.com/ny_local/2011/05/29/2011-05-29_student_who_got_lewd_pic_from_rep_anthony_weiners_twitter_account_denies_shes_hi.html.

Kifner, J. (2006, July 7). Hate groups are infiltrating the military, group asserts. Retrieved on August 7, 2011 from http://www.nytimes.com/2006/07/07/washington/07recruit.html.

Kilberg, W. J. (2002, Winter). Review of the Supreme Court's October 2001 term. Retrieved on November 25, 2009 from http://proquest.umi.com.library.keuka.edu/pqdweb?did=275383191&sid=4&Fmt=3&clientId=3663&RQT=309&VName=PQD.

King, M. & Shirek, J. (2007, May 9). Atlanta cop accused of rape. Retrieved on November 1, 2010 from http://www.11alive.com/news/article_news.aspx?storyid=96741.

King, N. (2007, September 18). Jury finds county employee firings illegal under Texas whistle-blower law. Retrieved on October 24, 2009 from http://search.ebscohost.com.library.keuka.edu/login.aspx?direct=true&db=nfh&AN=2W6171341579&site=ehost-live.

King Greenwood, J. (2007, November 14). Pittsburgh policeman charged with forgery. Retrieved on February 20, 2011 from http://web.ebscohost.com.library.keuka.edu/ehost/detail?hid=7&sid=ad66db90-f8fb-43a0-b3a0-a26957b3a8c0%40sessionmgr104&vid=5&bdata=JnNpdGU9ZWhvc3QtbGl2ZQ%3d%3d#db=nfh&AN=2W62W62099659730.

Kinnard, M. (2009, April 8). SC college sued for discriminating against whites. Retrieved on April 8, 2009 from http://www.goupstate.com/article/20090408/ARTICLES/904089943/1083/ARTICLES?Title=SC-college-sued-for-discriminating-against-whites.

Kintz, P. & Samyn, N. (2002, April). Use of alternative specimens: Drugs of abuse in saliva and doping agents in hair. Retrieved on January 18, 2010 from http://search.ebscohost.com.library.keuka.edu/login.aspx?direct=true&db=cmedm&AN=11897970&site=ehost-live.

Kirksey, L. A. & Smith, B. L. (1998, May). Granting a stamp of approval. *Security Management*, 62–69.

KIROTV.com (2010, April 29). Police: Craigslist ads tied to 2 home invasions, one deadly. Retrieved on September 5, 2010 from http://www.kirotv.com/news/23312992/detail.html.

Kitchen v. K-Mart Corporation (1997).

Kitzmiller, F. (2010, October 26). Officer fired after porn found on office computer. Retrieved on November 1, 2010 from http://www.nwfdailynews.com/articles/office-34290-officer-panama.html.

Klatell, J. M. (2009, February 11). Exclusive: Gangs spreading in the military. Retrieved on August 6, 2011 from http://www.cbsnews.com/stories/2007/07/28/eveningnews/main3107316.shtml.

Kleiman, L. S. & Benek-Rivera, J. (2010, September). A four-step model for teaching selection interviewing skills. Retrieved on July 27, 2011 from http://proquest.umi.com.library.keuka.edu/pqdweb?did=2142833731&sid=4&Fmt=2&clientId=3663&RQT=309&VName=PQD.

Kleiman, L. S. & White, C. S. (1991). Reference checking: A field survey of SHRM professionals. *Applied H.R.M. Research*, *2*(2), 84–95.

Klein, E. (n.d.). Employment tests: Get an edge. Retrieved on October 20, 2009 from http://www.asktheheadhunter.com/gv000802.htm.

Klein, J. S., Pappas, N. J., & Kim, J. Y. (2004, November). Compelled self-publication defamation. Retrieved on April 24, 2011 from http://www.weil.com/news/pubdetail.aspx?pub=8360.

Klein, K. E. (2010, January 13). Four legal pitfalls loom in 2010. Retrieved on March 16, 2010 from http://search.ebscohost.com.library.keuka.edu/login.aspx?direct=true&db=aph&AN=47568885&site=ehost-live.

Kleiss, K. (2009, September 25). Edmonton police tried to hide racist internal e-mail: Oversight body. Retrieved on October 25, 2009 from http://proquest.umi.com.library.keuka.edu/pqdweb?did=1867337531&sid=1&Fmt=3&cl ientId=3663&RQT=309&VName=PQD.

Klinzig, F., Vinner, E., Brassart, C., Houdain, E., Humbert, L., & Lhermitte, M. (2007). Hair analysis by LC-MS as evidence of Nalbuphine abuse by a nurse. Retrieved on January 18, 2010 from http://search.ebscohost.com.library.keuka.edu/login.aspx?direct=true&db=cmedm&AN=17389085&site=ehost-live.

Klotsche v. City of New York (1985).

Kmitch, J. (2010, November 17). Naperville tables police layoffs: But 6 officers are still scheduled to leave force after Monday. Retrieved on March 13, 2010 from http://www.dailyherald.com/article/20101116/news/711179625/.

Knight, W. (2007, July 17). What are your embarrassing Facebook pics? Retrieved on March 13, 2010 from http://www.newscientist.com/blog/technology/2007/07/what-are-your-embarassing-facebook-pics.html.

Knox, O. (2010, December 18). US congress votes to end military gay ban. Retrieved on January 18, 2011 from http://news.yahoo.com/s/afp/20101218/lf_afp/usmilitarygayspolitics_20101218211217.

KnoxNews.com (2008, January 18). Former trooper gets probation in porn-actress traffic stop. Retrieved on October 29, 2010 from http://www.knoxnews.com/news/2008/jan/18/former-trooper-gets-probation-porn-actress-traffic/.

Koch v. Cox (2007).

Koch v. Stanard (1992).

Koch, W. (2010, January 5). Study: Many sex offenders are kids themselves. Retrieved on October 13, 2010 from http://www.usatoday.com/news/nation/2010-01-03-kid-sex-offenders_N.htm.

Kochakian, C. (2008, October 9). Change in ADA gives disabled better chances in job-related suits. Retrieved on November 17, 2009 from http://proquest.umi.com.library.keuka.edu/pqdweb?did=1580125991&sid=1&Fmt=3&clientId=3663&RQT=309&VName=PQD.

Kohls, J. W. & Luke, L. K. (1977). *Background Investigation Manual—Guidelines for the Investigator* (2nd edn.). Retrieved on September 13, 2010 from http://web.ebscohost.com.library.keuka.edu/ehost/detail?vid=4&hid=105&sid=322c9a61-9e8d-40c3-96a0-ada73d8258bf%40sessionmgr113&bdata=JnNpdGU9ZWhvc3QtbGl2ZQ%3d%3d#db=sih&AN=SM075674.

Kohn, D. (2003, July 4). Millionaire boys club: Drugs and death in the suburbs. Retrieved on February 14, 2010 from http://www.cbsnews.com/stories/2002/05/07/48hours/main508255.shtml.

Kohn, D. (2004, July/August). Who is covered by HIPAA? Retrieved on November 20, 2009 from http://search.ebscohost.com.library.keuka.edu/login.aspx?direct=true&db=lxh&AN=14023770&site=ehost-live.

Koopmans, K. (2011, April 28). Police: Suspect tailgated officer's motorcycle. Retrieved on April 29, 2011 from http://www.kpic.com/news/120801394.html.

Koper, C. S., Maguire, E. R., & Moore, G. E. (2001, October). Hiring and retention issues in police agencies: Readings on the determinants of police strength, hiring, and retention of officers, and the federal cops program. Washington, DC: Urban Institute Justice Policy Center—Report to the National Institute of Justice Grant # NIJ 99-IJ-CX-0011.

Koppel, N. (2011, February 11). Judge Okays Walmart's firing of medical Marijuana user. Retrieved on June 1, 2011 from http://blogs.wsj.com/law/2011/02/11/judge-okays-walmarts-firing-of-medical-marijuana-user/.

Koppelman, T. (2011, February 17). Prosecutors using touch DNA in Waldo rape case. Retrieved on April 17, 2011 from http://www.fox4kc.com/news/wdaf-prosecutors-using-touch-dna-in-waldo-rape-case-20110217,0,7395125.story.

Korte, G. (2002, March 20). Police inquiry scorches Roach: He lied to investigators, report says. Retrieved on April 20, 2011 from http://www.enquirer.com/editions/2002/03/20/loc_1police_inquiry.html.

Kosan v. Utah Department of Corrections (2008).

Kotter, J. P. (1996). *Leading Change*. Boston, MA: Harvard Business School Press.

Kotz, P. (2010, October 29). Steven Spader on trial for hacking Kimberly Cates to death and trying to kill 11-year-old girl. Retrieved on March 23, 2011 from http://www.truecrimereport.com/2010/10/steven_spader_on_trial_for_hac.php.

Kouri, J. (2006, July 10). DoD investigator claims gangs are infiltrating the US military. Retrieved on August 6, 2011 from http://www.renewamerica.com/columns/kouri/060710.

Kovaleski, S. F. (2008, February 9). Old friends say drugs played bit part in Obama's young life. Retrieved on November 25, 2009 from http://search.ebscohost.com.library.keuka.edu/login.aspx?direct=true&db=nfh&AN=29331396&site=ehost-live.

KPCC Wire Services. (2009, November 4). Jury rejects gay ex-LAPD officer's discrimination lawsuit against city. Retrieved on September 27, 2010 from http://www.scpr.org/news/2009/11/04/jury-rejects-gay-ex-lapd-officers-discrimination-l/.

KPCC Wire Services. (2010, August 29). Pranksters turn to technology to fake emergency calls. Retrieved on April 30, 2011 from http://www.scpr.org/news/2010/08/29/pranksters-turn-technology-fake-emergency-calls/.

Kraft v. Police Commissioner of Boston (1995).

Krajewski, H. & Goffin, R. (2009, August 10). Choosing the right personality test for the job. Retrieved on October 21, 2009 from http://proquest.umi.com.library.keuka.edu/pqdweb?did=1846437611&sid=3&Fmt=3&clientId=3663&RQT=309&VName=PQD.

Kraska, P. B., Bussard, C. R., & Brent, J. J. (2010, April). Trafficking in bodily perfection: Examining the late-modern steroid marketplace and its criminalization. *Justice Quarterly*, *27*(2), 159–185.

Krause, K. (2010a, July 29). Dallas Sheriff's deputy investigates jailer twice. Retrieved on September 26, 2010 from http://crimeblog.dallasnews.com/archives/2010/07/dallas-sheriffs-deputy-investi-1.html.

Krause, K. (2010b, August 3). Tougher hiring rules suggested for Dallas County constables. Retrieved on September 26, 2010 from http://www.dallasnews.com/sharedcontent/dws/news/localnews/stories/0803dnmetconstables.1a82e284.html.

Krause, K. & Crawford, S. (2010, January 27). Dallas County constable's lieutenant, wife arrested on multiple felonies. Retrieved on September 26, 2010 from http://www.dallasnews.com/sharedcontent/dws/news/city/dallas/stories/012710dnmnetconstable.bd4c0d8d.html.

Kreimer, S. (2004, August 1). Getting around the no-reference rule: Some ex-employers have policy against evaluating work. Retrieved on November 21, 2009 from http://proquest.umi.com.library.keuka.edu/pqdweb?did=672056031&sid=1&Fmt=3&clientId=3663&RQT=309&VName=PQD.

Kreytak, S. (2009, November 21). Woman gets 40 years in sexual assault captured on video: Victim in January assault was a child. Retrieved on December 9, 2010 from http://www.statesman.com/news/content/news/stories/local/2009/11/21/1121garcia.html?cxtype=rss&cxsvc=7&cxcat=52.

Kreytak, S. (2010, June 20). Round rock man faces child porn charges: Timothy Cyrus Flores admitted assaulting young girl in Corpus Christi, Affidavit says. Retrieved on December 9, 2010 from http://www.statesman.com/news/local/round-rock-man-faces-child-porn-charges-759327.html.

Kristufek v. Hussman Foodservice Company (1993).

Krocka v. Branfield (1997).

Kroskob, L. (2010, October 4). 911 Abuse: Phony calls clog system. Retrieved on April 30, 2011 from http://proquest.umi.com.library.keuka.edu/pqdweb?did=2166850271&sid=1&Fmt=3&clientId=3663&RQT=309&VName=PQD.

KTLA.com (2010, July 14). OC rapist Greg Haidl to keep sex offender label: Haidl, Kyle Nachreiner and Keith Spann, wanted the court to lift a requirement that they register as sex offenders. Retrieved on February 11, 2011 from http://www.ktla.com/news/landing/ktla-greg-haidl,0,1950024.story.

KRQE.com (2010, October 28). Mora County deputy charged with DWI: Police: Breath test four times the legal limit. Retrieved on November 1, 2010 from http://www.krqe.com/dpp/news/crime/mora-county-deputy-charged-with-dwi.

KTVB.com (2010, January 4). Former deputy accused of kidnapping wife, stabbing mother in the eagle home. Retrieved on January 18, 2011 from http://www.ktvb.com/news/crime/Police-on-scene-of-a-reported-stabbing-in-Eagle-112913319.html.

Ku, M. & Musgrave, B. (2006, May 23). Candidate's record was cleaned up before vote: Charges were expunged for GOP judge-executive hopeful. Retrieved on February 5, 2011 from http://web.ebscohost.com.library.keuka.edu/ehost/detail?hid=13&sid=83ac1063-0972-4530-a77b-7200704592ca%40sessionmgr14&vid=8&bdata=JnNpdGU9ZWhvc3QtbGl2ZQ%3d%3d#db=nfh&AN=2W62W61029465789.

Kumho Tire Co. v. Carmichael (1999).

Kuntz, D. J. (n.d.). Laboratory perspective on additional drug testing and associated costs. Retrieved on August 8, 2011 from http://nac.samhsa.gov/DTAB/Presentations/Aug08/DavidKuntzDTAB0808.pdf.

Kuwik v. Starmark Star Marketing and Administration, Inc. (1993).

Kuzmits, F. E., Thacker, R. A., & Osbourn, M. A. (1991). Negligent hiring: Reducing the risk. *Employee Responsibilities and Rights Journal*, *4*(3), 203–214.

KVUE News (2008, December 16). Counselor accused of drug use, sex with juvenile Travis County inmate. Retrieved on November 1, 2010 from http://www.txcn.com/sharedcontent/dws/txcn/austin/stories/121608kvue_counselor_charges-cb.6c40f1d8.html.

Kwicien, J. (2010, April). Improving sales management effectiveness: Selection; hiring the right person has nothing to do with luck or gut feelings. It's the result of hard work and diligence in the candidate selection process. Retrieved on September 13, 2010 from http://proquest.umi.com.library.keuka.edu/pqdweb?index=0&did=1999484871&SrchMode=2&sid=5&Fmt=3&VInst=PROD&VType=PQD&RQT=309&VName=PQD&TS=1284424299&clientId=3663.

Kyles v. Whitley (1995).

Lachance v. Erickson (1998).

The Ladders (n.d.). Clean up your web trail checklist. Retrieved on June 5, 2011 from https://cdn.theladders.net/static/images/editorial/webchecklist09.0218.pdf.

LaDuca, R. (2010, November 24). Correction officer to stand trial next year in steroid case. Retrieved on March 19, 2011 from http://www.uticaod.com/latestnews/x1617323517/Correction-officer-to-stand-trial-next-year-in-steroid-case.

Lagorio, C. (2005, May 2). Judge accepts Abu Ghraib plea. Retrieved on August 17, 2010 from http://www.cbsnews.com/stories/2005/05/02/iraq/main692284.shtml.

Lagorio, C. (2006, July 30). Diploma mill calling: Continuing Ed without the Ed. Retrieved on April 14, 2011 from http://www.nytimes.com/2006/07/30/education/edlife/diplomamill.html.

LaGrange, R. L. (1993). *Policing American Society*. Chicago, IL: Nelson-Hall Publishers.

Lail, P. & Kale, K. D. (2005, June). Post-offer medical exam was premature. Retrieved on November 20, 2009 from http://search.ebscohost.com.library.keuka.edu/login.aspx?direct=true&db=buh&AN=17204046&site=ehost-live.

Lajoie, D. (2010, December 7). Bullying pervasive, expert warns. Retrieved on April 19, 2011 from http://proquest.umi.com.library.keuka.edu/pqdweb?did=2208793151&sid=2&Fmt=3&clientId=3663&RQT=309&VName=PQD.

Landale, A. (2006). Cutting the bull: An effective business writing approach. Retrieved on March 16, 2010 from http://proquest.umi.com.library.keuka.edu/pqdweb?did=1140281141&sid=3&Fmt=3&clientId=3663&RQT=309&VName=PQD.

Langton, L. & Planty, M. (2010, December). Victims of identity theft, 2008. Washington, DC: United States Department of Justice, Office of Justice Programs, Bureau of Justice Statistics.

Langworthy, R. H. & Travis, L. F. (1994). *Policing in America: A Balance of Forces*. New York: Macmillan Publishing Company.

Lankes, T. (2011, February 9). Five percent of city students graduate ready for college. Retrieved on February 9, 2011 from http://www.democratandchronicle.com/article/20110209/NEWS01/102090348/Five-percent-city-students-graduate-ready-college?odyssey=tab|topnews|text|Home.

Lanning v. South Eastern Pennsylvania Transit Authority—SEPTA (2002). Retrieved on October 22, 2009 from http://openjurist.org/308/f3d/286/lanning-v-southeastern-pennsylvania-transportation-authority-septa.

Larson, A. (2003, August). Obtaining or expunging a criminal record. Retrieved on February 6, 2011 from http://www.expertlaw.com/library/criminal/criminal_record.html#2.

Larson, G. E., Hammer, P. S., Conway, T. L., & Schmied, E. A. (2011, January). Predeployment and in-theater diagnoses of American military personnel serving in Iraq. Retrieved on April 17, 2011 from http://proquest.umi.com.library.keuka.edu/pqdweb?did=2311271801&sid=1&Fmt=2&clientId=3663&RQT=309&VName=PQD.

LATimes.com (1987, March 18). Police officer pleads innocent to having sex with teen-ager. Retrieved on December 6, 2010 from http://articles.latimes.com/1987-03-18/news/mn-7882_1_police-officer.

LATimes.com (1988, September 8). Local news in brief: Fugitive vows to fight extradition. Retrieved on February 14, 2011 from http://articles.latimes.com/1988-09-08/local/me-2285_1_extradition-fight-fugitive.

LATimes.com (2006, September 29). Police officer held in alleged molestation. Retrieved on December 6, 2010 from http://articles.latimes.com/2006/sep/29/local/me-iebriefs29.

Laudenslager, S. (1974, August). Providing legal assistance to small and rural law enforcement agencies, part 1—The regional legal advisor. Retrieved on October 30, 2009 from http://search.ebscohost.com.library.keuka.edu/login.aspx?direct=true&db=sih&AN=SM016738&site=ehost-live.

Lautenberg Amendment (1997).

Law and Order (2000a, April). Small towns struggle to find qualified officers. *Law and Order Magazine*, *48*(4), 6.

Law and Order (2000b, December). Community police officer exam: Assessing the total person for the job. *Law and Order Magazine*, *48*(12), 125.

Law and Order (2002, March). Voice stress analysis. *Law and Order Magazine*, *50*(3), 6.

Law and Order (2003, May). Certified forensic interviewer program. *Law and Order Magazine*, *51*(5), 42–45.

Law Enforcement Officers Safety Act (2004).

Leamon, J. A. (1999, August). Screening for counterproductivity. *The Police Chief Magazine*, *66*(8), 65–73. Copyright held by the International Association of Chiefs of Police, 515 North Washington Street, Alexandria, VA 22314 USA. Further reproduction without express written permission from IACP is strictly prohibited.

Leandra's Law (*Child Passenger Protection Act*) (2009).

Lederman, D. (2006, February 10). Registrars' group takes on diploma mills. Retrieved on April 14, 2011 from http://www.insidehighered.com/news/2006/02/10/aacrao.

Lee, C. B. (2006, March/April). Psychological testing for recruit screening. Retrieved on October 13, 2009 from http://proquest.umi.com.library.keuka.edu/pqdweb?did=1028926111&sid=4&Fmt=4&clientId=3663&RQT=309&VName=PQD.

Lee, H. K. (2009, June 11). Hayward cops' 'sexual conquests' prove costly. Retrieved on October 16, 2010 from http://www.sfgate.com/cgi-bin/article.cgi?file=/c/a/2009/06/11/BAPT184CKD.DTL.

Leff, L. & Wohlsen, M. (2010, March 25). California pot vote isn't just hippies versus cops. Retrieved on March 25, 2010 from http://news.yahoo.com/s/ap/20100325/ap_on_re_us/us_marijuana_legalization.

Legalize Arizona Workers Act (2007).

Leggett v. Northwest State College (1962).

Lehman, P. (2011, February 8). Bethlehem police officer suspended without pay after gun discharge. Retrieved on February 8, 2011 from http://www.mcall.com/news/local/bethlehem/mc-bethlehem-police-gun-suspend-20110207,0,5110651.story.

Lehman, W. E. K., Farabee, D. J., Holcom, M. L., & Simpson, D. D. (1995, Spring). Predictions of substance use in the workplace: Unique contributions of personal background and work environment variables. Retrieved on January 19, 2010 from http://search.ebscohost.com.library.keuka.edu/login.aspx?direct=true&db=aph&AN=9507231152&site=ehost-live.

Leite v. Providence (1978).

Lemire, J. (2011, April 1). ACS launching programs to prevent repeat of mistakes that lead to death of Marchella Pierce. Retrieved on April 7, 2011 from http://www.nydailynews.com/ny_local/2011/04/01/2011-04-01_acs_launching_programs_to_prevent_repeat_of_mistakes_that_lead_to_death_of_march.html.

Leonard, B. (1995, December). Reference-checking laws: Now what? Retrieved on October 23, 2003 from http://0-vnweb.hwwilsonweb.com.novacat.edu/hww/results_single.jthml?nn=7.

Leonard, T. (2011, March 2). Prince Andrew risks losing ambassador job as girl in underage sex case reveals meeting him. Retrieved on April 1, 2011 from http://www.dailymail.co.uk/news/article-1361296/Prince-Andrew-risks-ambassador-job-underage-sex-case-girl-reveals-meeting-him.html.

Leonel v. American Airlines, Inc. (2005).

LePere, R. (2002, October 8). Employers must follow guidelines for gathering personal information. Retrieved on November 17, 2009 from http://proquest.umi.com.library.keuka.edu/pqdweb?did=208209481&sid=1&Fmt=3&clientId=3663&RQT=309&VName=PQD.

Lepisto, S., Astedt-Kurki, P., Joronen, K., Luukkaala, T., & Paavilainen, E. (2010, June). Adolescents' experiences of coping with domestic violence. Retrieved on October 11, 2010 from http://web.ebscohost.com.library.keuka.edu/ehost/detail?vid=20&hid=6&sid=c11a669b-e675-487a-9271-e6576c348b8e%40sessionmgr12&bdata=JnNpdGU9ZWhvc3QtbGl2ZQ%3d%3d#db=cin20&AN=2010651894.

Lesce, T. (1998, October). Developing special investigations units. *Law and Order Magazine*, *46*(10), 175–178.

Leslie, K. & Garner, M. K. (2010, November 1). Credit checks of workers debated. Retrieved on February 26, 2011 from http://proquest.umi.com.library.keuka.edu/pqdweb?did=2177400321&sid=1&Fmt=3&clientId=3663&RQT=309&VName=PQD.

Lessenger, J. E. & Feinberg, S. D. (2008, January–February). Abuse of prescription and over-the-counter medications. Retrieved on January 20, 2010 from http://search.ebscohost.com.library.keuka.edu/login.aspx?direct=true&db=cmedm&AN=18178702&site=ehost-live.

Leung, R. (2004a, November 20). Does teen sex tape show rape? A night of sex and excess, caught on tape, leads to a rape trial. Retrieved on February 11, 2011 from http://www.cbsnews.com/stories/2004/11/17/48hours/main656245.shtml.

Leung, R. (2004b, December 10). Why did Eric kill? Dan Rather talks to teen killer about why he killed a 4-year-old boy. Retrieved on February 5, 2011 from http://www.cbsnews.com/stories/2004/12/10/48hours/main660314.shtml.

Leung, S. (1996, June 20). Ex-Boston officer accused of pension fraud. Retrieved on February 20, 2011 from http://proquest.umi.com.library.keuka.edu/pqdweb?did=16205402&sid=1&Fmt=3&clientId=3663&RQT=309&VName=PQD.

Levin, A. (2008, July 22). Facebook hell of young mother after profile is hijacked and pictures posted on porn website. Retrieved on August 17, 2010 from http://www.dailymail.co.uk/news/article-1036995/Facebook-hell-young-mother-profile-hijacked-pictures-posted-porn-website.html.

Levin, A. (2009, May 14). Airline: Pilot didn't disclose failed tests. *USA Today*, 3A.

Levin, S. & Goldsmith, S. (2011, March 26). ACS workers rally to support colleagues charged with homicide in Marchella Brett-Pierce death. Retrieved on April 7, 2011 from http://articles.nydailynews.com/2011-03-26/local/29363237_1_acs-workers-commissioner-john-mattingly-case-workers.

Levine, M. (2011, June 23). Source: Reservist suspected in military shootings self-radicalized through internet. Retrieved on June 29, 2011 from http://www.foxnews.com/politics/2011/06/23/sources-reservist-suspected-in-military-shootings-self-radicalized-through/.

Levine, M. & Griffith, J. (2011, July 28). AWOL soldier arrested in what police say was new Fort Hood terror plot. Retrieved on July 30, 2011 from http://www.foxnews.com/us/2011/07/28/exclusive-us-military-serviceman-arrested-in-second-alleged-attack-on-ft-hood/.

Levy, J. (1997a, October 10). New laws protect impaired workers from discrimination. Retrieved on November 17, 2009 from http://proquest.umi.com.library.keuka.edu/pqdweb?did=23663412&sid=1&Fmt=2&clientId=3663&RQT=309&VName=PQD.

Levy, J. (1997b, December 12). Clear job description key to hiring disabled workers. Retrieved on November 17, 2009 from http://proquest.umi.com.library.keuka.edu/pqdweb?did=23663412&sid=1&Fmt=2&clientId=3663&RQT=309&VName=PQD.

Lewis, D. E. (2005a, January 9). Screen test: Companies embrace personality profiles for prospective employees. Retrieved on November 17, 2009 from http://proquest.umi.com.library.keuka.edu/pqdweb?did=777498811&sid=1&Fmt=3&clientId=3663&RQT=309&VName=PQD.

Lewis, D. E. (2005b, July 27). Drug test biased against blacks, 7 ex-officers allege. Retrieved on January 24, 2010 from http://search.ebscohost.com.library.keuka.edu/login.aspx?direct=true&db=nfh&AN=2W61055353948&site=ehost-live.

Lewis v. Equitable Life Assurance Society of the United States (1986).

Lewis v. Goodie (1992).

Lichtenstein, B. B. & Plowman, D. A. (2009, August). The leadership of emergence: A complex systems leadership theory of emergence at successive organizational levels. Retrieved on October 24, 2009 from http://proquest.umi.com.library.keuka.edu/pqdweb?did=1778409691&sid=2&Fmt=2&clientId=3663&RQT=309&VName=PQD.

Lieber, R. (2010, June 1). Placing the blame as students are buried in debt. Retrieved on June 2, 2010 from http://finance.yahoo.com/college-education/article/109701/placing-the-blame-as-students-are-buried-in-debt?mod=edu-collegeprep.

Life (2002, September 17). Alleged Lackawanna terror cell. Retrieved on February 8, 2011 from http://www.life.com/image/1392483.

Lillsunde, P. (2008, April). Analytical techniques for drug detection in oral fluid. Retrieved on January 18, 2010 from http://search.ebscohost.com.library.keuka.edu/login.aspx?direct=true&db=cmedm&AN=18367978&site=ehost-live.

Lineberry, T. W. & Bostwick, J. M. (2006, January). Methamphetamine abuse: A perfect storm of complications. Retrieved on February 9, 2010 from http://search.ebscohost.com.library.keuka.edu/login.aspx?direct=true&db=cmedm&AN=16438482&site=ehost-live.

Linskey, A. (2010, February 10). Dixon sentenced on charges of perjury and embezzlement. Retrieved on February 9, 2010 from http://www.baltimoresun.com/news/maryland/baltimore-city/bal-dixon-sentenced0204,0,3904936.story.

Liptak, A. (2006, October 17). Expunged criminal records live to tell tales. Retrieved on February 5, 2011 from http://www.nacdl.org/public.nsf/mediasources/20061017a?OpenDocument.

Liptak, A. (2010, May 17). Extended civil commitment of sex offenders is upheld. Retrieved on November 25, 2010 from http://www.nytimes.com/2010/05/18/us/politics/18offenders.html.

Lisko, R. (2011, March). Agency policies imperative to disclose Brady v. Maryland material to prosecutors. *The Police Chief Magazine*, *78*(3), 12–13.

Litchford, J. M. (1993). Employment requirements of the Americans with Disabilities Act: Application to law enforcement officers. Retrieved on November from http://search.ebscohost.com.library.keuka.edu/login.aspx?direct=true&db=sih&AN=SM144292&site=ehost-live.

Litman v. Massachusetts Mutual Life Insurance Company (1984).

Littlejohn Shinder, D. (2003, December). Understanding legal issues. *Law and Order Magazine*, *51*(12), 38–44.

Liu, C. (2010, January 27). Officers uneasy as police layoffs loom. Retrieved on February 14, 2011 from http://www.kpho.com/news/22361705/detail.html.

Livingstone, S. (2005, June 8). Fight against steroids gaining muscle in high school athletes. Retrieved on April 13, 2011 from http://www.usatoday.com/sports/preps/2005-06-08-sports-weekly-steroids-report_x.htm.

Livshits, I., MacGee, J., & Tertilt, M. (2006, March 9). Consumer bankruptcy: A fresh start. Retrieved on March 9, 2011 from http://www.stanford.edu/~tertilt/research/bankruptcy.pdf.

LoBianco, T. (2011, August 13). Lawmaker allegedly answers male sex Ad. Retrieved on August 13, 2011 from http://www.journalgazette.net/article/20110813/NEWS07/308139936.

Lodge, B. (2010, February 22). Survey: Fraud likely to rise—workplace theft a concern. Retrieved on February 22, 2011 from http://proquest.umi.com.library.keuka.edu/pqdweb?did=1968064541&sid=3&Fmt=3&clientId=3663&RQT=309&VName=PQD.

Logsdon, A. (2009). Intelligence testing—Understanding intelligence testing for children. Retrieved on October 20, 2009 from http://learningdisabilities.about.com/od/glossar1/a/intelligencetes.htm.

Lohr, D. (n.d.). Death of innocence—The murder of young Shandra Sharer. Retrieved on March 24, 2011 from http://www.trutv.com/library/crime/notorious_murders/young/shanda_sharer/1.html.

Long, C. (2007, April). I need my space. Retrieved on March 14, 2010 from http://proquest.umi.com.library.keuka.edu/pqdweb?did=1271149751&sid=1&Fmt=3&clientId=3663&RQT=309&VName=PQD.

Longin v. Kelly (1995).

Lopez, V. (1995, October 29). Officers with glasses, contacts called a risk. Retrieved on November 25, 2009 from http://proquest.umi.com.library.keuka.edu/pqdweb?did=18771782&sid=1&Fmt=3&clientId=3663&RQT=309&VName=PQD.

Lorenz, A. (2009, August 20). Former Georgetown police sergeant denied parole. Retrieved on October 18, 2010 from http://www.statesman.com/blogs/content/shared-gen/blogs/austin/williamson/entries/2009/08/20/former_georgetown_pd_sergeant.html.

Loudon, B. J. (2011, January 26). Officers may sue Ontario County Sheriff's office. Retrieved on January 26, 2011 from http://www.democratandchronicle.com/article/20110126/NEWS01/101260339/1002/NEWS.

Louisiana Department of Public Safety Office of Motor Vehicles (2011, January 1). Classes of license and age requirements. Retrieved on April 2, 2011 from http://www.dps.state.la.us/Omv1.nsf/58c968bd569b099986256cdc000806eb/f49e283fc26019e8862564ae00546c22?OpenDocument.

Louisiana Revised Statutes

Lounsberry, E. (1992, April 10). City, police candidates see eye-to-eye; vision requirements may change due to lawsuit. Retrieved on November 25, 2009 from http://proquest.umi.com.library.keuka.edu/pqdweb?did=1365996391&sid=1&Fmt=3&clientId=3663&RQT=309&VName=PQD.

Lovett, K. (2009, November 8). Evolving evidence—Social media takes on larger role in courtrooms. Retrieved on March 13, 2010 from http://infoweb.newsbank.com.library.keuka.edu/iw-search/we/InfoWeb?p_product=NewsBank&p_theme=aggregated5&p_action=doc&p_docid=12C5FE45968C1458&p_docnum=6&p_queryname=2.

Lovett, K. (2010, July 12). New York State tallies 248 DWIS under Leandra's law; arrests reported in 48 of 62 counties. Retrieved on July 18, 2010 from http://www.nydailynews.com/ny_local/2010/07/12/2010-07-12_leandra_laws_in_overdrive_state_tallies_248_dwis_with_kids_in_car.html.

Lucio, V. (2009, July 3). SAPD officer charged with sex assault: Officer Gregory Mickel charged with sex assault, oppression. Retrieved on July 3, 2009 from http://www.ksat.com/news/19945092/detail.html.

Ludwig, M. (2009, July 9). Harassment complaint is reason UTSA's chief left. Retrieved on October 9, 2009 from http://www.mysanantonio.com/news/Sexual_harassment_allegations_led_UTSA_police_chief_to_resign.html.

Lukachick, J. (2010, September 22). Family relieved that Theresa Parker's remains have been found, Sheriff says. Retrieved on December 20, 2010 from http://www.timesfreepress.com/news/2010/sep/22/walker-county-sheriff-announcing-new-information-t/?breakingnews.

Lumadue, R. (2006, July). When graduate degrees prostitute the educational process: Degrees gone wild. Retrieved on April 7, 2011 from http://web.ebscohost.com.library.keuka.edu/ehost/detail?vid=7&hid=111&sid=8b68f380-de5e-409e-8eed-e2a570345a70%40sessionmgr113&bdata=JnNpdGU9ZWhvc3QtbGl2ZQ%3d%3d#db=aph&AN=21076509.

Lundstrom, M. & Stanton, S. (2009, March 26). Child protective services CPS hiring checks policy altered applicants with criminal past now reviewed at higher level. Retrieved on October 20, 2009 from http://proquest.umi.com.library.keuka.edu/pqdweb?index=21&did=1667862021&SrchMode=1&sid=1&Fmt=3&VInst=PROD&VType=PQD&RQT=309&VName=PQD&TS=1256092216&clientId=3663.

Lush, T. & Stacy, M. (2011, January 25). 2 Slain Florida law officers add to deadly toll for January: 14 Officers slain nationwide. Retrieved on February 1, 2011 from http://www.startribune.com/nation/114480729.html.

Lutter, R. W. (2005, November 1). Counterfeit drugs. Retrieved on February 12, 2010 from http://www.fda.gov/newsevents/testimony/ucm112670.htm.

Lutz, B. J. (2010, January 29). Boy, girl charged with child porn. Retrieved on October 24, 2010 from http://www.nbcchicago.com/news/local-beat/indiana-middle-school-sexting-82949612.html.

Lyle v. Waddle (1945).

Lyman, M. D. (2002). *Criminal Investigation: The Art and Science* (3rd edn.). Upper Saddle River, NJ: Prentice-Hall, Inc.

Lynch, R. G. (1998). *The Police Manager* (5th edn.). Cincinnati, OH: Anderson Publishing Company.

Lynem, J. N. (1999, February 25). Prison term won't end ex-cop's disability pay/$27,000 a year for San Jose man's gambling addiction. Retrieved on February 8, 2011 from http://articles.sfgate.com/1999-02-25/news/17679275_1_sentence-police-officer-disability.

Lyons, B. J. (2010, October 21). Parole insider tips Albany gang. Retrieved on October 24, 2010 from http://www.timesunion.com/default/article/Parole-insider-tips-Albany-gang-716093.php.

Machado, M. (2007, July 2). Polygraph uses body changes to detect lies. Retrieved on September 13, 2010 from http://web.ebscohost.com.library.keuka.edu/ehost/detail?vid=4&hid=105&sid=322c9a61-9e8d-40c3-96a0-ada73d8258bf%40sessionmgr113&bdata=JnNpdGU9ZWhvc3QtbGl2ZQ%3d%3d#db=nfh&AN=2W62W64047608421.

MacKay, H. (2009, January 4). Before hiring, hire an industrial psychologist. Retrieved on October 21, 2009 from http://proquest.umi.com.library.keuka.edu/pqdweb?did=1622075061&sid=3&Fmt=3&clientId=3663&RQT=309&VName=PQD.

MacIntosh, J. (2007, November 19). A new 'Jihad Jane': She's marine officer. Retrieved on March 13, 2010 from http://www.nypost.com/p/news/national/item_IAbbxV7tGgSbzeKRFvGHzI.

Maclachan, M. (2010, June 24). Former prison counselor says staffer in sex abuse suit was protected. Retrieved on October 13, 2010 from http://www.capitolweekly.net/article.php?xid=yxpzbw24p41nvg#.

Maer, P. (2010, September 15). Marijuana to blame for increased drug use in 2009, government report says. Retrieved on October 9, 2010 from http://www.cbsnews.com/8301-503544_162-20016614-503544.html.

Magin, P. J., May, J., McElduff, P., & Goode, S. M. (2011, February). Occupational violence in general practice: A whole-of-practice problem. Results of a cross-sectional study. Retrieved on April 19, 2011 from http://proquest.umi.com.library.keuka.edu/pqdweb?did=2296818231&sid=2&Fmt=3&clientId=3663&RQT=309&VName=PQD.

Magura, S., Sung-Yeon, K., & Shapiro, J. L. (1995, Fall). Measuring cocaine use by hair analysis among criminally-involved youth. Retrieved on January 18, 2010 from http://search.ebscohost.com.library.keuka.edu/login.aspx?direct=true&db=sih&AN=9512191473&site=ehost-live.

Mahan v. Am-Gard, Inc. (2003).

Maheshwari, S. R. (1993, May). The systems theory of organization. Retrieved on October 24, 2009 from http://proquest.umi.com.library.keuka.edu/pqdweb?did=1072858&sid=2&Fmt=2&clientId=3663&RQT=309&VName=PQD.

Maine Revised Statute

Maine.gov (2008, September 29). Accredited and non-accredited colleges and universities. Retrieved on April 13, 2011 from http://www.maine.gov/education/highered/Non-Accredited/non-accredited.htm#DL.

Malakate, A., Andriopoulos, C., & Gotsi, M. (2007, September). Assessing job candidates' creativity: Propositions and future research directions. Retrieved on July 27, 2011 from http://proquest.umi.com.library.keuka.edu/pqdweb?did=1322453371&sid=4&Fmt=2&clientId=3663&RQT=309&VName=PQD.

Malcolm, A. (2011, June 6). Anthony Weiner admits he lied about underpants photo; Twitter erupts with jokes. Retrieved on June 6, 2011 from http://latimesblogs.latimes.com/washington/2011/06/anthony-weiner-admits-he-lied-about-underpants-photo-twitter-erupts-with-jokes.html.

Malinowski, W. Z. (2010a, March 27). Cranston police officer fired for sex on duty. Retrieved on December 6, 2010 from http://www.projo.com/news/content/CRANSTON_POLICE_SEX_03-27-10_3CHTAUK_v22.3980bdc.html.

Malinowski, W. Z. (2010b, December 3). Judge upholds firing of Cranston officer for sex on duty. Retrieved on December 6, 2010 from http://www.projo.com/news/content/COP_FIRING_UPHELD_12-03-10_JBL9125_v9.2f1aedf.html.

Malone, J. D. (2010, July 13). Retired Bethlehem police sergeant Cheryl Ruth accused of stealing $19,000 from the force. Retrieved on February 8, 2011 from http://www.lehighvalleylive.com/bethlehem/index.ssf?/base/news-2/1278993908188660.xml&coll=3.

Man, G., Stoeber, B., & Walus, K. (2009, August). An assessment of sensing technologies for the detection of clandestine methamphetamine drug laboratories. Retrieved on February 9, 2010 from http://search.ebscohost.com.library.keuka.edu/login.aspx?direct=true&db=cmedm&AN=19428203&site=ehost-live.

Mandell, N. (2010, November 22). Former teacher Jennifer Riojas freed on $20,000 bond; accused of having sex with underage student. Retrieved on January 28, 2011 from http://www.nydailynews.com/news/national/2010/11/22/2010-11-22_former_teacher_jennifer_riojas_freed_on_20000_bond_accused_of_having_sex_with_un.html.

Manderson, D. (1999, Winter). Formalism and narrative in law and medicine: The debate over medical marijuana use. Retrieved on January 28, 2010 from http://search.ebscohost.com.library.keuka.edu/login.aspx?direct=true&db=sih&AN=1805075&site=ehost-live.

Manchikanti, L. (2007, May). National drug control policy and prescription drug abuse: Facts and fallacies. Retrieved on January 20, 2010 from http://search.ebscohost.com.library.keuka.edu/login.aspx?direct=true&db=cmedm&AN=17525776&site=ehost-live.

Mandell, N. (2010, November 21). Notre Dame accused of mishandling sexual assault investigation after college freshman's suicide. Retrieved on April 1, 2011 from http://articles.nydailynews.com/2010-11-21/news/27081936_1_university-police-county-police-student.

Mangan, D. (2010, October 9). NFL to probe Brett Favre's 'sexting' to jets reporter. Retrieved on October 13, 2010 from http://www.nypost.com/p/news/local/bombshell_nfl_probe_DxJO9QtruZzNSJeQzWMXZL.

Manguso v. Oceanside Unified School District (1984).

Manis, J., Archbold, C. A., & Hassell, K. D. (2008, Winter). Exploring the impact of police officer education level on allegations of police misconduct. Retrieved on March 28, 2010 from http://search.ebscohost.com.library.keuka.edu/login.aspx?direct=true&db=aph&AN=36610398&site=ehost-live.

Manley, R. (2009, June 26). Former Telfair Sheriff gets three years in prison. Retrieved on November 1, 2010 from http://www.macon.com/2009/06/26/759893/former-telfair-sheriff-gets-three.html.

Mann, C. (2011, June 13). Wash. State inmate Kevin Newland shot dead during forklift escape attempt. Retrieved on July 12, 2011 from http://www.cbsnews.com/8301-504083_162-20075702-504083.html.

Mann, D. (2001, July 6). Jury convicts ex-officer of coercing sex. Retrieved on November 1, 2010 from http://proquest.umi.com.library.keuka.edu/pqdweb?did=75041479&sid=1&Fmt=3&clientId=3663&RQT=309&VName=PQD.

Maready, J. (2008, March 21). 19 Arrested in child porn bust: 2 Suspects are still sought in Polk Sheriff's officer undercover operation. Retrieved on January 18, 2011 from http://www.theledger.com/article/20080321/NEWS/803210372.

Marion, N. E. & Oliver, W. M. (2006). *The Public Policy of Crime and Criminal Justice*. Upper Saddle River, NJ: Pearson Education, Inc.

Marken, G. A. (2006, Spring). Losing our most precious asset. Retrieved on March 16, 2010 from http://proquest.umi.com.library.keuka.edu/pqdweb?did=1130339891&sid=3&Fmt=3&clientId=3663&RQT=309&VName=PQD.

Marquay v. Eno (1995).

Marquet, C. T. & Peterson, L. J. B. (n.d.). Resume fraud: The top 10 lies. Retrieved on March 18, 2011 from http://www.marquetinternational.com/pdf/Resume%20Fraud-Top%20Ten%20Lies.pdf.

Marquet International Ltd. (2006–2011). Resume liars club. Retrieved on March 18, 2011 from http://www.marquetinternational.com/liars.htm.

Martenegara, V. & Kleiner, B. H. (2003). Effective employment screening in the American health care industry. Retrieved on February 16, 2010 from http://proquest.umi.com.library.keuka.edu/pqdweb?did=617913821&sid=1&Fmt=4&clientId=3663&RQT=309&VName=PQD.

Martin, J. (2003, December). Electronic crimefighting. *Law and Order Magazine*, *51*(12), 52–55.

Martin, P. (2002, May). Investigating internet fraud. *Law and Order Magazine*, *50*(5), 34–37.

Martin, R. (2011, August 16). Louisiana police: Father confesses to decapitating special needs son. Retrieved on August 16, 2011 from http://www.cnn.com/2011/CRIME/08/15/louisiana.child.killing/index.html?iref=obinsite.

Martin, S. L., Gibbs, D. A., Johnson, R. E., & Sullivan, K. (2010, November). Substance use by soldiers who abuse their spouses. Retrieved on April 16, 2011 from http://proquest.umi.com.library.keuka.edu/pqdweb?did=2200996001&sid=1&Fmt=2&clientId=3663&RQT=309&VName=PQD.

Martinelli, T. & Pollock, J. (2000, October). Law enforcement ethics, lawsuits, and liability: Defusing deliberate indifference. *The Police Chief Magazine*, *67*(10), 52.

Martinez, E. (2009, December 28). Prison guard Albert James Turner on the run after murdering wife, mother, says cops. Retrieved on November 1, 2010 from http://www.cbsnews.com/8301-504083_162-5025081-504083.html.

Martinez, E. (2010a, March 10). Amy Victoria Beck, middle school teacher, taught oral sex to 14-year-old, says cops. Retrieved on October 12, 2010 from http://www.cbsnews.com/8301-504083_162-20000238-504083.html.

Martinez, E. (2011a, March 10). Seaworld Toddler rape suspect now faces federal child pornography charge. Retrieved on May 27, 2011 from http://www.cbsnews.com/8301-504083_162-20041602-504083.html.

Martinez, J. (2010b, July 7). Bronx mother nixes manslaughter plea in Leandra Rosado's DWI death. Retrieved on July 18, 2010 from http://www.nydailynews.com/news/ny_crime/2010/07/07/2010-07-07_bx_ma_nixes_plea_in_girls_dwi_death.html.

Martinez, J. (2011b, February 19). Court says probationary cop who tested positive for cocaine can't have his job back. Retrieved on February 20, 2011 from http://www.nydailynews.com/ny_local/2011/02/19/2011-02-19_probationary_cop_cant_have_job_back_.html.

Martinez, M. (2011c, June 1). 'Walmart of Weed' to open in Arizona, promote growing your own. Retrieved on June 1, 2011 from http://edition.cnn.com/2011/US/06/01/arizona.marijuana.superstore/.

Martz, M. & Kapsidelis, K. (2008, August 19). Former VCU official says she did not give in to pressure to approve Monroe degree. Retrieved on August 15, 2010 from http://www.topix.com/forum/charlotte/TUFH9JO6M24KNE0PJ.

Marshall, R. (2010, August 1). Recent child pornography cases. Retrieved on October 24, 2010 from http://www.carrollcountytimes.com/news/local/article_ed6a865a-9d16-11df-9c06-001cc4c03286.html.

Marshall v. District of Columbia Government (1977).

Martucci, W. C. & Boatright, D. B. (1995, Summer). Immunity for employment references. *Employment Relations Today*, *22*(2), 119–123.

Maryland Department of Public Safety and Correctional Services (2011). Expungements. Retrieved on February 5, 2011 from http://www.dpscs.state.md.us/publicservs/expung.shtml.

Maryland Governor's Office of Crime Control and Prevention (2008). Maryland Statistical Analysis Center (MSAC). Retrieved on October 11, 2010 from http://www.goccp.maryland.gov/msac/msac.php.

Marzulli, J. (2010a, May 14). Cop pleads guilty to stealing heroin from drug dealers at gunpoint. Retrieved on May 14, 2010 from http://www.nydailynews.com/news/ny_crime/2010/05/14/2010-05-14_drugheist_guilty_plea_by_excop.html.

Marzulli, J. (2010b, October 19). Judge: No new hires until FDNY creates new exam that does not discriminate. Retrieved on April 14, 2011 from http://articles.nydailynews.com/2010-10-19/local/27078634_1_exam-racial-quotas-black-firefighters.

Marzulli, J. & McShane, L. (2009, March 6). 'Mafia Cops' Louis Eppolito, Stephen Caracappa sentenced to life in prison. Retrieved on November 1, 2010 from http://www.nydailynews.com/news/ny_crime/2009/03/06/2009-03-06_mafia_cops_louis_eppolito_stephen_caraca.html.

Marzulli, J., Shiffrel, S., & Gendar, A. (2008, October 31). NYPD cop Jorge Arbaje-Diaz arrested on charges he was part of cocaine robbery crew. Retrieved on July 13, 2011 from http://articles.nydailynews.com/2008-10-31/news/17911117_1_nypd-cop-crooked-cop-badge-and-handcuffs.

Maslanik, M. (2011, January 21). Greece man admits to having child porn. Retrieved on February 11, 2011 from http://www.greecepost.com/latestnews/x684399231/Greece-man-admits-to-having-child-porn.

Mason, P. L. (1998). Polygraph validity with urinalysis results as ground truth. Retrieved on January 24, 2010 from http://search.ebscohost.com.library.keuka.edu/login.aspx?direct=true&db=sih&AN=SM172192&site=ehost-live.

Mason v. Stock (1994).

Massachusetts Office of Student Financial Assistance (n.d.). Quinn Bill—Police career incentive pay program. Retrieved on March 19, 2011 from http://www.osfa.mass.edu/quinnbill/default.asp.

Massad, J. (2006, September 8). A.J. to review allegations on Swart: Police department's no. 2 hired without a background check. Retrieved on October 13, 2009 from http://web.ebscohost.com.library.keuka.edu/ehost/detail?vid=13&hid=8&sid=d30bed09-3932-47cc-9ef4-6811f3bac285%40sessionmgr4&bdata=JnNpdGU9ZWhvc3QtbGl2ZQ%3d%3d#db=nfh&AN=2W62W63396021525.

Massoni, M. (2009, February). Field training programs: Understanding adult learning styles. Retrieved on October 31, 2009 from http://proquest.umi.com.library.keuka.edu/pqdweb?did=1646136901&sid=1&Fmt=3&clientId=3663&RQT=309&VName=PQD.

Mateja, J. (2004, March 26). Educating companies to reality of negligent entrustment. Retrieved on November 15, 2009 from http://search.ebscohost.com.library.keuka.edu/login.aspx?direct=true&db=nfh&AN=2W70895531591&site=ehost-live.

Matt v. Pressley (2006).

Matter of Ajami, 22 I. & N. Dec. 949, 950 (BIA 1999).

Matter of Murray v. County of Nassau Civil Service Commission (2007).

Matteucci, M. (2005, November 25). PTO program lets officers learn at their own pace. Retrieved on October 31, 2009 from http://proquest.umi.com.library.keuka.edu/pqdweb?did=987085531&sid=2&Fmt=3&clientId=3663&RQT=309&VName=PQD.

Matteucci, M. (2009, October 19). Jailed cop had history of exposing himself. Retrieved on November 1, 2010 from http://www.ajc.com/news/jailed-cop-had-history-166511.html.

Matthews, C. (2009, December 1). Facebook and MySpace purge N.Y. sex offenders. Retrieved on December 1, 2009 from http://www.democratandchronicle.com/article/20091201/NEWS01/91201013/1002/RSS01.

Matsumoto, D., Hwang, H. S., Skinner, L., & Frank, M. (2011, June). Evaluating truthfulness and detecting deception. Retrieved on July 26, 2011 from http://proquest.umi.com.library.keuka.edu/pqdweb?did=2381119131&sid=2&Fmt=3&clientId=3663&RQT=309&VName=PQD.

Maugh, T. H. (2008, October 28). Study details sex-abuse rates of deployed female soldiers; 1 in 7 asked by the VA said they had been harassed or assaulted. Retrieved on April 16, 2011 from http://proquest.umi.com.library.keuka.edu/pqdweb?did=1583796381&sid=2&Fmt=3&clientId=3663&RQT=309&VName=PQD.

Mauriello, T. P. (2003). *Criminal Investigation Handbook: Strategy, Law, and Science*. Washington, DC: LexisNexis Group.

Maxwell, J. C. & Rutkowski, B. A. (2008, May). The prevalence of methamphetamine and amphetamine abuse in North America: A review of the indicators, 1992–2007. Retrieved on February 9, 2010 from http://search.ebscohost.com.library.keuka.edu/login.aspx?direct=true&db=cmedm&AN=18368603&site=ehost-live.

Mayer, M. J. (2009, September). ADA and the hiring process. *The Police Chief Magazine*, *76*(9), 14–15.

Mayfield v. Gleichert (1969).

Mayko, M. P. (2009, June 30). Supreme Court ruling could have local impact. Retrieved on October 26, 2009 from http://proquest.umi.com.library.keuka.edu/pqdweb?did=1769368981&sid=2&Fmt=3&clientId=3663&RQT=309&VName=PQD.

Maze, R. (2007, February 20). Rise in moral waivers troubles lawmaker. Retrieved on August 7, 2011 from http://www.armytimes.com/news/2007/02/apWaivedRecruits070213/.

McBride, D. (2010, August 29). Thibodaux officer accused of raping Nicholls student. Retrieved on October 28, 2010 from http://www.houmatoday.com/article/20100829/ARTICLES/100829260.

McCabe, S. E. (2007, December). Misperceptions of non-medical prescription drug use: A web survey of college students. Retrieved on January 28, 2010 from http://search.ebscohost.com.library.keuka.edu/login.aspx?direct=true&db=cmedm&AN=18242002&site=ehost-live.

McCabe, S. E. (2008, March). Screening for drug abuse among medical and nonmedical users of prescription drugs in a probability sample of college students. Retrieved on January 20, 2010 from http://search.ebscohost.com.library.keuka.edu/login.aspx?direct=true&db=cmedm&AN=18316659&site=ehost-live.

McCabe, S. E., Cranford, J. A., & West, B. T. (2008, October). Trends in prescription drug abuse and dependence, co-occurrence with other substance disorders, and treatment utilization: Results from two national surveys. Retrieved on January 20, 2010 from http://search.ebscohost.com.library.keuka.edu/login.aspx?direct=true&db=cmedm&AN=18632211&site=ehost-live.

McCabe v. Hoberman (1969).

McCall, W. (2010, April 23). Scouts must pay man $18.5M in punitive damages. Retrieved on April 23, 2010 from http://news.yahoo.com/s/ap/20100423/ap_on_re_us/us_boy_scouts_abuse.

McCarren, A. (2011, August 19). In DC, it's an all female heist in another flash mob robbery. Retrieved on August 27, 2011 from http://www.wusa9.com/news/article/163304/77/In-DC-Its-An-All-Female-Heist-In-Another-Flash-Mob-Robbery.

McCarthy v. Philadelphia Civil Service Commission (1976).

McCartney, S. M. (2005, March). General order 200: Recruitment and selection of police officer candidates. *General Orders Manual*. Warwick, RI: Warwick Police Department.

McClain, W. E. (1978). Summary of freedom of information and privacy laws of the 50 states. Retrieved on October 24, 2009 from http://search.ebscohost.com.library.keuka.edu/login.aspx?direct=true&db=sih&AN=SM055500&site=ehost-live.

McClean v. Kirby Co. (1992).

McCleskey v. Vericon Resources, Inc. (2003).

McConnell, C. R. (2000, December). Employment references: Walking scared between the minefield of defamation and the specter of negligent hiring. Retrieved on November 8, 2009 from http://search.ebscohost.com.library.keuka.edu/login.aspx?direct=true&db=cmedm&AN=11146876&site=ehost-live.

McConnell, C. R. (2007, October/December). Exchanging honest employment references: Tiptoeing between defamation and negligent hiring. Retrieved on November 8, 2009 from http://search.ebscohost.com.library.keuka.edu/login.aspx?direct=true&db=cmedm&AN=17992111&site=ehost-live.

McCord, L. B. (1999, Spring). Defamation vs. negligent referral. Retrieved on November 4, 2003 from http://gbr.pepperdine.edu/992/referral.html.

McCrink v. City of New York (1947).

McCue, C. & McNulty, P. J. (2003, December). Drugs, guns, and violence: Data mining. *Law and Order Magazine*, *51*(12), 34–36.

McCue, C., Smith, G. L., Diehl, R. L., Dabbs, D. F., McDonough, J. J., & Ferrara, P. B. (2001, October). Why DNA databases should include all felons. *The Police Chief Magazine*, *68*(10), 94–100.

McCullagh, D. (2008, March 20). FBI posts fake hyperlinks to snare child porn suspects. Retrieved on January 18, 2011 from http://news.cnet.com/8301-13578_3-9899151-38.html.

McCullagh, D. (2009a, February 26). Judge orders defendant to decrypt PGP-protected laptop. Retrieved on March 13, 2010 from http://news.cnet.com/8301-13578_3-10172866-38.html.

McCullagh, D. (2009b, March 17). Police blotter: Facebook photo convicts school aide of drinking charge. Retrieved on March 13, 2010 from http://news.cnet.com/8301-13578_3-10197908-38.html.

McCullagh, D. (2011, June 6). Rep. Weiner admits to Twitter, Facebook sex chats. Retrieved on June 6, 2011 from http://news.cnet.com/8301-31921_3-20069452-281/rep-weiner-admits-to-twitter-facebook-sex-chats/.

McCurley, C. & Snyder, H. N. (2004, July). Victims of violent juvenile crime. Juvenile Justice Bulletin, United States Department of Justice, Office of Justice Programs, Office of Juvenile Justice and Delinquency Programs, 1–7.

McCurley Bierlien, T. (2008, May 7). Judge sentences Orange Taylor to life for Laura Dickinson's murder. Retrieved on April 1, 2011 from http://blog.mlive.com/kzgazette/2008/05/judges_sentences_orange_taylor.html.

McDermott, M. M. (2009, May 6). Greece officer faces additional charges. Retrieved on May 7, 2009 from http://www.democratandchronicle.com/article/20090506/NEWS01/905060344/1002/NEWS/Greece+officer+faces+additional+charges.

McDermott v. Hughly (1989).

McDevitt, K. (2007, October 3). Police board to bulk up rules on officer steroid use: Changes in testing, prevention to come. Retrieved on January 18, 2010 from http://search.ebscohost.com.library.keuka.edu/login.aspx?direct=true&db=nfh&AN=2W62447780188&site=ehost-live.

McDonald v. Chicago (2010).

McDonnell, K. M. & Colaprete, F. A. (2010, March). Implementation of mentoring programs for community corrections officers in the parole environment. *Law Enforcement Executive Forum*, *10*(1), 57–82.

McGlone, T. (2011, January 16). As child porn activity grows, efforts to trap offenders do too. Retrieved on April 16, 2011 from http://proquest.umi.com.library.keuka.edu/pqdweb?did=2239168731&sid=1&Fmt=3&clientId=3663&RQT=309&VName=PQD.

McGonigle, P. (2011, February 14). Talking, texting while driving could raise your insurance rates. Retrieved on February 21, 2011 from http://www.whec.com/news/stories/S1972600.shtml?cat=565.

McGovern, K. L. (2008, March). Military members posing in sexually explicit photos. Retrieved on April 15, 2011 from http://proquest.umi.com.library.keuka.edu/pqdweb?did=1484186541&sid=3&Fmt=3&clientId=3663&RQT=309&VName=PQD.

McGreevy, P. (n.d.). LAPD sex scandal; eight assigned to explorer program subject to inquiry. Retrieved on December 6, 2010 from http://www.thefreelibrary.com/LAPD+SEX+SCANDAL%3B+EIGHT+ASSIGNED+TO+EXPLORER+PROGRAM+SUBJECT+OF…-a083817719.

McGreevy, P. (2010, October 1). Schwarzenegger signs bill reducing offense for marijuana possession. Retrieved on October 2, 2010 from http://latimesblogs.latimes.com/california-politics/2010/10/schwarzenegger-signs-bill-reducing-offense-for-marijuana-possession.html.

McGregor, D. (2011, January 14). Severe addiction to gambling is St. Maarten's public secret. Retrieved on February 8, 2011 from http://www.thedailyherald.com/islands/1-islands-news/12464-severe-addiction-to-gambling-is-st-maartens-public-secret.html.

McGregor, J. (2006, March 20). Background checks that never end. Retrieved on April 14, 2011 from http://web.ebscohost.com.library.keuka.edu/ehost/detail?vid=10&hid=106&sid=a5f33deb-ddb4-41a1-bfb7-88746339cbef%40sessionmgr115&bdata=JnNpdGU9ZWhvc3QtbGl2ZQ%3d%3d#db=buh&AN=20009028.

McGregor, K. (2009, August 11). Officer accused of 'Hiding The Facts.' Retrieved on April 14, 2011 from http://web.ebscohost.com.library.keuka.edu/ehost/detail?vid=7&hid=106&sid=a5f33deb-ddb4-41a1-bfb7-88746339cbef%40sessionmgr115&bdata=JnNpdGU9ZWhvc3QtbGl2ZQ%3d%3d#db=nfh&AN=200908111005723411.

McKay, M. J. (2009, February 11). Too close to the fire. Retrieved on July 30, 2011 from http://www.cbsnews.com/stories/2002/11/20/60II/main530103.shtml.

McKenna v. Fargo (1978).

McKinney, J. B. (2004). *Effective Financial Management in Public and Nonprofit Agencies* (3rd edn.). Westport, CT: Praeger Publishers.

McLaughlin, T. (2010, October 2). Sheriff's employees' racketeering trial begins Monday. Retrieved on October 22, 2010 from http://www.nwfdailynews.com/articles/sheriff-33521-trial-employees.html.

McMartin, C. P. K. (1981). Police legal advisor: A survey of the current state of the art and an examination of the benefit of the role to policing. Retrieved on October 30, 2009 from http://search.ebscohost.com.library.keuka.edu/login.aspx?direct=true&db=sih&AN=SM079726&site=ehost-live.

McMullen, C. (2008, November 30). Resume fraud. Retrieved on February 22, 2011 from http://proquest.umi.com.library.keuka.edu/pqdweb?did=1603581871&sid=3&Fmt=3&clientId=3663&RQT=309&VName=PQD.

McNary, T. (2009, October 20). Bible college officer stripped of certification: Bible college officer has history of exposing himself. Retrieved on November 1, 2010 from http://www.cbsatlanta.com/news/21345082/detail.html.

McNiff, E. (2010a, March 11). Net posse tracked Jihad Jane for three years: Civilian monitors warn of others like Jane on the net who are more dangerous. Retrieved on March 13, 2010 from http://abcnews.go.com/TheLaw/Technology/internet-monitors-tracked-jihad-jane-years/story?id=10069484.

McNiff, E. (2010b, June 8). Woman charged with adultery to challenge New York law. Retrieved on November 24, 2010 from http://abcnews.go.com/TheLaw/woman-charged-adultery-challenge-york-law/story?id=10857437.

McQuirk v. Donnelley (2000).

Means, R. (2007, December). The greatest liability reduction tool. *Law and Order Magazine*, *55*(12), 33–34.

Medick, E. M. (1997, November 22). New officer had her sights set on becoming a cop. Retrieved on November 25, 2009 from http://proquest.umi.com.library.keuka.edu/pqdweb?did=23204254&sid=1&Fmt=3&clientId=3663&RQT=309&VName=PQD.

MedicineNet.Com (2011). Definition of DNA. Retrieved on January 18, 2011 from http://www.medterms.com/script/main/art.asp?articlekey=3090.

Med-Tox Health Services (1999). Vision screening for law enforcement officers. Retrieved on November 25, 2009 from http://www.med-tox.com/poll.html.

Meeks, B. (2005, April 26). ACLU sues federal air marshal service: Marshals not allowed to exercise free speech, suit says. Retrieved on October 24, 2009 from http://www.msnbc.msn.com/id/7591272/.

Meese, E. & Ortmeier, P. J. (2004). *Leadership, Ethics, and Policing: Challenges of the 21st Century*. Upper Saddle River, NJ: Prentice-Hall, Inc.

Megerian, C. (2010, November 9). N.J. supreme court upholds civil commitment of sex offender who was denied therapy. Retrieved on November 25, 2010 from http://www.nj.com/news/index.ssf/2010/11/nj_supreme_court_upholds_civil.html.

Melchers, K. G., Lienhardt, N., Von Aarburg, M., & Kleinmann, M. (2011). Is more structure really better? A comparison of frame-of-reference training and descriptively anchored rating scales to improve interviewers' rating quality. Retrieved on July 27, 2011 from http://proquest.umi.com.library.keuka.edu/pqdweb?did=2303934421&sid=4&Fmt=2&clientId=3663&RQT=309&VName=PQD.

Mello, J. A. (1995, October). Personality screening in employment: Balancing information gathering and the law. Retrieved on October 22, 2009 from http://search.ebscohost.com.library.keuka.edu/login.aspx?direct=true&db=buh&AN=9601122297&site=ehost-live.

Memoli, M. A. (2010, December 9). Senate convicts federal judge Thomas Porteous of corruption and perjury: Among the charges was that the Louisiana judge lied to the Senate and the FBI during his 1994 appointment process. Retrieved on December 9, 2010 from http://www.latimes.com/news/politics/la-na-porteous-impeach-20101209,0,863537.story.

Memoli, M. A. & Susman, T. (2011, June 6). Anthony Weiner admits lying about online photos. Retrieved on June 6, 2011 from http://www.latimes.com/news/politics/la-pn-anthony-weiner-news-conference-20110606,0,1077360.story.

Memon, A. & Bull, R. (1991). The cognitive interview: Its origins, empirical support, evaluation, and practices. *Journal of Community and Applied Social Psychology*, *1*, 291–307.

Mendelson, J., Flower, K., Pletcher, M. J., & Galloway, G. P. (2008, August). Addiction to prescription opioids: Characteristics of the emerging epidemic and treatment with buprenorphine. Retrieved on January 20, 2010 from http://search.ebscohost.com.library.keuka.edu/login.aspx?direct=true&db=pdh&AN=pha-16-5-435&site=ehost-live.

Mendoza, M. (2003, June 25). Police allegedly molested teens in career program. Retrieved on December 6, 2010 from http://proquest.umi.com.library.keuka.edu/pqdweb?did=352768301&sid=1&Fmt=3&clientId=3663&RQT=309&VName=PQD.

Merillat v. Michigan State University (1995).

Messenger Post Newspaper (2009, September 10). Former Canandaigua police officer charged with felony DWI. Retrieved on September 10, 2009 from http://www.whec.com/news/stories/S1130620.shtml?cat=565.

Messenger Post Newspaper (2011, February 18). Police: Clifton springs man sent explicit text messages to underage girls. Retrieved on February 19, 2011 from http://www.greecepost.com/latestnews/x449515086/Police-Clifton-Springs-man-sent-explicit-text-messages-to-underage-girls.

Messner, E. (1981, July). Reactive entitlement in elective public office: A possible precursor to political corruption. Retrieved on November 26, 2009 from http://search.ebscohost.com.library.keuka.edu/login.aspx?direct=true&db=cmedm&AN=7294257&site=ehost-live.

Meyer, J. F. & Short, C. (1998, May). Investigating computer crime. *The Police Chief Magazine*, *65*(5), 28–35.

Mgbatogu, I. (2010, November 24). Man who slammed son to pavement charged with murder. Retrieved on April 19, 2011 from http://proquest.umi.com.library.keuka.edu/pqdweb?did=2222878421&sid=2&Fmt=3&clientId=3663&RQT=309&VName=PQD.

Michel, L. (1996, December 7). Officer is 1st to quit after drug testing. Retrieved on April 15, 2011 from http://proquest.umi.com.library.keuka.edu/pqdweb?did=17120886&sid=1&Fmt=3&clientId=3663&RQT=309&VName=PQD.

Michel, L. (1997, February 22). Two officers fired for drug, alcohol abuse. Retrieved on April 15, 2011 from http://proquest.umi.com.library.keuka.edu/pqdweb?did=13995903&sid=1&Fmt=3&clientId=3663&RQT=309&VName=PQD.

Michigan Courts (2010). Offense variables for crimes involving a controlled substance. Retrieved on February 12, 2010 from http://www.courts.michigan.gov/mji/Resources/sentencing-guidelines/PRINTGRID/controlled-substance.htm.

Mid-Atlantic Personnel Assessment Consortium (MAPAC) Weblink: http://www.ipacweb.org/mapac/index.htm.

Mieczkowski, T. (1995). Hair analysis as a drug detector. Retrieved on January 18, 2010 from http://www.ncjrs.gov/txtfiles/hair.txt.

Mieczkowski, T. (1997, April). Hair assays and urinalysis results for juvenile offenders. *National Institute of Justice Research Preview*, 1–2.

Mieczkowski, T., Lersch, K. M., & Kruger, M. (2002). Police drug testing, hair analysis, and the issue of race bias. *Criminal Justice Review*, *27*(1) 124–140.

Mieczkowski, T. & Newel, R. (1993a, June). Comparing hair and urine assays for cocaine and marijuana. Retrieved on January 18, 2010 from http://search.ebscohost.com.library.keuka.edu/login.aspx?direct=true&db=aph&AN=9309292301&site=ehost-live.

Mieczkowski, T. & Newel, R. (1993b, December). An evaluation of patterns of racial bias in hair assays for cocaine: Black and white arrestees compared. *Forensic Science International*, 63(1–3), 85–98.

Mieczkowski, T., Newel, R., & Wraight, B. (1998). Using hair analysis, urinalysis, and self-reports to estimate drug use in a sample of detained juveniles. *Substance Use and Misuse*, *33*(7), 1547–1567.

Mikkelsen, D. (2010, May 6). 4 Craigslist murder suspects behind bars. Retrieved on September 5, 2010 from http://www.king5.com/news/local/4th-Craigslist-murder-suspect-believed-to-be-in-the-area-92993619.html.

Milakovich, M. E. & Gordon, G. E. (2007). *Public Administration in America* (9th edn.). Belmont, CA: Thomson Wadsworth.

Miles, K. A. (2008, November 11). Restaurant's alcohol license yanked over Facebook pictures. Retrieved on March 13, 2010 from http://www.ajc.com/metro/content/metro/cobb/stories/2008/11/11/restaurant_alcohol_facebook.html.

Military.com (2011). USERRA overview. Retrieved on April 18, 2011 from http://www.military.com/benefits/legal-matters/userra/overview.

Millar, E. (2007, May 11). Vancouver University worldwide ordered to stop granting degrees: Raises questions about monitoring online universities. Retrieved on April 13, 2011 from http://www.macleans.ca/education/universities/article.jsp?content=20070511_131123_12988.

Miller, B. (2000, March 15). Applicants to file lawsuit over polygraph exams. Retrieved on October 13, 2009 from http://proquest.umi.com.library.keuka.edu/pqdweb?index=12&did=51044899&SrchMode=1&sid=4&Fmt=3&VInst=PROD&VType=PQD&RQT=309&VName=PQD&TS=1255437023&clientId=3663.

Miller, I. (2007, January). Drug test critics urge caution: Statistical probability of false positive finding demands follow-ups. Retrieved on January 24, 2010 from http://search.ebscohost.com.library.keuka.edu/login.aspx?direct=true&db=nfh&AN=2W62W6996888178&site=ehost-live.

Miller, C. & Barrett, G. V. (2008, Fall). The coachability and fakability of personality-based selection tests used for police selection. Retrieved on October 8, 2009 from http://www.entrepreneur.com/tradejournals/article/184643620.html.

Miller, G. D. & Fenton, J. W. (1991, March). Negligent hiring and criminal record information: A muddled area of employment law. *Labor Law Journal*, 186–192.

Miller, H. (2010, December 17). SMPD officer sentenced. Retrieved on February 8, 2011 from http://www.iberianet.com/articles/2010/12/17/news/doc4d0bee19314dc689248315.txt.

Miller, L. S. & Hess, K. M. (1994). *Community Policing: Theory and Practice*. St. Paul, MN: West Publishing Company.

Miller, J. (2008a, March 1). Police scandal grows to include possible misuse of money. Retrieved on November 1, 2010 from http://www.nytimes.com/2008/03/01/nyregion/01cops.html.

Miller, J. & Lehr, D. (2007, December). Writing tips to avoid career disaster. Retrieved on March 16, 2010 from http://proquest.umi.com.library.keuka.edu/pqdweb?did=1412701181&sid=3&Fmt=3&clientId=3663&RQT=309&VName=PQD.

Miller, T. (2008b, June 11). Monrovia police officer accused of sexual harassment. Retrieved on December 6, 2010 from http://beaconmedianews.com/2008/06/11/monrovia-police-officer-accused-of-sexual-harassment/.

Miller v. City of Springfield (1999).

Miller v. Pancucci (1992).

Millhorn, M., Monaghan, M., Montero, D., Reyes, M., Roman, T., Tollasken, R., & Walls, B. (2009, March). North Americans' attitudes toward illegal drugs. Retrieved on January 28, 2010 from http://search.ebscohost.com.library.keuka.edu/login.aspx?direct=true&db=sih&AN=37185893&site=ehost-live.

Milligan-Jensen v. Michigan Technological University (1992).

Mills, R. (2007, January 3). Police: Sheriff's cadet involved in gruesome beating. Retrieved on November 21, 2009 from http://search.ebscohost.com.library.keuka.edu/login.aspx?direct=true&db=nfh&AN=2W62W61212469654&site=ehost-live.

Mills, W. (2010, August 10). Two men accused of robbing and assaulting a police tipster appeared in court. Retrieved on September 5, 2010 from http://rochester.ynn.com/content/top_stories/513695/two-men-accused-of-robbing-and-assaulting-a-police-tipster-appeared-in-court/.

Mills-Senn, P. (2007, April). Weeding out bad seeds. Retrieved on October 13, 2009 from http://proquest.umi.com.library.keuka.edu/pqdweb?index=1&did=1295821761&SrchMode=1&sid=4&Fmt=4&VInst=PROD&VType=PQD&RQT=309&VName=PQD&TS=1255437023&clientId=3663.

Minnesota Judicial Branch Self Help Center (n.d.). Basics on criminal expungement. Retrieved on February 6, 2011 from http://www.mncourts.gov/selfhelp/?page=328.

Miranda v. Arizona (1966).

Missouri General Assembly (2009, August 28). Missouri revised statutes: Chapter 211 Juvenile courts Section 211.425. Retrieved on October 13, 2010 from http://www.moga.mo.gov/statutes/C200-299/2110000425.HTM.

Missouri Peace Officer Standards and Training (2009). Peace officer standards and training. Retrieved on October 20, 2009 from http://governor.mo.gov/boards/show/POST.

Missouri State Highway Patrol (2007a). Automated fingerprint identification system. Retrieved on September 21, 2010 from http://www.mshp.dps.mo.gov/MSHPWeb/PatrolDivisions/CRID/afisHistory.html.

Missouri State Highway Patrol (2007b). Missouri volunteer and employee criminal history service (vechs) program. Retrieved on September 21, 2010 from http://www.mshp.dps.mo.gov/MSHPWeb/PatrolDivisions/CRID/MoVECHSProgram.html.

Missouri State Highway Patrol Human Resources Division (2009). Trooper selection process description. Retrieved on October 21, 2009 from http://www.mshp.dps.mo.gov/MSHPWeb/PatrolDivisions/HRD/Trooper/selectionDesc.html.

Monell v. New York City Department of Social Services (1978).

Money Laundering Act (1986).

Monroe v. Pape (1961).

MonroeRising.com (2010, March 31). WWBBD? Retrieved on November 1, 2010 from http://monroerising.com/page/29/.

Montagna, M., Stramesi, C., Vignali, C., Groppi, A., & Polettini, A. (2000, January 10). Simultaneous hair testing for opiates, cocaine, and metabolytes by GC-MS: A survey of applicants for driving licenses with a history of drug use. Retrieved on January 18, 2010 from http://search.ebscohost.com.library.keuka.edu/login.aspx?Direct=true&db=cmedm&AN=10689569&site=ehost-live.

Montaldo, C. (2007, June 16). Ashley Reeves sees attacker sentenced. Retrieved on March 24, 2011 from http://crime.about.com/b/2007/06/16/ashley-reeves-sees-attacker-sentenced.htm.

Mook, J. R. (2002, Winter). Supreme Court does not allow disabled workers to place themselves in Harm's way. Retrieved on November 25, 2009 from http://proquest.umi.com.library.keuka.edu/pqdweb?did=275383201&sid=4&Fmt=3&clientId=3663&RQT=309&VName=PQD.

Moon v. Winfield (1974).

Mooney, T. (2010, March 5). 3 Providence officers arrested in drug sting. Retrieved on March 21, 2010 from http://www.projo.com/news/content/cops_busted_03-05-10_0AHLT3O_v20.3cf8038.html.

Moore and Associates v. Metropolitan Insurance Company (1980).

Moore, A. (2011, August 17). Man who allegedly cut officer faces attempted murder charges. Retrieved on August 18, 2011 from http://www.cbs8.com/story/15286652/man-who-allegedly-cut-officer-faces-attempted-murder-charges.

Moore, L. R. (2005, May). *Common Sense Police Supervision: Practical Tips for the First-Line Leader* (3rd. edn.) by Gerald W. Garner. Retrieved on October 25, 2009 from http://proquest.umi.com.library.keuka.edu/pqdweb?did=845913341&sid=2&Fmt=3&clientId=3663&RQT=309&VName=PQD.

Moore, M. G. (2009, October/December). A sad reminder that diploma mills are still with us. Retrieved on April 7, 2011 from http://web.ebscohost.com.library.keuka.edu/ehost/detail?vid=7&hid=111&sid=8b68f380-de5e-409e-8eed-e2a570345a70%40sessionmgr113&bdata=JnNpdGU9ZWhvc3QtbGl2ZQ%3d%3d#db=aph&AN=45542512.

Moore, M. H. & Stephens, D. W. (1991). *Beyond Command and Control: The Strategic Management of Police Departments*. Washington, DC: Police Executive Research Forum.

Moorhead, M. (2008, December 13). Drug deal deputy gets prison; a judge sentences former Sheriff's deputy Don Riggans to two years on federal drug charges. Retrieved on October 31, 2009 from http://proquest.umi.com.library.keuka.edu/pqdweb?did=1612475511&sid=1&Fmt=3&cl ientId=3663&RQT=309&VName=PQD.

Morgan, L. (2005, September 23). Steroid probe ensnarls prisons: Five corrections officers are charged as the investigation widens into some of the state's highest ranking prison officials. Retrieved on March 19, 2011 from http://www.sptimes.com/2005/09/23/State/Steroid_probe_ensnarl.shtml.

Moran, G. (2000, December 24). Database to let attorneys see conduct of officers. Retrieved on July 17, 2011 from http://faculty.law.lsu.edu/ccorcos/lawctr/sandiegopaper.htm.

Morgan, W. (2010, August 23). Weighing threats and rules of engagement in Afghanistan. Retrieved on April 16, 2011 from http://atwar.blogs.nytimes.com/2010/08/23/weighing-threats-and-rules-of-engagement-in-afghanistan/.

Morrell, A. (2004, September 16). Deputy faces child porn charges. *Democrat and Chronicle*.

Morlin, B. (2006, March 10). Fake diplomas sold globally: Operation based in Spokane made $4.7 million, Feds say. Retrieved on March 10, 2006 from http://www.hep.uiuc.edu/home/g-gollin/pigeons/morlin_spokesman_review_2006_03_13.htm.

Morris, K. (2008, June 2). Don't forget the background check. Retrieved on February 15, 2010 from http://proquest.umi.com.library.keuka.edu/pqdweb?did=1498067501&sid=1&Fmt=2&clientId=3663&RQT=309&VName=PQD.

Moskowitz, E. (2010, March 6). Sexting probed as child porn: Nude photo of girl reportedly sent. Retrieved on October 24, 2010 from http://www.boston.com/news/local/massachusetts/articles/2010/03/06/sexting_probed_as_child_porn/.

Moyer, M. & Dunphy, M. (2007, November). The candidate. Retrieved on November 21, 2009 from http://proquest.umi.com.library.keuka.edu/pqdweb?did=1389212841&sid=1&Fmt=4&clientId=3663&RQT=309&VName=PQD.

MSNBC.com (2008, February 5). Q&A: Impact of steroids on young athletes. Retrieved on April 13, 2011 from http://www.msnbc.msn.com/id/22994497/ns/health-kids_and_parenting/.

MSNBC.com (2009, April 22). Craigslist murder suspect held without bail. Retrieved on September 5, 2010 from http://www.msnbc.msn.com/id/30314735/.

MSNBC.com (2011, August 17). Expelled teen charged in plot to bomb school: He wanted 'more casualties than were suffered at Columbine,' Tampa police chief says. Retrieved on August 18, 2011 from http://www.msnbc.msn.com/id/44175557/ns/us_news-crime_and_courts/.

Mueller by Math v. Community Consolidated School District 54 (1989).

Muir, D. & Hopper, J. (2010, July 26). Who is Pvt. Bradley Manning? Retrieved on October 24, 2010 from http://abcnews.go.com/WN/wikileaks-case-pvt-bradley-manningss-alleged-role-leaking/story?id=11254454.

Mulick, S. (2006, August 31). Officer charged with assault against wife. Retrieved on April 19, 2011 from http://proquest.umi.com.library.keuka.edu/pqdweb?did=1116689841&sid=1&Fmt=3&clientId=3663&RQT=309&VName=PQD.

Mulkeen, D. (2008). Effective written communication: The foreign and commonwealth office approach. Retrieved on March 16, 2010 from http://proquest.umi.com.library.keuka.edu/pqdweb?did=1456934231&sid=3&Fmt=3&clientId=3663&RQT=309&VName=PQD.

Mullen v. County of Suffolk (2007).

Mulligan, J. E. (1995, December 15). Relatives of crash victim seek open pilot records. Retrieved on April 26, 2011 from http://proquest.umi.com.library.keuka.edu/pqdweb?did=31834999&sid=1&Fmt=3&clientId=3663&RQT=309&VName=PQD.

Mulvihill, G. (2010, March 12). Sharif Mobley, alleged NJ Al Qaeda terrorist, worked at five nuclear power plants before arrest. Retrieved on March 13, 2010 from http://www.huffingtonpost.com/2010/03/12/sharif-mobley-alleged-nj_n_496590.html.

Munsey, C. (2002, April 22). Ecstasy test sinks after flood of false positives. Retrieved on January 24, 2010 from http://search.ebscohost.com.library.keuka.edu/login.aspx?direct=true&db=mth&AN=6521581&site=ehost-live.

Muraskin, R. & Roberts, A. R. (2009). *Visions for Change: Crime and Justice in the Twenty-First Century* (5th edn.). Boston, MA: Pearson Education, Inc.

Murdock v. Dinsmoor (1989).

Murphy v. United Parcel Service, Inc. (1999).

Murphy, B. S. & Barlow, W. E. (1994, December). Negligent drug testing may lead to liability. Retrieved on January 24, 2010 from http://search.ebscohost.com.library.keuka.edu/login.aspx?direct=true&db=buh&AN=9412210756&site=ehost-live.

Murphy, J. (2006, January 24). Judgment in Jersey: High drama, big crowd: A top NYPD official gets hauled into traffic court across the river. Retrieved on October 29, 2010 from http://www.villagevoice.com/2006-01-24/news/judgment-in-jersey/.

Murray, B. T. (2009, October 13). FBI charges port authority police officer from NJ with fraud scheme. Retrieved on January 19, 2011 from http://www.nj.com/news/index.ssf/2009/10/fbi_charges_port_authority_pol.html.

Murray, S. & Light, J. (2010, November 26). Rebuilding lives after bankruptcy. Retrieved on February 25, 2011 from http://online.wsj.com/article/SB10001424052748703957804575602742718377682.html.

Mursch, B. (2008, July 31). Corrections officer charged in criminal sexual conduct case. Retrieved on November 3, 2010 from http://www.wistv.com/global/story.asp?s=8767873.

Mustian, J. (2010, April 23). Brookins guilty. Retrieved on September 20, 2010 from http://www.oaoa.com/news/brookins-46222-class-bodytext.html.

MyAddiction.com (2011). Gambling addiction statistics and facts. Retrieved on February 13, 2011 from http://www.myaddiction.com/education/articles/gambling_statistics.html.

MyFoxBoston.com (2011, May 26). K-9 officer starved dog to death. Retrieved on June 5, 2011 from http://www.myfoxboston.com/dpp/news/local/k-9-officer-starved-dog-to-death-20110524.

MyFoxOrlando.com (2009, June 4). Altamonte cop resigns. Retrieved on November 1, 2010 from http://www.myfoxorlando.com/dpp/news/seminole_news/060409maupin_resigns.

MySanAntonio.com (2007, August 30). Ex-S.A. cop guilty in sexual assault. Retrieved on October 18, 2010 from http://www.mysanantonio.com/news/MYSA083106_01A_cop_trial_verdict_309584c_html1035.html?showFullArticle=y.

Nadeau v. County of Ramsey (1979).

Nagle, M. (2008, May 19). Brief: Former Jax police sergeant seeking disability pay: Kelly Surratt claims post traumatic stress disorder caused his problems with alcohol. Retrieved on February 20, 2011 from http://web.ebscohost.com.library.keuka.edu/ehost/detail?hid=7&sid=ad66db90-f8fb-43a0-b3a0-a26957b3a8c0%40sessionmgr104&vid=6&bdata=JnNpdGU9ZWhvc3QtbGl2ZQ%3d%3d#db=nfh&AN=2W62W64115172281.

Nakashima, E. (2008, January 16). In child porn case, a digital dilemma: U.S. seeks to force suspect to reveal password to computer files. Retrieved on January 18, 2011 from http://www.washingtonpost.com/wp-dyn/content/article/2008/01/15/AR2008011503663.html.

Namuo, C. (2010, February 25). Man charged with having sex with teen, prostitution. Retrieved on October 22, 2010 from http://www.unionleader.com/article.aspx?headline=Man+charged+with+having+sex+with+teen%2C+prostitution&articleId=538ae32e-2d72-426a-a5af-47ae7fd98b03.

Napier, M. R. (2002, November). Criminal confessions: Overcoming the challenges—Interview and interrogation techniques. Retrieved on April 11, 2010 from http://findarticles.com/p/articles/mi_m2194/is_11_71/ai_94873351/.

Narramore, R. E. & Stephen, E. (1998, May). Hire smart: Develop a hiring strategy. *Law and Order Magazine*, *46*(5), 53–54.

NASA v. Nelson (2011).

NassauCountyNY.gov (2008, November 18). Prison guard convicted of rape, kidnapping, and robbery charges: Walters used his work-issued gun to rob women, force them into sexual acts. Retrieved on November 1, 2010 from http://www.nassaucountyny.gov/agencies/da/newsreleases/2008/111808walters.html.

NassauCountyNY.gov (2010, July 16). DA rice: BethPage pediatrician accused of videotaping naked young girls under guise of 'Medical Exams' punn videotaped female patients as young as 11-years-old. Retrieved on October 24, 2010 from http://www.nassaucountyny.gov/agencies/DA/NewsReleases/2010/071610punn.htm.

Nathan, A. J. (2000). At the intersection of domestic violence and guns: The public interest exception and the Lautenberg amendment. Retrieved on April 16, 2011 from http://web.ebscohost.com.library.keuka.edu/ehost/detail?vid=8&hid=111&sid=b3f5dc62-a935-427d-9ab9-e87305912346%40sessionmgr110&bdata=JnNpdGU9ZWhvc3QtbGl2ZQ%3d%3d#db=sih&AN=SN008942.

National Archive of Criminal Justice Data (n.d.). National crime victimization survey (NCVS) series. Retrieved on October 8, 2010 from http://www.icpsr.umich.edu/cocoon/NACJD/SERIES/00095.xml.

National Archives (2010, October). Instruction sheet for SF 180, request pertaining to military records. Retrieved on April 15, 2011 from http://www.archives.gov/research/order/standard-form-180.pdf.

National Archives (n.d.a). National personnel records center, St. Louis—Military personnel records. Retrieved on April 15, 2011 from http://www.archives.gov/st-louis/military-personnel/index.html.

National Archives (n.d.b). Veterans' service records—Start your military service record request. Retrieved on April 15, 2011 from http://www.archives.gov/veterans/military-service-records/.

National Association of Professional Background Screeners (NAPBS) (2011). Accreditation. Retrieved on August 2, 2011 from http://www.napbs.com/i4a/pages/index.cfm?pageid=3296.

National Association of Professional Background Screeners (NAPBS). Weblink: http://www.napbs.com/i4a/pages/index.cfm?pageid=1.

National Center for Children Exposed to Chronic Violence (2006, March 20). School violence. Retrieved on March 19, 2011 from http://www.nccev.org/violence/school.html.

National Center for Chronic Disease Prevention and Health Promotion (2010, June 3). Healthy youth! Health topics: Alcohol and drug use. Retrieved on March 19, 2011 from http://www.cdc.gov/HealthyYouth/alcoholdrug/index.htm.

National Center for Victims of Crime (2004, January). *Stalking*. Washington, DC: United States Department of Justice Office of Community Oriented Policing Services.

National Center on Shaken Baby Syndrome (n.d.). All about SBS/AHT. Retrieved on March 24, 2011 from http://www.dontshake.org/sbs.php?topNavID=3&subNavID=317.

National Child Abuse Protection Act of 1993 (1993, December 20). Retrieved on August 18, 2010 from http://www.ojjdp.ncjrs.gov/pubs/guidelines/appen-a.html.

National Counterterrorism Center (2010, February 1). About the national counterterrorism center. Retrieved on October 11, 2010 from http://www.nctc.gov/about_us/about_nctc.html.

National Criminal Justice Resource Center (2001, March). Executive summary—Juveniles who have sexually offended. Retrieved on October 13, 2010 from http://www.ncjrs.gov/html/ojjdp/report_juvsex_offend/sum.html.

National Drug Intelligence Center (2005, February). National drug threat assessment 2005: Steroids. Retrieved on April 13, 2011 from http://www.justice.gov/ndic/pubs11/12620/steroids.htm.

National Drug Intelligence Center and the Sexual Assault Services Office of George Mason University (2003, May). *Drug Facilitated Sexual Assault Resource Guide*. Johnstown, PA: Authors.

National Firearms Act (1934).

National Institute of Health (n.d.a). The economic costs of alcohol and drug abuse in the United States—1992. Retrieved on November 25, 2009 from http://www.drugabuse.gov/EconomicCosts/Chapter1.html#1.2.

National Institute of Health (n.d.b). The economic costs of alcohol and drug abuse in the united states—1992. Retrieved on November 25, 2009 from http://www.drugabuse.gov/EconomicCosts/Chapter5a.html#5.3.

National Insurance Crime Bureau (2011). About NICB. Retrieved on January 19, 2011 from https://www.nicb.org/about-nicb.

National Methamphetamine Training and Technical Assistance Center. (2009). Meth surpasses cocaine use as top drug in Mississippi. Retrieved on January 25, 2010 from http://www.nationalmethcenter.org/.

National Prohibition Act (1920).

National Registry of Workers Compensation Specialists (n.d.a). Reducing the risk of workers compensation claims begins with the hiring process. Retrieved on March 12, 2011 from http://www.nrwcs.com/hiring-process.

National Registry of Workers Compensation Specialists (n.d.b). Use pre-employment screening to cut workers' compensation losses. Retrieved on March 12, 2011 from http://www.nrwcs.com/pre-employment-screening.

National Treasury Employees Union v. Von Raab (1989).

National White Collar Crime Center (NW3C) (2011). Welcome. Retrieved on January 25, 2010 from http://www.nw3c.org/.

Navaretta v. Group Health, Inc. (1993).

Nazir v. United Airlines, Inc. (2009).

NBCNewYork.com (2010, August 5). Judge blocks FDNY hiring, rules "biased" test invalid. Retrieved on April 14, 2011 from http://www.nbcnewyork.com/news/local/Judge-Blocks-FDNY-Hiring-Rules-Test-Biased-Against-Blacks-Hispanics-100017859.html.

NBC-2.com (2006a, May 24). Decorated officers accused of having fake degrees. Retrieved on April 14, 2011 from http://www.nbc-2.com/story/10680855/decorated-officers-accused-of-having-fake-degrees.

NBC-2.com (2006b, July 17). Police officers fired over fake degrees. Retrieved on April 14, 2011 from http://www.nbc-2.com/story/10681541/police-officers-fired-over-fake-degrees.

Nebehay, S. (2011, February 11). Alcohol kills more than AIDS, TB or violence: Drinking causes more than 4 percent of deaths worldwide, WHO warns. Retrieved on February 13, 2011 from http://www.msnbc.msn.com/id/41529757/ns/health-addictions/.

Nebraska Code (2010). Chapter 28-crimes and punishment. Retrieved on February 12, 2010 from http://law.justia.com/nebraska/codes/s28index/s2804016000.html.

Neiwert, D. (2010, May 21). Two more police officers killed, two wounded in shootouts with apparent white supremacists. Retrieved on December 6, 2010 from http://crooksandliars.com/david-neiwert/two-more-police-officers-killed-two.

Nelson, J. (2010, December 10). Elizabeth smart's kidnapper found guilty in Utah. Retrieved on December 11, 2010 from http://www.reuters.com/article/idUSTRE6B94EG20101210.

Nelson, K. R. (1999, October). To select the best: A survey of selecting police officer applicants. *Law and Order Magazine*, *47*(10), 42–45.

Nelson, K. R. (2000, May). A tale of two cities: A comparison of background investigations. *Law and Order Magazine*, *48*(5), 85–88.

Neumerski v. Califano (1981).

Nevada Commission on Peace Officers' Standards and Training (2009). Nevada commission on peace officers' standards and training. Retrieved on October 20, 2009 from http://post.state.nv.us/.

New Hampshire Department of Safety Division of State Police (2010a). Support services bureau criminal records unit. Retrieved on September 7, 2010 from http://www.nh.gov/safety/divisions/nhsp/ssb/crimrecords/.

New Hampshire Department of Safety Division of State Police (2010b). Support services bureau recruitment and training unit probationary trooper recruitment. Retrieved on February 12, 2010 from http://www.nh.gov/safety/divisions/nhsp/ssb/recruitment/disquilifierexamples.html#p.

New York Fingerprinting Service (2008–2009). New York fingerprinting service. Retrieved on September 7, 2010 from http://www.newyorkfingerprinting.com/.

New York State Assembly. (n.d.). Brodsky seeks tougher sexual predators law: Civil commitment statute must be accompanied by restrictions on plea bargaining. Retrieved on October 13, 2010 from http://assembly.state.ny.us/member_files/092/20060209/.

New York State Civil Practice Law and Rules

New York State Civil Rights Law

New York State Civil Service Law

New York State Correction Law

New York State Criminal Procedure Law

New York State Department of Civil Servic (2006). *Understanding the Appointment Process for Police Officers*. Albany, NY: Author.

New York State Department of Motor Vehicles (2011a). Alcohol and drug violations. Retrieved on February 21, 2011 from http://www.nydmv.state.ny.us/alcohol-drug.htm.

New York State Department of Motor Vehicles (2011b). Driver license, learner permit, and non-driver photo ID card. Retrieved on April 2, 2011 from http://www.nydmv.state.ny.us/license.htm.

New York State Department of State (2009). Freedom of Information Law: Public Officers Law, article 6. Retrieved on July 7, 2009 from http://www.dos.state.ny.us/coog/foil2.html.

New York State Department of Taxation and Finance. Retrieved from http://www.tax.state.ny.us.

New York State Division of Criminal Justice Service (2010, May 24). DCJS honored for crime analysis center initiative. Retrieved on October 11, 2010 from http://criminaljustice.state.ny.us/pio/press_releases/2010-5-24_pressrelease.html.

New York State Division of Criminal Justice Services Bureau for Municipal Police (1991). *Basic Criminal Investigations Trainer's Manual*. Albany, NY: Author.

New York State Division of Criminal Justice Services Office of Public Safety (2002, January). *New York State Law Enforcement Accreditation Program Standards and Compliance Verification Manual*. Albany, NY: Author.

New York State Division of Criminal Justice Services Office of Public Safety (2010). History. Retrieved on February 13, 2010 from http://criminaljustice.state.ny.us/ops/accred/accred01.htm.

New York State Division of Human Rights (2007). Mission statement. Retrieved on November 7, 2009 from http://www.dhr.state.ny.us/mission.html.

New York State Division of State Police (2010). Pistol permits FAQs. Retrieved on September 22, 2010 from http://www.troopers.state.ny.us/faqs/Firearms/Permits.cfm.

New York State Education Law

New York State Family Court Act

New York State Human Rights Law

New York State Mental Hygiene Law

New York State Office of Mental Health (2009, January 5). Mental Hygiene Law—Admissions process. Retrieved on October 10, 2010 from http://www.omh.state.ny.us/omhweb/forensic/manual/html/mhl_admissions.htm.

New York State Penal Law

New York State Senate (2003). AO4690 summary. Retrieved on March 31, 2009 from http://assembly.state.ny.us/leg/?bn=A04690.

New York Times (1995, March 23). Inmate beats ex-trooper who faked prints. Retrieved on October 13, 2010 from http://web.ebscohost.com.library.keuka.edu/ehost/detail?vid=4&hid=110&sid=d99a6295-52d3-4c51-bbf2-3ca063d85b4a%40sessionmgr104&bdata=JnNpdGU9ZWhvc3QtbGl2ZQ%3d%3d#db=nfh&AN=29460559.

New York Times (1999, July 1). Officer is convicted of income tax fraud. Retrieved on February 20, 2011 from http://web.ebscohost.com.library.keuka.edu/ehost/detail?hid=119&sid=ad66db90-f8fb-43a0-b3a0-a26957b3a8c0%40sessionmgr104&vid=7&bdata=JnNpdGU9ZWhvc3QtbGl2ZQ%3d%3d#db=nfh&AN=29694463.

New York Times (2010, May 10). Bernard B. Kerik. Retrieved on April 16, 2011 from http://topics.nytimes.com/top/reference/timestopics/people/k/bernard_b_kerik/index.html.

New York Times (2011, February 11). Marijuana and medical Marijuana. Retrieved on June 1, 2011 from http://topics.nytimes.com/top/reference/timestopics/subjects/m/marijuana/index.html.

Newall, M. (2011, August 10). Three students surrender in old city mob attack. Retrieved on August 13, 2011 from http://www.philly.com/philly/news/breaking/20110810_Two_students_in_Old_City_mob_attack_surrender.html.

Newbern, A. E. (2000, October). Good cop, bad cop: Federal prosecution of state-legalized medical marijuana use after United States v. Lopez. Retrieved on January 28, 2010 from http://search.ebscohost.com.library.keuka.edu/login.aspx?direct=true&db=cmedm&AN=11475489&site=ehost-live.

Newbold, M. (2001, May). Officer liability for failure to disclose exculpatory evidence. *The Police Chief Magazine*, *68*(5), 10–13.

Newburn, T. & Webb, B. (1999). Understanding and preventing police corruption: Lessons from the literature. Retrieved on November 26, 2009 from http://search.ebscohost.com.library.keuka.edu/login.aspx?direct=true&db=sih&AN=SM180370&site=ehost-live.

Newman, G. R. (2003). *Check and Card Fraud*. Washington, DC: United States Department of Justice Office of Community Oriented Policing Services.

NewsAdvance.com (2009, October 27). Five Virginia correctional officers charged in dog fondling. Retrieved on November 1, 2010 from http://www2.newsadvance.com/news/2009/oct/27/five_virginia_correctional_officers_charged_in_dog-ar-207160/.

NewsChannel5.com (2010). Indictments released on Jackson County Sheriff's sex scandal. Retrieved on September 5, 2010 from http://www.newschannel5.com/Global/story.asp?S=6726896.

Nicholson, K. (2010, October 19). Denver police officer arrested as sex assault suspect. Retrieved on November 1, 2010 from http://www.denverpost.com/commented/ci_16377856?source=commented.

Nielsen, J. (2010, January 1). Accusations fly in feud involving lawmen, porn charges. Retrieved on April 19, 2011 from http://proquest.umi.com.library.keuka.edu/pqdweb?did=1931009851&sid=1&Fmt=3&clientId=3663&RQT=309&VName=PQD.

Nilsson v. City of Mesa (2007).

Nisperos, N. (2008, July 1). Chino officer placed on leave. Retrieved on October 31, 2009 from http://proquest.umi.com.library.keuka.edu/pqdweb?did=1503786771&sid=1&Fmt=3&cl ientId=3663&RQT=309&VName=PQD.

Nitz, A. (2009, July/August). Employee eligibility verification changes. Retrieved on March 16, 2010 from http://proquest.umi.com.library.keuka.edu/pqdweb?did=1807103511&sid=1&Fmt=2&clientId=3663&RQT=309&VName=PQD.

Nocera, K., Gendar, A., & McShane, L. (2009, September 19). Rogue cop likely to testify in Slay John Gotti Jr. ordered: DA Morgenthau's driver swears not a rat. Retrieved on April 22, 2010 from http://www.nydailynews.com/news/ny_crime/2009/09/19/2009-09-19_rogue_may_seal_jrs_fate_cop_likely_to_testify_he_was_driver_in_slay_gotti_ordere.html.

Nolan, J. (2010, May 28). Final witness says she had sex with chief master sergeant and his wife. Retrieved on January 25, 2011 from http://www.springfieldnewssun.com/news/crime/final-witness-says-she-had-sex-with-chief-master-sergeant-and-his-wife-734234.html.

Nolan v. Police Commissioner of Boston (1981).

Nolin, R. (2010, September 14). 911 Abuse can land callers in trouble frivolous calls waste dispatchers' time; special teams' performance all over spectrum v. OU. Retrieved on April 30, 2011 from http://proquest.umi.com.library.keuka.edu/pqdweb?did=2137982961&sid=1&Fmt=3&clientId=3663&RQT=309&VName=PQD.

Norman-Bloodsaw v. Lawrence Berkeley Laboratory (1998).

North Carolina Department of Crime Control and Public Safety (2009, June 18). The North Carolina criminal justice analysis center. Retrieved on October 11, 2010 from http://www.nccrimecon trol.org/Index2.cfm?a=000003,000011,000642.

North Carolina General Statutes

NorthCountryGazette.org (2007, March 16). Schenectady cop arrested in drug evidence scandal. Retrieved on October 29, 2010 from http://www.northcountrygazette.org/articles/2007/031607 EvidenceScandal.html.

NorthCountryGazette.org (2010, December 1). State court security officer in six-hour standoff. Retrieved on April 29, 2011 from http://www.northcountrygazette.org/2010/12/01/officer_standoff/.

Novack, J. (1995, December). What if the guy shoots somebody? Retrieved on October 23, 2003 from http://0-proquest.umi.com.novacat.nova.edu/pqdweb?index=20&did=000000008574514.

NPR.org (2007, July 2). Steroids' appeal reaches beyond pro athletes. Retrieved on April 13, 2011 from http://www.npr.org/templates/story/story.php?storyId=11654302.

NY.Gov (2010, June 1). Governor Paterson introduces all-crime DNA bill: Crime fighting initiative requires DNA sample for all penal law offenses—All five NYC district attorneys, state da's association, state police chief and crime victim advocates laud governor's proposal. Retrieved on July 18, 2010 from http://www.ny.gov/governor/press/060110DNA.html.

Oakley v. Flor-Shin, Inc. (1998).

Obabueki v. Choicepoint, Inc. (2002).

Obabueki v. International Business Machines Corporation (2002).

O'Callahan, T. (2006, February 28). Study: Almost half of resumes are bogus. Retrieved on September 12, 2010 from http://www.inc.com/news/articles/200602/resume.html.

Occupational Safety and Health Act (1970). Retrieved on March 29, 2010 from http://www.osha.gov/pls/oshaweb/owadisp.show_document?p_table=OSHACT&p_id=3359.

O'Connell, T. J. & Bou-Mattar, C. B. (2007, November 3). Long term Marijuana users seeking medical cannabis in California (2001–2007): Demographics, social characteristics, patterns of cannabis, and other drug use of 4117 applicants. Retrieved on January 28, 2010 from http://search.ebscohost.com.library.keuka.edu/login.aspx?direct=true&db=cmedm&AN=17980043&site=ehost-live.

O'Connor, C. (2010, March 25). Santa Rosa county Sheriff's office lieutenant charged with sexual battery. Retrieved on November 19, 2010 from http://navarrepress.com/news/13/1988-santa-rosa-county-sheriffs-office-lieutenant-charged-with-sexual-battery.

O'Connor, J. (2011, July 3). Jack Daniel Mccullough, man charged in 1957 murder of child, had history of abuse. Retrieved on July 4, 2011 from http://www.huffingtonpost.com/2011/07/04/jack-daniel-mccullough-ma_n_889719.html.

O'Connor, M. & Starks, C. (1999, December 7). Holiday hills, ex-cop sued in alleged sex case. Retrieved on November 1, 2010 from http://articles.chicagotribune.com/1999-12-07/news/9912070255_1_federal-court-police-force-woman.

O'Crowley, P. (2009, August 13). The sexting generation. Retrieved on October 14, 2010 from http://www.nj.com/insidejersey/index.ssf/2009/08/the_sexting_generation.html.

Office of Naval Intelligence (n.d.). Who we are. Retrieved on April 16, 2011 from http://www.oni.navy.mil/This_is_ONI/who_we_are.htm.

O'Hara, C. E. & O'Hara, G. L. (1981). *Fundamentals of Criminal Investigation* (5th edn.). Springfield, IL: Charles C. Thomas, Publishers, Limited.

O'Hara, J. (2007, January 19). Village's ex-police chief indicted; officials accuse him of taking $26,000 in Skaneateles parking meter money. Retrieved on October 8, 2010 from http://www.highbeam.com/doc/1G1-158021738.html.

O'Hara, J. (2009a, April 6). Parole officer stands trial of Perjury charges today in Syracuse. Retrieved on October 13, 2010 from http://www.syracuse.com/news/index.ssf/2009/04/parole_officer_stands_trial_on.html.

O'Hara, J. (2010, November 17). Welfare fraud raid in Onondaga County nets 41 arrests involving more than $600,000 in stolen benefits. Retrieved on November 18, 2010 from http://www.syracuse.com/news/index.ssf/2010/11/welfare_fraud_raid_nets_41_arr.html.

O'Hara, M. J. (2009b, Fall). Thinking before you speak: Avoid becoming a defendant in a defamation lawsuit. Retrieved on April 30, 2011 from http://www.muchshelist.com/avoid-becoming-a-defendant-in-a-defamation-lawsuit-blq.htm.

O'Hare, P. (2010, July 1). Pilot arrested on child porn charges: Houston-area man accused of having millions of images. Retrieved on October 24, 2010 from http://www.chron.com/disp/story.mpl/metropolitan/7089813.html.

O'Keefe, A. M. (1987). Case against drug testing. Retrieved on January 24, 2010 from http://search.ebscohost.com.library.keuka.edu/login.aspx?direct=true&db=sih&AN=SM109779&site=ehost-live.

O'Leary, L. R. (1976, November/December). Objectivity and job relatedness—Can we have our cake and eat it too. Retrieved on October 22, 2009 from http://proquest.umi.com.library.keuka.edu/pqdweb?did=1277045&sid=2&Fmt=2&clientId=3663&RQT=309&VName=PQD.

Olshan, J. & Sheehy, K. (2011, June 7). The dork knight: Weiner a 'caped crusader' in sext chats. Retrieved on June 7, 2011 from http://www.nypost.com/p/news/local/the_dork_knight_OYsymZ6kNMCxRRjZFtKanJ.

O'Quinn, K. (2004, June). Becoming a better communicator about writing. Retrieved on March 16, 2010 from http://proquest.umi.com.library.keuka.edu/pqdweb?did=653707671&sid=3&Fmt=3&clientId=3663&RQT=309&VName=PQD.

Office of National Drug Control Policy (2007). Teens and prescription drugs: An analysis of recent trends on the emerging drug threat. Retrieved on January 20, 2010 from http://search.ebscohost.com.library.keuka.edu/login.aspx?direct=true&db=eric&AN=ED495769&site=ehost-live.

Office of the Attorney General of the State of California (2010). Background checks. Retrieved on September 7, 2010 from http://www.ag.ca.gov/fingerprints/.

O'Hartigan v. Department of Personnel (1991).

Ohio Office of Criminal Justice Services (2003). 2003 *Ohio Peace Officers Task Analysis—Executive Summary*. Upper Columbus, OH: Author.

Oklahoma State Bureau of Investigation (2009). Law enforcement accreditation. Retrieved on October 22, 2009 from http://www.ok.gov/osbi/Administration/Accreditation/index.html.

Oldham, S. (2003, June). Are you leading? Retrieved on October 25, 2009 from http://proquest.umi.com.library.keuka.edu/pqdweb?did=355755951&sid=2&Fmt=3&clientId=3663&RQT=309&VName=PQD.

Oliver, P. (2002, December). Hiring in the spirit of service. *Law and Order Magazine*, *50*(12), 67–69.

Olson, B. (2011, March 8). Marshals wounded, suspect killed in St. Louis shooting. Retrieved on March 8, 2011 from http://www.reuters.com/article/2011/03/08/us-stlouis-marshals-idUSTRE7275I720110308.

Olson, R. & McEnroe, P. (2006, October 7). Fine had record expunged. Retrieved on February 5, 2011 from http://web.ebscohost.com.library.keuka.edu/ehost/detail?hid=13&sid=83ac1063-0972-4530-a77b-7200704592ca%40sessionmgr14&vid=8&bdata=JnNpdGU9ZWhvc3QtbGl2ZQ%3d%3d#db=nfh&AN=2W62W61875767132.

Omnibus Crime Control and Safe Streets Act (1968).

Omnibus Transportation Employee Testing Act (1991).

Onecle. (2006, November 21). Florida Crimes Code. Retrieved on February 12, 2010 from http://law.onecle.com/florida/crimes/831.31.html.

O'Neil, A. (1995, June 30). Ex-glendale fireman accused of Arson murders: Grand jury: John Orr pleads not guilty to indictment charges that he killed four people in a fire he allegedly set in 1984. Retrieved on July 30, 2011 from http://articles.latimes.com/1995-06-30/local/me-18875_1_grand-jury.

Open-Oregon.com (1999, October 13). Chapter 12: Defamation. Retrieved on April 28, 2011 from http://www.open-oregon.com/media-guide/chapter-12-defamation/.

Ord v. District of Columbia (2009).

Oregon Student Assistance Commission Office of Degree Authorization (n.d.). Unaccredited colleges. Retrieved on April 13, 2011 from http://www.osac.state.or.us/oda/unaccredited.aspx.

Orlando Sentinel (1989, December 9). Ormond man charged with raping minors. Retrieved on October 28, 2010 from http://articles.orlandosentinel.com/1989-12-09/news/8912093155_1_ehrhart-ormond-kersey.

OrlandoSentinel.com (2007, June 25). Cop accused in sex case. Retrieved on December 6, 2010 from http://articles.orlandosentinel.com/keyword/jennifer-hall.

Orrick, W. D. (2002, October). Calculating the cost of police turnover. *The Police Chief Magazine*, *69*(10), 100–103.

Orrick, D. (2008, March). Making recruitment and retention and priority. *Law and Order Magazine*, *56*(3), 26–28.

Orrick, D. (2009, December). Retaining police talent. *Law and Order Magazine*, *57*(12), 44–49.

Orrick, D. (2010, February). Recruiting during political unrest. *Law and Order Magazine*, *58*(2), 23–24.

Ortiz, B. (2007, May 26). Charges remain for unindicted, appeals court rules: Nicholasville man wanted record expunged after Grand Jury's decision. Retrieved on February 5, 2011 from http://web.ebscohost.com.library.keuka.edu/ehost/detail?hid=119&sid=83ac1063-0972-4530-a77b-7200704592ca%40sessionmgr14&vid=8&bdata=JnNpdGU9ZWhvc3QtbGl2ZQ%3d%3d#db=nfh&AN=2W62W6894656612.

Ortmeier, P. J. & Davis, J. J. (2012). *Police Administration: A Leadership Approach*. New York: McGraw-Hill, Inc.

O'Shea v. General Telephone Company (1987).

Osofsky, H. J., Dralle, P., & Greenleaf, W. (2001, January). Developing a partnership to enhance police recruitment and retention. *The Police Chief Magazine*, *68*(1), 38–46. Copyright held by the International Association of Chiefs of Police, Alexandria, VA. Further reproduction without express written permission from IACP is strictly prohibited.

Osorio, S. (2010, July 9). Erie Co. Deputy resigns after charges of relationship with inmate. Retrieved on November 1, 2010 from http://www.wkbw.com/news/local/28480474.html.

Ossad, J. (2011, April 1). Yale under federal investigation for alleged title IX violation. Retrieved on April 1, 2011 from http://www.cnn.com/2011/CRIME/04/01/connecticut.yale/.

Osterburg, J. W. & Ward, R. H. (2004). *Criminal Investigation: A Method for Reconstructing the Past* (4th edn.). Washington, DC: Mathew Bender and Company/LexisNexis Group.

Osterloh, J. D. & Becker, C. E. (1990, October–December). Chemical dependency and drug testing in the workplace. Retrieved on January 24, 2010 from http://search.ebscohost.com.library.keuka.edu/login.aspx?direct=true&db=cmedm&AN=2190418&site=ehost-live.

Ostrowe v. Lee (1931).

Ottesen, J. L. (2008). Put some punch in your pen. Retrieved on March 16, 2010 from http://proquest.umi.com.library.keuka.edu/pqdweb?did=1678497641&sid=3&Fmt=3&clientId=3663&RQT=309&VName=PQD.

OurAlzheimer's.com (2006, November 15). Mental status tests. Retrieved on October 20, 2009 from http://www.healthcentral.com/alzheimers/tests-10596-108.html.

Owen v. City of Independence, Missouri (1980).

Owens, D. (1995, March 3). Vision standards for troopers sparks lawsuit. Retrieved on November 25, 2009 from http://proquest.umi.com.library.keuka.edu/pqdweb?did=22961685&sid=1&Fmt=3&clientId=3663&RQT=309&VName=PQD.

Ozminkowski, R. J., Mark, T. L., Goetzel, R. Z., Blank, D., Walsh, J. M., & Cangianelli, L. (2003, February). Relationships between urinalysis testing for substance use, medical expenditures, and the occurrence of injuries at a large manufacturing firm. Retrieved on January 18, 2010 from http://search.ebscohost.com.library.keuka.edu/login.aspx?direct=true&db=aph&AN=9389413&site=ehost-live.

Pacula, R. L., Chriqui, J. F., Reichmann, D. A., & Terry-McElrath, Y. M. (2002). State medical marijuana laws: Understanding the laws and their limitations. Retrieved on January 28, 2010 from http://search.ebscohost.com.library.keuka.edu/login.aspx?direct=true&db=cmedm&AN=12532682&site=ehost-live.

Pagliery, J. (2009, March 28). Davie officer accused of raping teen. Retrieved on October 28, 2010 from http://www.palmbeachpost.com/news/content/state/epaper/2009/03/28/0328davie.html.

Palmiotto, M. J. (Ed.). (2001). *Police Misconduct: A Reader for the 21st Century*. Upper Saddle River, NJ: Prentice Hall Publishing.

Palotas, D. (2008, September 29). Joseph case: Who took him home? Retrieved on September 29, 2008 from http://rochester.ynn.com/print.cfm?id=65408.

Pam Lychner Sexual Offender Tracking and Identification Act (1996).

Papacosta, E. & Nassis, G. P. (2011, April 6). Saliva as a tool for monitoring steroid, peptide, and immune markers in sport and exercise science. Retrieved on April 13, 2011 from http://www.ncbi.nlm.nih.gov/pubmed/21474377.

Papadakis, M. A. & Wofsky, D. (2010, July 20). Plagiarism on personal statements: A disturbing symptom of a broader trend. Retrieved on September 13, 2010 from http://proquest.umi.com.library.keuka.edu/pqdweb?index=7&did=2097768141&SrchMode=2&sid=4&Fmt=2&VInst=PROD&VType=PQD&RQT=309&VName=PQD&TS=1284423867&clientId=3663.

Parascandola, R. (2007, October 3). New York police to randomly test officers for steroids. Retrieved on January 18, 2010 from http://search.ebscohost.com.library.keuka.edu/login.aspx?direct=true&db=nfh&AN=2W62W6536966118&site=ehost-live.

Parascandola, R. (2010a, October 8). Officer Daniel Zehrer's punishment for positive steroid test is delayed pension. Retrieved on February 20, 2011 from http://www.nydailynews.com/ny_local/2010/10/08/2010-10-08_druggie_cops_roid_to_retirement_just_got_tougher_as_his__pension_juiced.html?obref=obinsite.

Parascandola, R. (2010b, October 15). NYPD deputy inspector Steven Mauriello among five cops charged with tampering with crime reports. Retrieved on November 6, 2010 from http://www.nydailynews.com/news/ny_crime/2010/10/15/2010-10-15_nypd_deputy_inspector_steven_mauriello_charged_with_tampering_with_crime_reports.html.

Parker v. District of Columbia (1988).

Parker v. Williams (1988).

Parks, B. C. (2001, March). *Los Angeles Police Department Board of Inquiry into the Rampart Area Corruption Incident*. Los Angeles, CA: Los Angeles Police Department.

Parrish, D. M. (2007, June 5). Falsification of credentials in the research setting; scientific misconduct. Retrieved on September 11, 2010 from http://onlinelibrary.wiley.com/doi/10.1111/j.1748-720X.1996.tb01861.x/abstract.

Parsons, T. (2008, March 11). Panel upholds firing of Ark. Trooper. Retrieved on October 29, 2010 from http://www.usatoday.com/news/nation/2008-03-11-3664887186_x.htm.

Passalugo, A. (2010, July 18). Woman arrested under Leandra's law. Retrieved on July 18, 2010 from http://rochester.ynn.com/content/top_stories/511358/woman-arrested-under-leandra-s-law/.

Patane v. Broadmoor Hotel, Inc. (1985).

Patch v. Civil Service Commission of Des Moines (1980).

Patel, P. (2009, June). Expert's expect resume fraud to rise. Retrieved on February 22, 2011 from http://proquest.umi.com.library.keuka.edu/pqdweb?did=1748953341&sid=3&Fmt=2&clientId=3663&RQT=309&VName=PQD.

Patriot Act (2001).

Patterson, S. (2007, January 22). Can he deliver? Retrieved on October 25, 2009 from http://proquest.umi.com.library.keuka.edu/pqdweb?did=1198931721&sid=1&Fmt=2&clientId=3663&RQT=309&VName=PQD.

Patterson, S. (2011, March 23). Mother accused of scalding 4-year-old son.Retrieved on March 24, 2011 from http://rochester.ynn.com/content/top_stories/537565/mother-accused-of-scalding-4-year-old-son/.

Paybarah, A. (2008, March 24). Paterson admits past cocaine use. Retrieved on February 9, 2010 from http://www.observer.com/2008/paterson-admits-prior-cocaine-use.

Payne, D. M. (2002). *Police Liability*. Durham, NC: Carolina Academic Press.

Payroll Manager's Letter (2005a, June 21). DHS offers guidelines on form I-9 electronic storage and signatures. Retrieved on March 16, 2010 from http://search.ebscohost.com.library.keuka.edu/login.aspx?direct=true&db=buh&AN=17257086&site=ehost-live.

Payroll Manager's Letter (2005b, July 7). The long-awaited form I-9 is finally issued. Retrieved on March 16, 2010 from http://search.ebscohost.com.library.keuka.edu/login.aspx?direct=true&db=buh&AN=17608449&site=ehost-live.

Payroll Manager's Letter (2009, February 7). Government issues new form I-9. Retrieved on March 16, 2010 from http://search.ebscohost.com.library.keuka.edu/login.aspx?direct=true&db=buh&AN=36400254&site=ehost-live.

Payroll Manager's Report (2008, January). USCIS revises employment eligibility verification form I-9. Retrieved on March 16, 2010 from http://search.ebscohost.com.library.keuka.edu/login.aspx?direct=true&db=buh&AN=27872887&site=ehost-live.

Payroll Practitioner's Monthly (2006, August). Form I-9, no-match letters proposed rule changes. Retrieved on March 16, 2010 from http://search.ebscohost.com.library.keuka.edu/login.aspx?direct=true&db=buh&AN=21732968&site=ehost-live.

Peak, K., Evans, S., & Adams, F. (1998, April). Recruiting and testing criminal investigators: A job-related approach. *The Police Chief Magazine*, *65*(4), 165–168.

Peanick v. Reno (1995). Retrieved on October 23, 2009 from http://www.usdoj.gov/crt/emp/documents/peanick.htm.

Pear, R. (2005, June 7). Ruling limits prosecutions of people who violate law on privacy of medical records. Retrieved on August 18, 2010 from http://www.nytimes.com/2005/06/07/politics/07privacy.html?_r=1&ex=1275796800&en=fb3a3777ca7aa544&ei=5090&partner=rssuserland&emc=rss.

Pearson v. Simmonds Precision Products, Inc. (1993).

Peat, B. (2004). *From College to Career: A Guide for Criminal Justice Majors*. Boston, MA: Pearson Education, Inc.

Peck v. Siau (1992).

Pederson, B. J. (2009, April 10). Former South Tucson cop gets prison time in theft case. Retrieved on February 13, 2011 from http://web.ebscohost.com.library.keuka.edu/ehost/detail?hid=113&sid=c2c9c9fd-604a-40aa-8504-95895203904c%40sessionmgr114&vid=6&bdata=JnNpdGU9ZWhvc3QtbGl2ZQ%3d%3d#db=nfh&AN=2W62W63535385978.

Pedone, R. C. & Petil, G. A. (2011, January 10). Circuit court holds private employers permitted to reject applicants based on past bankruptcy filing; bar on termination and other discrimination for existing employees remains. Retrieved on March 9, 2011 from http://www.nixonpeabody.com/linked_media/publications/Employment_Law_Alert_01_10_2011.pdf.

Peltz, J. (2011, February 1). NY Juvenile worker gets prison for molesting girls. Retrieved on February 1, 2011 from http://www.seattlepi.com/national/1110ap_us_counselor_accused.html.

Peltz, J. & Long, C. (2010, April 19). Ex-NYPD officer goes on trial over cyclist crash. Retrieved on October 18, 2010 from http://abcnews.go.com/Technology/wireStory?id=10418424.

Pendleton Civil Service Reform Act (1883).

Pennsylvania Law Enforcement Accreditation Commission (2009, March). *Standards Manual*. Harrisburg, PA: Pennsylvania Law Enforcement Accreditation Commission.

People v. Gainey (2001).

People v. Rodriguez (2006).

People v. Rosario (1961).

Perez, A. J. (2010, May 12). Matthew Brown, former Red Wings exec, faces child pornography charge. Retrieved on October 24, 2010 from http://nhl.fanhouse.com/2010/05/12/former-red-wings-exec-faces-child-pornography-charge/.

Perez, E. (2007, October 3). Getting booked by Facebook: Police are finding, with help from networking sites, that students are incriminating themselves online. Retrieved on March 13, 2010 from http://www.jsonline.com/news/milwaukee/29260684.html.

Perez, R. (1993, November 19). Former police explorer finishes testimony in sex-charge trial. Retrieved on December 6, 2010 from http://articles.orlandosentinel.com/keyword/police-explorer.

Perez v. U.S. Postal Service (1993).

Perez-Pena, R. & Schweber, N. (2011, May 27). Newark officer is killed in a drive-by shooting. Retrieved on August 15, 2011 from http://www.nytimes.com/2011/05/28/nyregion/off-duty-newark-police-officer-shot-dead.html.

Perkins, K. (2003, May 19). Commentary: Smart hiring practices can reduce employer liability. Retrieved on November 17, 2009 from http://proquest.umi.com.library.keuka.edu/pqdweb?did=338304631&sid=1&Fmt=3&clientId=3663&RQT=309&VName=PQD.

Perry, P. M. (1994, October). ADA missteps: And how to avoid them. *Training*, *31*(10), 84–91.

Peters v. Bellinger (1959).

Peters, T. J. & Austin, N. (1985). *A Passion for Excellence: The Leadership Difference*. New York: Warner Books.

Peterson, I. (1999, May 12). 3 Officers found guilty of corruption. Retrieved on February 20, 2011 from http://query.nytimes.com/gst/fullpage.html?res=9907E5DA1731F931A15756C0A96F958260.

Peterson, M. (2010, February 17). Mineral Wells police officer arrested in string of commercial arsons. Retrieved on September 26, 2010 from http://crimeblog.dallasnews.com/archives/2010/02/mineral-wells-police-officer-a.html.

ThePetitionSite.com (2011). Fire San Marcos police officer Paul Stephens. Retrieved on June 5, 2011 from http://www.thepetitionsite.com/1/fire-san-marcos-police-officer-paul-stephens/.

Petrik v. New Hampshire Ins. Co. (1979).

Pew Research Center for the People and the Press (1998). Deconstructing distrust: How Americans view government. Retrieved on November 26, 2009 from http://search.ebscohost.com.library.keuka.edu/login.aspx?direct=true&db=sih&AN=SM171715&site=ehost-live.

Pfaelzer, M. R. & Berson, A. D. (1975, July). Police and public disorder intelligence—The Los Angeles experience. Retrieved on October 10, 2010 from http://web.ebscohost.com.library.keuka.edu/ehost/detail?vid=22&hid=17&sid=4c672b52-8d14-4332-a8cb-b1ff63c84f64%40sessionmgr11&bdata=JnNpdGU9ZWhvc3QtbGl2ZQ%3d%3d#db=sih&AN=SM037033.

Pfeiffer, R. (2009, January 11). Warning signs: Falls officer Ryan Warme was in trouble long before he became a cop. Retrieved on December 24, 2010 from http://tonawanda-news.com/local/x681751963/WARNING-SIGNS-Falls-Officer-Ryan-Warme-was-in-trouble-long-before-he-became-a-cop.

Philbin v. Trans Union Corporation (2001).

Philbrick v. County of Volusia (1996).

Phillips v. Edwin P. Stimpson Co., Inc. (1991).

Phillips, J. S. (2005). Synthetic validity. Retrieved on October 24, 2009 from http://search.ebscohost.com.library.keuka.edu/login.aspx?direct=true&db=buh&AN=14720961&site=ehost-live.

Phillips, J. S. (2005). Synthetic validity. Retrieved on October 24, 2009 from http://search.ebscohost.com.library.keuka.edu/login.aspx?direct=true&db=buh&AN=14720961&site=ehost-live.

Phillips-Sandy, M. (2011, February 10). Natalie Munroe suspended: Worst insults the teacher made about students. Retrieved on February 19, 2011 from http://www.aolnews.com/2011/02/10/natalie-munroe-suspended-the-worst-insults-the-teacher-made-abo/.

Phucas, K. (2011, April 8). Expanded DNA collection debated. Retrieved on April 17, 2011 from http://timesherald.com/articles/2011/04/08/news/doc4d9fb87e3ee13121593144.txt.

Pierce, D. & Ackerman, L. (2005, May 19). Data aggregators: A study of data quality and responsiveness. Retrieved on August 18, 2010 from www.csun.edu/~dwm3265/IS312/DataAggregatorsStudy.pdf.

Pignataro, T. J. (2010, October 14). Ex-Gowanda officer spared jail for misconduct. Retrieved on February 20, 2011 from http://www.buffalonews.com/city/police-courts/courts/article220172.ece.

Pileggi, J. (2010, July 2). Police investigate child porn video on Facebook. Retrieved on October 24, 2010 from http://www.myfoxny.com/dpp/news/local_news/police-investigate-child-porn-video-on-facebook-20100702.

Pina, A. A. (2010, May). Online diploma mills: Implications for legitimate distance education. Retrieved on April 7, 2011 from http://web.ebscohost.com.library.keuka.edu/ehost/detail?vid=7&hid=111&sid=8b68f380-de5e-409e-8eed-e2a570345a70%40sessionmgr113&bdata=JnNpdGU9ZWhvc3QtbGl2ZQ%3d%3d#db=aph&AN=49459731.

Pinkerton, J. (2010, July 3). Files shed more light on alleged HPD beating: 7 More officers appeal firings in case involving a 15-year-old suspect. Retrieved on October 28, 2010 from http://www.chron.com/disp/story.mpl/metropolitan/7092454.html.

Pittard v. Four Seasons Motor Inn, Inc. (1984).

Pitsch, M. (2009, April 21). Doyle plan would allow more young people to clear their criminal records. Retrieved on February 5, 2011 from http://web.ebscohost.com.library.keuka.edu/ehost/detail?hid=11&sid=83ac1063-0972-4530-a77b-7200704592ca%40sessionmgr14&vid=8&bdata=JnNpdGU9ZWhvc3QtbGl2ZQ%3d%3d#db=nfh&AN=2W61351048437.

Pleskac, T. J. & Busemeyer, J. R. (2011, April 21). Two-stage dynamic signal detection: A theory of choice, decision, and confidence. Retrieved on July 26, 2011 from http://web.ebscohost.com.library.keuka.edu/ehost/detail?vid=4&hid=122&sid=2d6b04cf-d2d8-474c-be2b-72912e7ffd9b%40sessionmgr113&bdata=JnNpdGU9ZWhvc3QtbGl2ZQ%3d%3d#db=pdh&AN=rev-118-1-56.

Pluskota v. Roadrunner Freight (1994).

Poe, M. (2005, May). How to beat a drug test. Retrieved on January 18, 2010 from http://search.ebscohost.com.library.keuka.edu/login.aspx?direct=true&db=lfh&AN=17277978&site=ehost-live.

Poinski, M. (2006, October 30). Other political officials' educational credentials have raised questions. Retrieved on April 13, 2011 from http://proquest.umi.com.library.keuka.edu/pqdweb?did=2083789211&sid=4&Fmt=3&clientId=3663&RQT=309&VName=PQD.

Police Benevolent Association Local 319 v. Township of Plainsboro (1998).

PoliceOne.com (2000, November 13). Webster Grove police fire three in sex case. Retrieved on December 6, 2010 from http://www.policeone.com/news/28888-Webster-Groves-police fire-three-in-sex-case/.

Polla, M., Stramesi, C., Pichini, S., Palmi, I., Vignali, C., & Dall'Olio, G. (2009, August 10). Hair testing is superior to urine to disclose cocaine consumption in driver's license regranting. Retrieved on January 18, 2010 from http://search.ebscohost.com.library.keuka.edu/login.aspx?direct=true&db=cmedm&AN=19446971&site=ehost-live.

Pollock, J. M. (2004). *Ethics in Crime and Justice: Dilemmas and Decisions* (4th edn.). Belmont, CA: Thomson Wadsworth.

Ponticas v. K.M.S. Investments (1983).

Porter, D. (2009, October 14). Port authority officer arrested on fraud charge. Retrieved on October 14, 2009 from http://www.philly.com/philly/news/20091014_Officer_of_Port_Authority_arrested.html.

Porter, G. G. (2011, March 16). Bullying victim Casey Heynes exacts revenge, gets suspended. Retrieved on March 18, 2011 from http://www.autismkey.com/bullying-victim-casey-heynes-exacts-revenge-gets-suspended/.

Porter, S. & Yuille, J. C. (1996, August). Language of deceit: An investigation of the verbal clues to deception in the interrogation context. Retrieved on July 24, 2011 from http://web.ebscohost.com.library.keuka.edu/ehost/detail?vid=5&hid=110&sid=e3273d33-5fa7-4328-bcbc-0764c45e691c%40sessionmgr110&bdata=JnNpdGU9ZWhvc3QtbGl2ZQ%3d%3d#db=sih&AN=SM164887.

Porto v. Town of Harrison (1984).

Post Wire Services (2011, March 4). Yale sex party under investigation, accusations of drinking and sex assault: Report. Retrieved on April 1, 2011 from http://www.nypost.com/p/news/national/yale_sex_party_under_investigation_oKZv8vgB7ohEF6LF7S9HjN.

Potter, N., James, M. S., Esposito, R., & Martinez, L. (2010, March 4). Pentagon shootout: Gunman killed after shooting two police officers. Retrieved on December 6, 2010 from http://abcnews.go.com/US/pentagon-shots-fired-police-officers-reported-injured/story?id=10014570.

Potts, C. (2010, May 28). Lazore pleads guilty to steroid charges. Retrieved on March 19, 2011 from http://www.uticaod.com/highlight/x11204616/Lazore-pleads-guilty-to-steroid-charges.

Powell, M. (2007, November 3). The long run: Loyal to Kerik, Giuliani missed warning signs. Retrieved on April 16, 2011 from http://www.nytimes.com/2007/11/03/us/politics/03kerik.html?ref=politics.

Powell v. Reno (1997).

PR Web. (2009, March 24). Struggle to find a job can increase when schools and employers don't recognize law. Retrieved on March 16, 2010 from http://www.prweb.com/releases/2009/03/prweb2247434.htm.

Pregnancy Discrimination Act

Preuitt, L. (2009, March 23). Fourth Oakland police officer dies. Retrieved on December 6, 2010 from http://www.nbcbayarea.com/news/local-beat/Two-Officers-Shot-in-Oakland.html.

Prieto, B. (2010, April 6). Apopka cop fired after latest arrest. Retrieved on November 1, 2010 from http://articles.orlandosentinel.com/2010-04-06/news/os-apopka-police-officer-arrested-20100406_1_officer-steve-popp-apopka-police-arrest.

Prison Rape Elimination Act (PREA) (2003).

Pritchett, P. (1992). *The Team Member Handbook for Teamwork.* Dallas, TX: Pritchett Publishing Company.

Privacy Act (1974).

Privacy Rights Clearing House (2006, October). Fact sheet 16c: FAQ on employment background checks. Retrieved on February 6, 2011 from http://www.privacyrights.org/fs/FS16c-FAQ-BkgChk-060928.htm.

Privacy Rights Clearing House (2010, October). Fact sheet 16a: Employment background checks in California: New focus on accuracy. Retrieved on February 6, 2011 from http://www.privacyrights.org/fs/fs16a-califbck.htm.

Privacy Rights Clearing House (2011, February). Fact sheet 16: Employment background checks: A jobseeker's guide. Retrieved on February 7, 2011 from http://www.privacyrights.org/fs/fs16-bck.htm.

ProCon.org (2010, January 26). Medical Marijuana. Retrieved on February 6, 2010 from http://medicalmarijuana.procon.org/viewresource.asp?resourceID=000881.

Prohaska, T. J. (2011, June 16). Former corrections officer pleads to knifepoint rape. Retrieved on June 26, 2011 from http://www.buffalonews.com/city/article455716.ece.

Psychemedics Corporation (2007). Frequently asked questions. Retrieved on January 25, 2010 from http://www.drugtestwithhair.com/questions.php#g3.

Public Personnel Management (2008, Winter). Police officer candidate background investigation: Law enforcement management's most effective tool for employing the most qualified candidate. Retrieved on October 9, 2009 from http://www.entrepreneur.com/tradejournals/article/54069613_1.html.

Puckett v. City of San Francisco (1962).

Pulkkinen, L. (2010a, March 15). Sex, drugs, and child porn at McNeil Island. Retrieved on October 24, 2010 from http://www.seattlepi.com/local/416372_predatorporn15.html.

Pulkkinen, L. (2010b, May 25). State: UW doctor traded painkiller addict drugs for sex. Retrieved on February 1, 2011 from http://www.seattlepi.com/local/420606_hudson25.html.

Pulkkinen, L. (2010c, December 16). Troopers busted with suspect diplomas sue state: Five troopers suspended without pay for 3–10 days claim they were defamed. Retrieved on March 19, 2011 from http://www.seattlepi.com/local/431875_troopers15.html.

Purdy, M. & Bergman, L. (2003, October 12). Unclear danger: Inside the Lackawanna terror case. Retrieved on February 8, 2011 from http://www.nytimes.com/2003/10/12/nyregion/12LACK.html.

Purdy v. Cole (1975).

Purpura, P. P. (2001). *Police and Community: Concepts and Cases.* Needham Heights, MA: Pearson Education—Allyn & Bacon.

Putney, L. (2011, January 19). Deal reached to avoid Jersey city police layoffs. Retrieved on February 14, 2011 from http://newyork.cbslocal.com/2011/01/19/deal-reached-to-avoid-jersey-city-police-layoffs/.

Quan, D. (2010, September 24). Investigation hits commercial child porn business. Retrieved on April 16, 2011 from http://proquest.umi.com.library.keuka.edu/pqdweb?did=2147088481&sid=1&Fmt=3&clientId=3663&RQT=309&VName=PQD.

Queally, J. & Friedman, A. (2010, November 30). Newark finalizes 167 police layoffs after union refuses Booker's pleas to return to negotiating table. Retrieved on February 14, 2011 from http://www.nj.com/news/index.ssf/2010/11/union_head_expects_167_newark.html.

Quill (1995, October 4). Hiring records open despite claims. Retrieved on October 24, 2009 from http://search.ebscohost.com.library.keuka.edu/login.aspx?direct=true&db=lfh&AN=9510015686&site=ehost-live.

Quill (1999, May). Disciplinary records ruled confidential. Retrieved on October 24, 2009 from http://search.ebscohost.com.library.keuka.edu/login.aspx?direct=true&db=lfh&AN=1881147&site=ehost-live.

Raab, S. (1985, September 24). Goodman assails police on recruit screenings. Retrieved on October 13, 2009 from http://web.ebscohost.com.library.keuka.edu/ehost/detail?vid=4&hid=7&sid=dab43474-f023-432f-841c-1b6c32a6afe5%40sessionmgr4&bdata=JnNpdGU9ZWhvc3QtbGl2ZQ%3d%3d#db=f5h&AN=30555933.

Rabon, D. (1992). *Interviewing and Interrogation*. Durham, NC: Carolina Academic Press.

Rabon, D. (1994). *Investigative Discourse Analysis*. Durham, NC: Carolina Academic Press.

Raby, J. (2011, March 13). 2 Va. deputies fatally shot, suspect killed. Retrieved on March 13, 2011 from http://news.yahoo.com/s/ap/20110314/ap_on_re_us/us_officers_shot_virginia;_ylt=AiM0Dtq80nrfCLNV9vLgHgpH2ocA;_ylu=X3oDMTNkcGE5cDlmBGFzc2V0A2FwLzIwMTEwMzE0L3VzX29mZmljZXJzX3Nob3RfdmlyZ2luaWEEY2NvZGUDbXBfZWNfOF8xMARjcG9zAzcEcG9zAzcEc2VjA3luX3RvcF9zdG9yaWVzBHNsawMydmFkZXB1dGllc2Y-.

Rachlin, H. (1997, May). Nassau County's police entrance exam. *Law and Order Magazine*, *45*(5), 72–82.

Rachlin, H. (2000, May). Available resources: Expanding research benefits investigators. *Law and Order Magazine*, *48*(5), 47–54.

Racketeer Influenced and Corrupt Organizations Act (RICO).

Raclin, D. & Asbury, J. (2006, September 29). Police officer arrested, suspected of sex crime. Retrieved on December 6, 2010 from http://www.pe.com/localnews/inland/stories/PE_News_Local_H_decker29.376aa70.html.

Radefeld, M. A. (2005, November 5). Commentary: Ever heard of the Lautenberg amendment? You're not alone. Retrieved on April 16, 2011 from http://web.ebscohost.com.library.keuka.edu/ehost/detail?vid=6&hid=111&sid=b3f5dc62-a935-427d-9ab9-e87305912346%40sessionmgr110&bdata=JnNpdGU9ZWhvc3QtbGl2ZQ%3d%3d#db=bwh&AN=L54143647DRMO.

Rae, M. (2008, May 7). Drug money fed Keno craving. Retrieved on February 13, 2011 from http://web.ebscohost.com.library.keuka.edu/ehost/detail?hid=9&sid=c2c9c9fd-604a-40aa-8504-95895203904c%40sessionmgr114&vid=6&bdata=JnNpdGU9ZWhvc3QtbGl2ZQ%3d%3d#db=nfh&AN=2008050710015O3047.

Rafilson, F. M. (2000, March). Candidate physical fitness testing: The need for legally defensible methodologies and outcomes. *Law and Order Magazine*, *48*(3), 99–101.

Rafilson, K. (1999, June). An alternate to conventional law enforcement written exams: The national criminal justice officer selection inventory. *Law and Order Magazine*, *47*(6), 83–88.

Ramde, D. (2011, February 24). Wis. man gets life sentence in slayings of 7 women: Milwaukee man sentenced to 7 consecutive life terms in killings of 7 women over 21 years. Retrieved on April 17, 2011 from http://abcnews.go.com/US/wireStory?id=12992071.

Ramker, G. F. (2006, July). Improving criminal history records for background checks, 2005. Washington, DC: United States Department of Justice, Office of Justice Programs, Bureau of Justice Statistics.

Ramos v. Equiserve (2005).

Ramsey, R. D. (2011, January). The art of interviewing final job candidates. Retrieved on July 17, 2011 from http://proquest.umi.com.library.keuka.edu/pqdweb?did=2219719221&sid=1&Fmt=3&clientId=3663&RQT=309&VName=PQD.

Randi W. v. Muroc Joint Unified School District (1997).

Rankin, B. (1998, May 20). Alleged tax scam by police officers not investigated Conyers tax preparer says he helped nearly 200 Atlanta and Fulton law enforcers to CHEAT the IRS, but department heads so far are not initiating probe. Retrieved on February 20, 2011 from http://proquest.umi.com.library.keuka.edu/pqdweb?did=29617160&sid=1&Fmt=3&clientId=3663&RQT=309&VName=PQD.

Rankin, K. (1999, July 12). Equal employment clarification. Retrieved on November 17, 2009 from http://proquest.umi.com.library.keuka.edu/pqdweb?did=43377346&sid=1&Fmt=3&clientId=3663&RQT=309&VName=PQD.

Rashbaum, W. K. (2005, April 22). Police corruption panel is losing its chairman. Retrieved on October 8, 2010 from http://query.nytimes.com/gst/fullpage.html?res=9D0CE7DF1431F931A15757C0A9639C8B63.

Ratliff v. City of Milwaukee (1986).

Ratcliffe, J. H. (2007). Integrated intelligence and crime analysis: Enhanced information management for law enforcement leaders. Retrieved on October 10, 2010 from http://web.ebscohost.com.library.keuka.edu/ehost/detail?vid=18&hid=11&sid=4c672b52-8d14-4332-a8cb-b1ff63c84f64%40sessionmgr11&bdata=JnNpdGU9ZWhvc3QtbGl2ZQ%3d%3d#db=cja&AN=CJA0400020000818.

Rea v. Federated Investors (2010).

Read, B. (2006, November 19). Online photos fell a college coach. Retrieved on March 13, 2010 from http://chronicle.com/blogPost/Online-Photos-Fell-a-College/7131/.

Read, J. M., Powell, M. B., Kebbell, M. R., & Milne, R. (2009, Winter). Investigative interviewing of suspected sex offenders: A review of what constitutes best practice. Retrieved on March 28, 2010 from http://search.ebscohost.com.library.keuka.edu/login.aspx?direct=true&db=aph&AN=44269207&site=ehost-live.

Read v. The Scott Fertilizer Co. (1998).

Reagle, C. (2009, September 23). Former MBTA K-9 officer charged with dog starvation back in court. Retrieved on April 30, 2011 from http://www.dailynewstranscript.com/state/x576518845/Former-MBTA-K-9-officer-charged-with-dog-starvation-back-in-court#axzz1L47ZdQp9.

Reagle, C. (2010, June 24). Trial set for former MBTA K-9 officer animal cruelty case: Lack of warrant weighs heavy on prosecutor's case. Retrieved on April 30, 2011 from http://www.wickedlocal.com/marion/news/x696772814/Trial-set-for-former-MBTA-K-9-officer-animal-cruelty-case#axzz1L48SK3Dq.

Real ID Act (2005).

Reaume, S. (2009, February). Improved hiring for child protective investigators. *Law and Order Magazine*, *57*(2), 19–24.

Reaves, B. A. & Hickman, M. J. (2004, March). *Law Enforcement and Administrative Statistics, 2000: Data for Individual and Local Agencies*. Washington, DC: United States Department of Justice, Office of Justice Programs, Bureau of Justice Statistics.

Redmond, L. (2007, June 30). Ex-Sheriff's cadet, pals jailed in vicious beating. Retrieved on July 30, 2011 from http://proquest.umi.com.library.keuka.edu/pqdweb?did=1297373481&sid=1&Fmt=3&clientId=3663&RQT=309&VName=PQD.

Redmond v. City of Overland Park (1987).

Reece, H. (2003, November). The keys to quality interviewing techniques. *Law and Order Magazine*, *51*(11), 66–69.

Reed v. Signode Corporation (1986).

Reed, M. (2009, December). How to address ICE strategy shift. Retrieved on March 16, 2010 from http://search.ebscohost.com.library.keuka.edu/login.aspx?direct=true&db=buh&AN=48276968&site=ehost-live.

Reeger, J. (2009, March 8). Online social sites good tool for police. Retrieved on March 13, 2010 from http://infoweb.newsbank.com.library.keuka.edu/iw-search/we/InfoWeb?p_product=NewsBank&p_theme=aggregated5&p_action=doc&p_docid=126D2546C8A8C818&p_docnum=23&p_queryname=3.

Regneir, J. (2010, May 18). MO—Former Sheriff's deputy (Damon Berti) charged with sexual assault. Retrieved on September 5, 2010 from http://sexoffenderissues.blogspot.com/2010/05/mo-former-sheriffs-deputy-damon-berti.html.

Rehabilitation Act (1973).

Reicher, L. (1996, November 19). The danger of employment recommendations. Retrieved on April 25, 2011 from http://www.reish.com/publications/article_detail.cfm?ARTICLEID=124.

Reilly, D. L. (2009, November 19). Choose wisely when using an employee to conduct your workplace investigation. Retrieved on February 21, 2010 from http://www.workplaceinvestigationsblog.com/tags/silva-v-lucky-stores/.

Reilly, L. (2004, March 18). Webshots incriminate students. Retrieved on March 13, 2010 from http://theloquitur.com/2004/03/18/webshotsincriminatestudents/.

Reintzell, J. F. (1997, January). When training saves lives. Retrieved on October 22, 2009 from http://proquest.umi.com.library.keuka.edu/pqdweb?did=10851609&sid=3&Fmt=3&clientId=3663&RQT=309&VName=PQD.

Renfro Drug Company v. Lawson (1942).

Rennison, C. M. & Welchans, S. (2000, May). *Intimate Partner Violence*. Washington, DC: United States Department of Justice, Office of Justice Programs, Bureau of Justice Statistics. NCJ 178247

Repa, B. K. (1999, October 21). Letters of recommendation. Retrieved on April 25, 2011 from http://www.inc.com/articles/1999/10/14694.html.

Resnick v. Blue Cross and Blue Shield of Missouri (1995).

Reuben, R. C. (1994, June). Employment lawyers rethink advice. Retrieved on October 23, 2003 from http://0-proquest.umi.com.novacat.nova.edu/pqdweb?index=23&did=000000008729528.

Reuters. (1998, May 7). Officer who posed for playboy leaves U.S. navy. Retrieved on April 15, 2011 from http://proquest.umi.com.library.keuka.edu/pqdweb?did=195939901&sid=1&Fmt=3&clientId=3663&RQT=309&VName=PQD.

Reynolds v. Arizona (1993).

Rhode Island General Law

Ricci v. Destefano (2009).

Richardson, J. F. (1980). Police in America—Functions and control (from history and crime, pp. 211–224, 1980, James A. Inciardi and Charles E. Faupel, eds.—See NCJ-74702). Retrieved on November 26, 2009 from http://search.ebscohost.com.library.keuka.edu/login.aspx?direct=true&db=sih&AN=SM074710&site=ehost-live.

Richert, G. (2011, April 6). Police say woman sold 1,000 pills a month. Retrieved on April 9, 2011 from http://www.wivb.com/dpp/news/crime/Police-say-woman-sold-1000-pills-a-month.

Richland School District v. Mabton School District (2002).

Richmond, R. (2009, March 26). Sexting may place teens at legal risk. Retrieved on October 14, 2010 from http://gadgetwise.blogs.nytimes.com/2009/03/26/sexting-may-place-teens-at-legal-risk/.

Richter, A. (2007, January 28). Matching the police to the populace. Retrieved on November 6, 2009 from http://proquest.umi.com.library.keuka.edu/pqdweb?did=1204111461&sid=2&Fmt=3&clientId=3663&RQT=309&VName=PQD.

Riggs, P. (2008, March). Non-medical use and abuse of commonly prescribed medications. Retrieved on January 20, 2010 from http://search.ebscohost.com.library.keuka.edu/login.aspx?direct=true&db=cmedm&AN=18267053&site=ehost-live.

Riley, K. J., Lu, N. T., & Taylor, B. G. (2000, Winter). Drug screening: A comparison of urinalysis results from two independent laboratories. Retrieved on January 18, 2010 from http://search.ebscohost.com.library.keuka.edu/login.aspx?direct=true&db=aph&AN=3017845&site=ehost-live.

Ring v. Fox (1977).

Ripley, A. (2007, September 28). A 9/11 survivor—Or 9/11 impostor. Retrieved on February 14, 2011 from http://www.time.com/time/nation/article/0,8599,1666594,00.html.

Ritch, V. R. (1997). *Background Investigation for Law Enforcement*. Raleigh, NC: Carolina Academic Press.

Rivera, R. & Baker, A. (2010a, July 16). Police cite help from stop-and-frisk data in 170 cases. Retrieved on October 10, 2010 from http://www.nytimes.com/2010/07/17/nyregion/17frisk.html.

Rivera, R. & Baker, A. (2010b, September 4). Mother of dead 4-year-old will face charges of drug possession and assault. Retrieved on April 7, 2011 from http://www.lexisnexis.com.library.keuka.edu/hottopics/lnacademic/?.

Rives, K. S. (2001, August 6). Some workers begin to challenge results of company drug tests. Retrieved on January 24, 2010 from http://search.ebscohost.com.library.keuka.edu/login.aspx?direct=true&db=nfh&AN=2W63855798631&site=ehost-live.

Rizzo, J. (2010, July 9). Buff state cop's sentencing is delayed; claims he was misled on plea deal. Retrieved on October 29, 2010 from http://www.wkbw.com/news/local/38833672.html.

Robbins, D. (2010, May 22). AP investigation: Texas man faked way into army. Retrieved on May 22, 2010 from http://news.yahoo.com/s/ap/us_army_infiltrator.

Robbins, S. P. (1995). *Supervision Today*. Englewood Cliffs, NJ: Prentice-Hall, Inc.

Roberg, R. R., Kuykendall, J., & Novak, K. (2002). *Police Management* (3rd edn.). Los Angeles, CA: Roxbury Publishing Company.

Roberg, R., Novak, K., & Cordner, G. (2005). *Police and Society* (3rd edn.). Los Angeles, CA: Roxbury Publishing Company.

Roberts, M. (2009, July 16). Former CSU top cop Dexter Yarbrough's past follows him. Retrieved on October 28, 2010 from http://blogs.westword.com/latestword/2009/07/former_csu_top_cop_dexter_yarb.php.

Robertson, J. (1999, September). The changing face of white-collar crime. *The Police Chief Magazine*, *66*(9), 24–26.

Robertson v. Baldwin (1897).

Robinson, C. (2009a, November 19). New York toughens drunken driving law. Retrieved on July 18, 2010 from http://www.cnn.com/2009/CRIME/11/19/new.york.dwi.law/index.html.

Robinson, M. (2008, October 25). Prosecutors widen Chicago police torture probe: Ex-Chicago homicide cops under scrutiny a federal prosecutors expand police torture probe. Retrieved on October 9, 2009 from http://abcnews.go.com/TheLaw/wireStory?id=6111074.

Robinson, M. (2009b, April 28). Deputy US marshal guilty of leaking secrets to mob. Retrieved on April 28, 2009 from http://news.yahoo.com/s/ap/20090428/ap_on_re_us/us_mob_trial.

Robinson, C. G., Fisbone, H., & Daley, R. (1982, January). American academy of police medicine. Retrieved on November 23, 2009 from http://search.ebscohost.com.library.keuka.edu/login.aspx?direct=true&db=sih&AN=SM083235&site=ehost-live.

Robinson v. City of Dallas (1975).

Robinson v. Lorillard Corporation (1971).

Robinson v. Shell Oil Co (1997).

Robson, S. (2006, December 7). FBI says U.S. criminal gangs are using military to spread their reach. Retrieved on August 6, 2011 from http://www.stripes.com/news/fbi-says-u-s-criminal-gangs-are-using-military-to-spread-their-reach-1.57718.

Rochesterathome.com (2008, October 1). Former police spokesman pleads guilty. Retrieved on January 19, 2011 from http://rochesterathome.com/dct/62/id/272128/mid/315/Former-Police-Spokesman-Pleads-Guilty.aspx.

Rodriguez, B. (2011, July 2). Police: Train ticket helps crack 1957 Ill. killing. Retrieved on July 4, 2011 from http://news.yahoo.com/police-train-ticket-helps-crack-1957-ill-killing-165142484.html.

Rodriguez-Herrera v. INS (1995).

Roe v. Cheyenne Mountain Conference Resort, Inc. (1997).

Roman, C. (2010, December). How to hire employees who live the mission. Retrieved on July 17, 2011 from http://proquest.umi.com.library.keuka.edu/pqdweb?did=2233653821&sid=1&Fmt=4&clientId=3663&RQT=309&VName=PQD.

Romer, P. A. (2009, August 21). Little River-Academy police chief resigns. Retrieved on September 26, 2010 from http://www.tdtnews.com/story/2009/08/21/60085/.

Rose, T. (2009, February 5). Concord settles sexual harassment lawsuit. Retrieved on October 31, 2009 from http://proquest.umi.com.library.keuka.edu/pqdweb?did=1639369501&sid=1&Fmt=3&cl ientId=3663&RQT=309&VName=PQD.

Rosen, L. S. (2010, March 17). Use of workers' compensation records: Extreme caution advised. Retrieved on March 12, 2011 from http://www.esrcheck.com/wordpress/2010/03/17/use-of-workers-compensation-records-extreme-caution-advised/. Used with permission of Les Rosen, President of Employment Screening Resources found at http://www.esrcheck.com/.

Rosen, R. (2007, April 25). *Essential Background Checks: An Introduction to the Why, Who, What, and How*. Morrisville, NC: National Association of Professional Background Screeners.

Rosner, B., Halcrow, A., & Levins, A. (2011, April 10). Corner office: Avoiding negligent supervision. Retrieved on April 21, 2011 from http://abcnews.go.com/Business/CornerOffice/story?id=87194&page=1.

Ross, B. (2007, November 20). Former cop Michael Farrell pleads guilty to online sex soliciting of a minor. Retrieved on October 29, 2010 from http://www.sfgate.com/cgi—http://www.nydailynews.com/news/ny_crime/2007/11/20/2007-11-20_former_cop_michael_farrell_pleads_guilty-2.html.

Ross, D. (2003). *Civil Liability in Criminal Justice* (3rd edn.). Cincinnati, OH: Anderson Publishing Company.

Ross, T. (2010, March 13). Lesbian Sgt. discharged after police tell military. Retrieved on March 14, 2010 from http://www.sfgate.com/cgi-bin/article.cgi?f=/n/a/2010/03/13/national/a105705S41.DTL.

Ross, B. & Schwartz, R. (2009, November 19). Major Hasan's e-mail: 'I Can't Wait to Join You' in afterlife: American official says accused shooter asked radical cleric when is Jihad appropriate? Retrieved on March 13, 2010 from http://abcnews.go.com/Blotter/major-hasans-mail-wait-join-afterlife/story?id=9130339.

Ross v. RagingWire Telecommunications, Inc. (2008).

Rosse, J. G., Ringer, R. C., & Miller, J. L. (1996, Summer). Personality and drug testing, an exploration of the perceived fairness of alternatives to urinalysis. Retrieved on October 22, 2009 from http://search.ebscohost.com.library.keuka.edu/login.aspx?direct=true&db=buh&AN=9605130432&site=ehost-live.

Rossi, D. (2010). 12 Years later, arrest relieves victims of attack: Woman narrowly escaped with her life. Retrieved on April 17, 2011 from http://www.kpho.com/news/26071647/detail.html.

Rostow, C. & Davis, R. (2002, May). Psychological screening. *Law and Order Magazine*, *50*(5), 100–106.

Rostow, C., Davis, R., Levy, J. P., & Brecknock, S. (2001, June). Civil liability and psychological services in law enforcement. *Police Chief Magazine*, *68*(6), 36–43.

Rowe, C. (2008, June 23). Juvenile sex offenders marked for life. Retrieved on October 13, 2010 from http://www.seattlepi.com/local/368007_youthoffenders23.html.

Rowe, M. (2009, April). Notes on a scandal: The official enquiry into deviance and corruption in New Zealand police. Retrieved on March 28, 2010 from http://search.ebscohost.com.library.keuka.edu/login.aspx?direct=true&db=aph&AN=37148161&site=ehost-live.

Ruggles, R. (1998, January 13). City must pay officer removed in '84. Retrieved on November 25, 2009 from http://proquest.umi.com.library.keuka.edu/pqdweb?did=25342638&sid=1&Fmt=3&clientId=3663&RQT=309&VName=PQD.

Rumberger.com (2008, May 22). The employer reference problem: How much, if anything, to disclose. Retrieved on April 21, 2011 from http://www.rumberger.com/?t=11&la=721&format=xml.

Runyon, B. (2010, November 28). Former Falmouth police dispatcher called attention to chief's contract. Retrieved on August 3, 2011 from http://www.capenews.net/communities/falmouth/news/756.

Ruud, W. (2000, June). Employer legal liability for employee workplace violence. Retrieved on July 6, 2009 from http://www.allbusiness.com/human-resources/workforce-management-conflict-resolution/651463-1.html.

Ryan, A. (2009, July 8). MBTA K-9 officer charged with animal cruelty. Retrieved on October 18, 2010 from http://www.boston.com/news/local/breaking_news/2009/07/mbta_k9_officer.html.

Ryan, A. M., Ployhart, R. E., & Friedel, L. A. (1998, April). Using personality testing to reduce adverse impact: A cautionary rule. Retrieved on October 22, 2009 from http://search.ebscohost.com.library.keuka.edu/login.aspx?direct=true&db=pdh&AN=apl-83-2-298&site=ehost-live.

Ryan, J. (2008, March 4). 'Sophisticated' child porn ring busted. Retrieved on October 24, 2010 from http://abcnews.go.com/TheLaw/story?id=4388379.

Ryan Evans, J. (2011, March 7). Mom kills son for potty training accident, then eats pizza. Retrieved on March 8, 2011 from http://thestir.cafemom.com/toddler/117162/mom_kills_son_for_potty?quick_picks=1&utm_medium=sem2&utm_source=outbrain&utm_campaign=outbrain&utm_content=outbrain_feb_test.

Sabatini, P. (2006, February 24). Fibs on resumes commonplace. Retrieved on May 18, 2010 from http://search.ebscohost.com.library.keuka.edu/login.aspx?direct=true&db=nfh&AN=2W62W61258278799&site=ehost-live.

Sabourin, M. (2007, February). The assessment of credibility: An analysis of truth and deception in a multiethnic environment. Retrieved on July 24, 2011 from http://proquest.umi.com.library.keuka.edu/pqdweb?did=1323649391&sid=5&Fmt=3&clientId=3663&RQT=309&VName=PQD.

Sack, S. M. (1995). From hiring to firing: The legal survival guide for employers. Retrieved on November 8, 2009 from http://smallbusiness.findlaw.com/bookshelf-hiring-firing/hfchp1_k.html.

Sacramento Metro News (2009, October 8). Former Kern County Sheriff's deputy sentenced to 57 months in prison for possession of child pornography. Retrieved on October 18, 2010 from http://www.sacmetronews.com/2009_10_01_archive.html.

Sacramento Police Department (n.d.). Background investigations. Retrieved on October 9, 2009 from http://my.starstream.net/tcfong/backgroundinvestigations.htm.

Sagall, R. (2005, April). Choosing a drug test panel: Concepts and considerations. Retrieved on January 24, 2010 from http://search.ebscohost.com.library.keuka.edu/login.aspx?direct=true&db=aph&AN=16881148&site=ehost-live.

Sager, S. (2010, April 8). Settlement reached in NJ priest sex assault case. Retrieved on April 9, 2010 from http://abclocal.go.com/wabc/story?section=news/local&id=7375989.

Saine v. Comcast Cablevision of Arkansas Inc. (2003).

Salit, R. & Milkovitz, A. (2010, September 30). Middletown soldier, wife found slain at fort hood; military. Retrieved on April 16, 2011 from http://proquest.umi.com.library.keuka.edu/pqdweb?did=2150746471&sid=3&Fmt=3&clientId=3663&RQT=309&VName=PQD.

Saltzman, J. (2007, April 26). Ex-celebrity stripper goes on trial for allegedly posing as licensed psychologist. Retrieved on April 13, 2011 from http://www.boston.com/news/globe/city_region/breaking_news/2007/04/former_celeb_st.html.

Saltzman, J., Cramer, M., & Ellement, J. R. (2009, April 21). Alleged 'Craigslist Killer' was heading to Foxwoods with fiancée. Retrieved on September 5, 2010 from http://www.boston.com/news/local/breaking_news/2009/04/bu_student_char.html.

Sampson, R. (2002a, May). Bullying in schools. Washington, DC: United States Department of Justice Office of Community Oriented Policing Services.

Sampson, R. (2002b). Misuse and abuse of 911. Retrieved on April 30, 2011 from http://www.popcenter.org/problems/911_abuse/.

Sampson, R. (2007, January). *Domestic Violence*. Washington, DC: United States Department of Justice Office of Community Oriented Policing Services.

San Antonio Express-News (2008, January 27). SAPD bent hiring rules. Retrieved on October 9, 2009 from http://www.mysanantonio.com/news/MYSA012708_01A_PoliceHiring_29e405f_html16144.html.

San Bernadino County Sheriff's Department (n.d.). San Bernadino County Sheriff's department pre-employment background interview questionnaire. Retrieved on July 25, 2011 from http://www.sheriffsjobs.com/PBIQ.pdf.

Sanchez, R. (2010, June 28). Teacher Stephanie Ragusa sentenced to 10 years in prison for sex with students. Retrieved on October 12, 2010 from http://abcnews.go.com/US/teacher-stephanie-ragusa-sentenced-10-years-sex-students/story?id=11036498.

Sandoval, V. A. (2003, October). Strategies to avoid interview contamination. Retrieved on July 24, 2011 from http://proquest.umi.com.library.keuka.edu/pqdweb?did=459552001&sid=4&Fmt=4&clientId=3663&RQT=309&VName=PQD.

Sandoval, V. A. & Adams, S. H. (2001, August). Subtle skills for building rapport: Using neuro-linguistic programming in the interview room. Retrieved on July 24, 2011 from http://www.au.af.mil/au/awc/awcgate/fbi/nlp_interviewing.htm.

Sanow, E. (2001, December). Improve by training? Selection? *Law and Order Magazine*, *49*(12), 4.

Sanow, E. (2002, February). Of Daubert and fingerprints. *Law and Order Magazine*, *50*(2), 4.

Santa Barbara Police Department (n.d). Police officer—Academy graduate. Retrieved on July 31, 2010 from http://www.santabarbaraca.gov/PagePrintVersion.htm?title=Police+Officer-Academy+Graduate&guid={27DAAD01-0EF3-4377-B649-94928FBB4CD9}.

Santana, S. (2009, July 31). Hollywood police chief: We're thoroughly investigating cover-up case. Retrieved on July 31, 2009 from http://www.sun-sentinel.com/news/broward/hollywood/sfl-hollywood-cops-fake-report-b072809,0,350771.story.

Sanz, C. (1995, October 2). A killer in blue. Retrieved on October 10, 2009 from http://www.people.com/people/archive/article/0,20101738,00.html.

Saunders, D. J. (2009, March 31). Obama—Just say no. Retrieved on November 25, 2009 from http://search.ebscohost.com.library.keuka.edu/login.aspx?direct=true&db=nfh&AN=37233661&site=ehost-live.

Sayles, L. R. & Strauss, G. (1981). *Managing Human Resources* (2nd edn.). Englewood Cliffs, NJ: Prentice-Hall, Inc.

Scahill, J. (2009, August 4). Blackwater founder implicated in murder. Retrieved on April 17, 2011 from http://www.thenation.com/article/blackwater-founder-implicated-murder.

Scaramella, G. L., Cox, S. M., & McCamey, W. P. (2011). *Introduction to Policing*. Thousand Oaks, CA: Sage Publications, Inc.

Schabner, D. (2011, February 19). Poughkeepsie shooting leaves cop, two others dead: A man allegedly shot a woman, grabbed a child, then exchanged gunfire with cops. Retrieved on February 20, 2011 from http://abcnews.go.com/US/poughkeepsie-shooting-leaves-cop-dead/story?id=12956407.

Schaper, D. (2006, March 20). Salvia: Legal herb hallucinogen draws teens, critics. Retrieved on January 23, 2011 from http://www.npr.org/templates/story/story.php?storyId=5290545.

Schapiro, R. (2011, May 27). Robin Pagoria, Florida Sheriff's deputy, busted for spanking girls and making porn films: Cops. Retrieved on May 27, 2011 from http://www.nydailynews.com/news/national/2011/05/27/2011-05-27_robin_pagoria_florida_sheriffs_deputy_busted_for_spanking_girls_and_making_porn_.html?r=topnews.

Schein, E. H. (1980). *Organizational Psychology* (3rd edn.). Englewood Cliffs, NJ: Prentice-Hall, Inc.

Schemo, D. J. (2008, June 29). Diploma mill concerns extend beyond fraud. Retrieved on April 9, 2011 from http://www.nytimes.com/2008/06/29/us/29diploma.html.

Scherwell, P. (2010, December 11). Salvia: More powerful than LSD, and legal. Retrieved on January 23, 2011 from http://www.telegraph.co.uk/health/healthnews/5090078/Salvia-more-powerful-than-LSD-and-legal.html.

Schloss, L. M. & Lahr, J. G. (2008, Winter). Watch your back: Smart hiring and proper background checks. *Employee Relations Journal*, *34*(3), 46–71.

Schmidt, M. S. (2010, January 21). Judge orders New York to correct bias in fire department. Retrieved on April 14, 2011 from http://www.nytimes.com/2010/01/22/nyregion/22vulcan.html?_r=1.

Schmidt, S. J. (2008, September 13). Jury finds former Alton police officer guilty on all counts: Committed crimes to feed gambling habit. Retrieved on February 20, 2011 from http://proquest.umi.com.library.keuka.edu/pqdweb?did=1554022421&sid=1&Fmt=3&clientId=3663&RQT=309&VName=PQD.

Schneider, M. & Somers, M. (2005, January 12). Organizations as complex adaptive systems: Implications of complexity theory for leadership research. Retrieved on October 26, 2009 from http://search.ebscohost.com.library.keuka.edu/login.aspx?direct=true&db=f5h&AN=21665158&site=ehost-live.

Schmalleger, F. (2007). *Criminal Justice Today: An Introductory Text for the 21st Century* (9th edn.). Upper Saddle River, NJ: Pearson Education, Inc.

Schmidt, B. (2010, June 30). Tualatin mayor's housemate arrested on child-pornography charges. Retrieved on October 24, 2010 from http://www.oregonlive.com/tualatin/index.ssf/2010/06/tualatin_mayors_roommate_arrested_on_child_pornography_charges.html.

Schmidt, H. (1998, May). The changing face of computer crime. *The Police Chief Magazine*, *65*(5), 38–45.

Schneider, M. F., Bailey, J. E., Cicero, T. J., Dart, R. C., Inciardi, J. A., Parrino, M., & Munoz, A. (2009, September). Integrating nine prescription opioid analgesics and/or four signal detection systems to summarize statewide prescription drug use in the United States in 2007. Retrieved on January 20, 2010 from http://search.ebscohost.com.library.keuka.edu/login.aspx?direct=true&db=cmedm&AN=19536784&site=ehost-live.

Schofield, D. L. (1998, August). Ensuring officer integrity and accountability recent court decisions. *FBI Law Enforcement Bulletin*, *67*(8), 28–32.

Schogol, M. (2005, January 12). Former trooper denied parole. Retrieved on October 13, 2009 from http://www.lexisnexis.com.library.keuka.edu/us/lnacademic/results/docview/docview.do?docLinkInd=true&risb=21_T7577964092&format=GNBFI&sort=RELEVANCE&startDocNo=1&resultsUrlKey=29_T7577964098&cisb=22_T7577964097&treeMax=true&treeWidth=0&csi=247189&docNo=25.

School Board of Nassau County, Florida v. Arline (1987).

Schor, E. (2008, April 21). US Army increases use of moral waivers to meet demand for troops. Retrieved on August 7, 2011 from http://www.guardian.co.uk/world/2008/apr/21/usa1.

Schorn, D. (2007, July 11). Campus cover-up in student's murder? Students were not informed young woman had been killed. Retrieved on April 1, 2011 from http://www.cbsnews.com/stories/2007/07/11/earlyshow/contributors/tracysmith/main3043779.shtml.

Schott, K. (2011, July 3). More than 5 decades later, Seattle man charged in abduction, slaying of sycamore girl. Retrieved on July 4, 2011 from http://www.daily-chronicle.com/2011/07/02/more-than-5-decades-later-seattle-man-charged-in-abduction-slaying-of-sycamore-girl/anq0p4s/.

Schouten, F. (2011, February 10). GOP Rep. Chris Lee resigns over shirtless photo on web. Retrieved on February 11, 2011 from http://www.usatoday.com/news/washington/2011-02-09-lee-resigns-amid-scandal_N.htm.

Schram, J. & Greene, L. (2010, December 15). WABC weather gal in 'rape' lie: Cops—Heidi charged with making up assault tale. Retrieved on December 16, 2010 from http://www.nypost.com/p/news/local/wabc_weather_gal_in_rape_lie_cops_Dt6rDzCTktzVPJ049g2YlO.

Schulte, S. (2010, September 30). Should police officers have college experience? Retrieved on March 19, 2011 from http://abclocal.go.com/wls/story?section=news/local&id=7695637.

Schwartz, R. (2009, July 18). Defamation in the Illinois workplace. Retrieved on April 25, 2011 from http://www.myemploymentlawyer.com/wiki/Defamation-in-the-Illinois-Workplace.htm.

Scott, M. D. (2008, May 11). Retired troopers investigate out of Canton home. Retrieved on October 13, 2009 from http://proquest.umi.com.library.keuka.edu/pqdweb?index=61&did=1476669631&SrchMode=1&sid=2&Fmt=3&VInst=PROD&VType=PQD&RQT=309&VName=PQD&TS=1255434330&clientId=3663.

Scott, M. S. (2004, August). *Rave Parties*. Washington, DC: United States Department of Justice Office of Community Oriented Policing Services.

Scott, M. S., Emerson, N. J., Antonacci, L. B., & Plant, J. B. (2006, February). *Drunk Driving*. Washington, DC: United States Department of Justice Office of Community Oriented Policing Services.

Scott, E. D. (2006a, June). Just(?) A true-false test: Applying signal detection theory to judgments of organizational dishonesty. Retrieved on July 26, 2011 from http://proquest.umi.com.library.keuka.edu/pqdweb?did=1043570521&sid=6&Fmt=4&clientId=3663&RQT=309&VName=PQD.

Scott, S. (2006b, June 24). City manager report to be aired: Police background check, now confidential, may be discussed at council meeting. Retrieved on October 13, 2009 from http://web.ebscohost.com.library.keuka.edu/ehost/detail?vid=12&hid=8&sid=d30bed09-3932-47cc-9ef4-6811f3bac285%40sessionmgr4&bdata=JnNpdGU9ZWhvc3QtbGl2ZQ%3d%3d#db=nfh&AN=2W62W63199577631.

Scott v. Harris (2007).

Scott v. Blanchet High School (1987).

Scrivner, E. (1994, October). Controlling police use of excessive force: The role of the police psychologist. Retrieved on February 13, 2010 from http://www.ncjrs.gov/txtfiles/ppsyc.txt.

Scrivner, E. (2006, January 26). *Innovations in Police Recruitment and Hiring: Hiring in the Spirit of Service*. Washington, DC: United States Department of Justice Office of Community Oriented Policing Service.

Scroggins, W. A., Thomas, S. L., & Morris, J. A. (2008, Summer). Psychological testing in personnel selection, part II: The refinement of methods and standards in employee selection. Retrieved on October 21, 2009 from http://proquest.umi.com.library.keuka.edu/pqdweb?did=1500727011&sid=3&Fmt=3&clientId=3663&RQT=309&VName=PQD.

Scully, J. L. (2011, April). Interviewing techniques for successful hiring. Retrieved on July 17, 2011 from http://proquest.umi.com.library.keuka.edu/pqdweb?did=2338265581&sid=3&Fmt=3&clientId=3663&RQT=309&VName=PQD.

Scuro, J. E. (2001, October). Predicting future dangerous activity. *Law and Order Magazine*, *49*(10), 22–24.

Scuro, J. E. (2002, May). Recent U.S. Supreme Court defines ADA disability. *Law and Order Magazine*, *50*(5), 16–18.

Scuro, J. E. (2003, July). RICO, money laundering and public corruption. *Law and Order Magazine*, *51*(7), 10–12.

Scuro, J. E. (2004, February). Supreme Court redefines affirmative action. *Law and Order Magazine*, *52*(2), 24–26.

SeaRiver Maritime, Inc. v. Industrial Medical Services, Inc. (1989).

Seattle Police Department (1995–2011). Seattle police department—Hiring process—Qualifications. Retrieved on September 23, 2011 from http://www.cityofseattle.net/police/jobs/hiring/qualifi cations.htm.

SecurityOnCampus.net. (2007, December 18). Eastern Michigan University faces largest ever Jeanne Clery Act fine of $357,500. Retrieved on April 1, 2011 from http://www.securityon-campus.net/index.php?option=com_content&view=article&id=174.&Itemid=79.

Seef, A. (2010, November 18). Sheriff's captain Catherine Mclaughlin charged with rape, official misconduct. Retrieved on November 18, 2010 from http://www.greecepost.com/latestnews/x151217467/Catherine-McLaughlin-Sheriffs-Captain-charged-with-rape-official-misconduct.

Seef, A. (2011a, January 12). Former Rochester police officer charged with tax fraud, grand larceny. Retrieved on January 12, 2011 from http://www.gateschilipost.com/latestnews/x471104343/Former-Rochester-police-officer-charged-with-tax-fraud-grand-larceny.

Seef, A. (2011b, February 5). Webster man charged after police find 60 pot plants. Retrieved on February 6, 2011 from http://www.greecepost.com/latestnews/x188778738/Webster-man-charged-after-police-find-60-pot-plants.

Seelye, K. Q. (2006, October 24). Barack Obama, asked about drug history, admits he inhaled—Americas—International Herald Tribune. Retrieved on February 20, 2011 from http://www.nytimes.com/2006/10/24/world/americas/24iht-dems.3272493.html.

Seigfried v. City of Easton (1992).

Selective Service System (2009a, June 26). Who must register chart. Retrieved on April 18, 2011 from http://www.sss.gov/PDFs/WhoMustRegisterChart.pdf.

Selective Service System (2009b, June 29). Who must register. Retrieved on April 18, 2011 from http://www.sss.gov/FSwho.htm.

Selekman, J. (2008, July–August). Gambling: Normal adolescent activity or pathologic addiction. *Pediatric Nursing*, *34*(4), 325–328.

Serpas, R. & Hagar, M. (2010, August). The untruthful employee: Is termination the only response. *The Police Chief Magazine*, *77*(8), 114–120.

Sewell, D. (2011, May 1). 4 Slain in Ohio; suspect dies in police shootout. Retrieved on May 1, 2011 from http://www.miamiherald.com/2011/05/01/2195710/4-slain-in-ohio-suspect-dies-in.html.

Sewell, J. D. (1999). *Controversial Issues in Policing*. Needham Heights, MA: Allyn & Bacon.

Sewell v. Town of Lake Hamilton (1998).

Shahid, A. (2011a, February 26). Toddler raped at Seaworld, Michael Grzybowicz being held without bail: Florida police. Retrieved on May 27, 2011 from http://www.nydailynews.com/news/national/2011/02/26/2011-02-26_toddler_raped_at_seaworld_michael_grzybowicz_being_held_without_bail_florida_pol.html?obref=obinsite.

Shahid, A. (2011b, May 27). Iraq vet and former U.S. Marine Jose Guerena gunned down in Arizona SWAT raid, video released. Retrieved on May 27, 2011 from http://www.nydailynews.com/news/national/2011/05/27/2011-05-27_iraq_vet_and_former_us_marine_jose_guerena_gunned_down_in_arizona_swat_raid_vide.html.

Shanks v. Allied Signal, Inc. (1999).

Shapiro, D. L. (2004, December). Response to Wright's analysis of when "Delayed" integrity occurs. Retrieved on July 24, 2011 from http://web.ebscohost.com.library.keuka.edu/ehost/detail?vid=8&hid=110&sid=e3273d33-5fa7-4328-bcbc-0764c45e691c%40sessionmgr110&bdata=JnNpdGU9ZWhvc3QtbGl2ZQ%3d%3d#db=buh&AN=15284059.

Sharon, M. (2007, December 10). Take note of changes to immigration form. Retrieved on March 16, 2010 from http://search.ebscohost.com.library.keuka.edu/login.aspx?direct=true&db=bwh&AN=27966757&site=ehost-live.

Sharp, A. (2003, September). Departmental divergences on marijuana use and new recruits. *Law and Order Magazine*, *51*(9), 80–84.

Sharp, A. (2004, December). Recruits and smoking. *Law and Order Magazine*, *52*(12), 52–55.

Sharp, B. (2009, July 12). Minorities mostly miss out on recent RPD hiring boon. Retrieved on February 20, 2011 from http://rocnow.com/article/local-news/2009907120348.

Shea, M. R. (2008a, April 8). Teacher pleads in sex case: Says he's not guilty of 4 felony charges. Retrieved on December 6, 2010 from http://www.modbee.com/2008/04/08/262750/teacher-pleads-in-sex-case.html.

Shea, M. R. (2008b, June 16). Police shoot, kill man who savagely beat toddler to death near Turlock: Driver stopped when he saw man slamming something into the road. Retrieved on April 18, 2011 from http://www.modbee.com/2008/06/16/330185/police-shoot-kill-man-who-savagely.html.

Sheetz, M. W. (2003, December). Reading between the lines: Steganography. *Law and Order Magazine*, *51*(12), 46–51.

Shepherd, C. & Kori, D. (2005, September). Style counsel. Retrieved on March 16, 2010 from http://proquest.umi.com.library.keuka.edu/pqdweb?did=909255761&sid=3&Fmt=4&clientId=3663&RQT=309&VName=PQD.

Sheridan, M. B. (2008, June 24). Recruits who failed checks were hired by capitol police. Retrieved on October 13, 2009 from http://proquest.umi.com.library.keuka.edu/pqdweb?index=52&did=1499479781&SrchMode=1&sid=2&Fmt=3&VInst=PROD&VType=PQD&RQT=309&VName=PQD&TS=1255433071&clientId=3663.

Sheridan, M. (2011a, January 10). Rachel Ann Hicks, 36, busted for cross-country trip to have sex with boy, 13, she met on Xbox: Cops. Retrieved on February 20, 2011 from http://www.nydailynews.com/news/national/2011/01/10/2011-01-10_rachel_ann_hicks_36_busted_for_cross country_trip_to_have_sex_with_boy_13_she_met.html?obref=obinsite.

Sheridan, M. (2011b, January 25). Loveland teacher, Courtney Bowles, busted for sex assault on student: Police. Retrieved on January 28, 2011 from http://www.nydailynews.com/news/national/2011/01/25/2011-01-25_loveland_teacher_courtney_bowles_busted_for_sex_assault_on_student_police.html?r=news/national.

Sheridan, M. (2011c, February 6). Gym teacher Stacy Schuler had sexual relations with high school football players: Authorities. Retrieved on February 20, 2011 from http://www.nydailynews.com/news/national/2011/02/06/2011-02-06_gym_teacher_stacy_schuler_had_sexual_relations_with_high_school_football_players.html?obref=obinsite.

Sheridan, M. (2011d, March 16). Biology teacher Carrie Shafer caught partially nude with 17-year-old student in Kentucky: Police. Retrieved on June 26, 2011 from http://www.nydailynews.com/news/national/2011/03/16/2011-03-16_biology_teacher_carrie_shafer_caught_partially_nude_with_17yearold_student_in_ke.html.

Sherman, M. (2009, June 29). White firefighters win Supreme Court appeal. Retrieved on June 29, 2009 from http://news.yahoo.com/s/ap/20090629/ap_on_go_su_co/us_supreme_court_firefighters_lawsuit.

Sherman, M. (2010a, June 17). High court: Go ahead, search cop's sexy texting: High court doesn't make cop's day, upholds search of sexy texting on department-owned pager. Retrieved on June 29, 2009 from http://finance.yahoo.com/news/High-court-Go-ahead-search-apf-468906243.html?x=0&.v=2.

Sherman, W. (2010b, November 9). Carlotta Brett-Pierce charged with murder in starvation, beating death of daughter Marchella, 4. Retrieved on April 7, 2011 from http://www.nydailynews.com/news/ny_crime/2010/11/09/2010-11-09_carlotta_brettpierce_charged_with_murder_in_starvation_beating_death_of_daughter.html.

Sherwyn, D., Eigen, Z. J., & Klausner, A. A. (2000, February). Interpreting the ADA and civil rights law. Retrieved on November 18, 2009 from http://proquest.umi.com.library.keuka.edu/pqdweb?did=51982577&sid=1&Fmt=3&clientId=3663&RQT=309&VName=PQD.

Shield Club v. City of Cleveland (1986).

Shirsat v. Mutual Pharmaceutical (1996).

Shulman, M. T. (2009, April 1). Employers can expect to encounter more cases of resume fraud. Retrieved on February 22, 2011 from http://proquest.umi.com.library.keuka.edu/pqdweb?did=1671195161&sid=3&Fmt=3&clientId=3663&RQT=309&VName=PQD.

Shumaker, T. A. (2003, November). Employee privacy versus employer rights. Retrieved on February 16, 2010 from http://proquest.umi.com.library.keuka.edu/pqdweb?did=500111621&sid=1&Fmt=2&clientId=3663&RQT=309&VName=PQD.

Siegel, L. J. (2006). *Criminology* (9th edn.). Belmont, CA: Thomson Wadsworth.

Siegert v. Gilley (1991).

Siemaszko, C. (2011, June 8). Pennsylvania man beats girlfriend's 2-year-old daughter 'for fun.' Retrieved on June 8, 2011 from http://www.nydailynews.com/news/national/2011/06/08/2011-06-08_pennsylvania_man_beats_girlfriends_2yearold_daughter_for_fun.html.

Sienkiewicz v. County of Santa Cruz (1987).

Silva v. Lucky Stores (1998).

Silver, J. D. & McNulty, T. (2003, August 7). City neighborhoods—Police layoff: Recent hires to be first to go and they're not happy. Retrieved on February 14, 2011 from http://www.post-gazette.com/neigh_city/20030807safetyC2.asp.

Silvera v. Orange County School Board (2001).

Simon, D. (2011, March 10). Glouco teacher's aide faces child-porn charges. Retrieved on August 13, 2011 from http://www.philly.com/philly/news/20110310_Glouco_teacher_s_aide_faces_child-porn_charges.html.

Simon, S. (2010, March 13). Paulin-Ramirez'z actions raised mother's concerns. Retrieved on March 13, 2010 from http://online.wsj.com/article/SB10001424052748704734304575119913693410050.html?mod=WSJ_hpp_MIDDLETopStories.

Simons, S. R. & Mawn, B. (2010, July). Bullying in the workplace—A qualitative study of newly registered nurses. Retrieved on February 5, 2011 from http://web.ebscohost.com.library.keuka.edu/ehost/detail?hid=21&sid=83ac1063-0972-4530-a77b-7200704592ca%40sessionmgr14&vid=4&bdata=JnNpdGU9ZWhvc3QtbGl2ZQ%3d%3d#db=c8h&AN=2010708185.

Simpson v. Western Graphics Corporation (1982).

Sina Corporation. (2010, March 13). Chinese official arrested after incriminating diary posted online. Retrieved on March 13, 2010 from http://english.sina.com/china/2010/0313/308666.html.

Sinclair-Bernadino, L. (2006). Negligent hiring doctrine opens more doors for pre-employment screening. Retrieved on November 8, 2009 from http://www.pimall.com/nais/n.hire.html.

Sindermann v. Civil Service (1995).

Singh, A. & Abraham, A. (2008, January). Neuro linguistic programming: A key to business excellence. Retrieved on July 24, 2011 from http://proquest.umi.com.library.keuka.edu/pqdweb?did=1438939261&sid=4&Fmt=2&clientId=3663&RQT=309&VName=PQD.

Singletary, M. (2010, November 1). Credit scores don't belong in job search. Retrieved on February 26, 2011 from http://proquest.umi.com.library.keuka.edu/pqdweb?did=2178300311&sid=1&Fmt=3&clientId=3663&RQT=309&VName=PQD.

Sinha, R. (2009, February 23). How companies bring a customer approach to employee hiring. Retrieved on October 11, 2009 from http://www.articlesbase.com/career-management-articles/how-companies-are-bringing-a-customer-approach-to-employee-hiring-785847.html.

Sisak, M. R. (2011, August 24). County fires deputy Sheriff after arrest. Retrieved on September 2, 2011 from http://standardspeaker.com/news/county-fires-deputy-sheriff-after-arrest-1.1192495#axzz1Vx5DdKWA.

Siuru, B. (1999, May). A simulator that shoots back. Retrieved on October 22, 2009 from http://proquest.umi.com.library.keuka.edu/pqdweb?did=40446286&sid=3&Fmt=4&clientId=3663&RQT=309&VName=PQD.

Six, J. (2008, February 15). Former Camden cop sentenced for giving gun to robber. Retrieved on October 28, 2010 from http://www.nj.com/south/index.ssf/2008/02/former_camden_cop_sentenced_fo.html.

Sixel, L. M. (2010, October 28). Working how's your credit score? Potential employers may be looking working: EEOC scrutinizes issue. Retrieved on February 26, 2011 from http://proquest.umi.com.library.keuka.edu/pqdweb?did=2174759081&sid=1&Fmt=3&clientId=3663&RQT=309&VName=PQD.

Skeel, S. (2006, April 3). US police departments having trouble finding recruits. Retrieved on October 12, 2009 from http://www.voanews.com/english/archive/2006-04/2006-04-03-voa60.cfm?moddate=2006-04-03.

Skinner v. Railway Labor Executives Association (1989).

Slack, D. (2006, December). Municipal officers fail hub screening 37 of 68 don't qualify to the Boston police. Retrieved on October 13, 2009 from http://proquest.umi.com.library.keuka.edu/pqdweb?index=3&did=1178424691&SrchMode=1&sid=4&Fmt=3&VInst=PROD&VType=PQD&RQT=309&VName=PQD&TS=1255437023&clientId=3663.

Slahor, S. (2010, March). "The" budget. *Law and Order Magazine*, *58*(3), 10.

Slowik, S. M. (2001, Spring). Objective pre-employment interviewing: Balancing recruitment. Selection, and retention goals. *Public Personnel Management*, *30*(1), 77–93.

Slowik, S. (2002, May). Selection systems and the smaller department. *Law and Order Magazine*, *50*(5), 112–116.

Slowik, S. (2003, July). Background checks on lateral hires. *Law and Order Magazine*, *51*(7), 98–102.

Slowik, S. M. (2005). ADA revisited: Current legal pre-employment interviewing and polygraph issues and solutions. Retrieved on November 21, 2009 from http://proquest.umi.com.library.keuka.edu/pqdweb?did=978646981&sid=1&Fmt=2&clientId=3663&RQT=309&VName=PQD.

Slowik, S. M. (2008). Forensic interviewing, polygraph, and child deception. *Polygraph, 37*(3), 216–227.

Smart v. Geren (2008).

Smith, A. (2009a, August). Nationwide I-9 audits reflect shift in enforcement strategy. Retrieved on March 16, 2010 from http://search.ebscohost.com.library.keuka.edu/login.aspx?direct=true&db=buh&AN=44234711&site=ehost-live.

Smith, E. D. (2004, November 28). Check before you hire. Retrieved on February 16, 2010 from http://proquest.umi.com.library.keuka.edu/pqdweb?did=838811641&sid=1&Fmt=2&clientId=3663&RQT=309&VName=PQD.

Smith, E. L. & Farole, D. J. (2009, October). Profile of intimate partner violence cases in large urban counties. Washington, DC: United States Department of Justice, Office of Justice Programs, Bureau of Justice Statistics. NCJ 228193

Smith, M., Segal, R., & Segal, J. (2008, November). Post-traumatic stress disorder (PTSD): Symptoms, treatment, and self-help. Retrieved on August 15, 2010 from http://helpguide.org/mental/post_traumatic_stress_disorder_symptoms_treatment.htm.

Smith, R. (2009b, February). Rewriters block: How to safely usher copy through the approval process. Retrieved on March 16, 2010 from http://proquest.umi.com.library.keuka.edu/pqdweb?did=1652561681&sid=3&Fmt=2&clientId=3663&RQT=309&VName=PQD.

Smith, T. (2000, September). Identity fraud: The hard lesson of higher education. *Law and Order Magazine, 48*(9), 101–105.

Smith, P. (2010a, October 3). California governor signs marijuana decriminalization bill: The bill reduces simple possession from a misdemeanor to an infraction. Retrieved on April 19, 2011 from http://www.alternet.org/drugs/148388/california_governor_signs_marijuana_decriminalization_bill/.

Smith, T. (2010b, August 27). Australian police, Facebook crack child porn ring. Retrieved on October 24, 2010 from http://www.physorg.com/news202103776.html.

Smith, G. T., McCarthy, D. M., & Zapolski, T. C. (2009, September). On the value of homogeneous constructs for construct validation, theory testing, and the description of psychopathology. Retrieved on October 21, 2009 from http://proquest.umi.com.library.keuka.edu/pqdweb?did=1864723121&sid=1&Fmt=2&clientId=3663&RQT=309&VName=PQD.

Smith v. Hireright Solutions, Inc. (2009).

Smith v. Holley (1992).

Snowden, L. L. & Fuss, T. (2000). A costly mistake: Inadequate police background investigations. *The Justice Professional, 13*, 359–375.

Snyder, C. (1996, August). The resume police. Retrieved on October 13, 2009 from http://web.ebscohost.com.library.keuka.edu/ehost/detail?vid=12&hid=8&sid=d30bed09-3932-47cc-9ef4-6811f3bac285%40sessionmgr4&bdata=JnNpdGU9ZWhvc3QtbGl2ZQ%3d%3d#db=f5h&AN=9702145972.

Snyder, H. N. (2003, December). Juvenile arrests. Juvenile Justice Bulletin, United States Department of Justice, Office of Justice Programs, Office of Juvenile Justice and Delinquency Programs, pp. 1–11.

Society for Human Resource Management (SHRM). Weblink: http://www.shrm.org/Pages/default.aspx.

Society of Financial Examiners (SOFE) (2011). Weblink: http://www.sofe.org/about/.

Socorro v. IMI Data Search, Inc. (2003).

Sokolove, B. A. & Field, M. W. (2002, January). The law enforcement candidate ride-along: A supplemental selection tool. *The Police Chief Magazine, 69*(1), 55–59.

Somerville, K. J. (2009, Summer). The military report card concerning domestic violence and sexual assault, including compliance with the Lautenberg amendment. Retrieved on April 16, 2011 from http://web.ebscohost.com.library.keuka.edu/ehost/detail?vid=8&hid=111&sid=b3f5dc62-a935-427d-9ab9-e87305912346%40sessionmgr110&bdata=JnNpdGU9ZWhvc3QtbGl2ZQ%3d%3d#db=aph&AN=46765631.

Sonnenberg, F. K. (1994). *Managing with a Conscience: How to Improve Performance through Integrity, Trust, and Commitment*. New York: McGraw-Hill, Inc.

Soto, J. (1998a). Avoiding the teeth of liability. *Law and Order Magazine*, *46*, 99–104.

Soto, J. (1998b, October). Informant operations: Direction and control of human sources of information. *Law and Order Magazine*, *46*(10), 93–100.

Soto v New York State Office of Mental Retardation and Developmental Disabilities (2010).

Souryal, S. S. (2003). *Ethics is Criminal Justice: In Search of the Truth* (3rd edn.). New York: HarperCollins Publishers.

South Carolina Highway Patrol (2009). Employment information. Retrieved on November 26, 2009 from http://www.schp.org/employment.asp.

Southeastern Apartments Management, Inc. v. Jackman (1999).

Spector, E. (1998). Liability for failure to disclose exculpatory information. *The Police Chief Magazine*, *65*, 12–14.

Spector, E. (2002, June). The model statutes project: Conducting background investigations. *The Police Chief Magazine*, *69*(6), 55–59.

Spector, E. (2008, April). Chief's counsel: Should police officer who lie be terminated as a matter of public policy. Retrieved on February 14, 2011 from http://www.policechiefmagazine.org/magazine/index.cfm?fuseaction=display_arch&article_id=1458&issue_id=42008.

Spector, J. (2010a, April 15). Carl Paladino beset by off-color e-mails. Retrieved on April 15, 2010 from http://www.democratandchronicle.com/article/20100415/NEWS01/4150348/1002/NEWS.

Spector, J. (2010b, August 16). Governor Paterson signs no-fault divorce bill. Retrieved on August 16, 2010 from http://www.democratandchronicle.com/article/20100816/NEWS01/8160322/1002/NEWS.

Spielman, F. & Main, F. (2010, January 6). Chicago police may scrap entrance exam: Fraternal Order of Police president mark Donahue said the idea "Sounds Too Stupid to Be True." Retrieved on May 5, 2011 from http://www.policeone.com/patrol-issues/articles/1986463-Chicago-police-may-scrap-entrance-exam/.

Spina, M. (2011, April 29). Inmate hurt trying to break up fighting officers: Loses tooth in scrap over bag of chips. Retrieved on May 1, 2011 from http://www.buffalonews.com/city/communities/eastern-erie/article406867.ece.

Srogi, K. (2006). Hair analysis as method for determination of level of drugs and pharmaceutical in human body: Review of chromatographic procedures. Retrieved on January 18, 2010 from http://search.ebscohost.com.library.keuka.edu/login.aspx?direct=true&db=aph&AN=19999968&site=ehost-live.

Staffing Industry Review Magazine (2010, December 14). Four top trends in background checks. Retrieved on February 21, 2011 from http://www.staffingindustry.com/me2/dirmod.asp?sid=9B6FFC446FF7486981EA3C0C3CCE4943&nm=&type=MultiPublishing&mod=PublishingTitles&mid=6EECC0FE471F4CA995CE2A3E9A8E4207&tier=4&id=A7A821EC79B740E2ACD620BC19096BF2.

Stamatis, D. H. (1996). *Total Quality Service: Principles, Practices, and Implementation*. Delray Beach, FL: St. Lucie Press.

Staples v. Rent-A-Center (2000).

State and Local Government on the Net (1995–2010). State employment sites. Retrieved on February 7, 2011 from http://www.statelocalgov.net/50states-jobs.cfm.

State of Minnesota By Spannaus v. Century Camera, Inc. (1981).

Stearns v. Gilchrist (1976).

Stein, A. (2010, July 20). Stoughton cop resigns after he left beat to see dwarf porn star. Retrieved on September 26, 2010 from http://www.enterprisenews.com/news/cops_and_courts/x1080706061/Stoughton-cop-lied-about-gun-left-beat-to-see-porn-star.

Stein, M. L. (1998, March 28). Cop records confidential. Retrieved on October 24, 2009 from http://search.ebscohost.com.library.keuka.edu/login.aspx?direct=true&db=aph&AN=435880&site=ehost-live.

Steinberg, J. (1993, October 12). Scars in a proud police force; troopers come to terms with evidence-tampering scandal. Retrieved on October 18, 2010 from http://www.nytimes.com/1993/10/12/nyregion/scars-proud-police-force-troopers-come-terms-with-evidence-tampering-scandal.html?sec=&spon=&pagewanted=all.

Stengle, J. (2011, July 29). Hood suspect defiant in court appearance. Retrieved on August 7, 2011 from http://www.armytimes.com/news/2011/07/ap-army-hood-naser-abdo-court-appearance-072911/.

Stepankowsky, A. (2009, October 30). Troopers with fake degrees suspended, not fired. Retrieved on March 19, 2011 from http://tdn.com/business/local/article_50cffe8b-80d5-503b-906e-d32462a91c07.html.

Stewart, N. & Craig, T. (2011, February 25). Sulaimon Brown, aide to D.C. Mayor, is fired after allegations of criminal record. Retrieved on April 16, 2011 from http://www.washingtonpost.com/wp-dyn/content/article/2011/02/24/AR2011022407597.html.

Stewart v. Jackson & Nash (1992).

Stirgus, E. (2000, October 29). Largo police explorer scandal inquiry ends with no charges. Retrieved on December 6, 2010 from http://www.sptimes.com/News/102900/TampaBay/Largo_police_Explorer.shtml.

Stohr, M. K. & Collins, P. A. (2009). *Criminal Justice Management: Theory and Practice in Justice-Centered Organizations*. New York: Oxford University Press, Inc.

Stokes, P. P. (2000, June). Is there a duty to disclose in employment references? (Honesty is the best policy). Retrieved on July 6, 2009 from http://www.allbusiness.com/legal/laws-government-regulations-employment/722564-1.html.

Stokes v. Bullins (1988).

Stokes v. Harris (2007).

Stone, G. (2009, March 13). 'Sexting' teens can go too far: Sending provocative images over cell phones is all the rage, but it can go all wrong. Retrieved on October 14, 2010 from http://abcnews.go.com/Technology/WorldNews/sexting-teens/story?id=6456834.

Stone v. Chelan County Sheriff's Department (1988).

Strandberg, K. W. (2000, November). Pointing investigators in the right direction: To successfully conduct online searchers, investigators need to know where to look. *The Law Enforcement Technology*, 48.

Strang, R. (2001, March). Recognizing and meeting Title III concerns in computer investigations. Retrieved on June 5, 2011 from http://www.justice.gov/criminal/cybercrime/usamarch2001_2.htm.

Stratton, S. N. (2002, August 5). Quinn Bill merits no badge of efficiency. Retrieved on March 19, 2011 from http://www.pioneerinstitute.org/pdf/020805_stratton.pdf.

Strauss, S. E., Tetroe, J., & Graham, I. (2009, August 4). Defining knowledge translation. Retrieved on October 27, 2009 from http://proquest.umi.com.library.keuka.edu/pqdweb?did=1809677351&sid=1&Fmt=3&clientId=3663&RQT=309&VName=PQD.

Strauss v. Hannig (1939).

Strausberg, C. (2002, May 20). McCann, Russell Rip $2.3 mil award. Retrieved on October 26, 2009 from http://proquest.umi.com.library.keuka.edu/pqdweb?did=583561421&sid=2&Fmt=3&clientId=3663&RQT=309&VName=PQD.

Strecher, V. G. (1997). *Planning Community Policing: Goal Specific Cases and Exercises*. Prospect Heights, IL: Waveland Press, Inc.

Strom, K. J. (2001, September). Hate crimes reported in NIBRS, 1997–1999. Washington, DC: United States Department of Justice, Office of Justice Programs, Bureau of Justice Statistics.

Struckhoff, D. R. (1994). American Sheriff. Retrieved on November 26, 2009 from http://search.ebscohost.com.library.keuka.edu/login.aspx?direct=true&db=sih&AN=SM152171&site=ehost-live.

Stuart, D. M. (2003, December). Domestic violence and sexual assault. *The Police Chief Magazine*, *70*(12), 28–30.

Suderman, A. (2011, February 23). The bigger scandal (updated). Retrieved on April 16, 2011 from http://www.washingtoncitypaper.com/blogs/looselips/2011/02/23/the-bigger-scandal/.

Suhr, B. (2011, January 24). Air force chief pleads guilty to sexual misconduct. Retrieved on January 25, 2011 from http://www.seattlepi.com/national/1110ap_us_air_force_harassment_charges.html.

Sullivan, B. (2006, May 3). Bob the writer, bob the molester. Retrieved on March 29, 2010 from http://redtape.msnbc.com/2006/05/bob_the_writer_.html.

Sullivan, J. (2008, October 20). Nine state patrol troopers put on leave in diploma-mill probe: Nine state troopers have been placed on administrative leave while the agency investigates whether they purchased falsified diplomas in order to get increased pay. Retrieved on March 19, 2011 from http://seattletimes.nwsource.com/html/localnews/2008289502_webdiplomas20m.html.

Sullivan, J. (2010, December 14). DNA leads to arrest in 1983 motel killing. Retrieved on April 17, 2011 from http://seattletimes.nwsource.com/html/localnews/2013680073_coldcase15m.html.

Sullivan, J. (2009, March 18). County settles sexual harassment lawsuit. *Daily Republic.*

Sullivan, L. (2011a, March 10). City agrees to lower test scores for police exam. Retrieved on April 14, 2011 from http://www.daytondailynews.com/news/dayton-news/city-agrees-to-lower-test-scores-for-police-exam-1103409.html.

Sullivan, L. (2011b, June 3). Married teacher Carrie Shafer caught partially naked with 17-year-old student cops a plea, avoids jail. Retrieved on June 26, 2011 from http://www.gadailynews.com/national/68059-married-teacher-carrie-shafer-caught-partially-naked-with-17-yr-old-student-cops-a-plea-avoids-jail.html.

Sulzberger, A. G. & Medina, J. (2011, January 17). Shooting suspect had been known to use potent, and legal, hallucinogen. Retrieved on January 23, 2011 from http://www.nytimes.com/2011/01/18/us/18salvia.html?src=twrhp.

Super, J. T. (2006, Fall). A survey of pre-employment psychological evaluation tests and procedures. Retrieved on October 13, 2009 from http://proquest.umi.com.library.keuka.edu/pqdweb?did=1174208971&sid=4&Fmt=2&clientId=3663&RQT=309&VName=PQD.

Suppan v. Kratzer (1995).

Surk, B. (2010, April 4). Dubai jail sentence upheld for UK kissing couple. Retrieved on April 4, 2010 http://news.yahoo.com/s/ap/20100404/ap_on_re_mi_ea/ml_dubai_kissing_case;_ylt=Aq9GxwaiK.ZcQBgkvCrxmK39xg8F;_ylu=X3oDMTNhMmQwazJ1BGFzc2V0A2FwLzI-wMTAwNDA0L21sX2R1YmFpX2tpc3NpbmdfY2FzZQRjY29kZQNtb3N0cG9wdWxhcgRjcG9zAzQEcG9zAzQEc2VjA3luX.

Susan M. Miron v. University of New Haven Police Department et al. (2007).

Sutton v. United Airlines (1999).

Sutton, R. I. (2007). *The No Asshole Rule*. New York: Warner Business Books.

Svaldi, A. (2011, February 13). Job loss, debt gain take toll in Colorado more individuals filed for bankruptcy protection in 2010: There were slightly fewer filings by businesses. Retrieved on February 22, 2011 from http://proquest.umi.com.library.keuka.edu/pqdweb?did=2265878201&sid=2&Fmt=3&clientId=3663&RQT=309&VName=PQD.

Swartz, N. (2005, January/February). Electronic I-9 forms not allowed. Retrieved on March 16, 2010 from http://search.ebscohost.com.library.keuka.edu/login.aspx?direct=true&db=lxh&AN=15615145&site=ehost-live.

Swearer v. Karoleski (1989).

Swift, A. (2006, May 21). Officer has to pay back raise after degree-mill probe: Popka's degree from Almeda University wasn't from an accredited school recognized by the Florida Department of Law Enforcement. Retrieved on April 14, 2011 from http://www.naplesnews.com/news/2006/may/21/officer_has_pay_back_raise_after_degreemill_probe/?local_news.

Szalavitz, M. (2011, July 11). U.S. rules that marijuana has no medical use. What does science say? Retrieved on July 20, 2011 from http://healthland.time.com/2011/07/11/u-s-rules-marijuana-has-no-medical-use-what-does-science-say/.

Szczesny, P. (2002, June). Suspect interviews: Asking for the necessary information. *Law and Order Magazine*, *50*(6), 126–128.

Tahmincioglu, E. (2010, March 17). Wal-Mart worker fired over medical marijuana: Joseph Casias, 29, has doctor's prescription for pot to treat his brain tumor. Retrieved on June 1, 2011 from http://www.msnbc.msn.com/id/35913492/ns/business-careers/t/wal-mart-worker-fired-over-medical-marijuana/.

Tallahassee Furniture Co., Inc. v. Harrison (1991).

Tandon, S. (2010, November 27). World braces for Wikileaks flood of US cables. Retrieved on November 27, 2010 from http://news.yahoo.com/s/afp/usdiplomacymilitaryinternetwikileaks.

Tanner, J. (2005, June). *Using Technology in the Supervision, Treatment, and Containment of Sex Offenders*. Seattle, WA: Innovative Technologies for Community Corrections Conference.

Tanner, S. (2010, March 5). Job applicant claims false positive for cocaine use. Retrieved on February 22, 2011 from http://chicagoemploymentattorneysblog.com/2010/03/job-applicant-claims-false-positive-for-cocaine-use.html.

Tansey, J. & O'Riordan, T. (1991). Cultural theory and risk: A review. *Health, Risk, and Society*, *1*(1), 71–90.

Tapper, J. & Miller, A. (2007, April 17). Teacher warned authorities about Va. tech shooter: Violent creative writing led teacher, students to fear potential violence. Retrieved on April 13, 2011 from http://abcnews.go.com/WNT/VATech/story?id=3050437&page=1.

Targeted News Service (2011a, February 16). Mclennan County Sheriff Larry Lynch conducts child support roundup. Retrieved on February 20, 2011 from http://proquest.umi.com.library.keuka.edu/pqdweb?did=2268490071&sid=1&Fmt=3&clientId=3663&RQT=309&VName=PQD.

Targeted News Service (2011b, July 16). New police officers hired. Retrieved on July 26, 2011 from http://proquest.umi.com.library.keuka.edu/pqdweb?did=2394456931&sid=2&Fmt=3&clientId=3663&RQT=309&VName=PQD.

Tavernise, S. (2010, November 22). Guilty verdict in Chandra Levy murder case. Retrieved on January 15, 2011 from http://www.nytimes.com/2010/11/23/us/23levy.html.

Tawney, M. (2008, December). Integrity testing… The selection tool of the future. *Law and Order Magazine*, *56*(12), 34–38.

Taylor, H. G. (1998, March–April). Analysis of the medical use of marijuana and its societal implications. Retrieved on January 28, 2010 from http://search.ebscohost.com.library.keuka.edu/login.aspx?direct=true&db=cmedm&AN=9654850&site=ehost-live.

Taylor, B., Kubu, B., Fridell, L., Rees, C., Jordan, T., & Cheney, J. (2005, December 30). *The Cop Crunch: Identifying Strategies for Dealing with the Recruiting and Hiring Crisis in Law Enforcement*. Washington, DC: Police Executive Research Forum.

Taylor, L. J., Moersch, B. J., & McClure Franklin, G. (2003, Fall). Applying the theory of constraints to a public safety hiring process. *Public Personnel Management*, *32*(3), 367–382.

Temponi, C., Bryant, M. D., & Fernandez, B. (2009, December 16). Integration of business function models into an aggregate enterprise systems model. Retrieved on October 24, 2009 from http://proquest.umi.com.library.keuka.edu/pqdweb?did=1738844761&sid=1&Fmt=2&clientId=3663&RQT=309&VName=PQD.

Tennessee Department of Commerce and Insurance. (2009). Law enforcement training academy. Retrieved on October 20, 2009 from http://www.state.tn.us/commerce/let/post/index.shtml.

Tennessee v. Garner (1985).

Terhune, C. (2008, June 9). The trouble with background checks: Employee screening has become a big business, but not always an accurate one. Retrieved on October 13, 2009 from http://www.lexisnexis.com.library.keuka.edu/us/lnacademic/search/homesubmitForm.do.

Tersine, R. J. & Jones, M. B. (1973, September). Models for examining organizations. Retrieved on October 24, 2009 from http://proquest.umi.com.library.keuka.edu/pqdweb?did=1186801&sid=2&Fmt=2&clientId=3663&RQT=309&VName=PQD.

TestCountry.org (2011). What are the popular drug test panels? Retrieved on August 8, 2011 from http://www.testcountry.org/what-are-the-popular-drug-test-panels.htm.

Tetrault, J. M., Desai, R. A., Becker, W. C., Fiellin, D. A., Concato, J., & Sullivan, L. E. (2008, February). Gender and non-medical use of prescription opioids: Results from a national US survey. Retrieved on January 28, 2010 from http://search.ebscohost.com.library.keuka.edu/login.aspx?direct=true&db=cmedm&AN=18042194&site=ehost-live.

Templeton, G. F., Schmidt, M. B., & Taylor, G. S. (2009, April). Managing the diffusion of organizational behavior. Retrieved on October 27, 2009 from http://proquest.umi.com.library.keuka.edu/pqdweb?did=1720911021&sid=2&Fmt=2&clientId=3663&RQT=309&VName=PQD.

Texas Commission on Law Enforcement Officer Standards and Education (2009a). Texas commission on law enforcement officer standards and education (TCLEOSE). Retrieved on October 20, 2009 from http://www.tcleose.state.tx.us/content/le_careers_non_tx.cfm.

Texas Commission on Law Enforcement Officer Standards and Education (2009b). Timeline of legislation and procedural changes affecting TCLEOSE (9/1/2007). Retrieved on November 6, 2009 from http://www.tcleose.state.tx.us/content/tcleose_history_timeline.cfm.

Texas Higher Education Coordinating Board (2011). Consumer protection. Retrieved on April 13, 2011 from http://www.thecb.state.tx.us/index.cfm?objectid=64E0A3FB-9466-60E5-07FE 4313341C8138.

Texas Occupations Code

Texas Skaggs, Inc. v. Joannides (1979).

The Aniston Star (2008, October 6). Editorial: The definition of moral crimes. Retrieved on February 7, 2010 from http://search.ebscohost.com.library.keuka.edu/login.aspx?direct=true&db=nfh&AN=2W61622217824&site=ehost-live.

TheAustralian.com (2011, March 15). Footage of bullying victim fighting back: A bullied student has been suspended for attacking his tormentor after video of the fight was posted online. Retrieved on March 18, 2011 from http://video.theaustralian.com.au/1842830630/Footage-of-bullying-victim-fighting-back.

The City of New York et al., v. The Patrolmen's Benevolent Association of the City of New York, Inc. et al., and The Sergeants' Benevolent Association of the City of York et al. (2009).

The Employment Law Post (2010, January 7). EEOC discrimination charges set record in 2009. Retrieved on February 20, 2010 from http://employmentlawpost.com/hrnews/2010/01/07/eeoc-discrimination-charges-set-records-in-2009/?TOPIC.

The Federal Register (2008, December 17). Documents acceptable for employment eligibility verification. Retrieved on March 16, 2010 from http://proquest.umi.com.library.keuka.edu/pqdweb?did=1613468001&sid=1&Fmt=3&clientId=3663&RQT=309&VName=PQD.

The Federal Register (2009, February 23). Employment authorization and verification of Aliens enlisting in the armed forces. Retrieved on March 16, 2010 from http://proquest.umi.com.library.keuka.edu/pqdweb?did=1649133891&sid=1&Fmt=3&clientId=3663&RQT=309&VName=PQD.

The Florida Senate. (2009). The 2009 Florida statutes—768.096 employer presumption against negligent hiring. Retrieved on November 15, 2009 from http://www.flsenate.gov/Statutes/index.cfm?App_mode=Display_Statute&Search_String=&URL=Ch0768/SEC096.HTM&Title=-%3E2009-%3ECh0768-%3ESection%20096#0768.096.

The IndyChannel.com (2009, November 18). Officer, corrections director arrested on felony charges: New Castle officers charged with 4 felony counts. Retrieved on November 1, 2010 from http://www.theindychannel.com/news/21657499/detail.html.

The New York Times (2009, February 6). Kwame M. Kilpatrick. Retrieved on February 9, 2010 from http://topics.nytimes.com/topics/reference/timestopics/people/k/kwame_m_kilpatrick/index.html.

The Police Chief Magazine (1997, June). The ADA and police hiring practices. *The Police Chief Magazine*, *64*(6), 24–29.

The Police Chief Magazine (2009, December). Opposition to label or classify marijuana as medicine. *The Police Chief Magazine*, *76*(12), 48.

The Police Executive (2003, September). Dallas police chief Terrell Bolton was fired on August 27th. *The Brass Key—The Police Executive*, *1*(12), 1–3.

The Record (2003, January 25). Former Parole officer receives probation. *The Record*. Bergen County, NJ.

The Smoking Gun (2011a, March 25). Federal agent targeted in phony degree probe: Grand jury investigating high-ranking DHS/ICE official. Retrieved on April 3, 2011 from http://www.thesmokinggun.com/documents/investigation/federal-agent-targeted-phony-degree-probe-123507.

The Smoking Gun (2011b, March 30). FBI targets prankster who harassed police: Suspect used Skype to place phony emergency calls. Retrieved on April 30, 2011 from http://www.thesmokinggun.com/documents/internet/fbi-targets-prankster-who-harassed-police-867530.

The Smoking Gun (2011c, April 1). Navy man targeted in child porn probe: Upon Afghanistan return, bomb disposal tech searched by NCIS. Retrieved on April 3, 2011 from http://www.thesmokinggun.com/documents/crime/navy-man-targeted-child-porn-probe-650831.

The Standard (1999, April 8). Former Toronto police officer charged with liquor store dupe in Tonawanda. Retrieved on February 20, 2011 from http://proquest.umi.com.library.keuka.edu/pqdweb?did=265314211&sid=1&Fmt=3&clientId=3663&RQT=309&VName=PQD.

The390.com (n.d.). Tonawanda man charged with distribution and possession of child pornography. Retrieved on July 12, 2011 from http://the390.com/buffalo-wny/tonawanda-man-charged-with-distribution-and-possession-of-child-pornography/comment-page-1#comment-5506.

Thibault, E. A., Lynch, L. M., & McBride, R. B. (2004). *Proactive Police Management* (6th edn.). Upper Saddle River, NJ: Pearson Education, Inc.

Thissen, P. (2009, August 10). Police officer sues Concord for sexual harassment. *Contra Cost Times*.

Thissen, P. (2010, April 23). As sexual harassment lawsuits pile up, Concord prepares for court fight. *Contra Cost Times*.

Thomas v. Corwin (2007).

Thomas, E. (2007, October 27). The scorched-earth obsession. Retrieved on July 31, 2011 from http://www.thedailybeast.com/newsweek/2007/10/27/the-scorched-earth-obsession.html.

Thomas, M. K. (2009, July 30). Know the law when you conduct background checks. Retrieved on October 13, 2009 from http://proquest.umi.com.library.keuka.edu/pqdweb?index=10&did=1810658551&SrchMode=2&sid=2&Fmt=3&VInst=PROD&VType=PQD&RQT=309&VName=PQD&TS=1255430936&clientId=3663.

Thomasson v. Valentine (1942).

Thomlinson v. Omaha (1995).

Thompson, C. (2011, February 10). NY Rep. Lee resigns after shirtless photo story. Retrieved on February 10, 2011 from http://news.yahoo.com/s/ap/20110210/ap_on_re_us/us_new_york_congressman_quits.

Thompson, M. (2006, August 10). Three on your side investigates: Mississippi diploma mills. Retrieved on April 14, 2011 from http://www.wlbt.com/Global/story.asp?S=5266042&nav=2CSf.

Thompson, M. (2009, November 18). Fort Hood: Were Hasan's warning signs ignored? Retrieved on December 8, 2009 from http://www.time.com/time/nation/article/0,8599,1940011,00.html.

Thompson v. Borg-Warner Protective Services (1996).

Thompson v. Chapel (1997).

Time.Com (1994, September 5). Evolution of the crime bill. Retrieved on October 19, 2009 from http://www.time.com/time/magazine/article/0,9171,981367,00.html.

Times Online (2007, October 9). Wisconsin gunman Tyler Peterson 'snapped over rebuff by ex-girlfriend.' Retrieved on March 29, 2009 from http://www.timesonline.co.uk/tol/news/world/us_and_americas/article2620258.ece.

Timmins, A. (2005, June 4). Not fit to serve and protect; police: Bench press, sit-ups keep many from the force. Retrieved on October 23, 2009 from http://proquest.umi.com.library.keuka.edu/pqdweb?did=849542551&sid=1&Fmt=3&clientId=3663&RQT=309&VName=PQD.

Timms, E. & Krause, K. (2010a, September 19). 3 Dozen Dallas County deputy constables hired despite troubling job histories. Retrieved on September 26, 2010 from http://www.dallasnews.com/sharedcontent/dws/dn/latestnews/stories/092010dnmetconstabledaytwo.299905e.html.

Timms, E. & Krause, K. (2010b, September 20). With legal loopholes, troubled pasts often not factor in hiring of Dallas County deputy constables. Retrieved on September 26, 2010 from http://www.dallasnews.com/sharedcontent/dws/dn/latestnews/stories/092010dnmetconstabledaytwo.299905e.html.

Timms, E. & Krause, K. (2010c, February 8). Dallas County deputy constable hired, promoted despite little experience. Retrieved on February 20, 2011 from http://web.ebscohost.com.library.keuka.edu/ehost/detail?hid=7&sid=ad66db90-f8fb-43a0-b3a0-a26957b3a8c0%40sessionmgr104&vid=5&bdata=JnNpdGU9ZWhvc3QtbGl2ZQ%3d%3d#db=nfh&AN=2W63147804235.

Tims, D. (2010a, March 16). State official says West Linn mayor Patti Galle violated law with voter's pamphlet information. Retrieved on March 18, 2010 from http://www.oregonlive.com/clackamascounty/index.ssf/2010/03/state_official_says_west_linn.html.

Tims, D. (2010b, March 17). Official calls West Linn mayor's college degree fake. Retrieved on March 18, 2010 from http://www.oregonlive.com/west-linn/index.ssf/2010/03/official_calls_west_linn_mayors_college_degree_fake.html.

Tingler v. City of Tampa (1981).

Tinsley, J. (2008, June 29). Careful, your next move may be seen by millions caught on tape—Thanks to technology, public eye is open wider than ever. Retrieved on March 14, 2010 from http://infoweb.newsbank.com.library.keuka.edu/iw-search/we/InfoWeb?p_product=NewsBank&p_theme=aggregated5&p_action=doc&p_docid=121A6616C71A5818&p_docnum=50&p_queryname=3.

Title 18, *U.S. Code 1028*. Fraud and related activity in connection with identification documents, authentication features, and information.

Title 42 of the *United States Code Section 1983*.

TMZ.com (2007, March 14). Celebrity designer sex bust—Not the first time. Retrieved on February 20, 2011 from http://www.tmz.com/2007/03/14/celebrity-designer-sex-bust-not-the-first-time/.

TMZ.com (2011, June 7). Weiner told porn start to lie, offered PR help. Retrieved on June 7, 2011 from http://www.tmz.com/2011/06/06/anthony-weiner-congressman-sex-text-twitter-kcover-up-Facebook-photo-women-admitted-wrongdoing-press-conference-penis-picture-apologized/.

Todd, B. (2001, September). The new face of high tech crime prevention in Tampa, Florida. *The Police Chief Magazine*, *68*(9), 32–34.

Tokasz, J. & Warner, G. (2010, August 21). The short life and long tortured death of Laura Cummings. Retrieved on April 9, 2011 from http://www.buffalonews.com/city/article36366.ece.

Tolle, N. L. (2007, May). Circuit court affirms damages award to plaintiff for discrimination under ADA. Retrieved on November 17, 2009 from http://proquest.umi.com.library.keuka.edu/pqdweb?did=1271156711&sid=1&Fmt=3&clientId=3663&RQT=309&VName=PQD.

Toppo, G. (2009, April 14). 10 Years later, the real story behind Columbine. Retrieved on August 18, 2011 from http://www.usatoday.com/news/nation/2009-04-13-columbine-myths_N.htm.

Toscano v. Greene Music (2004).

Town of Irondequoit, New York Police Department (2011). Town of Irondequoit, New York personal history statement. Irondequoit, NY: New York Police Department.

Town of Lee, 11 MLC 1274 (1984).

Townsend, S., Fanning, L., & O'Kennedy, R. (2008). Salivary analysis of drugs—Potential and difficulties. Retrieved on January 18, 2010 from http://search.ebscohost.com.library.keuka.edu/login.aspx?direct=true&db=aph&AN=32707108&site=ehost-live.

Tracy, B. (2007, June). The law of three. Retrieved on October 31, 2009 from http://proquest.umi.com.library.keuka.edu/pqdweb?did=1295540331&sid=1&Fmt=2&clientId=3663&RQT=309&VName=PQD.

Trahan, J. (2009, November 14). Fired Dallas County deputy gets 15 years for cocaine theft. Retrieved on February 20, 2011 from http://web.ebscohost.com.library.keuka.edu/ehost/detail?hid=7&sid=ad66db90-f8fb-43a0-b3a0-a26957b3a8c0%40sessionmgr104&vid=6&bdata=JnNpdGU9ZWhvc3QtbGl2ZQ%3d%3d#db=nfh&AN=2W6430528186.

Tran, M. (2002, November 7). Advisor to Anaheim police explorers faces charge of sex with recruit, 17. Retrieved on December 6, 2010 from http://articles.latimes.com/2002/nov/07/news/explorer07.

Trattner, M. H. (1982). Synthetic validity and its application to the uniform guidelines validation requirements. *Personnel Psychology*, *35*, 383–397.

Trautman, N. E. (2005). *Police Work: A Career Survival Guide* (2nd edn.). Upper Saddle River, NJ: Prentice-Hall, Inc.

Trautman, N. (2009, February 16). A crucial message for elected officials: A friend tells you what you need to hear. Retrieved on October 10, 2009 from http://www.lawofficer.com/news-and-articles/columns/Trautman/crucial_message_for_elected_officials.html;jsessionid=04E07EF9BEA1137E98D7379EC9BE1192.

Traynor, I. (1998, July 17). Children as young as 18 months abused by international network which police describe as one of the most extensive ever discovered. Retrieved on March 13, 2010 from http://www.lexisnexis.com.library.keuka.edu/us/lnacademic/results/docview/docview.do?docLinkInd=true&risb=21_T8805082670&format=GNBFI&sort=RELEVANCE&startDocNo=1&resultsUrlKey=29_T8805082675&cisb=22_T8805082674&treeMax=true&treeWidth=0&csi=138620&docNo=6.

Trial. (2003, February 1). Negligent hiring, retention and supervision: In the workplace, the past is prologue. Employers that haven't done their homework can be held liable for workers violent acts. Retrieved on March 30, 2009 from http://goliath.ecnext.com/coms2/gi_0199-2662255/Negligent-hiring-retention-and-supervision.html.

Tribble, D. A. (2001, May 1). The Health Insurance Portability and Accountability Act: Security and privacy requirements. Retrieved on November 20, 2009 from http://search.ebscohost.com.library.keuka.edu/login.aspx?direct=true&db=cmedm&AN=11351916&site=ehost-live.

Truesdale v. University of North Carolina (1988).

Truesdell, W. H. (2009). What's in a personnel file? (And what should not be). Retrieved on February 20, 2010 from http://www.management-advantage.com/products/free-personnel.htm.

Tucker, E. (2008, July 16). Facebook used as character evidence, lands some in jail. Retrieved on March 13, 2010 from http://www.usatoday.com/tech/webguide/internetlife/2008-07-19-facebook-trials_N.htm.

Tucker, R. (2010, November 5). Ban on credit checks for workers or job candidates has support. Retrieved on February 26, 2011 from http://proquest.umi.com.library.keuka.edu/pqdweb?did=2181098701&sid=1&Fmt=3&clientId=3663&RQT=309&VName=PQD.

Tuna, C. & Weinstein, K. J. (2008, November 18). Career journal: Vetting executives adds degree of difficulty—Rise in resume fraud reflects unevenness in background checks. Retrieved on February 22, 2011 from http://proquest.umi.com.library.keuka.edu/pqdweb?did=1596929851&sid=3&Fmt=3&clientId=3663&RQT=309&VName=PQD.

Tuohy, L. (2010, November 4). Coroner: NH woman alive for 32 machete, knife cuts. Retrieved on March 23, 2011 from http://www.boston.com/news/local/new_hampshire/articles/2010/11/04/coroner_nh_woman_alive_for_32_machete_knife_cuts/.

Turner, G. (2011, March 31). Man charged with tattooing, abusing 9-year-old boy. Retrieved on March 31, 2011 from http://rochester.ynn.com/content/top_stories/538456/man-charged-with-tattooing–abusing-9-year-old-boy/.

Turner, Y. C. (2000, February). "Decentralizing" the specialized unit function in small police agencies. *The Police Chief Magazine*, *67*(2), 50–51.

Tye v. Cincinnati (1992).

Uhl-Bein, M., Marion, R., & McKelvey, B. (2007, August). Complexity leadership theory: Shifting leadership from the industrial age to the knowledge era. Retrieved on October 26, 2009 from http://search.ebscohost.com.library.keuka.edu/login.aspx?direct=true&db=f5h&AN=25619058&site=ehost-live.

Unconsolidated Pennsylvania Statutes

UND.com (2001, December 14). Statement from George O'Leary. Retrieved on July 2, 2011 from http://www.und.com/sports/m-footbl/spec-rel/121401aab.html.

Uniform Code of Military Justice

Uniform Guidelines.com (n.d.). Uniform guidelines on employee selection procedures. Retrieved on October 7, 2009 from http://www.uniformguidelines.com/uniformguidelines.html#22.

Uniform Guidelines for Employee Selection Procedures (1978).

Uniformed Services Employment and Reemployment Rights Act (USERRA) (1994). United Press International. (2010, July 23). Report: Child porn users found at Pentagon. Retrieved on August 17, 2010 from http://www.upi.com/Top_News/US/2010/07/23/Report-Child-porn-users-found-at-Pentagon/UPI-99691279908892/.

United States Census Bureau (2008). Race data. Retrieved on August 17, 2010 from http://www.census.gov/population/www/socdemo/race/racefactcb.html.

United States Citizenship and Immigration Services (2009, July 31). Handbook for employers: Instructions for completing the I-9 (employment eligibility verification form) M-274. Washington, DC: Author. (*Note:* This document can be accessed online at www.uscis.gov/files/nativedocuments/m-274.pdf)

United States Coast Guard (2010, August 25). Drug testing and program requirements. Retrieved on August 8, 2011 from http://www.uscg.mil/nmc/drug_testing.asp.

United States Code

United States Congress, Office of Technology Assessment. (1990, September). The use of integrity tests for pre-employment screening (OTA-SET-442). Washington, DC: United States Government Printing Officer.

United States Courts (n.d.a). Officers and officer assistants: What professional standards apply to them. Retrieved on May 30, 2011 from http://www.uscourts.gov/FederalCourts/ProbationPretrialServices/Officers.aspx.

United States Courts (n.d.b). Officer and officer assistant essential job functions. Retrieved on May 30, 2011 from http://www.uscourts.gov/FederalCourts/ProbationPretrialServices/Officers/OfficerEssentialJobFunctions.aspx.

United States Courts (n.d.c). Officer and officer assistant medical requirements. Retrieved on May 30, 2011 from http://www.uscourts.gov/FederalCourts/ProbationPretrialServices/Officers/OfficerMedicalRequirements.aspx.

United States Department of Defense (2009a, August 20). Certificate of release or discharge from active duty (DD form 214/5 series). Retrieved on April 18, 2011 from http://www.dtic.mil/whs/directives/corres/pdf/133601p.pdf.

United States Department of Defense (2009b, November 20). Report of investigation. Retrieved on August 17, 2010 from http://www.dodig.mil/fo/Foia/PDFs/OperationFlickerReportsJuly2010pdf.pdf.

United States Department of Education (2010, May 5). Family Educational Rights and Privacy Act (FERPA). Retrieved on March 18, 2011 from http://www2.ed.gov/policy/gen/guid/fpco/ferpa/index.html.

United States Department of Health and Human Services (2009). Health information privacy—Summary of the HIPAA rule. Retrieved on November 17, 2009 from http://www.hhs.gov/ocr/privacy/hipaa/understanding/summary/index.html.

United States Department of Health and Human Services (2010, April). Mandatory reporters of child abuse and neglect: Summary of state laws. Retrieved on December 9, 2010 from http://www.childwelfare.gov/systemwide/laws_policies/statutes/manda.cfm.

United States Department of Homeland Security (2009, September 16). State and local fusion centers. Retrieved on October 11, 2010 from http://www.dhs.gov/files/programs/gc_1156877184684.shtm.

United States Department of Homeland Security Customs and Border Patrol (2008, January 16). FAQ's—Mandatory background investigation. Retrieved on October 20, 2009 from http://www.cbp.gov/xp/cgov/careers/apply/mandatory_back_invest.xml.

United States Department of Justice (1997, March 25). Questions and answers: The Americans with Disabilities Act. Retrieved on March 23, 2006 from www.usdoj.gov/crt/ada/copsq7a.htm.

United States Department of Justice (2001, January). *Principles for Promoting Police Integrity: Examples of Promising Police Practices and Policies*. Washington, DC: Author.

United States Department of Justice (2007a, January 19). Former San Antonio police officer sentenced for violating citizen's rights by sexual assault. Retrieved on October 18, 2010 from http://www.justice.gov/opa/pr/2007/January/07_crt_029.html.

United States Department of Justice (2007b, November 13). Former employee of CIA and FBI pleads guilty to conspiracy, unauthorized computer access, and naturalization fraud. Retrieved on October 15, 2009 from http://www.usdoj.gov/opa/pr/2007/November/07_nsd_910.html.

United States Department of Justice (2008a, May 16). Ringleader in Boston police corruption case sentenced to 26 years in prison. Retrieved on November 3, 2010 from http://boston.fbi.gov/dojpressrel/pressrel08/publiccorruption051608.htm.

United States Department of Justice (2008b, July 25). Omnibus Crime Control and Safe Streets Act of 1968 42 U.S.C. S 3789d. Retrieved on February 13, 2010 from http://www.justice.gov/crt/split/42usc3789d.php.

United States Department of Justice (2010). Project safe childhood. Retrieved on February 17, 2010 from http://www.projectsafechildhood.gov/.

United States Department of Justice (2011). Child exploitation and obscenity section (CEOS). Retrieved on January 11, 2011 from http://www.justice.gov/criminal/ceos/.

United States Department of Justice Bureau of Alcohol, Tobacco, Firearms, and Explosives. (2010, July 27). ATF (U) OMGs and the military 2010 update; ATF intelligence report. Retrieved on August 6, 2011 from http://info.publicintelligence.net/ATF-OMGmilitary2010.pdf.

United States Department of Justice Bureau of Justice Statistics (2004). Law enforcement statistics 2004. Retrieved on October 8, 2009 from http://www.ojp.usdoj.gov/bjs/lawenf.htm.

United States Department of Justice Bureau of Justice Statistics (2009, December 14). Terms & definitions: Criminal justice data improvement program. Retrieved on September 21, 2010 from http://bjs.ojp.usdoj.gov/index.cfm?ty=tdtp&tid=4.

United States Department of Justice Drug Enforcement Administration Office of Diversion Control. (2004, March). Steroid abuse in today's society. Retrieved on April 13, 2011 from http://www.deadiversion.usdoj.gov/pubs/brochures/steroids/professionals/.

United States Department of Justice Office of Justice Programs (1998, March). Violence by intimates: Analysis of data on crimes by current or former spouses, boyfriends, and girlfriends. Washington, DC: Author. NCJ-167237

United States Department of Justice, Office of Justice Programs, Office of Juvenile Justice and Delinquency Programs (1999, December). 1997 National youth gang survey. Washington, DC: Author. NCJ-167237.

United States Department of Justice Bureau Office of Public Affairs (2010, June 11). Three Baltimore city police department officers convicted in civil rights case. Retrieved on October 28, 2010 from http://www.justice.gov/opa/pr/2010/June/10-crt-685.html.

United States Department of Justice Civil Rights Division Disability Rights Section (n.d.). Questions and answers: The Americans with Disabilities Act and persons with HIV/AIDS. Retrieved on August 7, 2011 from http://www.ada.gov/pubs/hivqanda.txt.

United States Department of Justice Computer Crime and Intellectual Property Section Criminal Division (2009). Searching and seizing computers and obtaining electronic evidence in criminal investigations. Retrieved on June 5, 2011 from http://www.justice.gov/criminal/cybercrime/ssmanual/ssmanual2009.pdf.

United States Department of Justice United States Attorney Eastern District of Pennsylvania (2009, December 17). News release. Retrieved on August 13, 2011 from http://www.justice.gov/usao/pae/News/2009/dec/lacknerrelease.pdf.

United States Department of Labor (2000, February 10). Executive order 13145. Retrieved on November 22, 2009 from http://www.dol.gov/oasam/regs/statutes/eo13145.htm.

United States Department of State (2008). *Department of State Information Access Guide Manual.* Washington, DC: Author.

United States Department of the Interior (1998a, November 10). Crediting plan. Retrieved on July 17, 2011 from http://www.doi.gov/hrm/pmanager/st12e.html.

United States Department of the Interior (1998b, November 10). Interviews. Retrieved on July 17, 2011 from http://www.doi.gov/hrm/pmanager/st13c.html.

United States Department of the Interior (1998c, November 10). Job analysis. Retrieved on July 17, 2011 from http://www.doi.gov/hrm/pmanager/st12d.html.

United States Department of the Interior (1998d, November 10). Qualification standards. Retrieved on July 17, 2011 from http://www.doi.gov/hrm/pmanager/st12a.html.

United States Department of the Interior (1998e, November 10). Ranking interview. Retrieved on July 17, 2011 from http://www.doi.gov/hrm/pmanager/st13c2.html.

United States Department of the Interior (1998f, November 10). Selection interview. Retrieved on July 17, 2011 from http://www.doi.gov/hrm/pmanager/st13c1.html.

United States Department of the Interior (1998g, November 10). Uniform guidelines on employee selection procedures. Retrieved on October 19, 2009 from http://www.doi.gov/hrm/pmanager/st13d.html.

United States Department of State Foreign Affairs (2010). *United States Department of State Foreign Affairs Manual, Volume 9—Visas.* Washington, DC: Author.

United States Department of Transportation (2009). Office of drug and alcohol policy and compliance. Retrieved on January 28, 2010 from http://www.dot.gov/ost/dapc/.

United States Department of Transportation National Highway Traffic Safety Administration (2010, November). Traffic safety facts: Crash stats. Retrieved on February 21, 2011 from http://www-nrd.nhtsa.dot.gov/Pubs/811415.pdf.

United States Department Drug Enforcement Administration (n.d.). Title 21: Food and drugs, Chapter 13: Drug abuse prevention and control. Retrieved on December 1, 2009 from http://www.justice.gov/dea/pubs/csa.html.

United States Equal Employment Opportunity Commission (n.d.). Title VII of the civil rights act of 1964. Retrieved on September 20, 2010 from http://www.eeoc.gov/laws/statutes/titlevii.cfm.

United States Equal Employment Opportunity Commission (1978, October 13). Civil service reform act of 1978. Retrieved on October 20, 2009 from http://www.eeoc.gov/abouteeoc/35th/thelaw/civil_service_reform-1978.html.

United States Equal Employment Opportunity Commission (1987, February 2). EEOC notice N-915. Retrieved on July 26, 2011 from http://www.aele.org/law/Digests/empl157.html.

United States Equal Employment Opportunity Commission (1990, July 26). Titles I and V of the Americans with Disabilities Act of 1990 (ADA). Retrieved on November 17, 2009 from http://www.eeoc.gov/laws/statutes/ada.cfm.

United States Equal Employment Opportunity Commission (1991). The Americans with Disabilities Act: Your responsibilities as an employer. Washington, DC: Author.

United States Equal Employment Opportunity Commission (1997, March 25). EEOC enforcement guidance on the Americans with Disabilities Act and psychiatric disabilities. Retrieved on August 7, 2011 from http://www.eeoc.gov/policy/docs/psych.html.

United States Equal Employment Opportunity Commission (2000, July 27). Enforcement guidance: Disability-related inquiries and medical examinations of employees under the Americans with Disabilities Act (ADA). Retrieved on February 14, 2010 from http://www.eeoc.gov/policy/docs/guidance-inquiries.html#N_29_.

United States Equal Employment Opportunity Commission (2002, May). Americans with Disabilities Act: Questions and answers. Retrieved on November 22, 2009 from http://www.ada.gov/q&aeng02.htm.

United States Equal Employment Opportunity Commission (2006, September 11). Conviction records. Retrieved on March 12, 2011 from http://www.eeoc.gov/policy/docs/convict1.html.

United States Equal Employment Opportunity Commission (2008). ADA technical assistance manual addendum—Notice concerning the Americans with Disabilities Act of 2008. Retrieved on November 25, 2009 from http://www.eeoc.gov/policy/docs/adamanual_add.html.

United States Equal Employment Opportunity Commission (2009a). Laws enforced by EEOC. Retrieved on November 7, 2009 from http://www.eeoc.gov/laws/statutes/index.cfm.

United States Equal Employment Opportunity Commission (2009b, November 21). Section 902 definition of the term disability: Notice concerning the Americans with Disabilities Act of 2008. Retrieved on February 13, 2011 from http://www.eeoc.gov/policy/docs/902cm.html.

United States Equal Employment Opportunity Commission (2009c, February 17). Title VII of the Civil Rights Act of 1964. Retrieved on March 12, 2011 from http://archive.eeoc.gov/policy/vii.html.

United States Equal Employment Opportunity Commission (2010, September 17). Employment tests and selection procedures. Retrieved on September 19, 2010 from http://www.eeoc.gov/policy/docs/factemployment_procedures.html.

United States Food and Drug Administration (2006, April 20). Inter-agency advisory regarding claims that smoked marijuana is a medicine. Retrieved on February 7, 2010 from http://www.fda.gov/NewsEvents/Newsroom/PressAnnouncements/2006/ucm108643.htm.

United States General Accountability Office (2006, July). *National Sex Offender Registry: New Hires Data Has Potential for Updating Addresses of Convicted Sex Offenders*. Washington, DC: Author.

United States General Accounting Office (1998, May). Report to the honorable Charles B. Rangel, house of representatives—Law enforcement: Information on drug-related corruption. Washington, DC: Author.

United States Government Printing Office (1988). Employee Polygraph Protection Act of 1988. Washington, DC: Author.

United States Merit Systems Protection Board (2005, September). Reference checking in federal hiring: Making the call. Washington, DC: Author.

United States Office of Personnel Management (n.d.). Investigations. Retrieved on October 19, 2009 from http://www.opm.gov/Products_and_Services/Investigations/.

United States Securities and Exchange Commission (2007, July 17). Whistleblower Protection Act information. Retrieved on October 24, 2009 from http://www.sec.gov/eeoinfo/whistleblowers.htm.

United States v. Agurs (1976).

United States v. Baer (2003).

United States v. Bagley (1985).

United States v. Comstock (2010).

United States v. Flowers (2004).

United States v. Gloria (1974).

United States v. Henderson (2005).

United States v. Imperial Palace Inc. (2004).

United States v. Knox (1993).

United States v. Lopez (1995).

United States v. Morrison (2000).

United States v. Quality Terminal Services, LLC. (2009).

United States v. Scheffer (1998).

United States v. Smith (1970).
UPI.com (2011, April 27). Police officer who exposed himself fired. Retrieved on May 1, 2011 from http://www.upi.com/Odd_News/2011/04/27/Police-officer-who-exposed-himself-fired/UPI-31131303893000/#ixzz1KjryNH8A.
Urie, H. & Meltzer, E. (2011, August 7). Boulder weeds out its medical Marijuana industry. Retrieved on August 20, 2011 from http://proquest.umi.com.library.keuka.edu/pqdweb?did=2418910921&sid=2&Fmt=3&clientId=3663&RQT=309&VName=PQD.
U. S. Newswire (2005, August 2). Justice Department settles lawsuit regarding Delaware state police hiring practices. Retrieved on November 6, 2009 from http://proquest.umi.com.library.keuka.edu/pqdweb?did=876457221&sid=2&Fmt=3&clientId=3663&RQT=309&VName=PQD.
U. S. v. Virginia (1998). Retrieved on November 16, 2009 from http://lw.bna.com/lw/19980407/972045.htm.
U. S. Airways v. Barnett (2002).
USLegal.com (2011a). CODIS law and legal definition. Retrieved on January 18, 2011 from http://definitions.uslegal.com/c/codis/.
USLegal.com (2011b). Negligent supervision law and legal definition. Retrieved on April 21, 2011 from http://definitions.uslegal.com/n/negligent-supervision/.
Vaas, L. (2009, July 7). Employment background checks: Know your rights. Retrieved on February 21, 2011 from http://www.theladders.com/career-advice/employment-background-checks-your-rights.
Valdez v. Warner (1987).
Valentin v. Bootes (1998).
Vallee, P. (2006, February 10). Colleges use Facebook to incriminate students. Retrieved on March 13, 2010 from http://media.www.guilfordian.com/media/storage/paper281/news/2006/02/10/News/Colleges.Use.Facebook.To.Incriminate.Students-1610749.shtml.
Valot, S. (2010, March 15). Former OC assistant Sheriff Don Haidl sentenced. Retrieved on February 11, 2011 from http://www.scpr.org/news/2010/03/15/oc-haidl-sentence-03152010/.
Van Denburg, H. (2011, March 31). Mason Seckar's Wisconsin home raided by FBI over crank calls to cops. Retrieved on April 30, 2011 from http://blogs.citypages.com/blotter/2011/03/mason_seckar_fbi_crank_calls.php.
Van Derbeken, J. (2010, May 16). Police with problems are a problem for D.A. Retrieved on April 3, 2011 from http://articles.sfgate.com/2010-05-16/news/20900679_1_latest-woe-chronicle-exclusive.
Van Timmeren, C. (2010, September 20). Former Canandaigua academy teacher pleads guilty to endangering the welfare of a child. Retrieved on October 9, 2010 from http://www.whec.com/news/stories/S1751829.shtml?cat=566.
Van Horn, C. (2010, April 14). Stephanie Ragusa and Debra Lafave: What's wrong with Tampa teachers? Retrieved on October 9, 2010 from http://www.examiner.com/crime-in-tampa-bay/stephanie-ragusa-and-debra-lafave-what-s-wrong-with-tampa-teachers-videos.
Van-Go Transport Co., Inc. v. New York City Board of Education (1997).
The Vancouver Sun (2010, April 21). Vancouver police chief Jim Chu's statement on the arrest. Retrieved on April 30, 2011 from http://www.vancouversun.com/Vancouver+Police+Chief+statement+arrest/2935346/story.html.
Vanguard Justice Society v. Hughes (1979).
Vann, B. (1999, May 31). Louima trial: New York cop pleads guilty to immigrant's torture. Retrieved on October 9, 2009 from http://www.wsws.org/articles/1999/may1999/nyc-m31.shtml.
Varnum, C. (2009, January 13). Robbery suspect shot by off-duty cop dies. Retrieved on January 13, 2009 from http://images.google.com/imgres?imgurl=http://www.whec.com/whecimages/williams_christopher.jpg&imgrefurl=http://www.whec.com/article/stories/S740990.shtml%3Fcat%3D0&usg=__lrbiCPV6WLONpTIciacTJFTMc6A=&h=120&w=160&sz=4&hl=en&start=15&um=1&tbnid=WMLHAVKrogZubM:&tbnh=74&tbnw=98&prev=/images%3Fq%3Dgeorge%2Bmarkert%2Brochester%26um%3D1%26hl%3Den%26client%3Dfirefox-a%26rls%3Dorg.mozilla:en-US:official%26hs%3DOhp%26sa%3DG.

Vaughan, A. (2011, June 18). Teenage flash mob robberies on the rise. Retrieved on August 13, 2011 from http://www.foxnews.com/us/2011/06/18/top-five-most-brazen-flash-mob-robberies/.

Venugopal, J. (2009, October 13). Resume frauds have spiked with recession: Study says most job-seekers gave false information in February and March this year. Retrieved on February 22, 2011 from http://proquest.umi.com.library.keuka.edu/pqdweb?did=1879779881&sid=3&Fmt=3&clientId=3663&RQT=309&VName=PQD.

Verbano, S. (2011, April 25). Eugene police officer Chris Kilcullen fatally wounded: Memorial service to be held in Matthew Knight Arena for officer shot after routine traffic stop. Retrieved on April 29, 2011 from http://www.dailyemerald.com/news/eugene-police-officer-chris-kilcullen-fatally-wounded-1.2190786.

Verherke, J. H. (1998, Winter). Legal regulation of employment reference practices. *The University of Chicago Law Review*, *65*(1), 115–178.

Vick, K. (2008, July 27). The dark side of dreamland: Case against former Sheriff reveals underside of Orange County politics. Retrieved on February 11, 2011 from http://www.washingtonpost.com/wp-dyn/content/article/2008/07/26/AR2008072601875.html.

Village of Oak Lawn v. Illinois Human Rights Commission (1985).

Villano, M. (2006, March 19). Served as king of England, said the resume. Retrieved on September 12, 2010 from http://www.nytimes.com/2006/03/19/business/yourmoney/19advi.html?_r=1&ex=1143435600&en=ab9425570d5a463d&ei=5065&partner=MYWAY.

VinZant, N. (2011, March 6). Couple confesses to killing boy who wet his pants. Retrieved on March 8, 2011 from http://www.cfnews13.com/article/news/2011/march/214450/Couple-confesses-to-killing-boy-who-wet-his-pants.

Violence Against Women Act (1994).

Violent Crime Control and Law Enforcement Act (1994).

Virginia Commonwealth University (2008, September 5). Virginia Commonwealth University report to the southern association of colleges and schools. Richmond, VA: Author.

Virginia Law Enforcement Professional Standards Commission (2008). *Virginia Law Enforcement Accreditation Program Manual* (6th edn.). Richmond, VA: Author.

Viser, M. (2005, January 2). Racial goals unmet in 12 cities, towns; police, fire departments struggle to fulfill court mandates. Retrieved on November 6, 2009 from http://proquest.umi.com.library.keuka.edu/pqdweb?did=773208451&sid=2&Fmt=3&clientId=3663&RQT=309&VName=PQD.

Volet, S., Vauras, M., & Salonen, P. (2009, October). Self- and social regulation in learning contexts: An integrative perspective. Retrieved on October 24, 2009 from http://proquest.umi.com.library.keuka.edu/pqdweb?did=1884961341&sid=1&Fmt=2&clientId=3663&RQT=309&VName=PQD.

Volstead Act (1920).

Volunteers for Children Act: Public Law 105-251. Retrieved on October 13, 2009 from http://frwebgate.access.gpo.gov/cgi-bin/getdoc.cgi?dbname=105_cong_public_laws&docid=f:publ251.105.

Vostock, T. (2009, April 1). These People are F****** Disgusting. Retrieved on October 13, 2010 from http://www.nbcphiladelphia.com/news/archive/Philly-Cop-Alleged-Racist.html.

Vrij, A., Mann, S., Fisher, R. P., Leal, S., Milne, R., & Bull, R. (2007, August 13). Increasing cognitive load to facilitate lie detection: The benefit of recalling an event in reverse order. *Law and Human Behavior*, *32*, 253–265.

Vrij, A., Mann, S., Kristen, S., & Fisher, R. P. (2007, January 9). Cues to deception and ability to detect lies as a function of police interview styles. *Law and Human Behavior*, *31*, 499–518.

Walker, S. (1998). *Popular Justice: A History of American Criminal Justice* (2nd edn.). New York: Oxford University Press, Inc.

Walker, S. (1999). *The Police in America: An Introduction* (3rd edn.). Boston, MA: The McGraw-Hill Companies, Inc.

Walker, S. & Irlbeck, D. (2003, June). *Police Sexual Abuse of Teenage Girls: A 2003 Update on "Driving While Female."* Omaha, NE: University of Nebraska at Omaha.

Walker v. New York (1993).

Wall, C. (2009, December 15). Anthony Abbate, cop who beat bartender, has been fired: Unanimous decision finds Abbate guilty. Retrieved on November 3, 2010 from http://www.myfoxchicago.com/dpp/news/crime/anthony-abbate-discharged.

Waller, J. D. (2008, October 9). Criminal check changes proposed. Retrieved on November 21, 2009 from http://proquest.umi.com.library.keuka.edu/pqdweb?did=1570292051&sid=1&Fmt=3&clientId=3663&RQT=309&VName=PQD.

Waller, N. (2010, March 21). Bad credit history can crash your job search. *The Wall Street Journal as cited in The Providence Sunday Journal*, E5.

Walzer, P. (2007, May 4). Job seekers caught in the act of resume fraud. Retrieved on February 22, 2011 from http://proquest.umi.com.library.keuka.edu/pqdweb?did=1265829481&sid=3&Fmt=3&clientId=3663&RQT=309&VName=PQD.

Wallis, C. (2007, March 12). Casualty of war: Mental health. Retrieved on August 15, 2010 from http://www.time.com/time/nation/article/0,8599,1598474,00.html.

Wallman, B. (2009, October 20). Lauderdale police: For every officer who leaves, we lose $300k. Retrieved on October 31, 2009 from http://proquest.umi.com.library.keuka.edu/pqdweb?did=1884037241&sid=1&Fmt=3&clientId=3663&RQT=309&VName=PQD.

Walsh, J. (2008, December 10). Former police officer convicted in tax fraud scheme; Douglas Leiter, who left the Minneapolis police force in 2002, was one of three tax protestors found guilty of charges. Retrieved on February 20, 2011 from http://proquest.umi.com.library.keuka.edu/pqdweb?did=1613166631&sid=1&Fmt=3&clientId=3663&RQT=309&VName=PQD.

Walters, P. (2009, July 17). Group of officers sues Philly police over web site. Retrieved on October 28, 2010 from http://www.policeone.com/chiefs-sheriffs/articles/1856514-Group-of-officers-sues-Philly-police-over-web-site/.

Walton, M. (1986). *The Deming Management Method*. New York: Dodd, Mead, and Company.

Wambaugh, J. (2002). *Fire Lover*. New York: Harper Collins Publishers.

Wards Cove Packing v. Antonio (1989).

Ward, M. (2007, March 6). Youth commission official had history of porn, petty crime violations: Abuse claims, other infractions went on for years, records show. Retrieved on September 20, 2010 from http://www.statesman.com/news/content/region/legislature/stories/03/06/6brookins.html.

Ward, V. (2009, February 11). Esther Reed: How an ordinary girl faked her way into the Ivy League. Retrieved on February 11, 2011 from http://www.huffingtonpost.com/vicky-ward/esther-reed-how-an-ordina_b_166118.html.

Warner, D. (2011, March 8). Underage sex trial of former U. N. weapons official set. Retrieved on March 8, 2011 from http://www.reuters.com/article/2011/03/08/us-ritter-sex-idUSTRE7275E020110308.

Warner, W. J. (2005, April). Polygraph testing. Retrieved on October 13, 2009 from http://web.ebscohost.com.library.keuka.edu/ehost/detail?vid=14&hid=8&sid=d30bed09-3932-47cc-9ef4-6811f3bac285%40sessionmgr4&bdata=JnNpdGU9ZWhvc3QtbGl2ZQ%3d%3d#db=aph&AN=17200547.

Warrick, J. & Eggen, D. (2007, November 14). Agent admits fooling CIA, FBI faked past to get jobs, take secrets. Retrieved on October 13, 2009 from http://proquest.umi.com.library.keuka.edu/pqdweb?index=15&did=1748728391&SrchMode=2&sid=2&Fmt=3&VInst=PROD&VType=PQD&RQT=309&VName=PQD&TS=1255430937&clientId=3663.

Wartell, J. & La Vigne, N. G. (2004, May). *Prescription Fraud*. Washington, DC: United States Department of Justice Office of Community Oriented Policing Services.

Washington Association of Sheriffs and Police Chiefs (2007, May). *Law Enforcement Accreditation Standards Manual* (1st edn.). Lacey, WA: Washington Association of Sheriffs and Police Chiefs.

Washington Higher Education Coordinating Board (n.d.). Authorization and evaluation. Retrieved on April 13, 2011 from http://www.hecb.wa.gov/autheval/daa/daaindex.asp.

Washington State Criminal Justice Training Commission (2009). Peace officer certification. Retrieved on October 20, 2009 from https://fortress.wa.gov/cjtc/www/pocert/index.html.

Washington State Legislature (n.d.). RCW 69.50.410. Retrieved on February 12, 2010 from http://apps.leg.wa.gov/RCW/default.aspx?cite=69.50.410.

Washington State Legislature (2011, March 18). HB 2507—2005–2006 prohibiting false or misleading college degrees. Retrieved on March 18, 2011 from http://apps.leg.wa.gov/billinfo/summary.aspx?bill=2507&year=2006.

Washington State Patrol (n.d.a). *Be a Trooper: Washington State Patrol Now Hiring*. Olympia, WA: Human Resource Division Washington State Patrol.

Washington State Patrol (n.d.b). Cooper institute fitness standards. Retrieved on October 24, 2009 from http://www.wsp.wa.gov/employment/trooper.htm.

Washington State Patrol (n.d.c). How to become a trooper with the Washington State Patrol. Olympia, WA: Human Resource Division Washington State Patrol.

Washington Times (2011, March 7). Editorial: Firehouse flunkies—Justice Department puts political correctness over safety. Retrieved on February 7, 2010 from http://www.washingtontimes.com/news/2011/mar/7/firehouse-flunkies/.

Washington v. Davis (1976).

Washoe County Sheriff's Office (2009). Employment at the Washoe County Sheriff's Office. Retrieved on February 7, 2010 from http://www.washoesheriff.com/employment-main-page.htm.

Wassum v. City of Bellaire, Texas (1988).

Watkins, T. (2010a, February 2). Use of Twitter, Facebook rising among gang members. Retrieved on March 13, 2010 from http://www.lexisnexis.com.library.keuka.edu/us/lnacademic/results/docview/docview.do?docLinkInd=true&risb=21_T8805082670&format=GNBFI&sort=RELEVANCE&startDocNo=1&resultsUrlKey=29_T8805082675&cisb=22_T8805082674&treeMax=true&treeWidth=0&csi=147876&docNo=25.

Watkins, T. (2010b, May 20). 2 Police officers fatally shot in West Memphis, Arkansas. Retrieved on November 18, 2010 from http://articles.cnn.com/2010-05-20/justice/arkansas.2.police.killed_1_police-officers-suspects-bill-sadler?_s=PM:CRIME.

Watkins, T. (2011, January 28). LA chief apologizes for dragnet in shooting hoax. Retrieved on January 28, 2011 from http://news.yahoo.com/s/ap/20110128/ap_on_re_us/us_la_school_officer_shot;_ylt=AuORoz4J3mW8Oz26i_gTCgFH2ocA;_ylu=X3oDMTN-zYThiZ3NpBGFzc2V0Ay9zL2FwLzIwMTEwMTI4L2FwX29uX3J1X3VzL3VzX2xhX3NjaG9vbF9vZmZpY2VyX3Nob3QEY2NvZGUDbXBfZWNfOF8xMARjcG9zAzcEcG9zAzcEc2VjA3luX3RvcF9zdG9yaWVzBHNsawNsYWNoaWVmYXBvbG8-.

Watson v. City of Hialeah (1989).

Watson v. Fort Worth Bank and Trust (1988).

Watson, R. (2011, February 17). Police exam is a chance to alter culture. New York: The Buffalo News, C1.

Watson, S. T. (2010, March 15). How some cops cross the line: Hiring, training, monitoring, questioned amid misconduct. *The Buffalo News*, A1–A2.

WBZTV.com (2009, April 20). Pa. cop seen on video joking about murder victim. Retrieved on October 18, 2010 from http://wbztv.com/national/James.Cousins.caught.2.988779.html.

WCAX.com (2009, September 8). Vergennes police chief resigns. Retrieved on November 1, 2010 from http://www.wcax.com/Global/story.asp?S=11091237.

WDSU.com (2009, August 11). NOPD dismisses officer involved in bar brawl. Retrieved on November 1, 2010 from http://www.wdsu.com/r/20361514/detail.html.

Weathersbee, T. (2008, August 12). Sandwiches without sauce and other cases of 911 abuse. Retrieved on April 30, 2011 from http://proquest.umi.com.library.keuka.edu/pqdweb?did=1531097421&sid=1&Fmt=3&clientId=3663&RQT=309&VName=PQD.

Weaver, J. (2005, April 5). Steroid addiction a risk for young athletes: Withdrawal can cause depression, suicidal behavior. Retrieved on April 13, 2011 from http://www.msnbc.msn.com/id/7348758/ns/health-mental_health/.

Weber, T. J. & Horvath, F. (2008). Degrees of deception: Diploma mills and the polygraph examiner community—A recommendation for change. Retrieved on April 7, 2011 from http://web.ebscohost.com.library.keuka.edu/ehost/detail?vid=7&hid=111&sid=8b68f380-de5e-409e-8eed-e2a570345a70%40sessionmgr113&bdata=JnNpdGU9ZWhvc3QtbGl2ZQ%3d%3d.

Webster, M. (2009, March 6). Mexican drug cartel gang members in most American cities and our military. Retrieved on August 6, 2011 from http://www.renewamerica.com/columns/webster/090306.

Wefing, J. B. (2000). Employer drug testing: Disparate judicial and legislative responses. Retrieved on January 18, 2010 from http://search.ebscohost.com.library.keuka.edu/login.aspx?direct=true&db=aph&AN=3319884&site=ehost-live.

Weisel, D. L. (2005, August). *Analyzing Repeat Victimization*. Washington, DC: United States Department of Justice Office of Community Oriented Policing Services.

Weiss, D. (2001, December 15). By George, it's Blarney O'Leary admits resume is false, quits Irish. Retrieved on July 2, 2011 from http://articles.nydailynews.com/2001-12-15/sports/18354563_1_notre-dame-georgia-tech-press-conference.

Weiss, M. & Baker, M. (2011, February 21). Stepmother indicted in death of disabled girl. Retrieved on February 21, 2011 from http://news.yahoo.com/s/ap/20110222/ap_on_re_us/us_disabled_girl_killed;_ylt=AhDbIpKJj0uXZUW_RWJ0aVBH2ocA;_ylu=X3oDMTNiZzRpMXJrBGFzc2V0A2FwLzIwMTEwMjIyL3VzX2Rpc2FibGVkX2dpcmxfa2lsbGVkBGNjb2RlA21wX2VjXzhfMTAEY3BvcwM1BHBvcwM1BHNlYwN5bl90b3Bfc3RvcmllcwRzbGsDc3RlcG1vdGhlcmlu.

Weissberg, M. W. (1999). The reactive/non-reactive training controversy. *The Law Enforcement Trainer*, *14*, 10–47.

Weizel, R. (2008a, May 12). Stratford probes confidential breach. Retrieved on October 13, 2009 from http://proquest.umi.com.library.keuka.edu/pqdweb?index=48&did=1517809771&SrchMode=1&sid=2&Fmt=3&VInst=PROD&VType=PQD&RQT=309&VName=PQD&TS=1255433071&clientId=3663.

Weizel, R. (2008b, May 12). Council forwards anti-nepotism ordinance. Retrieved on October 13, 2009 from http://proquest.umi.com.library.keuka.edu/pqdweb?index=48&did=1517809771&SrchMode=1&sid=2&Fmt=3&VInst=PROD&VType=PQD&RQT=309&VName=PQD&TS=1255433071&clientId=3663.

Weizel, R. (2008c, July 25). Stratford PD fills ranks without Miron. Retrieved on October 13, 2009 from http://proquest.umi.com.library.keuka.edu/pqdweb?index=48&did=1517809771&SrchMode=1&sid=2&Fmt=3&VInst=PROD&VType=PQD&RQT=309&VName=PQD&TS=1255433071&clientId=3663.

Weizel, R. (2008d, March 29). Stratford police probe personnel links. Retrieved on November 21, 2009 from http://search.ebscohost.com.library.keuka.edu/login.aspx?direct=true&db=nfh&AN=2W62W62495059979&site=ehost-live.

Weizel, R. (2008e, April 11). Stratford leak of police info probed. Retrieved on November 21, 2009 from http://search.ebscohost.com.library.keuka.edu/login.aspx?direct=true&db=nfh&AN=2W62W63220054823&site=ehost-live.

Weizel, R. (2008f, October 2). McNeill appears before Stratford panel. Retrieved on November 21, 2009 from http://proquest.umi.com.library.keuka.edu/pqdweb?did=1566322611&sid=1&Fmt=3&cl ientId=3663&RQT=309&VName=PQD.

Weizel, R. (2009, June 16). Stratford mayor warned of cop hiring. Retrieved on October 13, 2009 from http://proquest.umi.com.library.keuka.edu/pqdweb?index=15&did=1748728391&SrchMode=2&sid=2&Fmt=3&VInst=PROD&VType=PQD&RQT=309&VName=PQD&TS=1255430937&clientId=3663.

Welchand, W. M. & Leinwand, D. (2010, March 8). Slowly, states are lessening limits on marijuana. Retrieved on March 9, 2010 from http://www.usatoday.com/news/nation/2010-03-08-marijuana_N.htm.

Weldon, J. A. (2003). "But, it was on my own time!" Professional consequences of off-duty behavior. Retrieved on February 7, 2010 from http://search.ebscohost.com.library.keuka.edu/login.aspx?direct=true&db=eric&AN=ED478388&site=ehost-live.

Wells v. Minor (1991).

Welsh Manufacturing v. Pinkerton's, Inc. (1984).

Welsh, W. N. & Harris, P. W. (2004). *Criminal Justice Policy and Planning* (2nd edn.). Albany, NY: LexisNexis Group.

Welsh-Huggins, A. (2011, January 1). Deputy, suspect dead in Ohio trailer park standoff. Retrieved on January 1, 2011 from http://www.daytondailynews.com/news/ohio-news/deputy-suspect-dead-in-ohio-trailer-park-standoff-1043327.html.

Wertz v. Wilson (1997).

WESH.com (2010, December 30). DNA identifies suspect in 1979 homicide: St. Cloud police arrest man in cold case. Retrieved on April 16, 2011 from http://www.wesh.com/r/26319284/detail.html.

Wetterich, C. (2007, October 31). Police chief not pleased with banding system; wants change to hiring process to get more minorities. Retrieved on November 6, 2009 from http://proquest.umi.com.library.keuka.edu/pqdweb?did=1375102311&sid=2&Fmt=3&clientId=3663&RQT=309&VName=PQD.

Wexler, A. & Wexler, S. (1992). Facts on compulsive gambling and addiction. Clearinghouse fact sheet. Retrieved on February 13, 2011 from http://web.ebscohost.com.library.keuka.edu/ehost/detail?hid=9&sid=c2c9c9fd-604a-40aa-8504-95895203904c%40sessionmgr114&vid=5&bdata=JnNpdGU9ZWhvc3QtbGl2ZQ%3d%3d#db=eric&AN=ED372337.

WFTV.com (2010a, February 1). Cop fired after investigation into "Inappropriate" messages. Retrieved on November 1, 2010 from http://www.wftv.com/news/24828806/detail.html.

WFTV.com (2010b, August 31). Police officer charged with sexual battery. Retrieved on October 28, 2010 from http://www.wftv.com/news/24828806/detail.html.

WGRZ.com (2011, April 7). Detective: "doctor shopping" helps dealers acquire painkillers. Retrieved on April 9, 2011 from http://www.wgrz.com/news/article/117424/37/Detective-Doctor-Shopping-Helps-Dealers-Acquire-Painkillers.

Whaley, M. (2009, July 23). UNC police chief heading to CSU. Retrieved on October 28, 2010 from http://www.denverpost.com/newsheadlines/ci_12894937?source=pkg.

WHDH.com (2003, March 5). Special report: What a waste: Quinn bill. Retrieved on March 19, 2011 from http://www1.whdh.com/features/articles/specialreport/A220/.

WHEC.Com (2009a, July 10). Former RPD captain facing sexual harassment charges. Retrieved on October 10, 2009 from http://www.whec.com/news/stories/S1022620.shtml?cat=566.

WHEC.Com (2009b, September 9). Former Canandaigua police officer charged with felony DWI. Retrieved on September 10, 2009 from http://www.whec.com/news/stories/S1130620.shtml?cat=565.

WHEC.Com (2010, December 10). Rochester man sentenced for coercion, enticement of a minor. Retrieved on December 10, 2010 from http://www.whec.com/news/stories/S1876568.shtml?cat=565.

WHEC.Com (2011, January 15). Tragedy at the U of R leaves one dead. Retrieved on April 13, 2011 from http://www.whec.com/news/stories/s1927154.shtml.

Whigham, J. (2010, September 2). Riviera police officer fired after internal investigation. Retrieved on September 5, 2010 from http://www.palmbeachpost.com/news/riviera-police-officer-fired-after-internal-investigation-894810.html.

WHIOTV.com (2007, December 6). Trotwood officer fired over pictures found on MySpace page. Retrieved on November 3, 2010 from http://www.whiotv.com/news/14793092/detail.html.

WHIOTV.com (2010, November 2). Versailles police officer fired for "Sexting." Retrieved on November 3, 2010 from http://www.whiotv.com/news/25610012/detail.html.

Whisenand, P. M. & Ferguson, R. F. (2005). *The Managing of Police Organizations* (6th edn.). Upper Saddle River, NJ: Prentice-Hall, Inc.

Whitacre, T. (2007, June). Behavioral interviewing-find your star. Retrieved on July 27, 2011 from http://proquest.umi.com.library.keuka.edu/pqdweb?did=1298920031&sid=4&Fmt=4&clientId=3663&RQT=309&VName=PQD.

White, D. (2011, February 7). N.Y. murder fugitive caught in Sarasota to stand trial. Retrieved on April 16, 2011 from http://www.heraldtribune.com/article/20110208/ARTICLE/102081061/2055/NEWS?Title=Trial-with-DNA-may-resolve-cold-case.

White, E. (2007, February 15). Air Force drill sergeant demoted for posing in Playboy photo spread. Retrieved on April 15, 2011 from http://proquest.umi.com.library.keuka.edu/pqdweb?did=1217733421&sid=2&Fmt=3&clientId=3663&RQT=309&VName=PQD.

White, M. B. (2008). Enhancing the problem-solving capacity of crime analysis units. Retrieved on October 11, 2010 from http://www.popcenter.org/tools/enhancing_capacity/.

White v. Blue Cross and Blue Shield of Massachusetts Inc. (2004).

White v. Kentuckiana Livestock Market, Inc. (2005).

Whitelaw, K. (2009, November 6). Massacre leaves 13 dead at Fort Hood. Retrieved on February 8, 2011 from http://www.npr.org/templates/story/story.php?storyId=120138496.

Whitney v. Warden

WIBW.Com (2010, February 10). Former corrections worker appeals sex offender registry requirement. Retrieved on November 1, 2010 from http://www.wibw.com/localnews/headlines/84041792.html.

Wieder v. Chemical Bank (1994).

Wikipedia (2007, August). Rampart scandal. Retrieved on October 9, 2009 from http://en.wikipedia.org/wiki/Rampart_scandal.

Wikipedia (2009, October 7). William M. Tweed. Retrieved on October 10, 2009 from http://en.wikipedia.org/wiki/William_M._Tweed.

Wikipedia (2010a, July 13). Revised NEO personality inventory. Retrieved on August 18, 2010 from http://en.wikipedia.org/wiki/Revised_NEO_Personality_Inventory.

Wikipedia (2010b, September 22). Concealed carry in the United States. Retrieved on September 22, 2010 from http://en.wikipedia.org/wiki/Concealed_carry_in_the_United_States.

Wikipedia (2011a, February 8). Gangs. Retrieved on February 8, 2011 from http://en.wikipedia.org/wiki/Gang.

Wikipedia (2011b, April 18). US military discharge. Retrieved on April 18, 2011 from http://en.wikipedia.org/wiki/Military_discharge#Entry_level_separation_.28ELS.29.

Wikipedia (2011c, May 9). Legal intoxicants. Retrieved on June 1, 2011 from http://en.wikipedia.org/wiki/Legal_intoxicants.

Wikipedia (2011d, June 1). Angie's list. Retrieved on June 5, 2011 from http://en.wikipedia.org/wiki/Angie%27s_List.

Wikipedia (2011e, June 4). Open source intelligence. Retrieved on June 5, 2011 from http://en.wikipedia.org/wiki/Open_source_intelligence.

Wilks v. DeBolt (1948).

Williams, C. (2010, June 29). Two Tampa police officers gunned down during early morning traffic stop: One person found, $75k reward for info on other. Retrieved on December 6, 2010 from http://www.abcactionnews.com/dpp/news/region_tampa/two-tampa-police-officers-murdered-during-early-morning-traffic-stop.

Williams, H. (2002, December). Core factors of police corruption across the world. *Forum on Crime and Society*, *2*(1), 86–99.

Williams, L. (2011, March 29). Barry Bonds' ex says he discussed steroid use. Retrieved on April 13, 2011 from http://articles.sfgate.com/2011-03-29/news/29356376_1_kimberly-bell-jeff-nedrow-effects-of-steroid-abuse.

Williams, R. & Macenka, J. (2009, May 20). Woman cleared in wreck; officer was going 98 mph. Retrieved on October 18, 2010 from http://proquest.umi.com.library.keuka.edu/pqdweb?did=1718818171&sid=4&Fmt=3&clientId=3663&RQT=309&VName=PQD.

Williams v. District of Columbia (1997).

Williams v. Feather Sound, Inc. (1980).
Williams v. Santana (2009).
Willing, R. (2006, November 21). Many DNA matches aren't acted on. Retrieved on April 17, 2011 from http://www.usatoday.com/news/nation/2006-11-20-dna-matches_x.htm.
Willing, R. & Watson, T. (2001, February 21). FBI portrays Robert Hanssen's double life. Retrieved on November 3, 2010 from http://www.usatoday.com/news/washington/2001-02-21-spydouble.htm#more.
Willis v. Roche Biomedical Laboratories, Inc. (1995).
Willon, P. (2009, September 17). LAPD opens new high-tech crime analysis center. Retrieved on October 11, 2010 from http://latimesblogs.latimes.com/lanow/2009/09/crime-lab.html.
Wilonsky, R. (2010, September 17). The police blotter: Dallas PD chief Brown fires five, releases details on in-custody death. Retrieved on September 27, 2010 from http://blogs.dallasobserver.com/unfairpark/2010/09/the_police_blotter_dallas_pd_c.php.
Wilson, C. (2011, February 1). Slain Indianapolis officer hailed as warrior. Retrieved on February 1, 2011 from http://www.seattlepi.com/national/1110ap_us_indianapolis_officer_shot.html.
Wilson, G. I. (2010a, December). Perspective on neurolinguistic programming (NLP). *The Police Chief Magazine*, *77*(12), 40–50.
Wilson, J. (2009, May 20). Record retention guidelines: Part 2, personnel records. Retrieved on February 20, 2010 from https://www.hrtools.com/insights/judith_wilson/record_retention_guidelines_part_2_personnel_records.aspx.
Wilson, J. (2010b, January 8). Record retention guidelines part 1: Pre-employment records. Retrieved on February 20, 2010 from https://www.hrtools.com/insights/judith_wilson/record_retention_guidelines.aspx.
Wilson, N. (2010c, Spring). Culture of rape. Retrieved on April 16, 2011 from http://proquest.umi.com.library.keuka.edu/pqdweb?did=2042655571&sid=2&Fmt=3&clientId=3663&RQT=309&VName=PQD.
Wilson v. City of Baton Rouge (2009).
Wilson v. Prudential Financial (2009).
Winston, C. N. (2005, July 25). The National Crime Information Center: A review and evaluation. Retrieved on August 18, 2010 from www.americanchecked.com/NCIC_Report_July25.pdf.
Winter, E. R. (2010a, February 1). How potential employees may use the web to write fake resumes. Retrieved on March 18, 2011 from http://www.bbb.org/us/post/how-potential-employees-may-use-the-web-to-write-fake-resumes-1214.
Winter, J. (2010b, April 27). Wikipedia distributing child porn, co-founder tells FBI. Retrieved on October 24, 2010 from http://www.foxnews.com/scitech/2010/04/27/wikipedia-child-porn-larry-sanger-fbi/.
Wisconsin Department of Justice (n.d.). Crime information bureau—Conducting criminal background checks. Retrieved on October 10, 2010 from http://www.doj.state.wi.us/dles/cib/crimback.asp.
Wise, D. (1995, May 22). Victims of Aldrich Ames. Retrieved on November 3, 2010 from http://www.time.com/time/magazine/article/0,9171,982988,00.html.
Wixted, J. T. & Mickes, L. (2010, October). A continuous dual-process model of remember/know judgments. Retrieved on July 26, 2011 from http://web.ebscohost.com.library.keuka.edu/ehost/detail?vid=4&hid=122&sid=2d6b04cf-d2d8-474c-be2b-72912e7ffd9b%40sessionmgr113&bdata=JnNpdGU9ZWhvc3QtbGl2ZQ%3d%3d#db=pdh&AN=rev-117-4-1025.
WLWT.com (2009, January 9). Cincinnati police officer sentenced to jail in records case. Retrieved on October 29, 2010 from http://www.wlwt.com/r/18445684/detail.html.
WMCTV.com (2011, June 27). Deputy jailer charged with sexual assault. Retrieved on June 28, 2011 from http://www.wmctv.com/story/14983981/deputy-jailer.
WMUR.com (2010, February 4). Pamela Smart says she's more than her 'Worst Mistake.' Retrieved on December 11, 2010 from http://www.wmur.com/r/22464822/detail.html.

WOAI.com (2010, June 15). Police suspected of cheating on promotion exams: Investigation into San Antonio police cheating on promotion exam. Retrieved on August 4, 2011 from http://www.woai.com/news/local/story/Police-suspected-of-cheating-on-promotion-exams/KpGBrCgp80mBBGJWmAg6qw.cspx.

Woestendiek, J. (1993, December 23). Things looking up for future firemen and department? Three men rejected for poor vision will enter the fire academy in '94. Retrieved on November 25, 2009 from http://proquest.umi.com.library.keuka.edu/pqdweb?did=1365052611&sid=10&Fmt=3&clientId=3663&RQT=309&VName=PQD.

Wolf, G. (1999, August). Developing performance criteria for pre-employment screenings. *The Police Chief Magazine*, *66*(8), 74–77.

Wolfbauer v. Office of Personnel Management (2008).

Wollack, Waibel, & Guenther, Inc. (1977). Interviewer's manual—A guide to the evaluation of police officer applicants. Retrieved on September 13, 2010 from http://web.ebscohost.com.library.keuka.edu/ehost/detail?vid=4&hid=105&sid=322c9a61-9e8d-40c3-96a0-ada73d8258bf%40sessionmgr113&bdata=JnNpdGU9ZWhvc3QtbGl2ZQ%3d%3d#db=sih&AN=SM050113.

Wong, D. (2011, February 11). Reno's police and fire departments start layoffs. Retrieved on February 14, 2011 from http://www.kolotv.com/home/headlines/Many_City_Workers_Receive_Pink_Slips_116024664.html?storySection=comments.

Wong, G. (2010, April 12). Ex-teacher pleads guilty to sex with teens. Retrieved on January 28, 2011 from http://articles.cnn.com/2010-04-12/justice/florida.teacher.student.sex_1_guilty-teen-underage-students?_s=PM:CRIME.

Wong, R. C., Tran, M., & Tung, J. K. (2005, June). Oral fluid tests: Effects of adulterants and foodstuffs. Retrieved on January 24, 2010 from http://search.ebscohost.com.library.keuka.edu/login.aspx?direct=true&db=sih&AN=17917664&site=ehost-live.

Wood, D. (2011a, January 3). Navy integrity vs. tradition: Should Capt. Honors have been fired over videos? Retrieved on January 4, 2011 from http://www.politicsdaily.com/2011/01/03/navy-integrity-vs-tradition-should-capt-honors-be-fired-over/.

Wood, S. (2011b, June 16). Cherry Hill dentist convicted of attempting sex with minor. Retrieved on August 13, 2011 from http://www.philly.com/philly/news/20110616_Cherry_Hill_dentist_convicted_of_attempting_sex_with_minor.html.

Woodford, K. C. & Woodford, T. J. (2006, Summer). The duty to accommodate a person who is perceived as disabled: Say it isn't so. Retrieved on November 17, 2009 from http://proquest.umi.com.library.keuka.edu/pqdweb?did=1082827291&sid=1&Fmt=3&clientId=3663&RQT=309&VName=PQD.

Woodland v. City of Houston (1991).

WoodTV.com (2009, June 26). State police layoffs take effect Sunday. Retrieved on February 14, 2011 from http://www.woodtv.com/dpp/news/michigan/State_Police_layoffs_take_effect_Sunday.

Woolnough, R. (2004, February 2). Office hours: Reading between the lines: When it comes to references, too much information can be as bad as too little. Retrieved on November 8, 2009 from http://proquest.umi.com.library.keuka.edu/pqdweb?did=536022811&sid=1&Fmt=3&clientId=3663&RQT=309&VName=PQD.

WorldNetDaily.com (2005, December 14). U.S. teacher sexpidemic spreading across planet: Long list of American rapists joined by female Australians. Retrieved on October 12, 2010 from http://www.wnd.com/news/article.asp?ARTICLE_ID=47895.

Wortham, J. (2009, August 20). More employers use networks to check out applicants. Retrieved on September 14, 2011 from http://bits.blogs.nytimes.com/2009/08/20/more-employers-use-social-networks-to-check-out-applicants/.

Wortley, R. & Smallbone, S. (2006, May). Child pornography on the internet. Washington, DC: United States Department of Justice Office of Community Oriented Policing Services.

Woska, W. J. (1991, September). Negligent employment practices. Retrieved on November 8, 2009 from http://search.ebscohost.com.library.keuka.edu/login.aspx?direct=true&db=sih&AN=5880826&site=ehost-live.

WPTV.com (2010, September 3). Riviera beach police officer terminated. Retrieved on November 1, 2010 from http://www.wptv.com/dpp/news/region_s_palm_beach_county/delray_beach/delray-beach-police-officer-terminated.

Wren, A. O., Clark, L., & Deriso, M. (2006, Spring). Employer beware: Truth-in-hiring may be the new standard in recruiting. Retrieved on February 16, 2010 from http://proquest.umi.com.library.keuka.edu/pqdweb?did=1160410661&sid=1&Fmt=4&clientId=3663&RQT=309&VName=PQD.

Wright, G. (2010, August 5). Pentagon case highlights need for HR to have clearer rules. Retrieved on August 17, 2010 from http://www.shrm.org/hrdisciplines/technology/Articles/Pages/HRPornRules.aspx.

Wright, T. (2009, July 29). Charges dropped against woman framed by cops: Police seen plotting to blame car accident on woman they hit. Retrieved on November 1, 2010 from http://www.nbcmiami.com/news/local-beat/Cops-Set-Up-Woman-After-Crash.html.

Wright v. Guarinello (1995).

WSBTV.com (2009, June 26). Woman alleges rape at Georgia police station. Retrieved on November 1, 2010 from http://www.officer.com/web/online/Internal-Affairs-News/Woman-Alleges-Rape-at-Georgia-Police-Station/5$47255.

WTMJ.com (2011, August 5). Witnesses describe mobs, some people claim racially-charged attacks. Retrieved on August 8, 2011 from http://www.todaystmj4.com/news/local/126825018.html.

Wu, A. H., Bristol, B., Sexton, K., Cassella-McLane, G., Holtman, V., & Hill, D. W. (1999). Adulteration of urine by "Urine Luck." Retrieved on January 18, 2010 from http://search.ebscohost.com.library.keuka.edu/login.aspx?direct=true&db=cmedm&AN=10388482&site=ehost-live.

WUSA9.com (2011a). Woodpecker-saving daughter costs mom $500: A woman in Fredericksburg is facing a $535 fine and possible jail time all because her daughter tried to save a baby woodpecker. Retrieved on August 28, 2011 from http://wusa9.com/video/1090121205001/0/Woodpecker-Saving-Daughter-Costs-Mom-500.

WUSA9.com (2011b). UPDATE: Woodpecker-saving girl's mom won't have to pay: The U.S. fish and wildlife service says the $500 citation was given in error and that it is correcting it. Retrieved on August 28, 2011 from http://wusa9.com/video/1091599018001/0/UPDATE-Woodpecker-Saving-Girls-Mom-Wont-Have-To-Pay.

Wyman, A. (2010, October 29). Melanson indicted in Fagiani's murder. Retrieved on April 17, 2011 from http://napavalleyregister.com/news/local/article_357db4d0-e3c6-11df-9dd7-001cc4c03286.html.

Wyoming Peace Officer Standards and Training (2009). Wyoming peace officer standards and training (P.O.S.T.). Retrieved on October 20, 2009 from http://attorneygeneral.state.wy.us/post.htm.

Yaniv, O. (2011, February 3). Conviction of mother of slain Marchella Pierce could hinge on young son's testimony. Retrieved on April 6, 2011 from http://articles.nydailynews.com/2011-02-03/news/27738725_1_testimony-beatings-monster-mom.

Yaniv, O. & Shapiro, R. (2011, March 25). Gruesome photos, bogus computer entries are key to homicide case against child welfare workers. Retrieved on April 4, 2011 from http://www.nydailynews.com/news/ny_crime/2011/03/25/2011-03-25_gruesome_evidence_acs.html?obref=obnetwork.

YNN Staff (2010, July 6). Former Greece police chief sentenced to prison. Retrieved on October 8, 2010 from http://rochester.ynn.com/content/top_stories/510089/former-greece-police-chief-sentenced-to-prison/.

YNN Staff (2011a, March 8). Man sentenced for trying to entice teen online. Retrieved on March 8, 2011 from http://rochester.ynn.com/content/top_stories/535955/man-sentenced-for-trying-to-entice-teen-online/.

YNN Staff (2011b, April 14). Grand jury hears case against couple accused of abusing child. Retrieved on April 14, 2011 from http://rochester.ynn.com/content/top_stories/539873/grand-jury-hears-case-against-couple-accused-of-abusing-child/

Young, D. E. (2011a, July 20). State Sen. Diane Savino pushes for legalization of medical Marijuana. Retrieved on July 20, 2011 from http://www.silive.com/news/index.ssf/2011/07/state_sen_diane_savino_pushes.html.

Young, J. R. (2009, February 6). How not to lose face on Facebook, for professors. Retrieved on June 19, 2010 from http://chronicle.com/article/How-Not-to-Lose-Face-on-Fac/24101/.

Young, K. (2007, March 18). New NS chief is being investigated. Retrieved on September 26, 2010 from http://jacksonvilleprogress.com/homepage/x154936326/New-NS-chief-is-being-investigated.

Young, M. (2000, February 20). Small business/drug free battle benefits everyone. Retrieved on November 25, 2009 from http://proquest.umi.com.library.keuka.edu/pqdweb?did=49871273&sid=1&Fmt=3&clientId=3663&RQT=309&VName=PQD.

Young, S. (2011b, February 4). Youtube video of bullying incident gets students arrested. Retrieved on February 5, 2011 from http://www.associatedcontent.com/article/7719236/youtube_video_of_bullying_incident.html.

Young v. City of Dimmitt (1989).

Young v. Providence (2005).

Yunker v. Honeywell, Inc. (1993).

Yusko, D. (2010, December 21). Incident leads to hate crime charges—Cops: Skidmore student used racial slur, smashed plate over victim's head. Retrieved on December 22, 2010 from http://www.timesunion.com/local/article/Incident-leads-to-hate-crime-charges-910882.php.

Zachary, M. K. (2001, February). Recent developments in employment testing: Part 1—Genetic testing. Retrieved on November 17, 2009 from http://proquest.umi.com.library.keuka.edu/pqdweb?did=67480002&sid=1&Fmt=3&clie ntId=3663&RQT=309&VName=PQD.

Zaniewski, A. (2010, September 3). Waterford police layoffs announced. Retrieved on February 14, 2011 from http://www.theoaklandpress.com/articles/2010/09/03/news/local_news/doc4c81470411e13819388254.txt.

Zappe, J. (2009, January 7). Add 'review background screening' to your list of resolutions. Retrieved on February 8, 2011 from http://www.ere.net/2009/01/07/add-review-background-screening-to-your-list-of-resolutions/.

Zash, C. & Quesinberry, J. (2010, February 2). Former Burlington police officer faces sex-related charges. Retrieved on December 6, 2010 from http://www.digtriad.com/news/local/article.aspx?storyid=136798&catid=57.

Zedlewski, E. & Murphy, M. B. (2006, January). DNA analysis for "minor" crimes: A major benefit for law enforcement. *National Institute of Justice Journal*, (253), 2–5.

Zehnder, I. (2010, November 16). Ohio teen found in basement, bound & gagged; 2 women, child still missing. Retrieved on December 11, 2010 from http://www.examiner.com/missing-persons-in-national/ohio-teen-found-basement-bound-gagged-2-women-child-still-missing.

Zeidner, R. (2007, October). How deep can you probe? Retrieved on February 22, 2011 from http://proquest.umi.com.library.keuka.edu/pqdweb?did=1341800941&sid=3&Fmt=3&clientId=3663&RQT=309&VName=PQD.

Zeigler, M. (2011a, August 26). RIT employee faces federal child porn charge. Retrieved on August 27, 2011 from http://www.democratandchronicle.com/article/20110826/NEWS01/110826023/RIT-employee-faces-federal-child-porn-charge?odyssey=mod|mostview.

Zeigler, M. (2011b, August 27). Irondequoit resident faces child porn charge. Retrieved on August 27, 2011 from http://www.democratandchronicle.com/article/20110827/NEWS01/108270326/Irondequoit-resident-faces-child-porn-charge?odyssey=mod|mostview.

Zeleny, J. (2007, December 13). Clinton aide sees problem for Obama. Retrieved on November 25, 2009 from http://search.ebscohost.com.library.keuka.edu/login.aspx?direct=true&db=nfh&AN=27920705&site=ehost-live.

Zerr v. Johnson (1995).

Zetter, K. (2005, March 11). Bad data fouls background checks. Retrieved on August 18, 2010 from http://www.wired.com/politics/security/news/2005/03/66856.

Zick, J. (2010, November 30). Former cop faces charges in weekend standoff. Retrieved on April 29, 2011 from http://www.the-leader.com/topstories/x1384148866/Former-cop-faces-charges-in-weekend-Elmira-standoff.

Zick, J. & Dunning, J. (2010, June 21). Father's day tragedy: Mother, infant stabbed to death; boy's dad held. Retrieved on April 18, 2011 from http://www.the-leader.com/features/x383297863/Father-s-Day-tragedy-Mother-infant-stabbed-to-death-boy-s-dad-held.

Zremski, J. (2011, February 25). New allegations against Lee. Retrieved on February 25, 2011 from http://www.buffalonews.com/topics/chris-lee/article351895.ece.

Zubak-Skees, C. (2010, September 17). Another year, another student prosecuted for child porn. Retrieved on January 11, 2011 from http://reportermag.com/article/09-17-2010/another-year-another-student-prosecuted-for-child-porn.

Zuk, R. (2009, February). The right kind of writing: Follow simple writing tenets to increase your likelihood of social media success. Retrieved on March 16, 2010 from http://proquest.umi.com.library.keuka.edu/pqdweb?did=1652561491&sid=3&Fmt=2&clientId=3663&RQT=309&VName=PQD.

Zulawski, D. E. & Wicklander, D. E. (1998, July). Interrogation: Understanding the process. *Law and Order Magazine*, *46*(7), 82–90.

Zuniga v. Sears, Roebuck, & Co. (1983).

Index

B

C

D

E

J

K

L

M

N

O

P

T

U

V

W